I0071524

Strategic
Management Communication

Compiled and Edited by:

Jonathan H. Westover, Ph.D.
Utah Valley University

First printed/published in 2014 in the USA
by HCI Press
as part of Leading Innovative Organizations series

Library of Congress Cataloging-in-Publication Data

Strategic Management Communication / Jonathan H. Westover, editor.
        p. cm. -- (Leading Innovative Organizations series)
ISBN-13: 978-0692325209; ISBN-10: 0692325204 (HCI Press)
1. Management Communication. 2. Organizational Strategy. I. Westover, Jonathan H.

Table of Contents

About the Editor

Dr. Jonathan H. Westover is an Associate Professor of Management and Associate Director of the Center for the Study of Ethics at Utah Valley University, specializing in international human resource management, organizational development, and community-engaged experiential learning. He is also a human resource development and performance management consultant. Already a recipient of numerous research, teaching, and service awards and fellowships early in his academic career, Jonathan also recently was named a Fulbright Scholar and was visiting faculty in the MBA program at Belarusian State University (Minsk, Belarus), and he is also a regular visiting faculty member in other graduate business programs in the U.S., UK, France, Poland, and China. Prior to his doctoral studies in the Sociology of Work and Organizations, Comparative International Sociology, and International Political Economy (University of Utah), he received his B.S. in Sociology (Research and Analysis emphasis, Business Management minor, Korean minor) and MPA (emphasis in Human Resource Management) from the Marriott School of Management at Brigham Young University. He also received graduate certificates in demography and higher education teaching during his time at the University of Utah. His ongoing research examines issues of globalization, labor transformation, work quality characteristics, and the determinants of job satisfaction cross-nationally.

Acknowledgements

This text was compiled, edited, and adapted from open source texts at http://www.saylor.org/books and created under a Creative Commons Attribution-NonCommercial ShareAlike 3.0 License without attribution as requested by the work's original creator or licensee. Please contact me for a free copy of the e-text. I would like to thank the many anonymous individuals who contributed their own wisdom and writing to this edited work, particularly those who contributed to the text *Business Communication for Success*. Of course, this text would not be possible without each of their important contributions. Most of all, I would like to publically thank my wife (Jacque) and my six wonderful children (Sara, Amber, Lia, Kaylie, David, and Brayden) for all of their love and support!

Preface

Strategic Management Communication (*SMC*) provides a comprehensive, integrated approach to the study and application of written and oral business communication to serve both student and professor.

This series features chapters with the following elements:
- Learning Objectives
- Introductory Exercises
- Clear expectations, relevant background, and important theories
- Practical, real-world examples
- Key Takeaways or quick internal summaries
- Key terms that are easily identified
- In-chapter assignments
- Post-chapter assessments linked to objectives and skills acquisition

Each chapter is self-contained, allowing for mix-and-match flexibility and custom or course-specific design. Each chapter focuses on clear objectives and skill demonstrations that can be easily linked to your syllabus and state or federal requirements. Additionally, each chapter features time-saving and learning-enhancement support for instructors and students.

SMC is designed to help students identify important information, reinforce for retention, and demonstrate mastery with a clear outcome product.

The text has three content categories:
1. Foundations
2. Process and products
3. Contexts

The first three chapters form the core foundation for the study of oral and written management communication. The next sequence of chapters focus on the process of writing, then oral performance with an emphasis on results. The final sequence focuses on contexts where business communication occurs, from interpersonal to intercultural, from groups to leadership.

In each of the process and product chapter sequences, the chapters follow a natural flow, from prewriting to revision, from preparation for a presentation to performance. Each sequence comes together in a concluding chapter that focuses on action—where we apply the skills and techniques of written or oral communication in business, from writing a letter to presenting a sales speech. These performances not only serve to reinforce real-world applications but also may serve as course assessments. All chapters are compartmentalized into sections so you can choose what you want to use and eliminate the rest.

Chapter 1:
Effective Business Communication

Communication leads to community, that is, to understanding, intimacy and mutual valuing.
  Rollo May
I know that you believe that you understood what you think I said, but I am not sure you realize that what you heard is not what I meant.
  Robert J. McCloskey, former State Department spokesman

Getting Started

INTRODUCTORY EXERCISES

1. Write five words that express what you want to do and where you want to be a year from now. Take those five words and write a paragraph that clearly articulates your responses to both "what" and "where."
2. Think of five words that express what you want to do and where you want to be five years from now. Share your five words with your classmates and listen to their responses. What patterns do you observe in the responses? Write a paragraph that addresses at least one observation.

Communication is an activity, skill, and art that incorporates lessons learned across a wide spectrum of human knowledge. Perhaps the most time-honored form of communication is storytelling. We've told each other stories for ages to help make sense of our world, anticipate the future, and certainly to entertain ourselves. The art of storytelling draws on your understanding of yourself, your message, and how you communicate it to an audience that is simultaneously communicating back to you. Your anticipation, reaction, and adaptation to the process will determine how successfully you are able to communicate. You were not born knowing how to write or even how to talk—but in the process of growing up, you have undoubtedly learned how to tell, and how not tell, a story out loud and in writing.

You didn't learn to text in a day and didn't learn all the codes—from LOL (laugh out loud) to BRB (be right back)—right away. In the same way, learning to communicate well requires you to read and study how others have expressed themselves, then adapt what you have learned to your present task—whether it is texting a brief message to a friend, presenting your qualifications in a job interview, or writing a business report. You come to this text with skills and an understanding that will provide a valuable foundation as we explore the communication process.

Effective communication takes preparation, practice, and persistence. There are many ways to learn communication skills; the school of experience, or "hard knocks," is one of them. But in the business environment, a "knock" (or lesson learned) may come at the expense of your credibility through a blown presentation to a client. The classroom environment, with a compilation of information and resources such as a text, can offer you a trial run where you get to try out new ideas and skills before you have to use them to communicate effectively to make a sale or form a new partnership. Listening to yourself, or perhaps the comments of others, may help you reflect on new ways to present, or perceive, thoughts, ideas and concepts. The net result is your growth; ultimately your ability to communicate in business will improve, opening more doors than you might anticipate.

As you learn the material in this text, each part will contribute to the whole. The degree to which you attend to each part will ultimately help give you the skills, confidence, and preparation to use communication in furthering your career.

1.1 Why Is It Important to Communicate Well?
LEARNING OBJECTIVES

1. Recognize the importance of communication in gaining a better understanding of yourself and others.
2. Explain how communication skills help you solve problems, learn new things, and build your career.

Communication is key to your success—in relationships, in the workplace, as a citizen of your country, and across your lifetime. Your ability to communicate comes from experience, and experience can be an effective teacher, but this text and the related business communication course will offer you a wealth of experiences gathered from professional speakers across their lifetimes. You can learn from the lessons they've learned and be a more effective communicator right out of the gate.

Business communication can be thought of as a problem solving activity in which individuals may address the following questions:

- What is the situation?
- What are some possible communication strategies?
- What is the best course of action?
- What is the best way to design the chosen message?
- What is the best way to deliver the message?

In this book, we will examine this problem solving process and help you learn to apply it in the kinds of situations you are likely to encounter over the course of your career.

Communication Influences Your Thinking about Yourself and Others

We all share a fundamental drive to communicate. Communication can be defined as the process of understanding and sharing meaning. [1] You share meaning in what you say and how you say it, both in oral and written forms. If you could not communicate, what would life be like? A series of never-ending frustrations? Not being able to ask for what you need or even to understand the needs of others?

Being unable to communicate might even mean losing a part of yourself, for you communicate your self-concept—your sense of self and awareness of who you are—in many ways. Do you like to write? Do you find it easy to make a phone call to a stranger or to speak to a room full of people? Perhaps someone told you that you don't speak clearly or your grammar needs improvement. Does that make you more or less likely to want to communicate? For some, it may be a positive challenge, while for others it may be discouraging. But in all cases, your ability to communicate is central to your self-concept.

Take a look at your clothes. What are the brands you are wearing? What do you think they say about you? Do you feel that certain styles of shoes, jewelry, tattoos, music, or even automobiles express who you are? Part of your self-concept may be that you express yourself through texting, or through writing longer documents like essays and research papers, or through the way you speak.

On the other side of the coin, your communications skills help you to understand others—not just their words, but also their tone of voice, their nonverbal gestures, or the format of their written documents provide you with clues about who they are and what their values and priorities may be. Active listening and reading are also part of being a successful communicator.

Communication Influences How You Learn

When you were an infant, you learned to talk over a period of many months. When you got older, you didn't learn to ride a bike, drive a car, or even text a message on your cell phone in one brief moment. You need to begin the process of improving your speaking and writing with the frame of mind that it will require effort, persistence, and self-correction.

You learn to speak in public by first having conversations, then by answering questions and expressing your opinions in class, and finally by preparing and delivering a "stand-up" speech. Similarly, you learn to write by first learning to read, then by writing and learning to think critically. Your speaking and writing are reflections of your thoughts, experience, and education. Part of that combination is your level of experience listening to other speakers, reading documents and styles of writing, and studying formats similar to what you aim to produce.

As you study business communication, you may receive suggestions for improvement and clarification from speakers and writers more experienced than yourself. Take their suggestions as challenges to improve; don't give up when your first speech or first draft does not communicate the message you intend. Stick with it until you get it right. Your success in communicating is a skill that applies to almost every field of work, and it makes a difference in your relationships with others.

Remember, luck is simply a combination of preparation and timing. You want to be prepared to communicate well when given the opportunity. Each time you do a good job, your success will bring more success.

Communication Represents You and Your Employer

You want to make a good first impression on your friends and family, instructors, and employer. They all want you to convey a positive image, as it reflects on them. In your career, you will represent your business or company in spoken and written form. Your professionalism and attention to detail will reflect positively on you and set you up for success.

In both oral and written situations, you will benefit from having the ability to communicate clearly. These are skills you will use for the rest of your life. Positive improvements in these skills will have a positive impact on your relationships, your prospects for employment, and your ability to make a difference in the world.

Communication Skills Are Desired by Business and Industry

Oral and written communication proficiencies are consistently ranked in the top ten desirable skills by employer surveys year after year. In fact, high-powered business executives sometimes hire consultants to coach them in sharpening their communication skills. According to the National Association of Colleges and Employers, [2] the following are the top five personal qualities or skills potential employers seek:

1. Communication skills (verbal and written)
2. Strong work ethic
3. Teamwork skills (works well with others, group communication)
4. Initiative
5. Analytical skills

Knowing this, you can see that one way for you to be successful and increase your promotion potential is to increase your abilities to speak and write effectively.

In September 2004, the National Commission on Writing for America's Families, Schools, and Colleges published a study on 120 human resource directors titled *Writing: A Ticket to Work…Or a Ticket Out, A Survey of Business Leaders*. [3] The study found that "writing is both a 'marker' of high-skill, high-wage, professional work and a 'gatekeeper' with clear equity implications," said Bob Kerrey, president of New School University in New York and chair of the commission. "People unable to express themselves clearly in writing limit their opportunities for professional, salaried employment." [4] On the other end of the spectrum, it is estimated that over forty million Americans are illiterate, or unable to functionally read or write. If you are reading this book, you may not be part of an at-risk group in need of basic skill development, but you still may need additional training and practice as you raise your skill level.

An individual with excellent communication skills is an asset to every organization. No matter what career you plan to pursue, learning to express yourself professionally in speech and in writing will help you get there.

KEY TAKEAWAY

Communication forms a part of your self-concept, and it helps you understand yourself and others, solve problems and learn new things, and build your career.

EXERCISES

1. Imagine that you have been hired to make "cold calls" to ask people whether they are familiar with a new restaurant that has just opened in your neighborhood. Write a script for the phone call. Ask a classmate to co-present as you deliver the script orally in class, as if you were making a phone call to the classmate. Discuss your experience with the rest of the class.
2. Imagine you have been assigned the task of creating a job description. Identify a job, locate at least two sample job descriptions, and create one. Please present the job description to the class and note to what degree communication skills play a role in the tasks or duties you have included.

[1] Pearson, J., & Nelson, P. (2000). *An introduction to human communication: understanding and sharing* (p. 6). Boston, MA: McGraw-Hill.
[2] National Association of Colleges and Employers. (2009). Frequently asked questions. Retrieved from http://www.naceweb.org/Press/Frequently_Asked_Questions.aspx?referal=
[3] National Commission on Writing for America's Families, Schools, and Colleges. (2004, September). *Writing: A Ticket to Work…Or a Ticket Out, A Survey of Business Leaders*. Retrieved fromhttp://www.writingcommission.org/pr/writing_for_employ.html
[4] The College Board. (2004, September). Writing skills necessary for employment, says big business: Writing can be a ticket to professional jobs, says blue-ribbon group. Retrieved fromhttp://www.writingcommission.org/pr/writing_for_employ.html

1.2 What Is Communication?
LEARNING OBJECTIVES

1. Define communication and describe communication as a process.
2. Identify and describe the eight essential components of communication.
3. Identify and describe two models of communication.

Many theories have been proposed to describe, predict, and understand the behaviors and phenomena of which communication consists. When it comes to communicating in business, we are often less interested in theory than in making sure our communications generate the desired results. But in order to achieve results, it can be valuable to understand what communication is and how it works.

Defining Communication

The root of the word "communication" in Latin is *communicare*, which means to share, or to make common. [1] Communication is defined as the process of understanding and sharing meaning. [2]

At the center of our study of communication is the relationship that involves interaction between participants. This definition serves us well with its emphasis on the process, which we'll examine in depth across this text, of coming to understand and share another's point of view effectively.

The first key word in this definition is process. A process is a dynamic activity that is hard to describe because it changes. [3] Imagine you are alone in your kitchen thinking. Someone you know (say, your mother) enters the kitchen and you talk briefly. What has changed? Now, imagine that your mother is joined by someone else, someone you haven't met before—and this stranger listens intently as you speak, almost as if you were giving a speech. What has changed? Your perspective might change, and you might watch your words more closely. The feedback or response from your mother and the stranger (who are, in essence, your audience) may cause you to reevaluate what you are saying. When we interact, all these factors—and many more—influence the process of communication.

The second key word is understanding: "To understand is to perceive, to interpret, and to relate our perception and interpretation to what we already know." [4] If a friend tells you a story about falling off a bike, what image comes to mind? Now your friend points out the window and you see a motorcycle lying on the ground. Understanding the words and the concepts or objects they refer to is an important part of the communication process.

Next comes the word sharing. Sharing means doing something together with one or more people. You may share a joint activity, as when you share in compiling a report; or you may benefit jointly from a resource, as when you and several coworkers share a pizza. In communication, sharing occurs when you convey thoughts, feelings, ideas, or insights to others. You can also share with yourself (a process called intrapersonal communication) when you bring ideas to consciousness, ponder how you feel about something, or figure out the solution to a problem and have a classic "Aha!" moment when something becomes clear.

Finally, meaning is what we share through communication. The word "bike" represents both a bicycle and a short name for a motorcycle. By looking at the context the word is used in and by asking questions, we can discover the shared meaning of the word and understand the message.

Eight Essential Components of Communication

In order to better understand the communication process, we can break it down into a series of eight essential components:

1. Source
2. Message
3. Channel
4. Receiver
5. Feedback
6. Environment
7. Context
8. Interference

Each of these eight components serves an integral function in the overall process. Let's explore them one by one.

Source

The source imagines, creates, and sends the message. In a public speaking situation, the source is the person giving the speech. He or she conveys the message by sharing new information with the audience. The speaker also conveys a message through his or her tone of voice, body language, and choice of clothing. The speaker begins by first determining the message—what to say and how to say it. The second step involves encoding the message by choosing just the right order or the perfect words to convey the intended meaning. The third step is to present or send the information to the receiver or audience. Finally, by watching for the audience's reaction, the source perceives how well they received the message and responds with clarification or supporting information.

Message

"The message is the stimulus or meaning produced by the source for the receiver or audience." [5] When you plan to give a speech or write a report, your message may seem to be only the words you choose that will convey your meaning. But that is just the beginning. The words are brought together with grammar and organization. You may choose to save your most important point for last. The message also consists of the way you say it—in a speech, with your tone of voice, your body language, and your appearance—and in a report, with your writing style, punctuation, and the headings and formatting you choose. In addition, part of the message may be the environment or context you present it in and the noise that might make your message hard to hear or see.

Imagine, for example, that you are addressing a large audience of sales reps and are aware there is a World Series game tonight. Your audience might have a hard time settling down, but you may choose to open with, "I understand there is an important game tonight." In this way, by expressing verbally something that most people in your audience are aware of and interested in, you might grasp and focus their attention.

Channel

"The channel is the way in which a message or messages travel between source and receiver." [6] For example, think of your television. How many channels do you have on your television? Each channel takes up some space, even in a digital world, in the cable or in the signal that brings the message of each channel to your home. Television combines an audio signal you hear with a visual signal you see. Together they convey the message to the receiver or audience. Turn off the volume on your television. Can you still understand what is happening? Many times you can, because the body language conveys part of the message of the show. Now turn up the volume but turn around so that you cannot see the television. You can still hear the dialogue and follow the story line.

Similarly, when you speak or write, you are using a channel to convey your message. Spoken channels include face-to-face conversations, speeches, telephone conversations and voice mail messages, radio, public address systems, and voice over Internet protocol (VoIP). Written channels include letters, memorandums, purchase orders, invoices, newspaper and magazine articles, blogs, e-mail, text messages, tweets, and so forth.

Receiver

"The receiver receives the message from the source, analyzing and interpreting the message in ways both intended and unintended by the source." [7] To better understand this component, think of a receiver on a football team. The quarterback throws the football (message) to a receiver, who must see and interpret where to catch the ball. The quarterback may intend for the receiver to "catch" his message in one way, but the receiver may see things differently and miss the football (the intended meaning) altogether.

As a receiver you listen, see, touch, smell, and/or taste to receive a message. Your audience "sizes you up," much as you might check them out long before you take the stage or open your mouth. The nonverbal responses of your listeners can serve as clues on how to adjust your opening. By imagining yourself in their place, you anticipate what you would look for if you were them. Just as a quarterback plans where the receiver will be in order to place the ball correctly, you too can recognize the interaction between source and receiver in a business communication context. All of this happens at the same time, illustrating why and how communication is always changing.

Feedback

When you respond to the source, intentionally or unintentionally, you are giving feedback. Feedback is composed of messages the receiver sends back to the source. Verbal or nonverbal, all these feedback signals allow the source to see how well, how accurately (or how poorly and inaccurately) the message was received. Feedback also provides an opportunity for the receiver or audience to ask for clarification, to agree or disagree, or to indicate that the source could make the message more interesting. As the amount of feedback increases, the accuracy of communication also increases. [8]

For example, suppose you are a sales manager participating in a conference call with four sales reps. As the source, you want to tell the reps to take advantage of the fact that it is World Series season to close sales on baseball-related sports gear. You state your message, but you hear no replies from your listeners. You might assume that this means they understood and agreed with you, but later in the month you might be disappointed to find that very few sales were made. If you followed up your message with a request for feedback ("Does this make sense? Do any of you have any questions?") you might have an opportunity to clarify your message, and to find out whether any of the sales reps believed your suggestion would not work with their customers.

Environment

"The environment is the atmosphere, physical and psychological, where you send and receive messages." [9] The environment can include the tables, chairs, lighting, and sound equipment that are in the room. The room itself is an example of the environment. The environment can also include factors like formal dress, which may indicate whether a discussion is open and caring or more professional and formal. People may be more likely to have an intimate conversation when they are physically close to each other, and less likely when they can only see each other from across the room. In that case, they may text each other, itself an intimate form of communication. The choice to text is influenced by the environment. As a speaker, your environment will impact and play a role in your speech. It's always a good idea to go check out where you'll be speaking before the day of the actual presentation.

Context

"The context of the communication interaction involves the setting, scene, and expectations of the individuals involved." [10] A professional communication context may involve business suits (environmental cues) that directly or indirectly influence expectations of language and behavior among the participants.

A presentation or discussion does not take place as an isolated event. When you came to class, you came from somewhere. So did the person seated next to you, as did the instructor. The degree to which the environment is formal or informal depends on the contextual expectations for communication held by the participants. The person sitting next to you may be used to informal communication with instructors, but this particular instructor may be used to verbal and nonverbal displays of respect in the academic environment. You may be used to formal interactions with instructors as well, and find your classmate's question of "Hey Teacher, do we have homework today?" as rude and inconsiderate when they see it as normal. The nonverbal response from the instructor will certainly give you a clue about how they perceive the interaction, both the word choices and how they were said.

Context is all about what people expect from each other, and we often create those expectations out of environmental cues. Traditional gatherings like weddings or quinceañeras are often formal events. There is a time for quiet social greetings, a time for silence as the bride walks down the aisle, or the father may have the first dance with his daughter as she is transformed from a girl to womanhood in the eyes of her community. In either celebration there may come a time for rambunctious celebration and dancing. You may be called upon to give a toast, and the wedding or quinceañera context will influence your presentation, timing, and effectiveness.

In a business meeting, who speaks first? That probably has some relation to the position and role each person has outside the meeting. Context plays a very important role in communication, particularly across cultures.

Interference

Interference, also called noise, can come from any source. "Interference is anything that blocks or changes the source's intended meaning of the message." [11] For example, if you drove a car to work or school, chances are you were surrounded by noise. Car horns, billboards, or perhaps the radio in your car interrupted your thoughts, or your conversation with a passenger.

Psychological noise is what happens when your thoughts occupy your attention while you are hearing, or reading, a message. Imagine that it is 4:45 p.m. and your boss, who is at a meeting in another city, e-mails you asking for last month's sales figures, an analysis of current sales projections, and the sales figures from the same month for the past five years. You may open the e-mail, start to read, and think, "Great—no problem—I have those figures and that analysis right here in my computer." You fire off a reply with last month's sales figures and the current projections attached. Then, at five o'clock, you turn off your computer and go home. The next morning, your boss calls on the phone to tell you he was inconvenienced because you neglected to include the sales figures from the previous years. What was the problem? Interference: by thinking about how you wanted to respond to your boss's message, you prevented yourself from reading attentively enough to understand the whole message.

Interference can come from other sources, too. Perhaps you are hungry, and your attention to your current situation interferes with your ability to listen. Maybe the office is hot and stuffy. If you were a member of an audience listening to an executive speech, how could this impact your ability to listen and participate?

Noise interferes with normal encoding and decoding of the message carried by the channel between source and receiver. Not all noise is bad, but noise interferes with the communication process. For example, your cell phone ringtone may be a welcome noise to you, but it may interrupt the communication process in class and bother your classmates.

Two Models of Communication

Researchers have observed that when communication takes place, the source and the receiver may send messages at the same time, often overlapping. You, as the speaker, will often play both roles, as source and receiver. You'll focus on the communication and the reception of your messages to the audience. The audience will respond in the form of feedback that will give you important clues. While there are many models of communication, here we will focus on two that offer perspectives and lessons for business communicators. Rather than looking at the source sending a message and someone receiving it as two distinct acts, researchers often view communication as a transactional process (Figure 1.3 "Transactional Model of Communication"), with actions often happening at the same time. The distinction between source and receiver is blurred in conversational turn-taking, for example, where both participants play both roles simultaneously.

Figure 1.3 Transactional Model of Communication

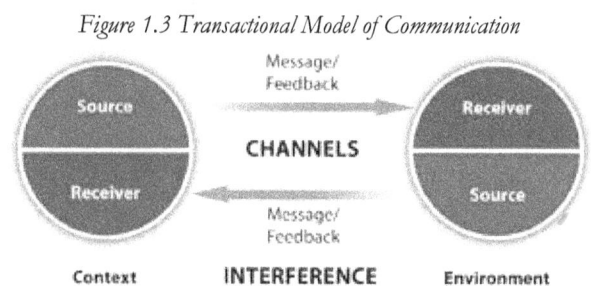

Researchers have also examined the idea that we all construct our own interpretations of the message. As the State Department quote at the beginning of this chapter indicates, what I said and what you heard may be different. In the constructivist model (Figure 1.4 "Constructivist Model of Communication"), we focus on the negotiated meaning, or common ground, when trying to describe communication. [12], [13]

Imagine that you are visiting Atlanta, Georgia, and go to a restaurant for dinner. When asked if you want a "Coke," you may reply, "sure." The waiter may then ask you again, "what kind?" and you may reply, "Coke is fine." The waiter then may ask a third time, "what kind of soft drink would you like?" The misunderstanding in this example is that in

Atlanta, the home of the Coca-Cola Company, most soft drinks are generically referred to as "Coke." When you order a soft drink, you need to specify what type, even if you wish to order a beverage that is not a cola or not even made by the Coca-Cola Company. To someone from other regions of the United States, the words "pop," "soda pop," or "soda" may be the familiar way to refer to a soft drink; not necessarily the brand "Coke." In this example, both you and the waiter understand the word "Coke," but you each understand it to mean something different. In order to communicate, you must each realize what the term means to the other person, and establish common ground, in order to fully understand the request and provide an answer.

Figure 1.4 Constructivist Model of Communication

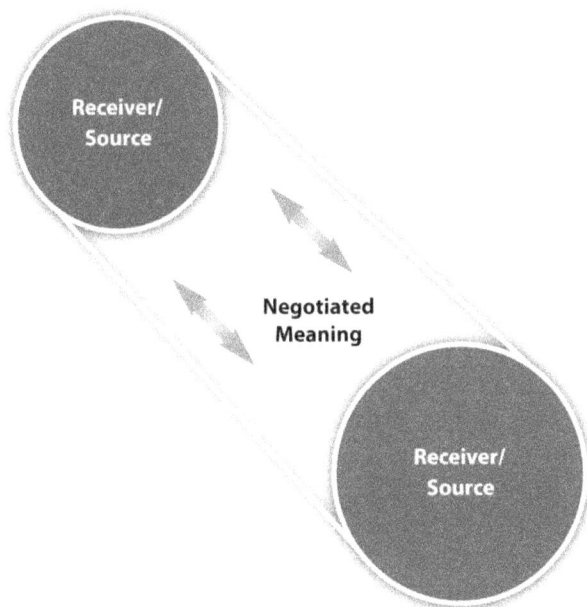

Because we carry the multiple meanings of words, gestures, and ideas within us, we can use a dictionary to guide us, but we will still need to negotiate meaning.

KEY TAKEAWAY

The communication process involves understanding, sharing, and meaning, and it consists of eight essential elements: source, message, channel, receiver, feedback, environment, context, and interference. Among the models of communication are the transactional process, in which actions happen simultaneously, and the constructivist model, which focuses on shared meaning.

EXERCISES

1. Draw what you think communication looks like. Share your drawing with your classmates.

2. List three environmental cues and indicate how they influence your expectations for communication. Please share your results with your classmates.

3. How does context influence your communication? Consider the language and culture people grew up with, and the role these play in communication styles.

4. If you could design the perfect date, what activities, places, and/or environmental cues would you include to set the mood? Please share your results with your classmates.

5. Observe two people talking. Describe their communication. See if you can find all eight components and provide an example for each one.

6. What assumptions are present in transactional model of communication? Find an example of a model of communication in your workplace or classroom, and provide an example for all eight components.

[1] Weekley, E. (1967). *An etymological dictionary of modern English* (Vol. 1, p. 338). New York, NY: Dover Publications.

[2] Pearson, J., & Nelson, P. (2000). *An introduction to human communication: Understanding and sharing* (p. 6). Boston, MA: McGraw-Hill.

[3] Pearson, J., & Nelson, P. (2000). *An introduction to human communication: Understanding and sharing.* Boston, MA: McGraw-Hill.

[4] McLean, S. (2003). *The basics of speech communication.* Boston, MA: Allyn & Bacon.

[5] McLean, S. (2005). *The basics of interpersonal communication* (p. 10). Boston, MA: Allyn & Bacon.

[6] McLean, S. (2005). *The basics of interpersonal communication* (p. 10). Boston, MA: Allyn & Bacon.

[7] McLean, S. (2005). *The basics of interpersonal communication* (p. 10). Boston, MA: Allyn & Bacon.

[8] Leavitt, H., & Mueller, R. (1951). Some effects of feedback on communication. *Human Relations, 4,* 401–410.

[9] McLean, S. (2005). *The basics of interpersonal communication* (p. 11). Boston, MA: Allyn & Bacon.

[10] McLean, S. (2005). *The basics of interpersonal communication* (p.11). Boston, MA: Allyn & Bacon.

[11] McLean, S. (2005). *The basics of interpersonal communication* (p. 11). Boston, MA: Allyn & Bacon.

[12] Pearce, W. B., & Cronen, V. (1980). *Communication, action, and meaning: The creating of social realities.* New York, NY: Praeger.

[13] Cronen, V., & Pearce, W. B. (1982). The coordinated management of meaning: A theory of communication. In F. E. Dance (Ed.), *Human communication theory* (pp. 61–89). New York, NY: Harper & Row.

1.3 Communication in Context
LEARNING OBJECTIVE

1. Identify and describe five types of communication contexts.

Now that we have examined the eight components of communication, let's examine this in context. Is a quiet dinner conversation with someone you care about the same experience as a discussion in class or giving a speech? Is sending a text message to a friend the same experience as writing a professional project proposal or a purchase order? Each context has an influence on the communication process. Contexts can overlap, creating an even more dynamic process. You have been communicating in many of these contexts across your lifetime, and you'll be able to apply what you've learned through experience in each context to business communication.

Intrapersonal Communication

Have you ever listened to a speech or lecture and gotten caught up in your thoughts so that, while the speaker continued, you were no longer listening? During a phone conversation, have you ever been thinking about what you are going to say, or what question you might ask, instead of listening to the other person? Finally, have you ever told yourself how you did after you wrote a document or gave a presentation? As you "talk with yourself" you are engaged in intrapersonal communication.

Intrapersonal communication involves one person; it is often called "self-talk." [1]Donna Vocate's [2] book on intrapersonal communication explains how, as we use language to reflect on our own experiences, we talk ourselves through situations. For example, the voice within you that tells you, "Keep on Going! I can DO IT!" when you are putting your all into completing a five-mile race; or that says, "This report I've written is pretty good." Your intrapersonal communication can be positive or negative, and directly influences how you perceive and react to situations and communication with others.

What you perceive in communication with others is also influenced by your culture, native language, and your world view. As the German philosopher Jürgen Habermas said, "Every process of reaching understanding takes place against the background of a culturally ingrained pre-understanding." [3]

For example, you may have certain expectations of time and punctuality. You weren't born with them, so where did you learn them? From those around you as you grew up. What was normal for them became normal for you, but not everyone's idea of normal is the same.

When your supervisor invites you to a meeting and says it will start at 7 p.m., does that mean 7:00 sharp, 7-ish, or even 7:30? In the business context, when a meeting is supposed to start at 9 a.m., is it promptly a 9 a.m.? Variations in time expectations depend on regional and national culture as well as individual corporate cultures. In some companies, everyone may be expected to arrive ten to fifteen minutes before the announced start time to take their seats and be ready to commence business at 9:00 sharp. In other companies, "meeting and greeting" from about 9 to 9:05 or even 9:10 is the norm. When you are unfamiliar with the expectations for a business event, it is always wise to err on the side of being punctual, regardless of what your internal assumptions about time and punctuality may be.

Interpersonal Communication

The second major context within the field of communication is interpersonal communication. Interpersonal communication normally involves two people, and can range from intimate and very personal to formal and impersonal. You may carry on a conversation with a loved one, sharing a serious concern. Later, at work, you may have a brief conversation about plans for the weekend with the security guard on your way home. What's the difference? Both scenarios involve interpersonal communication, but are different in levels of intimacy. The first example implies a trusting relationship established over time between two caring individuals. The second example level implies some previous familiarity, and is really more about acknowledging each other than any actual exchange of information, much like saying hello or goodbye.

Group Communication

Have you ever noticed how a small group of people in class sit near each other? Perhaps they are members of the same sports program, or just friends, but no doubt they often engage in group communication.

"Group communication is a dynamic process where a small number of people engage in a conversation." [4] Group communication is generally defined as involving three to eight people. The larger the group, the more likely it is to break down into smaller groups.

To take a page from marketing, does your audience have segments or any points of convergence/divergence? We could consider factors like age, education, sex, and location to learn more about groups and their general preferences as well as dislikes. You may find several groups within the larger audience, such as specific areas of education, and use this knowledge to increase your effectiveness as a business communicator.

Public Communication

In public communication, one person speaks to a group of people; the same is true of public written communication, where one person writes a message to be read by a small or large group. The speaker or writer may ask questions, and engage the audience in a discussion (in writing, examples are an e-mail discussion or a point-counter-point series of letters to the editor), but the dynamics of the conversation are distinct from group communication, where different rules apply. In a public speaking situation, the group normally defers to the speaker. For example, the boss speaks to everyone, and the sales team quietly listens without interruption.

This generalization is changing as norms and expectations change, and many cultures have a tradition of "call outs" or interjections that are not to be interpreted as interruptions or competition for the floor, but instead as affirmations. The boss may say, as part of a charged-up motivational speech, "Do you hear me?" and the sales team is expected to call back "Yes Sir!" The boss, as a public speaker, recognizes that intrapersonal communication (thoughts of the individual members) or interpersonal communication (communication between team members) may interfere with this classic public speaking dynamic of all to one, or the audience devoting all its attention to the speaker, and incorporate attention getting and engagement strategies to keep the sales team focused on the message.

Mass Communication

How do you tell everyone on campus where and when all the classes are held? Would a speech from the front steps work? Perhaps it might meet the need if your school is a very small one. A written schedule that lists all classes would be a better alternative. How do you let everyone know there is a sale on in your store, or that your new product will meet their needs, or that your position on a political issue is the same as your constituents? You send a message to as many people as you can through mass communication. Does everyone receive mass communication the same way the might receive a personal phone call? Not likely. Some people who receive mass mailings assume that they are "junk mail" (i.e., that they do not meet the recipients' needs) and throw them away unopened. People may tune out a television advertisement with a click of the mute button, delete tweets or ignore friend requests on Facebook by the hundreds, or send all unsolicited e-mail straight to the spam folder unread.

Mass media is a powerful force in modern society and our daily lives, and is adapting rapidly to new technologies. Mass communication involves sending a single message to a group. It allows us to communicate our message to a large number of people, but we are limited in our ability to tailor our message to specific audiences, groups, or individuals. As a business communicator, you can use multimedia as a visual aid or reference common programs, films, or other images that your audience finds familiar yet engaging. You can tweet a picture that is worth far more than 140 characters, and you are just as likely to elicit a significant response. By choosing messages or references that many audience members will recognize or can identify with, you can develop common ground and increase the appeal of your message.

Communication contexts include intrapersonal, interpersonal, group, public, and mass communication. Each context has its advantages and disadvantages, and its appropriate and inappropriate uses.

EXERCISES

1. Please recall a time when you gave a speech in front of a group. How did you feel? What was your experience? What did you learn from your experience?
2. If you were asked to get the attention of your peers, what image or word would you choose and why?
3. If you were asked to get the attention of someone like yourself, what image or word would you choose and why?
4. Make a list of mass communication messages you observe for a one hour period of time. Share your list with classmates.

[1] Wood, J. (1997). *Communication in our lives* (p. 22). Boston, MA: Wadsworth.
[2] Vocate, D. (Ed.). (1994). *Intrapersonal communication: Different voices, different minds.* Hillsdale, NJ: Lawrence Erlbaum.
[3] Habermas, J. (1984). *The theory of communicative action* (Vol. 1, p. 100). Boston, MA: Beacon Press.
[4] McLean, S. (2005). *The basics of interpersonal communication* (p. 14). Boston, MA: Allyn & Bacon.

1.4 Your Responsibilities as a Communicator
LEARNING OBJECTIVE

1. Discuss and provide several examples of each of the two main responsibilities of a business communicator.

Whenever you speak or write in a business environment, you have certain responsibilities to your audience, your employer, and your profession. Your audience comes to you with an inherent set of expectations that you will fulfill these responsibilities. The specific expectations may change given the context or environment, but two central ideas will remain: be prepared, and be ethical.

Communicator Is Prepared

As the business communicator's first responsibility, preparation includes several facets which we will examine: organization, clarity, and being concise and punctual.

Being prepared means that you have selected a topic appropriate to your audience, gathered enough information to cover the topic well, put your information into a logical sequence, and considered how best to present it. If your communication is a written one, you have written an outline and at least one rough draft, read it over to improve your writing and correct errors, and sought feedback where appropriate. If your communication is oral, you have practiced several times before your actual performance.

The Prepared Communicator Is Organized

Part of being prepared is being organized. Aristotle called this *logos*, or logic, and it involves the steps or points that lead your communication to a conclusion. Once you've invested time in researching your topic, you will want to narrow your focus to a few key points and consider how you'll present them. On any given topic there is a wealth of information; your job is to narrow that content down to a manageable level, serving the role of gatekeeper by selecting some information and "de-selecting," or choosing to not include other points or ideas.

You also need to consider how to link your main points together for your audience. Use transitions to provide signposts or cues for your audience to follow along. "Now that we've examined X, let's consider Y" is a transitional statement that provides a cue that you are moving from topic to topic. Your listeners or readers will appreciate your being well organized so that they can follow your message from point to point.

The Prepared Communicator Is Clear

You have probably had the unhappy experience of reading or listening to a communication that was vague and wandering. Part of being prepared is being clear. If your message is unclear, the audience will lose interest and tune you out, bringing an end to effective communication.

Interestingly, clarity begins with intrapersonal communication: you need to have a clear idea in your mind of what you want to say before you can say it clearly to someone else. At the interpersonal level, clarity involves considering your audience, as you will want to choose words and phrases they understand and avoid jargon or slang that may be unfamiliar to them.

Clarity also involves presentation. A brilliant message scrawled in illegible handwriting, or in pale gray type on gray paper, will not be clear. When it comes to oral communication, if you mumble your words, speak too quickly or use a monotonous tone of voice, or stumble over

certain words or phrases, the clarity of your presentation will suffer.

Technology also plays a part; if you are using a microphone or conducting a teleconference, clarity will depend on this equipment functioning properly—which brings us back to the importance of preparation. In this case, in addition to preparing your speech, you need to prepare by testing the equipment ahead of time.

The Prepared Communicator Is Concise and Punctual

Concise means brief and to the point. In most business communications you are expected to "get down to business" right away. Being prepared includes being able to state your points clearly and support them with clear evidence in a relatively straightforward, linear way.

It may be tempting to show how much you know by incorporating additional information into your document or speech, but in so doing you run the risk of boring, confusing, or overloading your audience. Talking in circles or indulging in tangents, where you get off topic or go too deep, can hinder an audience's ability to grasp your message. Be to the point and concise in your choice of words, organization, and even visual aids.

Being concise also involves being sensitive to time constraints. How many times have you listened to a speaker say "in conclusion" only to continue speaking for what seems like forever? How many meetings and conference calls have you attended that got started late or ran beyond the planned ending time? The solution, of course, is to be prepared to be punctual. If you are asked to give a five-minute presentation at a meeting, your coworkers will not appreciate your taking fifteen minutes, any more than your supervisor would appreciate your submitting a fifteen-page report when you were asked to write five pages. For oral presentations, time yourself when you rehearse and make sure you can deliver your message within the allotted number of minutes.

There is one possible exception to this principle. Many non-Western cultures prefer a less direct approach, where business communication often begins with social or general comments that a U.S. audience might consider unnecessary. Some cultures also have a less strict interpretation of time schedules and punctuality. While it is important to recognize that different cultures have different expectations, the general rule holds true that good business communication does not waste words or time.

Communicator Is Ethical

The business communicator's second fundamental responsibility is to be ethical. Ethics refers to a set of principles or rules for correct conduct. It echoes what Aristotle called *ethos*, the communicator's good character and reputation for doing what is right. Communicating ethically involves being egalitarian, respectful, and trustworthy—overall, practicing the "golden rule" of treating your audience the way you would want to be treated.

Communication can move communities, influence cultures, and change history. It can motivate people to take stand, consider an argument, or purchase a product. The degree to which you consider both the common good and fundamental principles you hold to be true when crafting your message directly relates to how your message will affect others.

The Ethical Communicator Is Egalitarian

The word "egalitarian" comes from the root "equal." To be egalitarian is to believe in basic equality: that all people should share equally in the benefits and burdens of a society. It means that everyone is entitled to the same respect, expectations, access to information, and rewards of participation in a group.

To communicate in an egalitarian manner, speak and write in a way that is comprehensible and relevant to all your listeners or readers, not just those who are "like you" in terms of age, gender, race or ethnicity, or other characteristics.

In business, you will often communicate to people with certain professional qualifications. For example, you may draft a memo addressed to all the nurses in a certain hospital, or give a speech to all the adjusters in a certain branch of an insurance company. Being egalitarian does not mean you have to avoid professional terminology that is understood by nurses or insurance adjusters. But it does mean that your hospital letter should be worded for all the hospital's nurses—not just female nurses, not just nurses working directly with patients, not just nurses under age fifty-five. An egalitarian communicator seeks to unify the audience by using ideas and language that are appropriate for all the message's readers or listeners.

The Ethical Communicator Is Respectful

People are influenced by emotions as well as logic. Aristotle named *pathos*, or passion, enthusiasm and energy, as the third of his three important parts of communicating after *logos* and *ethos*.

Most of us have probably seen an audience manipulated by a "cult of personality," believing whatever the speaker said simply because of how dramatically he or she delivered a speech; by being manipulative, the speaker fails to respect the audience. We may have also seen people hurt by sarcasm, insults, and other disrespectful forms of communication.

This does not mean that passion and enthusiasm are out of place in business communication. Indeed, they are very important. You can hardly expect your audience to care about your message if you don't show that you care about it yourself. If your topic is worth writing or speaking about, make an effort to show your audience why it is worthwhile by speaking enthusiastically or using a dynamic writing style. Doing so, in fact, shows respect for their time and their intelligence.

However, the ethical communicator will be passionate and enthusiastic without being disrespectful. Losing one's temper and being abusive are generally regarded as showing a lack of professionalism (and could even involve legal consequences for you or your employer). When you disagree strongly with a coworker, feel deeply annoyed with a difficult customer, or find serious fault with a competitor's product, it is important to express such sentiments respectfully. For example, instead of telling a customer, "I've had it with your complaints!" a respectful business communicator might say, "I'm having trouble seeing how I can fix this situation. Would you explain to me what you want to see happen?"

The Ethical Communicator Is Trustworthy

Trust is a key component in communication, and this is especially true in business. As a consumer, would you choose to buy merchandise from a company you did not trust? If you were an employer, would you hire someone you did not trust? Your goal as a communicator is to build a healthy relationship with your audience, and to do that you must show them why they can trust you and why the information you are about to give them is believable. One way to do this is to begin your message by providing some information about your qualifications and background, your interest in the topic, or your reasons for communicating at this particular time.

Your audience will expect that what you say is the truth as you understand it. This means that you have not intentionally omitted, deleted, or taken information out of context simply to prove your points. They will listen to what you say and how you say it, but also to what you don't say or do. You may consider more than one perspective on your topic, and then select the perspective you perceive to be correct, giving concrete reasons why you came to this conclusion. People in the audience may have considered or believe in some of the perspectives you consider, and your attention to them will indicate you have done your homework.

Being worthy of trust is something you earn with an audience. Many wise people have observed that trust is hard to build but easy to lose. A communicator may not know something and still be trustworthy, but it's a violation of trust to pretend you know something when you don't. Communicate what you know, and if you don't know something, research it before you speak or write. If you are asked a question to which you don't know the answer, say "I don't know the answer but I will research it and get back to you" (and then make sure you follow through later). This will go over much better with the audience than trying to cover by stumbling through an answer or portraying yourself as knowledgeable on an issue that you are not.

The "Golden Rule"

When in doubt, remember the "golden rule," which says to treat others the way you would like to be treated. In all its many forms, the golden rule incorporates human kindness, cooperation, and reciprocity across cultures, languages, backgrounds and interests. Regardless of where you travel, who you communicate with, or what your audience is like, remember how you would feel if you were on the receiving end of your communication, and act accordingly.

KEY TAKEAWAY

As a communicator, you are responsible for being prepared and being ethical. Being prepared includes being organized, clear, concise, and punctual. Being ethical includes being egalitarian, respectful, and trustworthy and overall, practicing the "golden rule."

EXERCISES

1. Recall one time you felt offended or insulted in a conversation. What contributed to your perception? Please share your comments with classmates.
2. When someone lost your trust, were they able earn it back? Please share your comments with classmates?
3. Does the communicator have a responsibility to the audience? Does the audience have a responsibility to the speaker? Why or why not? Please share your comments with classmates.

1.5 Additional Resources

- The International Association of Business Communicators (IABC) is a global network of communication professionals committed to improving organizational effectiveness through strategic communication. http://www.iabc.com
- Explore the Web site of the National Communication Association, the largest U.S. organization dedicated to communication. http://www.natcom.org
- Read The National Commission on Writing's findings about the importance of communication skills in business. http://www.writingcommission.org/pr/writing_for_employ.html
- The National Association of Colleges and Employers offers news about employment prospects for college graduates. http://www.naceweb.org
- Dale Carnegie, author of the classic *How to Win Friends and Influence People*, may have been one of the greatest communicators of the twentieth-century business world. The Dale Carnegie Institute focuses on giving people in business the opportunity to sharpen their skills and improve their performance in order to build positive, steady, and profitable results. http://www.dalecarnegie.com
- Purdue University's Online Writing Lab (OWL) provides a wealth of resources for writing projects. http://owl.english.purdue.edu
- To communicate ethically, check your facts. FactCheck is a nonpartisan project of the Annenberg Center for Public Policy at the University of Pennsylvania. http://www.factcheck.org
- To communicate ethically, check your facts. PolitiFact is a nonpartisan project of the St. Petersburg Times; it won a Pulitzer Prize in 2009. http://www.politifact.com

NOTES:

Chapter 2:
Delivering Your Message

Good communication is as stimulating as black coffee and just as hard to sleep after.

Anne Morrow Lindbergh

The meanings of words are not in the words; they are in us.

S. I. Hayakawa

Getting Started

INTRODUCTORY EXERCISES

1. Can you match the words to their meaning?

____ 1. phat	A. Weird, strange, unfair, or not acceptable
____ 2. dis	B. Something stupid or thoughtless, deserving correction
____ 3. wack	C. Excellent, together, cool
____ 4. smack	D. Old car, generally in poor but serviceable condition
____ 5. down	E. Insult, put down, to dishonor, to display disrespect
____ 6. hooptie	F. Get out or leave quickly
____ 7. my bad	G. Cool, very interesting, fantastic or amazing
____ 8. player	H. To be in agreement
____ 9. tight	I. Personal mistake
____ 10. jet	J. Person dating with multiple partners, often unaware of each other

2. Do people use the same language in all settings and contexts? Your first answer might be "sure," but try this test. For a couple of hours, or even a day, pay attention to how you speak, and how others speak: the words you say, how you say them, the pacing and timing used in each context. For example, at home in the morning, in the coffee shop before work or class, during a break at work with peers or a break between classes with classmates all count as contexts. Observe how and what language is used in each context and to what degree they are the same or different.

Answers

1. 1-C, 2-E, 3-A, 4-B, 5-H, 6-D, 7-I, 8-J, 9-G, 10-F

Successful business communication is often associated with writing and speaking well, being articulate or proficient with words. Yet, in the quote above, the famous linguist S. I. Hayakawa wisely observes that meaning lies within us, not in the words we use. Indeed, communication in this text is defined as the process of understanding and sharing meaning.[1] When you communicate you are sharing meaning with one or more other people—this may include members of your family, your community, your work community, your school, or any group that considers itself a group.

How do you communicate? How do you think? We use language as a system to create and exchange meaning with one another, and the types of words we use influence both our perceptions and others interpretation of our meanings. What kinds of words would you use to describe your thoughts and feelings, your preferences in music, cars, food, or other things that matter to you?

Imagine that you are using written or spoken language to create a bridge over which you hope to transport meaning, much like a gift or package, to your receiver. You hope that your meaning arrives relatively intact, so that your receiver receives something like what you sent. Will the package look the same to them on the receiving end? Will they interpret the package, its wrapping and colors, the way you intended? That depends.

What is certain is that they will interpret it based on their framework of experience. The package represents your words arranged in a pattern that both the source (you) and the receiver (your audience) can interpret. The words as a package try to contain the meaning and deliver it intact, but they themselves are not the meaning. That lies within us.

So is the package empty? Are the words we use empty? Without us to give them life and meaning, the answer is yes. Knowing what words will correspond to meanings that your audience holds within themselves will help you communicate more effectively. Knowing what meanings lie within you is your door to understanding yourself.

This chapter discusses the importance of delivering your message in words. It examines how the characteristics of language interact in ways that can both improve and diminish effective business communication. We will examine how language plays a significant role in how you perceive and interact with the world, and how culture, language, education, gender, race, and ethnicity all influence this dynamic process. We will look at ways to avoid miscommunication and focus on constructive ways to get your message delivered to your receiver with the meaning you intended.

[1] Pearson, J., & Nelson, P. (2000). *An introduction to human communication: Understanding and sharing.* Boston, MA: McGraw-Hill.

2.1 What Is Language?
LEARNING OBJECTIVES

1. Describe and define "language."
2. Describe the role of language in perception and the communication process.

Are you reading this sentence? Does it make sense to you? When you read the words I wrote, what do you hear? A voice in your head? Words across the internal screen of your mind? If it makes sense, then you may very well hear the voice of the author as you read along, finding meaning in these arbitrary symbols packaged in discrete units called words. The words themselves have no meaning except that which you give them.

For example, I'll write the word "home," placing it in quotation marks to denote its separation from the rest of this sentence. When you read that word, what comes to mind for you? A specific place? Perhaps a building that could also be called a house? Images of people or another time? "Home," like "love" and many other words, is quite individual and open to interpretation.

Still, even though your mental image of home may be quite distinct from mine, we can communicate effectively. You understand that each sentence has a subject and verb, and a certain pattern of word order, even though you might not be consciously aware of that knowledge. You weren't born speaking or writing, but you mastered—or, more accurately, are still mastering as we all are—these important skills of self-expression. The family, group, or community wherein you were raised taught you the code. The code came in many forms. When do you say "please" or "thank you," and when do you remain silent? When is it appropriate to communicate? If it is appropriate, what are the expectations and how do you accomplish it? You know because you understand the code.

We often call this code "language": a system of symbols, words, and/or gestures used to communicate meaning. Does everyone on earth speak the same language? Obviously, no. People are raised in different cultures, with different values, beliefs, customs, and different languages to express those cultural attributes. Even people who speak the same language, like speakers of English in London, New Delhi, or Cleveland, speak and interact using their own words that are community-defined, self-defined, and have room for interpretation. Within the United States, depending on the context and environment, you may hear colorful sayings that are quite regional, and may notice an accent, pace, or tone of communication that is distinct from your own. This variation in our use of language is a creative way to form relationships and communities, but can also lead to miscommunication.

Words themselves, then, actually hold no meaning. It takes you and me to use them to give them life and purpose. Even if we say that the dictionary is the repository of meaning, the repository itself has no meaning without you or me to read, interpret, and use its contents. Words change meaning over time. "Nice" once meant overly particular or fastidious; today it means pleasant or agreeable. "Gay" once meant happy or carefree; today it refers to homosexuality. The dictionary entry for the meaning of a word changes because we change how, when, and why we use the word, not the other way around. Do you know every word in the dictionary? Does anyone? Even if someone did, there are many possible meanings of the words we exchange, and these multiple meanings can lead to miscommunication.

Business communication veterans often tell the story of a company that received an order of machine parts from a new vendor. When they opened the shipment, they found that it contained a small plastic bag into which the vendor had put several of the parts. When asked what the bag was for, the vendor explained, "Your contract stated a thousand units, with maximum 2 percent defective. We produced the defective units and put them in the bag for you." If you were the one reading that contract, what would "defective" mean to you? We may use a word intending to communicate one idea only to have a coworker miss our meaning entirely.

Sometimes we want our meaning to be crystal clear, and at other times, less so. We may even want to present an idea from a specific perspective, one that shows our company or business in a positive light. This may reflect our intentional manipulation of language to influence meaning, as in choosing to describe a car as "preowned" or an investment as a "unique value proposition." We may also influence other's understanding of our words in unintentional ways, from failing to anticipate their response, to ignoring the possible impact of our word choice.

Languages are living exchange systems of meaning, and are bound by context. If you are assigned to a team that coordinates with suppliers from Shanghai, China, and a sales staff in Dubuque, Iowa, you may encounter terms from both groups that influence your team.

As long as there have been languages and interactions between the people who speak them, languages have borrowed words (or, more accurately, adopted—for they seldom give them back). Think of the words "boomerang," "limousine," or "pajama"; do you know which languages they come from? Did you know that "algebra" comes from the Arabic word "al-jabr," meaning "restoration"?

Does the word "moco" make sense to you? It may not, but perhaps you recognize it as the name chosen by Nissan for one of its cars. "Moco" makes sense to both Japanese and Spanish speakers, but with quite different meanings. The letters come together to form an arbitrary word that refers to the thought or idea of the thing in the semantic triangle (see Figure 2.9).

Figure 2.1 Semantic Triangle

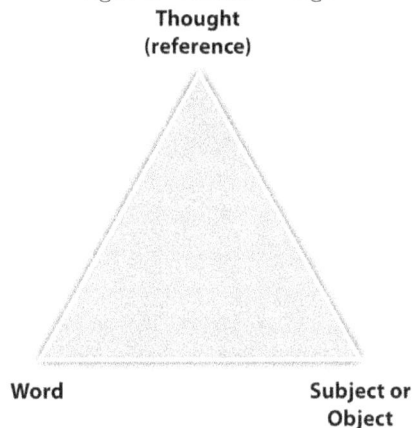

**Thought
(reference)**

Word   **Subject or
Object**

Source: Adapted from Ogden and Richards. [1]

This triangle illustrates how the word (which is really nothing more than a combination of four letters) refers to the thought, which then refers to the thing itself. Who decides what "moco" means? To the Japanese, it may mean "cool design," or even "best friend," and may be an apt name for a small, cute car, but to a Spanish speaker, it means "booger" or "snot"—not a very appealing name for a car.

Each letter stands for a sound, and when they come together in a specific way, the sounds they represent when spoken express the "word" that symbolizes the event. [2] For our discussion, the key word we need to address is "symbolizes." The word stands in for the actual event, but is not the thing itself. The meaning we associate with it may not be what we intended. For example, when Honda was contemplating the introduction of the Honda Fit, another small car, they considered the name "Fitta" for use in Europe. As the story

goes, the Swedish Division Office of Honda explained that "fitta" in Swedish is a derogatory term for female reproductive organ. The name was promptly changed to "Jazz."

The meaning, according to Hayakawa, [3] is within us, and the word serves as a link to meaning. What will your words represent to the listener? Will your use of a professional term enhance your credibility and be more precise with a knowledgeable audience, or will you confuse them?

KEY TAKEAWAY

Language is a system of words used as symbols to convey ideas, and it has rules of syntax, semantics, and context. Words have meaning only when interpreted by the receiver of the message.

EXERCISES

1. Using a dictionary that gives word origins, such as the *American Heritage College Dictionary*, *Merriam-Webster's Collegiate Dictionary*, or the *New Oxford American Dictionary*, find at least ten English words borrowed from other languages. Share your findings with your classmates.
2. Visit several English-language Web sites from different countries—for example, Australia, Canada, and the United States. What differences in spelling and word usage do you find? Discuss your results with your classmates.
3. From your viewpoint, how do you think thought influences the use of language? Write a one- to two-page explanation.
4. What is meant by *conditioned* in this statement: "people in Western cultures do not realize the extent to which their racial attitudes have been conditioned since early childhood by the power of words to ennoble or condemn, augment or detract, glorify or demean?" [4] Discuss your thoughts with a classmate.
5. Translations gone wrong can teach us much about words and meaning. Can you think of a word or phrase that just doesn't sound right when it was translated from English into another language, or vice versa? Share it with the class and discuss what a better translation would be.

[1] Odgen, C., & Richards, I. (1932). *The meaning of meaning: A study of the influence of language upon thought and of the science of symbolism.* New York, NY: Harcourt Brace & World.

[2] McLean, S. (2003). *The basics of speech communication.* Boston, MA: Allyn & Bacon.

[3] Hayakawa, S. I. (1978). *Language in thought and action.* Orlando, FL: Harcourt Brace Jovanovich.

[4] Moore, R. (2003). *Racism in the English language.* Boston, MA: Allyn & Bacon.

2.2 Messages
LEARNING OBJECTIVES

1. Describe three different types of messages and their functions.
2. Describe five different parts of a message and their functions.

Before we explore the principles of language, it will be helpful to stop for a moment and examine some characteristics of the messages we send when we communicate. When you write or say something, you not only share the meaning(s) associated with the words you choose, but you also say something about yourself and your relationship to the intended recipient. In addition, you say something about what the relationship means to you as well as your assumed familiarity as you choose formal or informal ways of expressing yourself. Your message may also carry unintended meanings that you cannot completely anticipate. Some words are loaded with meaning for some people, so that by using such words you can "push their buttons" without even realizing what you've done. Messages carry far more than the literal meaning of each word, and in this section we explore that complexity.

Primary Message Is Not the Whole Message
When considering how to effectively use verbal communication, keep in mind there are three distinct types of messages you will be communicating: primary, secondary, and auxiliary. [1]

Primary messages refer to the intentional content, both verbal and nonverbal. These are the words or ways you choose to express yourself and communicate your message. For example, if you are sitting at your desk and a coworker stops by to ask you a question, you may say, "Here, have a seat." These words are your primary message.

Even such a short, seemingly simple and direct message could be misunderstood. It may seem obvious that you are not literally offering to "give" a "seat" to your visitor, but to someone who knows only formal English and is unfamiliar with colloquial expressions, it may be puzzling. "Have a seat" may be much more difficult to understand than "please sit down."

Secondary messages refer to the unintentional content, both verbal and nonverbal. Your audience will form impressions of your intentional messages, both negative and positive, over which you have no control. Perceptions of physical attractiveness, age, gender, or ethnicity or even simple mannerisms and patterns of speech may unintentionally influence the message.

Perhaps, out of courtesy, you stand up while offering your visitor a seat; or perhaps your visitor has an expectation that you ought to do so. Perhaps a photograph of your family on your desk makes an impression on your visitor. Perhaps a cartoon on your bulletin board sends a message.

Auxiliary messages refer to the intentional and unintentional ways a primary message is communicated. This may include vocal inflection, gestures and posture, or rate of speech that influence the interpretation or perception of your message.

When you say, "Here, have a seat," do you smile and wave your hand to indicate the empty chair on the other side of your desk? Or do you look flustered and quickly lift a pile of file folders out of the way? Are your eyes on your computer as you finish sending an e-mail before turning your attention to your visitor? Your auxiliary message might be, "I'm glad you came by, I always enjoy exchanging ideas with you" or "I always learn something new when someone asks me a question." On the other hand, it might be, "I'll answer your question, but I'm too busy for a long discussion," or maybe even, "I wish you'd do your work and not bother me with your dumb questions!"

Parts of a Message
When you create a message, it is often helpful to think of it as having five parts:
1. Attention statement
2. Introduction
3. Body
4. Conclusion
5. Residual message
Each of these parts has its own function.

The attention statement, as you may guess, is used to capture the attention of your audience. While it may be used anywhere in your message, it is especially useful at the outset. There are many ways to attract attention from readers or listeners, but one of the most effective is the "what's in it for me" strategy: telling them how your message can benefit them. An attention statement like, "I'm going to explain how you can save up to $500 a year on car insurance" is quite likely to hold an audience's attention.

Once you have your audience's attention, it is time to move on to the introduction. In your introduction you will make a clear statement your topic; this is also the time to establish a relationship with your audience. One way to do this is to create common ground with the audience, drawing on familiar or shared experiences, or by referring to the person who introduced you. You may also explain why you chose to convey this message at this time, why the topic is important to you, what kind of expertise you have, or how your personal experience has led you to share this message.

After the introduction comes the body of your message. Here you will present your message in detail, using any of a variety of organizational structures. Regardless of the type of organization you choose for your document or speech, it is important to make your main points clear, provide support for each point, and use transitions to guide your readers or listeners from one point to the next.

At the end of the message, your conclusion should provide the audience with a sense of closure by summarizing your main points and relating them to the overall topic. In one sense, it is important to focus on your organizational structure again and incorporate the main elements into your summary, reminding the audience of what you have covered. In another sense, it is important not to merely state your list of main points again, but to convey a sense that you have accomplished what you stated you would do in your introduction, allowing the audience to have psychological closure.

The residual message, a message or thought that stays with your audience well after the communication is finished, is an important part of your message. Ask yourself of the following:

- What do I want my listeners or readers to remember?
- What information do I want to have the audience retain or act upon?
- What do I want the audience to do?

KEY TAKEAWAY

Messages are primary, secondary, and auxiliary. A message can be divided into a five-part structure composed of an attention statement, introduction, body, conclusion, and residual message.

EXERCISES

1. Choose three examples of communication and identify the primary message. Share and compare with classmates.
2. Choose three examples of communication and identify the auxiliary message(s). Share and compare with classmates.
3. Think of a time when someone said something like "please take a seat" and you correctly or incorrectly interpreted the message as indicating that you were in trouble and about to be reprimanded. Share and compare with classmates.
4. How does language affect self-concept? Explore and research your answer, finding examples that can serve as case studies.
5. Choose an article or opinion piece from a major newspaper or news Web site. Analyze the piece according to the five-part structure described here. Does the headline serve as a good attention statement? Does the piece conclude with a sense of closure? How are the main points presented and supported? Share your analysis with your classmates. For a further challenge, watch a television commercial and do the same analysis.

---

[1] Hasling, J. (1998). *Audience, message, speaker.* Boston, MA: McGraw-Hill.

2.3 Principles of Verbal Communication
LEARNING OBJECTIVE

1. Identify and describe five key principles of verbal communication.
2. Explain how the rules of syntax, semantics, and context govern language.
3. Describe how language serves to shape our experience of reality.

Verbal communication is based on several basic principles. In this section, we'll examine each principle and explore how it influences everyday communication. Whether it's a simple conversation with a coworker or a formal sales presentation to a board of directors, these principles apply to all contexts of communication.

Language Has Rules
Language is a code, a collection of symbols, letters, or words with arbitrary meanings that are arranged according to the rules of syntax and are used to communicate. [1]

In the first of the Note 2.1 "Introductory Exercises" for this chapter, were you able to successfully match the terms to their meanings? Did you find that some of the definitions did not match your understanding of the terms? The words themselves have meaning within their specific context or language community. But without a grasp of that context, "my bad" may have just sounded odd. Your familiarity with the words and phrases may have made the exercise easy for you, but it isn't an easy exercise for everyone. The words themselves only carry meaning if you know the understood meaning and have a grasp of their context to interpret them correctly.

There are three types of rules that govern or control our use of words. You may not be aware that they exist or that they influence you, but from the moment you put a word into text or speak it, these rules govern your communications. Think of a word that is all right to use in certain situations and not in others. Why? And how do you know?

Syntactic rules govern the order of words in a sentence. In some languages, such as German, syntax or word order is strictly prescribed. English syntax, in contrast, is relatively flexible and open to style. Still, there are definite combinations of words that are correct and incorrect in English. It is equally correct to say, "Please come to the meeting in the auditorium at twelve noon on Wednesday" or, "Please come to the meeting on Wednesday at twelve noon in the auditorium." But it would be incorrect to say, "Please to the auditorium on Wednesday in the meeting at twelve noon come."

Semantic rules govern the meaning of words and how to interpret them. [2] Semantics is the study of meaning in language. It considers what words mean, or are intended to mean, as opposed to their sound, spelling, grammatical function, and so on. Does a given statement refer to other statements already communicated? Is the statement true or false? Does it carry a certain intent? What does the sender or receiver need to know in order to understand its meaning? These are questions addressed by semantic rules.

Contextual rules govern meaning and word choice according to context and social custom. For example, suppose Greg is talking about his coworker, Carol, and says, "She always meets her deadlines." This may seem like a straightforward statement that would not vary according to context or social custom. But suppose another coworker asked Greg, "How do you like working with Carol?" and, after a long pause, Greg answered, "She always meets her deadlines." Are there factors in the context of the question or social customs that would influence the meaning of Greg's statement?

Even when we follow these linguistic rules, miscommunication is possible, for our cultural context or community may hold different meanings for the words used than the source intended. Words attempt to represent the ideas we want to communicate, but they are sometimes limited by factors beyond our control. They often require us to negotiate their meaning, or to explain what we mean in more than one way, in order to create a common vocabulary. You may need to state a word, define it, and provide an example in order to come to an understanding with your audience about the meaning of your message.

Our Reality Is Shaped by Our Language

What would your life be like if you had been raised in a country other than the one where you grew up? Malaysia, for example? Italy? Afghanistan? Or Bolivia? Or suppose you had been born male instead of female, or vice versa. Or had been raised in the northeastern United States instead of the Southwest, or the Midwest instead of the Southeast. In any of these cases, you would not have the same identity you have today. You would have learned another set of customs, values, traditions, other language patterns, and ways of communicating. You would be a different person who communicated in different ways.

You didn't choose your birth, customs, values, traditions, or your language. You didn't even choose to learn to read this sentence or to speak with those of your community, but somehow you accomplished this challenging task. As an adult, you can choose to see things from a new or diverse perspective, but what language do you think with? It's not just the words themselves, or even how they are organized, that makes communication such a challenge. Your language itself, ever changing and growing, in many ways determines your reality. [3] You can't escape your language or culture completely, and always see the world through a shade or tint of what you've been taught, learned, or experienced.

Suppose you were raised in a culture that values formality. At work, you pride yourself on being well dressed. It's part of your expectation for yourself and, whether you admit it or not, for others. Many people in your organization, however, come from less formal cultures, and they prefer business casual attire. You may be able to recognize the difference, and because humans are highly adaptable, you may get used to a less formal dress expectation, but it won't change your fundamental values.

Thomas Kuhn [4] makes the point that "paradigms, or a clear point of view involving theories, laws, and/or generalizations that provide a framework for understanding, tend to form and become set around key validity claims, or statements of the way things work." [5]The paradigm, or worldview, may be individual or collective. And paradigm shifts are often painful. New ideas are always suspect, and usually opposed, without any other reason than because they are not already common. [6]

As an example, consider the earth-heavens paradigm. Medieval Europeans believed that the Earth was flat and that the edge was to be avoided, otherwise you might fall off. For centuries after the acceptance of a "round earth" belief, the earth was still believed to be the center of the universe, with the sun and all planets revolving around it. Eventually, someone challenged the accepted view. Over time, despite considerable resistance to protect the status quo, people came to better understand the earth and its relationship to the heavens.

In the same way, the makers of the Intel microprocessor once thought that a slight calculation error, unlikely to negatively impact 99.9 percent of users, was better left as is and hidden. [7] Like many things in the information age, the error was discovered by a user of the product, became publicly known, and damaged Intel's credibility and sales for years. Recalls and prompt, public communication in response to similar issues are now the industry-wide protocol.

Paradigms involve premises that are taken as fact. Of course the Earth is the center of the universe, of course no one will ever be impacted by a mathematical error so far removed from most people's everyday use of computers, and of course you never danced the macarena at a company party. We now can see how those facts, attitudes, beliefs, and ideas of "cool" are overturned.

How does this insight lend itself to your understanding of verbal communication? Do all people share the same paradigms, words, or ideas? Will you be presenting ideas outside your audience's frame of reference? Outside their worldview? Just as you look back at your macarena performance, get outside your frame of reference and consider how to best communicate your thoughts, ideas, and points to an audience that may not have your same experiences or understanding of the topic.

By taking into account your audience's background and experience, you can become more "other-oriented," a successful strategy to narrow the gap between you and your audience. Our experiences are like sunglasses, tinting the way we see the world. Our challenge, perhaps, is to avoid letting them function as blinders, like those worn by working horses, which create tunnel vision and limit our perspective.

Language Is Arbitrary and Symbolic
As we have discussed previously, words, by themselves, do not have any inherent meaning. Humans give meaning to them, and their meanings change across time. The arbitrary symbols, including letters, numbers, and punctuation marks, stand for concepts in our experience. We have to negotiate the meaning of the word "home," and define it, through visual images or dialogue, in order to communicate with our audience.

Words have two types of meanings: denotative and connotative. Attention to both is necessary to reduce the possibility of misinterpretation. The denotative meaning is the common meaning, often found in the dictionary. The connotative meaning is often not found in the dictionary but in the community of users itself. It can involve an emotional association with a word, positive or negative, and can be individual or collective, but is not universal.

With a common vocabulary in both denotative and connotative terms, effective communication becomes a more distinct possibility. But what if we have to transfer meaning from one vocabulary to another? That is essentially what we are doing when we translate a message. In such cases, language and culture can sometimes make for interesting twists. The *New York Times* [8] noted that the title of the 1998 film *There's Something About Mary* proved difficult to translate when it was released in foreign markets. The movie was renamed to capture the idea and to adapt to local audiences' frame of reference: In Poland, where blonde jokes are popular and common, the film title (translated back to English for our use) was *For the Love of a Blonde*. In France, *Mary at All Costs* communicated the idea, while in Thailand *My True Love Will Stand All Outrageous Events* dropped the reference to Mary altogether.

Capturing our ideas with words is a challenge when both conversational partners speak the same language, but across languages, cultures, and generations the complexity multiplies exponentially.

Language Is Abstract
Words represent aspects of our environment, and can play an important role in that environment. They may describe an important idea or concept, but the very act of labeling and invoking a word simplifies and distorts our concept of the thing itself. This ability to simplify concepts makes it easier to communicate, but it sometimes makes us lose track of the specific meaning we are trying to convey through abstraction. Let's look at one important part of life in America: transportation.

Take the word "car" and consider what it represents. Freedom, status, or style? Does what you drive say something about you? To describe a car as a form of transportation is to consider one of its most basic and universal aspects. This level of abstraction means we lose individual distinctions between cars until we impose another level of labeling. We could divide cars into sedans (or saloon) and coupe (or coupé) simply by counting the number of doors (i.e., four versus two). We could also examine cost, size, engine displacement, fuel economy, and style. We might arrive at an American classic, the Mustang, and consider it for all these factors and its legacy as an accessible American sports car. To describe it in terms of transportation only is to lose the distinctiveness of what makes a Mustang a desirable American sports car.

Figure 2.2 Abstraction Ladder

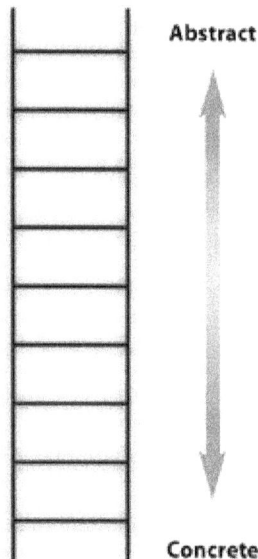

Source: Adapted from J. DeVito's Abstraction Ladder. [2]

We can see how, at the extreme level of abstraction, a car is like any other automobile. We can also see how, at the base level, the concept is most concrete. "Mustang," the name given to one of the best-selling American sports cars, is a specific make and model with specific markings; a specific size, shape, and range of available colors; and a relationship with a classic design. By focusing on concrete terms and examples, you help your audience grasp your content.

Language Organizes and Classifies Reality

We use language to create and express some sense of order in our world. We often group words that represent concepts by their physical proximity or their similarity to one another. For example, in biology, animals with similar traits are classified together. An ostrich may be said to be related to an emu and a nandu, but you wouldn't group an ostrich with an elephant or a salamander. Our ability to organize is useful, but artificial. The systems of organization we use are not part of the natural world but an expression of our views about the natural world.

What is a doctor? A nurse? A teacher? If a male came to mind in the case of the word "doctor" and a female came to mind in reference to "nurse" or "teacher," then your habits of mind include a gender bias. There was once a time in the United States where that gender stereotype was more than just a stereotype, it was the general rule, the social custom, the norm. Now it no longer holds true. More and more men are

training to serve as nurses. *Business Week* noted in 2008 that one-third of the U.S. physician workforce was female. [10]

We all use systems of classification to navigate through the world. Imagine how confusing life would be if we had no categories such as male/female, young/old, tall/short, doctor/nurse/teacher. These categories only become problematic when we use them to uphold biases and ingrained assumptions that are no longer valid. We may assume, through our biases, that elements are related when they have no relationship at all. As a result, our thinking is limited and our grasp of reality impaired. It is often easier to spot these biases in others, but it behooves us as communicators to become aware of them in ourselves. Holding them unconsciously will limit our thinking, our grasp of reality, and our ability to communicate successfully.

KEY TAKEAWAY

Language is a system governed by rules of syntax, semantics, and context; we use paradigms to understand the world and frame our communications.

EXERCISES

1. Write at least five examples of English sentences with correct syntax. Then rewrite each sentence, using the same words in an order that displays incorrect syntax. Compare your results with those of your classmates.

2. Think of at least five words whose denotative meaning differs from their connotative meaning. Use each word in two sentences, one employing the denotative meaning and the other employing the connotative. Compare your results with those of your classmates.

3. Do you associate meaning with the car someone drives? Does it say something about them? List five cars you observe people you know driving and discuss each one, noting whether you perceive that the car says something about them or not. Share and compare with classmates.

[1] Pearson, J., & Nelson, P. (2000). *An introduction to human communication: Understanding and sharing* (p. 54). Boston, MA: McGraw-Hill.

[2] Martinich, A. P. (Ed.). (1996). *The philosophy of language* (3rd ed.). Oxford, UK: Oxford University Press.

[3] Whorf, B. L. (1956). Science and linguistics. In J. B. Carroll (Ed.), *Language, thought and reality* (pp. 207–219). Cambridge, MA: MIT Press.

[4] Kuhn, T. (1996). *The structure of scientific revolutions* (3rd ed.). Chicago, IL: University of Chicago Press.

[5] McLean, S. (2003). *The basics of speech communication* (p. 50). Boston, MA: Allyn & Bacon.

[6] Ackerman, B. A. (1980). *Social justice in the liberal state*. New Haven, CT: Yale University Press.

[7] Emery, V. (1996). The Pentium chip story: A learning experience. Retrieved from http://www.emery.com/1e/pentium.htm

[8] Sterngold, J. (1998, November 15). Lost, and gained, in the translation. *New York Times*. Retrieved from http://www.nytimes.com

[9] DeVito, J. (1999). *Messages: building interpersonal communication skills* (p. 119). New York, NY: Addison Wesley Longman.

[10] Arnst, C. (2005, April 17). Are there too many women doctors? As an MD shortage looms, female physicians and their flexible hours are taking some of the blame. *Business Week*. Retrieved from http://www.businessweek.com/magazine/content/08_17/b4081104 183847.htm

2.4 Language Can be an Obstacle to Communication
LEARNING OBJECTIVES

1. Demonstrate six ways in which language can be an obstacle or barrier to communication.
2. Explain the differences between clichés, jargon, and slang.
3. Explain the difference between sexist or racist language and legitimate references to gender or race in business communication.

As you use language to make sense of your experiences, as part of our discussion, you no doubt came to see that language and verbal communication can work both for you and against you. Language allows you to communicate, but it also allows you to miscommunicate and misunderstand. The same system we use to express our most intimate thoughts can be frustrating when it fails to capture our thoughts, to represent what we want to express, and to reach our audience. For all its faults, though, it is the best system we have, and part of improving the communication process is the clear identification of where it breaks down. Anticipate where a word or expression may need more clarification and you will be on your way to reducing errors and improving verbal communication.

In an article titled "The Miscommunication Gap," Susan Washburn lists several undesirable results of poor communication in business: [1]

- Damaged relationships
- Loss of productivity
- Inefficiency and rework
- Conflict
- Missed opportunities
- Schedule slippage (delays, missed deadlines)
- Scope creep…or leap (gradual or sudden changes in an assignment that make it more complex and difficult than it was originally understood to be)
- Wasted resources
- Unclear or unmet requirements

In this section we discuss how words can serve either as a bridge, or a barrier, to understanding and communication of meaning. Our goals of effective and efficient business communication mean an inherent value of words and terms that keeps the bridge clear and free of obstacles.

Cliché

A cliché is a once-clever word or phrase that has lost its impact through overuse. If you spoke or wrote in clichés, how would your audience react? Let's try it. How do you react when you read this sentence: "A cliché is something to avoid like the plague, for it is nothing but a tired old war horse, and if the shoe were on the other foot you too would have an axe to grind"? As you can see, the problem with clichés is that they often sound silly or boring.

Clichés are sometimes a symptom of lazy communication—the person using the cliché hasn't bothered to search for original words to convey the intended meaning. Clichés lose their impact because readers and listeners tend to gloss over them, assuming their common meaning while ignoring your specific use of them. As a result, they can be obstacles to successful communication.

Jargon

Let's pretend you've been assigned to the task of preparing a short presentation on your company's latest product for a group of potential customers. It's a big responsibility. You only have one opportunity to get it right. You will need to do extensive planning and preparation, and your effort, if done well, will produce a presentation that is smooth and confident, looking simple to the casual audience member.

What words do you use to communicate information about your product? Is your audience familiar with your field and its specialized terms? As potential customers, they are probably somewhat knowledgeable in the field, but not to the extent that you and your coworkers are; even less so compared to the "techies" who developed the product. For your presentation to succeed, your challenge is to walk a fine line between using too much profession-specific language on the one hand, and "talking down" to your audience on the other hand.

While your potential customers may not understand all the engineering and schematic detail terms involved in the product, they do know what they and their organizations are looking for in considering a purchase. Your solution may be to focus on common ground—what you know of their past history in terms of contracting services or buying products from your company. What can you tell from their historical purchases? If your research shows that they place a high value on saving time, you can focus your presentation on the time-saving aspects of your new product and leave the technical terms to the user's manual.

Jargon is an occupation-specific language used by people in a given profession. Jargon does not necessarily imply formal education, but instead focuses on the language people in a profession use to communicate with each other. Members of the information technology department have a distinct group of terms that refer to common aspects in their field. Members of the marketing department, or advertising, or engineering, research, and development also have sets of terms they use within their professional community. Jargon exists in just about every occupation, independent of how much formal education is involved—from medicine and law; to financial services, banking, and insurance; to animal husbandry, auto repair, and the construction trades.

Whether or not to use jargon is often a judgment call, and one that is easier to make in speaking than in writing. In an oral context, we may be able to use a technical term and instantly know from feedback whether or not the receiver of the message "got it." If they didn't, we can define it on the spot. In written language, we lack that immediate response and must attend more to the context of receiver. The more we learn about our audience, the better we can tailor our chosen words. If we lack information or want our document to be understood by a variety of readers, it pays to use common words and avoid jargon.

Slang
Think for a moment about the words and expressions you use when you communicate with your best friends. If a coworker was to hang out with you and your friends, would they understand all the words you use, the music you listen to, the stories you tell and the way you tell them? Probably not, because you and your friends probably use certain words and expressions in ways that have special meaning to you.

This special form of language, which in some ways resembles jargon, is slang. Slang is the use of existing or newly invented words to take the place of standard or traditional words with the intent of adding an unconventional, nonstandard, humorous, or rebellious effect. It differs from jargon in that it is used in informal contexts, among friends or members of a certain age group, rather than by professionals in a certain industry.

If you say something is "phat," you may mean "cool," which is now a commonly understood slang word, but your coworker may not know this. As word "phat" moves into the mainstream, it will be replaced and adapted by the communities that use it.

Since our emphasis in business communication is on clarity, and a slang word runs the risk of creating misinterpretation,

it is generally best to avoid slang. You may see the marketing department use a slang word to target a specific, well-researched audience, but for our purposes of your general presentation introducing a product or service, we will stick to clear, common words that are easily understood.

Sexist and Racist Language
Some forms of slang involve put-downs of people belonging to various groups. This type of slang often crosses the line and becomes offensive, not only to the groups that are being put down, but also to others who may hear it. In today's workplace there is no place where sexist or racist language is appropriate. In fact, using such language can be a violation of company policies and in some cases antidiscrimination laws.

Sexist language uses gender as a discriminating factor. Referring to adult women as "girls" or using the word "man" to refer to humankind are examples of sexist language. In a more blatant example, several decades ago a woman was the first female sales representative in her company's sales force. The men resented her and were certain they could outsell her, so they held a "Beat the Broad" sales contest. (By the way, she won.) Today, a contest with a name like that would be out of the question.

Racist language discriminates against members of a given race or ethnic group. While it may be obvious that racial and ethnic slurs have no place in business communication, there can also be issues with more subtle references to "*those* people" or "you know how *they* are." If race or ethnicity genuinely enters into the subject of your communication—in a drugstore, for example, there is often an aisle for black hair care products—then naturally it makes sense to mention customers belonging to that group. The key is that mentioning racial and ethnic groups should be done with the same respect you would desire if someone else were referring to groups you belong to.

Euphemisms
In seeking to avoid offensive slang, it is important not to assume that a euphemism is the solution. A euphemism involves substituting an acceptable word for an offensive, controversial, or unacceptable one that conveys the same or similar meaning. The problem is that the audience still knows what the expression means, and understands that the writer or speaker is choosing a euphemism for the purpose of sounding more educated or genteel.

Euphemisms can also be used sarcastically or humorously—"H-E-double-hockey-sticks," for example, is a euphemism for "hell" that may be amusing in some contexts. If your friend has just gotten a new job as a janitor, you may jokingly ask, "How's my favorite sanitation engineer this morning?" But such humor is not always appreciated, and can convey disrespect even when none is intended.

Euphemistic words are not always disrespectful, however. For example, when referring to a death, it is considered polite in many parts of the United States to say that the person "passed" or "passed away," rather than the relatively insensitive word, "died." Similarly, people say, "I need to find a bathroom" when it is well understood they are not planning to take a bath.

Still, these polite euphemisms are exceptions to the rule. Euphemisms are generally more of a hindrance than a help to understanding. In business communication the goal is clarity, and the very purpose of euphemism is to be vague. To be clear, choose words that mean what you intend to convey.

Doublespeak
Doublespeak is the deliberate use of words to disguise, obscure, or change meaning. Doublespeak is often present in bureaucratic communication, where it can serve to cast a person or an organization in a less unfavorable light than plain language would do.

When you ask a friend, "How does it feel to be downsized?" you are using a euphemism to convey humor, possibly even dark humor. Your friend's employer was likely not joking, though, when the action was announced as a "downsizing" rather than as a "layoff" or "dismissal." In military communications, "collateral damage" is often used to refer to civilian deaths, but no mention of the dead is present. You may recall the "bailout" of the U.S. economy in 2008, which quickly came to be called the "rescue" and finally the "buy in" as the United States bought interests in nine regional and national banks. The meaning changed from saving an economic system or its institutions to investing in them. This change of terms, and the attempt to change the meaning of the actions, became common in comedy routines across the nation.

Doublespeak can be quite dangerous when it is used deliberately to obscure meaning and the listener cannot anticipate or predict consequences based on the (in)effective communication. When a medical insurance company says, "We insure companies with up to twenty thousand lives," is it possible to forget that those "lives" are people? Ethical issues quickly arise when humans are dehumanized and referred to as "objects" or "subjects." When genocide is referred to as "ethnic cleansing," is it any less deadly than when called by its true name?

If the meaning was successfully hidden from the audience, one might argue that the doublespeak was in fact effective. But our goal continues to be clear and concise communication with a minimum of misinterpretation. Learn to recognize doublespeak by what it does not communicate as well as what it communicates.

Each of these six barriers to communication contributes to misunderstanding and miscommunication, intentionally or unintentionally. If you recognize one of them, you can address it right away. You can redirect a question and get to essential meaning, rather than leaving with a misunderstanding that impacts the relationship. In business communication, our goal of clear and concise communication remains constant, but we can never forget that trust is the foundation for effective communication. Part of our effort must include reinforcing the relationship inherent between source and receiver, and one effective step toward that goal is to reduce obstacles to effective communication.

KEY TAKEAWAY

To avoid obstacles to communication, avoid clichés, jargon, slang, sexist and racist language, euphemisms, and doublespeak.

EXERCISES

1. Identify at least five common clichés and look up their origins. Try to understand how and when each phrase became a cliché. Share your findings with your classmates.
2. Using your library's microfilm files or an online database, look through newspaper articles from the 1950s or earlier. Find at least one article that uses sexist or racist language. What makes it racist or sexist? How would a journalist convey the same information today? Share your findings with your class.
3. Identify one slang term and one euphemism you know is used in your community, among your friends, or where you work. Share and compare with classmates.
4. How does language change over time? Interview someone older than you and someone younger than you and identify words that have changed. Pay special attention to jargon and slang words.
5. Is there ever a justifiable use for doublespeak? Why or why not? Explain your response and give some examples.
6. Can people readily identify the barriers to communication? Survey ten individuals and see if they accurately identify at least one barrier, even if they use a different term or word.

[1] Washburn, S. (2008, February). The miscommunication gap. *ESI Horizons, 9*(2). Retrieved fromhttp://www.esi-intl.com/public/Library/html/200802HorizonsArticle1.asp?UnityID=8522516.1290

2.5 Emphasis Strategies
LEARNING OBJECTIVES

1. Describe and define four strategies that can give emphasis to your message.
2. Demonstrate the effective use of visuals in an oral or written presentation.
3. Demonstrate the effective use of signposts, internal summaries and foreshadowing, and repetition in an oral or written presentation.

One key to communication is capturing and holding the audience's attention. No one likes to be bored, and no communicator likes to send boring messages. To keep your communications dynamic and interesting, it often helps to use specific strategies for emphasis. Let's examine some of these strategies and how to use them to strengthen your message.

Visual Communication

Adding the visual dimension to a document or speech can be an excellent way to hold your audience's interest and make your meaning clear. But be careful not to get carried away. Perhaps the most important rule to remember in using visuals is this: the visuals are to support your document or presentation, not to take the place of it. A picture may be worth a thousand words, but it is the words that really count. Make sure that your communication is researched, organized, and presented well enough to stand on its own. Whatever visuals you choose should be clearly associated with your verbal content, repeating, reinforcing, or extending the scope of your message.

Table 2.1 "Strategic Use of Visuals" lists some common types of visuals and gives examples of their strategic uses.

Table 2.1 Strategic Use of Visuals

Type	Purpose	Example(s)
Photograph, Video Clip, or Video Still	Show an actual person, event, or work of art.	*Figure 2.3* *Historic photo of U.S. troops raising the flag on Iwo Jima.* *Source: http://www.iwojima.com/raising/raisingb.htm*
Video Trailer, Video Still	Show the visual relationships among two or more things; a shape, a contrast in size, a process or how something works.	*Figure 2.4* *Diagram of a process or series of relationships.*

Type	Purpose	Example(s)
Bar Chart	Show the amount of one or more variables at different time intervals.	*Figure 2.5* *Different colored bars show the monthly dollar amount of sales closed by each of six sales associates for six months.*
Pie Chart	Show the percentages of the whole occupied by various segments.	*Figure 2.6* *"Pie slices" illustrate the market share held by competing products or companies.*
Line Graph	Show the change in one or more variables progressively across time.	*Figure 2.7* *Graph stock prices each day.*
Actual Object	Show the audience an item crucial to the discussion.	*Figure 2.8* *In a presentation on emergency preparedness, hold up a dust mask. In a presentation on auto safety, hold up a seatbelt.*

Signposts

Signposts (or indicators), are key words that alert the audience to a change in topic, a tangential explanation, an example, or a conclusion. Readers and listeners can sometimes be lulled into "losing their place"—forgetting what point is being made or how far along in the discussion the writer or speaker has gotten. You can help your audience avoid this by signaling to them when a change is coming. Common signposts include "on the one hand," "on the other hand," "the solution to this problem is," "the reason for this is," "for example," "to illustrate," and "in conclusion" or "in summary."

Internal Summaries and Foreshadowing

Like signposts, internal summaries and foreshadowing help the audience to keep track of where they are in the message. These strategies work by reviewing what has been covered and by highlighting what is coming next.

As a simple example, suppose you are writing or presenting information on how to assemble a home emergency preparedness kit. If you begin by stating that there are four main items needed for the kit, you are foreshadowing your message and helping your audience to watch or listen for four items. As you cover each of the items, you can say, "The first item," "The second item," "Now we've got X and Y in our kit; what else do we need? Our third item is," and so forth. These internal summaries help your audience keep track of progress as your message continues. (The four items, by the way, are water, nonperishable food, first aid supplies, and a dust mask.) [1]

With this strategy, you reinforce relationships between points, examples, and ideas in your message. This can be an effective strategy to encourage selective retention of your content.

Repetition

Saying the same word over and over may not seem like an effective strategy, but when used artfully, repetition can be an effective way to drive home your meaning and help your audience retain it in their memory. Many of history's greatest speakers have used repetition in speeches that have stood the test of time. For example, British Prime Minister Winston Churchill gave a speech in 1940 that is remembered as his "We Shall Fight" speech; in it he repeats the phrase "we shall fight" no fewer than six times. Similarly, in his famous "I Have a Dream" speech, Martin Luther King Jr. repeated the phrases "I have a dream" and "let freedom ring" with unforgettable effect.

Another form of repetition is indirect repetition: finding alternative ways of saying the same point or idea. Suppose your main point was, "global warming is raising ocean levels." You might go on to offer several examples, citing the level in each of the major oceans and seas while showing them on a map. You might use photographs or video to illustrate the fact that beaches and entire islands are going underwater. Indirect repetition can underscore and support your points, helping them stand out in the memory of your audience.

KEY TAKEAWAY

Emphasize your message by using visuals, signposts, internal summaries and foreshadowing, and repetition.

EXERCISES

1. Find a news article online or in a newspaper or magazine that uses several visuals. What do the visuals illustrate? Would the article be equally effective without them? Why or why not? Share your findings with your class.
2. Find an article or listen to a presentation that uses signposts. Identify the signposts and explain how they help the audience follow the article or presentation. Share your findings with your class.
3. Find the legend on a map. Pick one symbol and describe its use. Share and compare with the class.

[1] Federal Emergency Management Administration. (2009). Get a kit. Retrieved from http://www.ready.gov/america/getakit

2.6 Improving Verbal Communication
LEARNING OBJECTIVES

1. List and explain the use of six strategies for improving verbal communication.
2. Demonstrate the appropriate use of definitions in an oral or written presentation.
3. Understand how to assess the audience, choose an appropriate tone, and check for understanding and results in an oral or written presentation.

Throughout the chapter we have visited examples and stories that highlight the importance of verbal communication. To end the chapter, we need to consider how language can be used to enlighten or deceive, encourage or discourage, empower or destroy. By defining the terms we use and choosing precise words, we will maximize our audience's understanding of our message. In addition, it is important to consider the audience, control your tone, check for understanding, and focus on results. Recognizing the power of verbal communication is the first step to understanding its role and impact on the communication process.

Define Your Terms

Even when you are careful to craft your message clearly and concisely, not everyone will understand every word you say or write. As an effective business communicator, you know it is your responsibility to give your audience every advantage in understanding your meaning. Yet your presentation would fall flat if you tried to define each and every term—you would end up sounding like a dictionary.

The solution is to be aware of any words you are using that may be unfamiliar to your audience. When you identify an unfamiliar word, your first decision is whether to use it or to substitute a more common, easily understood word. If you choose to use the unfamiliar word, then you need to decide how to convey its meaning to those in your audience who are not familiar with it. You may do this in a variety of ways. The most obvious, of course, is to state the meaning directly or to rephrase the term in different words. But you may also convey the meaning in the process of making and supporting your points. Another way is to give examples to illustrate each concept, or use parallels from everyday life.

Overall, keep your audience in mind and imagine yourself in their place. This will help you to adjust your writing level and style to their needs, maximizing the likelihood that your message will be understood.

Choose Precise Words

To increase understanding, choose precise words that paint as vivid and accurate a mental picture as possible for your audience. If you use language that is vague or abstract, your meaning may be lost or misinterpreted. Your document or presentation will also be less dynamic and interesting than it could be.

Table 2.2 "Precisely What Are You Saying?" lists some examples of phrases that are imprecise and precise. Which one evokes a more dynamic image in your imagination?

Table 2.2 Precisely What Are You Saying?

The famous writer William Safire died in 2009; he was over seventy.	The former Nixon speech writer, language authority, and *New York Times* columnist William Safire died of pancreatic cancer in 2009; he was seventy-nine.
Clumber spaniels are large dogs.	The Clumber Spaniel Club of America describes the breed as a "long, low, substantial dog," standing 17 to 20 inches high and weighing 55 to 80 pounds.
It is important to eat a healthy diet during pregnancy.	Eating a diet rich in whole grains, fruits and vegetables, lean meats, low-fat dairy products can improve your health during pregnancy and boost your chances of having a healthy baby.
We are making good progress on the project.	In the two weeks since inception, our four-member team has achieved three of the six objectives we identified for project completion; we are on track to complete the project in another three to four weeks.
For the same amount spent, we expected more value added.	We have examined several proposals in the $10,000 range, and they all offer more features than what we see in the $12,500 system ABC Corp. is offering.
Officers were called to the scene.	Responding to a 911 call, State Police Officers Arellano and Chavez sped to the intersection of County Route 53 and State Highway 21.
The victim went down the street.	The victim ran screaming to the home of a neighbor, Mary Lee of 31 Orchard Street.
Several different color ways are available.	The silk jacquard fabric is available in ivory, moss, cinnamon, and topaz color ways.
This smartphone has more applications than customers can imagine.	At last count, the BlackBerry Tempest has more than 500 applications, many costing 99 cents or less; users can get real-time sports scores, upload videos to TwitVid, browse commuter train schedules, edit e-mails before forwarding, and find recipes—but so far, it doesn't do the cooking for you.
A woman was heckled when she spoke at a health care event.	On August 25, 2009, Rep. Frank Pallone (Democrat of New Jersey's 6th congressional district) hosted a "town hall" meeting on health care reform where many audience members heckled and booed a woman in a wheelchair as she spoke about the need for affordable health insurance and her fears that she might lose her home.

Consider Your Audience

In addition to precise words and clear definitions, contextual clues are important to guide your audience as they read. If you are speaking to a general audience and choose to use a word in professional jargon that may be understood by many—but not all—of the people in your audience, follow it by a common reference that clearly relates its essential meaning. With this positive strategy you will be able to forge relationships with audience members from diverse backgrounds. Internal summaries tell us what we've heard and forecast what is to come. It's not just the words, but also how people hear them that counts.

If you say the magic words "in conclusion," you set in motion a set of expectations that you are about to wrap it up. If, however, you introduce a new point and continue to speak, the audience will perceive an expectancy violation and hold you accountable. You said the magic words but didn't honor them. One of the best ways to display respect for your audience is to not exceed the expected time in a presentation or length in a document. Your careful attention to contextual clues will demonstrate that you are clearly considering your audience.

Take Control of Your Tone

Does your writing or speech sound pleasant and agreeable? Simple or sophisticated? Or does it come across as stuffy, formal, bloated, ironic, sarcastic, flowery, rude, or inconsiderate? Recognizing our own tone is not always easy, as we tend to read or listen from our own viewpoint and make allowances accordingly.

Once we have characterized our tone, we need to decide whether and how it can be improved. Getting a handle on how to influence tone and to make your voice match your intentions takes time and skill.

One useful tip is to read your document out loud before you deliver it, just as you would practice a speech before you present it to an audience. Sometimes hearing your own words can reveal their tone, helping you decide whether it is correct or appropriate for the situation.

Another way is to listen or watch others' presentations that have been described with terms associated with tone. Martin Luther King Jr. had one style while President Barack Obama has another. The writing in *The Atlantic* is far more sophisticated than the simpler writing in *USA Today*, yet both are very successful with their respective audiences. What kind of tone is best for your intended audience?

Finally, seek out and be receptive to feedback from teachers, classmates, and coworkers. Don't just take the word of one critic, but if several critics point to a speech as an example of pompous eloquence, and you don't want to come across in your presentation as pompous, you may learn from that example speech what to avoid.

Check for Understanding

When we talk to each other face-to-face, seeing if someone understood you isn't all that difficult. Even if they really didn't get it, you can see, ask questions, and clarify right away. That gives oral communication, particularly live interaction, a distinct advantage. Use this immediacy for feedback to your advantage. Make time for feedback and plan for it. Ask clarifying questions. Share your presentation with more than one person, and choose people that have similar characteristics to your anticipated audience.

If you were going to present to a group that you knew in advance was of a certain age, sex, or professional background, it would only make sense to connect with someone from that group prior to your actual performance to check and see if what you have created and what they expect are similar. In oral communication, feedback is core component of the communication model and we can often see it, hear it, and it takes less effort to assess it.

Be Results Oriented

At the end of the day, the assignment has to be complete. It can be a challenge to balance the need for attention to detail with the need to arrive at the end product—and its due date. Stephen Covey [1] suggests beginning with the end in mind as one strategy for success. If you have done your preparation, know your assignment goals, desired results, have learned about your audience and tailored the message to their expectations, then you are well on your way to completing the task. No document or presentation is perfect, but the goal itself is worthy of your continued effort for improvement.

Here the key is to know when further revision will not benefit the presentation and to shift the focus to test marketing, asking for feedback, or simply sharing it with a mentor or coworker for a quick review. Finding balance while engaging in an activity that requires a high level of attention to detail can be challenge for any business communicator, but it is helpful to keep the end in mind.

KEY TAKEAWAY

To improve communication, define your terms, choose precise words, consider your audience, control your tone, check for understanding, and aim for results.

EXERCISES

1. Choose a piece of writing from a profession you are unfamiliar with. For example, if you are studying biology, choose an excerpt from a book on fashion design. Identify several terms you are unfamiliar with, terms that may be considered jargon. How does the writer help you understand the meaning of these terms? Could the writer make them easier to understand? Share your findings with your class.

2. In your chosen career field or your college major, identify ten jargon words, define them, and share them with the class.

3. Describe a simple process, from brushing your teeth to opening the top of a bottle, in as precise terms as possible. Present to the class.

[1] Covey, S. (1989). *The seven habits of highly effective people.* New York, NY: Simon & Schuster.

2.7 Additional Resources

- Benjamin Lee Whorf was one of the twentieth century's foremost linguists. Learn more about his theories of speech behavior by visiting this site. http://grail.cba.csuohio.edu/~somos/whorf.html

- Visit Infoplease to learn more about the eminent linguist (and U.S. senator) S. I. Hayakawa. http://www.infoplease.com/ipa/A0880739.html

- Harvard psychology professor Steven Pinker is one of today's most innovative authorities on language. Explore reviews of books about language Pinker has published. http://pinker.wjh.harvard.edu/books/index.html

- Reference.com offers a wealth of definitions, synonym finders, and other guides to choosing the right words. http://dictionary.reference.com

- Visit Goodreads and learn about one of the best word usage guides, Bryan Garner's *Modern American Usage.* http://www.goodreads.com/book/show/344643.Garner_s_Modern_American_Usage

- Visit Goodreads and learn about one of the most widely used style manuals, *The Chicago Manual of Style.* http://www.goodreads.com/book/show/103362.The_Chicago_Manual_of_Style

- For in-depth information on how to present visuals effectively, visit the Web site of Edward Tufte, a Professor Emeritus at Yale University, where he taught courses in statistical evidence, information design, and interface design. http://www.edwardtufte.com/tufte/index

- The "I Have a Dream" speech by Martin Luther King Jr. is one of the most famous speeches of all time. View it on video and read the text. http://www.americanrhetoric.com/speeches/mlkihaveadream.htm

- The Religious Communication Association, an interfaith organization, seeks to promote honest, respectful dialogue reflecting diversity of religious beliefs. http://www.americanrhetoric.com/rca/index.html

- To learn more about being results oriented, visit the Web site of Stephen Covey, author of the best seller *The Seven Habits of Highly Effective People.* https://www.stephencovey.com

NOTES:

NOTES:

Chapter 3:
Understanding Your Audience

Your mind is like a parachute. It works best when it's open.
  Anonymous
To see an object in the world we must see it as something.
  Ludwig Wittgenstein
You will either step forward into growth or you will step back into safety.
  Abraham Maslow

Getting Started

INTRODUCTORY EXERCISES

1. In order to communicate with others, you need to know yourself. Please complete a personal inventory, a simple list of what comes to mind in these five areas:

- **Your knowledge**: What is your favorite subject?
- **Your skills**: What can you do?
- **Your experience**: What has been your experience writing to date?
- **Your interests**: What do you enjoy?
- **Your relationships**: Who is important to you?

2. To be a successful communicator, it is helpful to be conscious of how you view yourself and others. Please consider what groups you belong to, particularly in terms of race, ethnicity, or culture. Imagine that you had to communicate your perception of just one of these groups. Please choose five terms from the list below, and indicate the degree to which you agree or disagree that the term describes the group accurately.

Term	Describes the Group Accurately				
	1—Strongly disagree	2—Somewhat disagree	3—Neither agree nor disagree	4—Somewhat agree	5—Strongly agree
Independent					
Dependent					
Hardworking					
Lazy					
Progressive					
Traditional					
Sophisticated					
Simple					

Term	Describes the Group Accurately				
Creative					
Practical					

INTRODUCTORY EXERCISES (CONT.)

3. Now consider a group that you have little or no contact with. Please choose five terms (the same ones or different ones) and again indicate how accurately they describe the group. How do your results compare with those in Exercise 2? [1]

4. Please find the hidden message: [2]

Figure 3.1

D	U	E	O	E	F	T	E
L	O	C	Y	C	N	C	P
R	Y	R	W	N	I	E	R
O	E	E	O	E	E	P	U
W	V	P	H	U	V	S	O
R	I	U	S	L	I	R	Y

5. Connect the dots by drawing four straight lines, making sure not to lift your pen from the paper or retrace lines. [3]

Figure 3.2 Nine-Dot Problem

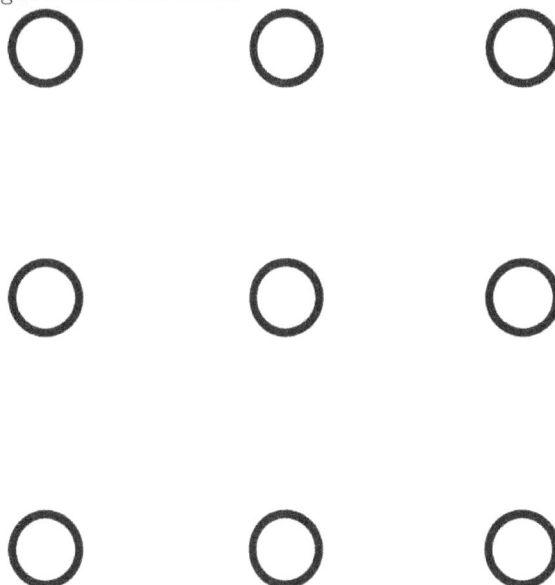

Communicating involves the translation of your thoughts and ideas to words. Speaking or writing involves sharing your perspective with others. If you talk to yourself, the action is a reflection of the communication process, but you play the role of audience. In your head, you may make sense of your words and their meaning, but when I hear what you said, what you meant may escape me. I might not "get it" because I don't know you, your references, your perspectives, your word choices, or your underlying meaning and motivation for speaking in the first place. In this chapter we'll discuss perspectives, and how people perceive information, as we learn how communication is an imperfect bridge to understanding. It requires our constant attention, maintenance, and effort.

Knowing your audience involves understanding others, and their perspectives, to see if they understand your words, examples, or the frames of reference you use to communicate your experiences, points, and conclusions. Ask yourself when you last had a miscommunication with someone. No doubt it was fairly recently, as it is for most people.

It's not people's fault that language, both verbal and nonverbal, is an imperfect system. We can, however, take responsibility for the utility and limitations of language to try to gain a better understanding of how we can communicate more effectively. As a communicator, consider both the role of the speaker and the audience and not only what and how you want to communicate but also what and how your audience needs you to communicate with them in order to present an effective message.

Figure 3.3 Solution to Introductory Exercise 5 (the "Nine-Dot Problem")

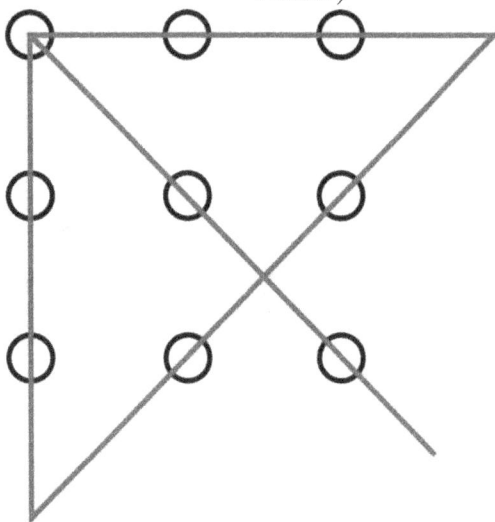

Take, for example, the word "love." Yes, we recognize those four little letters all in a row, but what does it really mean? You can use it to describe the feelings and emotions associated with your mother, a partner, or perhaps your dog. Or you might say you love chocolate cake. Does your use of the word in any given context allow the audience to get any

closer to what you mean by this word, "love"? The key here is context, which provides clues to how you mean the word and what its use means to you. The context allows you to close the gap between your meaning of "love" and what the receiver, or audience, has in their range of understanding of the same word. Your experiences are certainly different, but through clues, contexts, and attempts to understand each other's perspectives, we can often communicate more effectively.

This gives rise to an issue: how do I deal with twenty or twenty-five "perspectives" in a classroom or a reading audience of infinite size and try to narrow the gap with each audience member? Before we tackle this question, let's first follow the advice given by the character Polonius in Shakespeare's *Hamlet*: "To thine own self be true." This relates to the notion that you need to know yourself, or your perspective, before you can explore ways to know others and communicate more effectively. You will examine how you perceive stimuli, choosing some information over others, organizing the information according to your frame of reference, and interpreting it, deciding what it means to you and whether you should remember it or just ignore it and move on. We can recognize that not everyone tunes in to the same music, trends in clothing, or even classes, so experiences or stimuli can have different meanings. Still, we can find common ground and communicate effectively.

[1] Adapted from Gudykunst, W. (1994). Ethnocentrism scale and instructions. In *Bridging differences: Effective intergroup communication* (2nd ed., pp. 98–99). Thousand Oaks, CA: Sage.
[2] Adapted from McLean, S. (2003). *The basics of speech communication*. Boston, MA: Allyn & Bacon.
[3] Adapted from McLean, S. (2003). *The basics of speech communication*. Boston, MA: Allyn & Bacon.

3.1 Self-Understanding Is Fundamental to Communication
LEARNING OBJECTIVES

1. Describe the factors that contribute to self-concept.
2. Describe how the self-fulfilling prophecy works.

In the first of the Note 3.1 "Introductory Exercises" for this chapter, you listed terms to describe yourself. This exercise focuses on your knowledge, skills, experience, interests, and relationships. Your sense of self comes through in your oral and written presentations. Public communication starts with intrapersonal communication, or communication with yourself. You need to know what you want to say before you can say it to an audience.

Understanding your perspective can lend insight to your awareness, the ability to be conscious of events and stimuli. Awareness determines what you pay attention to, how you carry out your intentions, and what you remember of your activities and experiences each day. Awareness is a complicated and fascinating area of study. The way we take in information, give it order, and assign it meaning has long interested researchers from disciplines including sociology, anthropology, and psychology.

Your perspective is a major factor in this dynamic process. Whether you are aware of it or not, you bring to the act of reading this sentence a frame of mind formed from experiences and education across your lifetime. Imagine that you see a presentation about snorkeling in beautiful Hawaii as part of a travel campaign. If you have never been snorkeling but love to swim, how will your perspective lead you to pay attention to the presentation? If, however, you had a traumatic experience as a child in a pool and are now afraid of being under water, how will your perspective influence your reaction?

Learning to recognize how your perspective influences your thoughts is a key step in understanding yourself and preparing to communicate with others.

The communication process itself is the foundation for oral and written communication. Whether we express ourselves in terms of a live, face-to-face conversation or across a voice over Internet protocol (VoIP) chat via audio and visual channels, emoticons (:)), and abbreviations (IMHO [In My Humble Opinion]), the communication process remains the same. Imagine that you are at work and your Skype program makes the familiar noise indicating that someone wants to talk. Your caller ID tells you that it is a friend. You also know that you have the report right in front of you to get done before 5:00 p.m. Your friend is quite a talker, and for him everything tends to have a "gotta talk about it right now" sense of urgency. You know a little bit about your potential audience or conversational partner. Do you take the call? Perhaps you chat back "Busy, after 5," only to have him call again. You interpret the ring as his insistent need for attention, but you have priorities. You can choose to close the Skype program, stop the ringing, and get on with your report, but do you? Communication occurs on many levels in several ways.

Self-Concept

When we communicate, we are full of expectations, doubts, fears, and hopes. Where we place emphasis, what we focus on, and how we view our potential has a direct impact on our communication interactions. You gather a sense of self as you grow, age, and experience others and the world. At various times in your life, you have probably been praised for some

of your abilities and talents, and criticized for doing some things poorly. These compliments and criticisms probably had a deep impact on you. Much of what we know about ourselves we've learned through interaction with others. Not everyone has had positive influences in their lives, and not every critic knows what they are talking about, but criticism and praise still influence how and what we expect from ourselves.

Carol Dweck, a psychology researcher at Stanford University, states that "something that seems like a small intervention can have cascading effects on things we think of as stable or fixed, including extroversion, openness to new experience, and resilience." [1] Your personality and expressions of it, like oral and written communication, were long thought to have a genetic component. But, says Dweck, "More and more research is suggesting that, far from being simply encoded in the genes, much of personality is a flexible and dynamic thing that changes over the life span and is shaped by experience." [2] If you were told by someone that you were not a good speaker, know this: You can change. You can shape your performance through experience, and a business communication course, a mentor at work, or even reading effective business communication authors can result in positive change.

Attitudes, Beliefs, and Values

When you consider what makes you *you*, the answers multiply as do the questions. As a baby, you learned to recognize that the face in the mirror was your face. But as an adult, you begin to wonder what and who you are. While we could discuss the concept of self endlessly and philosophers have wrestled and will continue to wrestle with it, for our purposes, let's focus on self, which is defined as one's own sense of individuality, motivations, and personal characteristics. [3] We also must keep in mind that this concept is not fixed or absolute; instead it changes as we grow and change across our lifetimes.

One point of discussion useful for our study about ourselves as communicators is to examine our attitudes, beliefs, and values. These are all interrelated, and researchers have varying theories as to which comes first and which springs from another. We learn our values, beliefs, and attitudes through interaction with others. Table 3.1 "Attitudes, Beliefs, and Values" defines these terms and provides an example of each.

An attitude is your immediate disposition toward a concept or an object. Attitudes can change easily and frequently. You may prefer vanilla while someone else prefers peppermint, but if someone tries to persuade you of how delicious peppermint is, you may be willing to try it and find that you like it better than vanilla.

Table 3.1 Attitudes, Beliefs, and Values

	Definition	Changeable?	Example
Attitudes	Learned predispositions to a concept or object	Subject to change	I enjoyed the writing exercise in class today.
Beliefs	Convictions or expressions of confidence	Can change over time	This course is important because I may use the communication skills I am learning in my career.
Values	Ideals that guide our behavior	Generally long lasting	Effective communication is important.

Beliefs are ideas based on our previous experiences and convictions and may not necessarily be based on logic or fact. You no doubt have beliefs on political, economic, and religious issues. These beliefs may not have been formed through rigorous study, but you nevertheless hold them as important aspects of self. Beliefs often serve as a frame of reference through which we interpret our world. Although they can be changed, it often takes time or strong evidence to persuade someone to change a belief.

Values are core concepts and ideas of what we consider good or bad, right or wrong, or what is worth the sacrifice. Our values are central to our self-image, what makes us who we are. Like beliefs, our values may not be based on empirical research or rational thinking, but they are even more resistant to change than are beliefs. To undergo a change in values, a person may need to undergo a transformative life experience. For example, suppose you highly value the freedom to make personal decisions, including the freedom to choose whether or not to wear a helmet while driving a motorcycle. This value of individual choice is central to your way of thinking and you are unlikely to change this value. However, if your brother was driving a motorcycle without a helmet and suffered an accident that fractured his skull and left him with permanent brain damage, you might reconsider this value. While you might still value freedom of choice in many areas of life, you might become an advocate for helmet laws—and perhaps also for other forms of highway safety, such as stiffer penalties for cell-phone talking and texting while driving.

Self-Image and Self-Esteem
Your self-concept is composed of two main elements: self-image and self-esteem.

Your self-image is how you see yourself, how you would describe yourself to others. It includes your physical characteristics—your eye color, hair length, height, and so forth. It also includes your knowledge, experience, interests, and relationships. If these sound familiar, go back and look at the first of the Note 3.1 "Introductory Exercises" for this chapter. In creating the personal inventory in this exercise, you identified many characteristics that contribute to your self-image. In addition, image involves not just how you look but also your expectations of yourself—what you can be.

What is your image of yourself as a communicator? How do you feel about your ability to communicate? While the two responses may be similar, they indicate different things. Yourself-esteem is how you feel about yourself; your feelings of self-worth, self-acceptance, and self-respect. Healthy self-esteem can be particularly important when you experience a setback or a failure. Instead of blaming yourself or thinking, "I'm just no good," high self-esteem will enable you to persevere and give yourself positive messages like "If I prepare well and try harder, I can do better next time."

Putting your self-image and self-esteem together yields your self-concept: your central identity and set of beliefs about who you are and what you are capable of accomplishing. When it comes to communicating, your self-concept can play an important part. You may find that communicating is a struggle, or the thought of communicating may make you feel talented and successful. Either way, if you view yourself as someone capable of learning new skills and improving as you go, you will have an easier time learning to be an effective communicator. Whether positive or negative, your self-concept influences your performance and the expression of that essential ability: communication.

Looking-Glass Self
In addition to how we view ourselves and feel about ourselves, of course, we often take into consideration the opinions and behavior of others. Charles Cooley's [4] looking-glass self-reinforces how we look to others and how they view us, treat us, and interact with us to gain insight of our identity. We place an extra emphasis on parents, supervisors, and on those who have some degree of control over us when we look at others. Developing a sense of self as a communicator involves balance between constructive feedback from others and constructive self-affirmation. You judge yourself, as others do, and both views count.

Self-Fulfilling Prophecy

Now, suppose that you are treated in an especially encouraging manner in one of your classes. Imagine that you have an instructor who continually "catches you doing something right" and praises you for your efforts and achievements. Would you be likely to do well in this class and perhaps go on to take more advanced courses in this subject? In a psychology experiment that has become famous through repeated trials, several public school teachers were told that specific students in their classes were expected to do quite well because of their intelligence. [5] These students were identified as having special potential that had not yet "bloomed." What the teachers didn't know was that these "special potential" students were randomly selected. That's right: as a group, they had no more special potential than any other students.

Can you anticipate the outcome? As you may guess, the students lived up to their teachers' level of expectation. Even though the teachers were supposed to give appropriate attention and encouragement to all students, in fact they unconsciously communicated special encouragement verbally and nonverbally to the special potential students. And these students, who were actually no more gifted than their peers, showed significant improvement by the end of the school year. This phenomenon came to be called the "Pygmalion effect" after the myth of a Greek sculptor named Pygmalion, who carved a marble statue of a woman so lifelike that he fell in love with her—and in response to his love she did in fact come to life and marry him. [6], [7]

In more recent studies, researchers have observed that the opposite effect can also happen: when students are seen as lacking potential, teachers tend to discourage them or, at a minimum, fail to give them adequate encouragement. As a result, the students do poorly. [8]

When people encourage you, it affects the way you see yourself and your potential. Seek encouragement for your writing and speaking. Actively choose positive reinforcement as you develop your communication skills. You will make mistakes, but the important thing is to learn from them. Keep in mind that criticism should be constructive, with specific points you can address, correct, and improve.

The concept of a self-fulfilling prophecy, in which someone's behavior comes to match and mirror others' expectations, is not new. Robert Rosenthal, [9] a professor of social psychology at Harvard, has observed four principles while studying this interaction between expectations and performance:

1. We form certain expectations of people or events.
2. We communicate those expectations with various cues, verbal and nonverbal.
3. People tend to respond to these cues by adjusting their behavior to match the expectations.
4. The outcome is that the original expectation becomes true.
5.

KEY TAKEAWAY

You can become a more effective communicator by understanding yourself and how others view you: your attitudes, beliefs, and values; your self-concept; and how the self-fulfilling prophecy may influence your decisions.

EXERCISES

1. How would you describe yourself as a public speaker? Now, five, and ten years ago? Is your description the same or does it change across time? This business communication text and course can make a difference in what you might write for the category "one year from today."
2. How does your self-concept influence your writing? Write a one- to two-page essay on this topic and discuss it with a classmate.
3. Make a list of at least three of your strongly held beliefs. What are those beliefs based on? List some facts, respected authorities, or other evidence that support them. Share your results with your class.
4. What are some of the values held by people you know? Identify a target sample size (twenty is a good number) and ask members of your family, friends, and peers about their values. Compare your results with those of your classmates.
5. Make a list of traits you share with your family members. Interview them and see if anyone else in your family has shared them. Share and compare with your classmates.
6. What does the field of psychology offer concerning the self-fulfilling prophecy? Investigate the topic and share your findings.

[1] Begley, S. (2008, December 1). When DNA is not destiny. *Newsweek*, p. 14.

[2] Begley, S. (2008, December 1). When DNA is not destiny. *Newsweek*, p. 14.

[3] McLean, S. (2003). *The basics of speech communication*. Boston, MA: Allyn & Bacon.

[4] Cooley, C. (1922). *Human nature and the social order* (Rev. ed.). New York, NY: Scribners.

[5] Rosenthal, R., & Jacobson, L. (1968). *Pygmalion in the classroom*. New York, NY: Holt, Rinehart, & Winston.

[6] Rosenthal, R., & Jacobson, L. (1968). *Pygmalion in the classroom*. New York, NY: Holt, Rinehart, & Winston.

[7] Insel, P., & Jacobson, L. (1975). *What do you expect? An inquiry into self-fulfilling prophecies*. Menlo Park, CA: Cummings.

[8] Schugurensky, D. (Ed.). (2009). Selected moments of the 20th century. In *History of education: A work in progress*. Department of Adult Education, Community Development and Counselling Psychology, The Ontario Institute for Studies in Education of the University of Toronto (OISE/UT). Retrieved from http://fcis.oise.utoronto.ca/~daniel_sc/assignment1/1968rosenjacob.html. *Pygmalion in the Classroom* was followed by many other school-based studies that examined these mechanisms in detail from different perspectives. Prominent among the works on this subject conducted by U.S. scholars are Rist, R. C. (1970, August). Student social class and teacher expectations: The self-fulfilling prophecy in ghetto education. *Harvard Educational Review, 40*(3), 411–451; Anyon, J. (1980, Fall). Social class and the hidden curriculum of work. *Journal of Education, 162*(1), 67–92; Oakes, J. (1985). *Keeping track: How schools structure inequality*. Birmingham, NY: Vail-Ballou Press; and Sadker, M., & Sadker, D. (1994). *Failing at fairness: How America's schools cheat girls*. New York, NY: Macmillan Publishing Company.
[9] Rosnow, R., & Rosenthal, R. (1999). *Beginning behavioral research: A conceptual primer* (3rd ed.). Englewood Cliffs, NJ: Prentice Hall.

3.2 Perception
LEARNING OBJECTIVES

1. Describe the concept of perception.
2. Describe the process of selection and the factors that influence it.
3. Describe several principles of organization.
4. Explain how interpretation influences our perceptions.

Look at the fourth of the Note 3.1 "Introductory Exercises" for this chapter. If you deciphered the hidden message, how did you do it? You may have tried looking for words that were diagonal or backwards, using skills you learned solving similar puzzles in the past. While there are many ways to solve this puzzle, there is only one right answer. [1] Reading from right to left (not left to right), and bottom to top (not top to bottom), the hidden message reads: *Your perspective influences how you perceive your world*.

Where did you start reading on this page? The top left corner. Why not the bottom right corner, or the top right one? In English we read left to right, from the top of the page to the bottom. But not everyone reads the same. If you read and write Arabic or Hebrew, you will proceed from right to left. Neither is right or wrong, simply different. You may find it hard to drive on the *other* side of the road while visiting England, but for people in the United Kingdom, it is normal and natural.

We can extend this concept in many ways. Imagine that you are doing a sales presentation to a group where the average age is much older or younger than you. In terms of words to use to communicate ideas, references to music or movies, even expectations for behaviors when dating, their mental "road map" may be quite different from yours. Even though your sales message might focus on a product like a car, or a

service like car washing, preconceived ideas about both will need to be addressed.

For example, how many advertisements have you seen on television that have a song from specific time period, like the 1980s, or perhaps the 1960s? The music is a clear example of targeting a specific audience with something distinctive, like a familiar song. When speaking or writing, your style, tone, and word choice all influence the reader. The degree to which you can tailor your message to their needs will be associated with an increase in the overall effectiveness of your message. These differences in perspective influence communication and your ability to recognize not only your point of view but theirs will help you become "other-oriented" and improve communication.

Look at the puzzle again and see if you can *avoid* seeing the solution. It'll be hard because now that you know where it is, you have a mental road map that leads you to the solution. The mental state where you could not see it, or perceive it, is gone. Your audience has a mental road map that includes values, experiences, beliefs, strategies to deal with challenges, even scripts for behavioral expectations. You need to read the maps as closely as possibly in order to be able to communicate from common ground.

This discussion illustrates what the German philosopher Jürgen Habermas [2] calls preunderstanding, a set of expectations and assumptions from previous experience that we apply to a new problem or situation. We draw from our experiences to help guide us to our goal, even when the situations may be completely different. We "understand" before we experience because we predict or apply our mental template to what we think is coming.

Expectations affect our perceptions. If the teacher says, "I need to see you after class" your perception might involve thoughts like, "What have I done? Why me? What does he or she want?" and you may even think back to other times in similar situations. This may contribute to a negative perception of the meeting, and then you might be surprised to learn the teacher only wanted to tell you about a scholarship opportunity. The same idea applies to your audience. They will have certain expectations of you as a speaker.

"The customary forms and configurations (of communication) that members expect" are called conventions. [3] You've probably heard the terms "conventional," perhaps in relation to a "conventional oven." This use means a standard type oven with a heat source as opposed a microwave oven. Who decided that a stove, for example, would have burners on top and a front-opening door to the oven? Why four burners and not three, or two? Many modern stoves have ceramic burners that are integrated in to the top of the oven, or even into the top of a counter, separate from the oven. These new applications "stretch" the notion of what is the standard for a stove.

People use conventions to guide them every day. On which side of the plate will you find the spoon? In a formal place setting, the answer is "right." If, however, you are at a potluck supper, you may be handed a plate with all your utensils, including the spoon, just sitting on top. Or you might find a pile of spoons next to the plates and have to get one for yourself. In each case there are a set of conventions in place that we use to guide behavior and establish expectations. At a formal dinner, eating with your fingers might be unconventional or even rude. The same actions at a potluck might be the dominant convention, as in everyone is doing it. In business communication, conventions are always in place. The audience will have a set of expectations you need to consider, and you need to keep an open mind about the importance of those expectations; but you also need to achieve your goal of informing, persuading, or motivating them. If you are presenting a sales message and the results are zero sales, you'll have to take a long look at what you presented and develop alternative strategies. Providing a different perspective to your audience while adapting to their expectations and finding common ground is a good first step in gaining and maintaining their attention.

We often make assumptions about what others are communicating and connect the dots in ways that were not intended by the speaker. As a business communicator, your goal is to help the audience connect the dots in the way you intend while limiting alternative solutions that may confuse and divide the audience.

Taking care to make sure you understand before connecting your dots and creating false expectations is a positive way to prepare yourself for the writing process. Do you know what the assignment is? Are the goals and results clear? Do you know your audience? All these points reinforce the central theme that clear and concise communication is critical in business and industry.

Selection

Can you imagine what life would be like if you heard, saw, and felt every stimulus or activity in your environment all day long? It would be overwhelming. It is impossible to perceive, remember, process, and respond to every action, smell, sound, picture, or word that we see, hear, small, taste, or

touch. We would be lost paying attention to everything, being distracted by everything, and lack focus on anything.

In the same way, a cluttered message, with no clear format or way of discerning where the important information is located, can overwhelm the listener. It is handy, therefore, that we as humans can choose to pay attention to a specific stimulus while ignoring or tuning out others. This raises the question, however, of why we choose to pay attention to one thing over another. Since we cannot pay attention to everything at once, we choose to pay attention to what appears to be the most relevant for us.

This action of sorting competing messages, or choosing stimuli, is called selection. Selection is one very important part of perception and awareness. You select what to pay attention to based on what is important to you, or what you value, and that is different for each person. Let's pretend you're reading an article for class, or perhaps you're not as much reading but skimming or half-listening to the author's voice in your head, and only following along enough to get the main idea, as you do when you scan rather than read something word for word.

At the same time you are thinking about the attractive classmate who sits in the third row, wondering when it will be noon, and starting to think about what to eat for lunch. In this real-world example, we can quickly count the four stimuli you've selected to pay attention to, but not all of them receive equal attention at every moment. Perhaps your stomach starts to growl; while the mental image of the attractive classmate is indeed attractive, your stomach demands the center stage of your attention.

A stage is a useful way to think about your focus or attention. There are times when you see everything on the stage, the literal stage in terms of theater or the page you are reading now, in print or online. The stage refers to the setting, scene, and context of the communication interaction, and can be equally applied to written or oral communication. This page can be a stage, where objects, symbols, and words are placed to guide your attention in the same way an actor striding across a theater stage will compel you.

You may perceive everything happening at once—while your attention is divided, you still have a larger perspective. Suppose you have just come home from work and are standing by your kitchen table opening the day's mail. At the same time, you are planning what to cook for dinner and trying to get your dog leashed up to take a quick walk outside. You open a letter in a preprinted envelope whose return address is unfamiliar. The relationships between the words or characters are readily apparent. With one glance you can see that the letter is an introduction letter with a sales message, you assess that it doesn't interest you, and into the round file (garbage can) it goes.

If you were the author of that letter, you might be quite disappointed. How do you grasp a reader's attention? Part of the solution lies in your ability to help the reader select the key point or bit of information that will lead to "what else?" instead of "no, thanks."

The same lesson applies to public speaking, but the cues will be distinct. The audience won't throw you into the round file, but mentally they may ignore you and start planning what's for dinner, tuning you out. They may fidget, avoid eye contact, or even get up and walk out—all signs that your sales message was not well received.

There are other times where you are so focused on one character or part of the stage that you miss something going on the other side. In the same way, as you sit in your late-morning class and focus on your growling stomach, the instructor's voice becomes less of a focus until you hear laughter from your classmates. You look up to see and hear a friend say, "We can clearly see the power and the importance of nutrition and its impact on attention span," as he or she gestures in your direction. You notice that everyone is looking back at you and realize they too heard your stomach. Your focus and attention are important and constantly challenged.

As we follow the bouncing ball of attention, we see how selection involves focusing on one stimulus while limiting our attention on another, or ignoring it altogether. We do this as a matter of course.

The process of selection and ignoring has been discussed in both contexts of a learned behavior as well as something we are born with, as in instinct or preprogrammed behavioral patterns. Regardless of whether this process is instinctive or learned, we can easily see from the previous example how the speaker, to a degree, competes with internal and external stimuli.

Internal stimuli are those that arise from within one's self, such as being hungry. External stimuli involve stimulation from outside one's self, such as the image of the attractive classmate or the sound of the instructor's voice. As a communicator, your awareness of both of these sources of stimuli will help you recognize the importance or preparation, practice, and persistence as you prepare your message with them in mind. How will you help guide the audience's

thoughts about your topic? How will you build attention-getting features throughout your written work? How will you address issues like sleepiness when you cannot change the designated time of your speech, scheduled right after lunch? All these issues relate to the selection process, and to a degree the speaker can influence the perception of both internal and external stimuli.

Selection has three main parts: exposure, attention, and retention. [4] Selective exposure is both information we choose to pay attention to and information that we choose to ignore, or that is unavailable to us. For example, in a class you may have been required to view a student-created YouTube video presentation on which is better for you, Gatorade or water. As your levels of exposure to stimuli influence your decisions, you may think, "Oh, I've heard this before," and tune the speaker out. Selective attention involves focusing on one stimulus, like the image of an attractive classmate, and tuning out a competing stimulus, like the instructor's voice. Selective retention involves choosing to remember one stimulus over another.

You may be out walking and spot a friend from the same class. Your friend may say, "The program we had to watch for class said Gatorade has trans-fat in it. Do you think that's true?" and you may be at a loss, having no memory of hearing any such thing because, while you were present in your room, you were paying attention to other stimuli. Furthermore, you may not be a nutrition major like your friend so that the term "trans-fat" may not mean anything to you. To someone majoring in nutrition, it might be a common term used across their classes, but if you are an accounting major, you may not be familiar with the term. This illustrates how one aspect of selection, like exposure, can influence another aspect, like retention.

You might then think to yourself that the point in which you tuned out in the Gatorade program has something to do with this term and realize that as the speaker became technical about the nutritional and metabolic properties of Gatorade, you lost interest because you were unfamiliar with the terms being used. This highlights one aspect of a presentation that a speaker can focus on to influence the perception process. Not everyone in the audience will understand all the terminology, so by defining terms, providing visual aid cues, or speaking in common terms, you can make your topic and its presentation more accessible to a larger percentage of your audience.

Now, if you were asked to recall the basic properties of Gatorade after watching the program, could you? Even if you recall the general idea of the program, you may have a hard time remembering any specific property because you were focused on your hunger. Although you may have *heard* the words, you may not have chosen to *listen* to them. Hearing means you heard words, but listening implies you actively chose to listen to the program, processing the sounds, following the thread of discussion, making it easier for you to recall. This again illustrates the point that you chose one stimuli over another, in effect selecting what to pay attention to, and if the speaker was competing for your attention with more attractive, interesting or distracting stimuli, you probably just tuned him or her out, in effect deselecting them.

Organization

Organization is the process of sorting information into logical categories or series. We often take things we perceive and organize them into categories based on what we have perceived previously. Think back to the Gatorade video. Suppose the speaker started out with an attention statement and quickly moved to highlight three main points in the introduction. While the attention statement got you, by the second main point you were already starting to think, "This is going to be just another speech on how great Gatorade is for my body." You may think this because you have already heard other speakers presented similar information and you classify what you think this presentation is going to be in relation to your previous experiences.

But this speaker may have given some thought to the presentation and how to make it unique and interesting, and prepared their discussion on the nutritional aspects in more depth. As a result, the information may have been organized into categories like ingredients, how your body uses the ingredients, and what the net result is. The final conclusion might be that if you exercise and burn off the calories present in Gatorade, it might be a positive choice, but if you drink it just to drink it, then it will only provide you with empty calories just like any other soft drink.

Organization Schemes

The organization scheme used to create three categories focuses on nutrition and the process by which Gatorade's ingredients are used by the body. The conclusion creates two categories of consumers. This organization scheme can promote active listening and allow the audience to follow, but the speaker must take into account the possibility that an audience member might think, "Oh no, not again." To set this presentation apart from others the audience might have heard, the speaker could include a phrase like, "Is Gatorade always for you? Not necessarily. Let's look at…" which gains attention and penetrates a stereotype.

When you write a document or give a presentation, you may not be able to anticipate all the ways an audience might organize the information you present or how they might use it, but by investing time in seeing it from their perspective, you can improve your organization and be a more effective communicator.

For example, suppose you are assigned the task of writing a cost-benefit analysis report on a specific product currently in development. Do you already know the essential points you need to include and the common industry standards for this type of report? You may not know, but you have written an essay before and appreciate the need for organization. Your ability to organize information, taking something that you know or have experienced and applying it to new information, helps you make sense of your world.

Gestalt Principles of Organization

In the early twentieth century, some psychologists thought we could examine parts of things, much as a scientist would examine an atom, and make a whole and complete picture regardless of context. Their theory was that the setting and scene would not influence the picture or perspective. In response to this view, other psychologists developed what they called Gestalt principles—the German word "Gestalt" referring to the unified whole. According to Gestalt theory, context matters, and the whole is greater than the sum of the parts. What you see and how you see it matters, and you yourself play a role in that perception of organization.

In the fifth of the Note 3.1 "Introductory Exercises" for this chapter, you were asked to connect nine dots with four straight lines, without retracing any line. Did you find a solution? (A common solution appears at the end of this chapter.) The key to solving this puzzle is finding a way to "think outside the box"—in this case, to take your pencil outside the implied square, or box, formed by the three rows of dots. The physical configuration of the dots contributed to the illusion of the "box." But in fact there is no box, and our tendency to see one where one does not exist creates barriers to solving the puzzle. Gestalt theory states that we will perceive the nine dots as belonging to a whole—a group or set having a certain shape—whether or not that whole actually exists.

Gestalt principles apply not only to images or objects, but also to ideas and concepts. You can associate two or more bits of information in predictable ways, but your perspective can influence your view of the overall idea. We don't always have all the information we need to draw a conclusion, literally drawing a series of relationships to form a whole picture in our minds, so we often fill in the gaps. We guess and make logical leaps, even suspend disbelief, all in an effort to make sense of our experiences.

In your presentations, if you jump from topic to topic or go off on a tangent, what happens to the listener's ability to listen and follow you effectively? Why make barriers for your audience when you've worked so hard to get their attention? How does this relate to Gestalt principles? By failing to recognize our natural tendency to want ideas, shapes, or words to make sense, the author is confusing the reader. What happens when the reader is confused? He or she moves on to something else, and leaves your writing behind. The opposite of clear and concise, confused, and poorly organized writing can distract and defeat even the most motivated of readers. Table 3.2 "Gestalt Principles of Organization" lists some of the Gestalt organization principles.

Table 3.2 Gestalt Principles of Organization

Principle	Definition	Example
Proximity	Organization based on relationship of space to objects	Next to me on the beach, I see my daughter playing with her pail and shovel; in the middle distance, a trio of kayakers paddle by; farther away, I see several power boats, and in the far distance, the green shore of Long Island.
Continuity	Drawing connections between things that occur in sequence	I am beginning to notice a pattern in the absentee rate in our department. For the past year, more workers have been absent on the first Friday of the month than on other days. I expect we will again have many absences next Friday, as it is the first Friday of the month.
Similarity	Grouping things or concepts by properties they share	To make appliquéd candles, [5] you will need the following: Decorative material to appliqué: floral (fresh flowers, pine needles, or leaves), homey (dried beans or grains) or folksy (small nuts and bolts) Candle body: fat candles (at least 4" diameter to keep dried flowers away from flame), natural colored wax (sheets or chunks of beeswax or paraffin) Tools: a microwave flower press, a ½-inch paintbrush, a tin pie plate, a chip carving knife or v-tool
Uniformity/Homogeneity	Noting ways in which concepts or objects are alike	Armored personnel carriers include the Stryker, LAV, Pandur, M113 Armored Personnel Carrier, Amphibious Assault Vehicle, Expeditionary Fighting Vehicle, Grizzly APC, Rhino Runner, Bison (armored personnel carrier), and Mamba APC.
Figure and Ground	Emphasis on a single item that stands out from its surroundings	On a rock in Copenhagen Harbor stands the small statue of The Little Mermaid, a memorial to one of Denmark's most beloved citizens, Hans Christian Andersen.
Symmetry	Balancing objects or ideas equally from one side to the other	Representing the conservative viewpoint was *Wall Street Journal* correspondent John Emshwiller; the liberal viewpoint was argued by *New York Times* columnist Paul Krugman.
Closure	Tendency to use previous knowledge to fill in the gaps in an incomplete idea or picture	The wording of the memo was, "It is important for all employees to submit their health insurance enrollment selections no than November 1," but everyone understood that it should have said, "no later than November 1."

Let's examine some of the commonly used Gestalt principles: proximity, continuation, similarity, and closure.
It makes sense that we would focus first on things around us and the degree to which they are close to us and to each other. Proximity is the perceptual organization of information based on physical relationship of space to objects. In creating a scene for a play or movie, a stage designer knows that the audience will tend to pay attention

to objects in the foreground, unless special emphasis is added to objects farther away. This principle extends to people and daily life. Just because someone is walking down the street next to someone else, this does not necessarily mean they have a connection to each other—they are simply in close proximity.

We also see a similar tendency in the principle of continuity. We like things to be orderly, and our brain will see lines and movement where none exist. Examine Figure 3.5 "Continuity". What you see? Do you perceive two lines crossing one another? Or an X? The principle of continuity predicts that you would demonstrate a tendency to perceive continuous figures. The two lines cross one another, and you might even say from top to bottom or the reverse, when there is no motion indicated.

Figure 3.5 Continuity

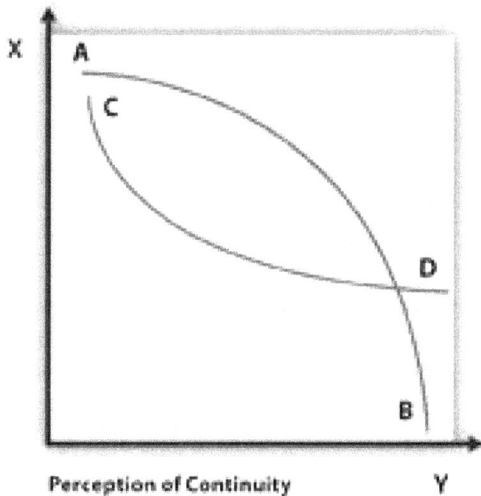

Perception of Continuity

Continuity can also lead to a well-known logical fallacy, or false belief, involving sequence and cause-effect relationships. If something happens after something else, does that mean that the first event caused the second event? You wish for rain and it rains. Connected? Logic and common sense would say no. You have a dream about a plane crash, and the next day there is a major airline crash. Did your dream cause the crash? Obviously not.

When objects or events are similar, we tend to group them together in our minds, again making the assumption that they are related by their common characteristics. Similarity is the perceptual organization of information based on perceived points of common characteristics across distinct items. For example, a horse, a mule, and a donkey are distinct, but we perceive them as being similar to one another.

The principle of closure underscores our tendency to use previous knowledge to fill in the gaps in an incomplete idea

or picture. If you are talking to a friend on your cell phone and the connection breaks up for a few seconds, you may miss some words, but you can grasp the main idea by automatically guessing what was said. You do this based on your previous history of communicating with your friend on similar topics. Do you always guess correctly? Of course not. Look at Figure 3.6.

Figure 3.6

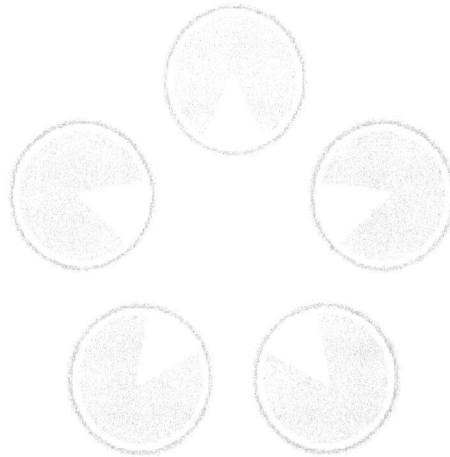

Do you see a ring of Pac-Man-like circles?

When we say we see a star, we don't really see one because there is no star. The five Pac-Man shapes in that arrangement, however, allow our mind to say, "If this was connected to this and that was connected to that, there would be a star." Sometimes the sense we make does not match reality, and we see a star where there is no star.

Sometimes we "fill in the blanks" without even being aware of it. When we speak on a topic and fail to clearly articulate a point or substantiate an assertion, we leave a "hole" in our presentation that the listener may or may not be aware of, but will predictably fill. This tendency to jump to conclusions may seem like a disadvantage, but it is only a disadvantage if you are unaware of it. If fact, it's a positive ability that allows us to infer and guess correctly, often in times of crisis when time is limited. But we don't always guess correctly. If your goal is to communicate your message to the audience, then by definition you don't want a "pothole" to interrupt, distract, or create a barrier that leads to misinterpretation.

Interpretation

After selection and organization, interpretation is the third step in the perception process. From your past experiences combined with your current expectations, you assign meaning to the current stimuli. If the word "college" for you has meaning, then what comes to mind? If a high school student has to take the PSAT (Preliminary Scholastic

Aptitude Test) in the morning, what does that word mean to him? Will his state of anxiety and anticipation over the importance of the exam and the unknown word of college influence how he responds to that word? If his parents ask, "Where are you planning on going to college?" when he is simply focused on the test that may influence his options, the word itself may take on a whole new meaning. It may invite issues of control ("Which college? You are going to the college we went to, right?") or of self-esteem ("Am I good enough to go to college?") to become associated with the word "college."

The word itself may shift in terms of meaning across time. Let's say the high school student did well on the PSAT and went to the same college as his parents. Is it the same college, or just the same location and buildings? It may have a tradition, but it is at the same time new and ever-changing, just like the students that arrive each year. Fast forward a couple of years and the college may represent a place where you studied, made friends, and came to know yourself. In a few more years, you may choose to become a member of the alumni association. The meaning of the word "college" can shift intrapersonally across time, and can mean different things to different groups.

Let's rewind and look back at a test gone bad, taken by a less than adequately prepared student from a household where there may not be sufficient resources to make the dream of college come true. The image of college may remain an image instead of a reality; a goal not attained. Structural barriers like socioeconomic status, parental and peer influences, and the need to work to support yourself or your family can all influence your decisions and perspective.

KEY TAKEAWAY

Perceptions are influenced by how we select, organize, and interpret words and ideas.

EXERCISES

1. Do a search on "M. C. Escher" or "tessellation art." How does Escher's work manipulate your perception? Share your opinions with your classmates.
2. Think of ways to describe something you know, such as what your home looks like. Organize the information using one of the Gestalt principles (e.g., proximity, similarity, continuity, or closure). Present the organized information to a classmate. Can your classmate tell which Gestalt principle you have used?
3. How does the process of perception limit our view, or expand it? Can we choose how to perceive things? Write a one- to two-page essay on this topic and discuss it with a classmate.

4. Think of a time when you jumped to a conclusion and later learned that it was incorrect. Write a brief summary of the experience. Share and compare with classmates.

[1] Adapted from McLean, S. (2003). *The basics of speech communication.* Boston, MA: Allyn & Bacon.
[2] Habermas, J. (1984). *The theory of communicative action* (Vol. 1). Boston, MA: Beacon Press.
[3] Kostelnick, C., & Roberts, D. (1998). *Designing visual language: Strategies for professional communicators.* Needham Heights, MA: Allyn & Bacon.
[4] Klopf, D. (1995). *Intercultural encounters: The fundamentals of intercultural communication* (2nd ed., p. 7). Englewood, CO: Morton.
[5] Ruffman, M. (2007, August 12). How to appliqué candles with flowers and other stuff. *ToolGirl, Mag Ruffman's Official Web Log.* Retrieved from http://www.toolgirl.com/toolgirl/2007/12/how-to-applique.html#more

3.3 Differences in Perception
LEARNING OBJECTIVE

1. Determine how perception differs between people.

Someone may say what you consider to be a simple exclamatory sentence—"Earn college credit while studying abroad!"—but a thought may come to mind: "How will I fit in as an outsider in a foreign country?" What makes you a member of a group? How you distinguish between those who belong in our family, group, or community and those who do not is central to our study of communication. Learning to see issues and experiences from multiple perspective can be a challenging task, but the effort is worth it. Increased understanding about each other can positively impact our communication and improve the degree to which we can share and understand meaning across languages, cultures, and divergent perspectives.

Why Don't We All See Eye to Eye?

People perceive things differently. We choose to select different aspects of a message to focus our attention based on what interests us, what is familiar to us, or what we consider important. Often, our listening skills could use improvement. Listening and thinking are directly related. When you are reading, what do you hear? When you are talking with someone, what do you hear? If the sound of your thoughts or voice is at least one of your answers, then communication is not occurring. Try to read this paragraph again without interruption. Your tendency might be to skim over the words, or to focus on key vocabulary, but if you allow your thoughts to stray from the text you are reading, even for a moment, you are interrupting your processing of the written word, or reading. Interruptions will impair your ability to understand and retain information, and make studying even harder.

In order to better understand perception, we will examine how you choose to pay attention, remember, and interpret messages within the communication process.

Individual Differences in Perception

Why do people perceive things in different ways? To answer the question, recall that we all engage in selection, or choosing some stimuli while ignoring others. We exist as individuals within a community, regardless of whether we are conscious of it. Do you like 80s music? Prefer the Beatles? Nothing before 2005? Your tastes in music involve the senses, and what you choose to experience is influenced by your context and environment. Your habits, values, and outlook on life are influenced by where you come from and where you are.
The attributes that cause people to perceive things differently are known as individual differences. Let's examine several of the most important ones.

Physical characteristics influence how we perceive and respond to information. You may be asked to design a sign that says, "Watch your head," which will be placed next to a six foot six inch overhang that is above floor level. While a few very tall people will have to worry about hitting their heads on the overhang, most people in the world are not that tall. Tall and short individuals will perceive this sign differently.

Your psychological state can also influence what you read and listen to, and why you do so. The emergency procedures binder on the wall next to the first aid kit doesn't mean much to you until a coworker falls and suffers some bad cuts and bruises. If you were asked to design the binder and its contents, could you anticipate a psychological state of anxiety that would likely be present when someone needed the information? If so, then you might use clear bullet lists, concise, declarative sentences, and diagrams to communicate clearly.

Your cultural background plays a significant role in what and how you perceive your world. You may be from a culture that values community. For example, the message across the advertisement reads: *Stand out from the crowd*. Given your cultural background, it may not be a very effective slogan to get your attention.

Our perceptual set involves our attitudes, beliefs, and values about the world. Perhaps you've heard the phrase, "Looking at the world through rose-colored glasses" and can even think of someone as an example. We experience the world through mediated images and mass communication. We also come to know one another interpersonally in groups. All these experiences help form our mental expectations of what is happening and what will happen.

Think about your brand preferences, your choice of transportation, your self-expression through your clothing, haircut, and jewelry—all these external symbols represent in some way how you view yourself within your community and the world. We can extend this perspective in many ways, both positive and negative, and see that understanding the perspective of the audience takes on new levels of importance.

KEY TAKEAWAY

Our perceptions are influenced by our individual differences and preconceived notions.

EXERCISES

1. When you watch a film with friends, make a point of talking about it afterward and listen to how each person perceived aspects of the film. Ask them each to describe it in ten words or less. Did they use the same words? Did you see it the same way, or differently? Did you catch all the points, frames of reference, values, or miss any information? What does this say about perception?
2. Think of a time when you misunderstood a message. What was your psychological state at the time? Do you think you would have understood the message differently if you had been in a different psychological state?
3. Think of a time when someone misunderstood your message. What happened and why? Share and compare with classmates.

3.4 Getting to Know Your Audience
LEARNING OBJECTIVE

1. Describe three ways to better understand and reach your audience.

Writing to your audience's expectations is key to your success, but how do you get a sense of your readers? Research, time, and effort. At first glance you may think you know your audience, but if you dig a little deeper you will learn more about them and become a better speaker.

Examine Figure 3.7 "Iceberg Model", often called the iceberg model. When you see an iceberg on the ocean, the great majority of its size and depth lie below your level of awareness. When you write a document or give a presentation, each person in your reading or listening audience is like the tip of an iceberg. You may perceive people of different ages, races, ethnicities, and genders, but those are only surface characteristics. This is your challenge. When you communicate with a diverse audience, you are engaging in intercultural communication. The more you learn about the audience, the better you will be able to navigate the waters, and your communication interactions, safely and effectively.

Figure 3.7 Iceberg Model

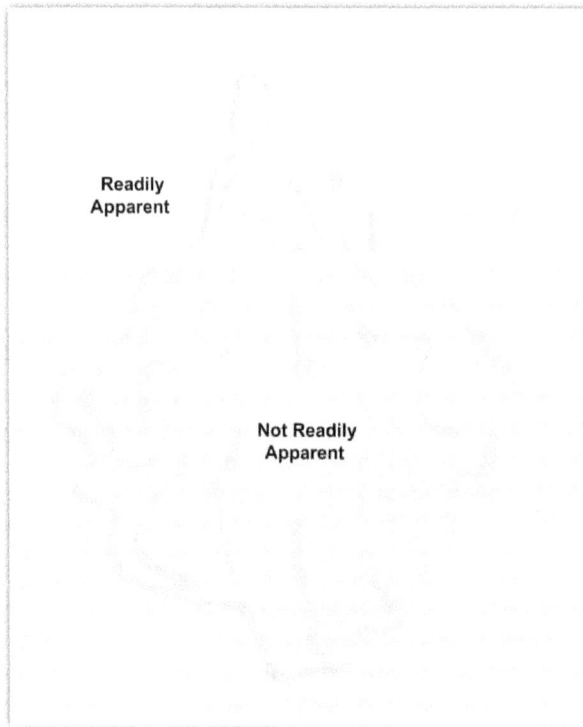

Readily Apparent

Not Readily Apparent

Theodore Roosevelt pointed out that "the most important single ingredient in the formula of success is knowing how to get along with people." Knowing your audience well before you speak is essential. Here are a few questions to help guide you in learning more about your audience:

- How big is the audience?
- What are their backgrounds, gender, age, jobs, education, and/or interests?
- Do they already know about your topic? If so, how much?
- Will other materials be presented or available? If so, what are they, what do they cover, and how do they relate to your message?
- How much time is allotted for your presentation, or how much space do you have for your written document? Will your document or presentation stand alone or do you have the option of adding visuals, audio-visual aids, or links?

Demographic Traits
Demographic traits refer to the characteristics that make someone an individual, but that he or she has in common

with others. For example, if you were born female, then your view of the world may be different from that of a male, and may be similar to that of many other females. Being female means that you share this "femaleness" trait with roughly half the world's population.

How does this demographic trait of being female apply to communication? For example, we might find that women tend to be more aware than the typical male of what it means to be capable of becoming pregnant, or to go through menopause. If you were giving a presentation on nutrition to a female audience, you would likely include more information about nutrition during pregnancy and during menopause than you would if your audience were male.

We can explore other traits by considering your audience's age, level of education, employment or career status, and various other groups they may belong to. Imagine that you are writing a report on the health risks associated with smoking. To get your message across to an audience of twelve-year-olds, clearly you would use different language and different examples than what you would use for an audience of adults age fifty-five and older. If you were writing for a highly educated audience—say, engineering school graduates—you would use much more scholarly language and rigorous research documentation than if you were writing for first-year college students.

Writing for readers in the insurance industry, you would likely choose examples of how insurance claims are affected by whether or not a policyholder smokes, whereas if you were writing for readers who are athletes, you would focus on how the human body reacts to tobacco. Similarly, if you were writing for a community newsletter, you would choose local examples, whereas if your venue was a Web site for parents, you might choose examples that are more universal.

Audiences tend to be interested in messages that relate to their interests, needs, goals, and motivations. Demographic traits can give us insight into our audience and allow for an audience-centered approach to your assignment that will make you a more effective communicator. [1]

Improving Your Perceptions of Your Audience
The better you can understand your audience, the better you can tailor your communications to reach them. To understand them, a key step is to perceive clearly who they are, what they are interested in, what they need, and what motivates them. This ability to perceive is important with audience members from distinct groups, generations, and even cultures. William Seiler and Melissa Beall [2] offer us six ways to improve our perceptions, and therefore improve our

communication, particularly in public speaking; they are listed in Table 3.3 "Perceptual Strategies for Success".

Table 3.3 Perceptual Strategies for Success

Perceptual Strategy	Explanation
Become an active perceiver	We need to actively seek out as much information as possible. Placing yourself in the new culture, group, or co-culture can often expand your understanding.
Recognize each person's unique frame of reference	We all perceive the world differently. Recognize that even though you may interact with two people from the same culture, they are individuals with their own set of experiences, values, and interests.
Recognize that people, objects, and situations change	The world is changing and so are we. Recognizing that people and cultures, like communication process itself, are dynamic and ever changing can improve your intercultural communication.
Become aware of the role perceptions play in communication	As we explored in Chapter 2 "Delivering Your Message", perception is an important aspect of the communication process. By understanding that our perceptions are not the only ones possible can limit ethnocentrism and improve intercultural communication.
Keep an open mind	The adage "A mind is like a parachute—it works best when open" holds true. Being open to differences can improve intercultural communication.
Check your perceptions	By learning to observe, and acknowledging our own perceptions, we can avoid assumptions, expand our understanding, and improve our ability to communicate across cultures.

Fairness in Communication

Finally, consider that your audience has several expectations of you. No doubt you have sat through a speech or classroom lecture where you asked yourself, "Why should I listen?" You have probably been assigned to read a document or chapter and found yourself wondering, "What does this have to do with me?" These questions are normal and natural for audiences, but people seldom actually state these questions in so many words or say them out loud.

In a report on intercultural communication, V. Lynn Tyler [3] offers us some insight into these audience expectations, which can be summarized as the need to be fair to your audience. One key fairness principle is reciprocity, or a relationship of mutual exchange and interdependence. Reciprocity has four main components: mutuality, nonjudgmentalism, honesty, and respect.

Mutuality means that the speaker searches for common ground and understanding with his or her audience, establishing this space and building on it throughout the speech. This involves examining viewpoints other than your own and taking steps to insure the speech integrates an inclusive, accessible format rather than an ethnocentric one. Nonjudgmentalism involves willingness to examine diverse ideas and viewpoints. A nonjudgmental communicator is open-minded, and able to accept ideas that may be strongly opposed to his or her own beliefs and values.

Another aspect of fairness in communication is honesty: stating the truth as you perceive it. When you communicate honestly, you provide supporting and clarifying information and give credit to the sources where you obtained the information. In addition, if there is significant evidence opposing your viewpoint, you acknowledge this and avoid concealing it from your audience.

Finally, fairness involves respect for the audience and individual members—recognizing that each person has basic rights and is worthy of courtesy. Consider these expectations of fairness when designing your message and you will more thoroughly engage your audience.

KEY TAKEAWAY

To better understand your audience, learn about their demographic traits, such as age, gender, and employment status, as these help determine their interests, needs, and goals. In addition, become aware of your perceptions and theirs, and practice fairness in your communications.

EXERCISES

1. List at least three demographic traits that apply to you. How does belonging to these demographic groups influence your perceptions and priorities? Share your thoughts with your classmates.
2. Think of two ways to learn more about your audience. Investigate them and share your findings with your classmates.
3. Think of a new group you have joined, or a new activity you have become involved in. Did the activity or group have an influence on your perceptions? Explain the effects to your classmates.
4. When you started a new job or joined a new group, to some extent you learned a new language. Please think of at least three words that outsiders would not know and share them with the class and provide examples.

[1] Beebe, S. [Steven], & Beebe, S. [Susan]. (1997). *Public speaking: An audience-centered approach* (3rd ed.). Boston, MA: Allyn & Bacon.
[2] Seiler, W., & Beall, M. (2000). *Communication: Making connections* (4th ed.). Boston, MA: Allyn & Bacon.
[3] Tyler, V. (1978). Report of the working groups of the second SCA summer conference on intercultural communication. In N. C. Asuncio-Lande (Ed.), *Ethical Perspectives and Critical Issues in Intercultural Communication* (pp. 170–177). Falls Church, VA: SCA.

3.5 Listening and Reading for Understanding
LEARNING OBJECTIVE

1. Explain the importance of becoming an active listener and reader.

As the popular author and Hollywood entrepreneur Wilson Mizner said, "A good listener is not only popular everywhere, but after a while he knows something." Learning to listen to your conversational partner, customer, supplier, or supervisor is an important part of business communication. Too often, instead of listening we mentally rehearse what we want to say. Similarly, when we read, we are often trying to multitask and therefore cannot read with full attention. Inattentive listening or reading can cause us to miss much of what the speaker is sharing with us.

Communication involves the sharing and understanding of meaning. To fully share and understand, practice active listening and reading so that you are fully attentive, fully present in the moment of interaction. Pay attention to both the actual words and for other clues to meaning, such as tone of voice or writing style. Look for opportunities for clarification and feedback when the time comes for you to respond, not before.

Active Listening and Reading

You've probably experienced the odd sensation of driving somewhere and, having arrived, have realized you don't remember driving. Your mind may have been filled with other issues and you drove on autopilot. It's dangerous when you drive like that, and it is dangerous in communication. Choosing to listen or read attentively takes effort. People communicate with words, expressions, and even in silence, and your attention to them will make you a better communicator. From discussions on improving customer service to retaining customers in challenging economic times, the importance of listening comes up frequently as a success strategy.

Here are some tips to facilitate active listening and reading:
- Maintain eye contact with the speaker; if reading, keep your eyes on the page.
- Don't interrupt; if reading, don't multitask.

- Focus your attention on the message, not your internal monologue.
- Restate the message in your own words and ask if you understood correctly.
- Ask clarifying questions to communicate interest and gain insight.

When the Going Gets Tough

Our previous tips will serve you well in daily interactions, but suppose you have an especially difficult subject to discuss, or you receive a written document delivering bad news. In a difficult situation like this, it is worth taking extra effort to create an environment and context that will facilitate positive communication.

Here are some tips that may be helpful:
- **Set aside a special time**. To have a difficult conversation or read bad news, set aside a special time when you will not be disturbed. Close the door and turn off the TV, music player, and instant messaging client.
- **Don't interrupt**. Keep silent while you let the other person "speak his piece." If you are reading, make an effort to understand and digest the news without mental interruptions.
- **Be nonjudgmental**. Receive the message without judgment or criticism. Set aside your opinions, attitudes, and beliefs.
- **Be accepting**. Be open to the message being communicated, realizing that acceptance does not necessarily mean you agree with what is being said.
- **Take turns**. Wait until it is your turn to respond, and then measure your response in proportion to the message that was delivered to you. Reciprocal turn-taking allows each person have his say.
- **Acknowledge**. Let the other person know that you have listened to the message or read it attentively.
- **Understand**. Be certain that you understand what your partner is saying. If you don't understand, ask for clarification. Restate the message in your own words.
- **Keep your cool**. Speak your truth without blaming. A calm tone will help prevent the conflict from escalating. Use "I" statements (e.g., "I felt concerned when I learned that my department is going to have a layoff") rather than "you" statements (e.g., "you want to get rid of some of our best people").

Finally, recognize that mutual respect and understanding are built one conversation at a time. Trust is difficult to gain and easy to lose. Be patient and keep the channels of communication open, as a solution may develop slowly over the course of many small interactions. Recognize that it is more valuable to maintain the relationship over the long term than to "win" in an individual transaction.

KEY TAKEAWAY

Part of being an effective communicator is learning to receive messages from others through active listening and reading.

EXERCISES

1. Pair up with a classmate and do a role-play exercise in which one person tries to deliver a message while the other person multitasks and interrupts. Then try it again while the listener practices active listening. How do the two communication experiences compare? Discuss your findings.

2. Select a news article and practice active reading by reading the article and summarizing each of its main points in your own words. Write a letter to the editor commenting on the article—you don't have to send it, but you may if you wish.

3. In a half-hour period of time, see if you can count how many times you are interrupted. Share and compare with your classmates.

3.6 Additional Resources

- Explore the Web site of the National Association for Self-Esteem. http://www.self-esteem-nase.org

- Forum Network offers a wealth of audio and video files of speeches on various topics. Listen to a lecture titled "Selective Attention: Neuroscience and the Art Museum" by Barbara Stafford, professor of art history, University of Chicago. http://forum-network.org/lecture/selective-attention-neuroscience-and-art-museum

- Explore the Web site of the journal *Perception*. http://www.perceptionweb.com

- Visit this About.com site to learn more about the Gestalt principles of perception.http://psychology.about.com/od/sensationandperception/ss/gestaltlaws_4.htm

- Visit About.com to read an article by Kendra Van Wagner on the Gestalt laws of perceptual organization. http://psychology.about.com/od/sensationandperception/ss/gestaltlaws.htm

- Visit the U.S. Environmental Protection Agency's site to read about demographic traits and their relationship to environmental issues. http://www.epa.gov/greenkit/traits.htm

- Philosophe.com offers a collection of articles about understanding your audience when you design a Web site. http://philosophe.com/understanding_users

- Read more about active listening on this MindTools page. http://www.mindtools.com/CommSkll/ActiveListening.htm

- Consider these academic survival tips provided by Chicago State University.http://www.csu.edu/engineeringstudies/acadsurvivaltips.htm

NOTES:

NOTES:

Chapter 4:
Effective Business Writing

However great…natural talent may be, the art of writing cannot be learned all at once.
  Jean-Jacques Rousseau
Read, read, read…Just like a carpenter who works as an apprentice and studies the master.
  William Faulkner
You only learn to be a better writer by actually writing.
  Doris Lessing

Getting Started

INTRODUCTORY EXERCISES

1. Take a moment to write three words that describe your success in writing.
2. Make a list of words that you associate with writing. Compare your list with those of your classmates.
3. Briefly describe your experience writing and include one link to something you like to read in your post.

Something we often hear in business is, "Get it in writing." This advice is meant to prevent misunderstandings based on what one person thought the other person said. But does written communication—getting it in writing—always prevent misunderstandings?

According to a *Washington Post* news story, a written agreement would have been helpful to an airline customer named Mike. A victim of an airport mishap, Mike was given vouchers for $7,500 worth of free travel. However, in accordance with the airline's standard policy, the vouchers were due to expire in twelve months. When Mike saw that he and his wife would not be able to do enough flying to use the entire amount before the expiration date, he called the airline and asked for an extension. He was told the airline would extend the deadline, but later discovered they were willing to do so at only 50 percent of the vouchers' value. An airline spokesman told the newspaper, "If [Mike] can produce a letter stating that we would give the full value of the vouchers, he should produce it." [1]

Yet, as we will see in this chapter, putting something in writing is not always a foolproof way to ensure accuracy and understanding. A written communication is only as accurate as the writer's knowledge of the subject and audience, and understanding depends on how well the writer captures the reader's attention.

This chapter addresses the written word in a business context. We will also briefly consider the symbols, design, font, timing, and related nonverbal expressions you make when composing a page or document. Our discussions will focus on effective communication of your thoughts and ideas through writing that is clear, concise, and efficient.

---

[1] Oldenburg, D. (2005, April 12). Old adage holds: Get it in writing. *Washington Post*, p. C10. Retrieved from http://www.washingtonpost.com/wp-dyn/articles/A45309-2005Apr11.html

4.1 Oral versus Written Communication
LEARNING OBJECTIVE

1. Explain how written communication is similar to oral communication, and how it is different.

The written word often stands in place of the spoken word. People often say "it was good to hear from you" when they receive an e-mail or a letter, when in fact they didn't *hear* the message, they *read* it. Still, if they know you well, they may mentally "hear" your voice in your written words. Writing a message to friends or colleagues can be as natural as talking to them. Yet when we are asked to write something, we often feel anxious and view writing as a more effortful, exacting process than talking would be.

Oral and written forms of communication are similar in many ways. They both rely on the basic communication process, which consists of eight essential elements: source, receiver, message, channel, receiver, feedback, environment, context, and interference. Table 4.1 "Eight Essential Elements of Communication" summarizes these elements and provides examples of how each element might be applied in oral and written communication.

As you can see from the applications in this example, at least two different kinds of interference have the potential to ruin a conference call, and the interference can exist regardless of whether the communication to plan the call is oral or written. Try switching the "Context" and "Interference" examples from Oral to Written, and you will see that mismatched expectations and time zone confusion can happen by phone or by e-mail. While this example has an unfavorable outcome, it points out a way in which oral and written communication processes are similar.

Table 4.1 Eight Essential Elements of Communication

Element of Communication	Definition	Oral Application	Written Application
1. Source	A source creates and communicates a message.	Jay makes a telephone call to Heather.	Jay writes an e-mail to Heather.
2. Receiver	A receiver receives the message from the source.	Heather listens to Jay.	Heather reads Jay's e-mail.
3. Message	The message is the stimulus or meaning produced by the source for the receiver.	Jay asks Heather to participate in a conference call at 3:15.	Jay's e-mail asks Heather to participate in a conference call at 3:15.
4. Channel	A channel is the way a message travels between source and receiver.	The channel is the telephone.	The channel is e-mail.
5. Feedback	Feedback is the message the receiver sends in response to the source.	Heather says yes.	Heather replies with an e-mail saying yes.
6. Environment	The environment is the physical atmosphere where the communication occurs.	Heather is traveling by train on a business trip when she receives Jay's phone call.	Heather is at her desk when she receives Jay's e-mail.
7. Context	The context involves the psychological expectations of the source and receiver.	Heather expects Jay to send an e-mail with the call-in information for the call. Jay expects to do so, and does.	Heather expects Jay to dial and connect the call. Jay expects Heather to check her e-mail for the call-in information so that she can join the call.
8. Interference	Also known as noise, interference is anything that blocks or distorts the communication process.	Heather calls in at 3:15, but she has missed the call because she forgot that she is in a different time zone from Jay.	Heather waits for a phone call from Jay at 3:15, but he doesn't call.

Another way in which oral and written forms of communication are similar is that they can be divided into verbal and nonverbal categories. Verbal communication involves the words you say, and nonverbal communication involves how you say them—your tone of voice, your facial expression, body language, and so forth. Written communication also involves verbal and nonverbal dimensions. The words you choose are the verbal dimension. How you portray or display them is the nonverbal dimension, which can include the medium (e-mail or a printed document), the typeface or font, or the appearance of your signature on a letter. In this sense, oral and written communication are similar in their approach even as they are quite different in their application.

The written word allows for a dynamic communication process between source and receiver, but is often asynchronous, meaning that it occurs at different times. When we communicate face-to-face, we get immediate feedback, but our written words stand in place of that interpersonal interaction and we lack that immediate

response. Since we are often not physically present when someone reads what we have written, it is important that we anticipate the reader's needs, interpretation, and likely response to our written messages.

Suppose you are asked to write a message telling clients about a new product or service your company is about to offer. If you were speaking to one of them in a relaxed setting over coffee, what would you say? What words would you choose to describe the product or service, and how it may fulfill the client's needs? As the business communicator, you must focus on the words you use and how you use them. Short, simple sentences, in themselves composed of words, also communicate a business style. In your previous English classes you may have learned to write eloquently, but in a business context, your goal is clear, direct communication. One strategy to achieve this goal is to write with the same words and phrases you use when you talk. However, since written communication lacks the immediate feedback that is present in an oral conversation, you need to choose words and phrases even more carefully to promote accuracy, clarity, and understanding.

KEY TAKEAWAY

Written communication involves the same eight basic elements as oral communication, but it is often asynchronous.

EXERCISES

1. Review the oral and written applications in Table 4.1 "Eight Essential Elements of Communication" and construct a different scenario for each. What could Jay and Heather do differently to make the conference call a success?
2. Visit a business Web site that has an "About Us" page. Read the "About Us" message and write a summary in your own words of what it tells you about the company. Compare your results with those of your classmates.
3. You are your own company. What words describe you? Design a logo, create a name, and present your descriptive words in a way that gets attention. Share and compare with classmates.

4.2 How Is Writing Learned?
LEARNING OBJECTIVE

1. Explain how reading, writing, and critical thinking contribute to becoming a good writer.

You may think that some people are simply born better writers than others, but in fact writing is a reflection of experience and effort. If you think about your successes as a writer, you may come up with a couple of favorite books, authors, or teachers that inspired you to express yourself. You may also recall a sense of frustration with your previous writing experiences. It is normal and natural to experience a sense of frustration at the *perceived* inability to express oneself. The emphasis here is on your perception of yourself as a writer as one aspect of how you communicate. Most people use oral communication for much of their self-expression, from daily interactions to formal business meetings. You have a lifetime of experience in that arena that you can leverage to your benefit in your writing. Reading out loud what you have written is a positive technique we'll address later in more depth.

Martin Luther King Jr.'s statement, "Violence is the language of the unheard" emphasizes the importance of finding one's voice, of being able to express one's ideas. Violence comes in many forms, but is often associated with frustration born of the lack of opportunity to communicate. You may read King's words and think of the Civil Rights movement of the

1960s, or perhaps of the violence of the 9/11 terrorist attacks, or of wars happening in the world today. Public demonstrations and fighting are expressions of voice, from individual to collective. Finding your voice, and learning to listen to others, is part of learning to communicate.

You are your own best ally when it comes to your writing. Keeping a positive frame of mind about your journey as a writer is not a cliché or simple, hollow advice. Your attitude toward writing can and does influence your written products. Even if writing has been a challenge for you, the fact that you are reading this sentence means you perceive the importance of this essential skill. This text and our discussions will help you improve your writing, and your positive attitude is part of your success strategy.

There is no underestimating the power of effort when combined with inspiration and motivation. The catch then is to get inspired and motivated. That's not all it takes, but it is a great place to start. You were not born with a key pad in front of you, but when you want to share something with friends and text them, the words (or abbreviations) come almost naturally. So you recognize you have the skills necessary to begin the process of improving and harnessing your writing abilities for business success. It will take time and effort, and the proverbial journey starts with a single step, but don't lose sight of the fact that your skillful ability to craft words will make a significant difference in your career.

Reading

Reading is one step many writers point to as an integral step in learning to write effectively. You may like Harry Potter books or be a Twilight fan, but if you want to write effectively in business, you need to read business-related documents. These can include letters, reports, business proposals, and business plans. You may find these where you work or in your school's writing center, business department, or library; there are also many Web sites that provide sample business documents of all kinds. Your reading should also include publications in the industry where you work or plan to work, such as *Aviation Week*, *Info World*, *Journal of Hospitality*, *International Real Estate Digest*, or *Women's Wear Daily*, to name just a few. You can also gain an advantage by reading publications in fields other than your chosen one; often reading outside your niche can enhance your versatility and help you learn how other people express similar concepts. Finally, don't neglect general media like the business section of your local newspaper, and national publications like the *Wall Street Journal*, *Fast Company*, and the *Harvard Business Review*. Reading is one of the most useful lifelong habits you can practice to boost your business communication skills.

In the "real world" when you are under a deadline and production is paramount, you'll be rushed and may lack the time to do adequate background reading for a particular assignment. For now, take advantage of your business communication course by exploring common business documents you may be called on to write, contribute to, or play a role in drafting. Some documents have a degree of formula to them, and your familiarity with them will reduce your preparation and production time while increasing your effectiveness. As you read similar documents, take notes on what you observe. As you read several sales letters, you may observe several patterns that can serve you well later on when it's your turn. These patterns are often called conventions, or conventional language patterns for a specific genre.

Writing

Never lose sight of one key measure of the effectiveness of your writing: the degree to which it fulfills readers' expectations. If you are in a law office, you know the purpose of a court brief is to convince the judge that certain points of law apply to the given case. If you are at a newspaper, you know that an editorial opinion article is supposed to convince readers of the merits of a certain viewpoint, whereas a news article is supposed to report facts without bias. If you are writing ad copy, the goal is to motivate consumers to make a purchase decision. In each case, you are writing to a specific purpose, and a great place to start when considering what to write is to answer the following question: what are the readers' expectations?

When you are a junior member of the team, you may be given clerical tasks like filling in forms, populating a database, or coordinating appointments. Or you may be assigned to do research that involves reading, interviewing, and note taking. Don't underestimate these facets of the writing process; instead, embrace the fact that writing for business often involves tasks that a novelist might not even recognize as "writing." Your contribution is quite important and in itself is an on-the-job learning opportunity that shouldn't be taken for granted.

When given a writing assignment, it is important to make sure you understand what you are being asked to do. You may read the directions and try to put them in your own words to make sense of the assignment. Be careful, however, not to lose sight of what the directions say versus what you think they say. Just as an audience's expectations should be part of your consideration of how, what, and why to write, the instructions given by your instructor, or in a work situation by your supervisor, establish expectations. Just as you might ask a mentor more about a business writing assignment at work, you need to use the resources available to you to maximize your learning opportunity. Ask the professor to clarify any points you find confusing, or perceive more than one way to interpret, in order to better meet the expectations. Before you write an opening paragraph, or even the first sentence, it is important to consider the overall goal of the assignment. The word *assignment* can apply equally to a written product for class or for your employer. You might make a list of the main points and see how those points may become the topic sentences in a series of paragraphs. You may also give considerable thought to whether your word choice, your tone, your language, and what you want to say is in line with your understanding of your audience. We briefly introduced the writing process previously, and will visit it in depth later in our discussion, but for now writing should about exploring your options. Authors rarely have a finished product in mind when they start, but once you know what your goal is and how to reach it, you writing process will become easier and more effective.

Constructive Criticism and Targeted Practice

Mentors can also be important in your growth as a writer. Your instructor can serve as a mentor, offering constructive criticism, insights on what he or she has written, and life lessons about writing for a purpose. Never underestimate the mentors that surround you in the workplace, even if you are currently working in a position unrelated to your desired career. They can read your rough draft and spot errors, as well as provide useful insights. Friends and family can also be helpful mentors—if your document's meaning is clear to someone not working in your business, it will likely also be clear to your audience.

The key is to be open to criticism, keeping in mind that no one ever improved by repeating bad habits over and over. Only when you know what your errors are—errors of grammar or sentence structure, logic, format, and so on—can you correct your document and do a better job next time. Writing can be a solitary activity, but more often in business settings it is a collective, group, or team effort. Keep your eyes and ears open for opportunities to seek outside assistance before you finalize your document.

Learning to be a successful business writer comes with practice. Targeted practice, which involves identifying your weak areas and specifically working to improve them, is especially valuable. In addition to reading, make it a habit to write, even if it is not a specific assignment. The more you practice writing the kinds of materials that are used in your line of work, the more writing will come naturally and become an easier task—even on occasions when you need to work under pressure.

Critical Thinking

Critical thinking means becoming aware of your thinking process. It's a human trait that allows us to step outside what we read or write and ask ourselves, "Does this really make sense?" "Are there other, perhaps better, ways to explain this idea?" Sometimes our thinking is very abstract and becomes clear only through the process of getting thoughts down in words. As a character in E. M. Forster's *Aspects of the Novel* said, "How can I tell what I think till I see what I say?" [1] Did you really write what you meant to, and will it be easily understood by the reader? Successful writing forms a relationship with the audience, reaching the reader on a deep level that can be dynamic and motivating. In contrast, when writing fails to meet the audience's expectations, you already know the consequences: they'll move on.

Learning to write effectively involves reading, writing, critical thinking, and hard work. You may have seen *The Wizard of Oz* and recall the scene when Dorothy discovers what is behind the curtain. Up until that moment, she believed the Wizard's powers were needed to change her situation, but now she discovers that the power is her own. Like Dorothy, you can discover that the power to write successfully rests in your hands. Excellent business writing can be inspiring, and it is important to not lose that sense of inspiration as we deconstruct the process of writing to its elemental components.

You may be amazed by the performance of Tony Hawk on a skateboard ramp, Mia Hamm on the soccer field, or Michael Phelps in the water. Those who demonstrate excellence often make it look easy, but nothing could be further from the truth. Effort, targeted practice, and persistence will win the day every time. When it comes to writing, you need to learn to recognize clear and concise writing while looking behind the curtain at how it is created. This is not to say we are going to lose the magic associated with the best writers in the field. Instead, we'll appreciate what we are reading as we examine how it was written and how the writer achieved success.

KEY TAKEAWAY

Success in writing comes from good habits: reading, writing (especially targeted practice), and critical thinking.

EXERCISES

1. Interview one person whose job involves writing. This can include writing e-mails, reports, proposals, invoices, or any other form of business document. Where did this person learn to write? What would they include as essential steps to learning to write for success in business? Share your results with a classmate.

2. For five consecutive days, read the business section of your local newspaper or another daily paper. Write a one-page summary of the news that makes the most impression on you. Review your summaries and compare them with those of your classmates.

3. Practice filling out an online form that requires writing sentences, such as a job application for a company that receives applications online. How does this kind of writing compare with the writing you have done for other courses in the past? Discuss your thoughts with your classmates.

---

[1] Forster, E. M. (1976). *Aspects of the novel* (p. 99). Oliver Stallybrass (Ed.). Harmondsworth, UK: Penguin.

4.3 Good Writing
LEARNING OBJECTIVES

1. Identify six basic qualities that characterize good business writing.
2. Identify and explain the rhetorical elements and cognate strategies that contribute to good writing.

One common concern is to simply address the question, what is good writing? As we progress through our study of written business communication we'll try to answer it. But recognize that while the question may be simple, the answer is complex. Edward P. Bailey [1] offers several key points to remember.

Good business writing
- follows the rules,
- is easy to read, and
- attracts the reader.

Let's examine these qualities in more depth.

Bailey's first point is one that generates a fair amount of debate. What are the rules? Do "the rules" depend on audience expectations or industry standards, what your English teacher taught you, or are they reflected in the amazing writing of authors you might point to as positive examples? The answer is "all of the above," with a point of clarification. You may find it necessary to balance audience expectations with industry standards for a document, and may need to find a balance or compromise. Bailey [2] points to common sense as one basic criterion of good writing, but common sense is a product of experience. When searching for balance, reader understanding is the deciding factor. The correct use of a semicolon may not be what is needed to make a sentence work. Your reading audience should carry extra attention in everything you write because, without them, you won't have many more writing assignments.

When we say that good writing follows the rules, we don't mean that a writer cannot be creative. Just as an art student needs to know how to draw a scene in correct perspective before he can "break the rules" by "bending" perspective, so a writer needs to know the rules of language. Being well versed in how to use words correctly, form sentences with proper grammar, and build logical paragraphs are skills the writer can use no matter what the assignment. Even though some business settings may call for conservative writing, there are other areas where creativity is not only allowed but mandated. Imagine working for an advertising agency or a software development firm; in such situations success comes from expressing new, untried ideas. By following the rules of language and correct writing, a writer can express those creative ideas in a form that comes through clearly and promotes understanding.

Similarly, writing that is easy to read is not the same as "dumbed down" or simplistic writing. What is easy to read? For a young audience, you may need to use straightforward, simple terms, but to ignore their use of the language is to create an artificial and unnecessary barrier. An example referring to Miley Cyrus may work with one reading audience and fall flat with another. Profession-specific terms can serve a valuable purpose as we write about precise concepts. Not everyone will understand all the terms in a profession, but if your audience is largely literate in the terms of the field, using industry terms will help you establish a relationship with your readers.

The truly excellent writer is one who can explain complex ideas in a way that the reader can understand. Sometimes ease of reading can come from the writer's choice of a brilliant illustrative example to get a point across. In other situations, it can be the writer's incorporation of definitions into the text so that the meaning of unfamiliar words is clear. It may also be a matter of choosing dynamic, specific verbs that make it clear what is happening and who is carrying out the action. Bailey's third point concerns the interest of the reader. Will they want to read it? This question should guide much of what you write. We increasingly gain information from our environment through visual, auditory, and multimedia channels, from YouTube to streaming audio, and to watching the news online. Some argue that this has led to a decreased attention span for reading, meaning that writers need to appeal to readers with short, punchy sentences and catchy phrases. However, there are still plenty of people who love to immerse themselves in reading an interesting article, proposal, or marketing piece.

Perhaps the most universally useful strategy in capturing your reader's attention is to state how your writing can meet the reader's needs. If your document provides information to answer a question, solve a problem, or explain how to increase profits or cut costs, you may want to state this in the beginning. By opening with a "what's in it for me" strategy, you give your audience a reason to be interested in what you've written.

More Qualities of Good Writing
To the above list from Bailey, let's add some additional qualities that define good writing. Good writing

* meets the reader's expectations,
* is clear and concise,
* is efficient and effective.

To meet the reader's expectations, the writer needs to understand who the intended reader is. In some business situations, you are writing just to one person: your boss, a coworker in another department, or an individual customer or vendor. If you know the person well, it may be as easy for you to write to him or her as it is to write a note to your parent or roommate. If you don't know the person, you can at least make some reasonable assumptions about his or her expectations, based on the position he or she holds and its relation to your job.

In other situations, you may be writing a document to be read by a group or team, an entire department, or even a large number of total strangers. How can you anticipate their expectations and tailor your writing accordingly? Naturally you want to learn as much as you can about your likely audience. How much you can learn and what kinds of information will vary with the situation. If you are writing Web site content, for example, you may never meet the people who will visit the site, but you can predict why they would be drawn to the site and what they would expect to read there. Beyond learning about your audience, your clear understanding of the writing assignment and its purpose will help you to meet reader expectations.

Our addition of the fifth point concerning clear and concise writing reflects the increasing tendency in business writing to eliminate error. Errors can include those associated with production, from writing to editing, and reader response. Your twin goals of clear and concise writing point to a central goal across communication: fidelity. This concept involves our goal of accurately communicating all the intended information with a minimum of signal or message breakdown or misinterpretation. Designing your documents, including writing and presentation, to reduce message breakdown is an important part of effective business communication.

This leads our discussion to efficiency. There are only twenty-four hours in a day and we are increasingly asked to do more with less, with shorter deadlines almost guaranteed. As a writer, how do you meet ever-increasing expectations? Each writing assignment requires a clear understanding of the goals and desired results, and when either of these two aspects is unclear, the efficiency of your writing can be compromised. Rewrites require time that you may not have, but will have to make if the assignment was not done correctly the first time. As we have discussed previously, making a habit of reading similar documents prior to beginning your process of writing can help establish a mental template of your desired product. If you can see in your mind's eye what you want to write, and have the perspective of similar documents combined with audience's needs, you can write more efficiently. Your written documents are products and will be required on a schedule that impacts your coworkers and business. Your ability to produce effective documents efficiently is a skill set that will contribute to your success.

Our sixth point reinforces this idea with an emphasis on effectiveness. What is effective writing? It is writing that succeeds in accomplishing its purpose. Understanding the purpose, goals, and desired results of your writing assignment will help you achieve this success. Your employer may want an introductory sales letter to result in an increase in sales leads, or potential contacts for follow-up leading to sales. Your audience may not see the document from that perspective, but will instead read with the mindset of, "How does this help me solve X problem?" If you meet both goals, your writing is approaching effectiveness. Here, effectiveness is qualified with the word "approaching" to point out that writing is both a process and a product, and your writing will continually require effort and attention to revision and improvement.

Rhetorical Elements and Cognate Strategies

Another approach to defining good writing is to look at how it fulfills the goals of two well-known systems in communication. One of these systems comprises the three classical elements of rhetoric, or the art of presenting an argument. These elements are *logos* (logic), *ethos* (ethics and credibility), and *pathos* (emotional appeal), first proposed by the ancient Greek teacher Aristotle. Although rhetoric is often applied to oral communication, especially public speaking, it is also fundamental to good writing.

A second set of goals involves what are called cognate strategies, or ways of promoting understanding, [3] developed in recent decades by Charles Kostelnick and David Rogers. Like rhetorical elements, cognate strategies can be applied to public speaking, but they are also useful in developing good writing. Table 4.2 "Rhetorical Elements and Cognate Strategies" describes these goals, their purposes, and examples of how they may be carried out in business writing.

Table 4.2 Rhetorical Elements and Cognate Strategies

Aristotle's Rhetorical Elements	Cognate Strategies	Focus	Example in Business Writing
	Clarity	Clear understanding	An announcement will be made to the company later in the week, but I wanted to tell you personally that as of the first of next month, I will be leaving my position to accept a three-year assignment in our Singapore office. As soon as further details about the management of your account are available, I will share them with you.
	Conciseness	Key points	In tomorrow's conference call Sean wants to introduce the new team members, outline the schedule and budget for the project, and clarify each person's responsibilities in meeting our goals.
Logos	Arrangement	Order, hierarchy, placement	Our department has matrix structure. We have three product development groups, one for each category of product. We also have a manufacturing group, a finance group, and a sales group; different group members are assigned to each of the three product categories. Within the matrix, our structure is flat, meaning that we have no group leaders. Everyone reports to Beth, the department manager.

Aristotle's Rhetorical Elements	Cognate Strategies	Focus	Example in Business Writing
Ethos	Credibility	Character, trust	Having known and worked with Jesse for more than five years, I can highly recommend him to take my place as your advisor. In addition to having superb qualifications, Jesse is known for his dedication, honesty, and caring attitude. He will always go the extra mile for his clients.
	Expectation	Norms and anticipated outcomes	As is typical in our industry, we ship all merchandise FOB our warehouse. Prices are exclusive of any federal, state, or local taxes. Payment terms are net 30 days from date of invoice.
	Reference	Sources and frames of reference	According to an article in *Business Week* dated October 15, 2009, Doosan is one of the largest business conglomerates in South Korea.
Pathos	Tone	Expression	I really don't have words to express how grateful I am for all the support you've extended to me and my family in this hour of need. You guys are the best.
	Emphasis	Relevance	It was unconscionable for a member of our organization to shout an interruption while the president was speaking. What needs to happen now—and let me be clear about this—is an immediate apology.
	Engagement	Relationship	Faithful soldiers pledge never to leave a fallen comrade on the battlefield.

KEY TAKEAWAY

Good writing is characterized by correctness, ease of reading, and attractiveness; it also meets reader expectations and is clear, concise, efficient, and effective. Rhetorical elements (*logos*, *ethos*, and *pathos*) and cognate strategies (clarity, conciseness, arrangement, credibility, expectation, reference, tone, emphasis, and engagement) are goals that are achieved in good business writing.

EXERCISES

1. Choose a piece of business writing that attracts your interest. What made you want to read it? Share your thoughts with your classmates.
2. Choose a piece of business writing and evaluate it according to the qualities of good writing presented in this section. Do you think the writing qualifies as "good"? Why or why not? Discuss your opinion with your classmates.
3. Identify the ethos, pathos, and logos in a document. Share and compare with classmates.

[1] Bailey, E. (2008). *Writing and speaking.* New York, NY: McGraw-Hill.
[2] Bailey, E. (2008). *Writing and speaking.* New York, NY: McGraw-Hill.
[3] Kostelnick, C., & Roberts, D. (1998). *Designing visual language: Strategies for professional communicators* (p. 14). Needham Heights, MA: Allyn & Bacon.

4.4 Style in Written Communication
LEARNING OBJECTIVES

1. Describe and identify three styles of writing.
2. Demonstrate the appropriate use of colloquial, casual, and formal writing in at least one document of each style.

One way to examine written communication is from a structural perspective. Words are a series of symbols that communicate meaning, strung together in specific patterns that are combined to communicate complex and compound meanings. Nouns, verbs, adjectives, adverbs, prepositions, and articles are the building blocks you will use when composing written documents. Misspellings of individual words or grammatical errors involving misplacement or incorrect word choices in a sentence, can create confusion, lose meaning, and have a negative impact on the reception of your document. Errors themselves are not inherently bad, but failure to recognize and fix them will reflect on you, your company, and limit your success. Self-correction is part of the writing process.

Another way to examine written communication is from a goals perspective, where specific documents address stated (or unstated) goals and have rules, customs, and formats that are anticipated and expected. Violations of these rules, customs, or formats—whether intentional or unintentional—can also have a negative impact on the way your document is received.

Colloquial, casual, and formal writing are three common styles that carry their own particular sets of expectations. Which style you use will depend on your audience, and often whether your communication is going to be read only by those in your company (internal communications) or by those outside the organization, such as vendors, customers or clients (external communications). As a general rule, external communications tend to be more formal, just as corporate letterhead and business cards—designed for presentation to the "outside world"—are more formal than the e-mail and text messages that are used for everyday writing within the organization.

Style also depends on the purpose of the document and its audience. If your writing assignment is for Web page content, clear and concise use of the written word is essential. If your writing assignment is a feature interest article for an online magazine, you may have the luxury of additional space and word count combined with graphics, pictures, embedded video or audio clips, and links to related topics. If your writing assignment involves an introductory letter represented on a printed page delivered in an envelope to a potential customer, you won't have the interactivity to enhance your writing, placing an additional burden on your writing and how you represent it.

Colloquial

Colloquial language is an informal, conversational style of writing. It differs from standard business English in that it often makes use of colorful expressions, slang, and regional phrases. As a result, it can be difficult to understand for an English learner or a person from a different region of the country. Sometimes colloquialism takes the form of a word difference; for example, the difference between a "Coke," a "tonic," a "pop, and a "soda pop" primarily depends on where you live. It can also take the form of a saying, as Roy Wilder Jr. discusses in his book *You All Spoken Here: Southern Talk at Its Down-Home Best.* [1] Colloquial sayings like "He could mess up a rainstorm" or "He couldn't hit the ground if he fell" communicate the person is inept in a colorful, but not universal way. In the Pacific Northwest someone might "mosey," or walk slowly, over to the "café," or bakery, to pick up a "maple bar"—a confection known as a "Long John doughnut" to people in other parts of the United States.

Colloquial language can be reflected in texting:

"ok fwiw i did my part n put it in where you asked but my ?
is if the group does not participate do i still get credit for my

part of what i did n also how much do we all have to do i mean
i put in my opinion of the items in order do i also have to reply
to the other team members or what? Thxs"

We may be able to grasp the meaning of the message, and understand some of the abbreviations and codes, but when it comes to business, this style of colloquial text writing is generally suitable only for one-on-one internal communications between coworkers who know each other well (and those who do not judge each other on spelling or grammar). For external communications, and even for group communications within the organization, it is not normally suitable, as some of the codes are not standard, and may even be unfamiliar to the larger audience.

Colloquial writing may be permissible, and even preferable, in some business contexts. For example, a marketing letter describing a folksy product such as a wood stove or an old-fashioned popcorn popper might use a colloquial style to create a feeling of relaxing at home with loved ones. Still, it is important to consider how colloquial language will appear to the audience. Will the meaning of your chosen words be clear to a reader who is from a different part of the country? Will a folksy tone sound like you are "talking down" to your audience, assuming that they are not intelligent or educated enough to appreciate standard English? A final point to remember is that colloquial style is not an excuse for using expressions that are sexist, racist, profane, or otherwise offensive.

Casual

Casual language involves everyday words and expressions in a familiar group context, such as conversations with family or close friends. The emphasis is on the communication interaction itself, and less about the hierarchy, power, control, or social rank of the individuals communicating. When you are at home, at times you probably dress in casual clothing that you wouldn't wear in public—pajamas or underwear, for example. Casual communication is the written equivalent of this kind of casual attire. Have you ever had a family member say something to you that a stranger or coworker would never say? Or have you said something to a family member that you would never say in front of your boss? In both cases, casual language is being used. When you write for business, a casual style is usually out of place. Instead, a respectful, professional tone represents you well in your absence.

Formal

In business writing, the appropriate style will have a degree of formality. Formal language is communication that focuses on professional expression with attention to roles, protocol, and appearance. It is characterized by its vocabulary and syntax, or the grammatical arrangement of words in a sentence. That is, writers using a formal style tend to use a more sophisticated vocabulary—a greater variety of words, and more words with multiple syllables—not for the purpose of throwing big words around, but to enhance the formal mood of the document. They also tend to use more complex syntax, resulting in sentences that are longer and contain more subordinate clauses.

The appropriate style for a particular business document may be very formal, or less so. If your supervisor writes you an e-mail and you reply, the exchange may be informal in that it is fluid and relaxed, without much forethought or fanfare, but it will still reflect the formality of the business environment. Chances are you will be careful to use an informative subject line, a salutation ("Hi [supervisor's name]" is typical in e-mails), a word of thanks for whatever information or suggestion she provided you, and an indication that you stand ready to help further if need be. You will probably also check your grammar and spelling before you click "send."

A formal document such as a proposal or an annual report will involve a great deal of planning and preparation, and its style may not be fluid or relaxed. Instead, it may use distinct language to emphasize the prestige and professionalism of your company. Let's say you are going to write a marketing letter that will be printed on company letterhead and mailed to a hundred sales prospects. Naturally you want to represent your company in a positive light. In a letter of this nature you might write a sentence like "The Widget 300 is our premium offering in the line; we have designed it for ease of movement and efficiency of use, with your success foremost in our mind." But in an e-mail or a tweet, you might use an informal sentence instead, reading "W300—good stapler."

Writing for business often involves choosing the appropriate level of formality for the company and industry, the particular document and situation, and the audience.

KEY TAKEAWAY

The best style for a document may be colloquial, casual, informal, or formal, depending on the audience and the situation.

EXERCISES

1. Refer back to the e-mail or text message example in this section. Would you send that message to your professor? Why or why not? What normative expectations concerning professor-student communication are there and where did you learn them? Discuss your thoughts with your classmates.

2. Select a business document and describe its style. Is it formal, informal, or colloquial? Can you rewrite it in a different style? Share your results with a classmate.

3. List three words or phrases that you would say to your friends. List three words or phrases that communicate similar meanings that you would say to an authority figure. Share and compare with classmates.

4. When is it appropriate to write in a casual tone? In a formal tone? Write a one- to two-page essay on this topic and discuss it with a classmate.

5. How does the intended audience influence the choice of words and use of language in a document? Think of a specific topic and two specific kinds of audiences. Then write a short example (250–500 words) of how this topic might be presented to each of the two audiences.

[1] Wilde, J., Jr. (2003). *You all spoken here: Southern talk at its down-home best.* Athens: University of Georgia Press.

4.5 Principles of Written Communication
LEARNING OBJECTIVES

1. Understand the rules that govern written language.
2. Understand the legal implications of business writing.

You may not recall when or where you learned all about nouns, verbs, adjectives, adverbs, prepositions, articles, and phrases, but if you understand this sentence we'll take for granted that you have a firm grasp of the basics. But even professional writers and editors, who have spent a lifetime navigating the ins and outs of crafting correct sentences, have to use reference books to look up answers to questions of grammar and usage that arise in the course of their work. Let's examine how the simple collection of symbols called a word can be such a puzzle.

Words Are Inherently Abstract

There is no universally accepted definition for love, there are many ways to describe desire, and there are countless ways to draw patience. Each of these terms is a noun, but it's an abstract noun, referring to an intangible concept.

While there are many ways to define a chair, describe a table, or draw a window, they each have a few common characteristics. A chair may be made from wood, crafted in a Mission style, or made from plastic resin in one solid piece in nondescript style, but each has four legs and serves a common function. A table and a window also have common characteristics that in themselves form a basis for understanding between source and receiver. The words "chair," "table," and "window" are concrete terms, as they describe something we can see and touch.

Concrete terms are often easier to agree on, understand, or at least define the common characteristics of. Abstract terms can easily become even more abstract with extended discussions, and the conversational partners may never agree on a common definition or even a range of understanding.

In business communication, where the goal is to be clear and concise, limiting the range of misinterpretation, which type of word do you think is preferred? Concrete terms serve to clarify your writing and more accurately communicate your intended meaning to the receiver. While all words are abstractions, some are more so than others. To promote effective communication, choose words that can be easily referenced and understood.

Words Are Governed by Rules

Perhaps you like to think of yourself as a free spirit, but did you know that all your communication is governed by rules? You weren't born knowing how to talk, but learned to form words and sentences as you developed from infancy. As you learned language, you learned rules. You learned not only what a word means in a given context, and how to pronounce it; you also learned the social protocol of when to use it and when not to. When you write, your words represent you in your absence. The context may change from reader to reader, and your goal as an effective business communicator is to get your message across (and some feedback) regardless of the situation.

The better you know your audience and context, the better you can anticipate and incorporate the rules of how, what, and when to use specific words and terms. And here lies a paradox. You may think that, ideally, the best writing is writing that is universally appealing and understood. Yet the more you design a specific message to a specific audience or context, the less universal the message becomes. Actually, this is neither a good or bad thing in itself. In fact, if you didn't target your messages, they wouldn't be nearly as effective. By understanding this relationship of a universal or specific appeal to an audience or context, you can look beyond vocabulary and syntax and focus on the reader. When considering a communication assignment like a sales letter, knowing the intended audience gives you insight to the explicit and implicit rules.

All words are governed by rules, and the rules are vastly different from one language and culture to another. A famous example is the decision by Chevrolet to give the name "Nova" to one of its cars. In English, nova is recognized as coming from Latin meaning "new"; for those who have studied astronomy, it also refers to a type of star. When the Chevy Nova was introduced in Latin America, however, it was immediately ridiculed as the "car that doesn't go." Why? Because "*no va*" literally means "doesn't go" in Spanish.

By investigating sample names in a range of markets, you can quickly learn the rules surrounding words and their multiple meaning, much as you learned about subjects and objects, verbs and nouns, adjectives and adverbs when you were learning language. Long before you knew formal grammar terms, you observed how others communicate and learned by trial and error. In business, error equals inefficiency, loss of resources, and is to be avoided. For Chevrolet, a little market research in Latin America would have gone a long way.

Words Shape Our Reality

Aristotle is famous for many things, including his questioning of whether the table you can see, feel, or use is real. [1] This may strike you as strange, but imagine that we are looking at a collection of antique hand tools. What are they? They are made of metal and wood, but what are they used for? The words we use help us to make sense of our reality, and we often use what we know to figure out what we don't know. Perhaps we have a hard time describing the color of the tool, or the table, as we walk around it. The light itself may influence our perception of its color. We may lack the vocabulary to accurately describe to the color, and instead say it is "like a" color, but not directly describe the color itself. [2] The color, or use of the tool, or style of the table are all independent of the person perceiving them, but also a reflection of the person perceiving the object.

Clear and concise communication involves anticipation of this inability to label a color or describe the function of an antique tool by constructing meaning. Anticipating the language that the reader may reasonably be expected to know, as well as unfamiliar terms, enables the writer to communicate in a way that describes with common reference points while illustrating the new, interesting, or unusual. Promoting understanding and limiting misinterpretations are key goals of the effective business communicator.

Your letter introducing a new product or service relies, to an extent, on your preconceived notions of the intended audience and their preconceived notions of your organization and its products or services. By referencing common ground, you form a connection between the known and the unknown, the familiar and the new. People are more likely to be open to a new product or service if they can reasonably relate it to one they are familiar with, or with which they have had good experience in the past. Your initial measure of success is effective communication, and your long term success may be measured in the sale or new contract for services.

Words and Your Legal Responsibility

Your writing in a business context means that you represent yourself and your company. What you write and how you write it can be part of your company's success, but can also expose it to unintended consequences and legal responsibility. When you write, keep in mind that your words will keep on existing long after you have moved on to other projects. They can become an issue if they exaggerate, state false claims, or defame a person or legal entity such as a competing company. Another issue is plagiarism, using someone else's writing without giving credit to the source. Whether the "cribbed" material is taken from a printed book, a Web site, or a blog, plagiarism is a violation of copyright law and may also violate your company policies. Industry standards often have legal aspects that must be respected and cannot be ignored. For the writer this can be a challenge, but it can be a fun challenge with rewarding results.

The rapid pace of technology means that the law cannot always stay current with the realities of business communication. Computers had been in use for more than twenty years before Congress passed the Digital Millennium Copyright Act of 1998, the first federal legislation to "move the nation's copyright law into the digital age." [3] Think for a moment about the changes in computer use that have taken place since 1998, and you will realize how many new laws are needed to clarify what is fair and ethical, what should be prohibited, and who owns the rights to what.

For example, suppose your supervisor asks you to use your Facebook page or Twitter account to give an occasional "plug" to your company's products. Are you obligated to comply? If you later change jobs, who owns your posts or tweets—are they yours, or does your now-former employer have a right to them? And what about your network of "friends"? Can your employer use their contact information to send marketing messages? These and many other questions remain to be answered as technology, industry practices, and legislation evolve. [4]

"Our product is better than X company's product. Their product is dangerous and you would be a wise customer to choose us for your product solutions."

What's wrong with these two sentences? They may land you and your company in court. You made a generalized claim of one product being better than another, and you stated it as if it were a fact. The next sentence claims that your competitor's product is dangerous. Even if this is true, your ability to prove your claim beyond a reasonable doubt may be limited. Your claim is stated as fact again, and from the other company's perspective, your sentences may be considered libel or defamation.

Libel is the written form of defamation, or a false statement that damages a reputation. If a false statement of fact that concerns and harms the person defamed is published—including publication in a digital or online environment—the author of that statement may be sued for libel. If the person defamed is a public figure, they must prove malice or the intention to do harm, but if the victim is a private person, libel applies even if the offense cannot be proven to be malicious. Under the First Amendment you have a right to express your opinion, but the words you use and how you use them, including the context, are relevant to their interpretation as opinion versus fact. Always be careful to qualify what you write and to do no harm.

KEY TAKEAWAY

Words are governed by rules and shape our reality. Writers have a legal responsibility to avoid plagiarism and libel.

EXERCISES

1. Define the word "chair." Describe what a table is. Draw a window. Share, compare, and contrast results with classmates
2. Define love. Describe desire. Draw patience.
3. Identify a target audience and indicate at least three words that you perceive would be appropriate and effective for that audience. Identify a second audience (distinct from the first) and indicate three words that you perceive would be appropriate and effective. How are the audiences and their words similar or different? Compare your results with those of your classmates.
4. Create a sales letter for an audience that comes from a culture other than your own. Identify the culture and articulate how your message is tailored to your perception of your intended audience. Share and compare with classmates.
5. Do an online search on "online libel cases" and see what you find. Discuss your results with your classmates.
6. In other examples beyond the grammar rules that guide our use of words, consider the online environment. Conduct a search on the word "netiquette" and share your findings.

[1] Aristotle. (1941). De anima. In R. McKeon (Ed.), *The basic works of Aristotle* (J. A. Smith, Trans.). New York, NY: Random House.
[2] Russell, B. (1962). *The problems of philosophy* (28th ed., p. 9). Oxford, UK: Oxford University Press. (Original work published 1912)
[3] United States Copyright Office (1998). Executive summary: Digital millennium copyright act. Washington, DC: U.S. Government Printing Office. Retrieved

fromhttp://www.copyright.gov/reports/studies/dmca/dmca_executive.ht ml

[4] Tahmincioglu, E. (2009, October 11). Your boss wants you on Twitter: Companies recognizing value of having workers promote products. MSNBC Careers. Retrieved fromhttp://www.msnbc.msn.com/id/33090717/ns/business-careers

4.6 Overcoming Barriers to Effective Written Communication
LEARNING OBJECTIVE

1. Describe some common barriers to written communication and how to overcome them.

In almost any career or area of business, written communication is a key to success. Effective writing can prevent wasted time, wasted effort, aggravation, and frustration. The way we communicate with others both inside of our business and on the outside goes a long way toward shaping the organization's image. If people feel they are listened to and able to get answers from the firm and its representatives, their opinion will be favorable. Skillful writing and an understanding of how people respond to words are central to accomplishing this goal.

How do we display skillful writing and a good understanding of how people respond to words? Following are some suggestions.

Do Sweat the Small Stuff

Let us begin with a college student's e-mail to a professor:

"i am confused as to why they are not due intil 11/10 i mean the calender said that they was due then so thats i did them do i still get credit for them or do i need to due them over on one tape? please let me know thanks. also when are you grading the stuff that we have done?"

What's wrong with this e-mail? What do you observe that may act as a barrier to communication? Let's start with the lack of formality, including the fact that the student neglected to tell the professor his or her name, or which specific class the question referred to. Then there is the lack of adherence to basic vocabulary and syntax rules. And how about the lower case "i's" and the misspellings?

One significant barrier to effective written communication is failure to sweat the small stuff. Spelling errors and incorrect grammar may be considered details, but they reflect poorly on you and, in a business context, on your company. They imply either that you are not educated enough to know you've made mistakes or that you are too careless to bother correcting them. Making errors is human, but making a habit of producing error-filled written documents makes negative

consequences far more likely to occur. When you write, you have a responsibility to self-edit and pay attention to detail. In the long run, correcting your mistakes before others see them will take less time and effort than trying to make up for mistakes after the fact.

Get the Target Meaning
How would you interpret this message?

"You must not let inventory build up. You must monitor carrying costs and keep them under control. Ship any job lots of more than 25 to us at once."

Bypassing involves the misunderstanding that occurs when the receiver completely misses the source's intended meaning. Words mean different things to different people in different contexts. All that difference allows for both source and receiver to completely miss one another's intended goal. Did you understand the message in the example? Let's find out. Jerry Sullivan, in his article *Bypassing in Managerial Communication*, [1] relates the story of Mr. Sato, a manager from Japan who is new to the United States. The message came from his superiors at Kumitomo America, a firm involved with printing machinery for the publishing business in Japan. Mr. Sato delegated the instructions (in English as shown above) to Ms. Brady, who quickly identified there were three lots in excess of twenty-five and arranged for prompt shipment.

Six weeks later Mr. Sato received a second message:

"Why didn't you do what we told you? Your quarterly inventory report indicates you are carrying 40 lots which you were supposed to ship to Japan. You must not violate our instructions."

What's the problem? As Sullivan relates, it is an example of one word, or set of words, having more than one meaning. [2] According to Sullivan, in Japanese "more than x" includes the reference number twenty-five. In other words, Kumitomo wanted all lots with twenty-five or more to be shipped to Japan. Forty lots fit that description. Ms. Brady interpreted the words as written, but the cultural context had a direct impact on the meaning and outcome.

You might want to defend Ms. Brady and understand the interpretation, but the lesson remains clear. Moreover, cultural expectations differ not only internationally, but also on many different dimensions from regional to interpersonal. Someone raised in a rural environment in the Pacific Northwest may have a very different interpretation of meaning from someone from New York City. Take, for example, the word "downtown." To the rural resident, downtown refers to the center or urban area of any big city.

To a New Yorker, however, downtown may be a direction, not a place. One can go uptown or downtown, but when asked, "Where are you from?" the answer may refer to a borough ("I grew up in Manhattan") or a neighborhood ("I'm from the East Village").

This example involves two individuals who differ by geography, but we can further subdivide between people raised in the same state from two regions, two people of the opposite sex, or two people from different generations. The combinations are endless, as are the possibilities for bypassing. While you might think you understand, requesting feedback and asking for confirmation and clarification can help ensure that you get the target meaning.

Sullivan also notes that in stressful situations we often think in terms of either/or relationships, failing to recognize the stress itself. This kind of thinking can contribute to source/receiver error. In business, he notes that managers often incorrectly assume communication is easier than it is, and fail to anticipate miscommunication. [3]

As writers, we need to keep in mind that words are simply a means of communication, and that meanings are in people, not the words themselves. Knowing which words your audience understands and anticipating how they will interpret them will help you prevent bypassing.

Consider the Nonverbal Aspects of Your Message
Let's return to the example at the beginning of this section of an e-mail from a student to an instructor. As we noted, the student neglected to identify himself or herself and tell the instructor which class the question referred to. Format is important, including headers, contact information, and an informative subject line.

This is just one example of how the nonverbal aspects of a message can get in the way of understanding. Other nonverbal expressions in your writing may include symbols, design, font, and the timing of delivering your message.

Suppose your supervisor has asked you to write to a group of clients announcing a new service or product that directly relates to a service or product that these clients have used over the years. What kind of communication will your document be? Will it be sent as an e-mail or will it be a formal letter printed on quality paper and sent by postal mail? Or will it be a tweet, or a targeted online ad that pops up when these particular clients access your company's Web site? Each of these choices involves an aspect of written communication that is nonverbal. While the words may communicate a formal tone, *the font may not*. The paper chosen to represent your company influences the perception of it. An e-mail may indicate that it is less than formal and be easily deleted.

As another example, suppose you are a small business owner and have hired a new worker named Bryan. You need to provide written documentation of asking Bryan to fill out a set of forms that are required by law. Should you send an e-mail to Bryan's home the night before he starts work, welcoming him aboard and attaching links to IRS form W-4 and Homeland Security form I-9? Or should you wait until he has been at work for a couple of hours, then bring him the forms in hard copy along with a printed memo stating that he needs to fill them out? There are no right or wrong answers, but you will use your judgment, being aware that these nonverbal expressions are part of the message that gets communicated along with your words.

Review, Reflect, and Revise
Do you review what you write? Do you reflect on whether it serves its purpose? Where does it miss the mark? If you can recognize it, then you have the opportunity to revise.

Writers are often under deadlines, and that can mean a rush job where not every last detail is reviewed. This means more mistakes, and there is always time to do it right the second time. Rather than go through the experience of seeing all the mistakes in your "final" product and rushing off to the next job, you may need to focus more on the task at hand and get it done correctly the first time. Go over each step in detail as you review.

A mental review of the task and your performance is often called reflection. Reflection is not procrastination. It involves looking at the available information and, as you review the key points in your mind, making sure each detail is present and perfect. Reflection also allows for another opportunity to consider the key elements and their relationship to each other.

When you revise your document, you change one word for another, make subtle changes, and improve it. Don't revise simply to change the good work you've completed, but instead look at it from the perspective of the reader—for example, how could this be clearer to them? What would make it visually attractive while continuing to communicate the message? If you are limited to words only, then does each word serve the article or letter? No extras, but just about right.

KEY TAKEAWAY

To overcome barriers to communication, pay attention to details; strive to understand the target meaning; consider your nonverbal expressions; and review, reflect, and revise.

EXERCISES

1. Review the example of a student's e-mail to a professor in this section, and rewrite it to communicate the message more clearly.
2. Write a paragraph of 150–200 words on a subject of your choice. Experiment with different formats and fonts to display it and, if you wish, print it. Compare your results with those of your classmates.
3. How does the purpose of a document define its format and content? Think of a specific kind of document with a specific purpose and audience. Then create a format or template suitable to that document, purpose, and audience. Show your template to the class or post it on a class bulletin board.
4. Write one message of at least three sentences with at least three descriptive terms and present it to at least three people. Record notes about how they understand the message, and to what degree their interpretations are the same of different. Share and compare with classmates.

[1] Sullivan, J., Kameda, N., & Nobu, T. (1991). Bypassing in managerial communication. *Business Horizons, 34*(1), 71–80.
[2] Sullivan, J., Kameda, N., & Nobu, T. (1991). Bypassing in managerial communication. *Business Horizons, 34*(1), 71–80.
[3] Sullivan, J., Kameda, N., & Nobu, T. (1991). Bypassing in managerial communication. *Business Horizons, 34*(1), 71–80.

4.7 Additional Resources

- Visit AllYouCanRead.com for a list of the top ten business magazines. http://www.allyoucanread.com/top-10-business-magazines
- The Wall Street Executive Library presents a comprehensive menu of business Web sites, publications, and other resources. http://www.executivelibrary.com
- The Web site 4hb.com (For Home Business) provides many sample business documents, as well as other resources for the small business owner. http://www.4hb.com/index.html
- The Business Owner's Toolkit provides sample documents in more than a dozen categories from finance to marketing to worker safety. http://www.toolkit.com/tools/index.aspx
- Words mean different things to different people—especially when translated from one language to another.

Visit this site for a list of car names "*que no va*" (that won't go) in foreign languages. http://www.autoblog.com/2008/04/30/nissan-360-the-otti-and-the-moco
- Visit "Questions and Quandaries," the *Writer's Digest* blog by Brian Klems, for a potpourri of information about writing. http://blog.writersdigest.com/qq
- Appearance counts. Read an article by communications expert Fran Lebo on enhancing the nonverbal aspects of your document. http://ezinearticles.com/?The-Second-Law-of-Business-Writing---Appearance-Counts&id=3039288
- Visit this site to access the Sullivan [1] article on bypassing in managerial communication.http://findarticles.com/p/articles/mi_m1038/is_n1_v34/ai_10360317

[1] Sullivan, J., Kameda, N., & Nobu, T. (1991). Bypassing in managerial communication. *Business Horizons, 34*(1), 71–80.

NOTES:

NOTES:

Chapter 5:
Writing Preparation

Before you write, think.
  William Arthur Ward

Getting Started

INTRODUCTORY EXERCISES

1. Identify a career you are interested in pursuing and do an online search for information about it, taking note of the number of results returned and a couple of the top ten sources. Compare your results with those of your classmates.
2. Visit your college or university library. Familiarize yourself with the resources available to business writers and choose one resource that you find especially valuable. Write a short summary of the resource to share with your classmates, explaining why you chose this resource.
3. In a business setting, describe some circumstances where it would it be appropriate to send a message by instant messaging, or by e-mail, or in a printed memo. Ask some colleagues or coworker what they consider the best option and why, and share the results with the class.

No matter who you are, you were not born speaking English (or any other language), and were certainly not born writing. You learned to speak and to write and, like all humans, your skill in speaking and writing can continue to improve and adapt across your lifetime. The awareness of this simple fact should encourage you. If your writing has been well received in the past, congratulations. It may be that your skill in producing college-level essays has served you well. Still, the need for learning to produce clear, concise business writing may be a new skill for you. Even seasoned professional business communicators find it a challenge to present complex and dynamic relationships in a way that the audience can grasp at a glance, on a first read, or with minimal effort. If your writing has not been as well received in the past as you would like, this chapter will help you see the process from a perspective where attention to specific steps can lead to overall success.

In addition to your previous experiences, you will necessarily draw on the writing of others as you prepare for your writing effort. If you have ever fallen asleep on your textbook, you know that trying to absorb many pages of reading in a single session is not the best strategy for studying. In the same way, as you prepare to write a business document, you know that

using the first search result listed on Google or Yahoo! is not the best strategy for success. You may be tempted to gather only the information that is most readily available, or that which confirms your viewpoint, but you will sell yourself short and may produce an inferior piece of writing.

Instead, you need to determine the purpose of your writing project; search for information, facts, and statistics to support your purpose; and remain aware of information that contradicts the message you are aiming to convey. Think of it as an exercise program. If you only do the easy exercises, and nothing else, you may develop a single muscle group, but will never gain real strength. What kinds of skills, or strengths, will you need in order to write well enough to succeed in your career? Solid research skills combined with effective preparation for writing involve a range of skill sets that require time and practice. The degree to which you make the extra effort will pay dividends throughout your career.

5.1 Think, Then Write: Writing Preparation
LEARNING OBJECTIVES

1. Explain why preparation is important in business writing.
2. Think critically and employ strategies to overcome common fears of writing.

"How do I prepare myself for writing?" is a common question and one that has no single correct answer. When do you do your best work? Whatever your work or task may be, it doesn't have to be writing. Some people work best in the morning, others only after their daily dose of coffee. Still others burn the midnight oil and work well late into the night while their colleagues lose their productive edge as the sun sets. "To thine own self be true," is a great idea when you have the freedom to choose when you work, but increasingly our lives are governed by schedules and deadlines that we do not control. You may have a deadline that requires you to work late at night when you recognize that you are far more productive early in the morning. If you can, consider one important step to writing success: know when you are most productive. If you cannot choose your timing, then dedication and perseverance are required. The job must be completed and the show must go on. Your effort demonstrates self-control and forbearance (as opposed to impatience and procrastination) and implies professionalism. To be productive, you have to be alert, ready to work, and can accomplish tasks with relative ease. You will no doubt recognize that sometimes tasks take a lot longer, the solution is much harder to find, and you may find work more frustrating at other times. If you have the option, try to adjust your schedule so the writing tasks before you can be tackled at times when you are most productive, where your ability to concentrate is best, and when you are your most productive. If you don't have the option, focus clearly on the task before you.

Every individual is different, and what works for one person may be ineffective for someone else. One thing that professional writers agree on, however, is that you don't need to be in the "right mood" to write—and that, in fact, if you wait for the right mood to strike, you will probably never get started at all. Ernest Hemingway, who wrote some of the most famous novels of the twentieth century as well as hundreds of essays, articles, and short stories, advised writers to "work every day. No matter what has happened the day or night before, get up and bite on the nail." [1]

In order for your work to be productive, you will need to focus your attention on your writing. The stereotype of the writer tucked away in an attic room or a cabin in the woods, lost in the imaginary world created by the words as they flow onto the page, is only a stereotype. Our busy lives involve constant interruption. In a distraction-prone business environment, much of your writing will be done while colleagues are talking on the phone, having face-to-face conversations as they walk by, and possibly stopping at your desk to say hello or ask a question. Your phone may ring or you may have incoming instant messages (IMs) that need to be answered quickly. These unavoidable interruptions make it even more important to develop a habit of concentrating when you write.

The mind has been likened to a brace of wild horses; if you have ever worked with horses, you know they each have a mind of their own. Taken individually they can be somewhat manageable, but together they can prove to be quite a challenge. Our minds can multitask and perform several tasks simultaneously, but we can also get easily distracted. We can get sidetracked and lose valuable time away from our designated task. Our ability to concentrate is central to our ability to write effectively, whether we work alone or as part of a team.

In many business situations, you may not be writing solo but instead collaborating on a document with various coworkers, vendors, or customers. The ability to concentrate is perhaps even more important in these group writing situations. [2] In this discussion, we'll consider the writing process from a singular perspective, where you are personally responsible for

planning, researching, and producing a product of writing. In other areas of this text we also consider the collaborative process, its strengths and weaknesses, and how to negotiate and navigate the group writing process.

Thinking Critically

As you approach your writing project, it is important to practice the habit of thinking critically. Critical thinking can be defined as "self-directed, self-disciplined, self-monitored, and self-corrective thinking." [3] It is the difference between watching television in a daze versus analyzing a movie with attention to its use of lighting, camera angles, and music to influence the audience. One activity requires very little mental effort, while the other requires attention to detail, the ability to compare and contrast, and sharp senses to receive all the stimuli.

As a habit of mind, critical thinking requires established standards and attention to their use, effective communication, problem solving, and a willingness to acknowledge and address our own tendency for confirmation bias, egocentrism, and sociocentrism. We'll use the phrase "habit of mind" because clear, critical thinking is a habit that requires effort and persistence. People do not start an exercise program, a food and nutrition program, or a stop-smoking program with 100 percent success the first time. In the same way, it is easy to fall back into lazy mental short cuts, such as "If it costs a lot, it must be good," when in fact the statement may very well be false. You won't know until you gather information that supports (or contradicts) the assertion.

As we discuss getting into the right frame of mind for writing, keep in mind that the same recommendations apply to reading and research. If you only pay attention to information that reinforces your existing beliefs and ignore or discredit information that contradicts your beliefs, you are guilty of confirmation bias. [4] As you read, research, and prepare for writing, make an effort to gather information from a range of reliable sources, whether or not this information leads to conclusions you didn't expect. Remember that those who read your writing will be aware of, or have access to, this universe of data as well and will have their own confirmation bias. Reading and writing from an audience-centered view means acknowledging your confirmation bias and moving beyond it to consider multiple frames of references, points of view, and perspectives as you read, research, and write.

Egocentrism and sociocentrism are related concepts to confirmation bias. Egocentrism can be defined as the use of self-centered standards to determine what to believe and what to reject. Similarly, sociocentrism involves the use of society-centered standards. [5] Both ways of thinking create an "us versus them" relationship that can undermine your credibility and alienate readers who don't share your viewpoint.

This leads to confirmation bias and groupthink, resulting in false conclusions with little or no factual support for a belief. If a person believes the earth is flat and never questions that belief, it serves as an example of egocentric thinking. The person believes it is true even though he has never questioned why he believes it. If the person decides to look for information but only finds information that supports his pre-existing belief, ignoring or discrediting information that contradicts that belief, he is guilty of confirmation bias. If he believes the earth is flat because everyone in his group or community believes it, even though he himself has never questioned or confirmed the belief, he is guilty of sociocentrism.

In each case, the false thinking strategy leads to poor conclusions. Watch out for your tendency to read, write, and believe that which reflects only what you think you know without solid research and clear, critical thinking.

Overcoming Fear of Writing
For many people, one of the most frightening things in life is public speaking. For similar reasons, whether rational or irrational, writing often generates similar fears. There is something about exposing one's words to possible criticism that can be truly terrifying. In this chapter, we are going to break down the writing process into small, manageable steps that, in turn, will provide you with a platform for success. To take advantage of these steps, you need to acknowledge any reluctance or fear that may be holding you back, and bring your interests and enthusiasm to this discussion on writing.

Having a positive attitude about writing in general, and your effort, is also a key ingredient to your success. If you approach a writing assignment with trepidation and fear, you will spend your valuable time and attention in ways that do not contribute positively to your writing. People often fear the writing process because of three main reasons:
1. Negative orientation
2. Risk of failure
3. Fear of the unknown

Let's take each reason in turn. Negative orientation means the writer has a pre-existing negative association or view of the task or activity. We tend to like people who like us, [6] tend to pursue activities where we perceive rewards and appreciation for our efforts, and are more likely to engage in activities where we perceive we are successful. Conversely, we tend to

not like people who we perceive as not like us, tend to ignore or avoid activities where we perceive we are not appreciated or are not rewarded, and are less likely to engage in activities where we perceive we are not successful. For some writers, previous experiences have led to a pre-existing association with writing. That association may be positive if they have been encouraged, affirmed, or rewarded as they demonstrated measurable gain. That association may also be negative if efforts have been met with discouraging feedback, a lack of affirmation, or negative reinforcement.

Effective business writing is a highly valued skill, and regardless of the degree to which writing will be a significant aspect of your designated job duties, your ability to do it well will be a boost to your career. If you have a negative orientation toward writing, admitting this fact is an important first step. Next, we need to actively seek ways to develop your skills in ways that will demonstrate measurable gain and lead to positive affirmation. Not everyone develops in the same way on the same schedule, and measurable gain means that from one writing assignment to the next you can demonstrate positive progress. In an academic setting, measurable gain is one of your clear goals as a writer. In a business or industry setting, you may lack the time to revise and improve, meaning that you will need to get it right the first time. Take advantage of the academic setting to set positive, realistic goals to improve your writing. Surround yourself with resources, including people who will help you reach your goal. If your college or university has a writing center, take advantage of it. If it does not, seek out assistance from those whose writing has been effective and well received.

It is a given that you do not want to fail. Risk of failure is a common fear across public speaking and writing situations, producing predictable behavioral patterns we can recognize, address, and resolve. In public speaking, our minds may go blank at the start of a presentation as we confront our fear of failure. In writing, we may experience a form of blankness often referred to as "writer's block"—the overwhelming feeling of not knowing what to write or where to start—and sit helplessly waiting for our situation to change.

But we have the power to change our circumstances and to overcome our risk of failure. You may be familiar with the concept of a rough draft, but it may compete in your mind with a desire for perfection. Writing is a dynamic process, a reflection of the communication process itself. It won't be perfect the first time you attempt it. Awareness that your rough draft serves a purpose, but doesn't represent your final product, should serve in the same way a rehearsal for a speech serves a speaker. You get a second (or third) chance to get it right. Use this process to reduce your fear of failure and let go of your perfectionist tendencies, if only for a moment. Your desire for perfection will serve you well when it comes to polishing your finished document, but everything has its time and place. Learning where and when to place your effort is part of writing preparation.

Finally, we often fear the unknown. It is part of being human, and is reflected across all contexts, including public speaking and writing. If you have never given a speech before, your first time on stage can be quite an ordeal. If you have never written a formal business report, your fear of the unknown is understandable. How can you address this fear? Make the unknown known. If we take the mystery out of the process and product, we can see it for its essential components, its organizational pattern, and start to see how our product may look before we even start to produce it. In many organizations, you can ask your supervisor or coworkers for copies of similar documents to the one you have been assigned, even if the content is quite different. If this is not an option, simply consider the way most documents in your company are written—even something as basic as an interoffice e-mail will provide some clues. Your goal is to become familiar with the type of document and to examine several successful examples. Once you see a couple of reports, you will have a better feel for what you have to produce and the unknown will be far less mysterious.

KEY TAKEAWAY

There are several reasons why people fear writing, but there are also several strategies to reduce or eliminate those fears.

EXERCISES

1. How would you describe your orientation to writing? Where does this orientation come from? Discuss your thoughts with a classmate.
2. If you could identify one aspect of your writing you would like to improve, what would it be and why? Write a one- two-page essay on this subject.
3. What kinds of writing do you like? Dislike? Explain why and provide an example of each. Share and compare with the class.
4. Who is your favorite author? What do you like about her or his writing? Discuss your opinion with a classmate.

[1] Hemingway, E. (1999). *Ernest Hemingway on writing* (L. W. Phillips, Ed.). New York, NY: Simon & Schuster Adult Publishing Group.
[2] Nickerson, R. S., Perkins, D. N., & Smith, E. E. (1985). *The teaching of thinking*. Hillsdale, NJ: Lawrence Erbaum Associates.
[3] Paul, R., & Elder, L. (2007). *The miniature guide to critical thinking: Concepts and tools*. Dillon Beach, CA: The Foundation for Critical Thinking Press.
[4] Gilovich, T. (1993). *How we know what isn't so: The fallibility of human reason in everyday life*. New York, NY: The Free Press.
[5] Paul, R., & Elder, L. (2007). *The miniature guide to critical thinking: Concepts and tools*. Dillon Beach, CA: The Foundation for Critical Thinking Press.

[6] Gudykunst, W. B., & Kim, Y. Y. (1997). *Communicating with strangers: An approach to intercultural communication* (3rd ed.). New York, NY: McGraw-Hill.

5.2 A Planning Checklist for Business Messages
LEARNING OBJECTIVES

1. Understand who, what, where, when, why, and how as features of writing purpose.
2. Describe the planning process and essential elements of a business document.

John Thill and Courtland Bovee, [1] two leading authors in the field of business communication, have created a checklist for planning business messages. The following twelve-item checklist, adapted here, serves as a useful reminder of the importance of preparation in the writing process:

1. Determine your general purpose: are you trying to inform, persuade, entertain, facilitate interaction, or motivate a reader?
2. Determine your specific purpose (the desired outcome).
3. Make sure your purpose is realistic.
4. Make sure your timing is appropriate.
5. Make sure your sources are credible.
6. Make sure the message reflects positively on your business.
7. Determine audience size.
8. Determine audience composition.
9. Determine audience knowledge and awareness of topic.
10. Anticipate probable responses.
11. Select the correct channel.
12. Make sure the information provided is accurate, ethical, and pertinent.

Throughout this chapter we will examine these various steps in greater detail.

Determining Your Purpose

Preparation for the writing process involves purpose, research and investigation, reading and analyzing, and adaptation. In the first section we consider how to determine the purpose of a document, and how that awareness guides the writer to effective product.

While you may be free to create documents that represent yourself or your organization, your employer will often have direct input into their purpose. All acts of communication have general and specific purposes, and the degree to which you can identify these purposes will influence how effective your writing is. General purposes involve the overall goal of the communication interaction: to inform, persuade, entertain, facilitate interaction, or motivate a reader. The general purpose influences the presentation and expectation for feedback. In an informative message—the most common type of writing in business—you will need to cover several predictable elements:

- Who
- What
- When
- Where
- How
- Why (optional)

Some elements may receive more attention than others, and they do not necessarily have to be addressed in the order you see here. Depending on the nature of your project, as a writer you will have a degree of input over how you organize them. Note that the last item, *Why*, is designated as optional. This is because business writing sometimes needs to report facts and data objectively, without making any interpretation or pointing to any cause-effect relationship. In other business situations, of course, identifying why something happened or why a certain decision is advantageous will be the essence of the communication.

In addition to its general purpose (e.g., to inform, persuade, entertain, or motivate), every piece of writing also has at least one specific purpose, which is the intended outcome; the result that will happen once your written communication has been read.

For example, imagine that you are an employee in a small city's housing authority and have been asked to draft a letter to city residents about radon. Radon is a naturally occurring radioactive gas that has been classified by the United States Environmental Protection Agency as a health hazard. In the course of a routine test, radon was detected in minimal levels in an apartment building operated by the housing authority. It presents a relatively low level of risk, but because the incident was reported in the local newspaper, the mayor has asked the housing authority director to be proactive in informing all the city residents of the situation.

The general purpose of your letter is to inform, and the specific purpose is to have a written record of informing all city residents about how much radon was found, when, and where; where they can get more information on radon; and the date, time, and place of the meeting. Residents may read the information and attend or they may not even read the letter. But once the letter has been written, signed, and distributed, your general and specific purposes have been accomplished.

Now imagine that you begin to plan your letter by applying the above list of elements. Recall that the letter informs

residents on three counts: (1) the radon finding, (2) where to get information about radon, and (3) the upcoming meeting. For each of these pieces of information, the elements may look like the following:

1. Radon Finding
   o Who: The manager of the apartment building (give name)
   o What: Discovered a radon concentration of 4.1 picocuries per liter (pCi/L) and reported it to the housing authority director, who informed the city health inspector, environmental compliance office, and mayor
   o When: During the week of December 15
   o Where: In the basement of the apartment building located at (give address)
   o How: In the course of performing a routine annual test with a commercially available do-it-yourself radon test kit
2. Information about radon
   o Who: According to the city health inspector and environmental compliance officer
   o What: Radon is a naturally occurring radioactive gas that results from the breakdown of uranium in soil; a radon test level above 4.0 pCi/L may be cause for concern
   o When: Radon levels fluctuate from time to time, so further testing will be done; in past years, test results were below 4.0 pCi/L
   o Where: More information is available from the U.S. Environmental Protection Agency or the state radon office
   o How: By phone, mail, or on the Internet (provide full contact information for both sources)
   o Why: To become better informed and avoid misunderstandings about radon, its health risks, and the meaning of radon test results
3. City meeting about radon
   o Who: All city residents are welcome
   o What: Attend an informational meeting where the mayor, director of the housing authority, city health inspector, and city environmental compliance officer will speak and answer questions
   o When: Monday, January 7, at 7 p.m.
   o Where: City hall community room
   o Why: To become better informed and avoid misunderstandings about radon, its health risks, and the meaning of radon test results

Once you have laid out these elements of your informative letter, you have an outline from which it will be easy to write the actual letter.

Your effort serves as a written record of correspondence informing them that radon was detected, which may be one of the specific or primary purposes. A secondary purpose may be to increase attendance at the town hall meeting, but you will need feedback from that event to determine the effectiveness of your effort.

Now imagine that instead of being a housing authority employee, you are a city resident who receives that informative letter, and you happen to operate a business as a certified radon mitigation contractor. You may decide to build on this information and develop a persuasive message. You may draft a letter to the homeowners and landlords in the neighborhood near the building in question. To make your message persuasive, you may focus on the perception that radiation is inherently dangerous and that no amount of radon has been declared safe. You may cite external authorities that indicate radon is a contributing factor to several health ailments, and even appeal to emotions with phrases like "protect your children" and "peace of mind." Your letter will probably encourage readers to check with the state radon office to verify that you are a certified contractor, describe the services you provide, and indicate that friendly payment terms can be arranged.

Credibility, Timing, and Audience
At this point in the discussion, we need to visit the concept of credibility. Credibility, or the perception of integrity of the message based on an association with the source, is central to any communication act. If the audience perceives the letter as having presented the information in an impartial and objective way, perceives the health inspector's and environmental compliance officer's expertise in the field as relevant to the topic, and generally regards the housing authority in a positive light, they will be likely to accept your information as accurate. If, however, the audience does not associate trust and reliability with your message in particular and the city government in general, you may anticipate a lively discussion at the city hall meeting.

In the same way, if the reading audience perceives the radon mitigation contractor's letter as a poor sales pitch without their best interest or safety in mind, they may not respond positively to its message and be unlikely to contact him about any possible radon problems in their homes. If, however, the sales letter squarely addresses the needs of the audience and effectively persuades them, the contractor may look forward to a busy season.

Returning to the original housing authority scenario, did you consider how your letter might be received, or the fear it may have generated in the audience? In real life you don't get a second chance, but in our academic setting, we can go back and take more time on our assignment, using the twelve-item checklist we presented earlier. Imagine that you are the mayor or the housing authority director. Before you assign an employee to send a letter to inform residents about the radon finding, take a moment to consider how realistic your purpose is. As a city official, you may want the letter to serve as a record that residents were informed of the radon finding, but will that be the only outcome? Will people be even more concerned in response to the letter than they were when the item was published in the newspaper? Would a persuasive letter serve the city's purposes better than an informative one?

Another consideration is the timing. On the one hand, it may be important to get the letter sent as quickly as possible, as the newspaper report may have already aroused concerns that the letter will help calm. On the other hand, given that the radon was discovered in mid-December, many people are probably caught up in holiday celebrations. If the letter is mailed during the week of Christmas, it may not get the attention it deserves. After January 1, everyone will be paying more attention to their mail as they anticipate the arrival of tax-related documents or even the dreaded credit card statement. If the mayor has scheduled the city hall meeting for January 7, people may be unhappy if they only learn about the meeting at the last minute. Also consider your staff; if many of them will be gone over the holidays, there may not be enough staff in place to respond to phone calls that will likely come in response to the letter, even though the letter advises residents to contact the state radon office and the Environmental Protection Agency.

Next, how credible are the sources cited in the letter? If you as a housing authority employee have been asked to draft it, to whom should it go once you have it written? The city health inspector and environmental compliance officer are mentioned as sources; will they each read and approve the letter before it is sent? Is there someone at the county, state, or even the federal level who can, or should, check the information before it is sent?

The next item on the checklist is to make sure the message reflects positively on your business. In our hypothetical case, the "business" is city government. The letter should acknowledge that city officials and employees are servants of the taxpayers. "We are here to serve you" should be expressed, if not in so many words, in the tone of the letter. The next three items on the checklist are associated with the audience profile: audience size, composition, knowledge, and awareness of the topic. Since your letter is being sent to all city residents, you likely have a database from which you can easily tell how many readers constitute your audience. What about audience composition? What else do you know about the city's residents? What percentage of households includes children? What is the education level of most of the residents? Are there many residents whose first language is not English; if so, should your letter be translated into any other languages? What is the range of income levels in the city? How well informed are city residents about radon? Has radon been an issue in any other buildings in the city in recent years? The answers to these questions will help determine how detailed the information in your letter should be.

Finally, anticipate probable responses. Although the letter is intended to inform, could it be misinterpreted as an attempt to "cover up" an unacceptable condition in city housing? If the local newspaper were to reprint the letter, would the mayor be upset? Is there someone in public relations who will be doing media interviews at the same time the letter goes out? Will the release of information be coordinated, and if so by whom?

One additional point that deserves mention is the notion of decision makers. Even if your overall goal is to inform or persuade, the basic mission is to simply communicate. Establishing a connection is a fundamental aspect of the communication audience, and if you can correctly target key decision makers you increase your odds for making the connection with those you intend to inform or persuade. Who will open the mail, or e-mail? Who will act upon it? The better you can answer those questions, the more precise you can be in your writing efforts.

In some ways this is similar to asking your professor to write a letter of recommendation for you, but to address it to "to whom it may concern." If you can provide a primary contact name for the letter of recommendation it will increase its probable impact on the evaluation process. If your goal is to get a scholarship or a job offer, you want to take the necessary steps to increase your positive impact on the audience.

Communication Channels

Purpose is closely associated with channel. We need to consider the purpose when choosing a channel. From source to receiver, message to channel, feedback to context, environment, and interference, all eight components play a role in the dynamic process. While writing often focuses on an understanding of the receiver (as we've discussed) and defining the purpose of the message, the channel—or the "how" in the communication process—deserves special mention.

So far, we have discussed a simple and traditional channel of written communication: the hardcopy letter mailed in a standard business envelope and sent by postal mail. But in today's business environment, this channel is becoming increasingly rare as electronic channels become more widely available and accepted.

When is it appropriate to send an instant message (IM) or text message versus a conventional e-mail or fax? What is the difference between a letter and a memo? Between a report and a proposal? Writing itself is the communication medium, but each of these specific channels has its own strengths, weaknesses, and understood expectations that are summarized in Table 5.1 "Written Communication Channels".

By choosing the correct channel for a message, you can save yourself many headaches and increase the likelihood that your writing will be read, understood, and acted upon in the manner you intended.

Our discussion of communication channels would not be complete without mentioning the issues of privacy and security in electronic communications. The American Management Association [2] estimates that about two thirds of employers monitor their employees' electronic communications or Internet use. When you call and leave a voice message for a friend or colleague at work, do you know where your message is stored? There was a time when the message may have been stored on an analog cassette in an answering machine, or even on a small pink handwritten note which a secretary deposited in your friend's in-box. Today the "where" is irrelevant, as the in-box is digital and can be accessed from almost anywhere on the planet. That also means the message you left, with the representation of your voice, can be forwarded via e-mail as an attachment to anyone. Any time you send an IM, text, or e-mail or leave a voice message, your message is stored on more than one server, and it can be intercepted or forwarded to persons other than the intended receiver. Are you ready for your message to be broadcast to the world? Do your words represent you and your business in a positive light?

Table 5.1 Written Communication Channels

Channel	Strengths	Weaknesses	Expectations	When to Choose
IM or Text Message	Very fast Good for rapid exchanges of small amounts of information Inexpensive	Informal Not suitable for large amounts of information Abbreviations lead to misunderstandings	Quick response	Informal use among peers at similar levels within an organization You need a fast, inexpensive connection with a colleague over a small issue and limited amount of information
E-mail	Fast Good for relatively fast exchanges of information "Subject" line allows compilation of many messages on one subject or project Easy to distribute to multiple recipients Inexpensive	May hit "send" prematurely May be overlooked or deleted without being read "Reply to all" error "Forward" error Large attachments may cause the e-mail to be caught in recipient's spam filter	Normally a response is expected within 24 hours, although norms vary by situation and organizational culture	You need to communicate but time is not the most important consideration You need to send attachments (provided their file size is not too big)
Fax	Fast Provides documentation	Receiving issues (e.g., the receiving machine may be out of paper or toner) Long distance telephone charges apply Transitional telephone-based technology losing popularity to online information exchange	Normally, a long (multiple page) fax is not expected	You want to send a document whose format must remain intact as presented, such as a medical prescription or a signed work order Allows use of letterhead to represent your company
Memo	Official but less formal than a letter Clearly shows who sent it, when, and to whom	Memos sent through e-mails can get deleted without review Attachments can get removed by spam filters	Normally used internally in an organization to communicate directives from management on policy and procedure, or documentation	You need to communicate a general message within an organization
Letter	Formal Letterhead represents your company and adds credibility	May get filed or thrown away unread Cost and time involved in printing, stuffing, sealing, affixing postage, and travel through the postal system	Specific formats associated with specific purposes	You need to inform, persuade, deliver bad news or negative message, and document the communication
Report	Significant time for preparation and production	Requires extensive research and documentation	Specific formats for specific purposes; generally reports are to inform	You need to document the relationship(s) between large amounts of data to inform an internal or external audience
Proposal	Significant time for preparation and production	Requires extensive research and documentation	Specific formats for specific purposes; generally proposals are to persuade	You need to persuade an audience with complex arguments and data

Newsweek columnist Jennifer Ordoñez raises this question when she writes, "For desk jockeys everywhere, it has become as routine as a tour of the office-supply closet: the consent form attesting that you understand and accept that any e-mails you write, Internet sites you visit or business you conduct on your employer's computer network are subject to inspection." [3] As you update your Facebook page, get LinkedIn, Twitter, text, and IM, you leave an electronic trail of "bread crumbs" that merge personal and professional spheres, opening up significant issues of privacy. In our discussion we address research for specific business document production, and all the electronic research conducted is subject to review. While the case law is evolving as the technology we use to interface expands, it is wise to consider that anything you write or record can and will be stored for later retrieval by people for whom your message was not initially intended.

In terms of writing preparation, you should review any electronic communication before you send it. Spelling and grammatical errors will negatively impact your credibility. With written documents we often take time and care to get it right the first time, but the speed of IM, text, or e-mail often deletes this important review cycle of written works. Just because the document you prepare in IM is only one sentence long doesn't mean it can't be misunderstood or expose you to liability. Take time when preparing your written messages, regardless of their intended presentation, and review your work before you click "send."

KEY TAKEAWAY

Choose the most effective channel for your document and consider the possible ramifications of what you have written before you send it.

EXERCISES

1. Write a one-page letter to a new customer introducing a new product or service. Compare your result to the letters your classmates wrote. What do the letters have in common? How do they differ from one another?
2. Write a memo that addresses a new norm or protocol, such as the need to register with a new company that will be handling all the organization's business-related travel, with specific expectations including what information is needed, when, and to whom.
3. Make a list of the written communication that you read, skim, or produce in a one day. Please share your results with the class.

[1] Thill, J. V., & Bovee, C. L. (2004). *Business communication today* (8th ed.). Upper Saddle River, NJ: Prentice Hall.

[2] American Management Association. (2007). *Electronic monitoring & surveillance survey: Over half of all employers combined fire workers for e-mail & Internet abuse.* Retrieved from http://press.amanet.org/press-releases/177/2007-electronic-monitoring-surveillance-survey
[3] Ordoñez, J. (2008, July 14). *The technologist: They can't hide their pryin' eyes.* Retrieved from http://www.newsweek.com/id/143737

5.3 Research and Investigation: Getting Started
LEARNING OBJECTIVES

1. Compare and contrast ways of knowing your reading audience.
2. Conduct research and investigation to gather information.

Clearly, not every piece of business writing requires research or investigation. If you receive an e-mail asking for the correct spelling of your boss's name and her official title, you will probably be able to answer without having to look anything up. But what if the sender of the e-mail wants to know who in your company is the decision maker for purchasing a certain supply item? Unless you work for a very small company, you will likely have to look through the organizational chart, and possibly make a phone call or two, before you are able to write an e-mail answering this question. There—you have just done the research for a piece of business writing.

Even if you need to write something much more complex than an e-mail, such as a report or proposal, research does not have to be all about long hours at a library. Instead, start by consulting with business colleagues who have written similar documents and ask what worked, what didn't work, what was well received by management and the target audience. Your efforts will need to meet similar needs. Your document will not stand alone but will exist within a larger agenda. How does your proposed document fit within this agenda at your place of work, within the larger community, or with the target audience? It's worth noting that the word "investigation" contains the word "invest." You will need to invest your time and effort to understand the purpose and goal of your proposed document.

Before you go to the library, look over the information sources you already have in hand. Do you regularly read a magazine that relates to the topic? Was there an article in the newspaper you read that might work? Is there a book, CD-ROM or mp3 that has information you can use? Think of what you want the audience to know and how you could show it to them. Perhaps a famous quote or a line from a poem may make an important contribution to your document. You might even know someone that has experience in the area you want to research, someone who has been involved with skydiving locally for his or her whole life. Consider how you are going to tell and show your audience what your document is all about.

Once you have an assignment or topic, know your general and specific purposes, and have good idea of your reader's expectations, it's time to gather information. Your best sources may be all around you, within your business or organization. Information may come from reports from the marketing department or even from a trusted and well-versed colleague, but you will still need to do your homework. After you have written several similar documents for your organization, you may have your collection of sample documents, but don't be tempted to take shortcuts and "repurpose" existing documents to meet a tight deadline. Creating an original work specifically tailored to the issue and audience at hand is the best approach to establish credibility, produce a more effective document, and make sure no important aspect of your topic is left out.

Narrowing Your Topic

By now you have developed an idea of your topic, but even with a general and specific purpose, you may still have a broad subject that will be a challenge to cover within the allotted time before the deadline. You might want to revisit your purpose and ask yourself, how specific is my topic?

Imagine that you work for a local skydiving training facility. Your boss has assembled a list of people who might be candidates for skydiving and asks you to write a letter to them. Your general purpose is to persuade, and your specific purpose is to increase the number of students enrolled in classes. You've decided that skydiving is your topic area and you are going to tell your audience how exhilarating the experience is, discuss the history and basic equipment, cover the basic requirements necessary to go on a first jump, and provide reference information on where your audience could go to learn more (links and Web sites, for example).

But at this point you might find that a one-page letter simply is not enough space for the required content. Rather than expand the letter to two pages and risk losing the reader, consider your audience and what they might want to learn. How can you narrow your topic to better consider their needs? As you edit your topic, considering what the essential information is and what can be cut, you'll come to focus on the key points naturally and reduce the pressure on yourself to cover too much information in a limited space environment.

Perhaps starting with a testimony about a client's first jump, followed by basic equipment and training needed, and finally

a reference to your organization may help you define your document. While the history may be fascinating, and may serve as a topic in itself for another day, it may add too much information in this persuasive letter. Your specific purpose may be to increase enrollment, but your general goal will be to communicate goodwill and establish communication. If you can get your audience to view skydiving in a positive light and consider the experience for themselves, or people they know, you have accomplished your general purpose.

Focus on Key Points

As a different example, let's imagine that you are the office manager for a pet boarding facility that cares for dogs and cats while their owners are away. The general manager has asked you to draft a memo to remind employees about safety practices. Your general purpose is twofold: to inform employees about safety concerns and to motivate them to engage in safe work practices. Your specific purpose is also twofold: to prevent employees from being injured or infected with diseases on the job, and to reduce the risk of the animal patients being injured or becoming sick while in your care.

You are an office manager, not a veterinary or medical professional, and clearly there are volumes written about animal injuries and illnesses, not to mention entire schools devoted to teaching medicine to doctors who care for human patients. In a short memo you cannot hope to cover all possible examples of injury or illness. Instead, focus on the following behaviors and situations you observe:

- Do employees wash their hands thoroughly before and after contact with each animal?
- Are hand-washing facilities kept clean and supplied with soap and paper towels?
- When cleaning the animals' cages, do employees wear appropriate protection such as gloves?
- What is the procedure for disposing of animal waste, and do all employees know and follow the procedure?
- When an animal is being transferred from one cage to another, are there enough staff members present to provide backup assistance in case the animal becomes unruly?
- What should an employee do if he or she is bitten or scratched?
- What if an animal exhibits signs of being ill?
- Have there been any recent incidents that raised concerns about safety?

Once you have posed and answered questions like these, it should be easier to narrow down the information so that the result is a reasonably brief, easy to read memo that will get employees' attention and persuade them to adopt safe work practices.

Planning Your Investigation for Information

Now let's imagine that you work for a small accounting firm whose president would like to start sending a monthly newsletter to clients and prospective clients. He is aware of newsletter production service vendors that provide newsletters to represent a particular accounting firm. He has asked you to compile a list of such services, their prices and practices, so that the firm can choose one to employ.

If you are alert, you will begin your planning immediately, while your conversation with the president is still going on, as you will need more information before you can gauge the scope of the assignment. Approximately how many newsletter vendors does your president want to know about—is three or four enough? Would twenty be too many? Is there a set budget figure that the newsletter cost must not exceed? How soon does your report need to be done?

Once you have these details, you will be able to plan when and where to gather the needed information. The smartest place to begin is right in your office. If the president has any examples of newsletters he has seen from other businesses, you can examine them and note the contact information of the companies that produced them. You may also have an opportunity to ask coworkers if they know or even have copies of any such newsletters.

Assuming that your president wants to consider more than just a couple of vendors, you will need to expand your search. The next logical place to look is the Internet. In some companies, employees have full Internet access from their office computers; other companies provide only a few terminals with Internet access. Some workplaces allow no Internet access; if this is the case, you can visit your nearest public library.

As anyone who has spent an entire evening aimlessly Web surfing can attest, the Internet is a great place to find loads and loads of interesting but irrelevant information. Knowing what questions you are seeking to answer will help you stay focused on your report's topic, and knowing the scope of the report will help you to decide how much research time to plan in your schedule.

Staying Organized

Once you open up a Web browser such as Google and type in a search parameter like "newsletter production," you will have a wealth of information to look at. Much of it may be irrelevant, but even the information that fits with your project will be so much that you will be challenged to keep track of it.

Perhaps the most vital strategy for staying organized while doing online research is to open a blank page in your word processor and title it "Sources." Each time you find a Web page that contains what you believe may be useful and relevant information, copy the URL and paste it on this Sources page. Under the URL, copy and paste a paragraph or two as an example of the information you found on this Web page. Err on the side of listing too many sources; if in doubt about a source, list it for the time being—you can always discard it later. Having these source URLs and snippets of information all in one place will save you a great deal of time and many headaches later on.

As you explore various Web sites of companies that provide newsletter production services, you will no doubt encounter new questions that your president did not answer in the original conversation:

- Does the newsletter need to be printed on paper and mailed? Or would an e-mail newsletter be acceptable, or even preferable?
- Does your firm want the newsletter vendor to write all of the content customized to your firm, provide a menu of pre-existing articles for your firm to choose from, or let your firm provide some—or even all—of the content?
- What are the advantages and disadvantages of these various options?

You also realize that in order to get any cost estimates, even when the above questions are settled, you will need to know the desired length of the newsletter (in pages or in words), and how many recipients are on your firm's mailing list. At this point in your research and investigation, it may make sense to give your president an informal interim report, summarizing what you have found out and what additional questions need to be answered.

Having a well-organized list of the information you have assembled, the new questions that have arisen, and the sources where you found your information will allow you to continue researching effectively as soon as you have gotten answers and more specific direction from your president.

KEY TAKEAWAY

To make a writing project manageable, narrow your topic, focus on key points, plan your investigation for information, and stay organized as you go along.

EXERCISES

1. Think of a time when someone asked you to gather information to make a decision, whether for work, school, or in your personal life. How specific was the request? What did you need to know before you could determine how much and what kind of information to gather? Discuss your answer with those of your classmates.
2. Make a list of all the ways you procrastinate, noting how much time is associated with each activity or distraction. Share and compare your results with a classmate.
3. You are the manager. Write an e-mail requesting an employee to gather specific information on a topic. Give clear directions and due date(s). Please share your results with the class.
4. How do you prepare yourself for a writing project? How do others? What strategies work best for you? Survey ten colleagues or coworkers and compare your results with your classmates.

5.4 Ethics, Plagiarism, and Reliable Sources
LEARNING OBJECTIVE

1. Understand how to be ethical, avoid plagiarism, and use reputable sources in your writing.

Unlike writing for personal or academic purposes, your business writing will help determine how well your performance is evaluated in your job. Whether you are writing for colleagues within your workplace or outside vendors or customers, you will want to build a solid, well-earned favorable reputation for yourself with your writing. Your goal is to maintain and enhance your credibility, and that of your organization, at all times.

Make sure as you start your investigation that you always question the credibility of the information. Sources may have no reviews by peers or editor, and the information may be misleading, biased, or even false. Be a wise information consumer.

Business Ethics
Many employers have a corporate code of ethics; even if your employer does not, it goes without saying that there are laws governing how the company can and cannot conduct business. Some of these laws apply to business writing. As an example, it would be not only unethical but also illegal to send out a promotional letter announcing a special sale on an item that ordinarily costs $500, offering it for $100, if in fact you have only one of this item in inventory. When a retailer does this, the unannounced purpose of the letter is to draw customers into the store, apologize for running out of the sale item, and urge them to buy a similar item for $400. Known as "bait and switch," this is a form of fraud and is punishable by law.

Let's return to our previous newsletter scenario to examine some less clear-cut issues of business ethics. Suppose that, as you confer with your president and continue your research on newsletter vendors, you remember that you have a cousin who recently graduated from college with a journalism degree. You decide to talk to her about your project. In the course of the conversation, you learn that she now has a job working for a newsletter vendor. She is very excited to hear about your firm's plans and asks you to make her company "look good" in your report.

You are now in a situation that involves at least two ethical questions:
1. Did you breach your firm's confidentiality by telling your cousin about the plan to start sending a monthly newsletter?
2. Is there any ethical way you can comply with your cousin's request to show her company in an especially favorable light?

On the question of confidentiality, the answer may depend on whether you signed a confidentiality agreement as a condition of your employment at the accounting firm, or whether your president specifically told you to keep the newsletter plan confidential. If neither of these safeguards existed, then your conversation with your cousin would be an innocent, unintentional and coincidental sharing of information in which she turned out to have a vested interest. As for representing her company in an especially favorable light—you are ethically obligated to describe all the candidate vendors according to whatever criteria your president asked to see. The fact that your cousin works for a certain vendor may be an asset or a liability in your firm's view, but it would probably be best to inform them of it and let them make that judgment.

As another example of ethics in presenting material, let's return to the skydiving scenario we mentioned earlier. Because you are writing a promotional letter whose goal is to increase enrollment in your skydiving instruction, you may be tempted to avoid mentioning information that could be perceived as negative. If issues of personal health condition or accident rates in skydiving appear to discourage rather than encourage your audience to consider skydiving, you may be tempted to omit them. But in so doing, you are not presenting an accurate picture and may mislead your audience.

Even if your purpose is to persuade, deleting the opposing points presents a one-sided presentation. The audience will naturally consider not only what you tell them but also what you are not telling them, and will raise questions. Instead, consider your responsibility as a writer to present information you understand to be complete, honest, and ethical. Lying by omission can also expose your organization to liability. Instead of making a claim that skydiving is completely safe, you may want to state that your school complies with the safety guidelines of the United States Parachute Association. You might also state how many jumps your school has completed in the past year without an accident.

Giving Credit to Your Sources

You have photos of yourself jumping but they aren't very exciting. Since you are wearing goggles to protect your eyes and the image is at a distance, who can really tell if the person in the picture is you or not? Why not find a more exciting photo on the Internet and use it as an illustration for your letter? You can download it from a free site and the "fine print" at the bottom of the Web page states that the photos can be copied for personal use.

Not so fast—do you realize that a company's promotional letter does not qualify as personal use? The fact is that using the photo for a commercial purpose without permission from the photographer constitutes an infringement of copyright law; your employer could be sued because you decided to liven up your letter by taking a shortcut. Furthermore, falsely representing the more exciting photo as being your parachute jump will undermine your company's credibility if your readers happen to find the photo on the Internet and realize it is not yours.

Just as you wouldn't want to include an image more exciting than yours and falsely state that it is your jump, you wouldn't want to take information from sources and fail to give them credit. Whether the material is a photograph, text, a chart or graph, or any other form of media, taking someone else's work and representing it as your own is plagiarism. Plagiarism is committed whether you copy material verbatim, paraphrase its wording, or even merely take its ideas—if you do any of these things—without giving credit to the source. This does not mean you are forbidden to quote from your sources. It's entirely likely that in the course of research you may find a perfect turn of phrase or a way of communicating ideas that fits your needs perfectly. Using it in your writing is fine, provided that you credit the source fully enough that your readers can find it on their own. If you fail to take careful notes, or the sentence is present in your writing but later fails to get accurate attribution, it can have a negative impact on you and your organization. That is why it is important that

when you find an element you would like to incorporate in your document, in the same moment as you copy and paste or make a note of it in your research file, you need to note the source in a complete enough form to find it again.

Giving credit where credit is due will build your credibility and enhance your document. Moreover, when your writing is authentically yours, your audience will catch your enthusiasm, and you will feel more confident in the material you produce. Just as you have a responsibility in business to be honest in selling your product of service and avoid cheating your customers, so you have a responsibility in business writing to be honest in presenting your idea, and the ideas of others, and to avoid cheating your readers with plagiarized material.

Challenges of Online Research

Earlier in the chapter we have touched on the fact that the Internet is an amazing source of information, but for that very reason, it is a difficult place to get information you actually need. In the early years of the Internet, there was a sharp distinction between a search engine and a Web site. There were many search engines competing with one another, and their home pages were generally fairly blank except for a search field where the user would enter the desired search keywords or parameters. There are still many search sites, but today, a few search engines have come to dominate the field, including Google and Yahoo! Moreover, most search engines' home pages offer a wide range of options beyond an overall Web search; buttons for options such as news, maps, images, and videos are typical. Another type of search engine performs a metasearch, returning search results from several search engines at once.

When you are looking for a specific kind of information, these relatively general searches can still lead you far away from your desired results. In that case, you may be better served by an online dictionary, encyclopedia, business directory, or phone directory. There are also specialized online databases for almost every industry, profession, and area of scholarship; some are available to anyone, others are free but require opening an account, and some require paying a subscription fee. For example, http://www.zillow.com allows for in-depth search and collation of information concerning real estate and evaluation, including the integration of public databases that feature tax assessments and ownership transfers. Table 5.2 "Some Examples of Internet Search Sites" provides a few examples of different kinds of search sites.

At the end of this chapter, under "Additional Resources," you will find a list of many Web sites that may be useful for business research.

Table 5.2 Some Examples of Internet Search Sites

Description	URL
General Web searches that can also be customized according to categories like news, maps, images, video	http://altavista.com http://www.google.com http://go.com http://www.itools.com/research-it http://www.live.com http://www.yahoo.com
Metasearch engines	http://www.dogpile.com http://www.info.com http://www.metacrawler.com http://www.search.com http://www.webcrawler.com
Dictionaries and encyclopedias	http://www.britannica.com http://dictionary.reference.com http://encarta.msn.com http://www.encyclopedia.com http://www.merriam-webster.com http://en.wikipedia.org/wiki/Main_Page
Very basic information on a wide range of topics	http://www.about.com http://www.answers.com http://wiki.answers.com
To find people or businesses in white pages or yellow pages listings	http://www.anywho.com http://www.peoplelookup.com http://www.switchboard.com http://www.whitepages.com http://www.yellowpages.com
Specialized databases—may be free, require registration, or require a paid subscription	http://www.apa.org/psycinfo http://clinicaltrials.gov/ct/screen/AdvancedSearch http://medline.cos.com http://www.northernlight.com http://www.zillow.com

Evaluating Your Sources

One aspect of Internet research that cannot be emphasized enough is the abundance of online information that is incomplete, outdated, misleading, or downright false. Anyone can put up a Web site; once it is up, the owner may or may not enter updates or corrections on a regular basis. Anyone can write a blog on any subject, whether or not that person actually has any expertise on that subject. Anyone who wishes to contribute to a Wikipedia article can do so—although the postings are moderated by editors who have to register and submit their qualifications. In the United States, the First Amendment of the Constitution guarantees freedom of expression. This freedom is restricted by laws prohibiting libel (false accusations against a person) and indecency, especially child pornography, but those laws are limited in scope and sometimes difficult to enforce. Therefore, it is always important to look beyond the surface of a site to assess who sponsors it, where the information displayed came from, and whether the site owner has a certain agenda.

When you write for business and industry you will want to draw on reputable, reliable sources—printed as well as electronic ones—because they reflect on the credibility of the message and the messenger. Analyzing and assessing information is an important skill in the preparation of writing, and here are six main points to consider when evaluating a document, presentation, or similar source of information. [1] In general, documents that represent quality reasoning have the following traits:

- A clearly articulated purpose and goal
- A question, problem, or issue to address
- Information, data, and evidence that is clearly relevant to the stated purpose and goals
- Inferences or interpretations that lead to conclusions based on the presented information, data, and evidence
- A frame of reference or point of view that is clearly articulated
- Assumptions, concepts, and ideas that are clearly articulated

An additional question that is central to your assessment of your sources is how credible the source is. This question is difficult to address even with years of training and expertise. You may have heard of academic fields called "disciplines," but may not have heard of each field's professors called "disciples." Believers, keepers of wisdom, and teachers of tomorrow's teachers have long played a valuable role establishing, maintaining, and perpetuating credibility. Academics have long cultivated an understood acceptance of the role of objective, impartial use of the scientific method to determine validity and reliability. But as research is increasingly dependent on funding, and funding often brings specific points of view and agendas with it, pure research can be—and has been—compromised. You can no longer simply assume that "studies show" something without awareness of who conducted the study, how was it conducted, and who funded the effort. This may sound like a lot of investigation and present quite a challenge, but again it is worth the effort.

Information literacy is an essential skill set in the process of writing. As you learn to spot key signs of information that will not serve to enhance your credibility and contribute to your document, you can increase your effectiveness as you research and analyze your resources. For example, if you were researching electronic monitoring in the workplace, you might come upon a site owned by a company that sells workplace electronic monitoring systems. The site might give many statistics illustrating what percentage of employers use electronic monitoring, what percentage of employees use the Internet for nonwork purposes during work hours, what percentage of employees use company e-mail for personal

messages, and so on. But the sources of these percentage figures may not be credited. As an intelligent researcher, you need to ask yourself, did the company that owns the site perform its own research to get these numbers? Most likely it did not—so why are the sources not cited? Moreover, such a site would be unlikely to mention any court rulings about electronic monitoring being unnecessarily invasive of employees' privacy. Less biased sources of information would be the American Management Association, the U.S. Department of Labor, and other not-for-profit organizations that study workplace issues.

The Internet also encompasses thousands of interactive sites where readers can ask and answer questions. Some sites, like Askville by Amazon.com, WikiAnswers, and Yahoo! Answers, are open to almost any topic. Others, like ParentingQuestions and WebMD, deal with specific topics. Chat rooms on bridal Web sites allow couples who are planning a wedding to share advice and compare prices for gowns, florists, caterers, and so on. Reader comment sites like Newsvine facilitate discussions about current events. Customer reviews are available for just about everything imaginable, from hotels and restaurants to personal care products, home improvement products, and sports equipment. The writers of these customer reviews, the chat room participants, and the people who ask and answer questions on many of these interactive sites are not experts, nor do they pretend to be. Some may have extreme opinions that are not based in reality. Then, too, it is always possible for a vendor to "plant" favorable customer reviews on the Internet to make its product look good. Although the "terms of use" which everyone registering for interactive sites must agree to usually forbid the posting of advertisements, profanity, or personal attacks, some sites do a better job than others in monitoring and deleting such material. Nevertheless, if your business writing project involves finding out how the "average person" feels about an issue in the news, or whether a new type of home exercise device really works as advertised, these comment and customer review sites can be very useful indeed.

It may seem like it's hard work to assess your sources, to make sure your information is accurate and truthful, but the effort is worth it. Business and industry rely on reputation and trust (just as we individuals do) in order to maintain healthy relationships. Your document, regardless of how small it may appear in the larger picture, is an important part of that reputation and interaction.

KEY TAKEAWAY

Evaluating your sources is a key element of the preparation process in business writing. To avoid plagiarism, always record your sources so that you can credit them in your writing.

EXERCISES

1. Before the Internet improved information access, how did people find information? Are the strategies they used still valid and how might they serve you as a business writer? Interview several people who are old enough to have done research in the "old days" and report your findings.
2. Visit the Web site of the United States Copyright Office at http://www.copyright.gov. Find something on the Web site that you did not know before reviewing it and share it with your classmates.
3. On the United States Copyright Office Web site at http://www.copyright.gov view the multimedia presentation for students and teachers, "Taking the Mystery out of Copyright." Download the "Copyright Basics" document and discuss it with your class.
4. Look over the syllabus for your business communication course and assess the writing assignments you will be completing. Is all the information you are going to need for these assignments available in electronic form? Why or why not?
5. Does the fact that Internet search results are often associated with advertising influence your research and investigation? Why or why not? Discuss with a classmate.
6. Find an example of a bogus or less than credible Web site. Indicate why you perceive it to be untrustworthy, and share it with your classmates.
7. Visit the parody Web site The Onion at http://www.theonion.com and find one story that you think has plausible or believable elements. Share your findings with the class.

[1] Adapted from Paul, R., & Elder, L. (2007). *The miniature guide to critical thinking: Concepts and tools*. Dillon Beach, CA: The Foundation for Critical Thinking Press.

5.5 Completing Your Research and Investigation
LEARNING OBJECTIVE

1. Demonstrate your ability to manage your time and successfully conduct research and investigation for a writing assignment.

Once you become immersed in your sources, it can be easy to get carried away in the pursuit of information and lose sight of why you are doing all this research and investigation. As a responsible writer, you will need to plan not only how

you will begin your information gathering, but also how you will bring it to a conclusion.

Managing Your Time

Given the limited time for research involved in most business writing, how can you make the most of your information-gathering efforts? Part of learning to write effectively involves learning to read quickly and efficiently while conducting research. You are not required to read each word, and if you did, you would slow yourself down greatly. At the same time, if you routinely skip large sections of print and only focus on the bullet lists, you may miss valuable examples that could inspire you in your writing.

How can you tell when to skim and when to pay attention to detail? One strategy is to look for abstracts (or brief summaries of information) before you commit time to reading an article all the way through. Look for indexes to identify key terms you might want to cover before eliminating them as you narrow your topic.

As we mentioned earlier in this chapter, it is smart to make a list of your sources as you search; you may also want to bookmark pages with your Web browser. Sometimes a source that does not look very promising may turn out to offer key information that will drive home an important point in your document. If you have done a good job of recording your sources, it will be easy to go back to a site or source that at first you passed over, but now think may make a relevant contribution.

Compiling Your Information

Patricia Andrews, James Andrews, and Glen Williams [1] provide a useful outline of a process to consider when compiling your information. Compiling involves composing your document out of materials from other documents or sources. This process has seven major steps, adapted from the Andrews, Andrews, and Williams [2] model, which we will consider: sensitivity, exposure, assimilation and accommodation, incubation, incorporation, production and revision.

Let's say your letter introducing skydiving to a new audience was relatively successful and the regional association asks you to write a report on the status of skydiving services in your region, with the hope that the comprehensive guide may serve to direct and enhance class enrollment across the region. Your task has considerably expanded and involves more research, but given the opportunity this assignment presents, you are excited at the challenge. As you begin to research, plan, and design the document, you will touch on the process of compiling information. If you are aware of each step, your task can be accomplished effectively and efficiently.

Sensitivity refers to your capacity to respond to stimulation, being excited, responsive or susceptible to new information. This starts with a self-inventory of your current or past interests and activities. If you are intrigued by a topic or area of interest, your enthusiasm will carry through to your document and make it more stimulating for your reading audience. You may not have considered, or even noticed elements or ideas associated with your topic, but now that you have begun the process of investigation, you see them everywhere. For example, have you ever heard someone say a word or phrase that you never heard before, but now that you are familiar with it, you hear it everywhere? This same principle applies to your sensitivity to ideas related to your topic. You'll notice information and it will help you as you develop your awareness of your topic and the many directions you could take the speech. Cognitive psychologist use the term priming to refer to this excited state of awareness. [3]

Exposure involves your condition of being presented views, ideas, or experiences made known to you through direct experience. If you are going to select a topic on flying but have never flown before, your level of exposure may be low. Your level of awareness may be high, however, in terms of the importance of security on airplanes after reading about, watching on television, or hearing on the radio stories after the events of September 11, 2001. You may decide to expose yourself to more information through a range of sources as you investigate the topic of airline security. And the more you become exposed to the issues, processes, and goals of your topic, the more likely you are to see areas of interest, new ideas that might fit in your speech, and form patterns of awareness you did not perceive earlier. We have previously discussed at length the importance of selection as a stage in the perceptual process, and selective exposure is one way you gain awareness. You may want to revisit this chapter as you develop your topic or choose where to look for information or decide what kinds of information to expose yourself to as you research your topic.

Assimilation and accommodation refer to the processes by which you assimilate (or integrate) new ideas into your thinking patterns and accommodate (or adopt, adapt, or filter out) new sources of information as they relate to your goal. You may have had preconceived notions or ideas about airline security before you began your investigation, but new information has changed the way you view your topic. You might also find issues (e.g., right to privacy) that may be points of conflict with your beliefs as you review information.

This stage is important to the overall process of developing your topic, and it takes time. You need time to be able to contemplate, review, and reflect on how the new information fits or fails to connect clearly to your chosen topic.

Incubation is the process by which you cause an idea or ideas to develop in your mind. This might not happen all at once, and you might spend time thinking about the new information, directions, or ways you might develop or focus your topic. Consider the meaning of the word as it relates to chickens and eggs. An egg may be produced, but it needs time and a warm environment to develop. You might have an idea, but you need to create an environment for it to develop. This might involve further investigation and exploration, or it may involve removing yourself from active research to "digest" or "incubate" what you have already learned. You may feel stuck on an idea or perceive an inability to move on in the development of your ideas or topic, and giving it a rest may be the best course of action. You may also find that just when you least expect it, an idea, fully formed, flashes in your mind and you think, "Why didn't I see that before?" Before the idea escapes you, write it down and make sure you can refer to it later.

Incorporation refers to the process by which you bring the information into a whole or complete topic. By now you have investigated, chosen some information over others, and have started to see how the pieces will come together. Your perceptions of how the elements come together will form the basis for your development of the organization of your document. It will contribute to the *logos*, or logic, of your thought and its representation in your document, and help you produce a coherent, organized message that your audience can follow clearly.

Production involves the act of creating your document from the elements you have gathered. You may start to consider what comes first, what goes last, and how you will link your ideas and examples together. You may find that you need additional information and need to go back to your notes that you have taken to find the source quickly and easily. You may also start to communicate with friends, sharing some of the elements or even practicing the first drafts of your document, learning where the connections are clear and where they need work.

Revision is the process by which you look over again in order to correct or improve your message. You will notice elements that need further investigation, development, or additional examples and visual aids as you produce your document. This is an important step to the overall production of your message, much like revising an essay for an English course.

The first time you said, thought, or wrote something it may have made sense to you, but upon reflection and after trying an idea out, you need it to be revised in order to work effectively as part of your document. You may revisit the place in which you started (and start all speeches) by reconsidering the rhetorical situation and see if what you have produces is in line with the expectations of the audience. Your awareness of the content, audience, and purpose of the rhetorical situation will guide you through the revision process and contribute to the production of a more effective document.

Once you have gathered what you think is enough material—or, perhaps, once your eyes begin to glaze over—take a step back and return to the general and specific purpose of the document you set out to write. Look again at the basic elements (i.e., who, what, when, etc.) and fill in the "answers" based on what you have found. It is not unusual at this stage to have some "holes" in the information that require more research to fill. You may also realize that your research findings have disproved part or even all of your original agenda, making it necessary to change your message significantly.

Leave enough time before your deadline so that you can sketch out a detailed outline and rough draft of your document and leave it alone for at least a day. When you look at it again, it will probably be clear which additional details need more support, and you can perform targeted research to fill in those gaps.

KEY TAKEAWAY

Be mindful of your result and your time frame as you conduct your research and investigation. Allow enough time to let the writing rest before you return to it and make revisions.

EXERCISES

1. Choose a topic related to a career that interests you and think about how you would research that topic on the Internet. Set a timer for fifteen minutes. Ready, set, go! At the end of fifteen minutes, review the sources you have recorded in your list and think about the information you have found. How well did you use your limited time? Could you do better next time? Try it again.
2. Complete an Internet search of your name and report your findings to the class.
3. Complete an Internet search of your favorite product or service and report your findings to the class.
4. You've been assigned to a marketing team tasked to engage an audience just like you. Make a list of what services or products your target audience would find

attractive. Pick one and develop a slogan that is sure to get attention. Share your results with the class.

[1] Andrews, P. H., Andrews, J., & Williams, G. (1999). *Public speaking: Connecting you and your audience.* Boston, MA: Houghton Mifflin Company.
[2] Andrews, P. H., Andrews, J., & Williams, G. (1999). *Public speaking: Connecting you and your audience.* Boston, MA: Houghton Mifflin Company.
[3] Yaniv, I., & Meyer, D. (1987). Activation and metacognition of inaccessible stored information: potential bases for incubation effects in problem loving. *Journal of Experimental Psychology: Learning, Memory, and Cognition, 13*, 187–205.

5.6 Reading and Analyzing
LEARNING OBJECTIVES

1. Understand different types of reading and analyzing that business documents encounter.
2. Demonstrate how to write for skimming and for analytical reading in at least one written document of each kind.

When you read, do you read each and every word? Do you skim over the document and try to identify key terms and themes? Do you focus on numbers and statistics, or ignore the text and go straight to the pictures or embedded video? Because people read in many diverse ways, you as a writer will want to consider how your audience may read and analyze your document.

Ever since Benjamin Franklin said that "time is money," [1] business managers have placed a high value on getting work done quickly. Many times, as a result, a document will be skimmed rather than read in detail. This is true whether the communication is a one-paragraph e-mail or a twenty-page proposal. If you anticipate that your document will be skimmed, it behooves you to make your main points stand out for the reader.

In an e-mail, use a "subject" line that tells the reader the gist of your message before he or she opens it. For example, the subject line "3 p.m. meeting postponed to 4 p.m." conveys the most important piece of information; in the body of the e-mail you may explain that Wednesday's status meeting for the XYZ project needs to be postponed to 4 p.m. because of a conflict with an offsite luncheon meeting involving several XYZ project team members. If you used the subject line "Wednesday meeting" instead, recipients might glance at their in-box, think, "Oh, I already know I'm supposed to attend that meeting," and not read the body of the message. As a result, they will not find out that the meeting is postponed.

For a longer piece of writing such as a report or proposal, here are some techniques you can use to help the reader grasp key points.

- Present a quick overview, or "executive summary," at the beginning of the document.

- Use boldface headings as signposts for the main sections and their subsections.

- Where possible, make your headings informative; for example, a heading like "Problem Began in 1992" is more informative than one that says "Background."

- Within each section, begin each paragraph with a topic sentence that indicates what the paragraph discusses.

- When you have a list of points, questions, or considerations, format them with bullets rather than listing them in sentences.

- The "bottom line," generally understood to mean the total cost of a given expenditure or project, can also refer to the conclusions that the information in the report leads to. As the expression indicates, these conclusions should be clearly presented at the end of the document, which is the place where the time-pressed reader will often turn immediately after reading the first page.

Imagine how unhappy you would be if you submitted a report and your audience came away with a message completely different from what you had intended. For example, suppose your manager is considering adopting a specific new billing system in your office and has asked you to report on the pros and cons of this system. You worked hard, gathered plenty of information, and wrote a detailed report which, in your opinion, gave strong support for adopting the new system. However, the first few pages of your report described systems other than the one under consideration. Next, you presented the reasons not to implement the new system. Throughout the report, embedded in the body of several different paragraphs, you mentioned the advantages offered by the new system; but they were not grouped together so that you could emphasize them with a heading or other signpost for the reader. At the end of the report, you reviewed the current billing system and stated that few problems were encountered with it.

When you delivered your report, the manager and colleagues who received it missed your most important information and decided not to consider the new system any further. Worse, your manager later criticized you for spending too much time on the report, saying it was not very informative. Situations like this can be avoided if you provide a clear organizational framework to draw your reader's attention to your main points.

Analyzing is distinct from reading. When you read, you attempt to grasp the author's meaning via words and symbols, and you may come away with a general emotional feeling about what the writer has written instead of an arsenal of facts. When you analyze a document, you pay more attention to how the author assembled the information to present a coherent message. Business writing often involves communication via words and symbols in ways that meet audience expectations; in many cases, the audience needs to be able to analyze the content, and reading is secondary. For this reason, a solid organizational pattern will greatly enhance your document's effectiveness.

KEY TAKEAWAY

Logical organization is important to promote reader understanding and analysis.

EXERCISES

1. Take a news article and mark it up to reveal its organizational structure. Does it have an informative opening paragraph? Does each additional paragraph begin with a topic sentence? Does it use subheadings? Is there a conclusion that follows logically from the information presented?

2. Find an article that you do not like and review it. State specific reasons why you dislike it and share your opinion with your classmates.

3. Find an article that you do like and review it. State specific reasons why you like it and share your opinion with your classmates.

4. You've been assigned to a sales team that has not been performing at optimal levels. Develop an incentive program to improve the team's performance. Present your idea to the class.

[1] Franklin, B. (1748). *Advice to a young tradesman, written by an old one.* Philadelphia, PA: B. Franklin and D. Hall.

5.7 Additional Resources

- The Library of Congress is the nation's oldest federal cultural institution and serves as the research arm of the U.S. Congress. It is also the largest library in the world, with millions of books, recordings, photographs, maps, and manuscripts in its collections. http://www.loc.gov/index.html

- The Copyright Office of the Library of Congress offers a wide variety of resources for understanding copyright law and how to avoid plagiarism. http://www.copyright.gov

- The Learning Center is designed to help educators and students develop a better sense of what plagiarism means in the information age, and to teach the planning, organizational, and citation skills essential for producing quality writing and research. http://www.plagiarism.org/learning_center/home.html

- The New York Public Library's Science, Industry, and Business Library (SIBL) is the nation's largest public information center devoted solely to science and business. http://www.nypl.org/research/sibl
- The Lippincott Library serves the Wharton School of the University of Pennsylvania, one of the world's top business schools. http://www.library.upenn.edu/lippincott
- Thunderbird School of Global Management operates Thunderbird Knowledge Network, an interactive forum on contemporary business issues delivered in stories, columns, videos, podcasts, and blogs. http://knowledgenetwork.thunderbird.edu/research
- The *Wall Street Journal* is one of the most widely read sources of business news. http://online.wsj.com/home-page
- Personalize your business news and analysis with *Business Week*'s member service, Business Exchange. http://bx.businessweek.com
- INSEAD: The Business School for the World, one of the largest and most highly regarded schools for MBA, Executive MBA, and PhD degrees in business, makes its library resources available online. http://www.insead.edu/library/index.cfm
- As an example of an industry trade association, the Association of Construction Project Managers (ACPM) is a voluntary association of specialist project management professionals working in the built environment. http://www.acpm.co.za
- The United States Government's Small Business Administration has a mandate to aid, counsel, assist and protect the interests of small business concerns, to preserve free competitive enterprise, and to maintain and strengthen the overall economy of our nation. http://www.sba.gov
- The U.S. Department of Labor's Occupational Safety and Health Administration (OSHA) sets the standards and conducts inspections to ensure safety and prevent accidents in the workplace. http://www.osha.gov
- The Society for Human Resource Management is a key source of news and information on HR topics. http://www.shrm.org/Pages/default.aspx
- The Chicago Board of Trade, the world's oldest futures and options exchange, trades treasury bonds, corn, soybean, wheat, gold, silver, and other commodities. http://www.cbot.com
- Yahoo! Finance is a useful site for tracking the Dow, S&P 500, and other major stock indices in the United States and abroad; it also has areas for financial news, investing, and personal finance. http://finance.yahoo.com
- The *Occupational Outlook Handbook*, published every two years by the U.S. Bureau of Labor Statistics, describes hundreds of different types of jobs, the training and education each job requires, the typical earnings in that job, and more. http://www.bls.gov/OCO
- CareerBuilder.com, which describes itself as the largest online job search site, offers a vast online and print network to help job seekers connect with employers. http://www.careerbuilder.com
- According to its Web site, *Fast Company* "sets the agenda, charting the evolution of business through a unique focus on the most creative individuals sparking change in the marketplace." http://www.fastcompany.com
- LinkedIn, which has been described as the professional counterpart to social networking sites such as Facebook are an interconnected network of experienced professionals from around the world, representing 170 industries and 200 countries. http://www.linkedin.com
- Intuit, maker of QuickBooks, Quicken, TurboTax, and other accounting software, provides a small business information center on its Web site. What would you expect to find here that is different from the resources a noncommercial source would offer? http://smallbusiness.intuit.com

NOTES:

Chapter 6:
Writing

Although I usually think I know what I'm going to be writing about, what I'm going to say, most of the time it doesn't happen that way at all. At some point I get misled down a garden path, I get surprised by an idea that I hadn't anticipated getting, which is a little bit like being in a laboratory.

  Lewis Thomas

Getting Started

INTRODUCTORY EXERCISES

1. Match each statement in the left column with the most appropriate mode of communication in the right column, and note why.

___ 1. Need the sales figures for the last month available in three days	A. Text message or instant message (IM)
___ 2. Inform department employees of face-to-face (F2F) meeting next month	B. E-mail
___ 3. International client requests price quote	C. Fax
___ 4. Assigned to investigate partnership with supplier to codevelop a new product	D. Report

___ 5. Need to inform employee of a discrepancy in their expense report	E. Proposal
___ 6. Need to facilitate meeting with two department managers from two distinct time zones.	F. Face-to-face (F2F) meeting, interpersonal interaction
___ 7. Need to follow up with customer post sale	G. F2F meeting, group or team
___ 8. Need to contact new prospective customer	H. Meeting (mediated), teleconference or videoconference

There are no right or wrong answers to this matching exercise, but there are strengths and weaknesses associated with each mode. Does the information need to be received as soon as possible? Will the document require time and preparation? Will the result be comprehensive and require visual representation of data, trends, and their relationships(s)? Associate each statement with what you consider the most appropriate model of communication and note why. Discuss your responses with your classmates.

2. These sentences focus on some of the most common errors in English. Can you fill in the blanks correctly?

1. *accept* or *except*	The office will _____ applications until 5 p.m. on the 31st.	accept	Attendance is required for all employees _____ supervisors.	except
2. *affect* or *effect*	To _____ the growth of plants, we can regulate the water supply.	affect	A lack of water has a predictable _____ on most plants.	effect
3. *e.g.* or *i.e.*	Please order 2,000 imprinted giveaways (_____, pens or coffee mugs)	e.g.	Charge them to my account (_____, account #98765).	i.e.
4. *its* or *it's*	The department surpassed _____ previous sales record this quarter.	its	_____ my opinion that we reached peak oil in 2008.	It's
5. *lay* or *lie*	Please _____ the report on the desk.	lay	The doctor asked him to _____ down on the examination table.	lie
6. *pressure* or *pressurize*	We need to _____ the liquid nitrogen tanks.	pressurize	It might be possible to _____ him to resign.	pressure
7. *principle* or *principal*	It's the basic _____ of farming: no water, no food.	principle	The _____ reason for the trip is to attend the sales meeting.	principal

8. *regardless* or *irregardless*	_____ of what we do, gas prices are unlikely to go back down.	Regardless	_____ of your beliefs, please try to listen with an open mind.	Regardless (*irregardless* is not a standard word; see your dictionary)
9. *than* or *then*	This year's losses were worse _____ last year's.	than	If we can cut our costs, _____ it might be possible to break even.	then
10. *that* or *which*	_____ type of marketing data did you need?	Which	Karen misplaced the report, _____ caused a delay in making a decision.	which
	There are several kinds of data _____ could be useful.	that		
11 *there their,* or *they're*	The report is _____, in the top file drawer.	there	_____ strategic advantage depends on a wide distribution network.	Their
	_____ planning to attend the sales meeting in Pittsburgh.	They're		
12. *to too,* or *two*	Customers need _____ drive slower if they want to save gas.	to	After sales meeting, you should visit customers in the Pittsburgh area _____.	too
	In fact, the _____ of you should make some customer visits together.	two		
13. *uninterested* or *disinterested*	He would be the best person to make a decision, since he isn't biased and is relatively _____ in the outcome.	disinterested	The sales manager tried to speak dynamically, but the sales reps were simply _____ in what he had to say.	uninterested
14. *who, whom, who's,* or *whose*	_____ truck is that?	Whose	_____ going to pay for the repairs?	Who's
	_____ will go to the interview?	Who	To _____ should we address the thank-you note?	whom
15 *your* or *you're*	My office is bigger than _____ cubicle.	your	_____ going to learn how to avoid making these common mistakes in English.	You're

If all the world is a stage then you, as a business writer, must be the script writer, correct? Actually, those who employ you, specify your job duties, manage the business, and designate which problems you are to solve are more like the script writers, directors, and producers. So what role does that leave you as a business writer? Actor. You may not be seen "on stage" by the suppliers you write, the departments you inform with your reports, or the customers you serve, but your writing represents you and your organization. As an actor must learn his or her lines, you too must learn the role of a business writer within the context of your business or organization. It may well be that you are allowed a degree of improvisation and creativity when you interpret your role, or it could be the case that many of the written documents you will produce follow a standard template, much like a script, that designates your lines before the writing process begins. Knowing your place on stage and how it relates to your business is an important aspect of business writing best not ignored.

This chapter focuses on several strategies for success when it comes to the creative process of writing, and your awareness of these skills will prove invaluable as your responsibility increases and your ability to shape documents develops. Never lose sight of the fact that each document exists with a universe of relationships and interaction; it does not stand alone. Also remember that what you write today, particularly if you "publish" it on the Internet, will be there for years to come. Always consider how your words will represent you and your organization when you are not there to clarify, defend, or correct them. Your audience will have expectations of you, as will your employer, and as an effective business writer you know that one key to success is meeting these expectations.

Creative writing for exposition, narration, and self-expression is an important part of writing, but in the business context you have a role, job duties, and responsibilities both internal and external to your organization. Your mastery of clear and concise writing will directly affect the interpretation, and misinterpretation, of your message. Your goal remains to reduce misunderstandings through the effective and efficient use of words in business documents, and the well-known mandate to "Omit needless words" [1] stands true. Up to this point you have been preparing to write, but now the moment has come for performance.

---

[1] Strunk, W., Jr., & White, E. B. (1979). *The elements of style* (3rd ed.). New York, NY: Macmillian.

6.1 Organization
LEARNING OBJECTIVES

1. Understand how to develop and organize content in patterns that are appropriate for your document and audience.
2. Demonstrate your ability to order, outline, and emphasize main points in one or more written assignments.
3. Demonstrate how to compose logically organized paragraphs, sentences, and transitions in one or more written assignments.

The purpose of business writing is to communicate facts and ideas. In order to accomplish that purpose, each document has key components that need to be present in order for your reading audience to understand the message. These elements may seem simple to the point that you may question how any writer could neglect them. But if you take note of how often miscommunication and misunderstanding happen, particularly in written communications, you will realize that it happens all the time. Omission or neglect may be intentional, but it is often unintentional; the writer assumes (wrongly) that the reader will easily understand a concept, idea, or the meaning of the message. From background to language, culture to education, there are many variables that come into play and make effective communication a challenge. The degree to which you address these basic elements will increase the effectiveness of your documents. Each document must address the following:

- Who
- What
- When
- Where
- How
- (and sometimes) Why

If you have these elements in mind as you prepare your document, it will be easier to decide what to write and in what order. They will also be useful when you are reviewing your document before delivering it. If your draft omits any one of these elements or addresses it in an unclear fashion, you will know what you need to do to fix it.

Another way to approach organizing your document is with the classical proofs known as *ethos*, *logos*, and *pathos*. Ethos, or your credibility, will come through with your choice of sources and authority on the subject(s). Your logos, or the logic of your thoughts represented across the document, will allow the reader to come to understand the relationships among who, what, where, when, and so forth. If your readers cannot follow your logic they will lose interest, fail to understand your message, and possibly not even read it at all. Finally, your pathos, or passion and enthusiasm, will be reflected in your design and word choices. If your document fails to convey enthusiasm for the subject, how can you expect the reader to be interested? Every document, indeed every communication, represents aspects of these classical elements.

General Purpose and Thesis Statements
No matter what your business writing project involves, it needs to convey some central idea. To clarify the idea in your mind and make sure it comes through to your audience, write a thesis statement. A thesis statement, or central idea, should be short, specific, and to the point. Steven Beebe and Susan Beebe [1] recommend five guiding principles when considering your thesis statement. The thesis statement should
1. be a declarative statement;
2. be a complete sentence;
3. use specific language, not vague generalities;
4. be a single idea;
5. reflect consideration of the audience.

This statement is key to the success of your document. If your audience has to work to find out what exactly you are talking about, or what your stated purpose or goal is, they will be less likely to read, be influenced, or recall what you have written. By stating your point clearly in your introduction, and then referring back to it in the body of the document and at the end, you will help your readers to understand and remember your message.

Organizing Principles

Once you know the basic elements of your message, you need to decide in what order to present them to your audience. A central organizing principle will help you determine a logical order for your information. One common organizing principle is chronology, or time: the writer tells what happened first, then what happened next, then what is happening now, and, finally, what is expected to happen in the future. Another common organizing principle is comparison: the writer describes one product, an argument on one side of an issue, or one possible course of action; and then compares it with another product, argument, or course of action.

As an example, let's imagine that you are a business writer within the transportation industry and you have been assigned to write a series of informative pieces about an international initiative called the "TransAmerica Transportation System Study." Just as the First Transcontinental Railroad once unified the United States from east to west, which was further reinforced by the Interstate Highway System, the proposed TransAmerica Transportation System will facilitate integrating the markets of Mexico, the United States, and Canada from north to south. Rail transportation has long been an integral part of the transportation and distribution system for goods across the Americas, and its role will be important in this new system.

In deciding how to organize your report, you have several challenges and many possibilities of different organizing principles to use. Part of your introduction will involve a historical perspective, and a discussion of the events that led from the First Transcontinental Railroad to the TransAmerica Transportation System proposal. Other aspects will include comparing the old railroad and highway systems to the new ones, and the transformative effect this will have on business and industry. You will need to acknowledge the complex relationships and challenges that collaboration has overcome, and highlight the common benefits. You will be called on to write informative documents as part of a public relations initiative, persuasive essays to underscore the benefits for those who prefer the status quo, and even write speeches for celebrations and awards.

Table 6.1 "Organizing Principles" lists seventeen different organizing principles and how they might be applied to various pieces you would write about the TransAmerican Transportation System. The left column provides the name of the organizing principle. The center column explains the process of organizing a document according to each principle, and the third column provides an example.

Table 6.1 Organizing Principles

Organizing Principle	Explanation of Process	Example
1. Time (Chronological)	Structuring your document by time shows a series of events or steps in a process, which typically has a beginning, middle, and end. "Once upon a time stories" follow a chronological pattern.	Before the First Transcontinental Railroad, the events that led to its construction, and its impact on early America. Additional examples may include the national highway projects and the development of reliable air freight. Now we can consider the TransAmerica Transportation System and the similar and distinct events that led us to today.
2. Comparison	Structuring your document by comparison focuses on the similarities and/or differences between points or concepts.	A comparison of pre– and post–First Transcontinental Railroad America, showing how health and life expectancy improved with the increased access to goods and services. Another example could be drawn from air freight, noting that organ donation in one part of the country can now save a life in another state or on the opposite coast.

Organizing Principle	Explanation of Process	Example
		In a similar way, the TransAmerica Transportation System will improve the lives of the citizens of Mexico, the United States, and Canada.
3. Contrast	Structuring your document by using contrasting points highlights the differences between items and concepts.	A contrast of pre– and post–First Transcontinental Railroad America showing how much time it took to communicate via letter, or how long it took to move out West. Just in time delivery and the modern highway system and trucking may serve as an example for contrast. The TransAmerica Transportation System will reduce customs clearing time while increasing border security along the distribution network.
4. Cause and Effect	Structuring your document by cause and effect structuring establishes a relationship between two events or situations, making the connection clear.	The movement of people and goods out West grew considerably from 1750 to 1850. With the availability of a new and faster way to go West, people generally supported its construction. Both the modern highway and air transportation systems may serve as examples, noting how people, goods, and services can be delivered in drastically reduced time frames. Citizens of all three countries involved have increasingly been involved in trade, and movement across common borders through the TransAmerica Transportation System will enable the movement of goods and services with great efficiency.
5. Problem and Solution	Structuring your document by problem and solution means you state the problem and detail how it was solved. This approach is effective for persuasive speeches.	Manufacturers were producing better goods for less money at the start of the Industrial Revolution, but they lacked a fast and effective method of getting their goods to growing markets. The First Transcontinental Railroad gave them speed, economy, and access to new markets. Highways and air routes have dramatically increased this trend. In a similar way, this new system is the next evolutionary step in the integration and growth of our common marketplaces.
6. Classification (Categorical)	Structuring your document by classification establishes categories.	At the time the United States considered the First Transcontinental Railroad, there were three main types of transportation: by water, by horse, and by foot. Now rail, road, and air transportation are the norm across business and industry.
7. Biographical	Structuring your document by biography means examining specific people as they relate to the central topic.	1804: Lewis and Clark travel 4,000 miles in over two years across America 1862: President Lincoln signs the Pacific Railroad Act 1876: The Transcontinental Express from New York arrives in San Francisco with a record-breaking time of 83 hours and 39 minutes

Organizing Principle	Explanation of Process	Example
		2009: President Obama can cross America by plane in less than 5 hours So why shouldn't the ratio of time from import to consumer be reduced?
8. Space (Spatial)	Structuring your document by space involves the parts of something and how they fit to form the whole.	A train uses a heat source to heat water, create steam, and turn a turbine, which moves a lever, causing a wheel to move on a track. A package picked up from an office in New York in the morning is delivered to another in Los Angeles in the afternoon. From a Pacific port in Northern Mexico to a market in Chicago or Canada, this system unifies the movement of goods and services.
9. Ascending and Descending	Structuring your document by ascending or descending order involves focusing on quantity and quality. One good story (quality) leads to the larger picture, or the reverse.	A day in the life of a traveler in 1800. Incremental developments in transportation to the present, expressed through statistics, graphs, maps, and charts. A day in the life of a traveler in 1960, 1980, or even 2000, with visual examples of changes and trends may also contribute to the document. A day in the life of a traveler in 2009 compared to the relatively slow movement of goods and services, constrained by an antiquated transportation network that negatively impacts efficiency.
10. Psychological	It is also called "Monroe's Motivated Sequence." [2] Structuring your document on the psychological aspects of the audience involves focusing on their inherent needs and wants. See Maslow [3] and Schutz. [4] The author calls *attention* to a *need*, then focuses on the satisfaction of the need, *visualization* of the solution, and ends with a proposed or historical *action*. Useful for a persuasive message.	When families in the year 1800 went out West, they rarely returned to see family and friends. The country as a whole was an extension of this distended family, separated by time and distance. The railroad, the highways, and air travel brought families and the country together. In the same way, common markets already exist across the three countries, but remain separated by time, distance, and an antiquated system scheduled for significant improvement.
11. Elimination	Structuring your document using the process of elimination involves outlining all the possibilities.	The First Transcontinental Railroad helped pave the way for the destruction of the Native American way of life in 1870. After examining treaties, relocation and reservations, loss of the buffalo, disease, and war, the railroad can be accurately considered the catalyst for the end of an era. From the lessons of history we can learn to protect and preserve our distinct cultures, languages, and sovereign territories as we integrate a common transportation system for our mutual benefit and security.
12. Example	Structuring your document by example involves providing vivid, specific examples (as opposed to	Just as it once took weeks, even months, for a simple letter to move from coast to coast, goods and services

Organizing Principle	Explanation of Process	Example
	abstract representations of data) to support main points.	have had a long and arduous process from importation to market. For example, the popular Christmas toy X, imported to Mexico from China in September, may well not be on store shelves by December 25 under the old system. Now it can move from importation to market in under two weeks.
13. Process and Procedure	Structuring your document by process and procedure is similar to the time (chronological) organizational pattern with the distinction of steps or phases that lead to a complete end goal. This is often referred to as the "how-to" organizational pattern.	From conception to design, manufacturing to packaging, to transportation and inspection, to sales and sales support, let's examine how the new transportation system facilitates increased efficiency in delivery to market and product support.
14. Point Pattern	Structuring your document in a series of points allows for the presentation of diverse assertions to be aligned in a cohesive argument with clear support.	The TransAmerica Transportation System offers several advantages: security, speed, efficiency, and cost reduction.
15. Definition	Structuring your document with a guiding definition allows for a clear introduction of terms and concepts while reducing the likelihood of misinterpretation.	The TransAmerica Transportation System can be defined by its purpose, its integrated components, and its impact on the secure movement of goods and services across common borders.
16. Testimonial	Structuring your document around a testimony, or first person account of an experience, can be an effective way to make an abstract concept clearer to an audience.	According to Ms. X, owner of InterCountry Trading Company, it previously took 12 weeks to import, clear, and deliver a product from Mexico to the United States, and an additional four weeks to take delivery in Canada. Now the process takes less than two weeks.
17. Ceremonial (Events, Ceremonies, or Celebrations)	Structuring your document by focusing on the following: Thanking dignitaries and representatives The importance of the event The relationship of the event to the audience Thanking the audience for participation in the event, ceremony, or celebration	Thanking the representatives, builders, and everyone involved with the construction of the TransAmerica Transportation System. The railroad will unite America, and bring us closer in terms of trade, communication, and family. Thank you for participating in today's dedication.

Outlines

Chances are you have learned the basic principles of outlining in English writing courses: an outline is a framework that organizes main ideas and subordinate ideas in a hierarchical series of roman numerals and alphabetical letters. The right column of Table 6.2 "Outline 1" presents a generic outline in a classical style. In the left column, the three main structural elements of an informative document are tied to the outline. Your task is to fill in the right column outline with the actual ideas and points you are making in your writing project. Feel free to adapt and tailor it to your needs, depending on the specifics of your report, letter, or other document.

Table 6.2 Outline 1

Introduction	Main Idea
Body	I. Main idea: Point 1 Subpoint 1 A.1 specific information 1 A.2 specific information 2
Body	II. Main idea: Point 2 Subpoint 1 B.1 specific information 1 B.2 specific information 2

Introduction	Main Idea
	III. Main idea: Point 3 Subpoint 1 C.1 specific information 1 C.2 specific information 2
Conclusion	Summary: Main points 1–3

Table 6.3 "Outline 2" presents an alternate outline form that may be more suitable for brief documents like letters and e-mails. You can use this format as a model or modify it as needed.

Table 6.3 Outline 2

1	Introduction	General purpose, statement, or thesis statement
2	Body	Point 1:
		Point 2:
		Point 3:
3	Conclusion	Summarize main points

Paragraphs

Paragraphs are how we package information in business communication, and the more efficient the package, the easier the meaning can be delivered.

You may wish to think of each paragraph as a small essay within a larger information platform, defined by a guiding thesis and an organizing principle. The standard five-paragraph essay format used on college term papers is mirrored in individual paragraphs. Often college essays have minimum or maximum word counts, but paragraphs hardly ever have established limits. Each paragraph focuses on one central idea. It can be as long or as short as it needs to be to get the message across, but remember your audience and avoid long, drawn-out paragraphs that may lose your reader's attention.

Just as a document generally has an introduction, body, and conclusion, so does a paragraph. Each paragraph has one idea, thought, or purpose that is stated in an introductory sentence. This is followed by one or more supporting sentences and concluded with a summary statement and transition or link to the next idea, or paragraph. Let's address each in turn:

- The topic sentence states the main thesis, purpose, or topic of the paragraph; it defines the subject matter to be addressed in that paragraph.
- Body sentences support the topic sentence and relate clearly to the subject matter of the paragraph and overall document. They may use an organizing principle similar to that of the document itself (chronology, contrast, spatial) or introduce a related organizing principle (point by point, process or procedure).
- The conclusion sentence brings the paragraph to a close; it may do this in any of several ways. It may reinforce the paragraph's main point, summarize the relationships among the body sentences, and/or serve as a transition to the next paragraph.

Effective Sentences

We have talked about the organization of documents and paragraphs, but what about the organization of sentences? You have probably learned in English courses that each sentence needs to have a subject and a verb; most sentences also have an object. There are four basic types of sentences: declarative, imperative, interrogative, and exclamatory. Here are some examples:

- **Declarative** – You are invited to join us for lunch.
- **Imperative** – Please join us for lunch.
- **Interrogative** – Would you like to join us for lunch?
- **Exclamatory** – I'm so glad you can join us!

Declarative sentences make a statement, whereas interrogative sentences ask a question. Imperative sentences convey a command, and exclamatory sentences express a strong emotion. Interrogative and exclamatory sentences are easy to identify by their final punctuation, a question mark and an exclamation point, respectively. In business writing, declarative and imperative sentences are more frequently used.

There are also compound and complex sentences, which may use two or more of the four basic types in combination:

1. *Simple sentence.* Sales have increased.
2. *Compound sentence.* Sales have increased and profits continue to grow.
3. *Complex sentence.* Sales have increased and we have the sales staff to thank for it.
4. *Compound complex sentence.* Although the economy has been in recession, sales have increased, and we have sales staff to thank for it.

In our simple sentence, "sales" serves as the subject and "have increased" serves as the verb. The sentence can stand alone because it has the two basic parts that constitute a sentence. In our compound sentence we have two independent clauses that could stand alone; they are joined by the conjunction "and." In our complex sentence, we have an independent clause, which can stand on its own, combined with a fragment (not a sentence) or dependent clause which, if it were not joined to the independent clause, would not make any sense. The fragment "and we have the sales staff to thank" on its own would have us asking "for what?" as the subject is absent. Complex compound sentences combine a mix of independent and dependent clauses, and at least one of the clauses must be dependent.

The ability to write complete, correct sentences is like any other skill—it comes with practice. The more writing you do, as you make an effort to use correct grammar, the easier it will become. Reading audiences, particularly in a business context, will not waste their time on poor writing and will move on. Your challenge as an effective business writer is to know what you are going to write and then to make it come across, via words, symbols, and images, in a clear and concise manner.

Sentences should avoid being vague and focus on specific content. Each sentence should convey a complete thought; a vague sentence fails to meet this criteria. The reader is left wondering what the sentence was supposed to convey.

- Vague – We can facilitate solutions in pursuit of success by leveraging our core strengths.
- Specific – By using our knowledge, experience, and capabilities, we can achieve the production targets for the coming quarter.

Effective sentences also limit the range and scope of each complete thought, avoiding needless complexity. Sometimes writers mistakenly equate long, complex sentences with excellence and skill. Clear, concise, and often brief sentences serve to communicate ideas and concepts in effective and efficient ways that complex, hard-to-follow sentences do not.

- *Complex.* Air transportation features speed of delivery in ways few other forms of transportation can match, including tractor-trailer and rail, and is readily available to the individual consumer and the corporate client alike.
- *Clear.* Air transportation is accessible and faster than railroad or trucking.

Effective sentences are complete, containing a subject and a verb. Incomplete sentences—also known as sentence fragments—demonstrate a failure to pay attention to detail. They often invite misunderstanding, which is the opposite of our goal in business communication.

- Fragments – Although air transportation is fast. Costs more than trucking.
- Complete – Although air transportation is fast, it costs more than trucking.

Effective business writing avoids bureaucratic language and phrase that are the hallmark of decoration. Decoration is a reflection of ritual, and ritual has its role. If you are the governor of a state, and want to make a resolution declaring today as HIV/AIDS Awareness Day, you are allowed to start the document with "Whereas" because of its ritual importance. Similarly, if you are writing a legal document, tradition calls for certain standard phrases such as "know all men by these presents." However, in standard business writing, it is best to refrain from using bureaucratic phrases and ritualistic words that decorate and distract the reader from your clear, essential meaning. If the customer, client, or supplier does not understand the message the first time, each follow-up attempt to clarify the meaning through interaction is a cost. Table 6.4 "Bureaucratic Phrases and Standard Alternatives" presents a few examples of common bureaucratic phrases and standard English alternatives.

Table 6.4 Bureaucratic Phrases and Standard Alternatives

Bureaucratic Phrase	Standard English Alternatives
At the present time	Now, today
Concerning the matter of	Regarding, about
Despite the fact that	Although, while, even though
Due to the fact that	Because, since, as
Implement an investigation of	Find out, investigate
Inasmuch as	Because, since, as
It has been suggested	[name of person or organization] has suggested, said, or stated
It is believed that	[name of person or organization] believes, thinks, or says that
It is the opinion of the author	I believe, I think, in my opinion
Until such time as	Until, when
With the exception of	Except, apart from

In oral communication, repetition can be an effective strategy to reinforce a message, but in written communication it adds needless length to a document and impairs clarity.

- Redundant – In this day and age air transportation by air carrier is the clear winner over alternative modes of conveyance for speed and meeting tight deadlines.

- Clear – Today air transportation is faster than other methods.

When a writer states that something is a "true fact," a group achieved a "consensus of opinion," or that the "final outcome" was declared, the word choices reflect an unnecessary redundancy. A fact, consensus, or outcome need not be qualified with words that state similar concepts. If it is fact, it is true. A consensus, by definition, is formed in a group from diverse opinions. An outcome is the final result, so adding the word "final" repeats the fact unnecessarily.

In business writing we seek clear and concise writing that speaks for itself with little or no misinterpretation. The more complex a sentence becomes, the easier it is to lose track of its meaning. When we consider that it may read by someone for whom English is a second language, the complex sentence becomes even more problematic. If we consider its translation, we add another layer of complexity that can lead to miscommunication. Finally, effective sentences follow the KISS formula for success: Keep It Simple—Simplify!

Transitions

If you were going to build a house, you would need a strong foundation. Could you put the beams to hold your roof in place without anything to keep them in place? Of course not; they would fall down right away. In the same way, the columns or beams are like the main ideas of your document. They need to have connections to each other so that they become interdependent and stay where you want them so that your house, or your writing, doesn't come crashing down.

Transitions involve words or visual devices that help the audience follow the author's ideas, connect the main points to each other, and see the relationships you've created in the information you are presenting. They are often described as bridges between ideas, thought or concepts, providing some sense of where you've been and where you are going with your document. Transitions guide the audience in the progression from one significant idea, concept, or point to the next. They can also show the relationships between the main point and the support you are using to illustrate your point, provide examples for it, or refer to outside sources. Table 6.5 "Types of Transitions in Writing" is a summary of fourteen different types of transitions. Consider them as you contemplate how to bring together your information and make notes on your outline.

Table 6.5 Types of Transitions in Writing

Type	Definition	Examples
1. Internal Previews	An **internal preview** is a brief statement referring to a point you are going to make. It can forecast or foreshadow a main point in your document.	If we look ahead to, next we'll examine, now we can focus our attention on, first we'll look at, then we'll examine
2. Signposts	A **signpost** alerts the audience you are moving from one topic to the next. Sign posts or signal words draw attention to themselves and focus the audience's attention.	Stop and consider, we can now address, turning from/to, another, this reminds me of, I would like to emphasize
3. Internal Summaries	An **internal summary** briefly covers information or alludes to information introduced previously. It can remind an audience of a previous point and reinforce information covered in your document.	As I have said, as we have seen, as mentioned earlier, in any event, in conclusion, in other words, in short, on the whole, therefore, to summarize, as a result, as has been noted previously,
4. Sequence	A **sequence transition** outlines a hierarchical order or series of steps in your document. It can illustrate order or steps in a logical process.	First…second…third, furthermore, next, last, still, also, and then, besides, finally
5. Time	A **time transition** focuses on the chronological aspects of your order. Particularly useful in an article	Before, earlier, immediately, in the meantime, in the past, lately, later, meanwhile, now, presently, shortly,

Type	Definition	Examples
	utilizing a story, this transition can illustrate for the audience progression of time.	simultaneously, since, so far, soon as long as, as soon as, at last, at length, at that time, then, until, afterward
6. Addition	An **addition or additive transition** contributes to a previous point. This transition can build on a previous point and extend the discussion.	Additionally, not to mention, in addition to, furthermore, either, neither, besides, on, in fact, as a matter of fact, actually, not only, but also, as well as
7. Similarity	A **transition by similarity** draws a parallel between two ideas, concepts or examples. It can indicate a common area between points for the audience.	In the same way, by the same token, equally, similarly, just as we have seen, in the same vein
8. Comparison	A **transition by comparison** draws a distinction between two ideas, concepts or examples. It can indicate a common or divergent area between points for the audience.	Like, in relation to, bigger than, the fastest, larger than, than any other, is bigger than, both, either...or, likewise
9. Contrast	A **transition by contrast** draws a distinction of difference, opposition, or irregularity between two ideas, concepts or examples. This transition can indicate a key distinction between points for the audience.	But, neither...nor, however on the other hand, although, despite, even though, in contrast, in spite of, on the contrary conversely, unlike, while instead, nevertheless, nonetheless, regardless, still, though, yet, although
Type	Definition	Examples
10. Cause and Effect, Result	A **transition by cause and effect or result** illustrates a relationship between two ideas, concepts or examples and may focus on the outcome or result. It can illustrate a relationship between points for the audience.	As a result, because, consequently, for this purpose, accordingly, so, then, therefore, thereupon, thus, to this end, for this reason, as a result, because , therefore, consequently, as a consequence, and the outcome was
11. Examples	A **transition by example** illustrates a connection between a point and an example or examples. You may find visual aids work well with this type of transition.	In fact, as we can see, after all, even, for example, for instance, of course, specifically, such as, in the following example, to illustrate my point
12. Place	A **place transition** refers to a location, often in a spatially organized essay, of one point of emphasis to another. Again, visual aids work well when discussing physical location with the reading audience.	opposite to, there, to the left, to the right, above, adjacent to, elsewhere, far, farther on, below, beyond, closer to, here, near, nearby, next to
13. Clarification	A **clarification transition** restates or further develops a main idea or point. It can also serve as a signal to a key point.	To clarify, that is, I mean, in other words, to put it another way that is to say, to rephrase it, in order to explain, this means
14. Concession	A **concession transition** indicates knowledge of contrary information. It can address a perception the audience may hold and allow for clarification.	We can see that while, although it is true that, granted that, while it may appear that, naturally, of course, I can see that, I admit that while

KEY TAKEAWAY

Organization is the key to clear writing. Organize your document using key elements, an organizing principle, and an outline. Organize your paragraphs and sentences so that your audience can understand them, and use transitions to move from one point to the next.

1. What functions does organization serve in a document? Can they be positive or negative? Explain and discuss with a classmate.

2. Create an outline from a sample article or document. Do you notice an organizational pattern? Explain and discuss with a classmate.

3. Which of the following sentences are good examples of correct and clear business English? For sentences needing improvement, describe what is wrong and write a sentence that corrects the problem. Discuss your answers with your classmates.

   a. Marlys has been chosen to receive a promotion next month.

   b. Because her work is exemplary.

   c. At such time as it becomes feasible, it is the intention of our department to facilitate a lunch meeting to congratulate Marlys

   d. As a result of budget allocation analysis and examination of our financial condition, it is indicated that salary compensation for Marlys can be increased to a limited degree.

   e. When will Marlys's promotion be official?

   f. I am so envious!

   g. Among those receiving promotions, Marlys, Bob, Germaine, Terry, and Akiko.

   h. The president asked all those receiving promotions come to the meeting.

   i. Please attend a meeting for all employees who will be promoted next month.

   j. Marlys intends to use her new position to mentor employees joining the firm, which will encourage commitment and good work habits.

Find an example of a poor sentence or a spelling or grammar error that was published online or in print and share your finding with the class.

[1] Beebe, S. [Steven], & Beebe, S. [Susan]. (1997). *Public speaking: An audience-centered approach* (3rd ed., pp. 121–122). Boston, MA: Allyn & Bacon.
[2] Ayres, J., & Miller, J. (1994). *Effective public speaking* (4th ed., p. 274). Madison, WI: Brown &Benchmark.
[3] Maslow, A. (1970). *Motivation and personality* (2nd ed.). New York, NY: Harper & Row.
[4] Schutz, W. (1966). *The interpersonal underworld*. Palo Alto, CA: Science and Behavior Books.

6.2 Writing Style
LEARNING OBJECTIVE

1. Demonstrate your ability to prepare and present information using a writing style that will increase understanding, retention, and motivation to act.

You are invited to a business dinner at an expensive restaurant that has been the top-rated dining establishment in your town for decades. You are aware of the restaurant's dress code, which forbids casual attire such as jeans, T-shirts, and sneakers. What will you wear? If you want to fit in with the other guests and make a favorable impression on your hosts, you will choose a good quality suit or dress (and appropriately dressy shoes and accessories). You will avoid calling undue attention to yourself with clothing that is overly formal—an evening gown or a tuxedo, for example—or that would distract from the business purpose of the occasion by being overly revealing or provocative. You may feel that your freedom to express yourself by dressing as you please is being restricted, or you may appreciate the opportunity to look your best. Either way, adhering to these style conventions will serve you well in a business context.

The same is true in business writing. Unlike some other kinds of writing such as poetry or fiction, business writing is not an opportunity for self-expression. Instead it calls for a fairly conservative and unadorned style. Writing style, also known as voice or tone, is the manner in which a writer addresses the reader. It involves qualities of writing such as vocabulary and figures of speech, phrasing, rhythm, sentence structure, and paragraph length. Developing an appropriate business writing style will reflect well on you and increase your success in any career.

Formal versus Informal

There was a time when many business documents were written in third person to give them the impression of objectivity. This formal style was often passive and wordy. Today it has given way to active, clear, concise writing, sometimes known as "Plain English." [1] As business and industry increasingly trade across borders and languages, writing techniques that obscure meaning or impede understanding can cause serious problems. Efficient writing styles have become the norm. Still, you will experience in your own writing efforts this "old school versus new school" writing debate over abbreviations, contractions, and the use of informal language in what was once considered a formal business context. Consider the following comparison of informal versus formal and bureaucratic styles.

Bureaucratic: Attached is the latest delivery data represented in topographical forms pursuant to the directive ABC123 of the air transportation guide supplied by the Federal Aviation Administration in September of 2008.

- Formal – Please note the attached delivery data for July 2009.

- Informal – Here's the delivery data for last month.

While it is generally agreed that bureaucratic forms can obscure meaning, there is a debate on the use of formal versus informal styles in business communication. Formal styles often require more detail, adhere to rules of etiquette, and avoid shortcuts like contractions and folksy expressions. Informal styles reflect everyday speech patterns and may include contractions and colloquial expressions. Many managers prefer not to see contractions in a formal business context. Others will point out that a comma preceding the last item in a series (known as the "serial comma") is the standard, not the exception. Some will make a general recommendation that you should always "keep it professional." Here lies the heart of the debate: what *is* professional writing in a business context? If you answered "it depends," you are correct.

Keep in mind that audiences have expectations and your job is to meet them. Some business audiences prefer a fairly formal tone. If you include contractions or use a style that is too casual, you may lose their interest and attention; you may also give them a negative impression of your level of expertise. If, however, you are writing for an audience that expects informal language, you may lose their interest and attention by writing too formally; your writing may also come across as arrogant or pompous. It is not that one style is better than the other, but simply that styles of writing vary across a range of options. Business writing may need to meet legal standards and include references, as we see in the bureaucratic example above, but that is generally not the norm for communications within an organization. The skilled business writer will know his or her audience and will adapt the message to best facilitate communication. Choosing the right style can make a significant impact on how your writing is received.

You may hear reference to a conversational tone in writing as one option in business communication. A conversational tone, as the name implies, resembles oral communication in style, tone, and word choice. It can be appropriate for some audiences, and may serve you well in specific contexts, but it can easily come across as less than professional.

If you use expressions that imply a relationship or a special awareness of information such as "you know," or "as we discussed," without explaining the necessary background, your writing may be seen as overly familiar, intimate, or even secretive. Trust is the foundation for all communication interactions and a careless word or phrase can impair trust.

If you want to use humor, think carefully about how your audience will interpret it. Humor is a fragile form of communication that requires an awareness of irony, of juxtaposition, or a shared sense of attitudes, beliefs, and values. Different people find humor in different situations, and what is funny to one person may be dull, or even hurtful, to someone else.

Although there are business situations such as an interview or a performance self-evaluation where you need to state your accomplishments, in general business writing it is best to avoid self-referential comments that allude to your previous successes. These can come across as selfish or arrogant. Instead, be generous in giving credit where credit is due. Take every opportunity to thank your colleagues for their efforts and to acknowledge those who contributed good ideas.

Jargon is a vocabulary that has been developed by people in a particular group, discipline, or industry, and it can be a useful shorthand as long as the audience knows its meaning. For example, when writing for bank customers, you could refer to "ATM transactions" and feel confident that your readers would know what you meant. It would be unnecessary and inappropriate to write "Automated Teller Machine transactions." Similarly, if you were working in a hospital, you would probably use many medical terms in your interactions with other medical professionals. However, if you were a hospital employee writing to a patient, using medical jargon would be inappropriate, as it would not contribute to the patient's understanding.

Finally, in a business context, remember that conversational style is not an excuse to use poor grammar, disrespectful or offensive slang, or profanity. Communication serves as the bridge between minds and your written words will represent you in your absence. One strategy when trying to use a conversation tone is to ask yourself, "Would I say it in this way to their face?" A follow-up question to consider is, "Would I say it in this way in front of everyone?" Your professional use of language is one the hallmark skills in business, and the degree to which you master its use will reflect itself in your success. Take care, take time, and make sure what you write communicates a professional tone that positively represents you and your organization.

Introductions: Direct and Indirect
Sometimes the first sentence is the hardest to write. When you know the two main opening strategies it may not make it any easier, but it will give a plan and form a framework. Business documents often incorporate one of two opening strategies regardless of their organizational pattern. The direct pattern states the main purpose directly, at the

beginning, and leaves little room for misinterpretation. The indirect pattern, where you introduce your main idea after the opening paragraph, can be useful if you need a strong opening to get the attention of what you perceive may be an uninterested audience. Normally, if you expect a positive response from the reader you will choose a direct opening, being clear from the first sentence about your purpose and goal. If you do not expect a positive reception, or have to deliver bad news, you may want to be less direct. Each style has its purpose and use; the skilled business writer will learn to be direct and be able to present bad news with a positive opening paragraph.

Adding Emphasis

There are times when you will want to add emphasis to a word, phrase, or statistic so that it stands out from the surrounding text. The use of visual aids in your writing can be an excellent option, and can reinforce the written discussion. For example, if you write that sales are up 4 percent over this time last year, the number alone may not get the attention it deserves. If, however, near the text section you feature a bar graph demonstrating the sales growth figures, the representation of the information in textual and graphical way may reinforce its importance.

As you look across the top of your word processing program you may notice **bold**, *italics*, underline, highlights, your choice of colors, and a host of interesting fonts. Although it can be entertaining to experiment with these visual effects, do not use them just for the sake of decoration. Consistency and branding are important features of your firm's public image, so you will want the visual aspects of your writing to support that image. Still, when you need to highlight an important fact or emphasize a key question in a report, your readers will appreciate your use of visual effects to draw their attention. Consider the following examples:

- Bullets can be effective when used with discretion.
  Take care when using the following:
    i. Numbers
    ii. With subheadings
    iii. In serial lists
    iv. As they can get
    v. A bit overwhelming to the point where
    vi. The reader loses his or her interest

Emphasis can be influenced by your choice of font. Serif fonts, such as Times New Roman and Garamond, have decorative ends that make the font easy to read. Sans serif fonts, like Arial, lack these visual cues and often serve better as headers.

You can also vary the emphasis according to where you place information within a sentence:

- *Maximum emphasis.* Sales have increased across the United States because of our latest promotion efforts in our largest and most successful market.
- *Medium emphasis.* Because of our latest promotion efforts in our largest and most successful market, sales have increased across the United States.
- *Minimum emphasis.* The United States, which has experienced a sales increase, is our largest and most successful market.

The information at end of the sentence is what people often recall, and is therefore normally considered the location of maximum emphasis. The second best position for recall is the beginning of the sentence, while the middle of the sentence is the area with the least recall. If you want to highlight a point, place it at the beginning or end of the sentence, and if you want to deemphasize a point, the middle is your best option. [2]

Active versus Passive Voice

You want your writing to be engaging. Which sentence would you rather read?

- A – All sales orders are processed daily by Mackenzie.
- B – Mackenzie processes all sales orders daily.

Most readers prefer sentence B, but why? You'll recall that all sentences have a subject and a verb, but you may not have paid much attention to their functions. Let's look at how the subject and verb function in these two sentences. In sentence A, the subject is "Mackenzie," and the subject is the doer of the action expressed by the verb (processes). In sentence A, the subject is "sales orders," and the subject is the receiver of the action expressed by the verb (are processed). Sentence A is written in active voice—a sentence structure in which the subject carries out the action. Sentence B is written in passive voice—a sentence structure in which the subject receives the action.

Active sentences tend to be shorter, more precise, and easier to understand. This is especially true because passive sentences can be written in ways that do not tell the reader who the doer of the action is. For example, "All sales orders are processed daily" is a complete and correct sentence in passive voice.

Active voice is the clear choice for a variety of contexts, but not all. When you want to deemphasize the doer of the action, you may write, "Ten late arrivals were recorded this month" and not even mention who was late. The passive form doesn't place blame or credit, so it can be more diplomatic in some contexts. Passive voice allows the writer to avoid personal references or personal pronouns (he, she, they) to create a more objective tone. There are also situations where the doer of the action is unknown, as in "graffiti was painted on the side of our building last night."

Overall, business communication resources tend to recommend active voice as the preferred style. Still, the styles themselves are not the problem or challenge, but it is how we use them that matters. A skilled business writer will see both styles as options within a range of choices and learn to distinguish when each style is most appropriate to facilitate communication.

Commonly Confused Words

The sentences in Table 6.6 "Common Errors in English" focus on some of the most common errors in English. You may recall this exercise from the introduction of this chapter. How did you do? Visit the "Additional Resources" section at the end of the chapter for some resources on English grammar and usage.

Table 6.6 Common Errors in English

1. *accept* or *except*	The office will _____ applications until 5 p.m. on the 31st.	accept	Attendance is required for all employees _____ supervisors.	except
2. *affect* or *effect*	To _____ the growth of plants, we can regulate the water supply.	affect	A lack of water has a predictable _____ on most plants.	effect
3. *e.g.* or *i.e.*	Please order 2,000 imprinted giveaways (_____, pens or coffee mugs)	e.g.	Charge them to my account (_____, account #98765).	i.e.
4. *its* or *it's*	The department surpassed _____ previous sales record this quarter.	its	_____ my opinion that we reached peak oil in 2008.	It's
5. *lay* or *lie*	Please _____ the report on the desk.	lay	The doctor asked him to _____ down on the examination table.	lie
6. *pressure* or *pressurize*	We need to _____ the liquid nitrogen tanks.	pressurize	It might be possible to _____ him to resign.	pressure
7. *principle* or *principal*	It's the basic _____ of farming: no water, no food.	principle	The _____ reason for the trip is to attend the sales meeting.	principal
8. *regardless* or *irregardless*	_____ of what we do, gas prices are unlikely to go back down.	Regardless	_____ of your beliefs, please try to listen with an open mind.	Regardless (*Irregardless* is not a standard word; see your dictionary)
9. *than* or *then*	This year's losses were worse _____ last year's.	than	If we can cut our costs, _____ it might be possible to break even.	then
10. *that* or *which*	_____ type of marketing data did you need?	Which	Karen misplaced the report, _____ caused a delay in making a decision.	which

	There are several kinds of data _____ could be useful.	that			
11 *there their*, or *they're*	The report is _____, in the top file drawer.	there	_____ strategic advantage depends on a wide distribution network.	Their	
	_____ planning to attend the sales meeting in Pittsburgh.	They're			
12. *to*, *too*, or *two*	Customers need _____ drive slower if they want to save gas.	to	After sales meeting, you should visit customers in the Pittsburgh area _____.	too	
	In fact, the _____ of you should make some customer visits together.	two			
13. *uninterested* or *disinterested*	He would be the best person to make a decision, since he isn't biased and is relatively _____ in the outcome.	disinterested	The sales manager tried to speak dynamically, but the sales reps were simply _____ in what he had to say.	uninterested	
14. *who*, *whom*, *who's*, or *whose*	_____ truck is that?	Whose	_____ going to pay for the repairs?	Who's	
	_____ will go to the interview?	Who	To _____ should we address the thank-you note?	whom	
15 *your* or *you're*	My office is bigger than _____ cubicle.	your	_____ going to learn how to avoid making these common mistakes in English.	You're	

Making Errors at the Speed of Light

In business and industry there is increasing pressure to produce under deadlines that in some respects have been artificially accelerated by the immediacy inherent in technological communication devices. If you receive an e-mail or text message while you are in the middle of studying a complex problem, you may be tempted to "get it out of the way" by typing out a quick reply, but in your haste you may fail to qualify, include important information, or even check to make sure you have hit "Reply" and not "Reply to All" or even "Delete." Take care to pause and review your text message, e-mail, or document before you consider it complete. Here is a quick electronic communication do/don't list to keep in mind before you click "send."

Do remember the following:

- Everything you access via an employer's system is subject to inspection.

- Everything you write or record reflects you and your business or organization, even if it is stored in a Google or Yahoo! account.
- Respect personal space by not forwarding every e-mail you think is funny.
- Use a concise but relevant and informative phrase for the subject line.
- E-mail the receiver before sending large attachments, as they may exceed the limit of the receiver's in-box.
- Attach your intended attachments.

KEY TAKEAWAY

An appropriate business writing style can be formal or informal, depending on the context, but it should always reflect favorably on the writer and the organization.

EXERCISES

1. Select at least three examples of writing from different kinds of sources, such as a government Web site, a textbook, a popular magazine, and a novel. According to the style characteristics discussed in this section, how would you characterize the style of each? Select a paragraph to rewrite in a different style—for example, if the style is formal, make it informal; if the selection is written in active voice, make it passive. Discuss your results with your classmates.

2. What are some qualities of a good business writing style? What makes certain styles more appropriate for business than others? Discuss your thoughts with a classmate.

3. Find an example of formal writing and write an informal version. Please share with your classmates.

4. Find an example of informal writing and write a formal version. Please share with your classmates

5. You are assigned to a work team that has to come up with a formal declaration and an informal explanation for the declaration. The declaration could be a memo indicating that your business will be observing a holiday (each team should have a different holiday).

6. How would you characterize your writing style? Do you need to make modifications to make your style suitable for business writing? Write a one- to two-page essay on this subject.

[1] Bailey, E. P. (2008). *Plain English at work: A guide to business writing and speaking*. New York, NY: McGraw-Hill.

[2] McLean, S. (2003). *The basics of speech communication*. Boston, MA: Allyn & Bacon.

6.3 Making an Argument
LEARNING OBJECTIVES

1. Demonstrate how to form a clear argument with appropriate support to persuade your audience.

2. Recognize and understand inherent weaknesses in fallacies.

According to the famous satirist Jonathan Swift, "Argument is the worst sort of conversation." You may be inclined to agree. When people argue, they are engaged in conflict and it's usually not pretty. It sometimes appears that way because people resort to fallacious arguments or false statements, or they simply do not treat each other with respect. They get defensive, try to prove their own points, and fail to listen to each other.

But this should not be what happens in written argument. Instead, when you make an argument in your writing, you will want to present your position with logical points, supporting each point with appropriate sources. You will want to give your audience every reason to perceive you as ethical and trustworthy. Your audience will expect you to treat them with respect, and to present your argument in a way that does not make them defensive. Contribute to your credibility by building sound arguments and using strategic arguments with skill and planning.

In this section we will briefly discuss the classic form of an argument, a more modern interpretation, and finally seven basic arguments you may choose to use. Imagine that these are tools in your toolbox and that you want to know how each is effectively used. Know that the people who try to persuade you—from telemarketers to politicians—usually have these tools at hand.

Let's start with a classical rhetorical strategy. It asks the rhetorician, speaker, or author to frame arguments in the following steps:

Table 6.7 Classical Rhetorical Strategy

1. Exordium	Prepares the audience to consider your argument
2. Narration	Provides the audience with the necessary background or context for your argument
3. Proposition	Introduces your claim being argued in the document
4. Confirmation	Offers the audience evidence to support your argument
5. Refutation	Introduces to the audience and then discounts or refutes the counterarguments or objections
6. Peroration	Your conclusion of your argument

This is a standard pattern in rhetoric and you will probably see it in both speech and English courses. The pattern is useful to guide you in preparing your document and can serve as a valuable checklist to insure you are prepared. While this formal pattern has distinct advantages, you may not see it used exactly as indicated here on a daily basis. What may be more familiar to you is Stephen Toulmin's rhetorical strategy, which focuses on three main elements (see Table 6.8 "Toulmin's Three-Part Rhetorical Strategy"). [1]

Toulmin's rhetorical strategy is useful in that it makes the claim explicit, clearly illustrates the relationship between the claim and the data, and allows the reader to follow the writer's reasoning. You may have a good idea or point, but your audience will want to know how you arrived at that claim or viewpoint. The warrant addresses the inherent and often unsaid question, "Why is this data so important to your topic?" In so doing, it helps you to illustrate relationships between information for your audience.

Table 6.8 Toulmin's Three-Part Rhetorical Strategy

Element	Description	Example
1. Claim	Your statement of belief or truth	It is important to spay or neuter your pet.
2. Data	Your supporting reasons for the claim	Millions of unwanted pets are euthanized every year.
3. Warrant	You create the connection between the claim and the supporting reasons	Pets that are spayed or neutered do not reproduce, preventing the production of unwanted animals.

Effective Argumentation Strategies: GASCAP/T

Here is a useful way of organizing and remembering seven key argumentative strategies:

1. Argument by **G**eneralization
2. Argument by **A**nalogy
3. Argument by **S**ign
4. Argument by **C**onsequence
5. Argument by **A**uthority
6. Argument by **P**rinciple
7. Argument by **T**estimony

Richard Fulkerson notes that a single strategy is sufficient to make an argument some of the time, but it is often better to combine several strategies to make an effective argument. [2] He organized the argumentative strategies in this way to compare the differences, highlight the similarities, and allow for their discussion. This model, often called by its acronym GASCAP, is a useful strategy to summarize six key arguments and is easy to remember. Here we have adapted it, adding one argument that is often used in today's speeches and presentations, the argument by testimony. Table 6.9 "GASCAP/T Strategies" presents each argument, provides a definition of the strategy and an example, and examines ways to evaluate each approach.

Table 6.9 GASCAP/T Strategies

	Argument by	Claim	Example	Evaluation
G	Generalization	Whatever is true of a good example or sample will be true of everything like it or the population it came from.	If you can vote, drive, and die for your country, you should also be allowed to buy alcohol.	STAR System: For it to be reliable, we need a (S) sufficient number of (T) typical, (A) accurate, and (R) reliable examples.
A	Analogy	Two situations, things or ideas are alike in observable ways and will tend to be alike in many other ways	Alcohol is a drug. So is tobacco. They alter perceptions, have an impact physiological and psychological systems, and are federally regulated substances.	Watch for adverbs that end in "ly," as they qualify, or lessen the relationship between the examples. Words like "probably," "maybe," "could, "may," or "usually" all weaken the relationship.
S	Sign	Statistics, facts, or cases indicate meaning, much like a stop sign means "stop."	Motor vehicle accidents involving alcohol occur at significant rates among adults of all ages in the United States.	Evaluate the relationship between the sign and look for correlation, where the presenter says what the facts "mean." Does the sign say that? Does it say more? What is not said? Is it relevant?
C	Cause	If two conditions always appear together, they are causally related.	The U.S. insurance industry has been significantly involved in state and national legislation requiring proof of insurance, changes in graduated driver's licenses, and the national	Watch out for "after the fact, therefore because of the fact" (*post hoc, ergo propter hoc*) thinking. There might not be a clear connection, and it might not be the whole picture. Mothers Against Drunk Driving

	Argument by	Claim	Example	Evaluation
			change in the drinking age from age 18 to age 21.	might have also been involved with each example of legislation.
A	Authority	What a credible source indicates is probably true.	According to the National Transportation Safety Board, older drivers are increasingly involved in motor vehicle accidents.	Is the source legitimate and is their information trustworthy? Institutes, boards, and people often have agendas and distinct points of view.
P	Principle	An accepted or proper truth	The change in the drinking age was never put to a vote. It's not about alcohol, it's about our freedom of speech in a democratic society.	Is the principle being invoked generally accepted? Is the claim, data or warrant actually related to the principle stated? Are there common exceptions to the principle? What are the practical consequences of following the principle in this case?
T	Testimony	Personal experience	I've lost friends from age 18 to 67 to alcohol. It impacts all ages, and its effects are cumulative. Let me tell you about two friends in particular.	Is the testimony authentic? Is it relevant? Is it representative of other's experiences? Use the STAR system to help evaluate the use of testimony.

Evidence

Now that we've clearly outlined several argument strategies, how do you support your position with evidence or warrants? If your premise or the background from which you start is valid, and your claim is clear and clearly related, the audience will naturally turn their attention to "prove it." This is where the relevance of evidence becomes particularly important. Here are three guidelines to consider in order to insure your evidence passes the "so what?" test of relevance in relation to your claim. Make sure your evidence has the following traits:

1. *Supportive.* Examples are clearly representative, statistics are accurate, testimony is authoritative, and information is reliable.
2. *Relevant.* Examples clearly relate to the claim or topic, and you are not comparing "apples to oranges."
3. *Effective.* Examples are clearly the best available to support the claim, quality is preferred to quantity, there are only a few well-chosen statistics, facts, or data.

Appealing to Emotions

While we've highlighted several points to consider when selecting information to support your claim, know that Aristotle strongly preferred an argument based in logic over emotion. Can the same be said for your audience, and to what degree is emotion and your appeal to it in your audience a part of modern life?

Emotions are a psychological and physical reaction, such as fear or anger, to stimuli that we experience as a feeling. Our feelings or emotions directly impact our own point of view and readiness to communicate, but also influence how, why, and when we say things. Emotions influence not only how you say or what you say, but also how you hear or what you hear. At times, emotions can be challenging to control. Emotions will move your audience, and possibly even move you, to change or act in certain ways.

Aristotle thought the best and most preferable way to persuade an audience was through the use of logic, free of emotion. He also recognized that people are often motivated, even manipulated, by the exploitation of their emotions. In a business context, we still engage in this debate, demanding to know the facts separate from personal opinion or agenda, but see the use of emotional appeal to sell products.

Marketing experts are famous for creating a need or associating an emotion with a brand or label in order to sell it. You will speak the language of your audience in your document, and may choose to appeal to emotion, but you need to consider how the strategy works, as it may be considered a tool that has two edges.

If we think of the appeal to emotion as a knife, we can see it has two edges. One edge can cut your audience, and the other can cut you. If you advance an appeal to emotion in your document on spaying and neutering pets, and discuss the millions of unwanted pets that are killed each year, you may elicit an emotional response. If you use this approach repeatedly, your audience may grow weary of this approach, and it will lose its effectiveness. If you change your topic to the use of animals in research, the same strategy may apply, but repeated attempts to elicit an emotional response may backfire (i.e., in essence "cutting" you) and produce a negative response called "emotional resistance."

Emotional resistance involves getting tired, often to the point of rejection, of hearing messages that attempt to elicit an emotional response. Emotional appeals can wear out the audience's capacity to receive the message. As Aristotle outlined, ethos (credibility), logos (logic), and pathos (passion, enthusiasm, and emotional response) constitute the building blocks of any document. It's up to you to create a balanced document, where you may appeal to emotion, but choose to use it judiciously.

On a related point, the use of an emotional appeal may also impair your ability to write persuasively or effectively. For example, if you choose to present an article about suicide to persuade people against committing it and you start showing a photo of your brother or sister that you lost to suicide, your emotional response may cloud your judgment and get in the way of your thinking. Never use a personal story, or even a story of someone you do not know, if the inclusion of that story causes you to lose control. While it's important to discuss relevant topics, you need to assess your relationship to the message. Your documents should not be an exercise in therapy. Otherwise, you will sacrifice ethos and credibility, even your effectiveness, if you "lose it" because you are really not ready to discuss the issue.

Recognizing Fallacies

"Fallacy" is another way of saying false logic. Fallacies or rhetorical tricks deceive your audience with their style, drama, or pattern, but add little to your document in terms of substance. They are best avoided because they can actually detract from your effectiveness. There are several techniques or "tricks" that allow the writer to rely on style without offering substantive argument, to obscure the central message, or twist the facts to their own gain. Table 6.10 "Fallacies" examines the eight classical fallacies. Learn to recognize them so they can't be used against you, and learn to avoid using them with your audience.

Table 6.10 Fallacies

Fallacy	Definition	Example
1. Red Herring	Any diversion intended to distract attention from the main issue, particularly by relating the issue to a common fear.	It's not just about the death penalty; it's about the victims and their rights. You wouldn't want to be a victim, but if you were, you'd want justice.
2. Straw Man	A weak argument set up to easily refute and distract attention from stronger arguments.	Look at the idea that criminals who commit murder should be released after a few years of rehabilitation. Think of how unsafe our streets would be then!
3. Begging the Question	Claiming the truth of the very matter in question, as if it were already an obvious conclusion.	We know that they will be released and unleashed on society to repeat their crimes again and again.
4. Circular Argument	The proposition is used to prove itself. Assumes the very thing it aims to prove. Related to begging the question.	Once a killer, always a killer.
5. Ad Populum	Appeals to a common belief of some people, often prejudicial, and states everyone holds this belief. Also called the bandwagon fallacy, as people "jump on the bandwagon" of a perceived popular view.	Most people would prefer to get rid of a few "bad apples" and keep our streets safe.
6. Ad Hominem or "Argument against the Man"	Argument against the man instead of his message. Stating that someone's argument is wrong solely because of something about the person rather than about the argument itself.	Our representative is a drunk and philanderer. How can we trust him on the issues of safety and family?

Fallacy	Definition	Example
7. Non Sequitur or "It Does Not Follow"	The conclusion does not follow from the premises. They are not related.	Since the liberal 1960s, we've seen an increase in convicts who got let off death row.
8. Post Hoc Ergo Propter Hoc or "After This, Therefore because of This"	It is also called a coincidental correlation.	Violent death rates went down once they started publicizing executions.

Ethical Considerations in Persuasion

In his book *Ethics in Human Communication*, Richard Johannesen offers eleven points to consider when communicating. Although they are related to public speaking, they are also useful in business writing. You may note that many of his cautions are clearly related to the fallacies we've discussed. His main points reiterate many of the points across this chapter and should be kept in mind as you prepare, and present, your persuasive message. [3]

Do not:

- use false, fabricated, misrepresented, distorted, or irrelevant evidence to support arguments or claims;
- intentionally use unsupported, misleading, or illogical reasoning;
- represent yourself as informed or an "expert" on a subject when you are not;
- use irrelevant appeals to divert attention from the issue at hand;
- ask your audience to link your idea or proposal to emotion-laden values, motives, or goals to which it is actually not related;
- deceive your audience by concealing your real purpose, your self-interest, the group you represent, or your position as an advocate of a viewpoint;
- distort, hide, or misrepresent the number, scope, intensity, or undesirable features of consequences or effects;
- use emotional appeals that lack a supporting basis of evidence or reasoning;
- oversimplify complex, gradation-laden situations into simplistic, two-valued, either-or, polar views or choices;
- pretend certainty where tentativeness and degrees of probability would be more accurate;
- advocate something that you yourself do not believe in.

Aristotle said the mark of a good person, well spoken, was a clear command of the faculty of observing in any given case the available means of persuasion. He discussed the idea of perceiving the various points of view related to a topic and their thoughtful consideration. While it's important to be able to perceive the complexity of a case, you are not asked to be a lawyer and defend a client.

In your message to persuade, consider honesty and integrity as you assemble your arguments. Your audience will appreciate your thoughtful consideration of more than one view and your understanding of the complexity of the issue, thus building your ethos, or credibility, as you present your document. Be careful not to stretch the facts, or assemble them only to prove your point; instead, prove the argument on its own merits. Deception, coercion, intentional bias, manipulation and bribery should have no place in your message to persuade.

KEY TAKEAWAY

The art of argument in writing involves presenting supportive, relevant, effective evidence for each point and doing it in a respectful and ethical manner.

EXERCISES

1. Select a piece of persuasive writing such as a newspaper op-ed essay, a magazine article, or a blog post. Examine the argument, the main points, and how the writer supports them. Which strategies from the foregoing section does the writer use? Does the writer use any fallacies or violate any ethical principles? Discuss your results with your classmates.
2. Find one slogan or logo that you perceive as persuasive and share it with your classmates.
3. Find an example of a piece of writing that appears to want to be persuasive, but doesn't get the job done. Write a brief review and share it with classmates.
4. In what ways might the choice of how to organize a document involve ethics? Explain your response and discuss it with your class.

[1] Toulmin, S. (1958). *The uses of argument*. New York, NY: Cambridge University Press.

[2] Fulkerson, R. (1996). The Toulmin model of argument and the teaching of composition. In E. Barbara, P. Resch, & D. Tenney (Eds.), *Argument*

revisited: argument redefined: negotiating meaning the composition classroom (pp. 45–72). Thousand Oaks, CA: Sage.

[3] Johannesen, R. (1996). *Ethics in human communication* (4th ed.). Prospect Heights, IL: Waveland Press.

6.4 Paraphrase and Summary versus Plagiarism

LEARNING OBJECTIVES

1. Understand the difference between paraphrasing or summarizing and plagiarism.
2. Demonstrate how to give proper credit to sources that are quoted verbatim, and sources whose ideas are paraphrased or summarized.
3. Demonstrate your ability to paraphrase in one or more written assignments.

Even if you are writing on a subject you know well, you will usually get additional information from other sources. How you represent others' ideas, concepts, and words is critical to your credibility and the effectiveness of your document. Let's say you are reading a section of a document and find a point that relates well to your current writing assignment. How do you represent what you have read in your work? You have several choices.

One choice is simply to reproduce the quote verbatim, or word for word, making sure that you have copied all words and punctuation accurately. In this case, you will put quotation marks around the quoted passage (or, if it is more than about fifty words long, inset it with wider margins than the body of your document) and give credit to the source. The format you use for your source citation will vary according to the discipline or industry of your audience; common formats include APA (American Psychological Association), MLA (Modern Language Association), and CMS (Chicago Manual of Style).

Another common strategy in business writing is to paraphrase, or rewrite the information in your own words. You will relate the main point, but need to take care not to copy the original. You will give credit where credit is due, but your citation will be more informal, such as "A *Wall Street Journal* article dated July 8, 2009, described some of the disagreements among G-8 nations about climate change." Here are several steps that can help you paraphrase a passage while respecting its original author:

1. Read the passage out loud, paying attention to the complete thought rather than the individual words.
2. Explain the concept in your own words to a friend or colleague, out loud, face-to-face.
3. Write the concept in your own words, and add one or more illustrative examples of the concept that are meaningful to you.

4. Reread the original passage and see how your version compares with it in terms of grammar, word choice, example, and conveyance of meaning.
5. If your writing parrots the original passage or merely substitutes synonyms for words in the original, return to step one and start over, remembering that your goal is to express the central concepts, not to "translate" one word into another.
6. When you are satisfied that your expression of the concept can stand on its own merit, include it in your document and cite the original author as the source of the idea.

Summarizing information is another common way of integrating information into your original work that requires care and attention to detail. To summarize is to reduce a concept, idea, or data set to its most basic point or element. You may have a literature survey to summarize related information in the field under consideration, or a section on background to serve a similar purpose. Suppose you are reporting on a business situation and it occurs to you that one of Shakespeare's plays has a plot that resembles your situation. You may wish to summarize the Shakespeare play in a few sentences before drawing parallels between it and your current situation. This may help readers to remember and understand your report. Regardless of how or where you incorporate a summary within your document, give attention to its original context and retain its essential meaning free of distortion in the new context of your writing.

Because summarizing is an act of reductionism, some of the original richness in detail that surrounds the original will be necessarily lost. Think of a photograph you have taken in the past that featured several people you know. Using a software program that allows you to modify and manipulate the image, draw a box around only one face. Delete the rest of the contents of the photo so only the information in the box remains. Part of the photo is intact, and one person has become the focal point for the image, but the context has been lost. In the same way, if you focus on one statistic, one quote, or one idea and fail to capture its background you will take the information out of context. Context is one of the eight components of communication, and without it, the process breaks down. While you cannot retain all the definition and detail of the original context in a brief summary, effort to represent the essential point within its context is essential or you risk distortion of the original meaning.

Unlike quoting or paraphrasing, summarizing is something you can—and will—also do to the material you have written. You may start your document with a summary of the background that gives the document purpose. Formal business reports often begin with an executive summary, and scientific articles usually begin with an abstract; both of these serve as a brief preview of the information in the full document. You may write a brief internal summary after each main discussion point in a lengthy document; this will serve to remind your reader of the discussion to date and to establish the context for the upcoming point. Finally, a summary is a very common, and often effective, way to conclude a document. Ending your writing with a summary helps your reader to remember your main points.

Plagiarism is neither paraphrasing nor summarizing information from other works. Plagiarism is representing another's work as your own. Professional standards, which are upheld in all fields from architecture to banking to zoology, all involve the elements of authenticity and credibility. Credit is given where credit is due, authorities in the field are appropriately cited or referenced, and original writing is expected to be exactly that. Patch writing, or the verbatim cut-and-paste insertion of fragments, snippets, or small sections of other publications into your own writing without crediting the sources, is plagiarism. Wholesale copying of other works is also plagiarism. Both destroy your professional credibility, and fail to uphold common professional standards.

Colleges and universities have policies against plagiarism, and within business and industry, the negative impact on credibility and careers often exceeds any academic punishment. There is no shame in quoting someone else's work while giving credit, nor in paraphrasing a point correctly or summarizing the research results of a study you did not perform; but there are significant consequences to representing other's ideas as your own.

Aside from the fear of punishment, a skilled business writer should recognize that intellectual theft is wrong. You may be tempted to borrow a sentence; however, know your document will be represented in many ways across time, and more than one career has been destroyed by plagiarism discovered years after the fact. The accomplished business writer should take as a compliment the correct citation and reference of their work. The novice business writer should learn by example but refrain from cut and paste strategies to complete a document.

In a world where most modern documents are accessible in some form online, the ability to cross-reference information with a couple of key strokes makes plagiarism a self-defeating solution when better alternatives exist. Quote and give credit, link to related documents with permission, paraphrase and summarize with citation, but do not plagiarize.

KEY TAKEAWAY

There is nothing wrong with quoting, paraphrasing, and summarizing with credit to your original source, but presenting someone else's work as if it were your own is plagiarism.

EXERCISES

1. Select a piece of writing such as an essay from a Web site, a book chapter, or a newspaper or magazine article. Write a paraphrase of a portion of it. Write a brief summary of the entire piece. Note the difference between the two techniques. Giving credit to the original piece, discuss your paraphrase and summary with your classmates.

2. Find an example of an advertisement you perceive as particularly effective and write a one-sentence summary. Share the advertisement and your one-sentence summary with the class.

3. Find an example of an advertisement you perceive as particularly ineffective and write a one-sentence summary. Share the advertisement and your one sentence review with the class.

4. Find a case where plagiarism or misrepresentation had consequences in the business world. Share your findings and discuss with classmates.

6.5 Additional Resources

- Read an informative article about outlines and get a sample outline template. http://www.essaywritinghelp.com/outline.htm

- This Writing Tutorials site from John Jay College of Criminal Justice offers a menu of tools for composing a thesis statement, an outline, well-constructed paragraphs, and more. http://resources.jjay.cuny.edu/erc/writing/index.php.

- This RefDesk.com page offers a compendium of different resources for English grammar and usage. http://www.refdesk.com/factgram.html

- Read an article on avoiding bureaucratic language by marketing strategist David Meerman Scott. http://www.econtentmag.com/Articles/ArticleReader.aspx?ArticleID=14538&ContextSubtypeID=12

- Garbl's Wordy Phrases presents a list of bureaucratic phrases to avoid and their standard English alternatives. http://home.comcast.net/~garbl/stylemanual/phrases.htm

- This University of North Carolina site provides a handout on writing arguments.

http://www.unc.edu/depts/wcweb/handouts/argume
nt.html
- Read about logic in argumentative writing on Purdue University's Online Writing Lab (OWL). http://owl.english.purdue.edu/owl/resource/659/01

- The College Board Web site provides a robust guide for how to avoid plagiarism.http://www.collegeboard.com/student/plan/college-success/10314.html

NOTES:

Chapter 7:
Revising and Presenting Your Writing

I'm not a very good writer, but I'm an excellent rewriter.
  James A. Michener
Half my life is an act of revision.
  John Irving

Getting Started

INTRODUCTORY EXERCISES

1. Find an article you read online and review it, noting at least one area that would benefit from revision. Please share your results with classmates.
2. Exchange draft revisions of a document prepared for a class or work assignment with a classmate or colleague. Note at least one strength and one area for improvement, Provide feedback to the writer.

One of the hardest tests to pass is the one of peer review. In the academic environment, professors conduct research, learn lessons, and share their findings by contributing articles for professional journals. Each academic journal article undergoes peer review, or evaluation by colleagues in the same field as the professor who wrote the article. These evaluations, often conducted by leaders in each field, do not only consider the value of the writer's findings. They also evaluate the mechanics of the document (spelling and grammar) and its presentation, organization, and design. The first time a scholar submits an article for peer review, he or she can expect rejections and liberal use of the red pen.

You may not experience such a rigorous and vigorous review of your writing, but in many ways the world of business is equally challenging. Academic publications ultimately value solid findings that contribute to the field or discipline. Business writing ultimately values writing that produces results or outcomes in environments where you do not have the luxury of controlling the variables, designing the context, or limiting the scope of your inquiry. Your business document will be evaluated by people you never met or even anticipated would read it, and errors will have a negative impact on its performance.

In every career, industry, and profession, today's business climate is a results-oriented environment. Regardless of what you write, there exists the possibility, even probability, that misunderstandings and miscommunications can and will occur. Although you will not always have control over the importance of the ideas you are assigned to communicate in your writing, there is one thing you can control: errors. If you avoid mistakes, both in the document itself and in the way your audience interprets your message, your document will have its best chance of success. To this end a thorough revision is an important part of your writing process.

As you review and evaluate documents, those written by you and others, you will need to keep in mind the three goals of being correct, clear, and concise. Next you will have to focus on effectiveness and efficiency, recognizing that in a climate of increasing demands and limited resources like time, you need to get it right the first time.

The environment of a business writer can be stressful, but it can also be rewarding. Recognition from your peers—suppliers, internal department colleagues, or customers—can make it all worthwhile. Still, the reward in terms of acknowledgement may come in the form of silence. When your document clearly meets expectations and accomplishes its goal, the outcome may be the absence of error or misinterpretation, a rare occasion that often goes unheralded. As a business writer you need to value your work and note what works. When it does, take pride in your hard work in effort. You may not always be celebrated for your error-free documents that communicate concepts and ideas clearly, but know that they are successful, and their success is your success.

7.1 General Revision Points to Consider
LEARNING OBJECTIVES

1. Discuss the process of revision
2. List three general elements of every document that require revision

Just when you think the production of your document is done, the revision process begins. Runners often refer to "the wall," where the limits of physical exertion are met and exhaustion is imminent. The writing process requires effort, from overcoming writer's block to the intense concentration composing a document often involves. It is only natural to have a sense of relief when your document is drafted from beginning to end. This relief is false confidence, though. Your document is not complete, and in its current state it could, in fact, do more harm than good. Errors, omissions, and unclear phrases may lurk within your document, waiting to reflect poorly on you when it reaches your audience. Now is not time to let your guard down, prematurely celebrate, or to mentally move on to the next assignment. Think of the revision process as one that hardens and strengthens your document, even though it may require the sacrifice of some hard-earned writing.

General revision requires attention to content, organization, style, and readability. These four main categories should give you a template from which to begin to explore details in depth. A cursory review of these elements in and of itself is insufficient for even the briefest review. Across this chapter we will explore ways to expand your revision efforts to cover the common areas of weakness and error. You may need to take some time away from your document to approach it again with a fresh perspective. Writers often juggle multiple projects that are at different stages of development. This allows the writer to leave one document and return to another without losing valuable production time. Overall, your goal is similar to what it was during your writing preparation and production: a clear mind.

Evaluate Content

Content is only one aspect of your document. Let's say you were assigned a report on the sales trends for a specific product in a relatively new market. You could produce a one-page chart comparing last year's results to current figures and call it a day, but would it clearly and concisely deliver content that is useful and correct? Are you supposed to highlight trends? Are you supposed to spotlight factors that contributed to the increase or decrease? Are you supposed to include projections for next year? Our list of questions could continue, but for now let's focus on content and its relationship to the directions. Have you included the content that corresponds to the given assignment, left any information out that may be necessary to fulfill the expectations, or have you gone beyond the assignment directions? Content will address the central questions of who, what, where, when, why and how within the range and parameters of the assignment.

Evaluate Organization

Organization is another key aspect of any document. Standard formats that include an introduction, body, and conclusion may be part of your document, but did you decide on a direct or indirect approach? Can you tell? A direct approach will announce the main point or purpose at the beginning, while an indirect approach will present an introduction before the main point. Your document may use any of a wide variety of organizing principles, such as chronological, spatial, compare/contrast. Is your organizing principle clear to the reader?

Beyond the overall organization, pay special attention to transitions. Readers often have difficulty following a document if the writer makes the common error of failing to make one point relevant to the next, or to illustrate the relationships between the points. Finally, your conclusion should mirror your introduction and not introduce new material.

Evaluate Style

Style is created through content and organization, but also involves word choice and grammatical structures. Is your document written in an informal or formal tone, or does it present a blend, a mix, or an awkward mismatch? Does it provide a coherent and unifying voice with a professional tone? If you are collaborating on the project with other writers or contributors, pay special attention to unifying the document across the different authors' styles of writing. Even if they were all to write in a professional, formal style, the document may lack a consistent voice. Read it out loud—can you tell who is writing what? If so, that is a clear clue that you need to do more revising in terms of style.

Evaluate Readability

Readability refers to the reader's ability to read and comprehend the document. A variety of tools are available to make an estimate of a document's reading level, often correlated to a school grade level. If this chapter has a reading level of 11.8, it would be appropriate for most readers in the eleventh grade. But just because you are in grade thirteen, eighteen, or twenty-one doesn't mean that your audience, in their everyday use of language, reads at a postsecondary level. As a business writer, your goal is to make your writing clear and concise, not complex and challenging.

You can often use the "Tools" menu of your word processing program to determine the approximate reading level of your document. The program will evaluate the number of characters per word, add in the number of words per sentence, and come up with a rating. It may also note the percentage of passive sentences, and other information that will allow you to evaluate readability. Like any computer-generated rating, it should serve you as one point of evaluation, but not the only point. Your concerted effort to choose words you perceive as appropriate for the audience will serve you better than any computer evaluation of your writing.

KEY TAKEAWAY

The four main categories—content, organization, style, and readability—provide a template for general revision.

EXERCISES

1. Select a document, such as an article from a Web site, newspaper, magazine, or a piece of writing you have completed for a course. Evaluate the document according to the four main categories described in this section. Could the document benefit from revision in any of these areas? Discuss your findings with your classmates.

2. Interview a coworker or colleague and specifically ask how much time and attention they dedicate to the revision process of their written work. Compare your results with classmates.

3. Find a particularly good example of writing according to the above criteria. Review it and share it with your classmates.

4. Find a particularly bad example of writing according to the above criteria. Review it and share it with your classmates.

7.2 Specific Revision Points to Consider
LEARNING OBJECTIVE

1. List six specific elements of every document to check for revision

When revising your document, it can be helpful to focus on specific points. When you consider each point in turn, you will be able to break down the revision process into manageable steps. When you have examined each point, you can be confident that you have avoided many possible areas for errors. Specific revision requires attention to the following:

- Format
- Facts
- Names
- Spelling
- Punctuation
- Grammar

Let's examine these characteristics one by one.

Format

Format is an important part of the revision process. Format involves the design expectations of author and audience. If a letter format normally designates a date at the top, or the sender's address on the left side of the page before the salutation, the information should be in the correct location. Formatting that is messy or fails to conform to the company style will reflect poorly on you before the reader even starts to read it. By presenting a document that is properly formatted according to the expectations of your organization and your readers, you will start off making a good impression.

Facts

Another key part of the revision process is checking your facts. Did you know that news organizations and magazines employ professional fact-checkers? These workers are responsible for examining every article before it gets published and consulting original sources to make sure the information in the article is accurate. This can involve making phone calls to the people who were interviewed for the article—for example, "Mr. Diaz, our report states that you are thirty-nine years old. Our article will be published on the fifteenth. Will that be your correct age on that date?" Fact checking also involves looking facts up in encyclopedias, directories, atlases, and other standard reference works; and, increasingly, in online sources.

While you can't be expected to have the skills of a professional fact-checker, you do need to reread your writing with a critical eye to the information in it. Inaccurate content can expose you and your organization to liability, and will create far more work than a simple revision of a document. So, when you revise a document, ask yourself the following:

- Does my writing contain any statistics or references that need to be verified?
- Where can I get reliable information to verify it?

It is often useful to do independent verification—that is, look up the fact in a different source from the one where you first got it. For example, perhaps a colleague gave you a list of closing averages for the Dow Jones Industrial on certain dates. You still have the list, so you can make sure your document agrees with the numbers your colleague provided. But what if your colleague made a mistake? The Web sites of the *Wall Street Journal* and other major newspapers list closings for "the Dow," so it is reasonably easy for you to look up the numbers and verify them independently.

Names

There is no more embarrassing error in business writing than to misspell someone's name. To the writer, and to some readers, spelling a name "Michelle" instead of "Michele" may seem like a minor matter, but to Michele herself it will make a big difference. Attribution is one way we often involve a person's name, and giving credit where credit is due is essential. There are many other reasons for including someone's name, but regardless of your reasons for choosing to focus on them, you need to make sure the spelling is correct. Incorrect spelling of names is a quick way to undermine your credibility; it can also have a negative impact on your organization's reputation, and in some cases it may even have legal ramifications.

Spelling

Correct spelling is another element essential for your credibility, and errors will be glaringly obvious to many readers. The negative impact on your reputation as a writer, and its perception that you lack attention to detail or do not value your work, will be hard to overcome. In addition to the negative personal consequences, spelling errors can become factual errors and destroy the value of content. This may lead you to click the "spell check" button in your word processing program, but computer spell-checking is not enough. Spell checkers have improved in the years since they were first invented, but they are not infallible. They can and do make mistakes.

Typically, your incorrect word may in fact be a word, and therefore, according to the program, correct. For example, suppose you wrote, "The major will attend the meeting" when you meant to write "The mayor will attend the meeting." The program would miss this error because "major" is a word, but your meaning would be twisted beyond recognition.

Punctuation

Punctuation marks are the traffic signals, signs, and indications that allow us to navigate the written word. They serve to warn us in advance when a transition is coming or the complete thought has come to an end. A period indicates the thought is complete, while a comma signals that additional elements or modifiers are coming. Correct signals will help your reader follow the thoughts through sentences and paragraphs, and enable you to communicate with maximum efficiency while reducing the probability of error. [1]

Table 7.1 "Punctuation Marks" lists twelve punctuation marks that are commonly used in English in alphabetical order along with an example of each.

Table 7.1 Punctuation Marks

	Symbol	Example
Apostrophe	'	Michele's report is due tomorrow.
Colon	:	This is what I think: you need to revise your paper.
Comma	,	The report advised us when to sell, what to sell, and where to find buyers.
Dash	—	This is more difficult than it seems—buyers are scarce when credit is tight.
Ellipsis	…	Lincoln spoke of "a new nation…dedicated to the proposition that all men are created equal."
Exclamation Point	!	How exciting!
Hyphen	-	The question is a many-faceted one.
Parentheses	( )	To answer it (or at least to begin addressing it) we will need more information.
Period	.	The answer is no. Period. Full stop.
Question Mark	?	Can I talk you into changing your mind?
Quotation Marks	" "	The manager told him, "I will make sure Renée is available to help you."
Semicolon	;	Theresa was late to the meeting; her computer had frozen and she was stuck at her desk until a tech rep came to fix it.

It may be daunting to realize that the number of possible punctuation errors is as extensive as the number of symbols and constructions available to the author. Software program may catch many punctuation errors, but again it is the committed writer that makes the difference. Here we will provide details on how to avoid mistakes with three of the most commonly used punctuation marks: the comma, the semicolon, and the apostrophe.

Commas

The comma is probably the most versatile of all punctuation marks. This means you as a writer can use your judgment in many cases as to whether you need a comma or not. It also means that the possible errors involving commas are many. Commas are necessary some of the time, but careless writers often place a comma in a sentence where it is simply not needed.

Commas are used to separate two independent clauses joined by a conjunction like "but," "and," and "or."

Example
The advertising department is effective, but don't expect miracles in this business climate.

Commas are not used simply to join two independent clauses. This is known as the comma splice error, and the way to correct it is to insert a conjunction after the comma.

Examples
The advertising department is effective, the sales department needs to produce more results.
The advertising department is effective, *but* the sales department needs to produce more results.

Commas are used for introductory phrases and to offset clauses that are not essential to the sentence. If the meaning would remain intact without the phrase, it is considered nonessential.

Examples
After the summary of this year's sales, the sales department had good reason to celebrate.
The sales department, *last year's winner of the most productive award*, celebrated their stellar sales success this year.
The sales department celebrated their stellar sales success this year.

Commas are used to offset words that help create unity across a sentence like "however" and "therefore."

Examples
The sales department discovered, *however*, that the forecast for next year is challenging.
However, the sales department discovered that the forecast for next year is challenging.

Commas are often used to separate more than one adjective modifying a noun.

Example
The sales department discovered the *troublesome, challenging* forecast for next year.

Commas are used to separate addresses, dates, and titles; they are also used in dialogue sequences.

Examples
John is from Ancud, Chile.
Katy was born on August 2, 2002.
Mackenzie McLean, D. V., is an excellent veterinarian.
Lisa said, "When writing, omit needless words."

Semicolons

Semicolons have two uses. First, they indicate relationships among groups of items in a series when the individual items are separated by commas. Second, a semicolon can be used to join two independent clauses; this is another way of avoiding the comma splice error mentioned above. Using a semicolon this way is often effective if the meaning of the two independent clauses is linked in some way, such as a cause-effect relationship.

Examples
Merchandise on order includes women's wear such as sweaters, skirts, and blouses; men's wear such as shirts, jackets, and slacks; and outwear such as coats, parkas, and hats.
The sales campaign was successful; without its contributions our bottom line would have been dismal indeed.

Apostrophes

The apostrophe, like the semicolon, has two uses: it replaces letters omitted in a contraction, and it often indicates the possessive.

Because contractions are associated with an informal style, they may not be appropriate for some professional writing. The business writer will—as always—evaluate the expectations and audience of the given assignment.

Examples
It's great news that sales were up. *It is* also good news that *we've* managed to reduce our advertising costs.

When you indicate possession, pay attention to the placement of the apostrophe. Nouns commonly receive "'s" when they are made possessive. But plurals that end in "s" receive a hanging apostrophe when they are made possessive, and the word "it" forms the possessive ("its") with no apostrophe at all.

Examples
Mackenzie's sheep are ready to be sheared.
The parents' meeting is scheduled for Thursday.
We are willing to adopt a dog that has already had its shots.

Grammar

Learning to use good, correct standard English grammar is more of a practice than an event, or even a process. Grammar involves the written construction of meaning from words and involves customs that evolve and adapt to usage over time. Because grammar is always evolving, none of us can sit back and rest assured that we "know" how to write with proper grammar. Instead, it is important to write and revise with close attention to grammar, keeping in mind that grammatical errors can undermine your credibility, reflect poorly on your employer, and cause misunderstandings.

Jean Wyrick has provided a list of common errors in grammar to watch out for, which we have adapted here for easy reference. [2] In each case, the error is in *italics* and the *[correct form]* is italicized within square bracket.

Subject-Verb Agreement

The subject and verb should agree on the number under consideration. In faulty writing, a singular subject is sometimes mismatched with a plural verb form, or vice versa.

Examples
Sales have not been consistent and they *doesn't [do not]* reflect your hard work and effort.
The president appreciates your hard work and *wish [wishes]* to thank you.

Verb Tense

Verb tense refers to the point in time where action occurs. The most common tenses are past, present, and future. There is nothing wrong with mixing tenses in a sentence if the action is intended to take place at different times. In faulty or careless writing, however, they are often mismatched illogically.

Examples
Sharon was under pressure to finish the report, so she *uses [used]* a shortcut to paste in the sales figures.
The sales department holds a status meeting every week, and last week's meeting *will be [was]* at the Garden Inn.

Split Infinitive

The infinitive form of verb is one without a reference to time, and in its standard form it includes the auxiliary word "to," as in "to write is to revise." It has been customary to keep the "to" next to the verb; to place an adverb between them is known as splitting the infinitive. Some modern writers do this all the time (for example, "to boldly go…"), and since all grammar is essentially a set of customs that govern the written word, you will need to understand what the custom is where you work. If you are working with colleagues trained across the last fifty years, they may find split infinitives annoying. For this reason, it's often best to avoid splitting an infinitive wherever you can do so without distorting the meaning of the sentence.

Examples
The Marketing Department needs assistance *to accurately understand our readers [to understand our readers accurately]*.
David pondered *how to best revise [how best to revise]* the sentence.

Double Negative

A double negative uses two negatives to communicate a single idea, duplicating the negation. In some languages, such as Spanish, when the main action in the sentence is negative, it is correct to express the other elements in the sentence negatively as well. However, in English, this is incorrect. In addition to sounding wrong (you can often hear the error if you read the sentence out loud), a double negative in English causes an error in logic, because two negatives cancel each other out and yield a positive. In fact, the wording of ballot measures is often criticized for confusing voters with double negatives.

Examples
John *doesn't need no [any]* assistance with his sales presentation. [Or *John needs no assistance with his sales presentation.*]
Jeri *could not find no [any]* reason to approve the request. [Or *Jeri could find no reason to approve the request.*]

Irregular Verbs

Most verbs represent the past with the addition of the suffix "ed," as in "ask" becomes "asked." Irregular verbs change a vowel or convert to another word when representing the past tense. Consider the irregular verb "to go"; the past tense is "went," not "goed."

Examples
The need *arised [arose]* to seek additional funding.
Katy *leaped [leapt]* onto the stage to introduce the presentation.

Commas in a Series

A comma is used to separate the items in a series, but in some writing styles the comma is omitted between the final two items of the series, where the conjunction joins the last and next-to-last items. The comma in this position is known as the "serial comma." The serial comma is typically required in academic writing and typically omitted in journalism. Other writers omit the serial comma if the final two items in the series have a closer logical connection than the other items. In business writing, you may use it or omit it according to the prevailing style in your organization or industry. Know your audience and be aware of the rule.

Examples
Lisa is an amazing wife, mother, teacher, *gardener, and editor.*
Lisa is an amazing wife, mother teacher, *gardener and editor.*
Lisa is an amazing teacher, editor, gardener, *wife and mother.*

Faulty Comparisons

When comparing two objects by degree, there should be no mention of "est," as in "biggest" as all you can really say is that one is bigger than the other. If you are comparing three or more objects, then "est" will accurately communicate which is the "biggest" of them all.

Examples
Between the twins, Mackenzie is the *fastest [faster]* of the two.
Among our three children, Mackenzie is the *tallest.*

Dangling Modifiers

Modifiers describe a subject in a sentence or indicate how or when the subject carried out the action. If the subject is omitted, the modifier intended for the subject is left dangling or hanging out on its own without a clear relationship to the sentence. Who is doing the seeing in the first sentence?

Examples
Seeing the light at the end of the tunnel, celebrations were in order.
Seeing the light at the end of the tunnel, *we decided* that celebrations were in order.

Misplaced Modifiers

Modifiers that are misplaced are not lost, they are simply in the wrong place. Their unfortunate location is often far from the word or words they describe, making it easy for readers to misinterpret the sentence.

Examples
Trying to avoid the deer, *the tree hit my car.*
My car hit the tree when I tried to avoid a deer in the road.

KEY TAKEAWAY

By revising for format, facts, names, spelling, punctuation, and grammar, you can increase your chances of correcting many common errors in your writing.

EXERCISES

1. Select a news article from a news Web site, newspaper, or magazine. Find as many facts in the article as you can that could require fact-checking. Then check as many of these facts as you can, using sources available to you in the library and on the Internet. Did you find any errors in the article? Discuss your findings with your classmates.
2. Find an example of an assertion without attribution and share it with classmates.
3. Find an example of an error in a published document and share it with classmates.
4. Interview a coworker or colleague and specifically ask them to share a story where an error got past them during the revision process and made it to print or publication. How did they handle it? How much time did it take to correct? What did they learn from the experience? Compare your results with classmates.

[1] Strunk, W., Jr., & White, E. B. (1979). *The elements of style* (3rd ed.). New York, NY: Macmillian.
[2] Wyrick, J. (2008). *Steps to writing well* (10th ed.). Boston, MA: Thomson Wadsworth.

7.3 Style Revisions

LEARNING OBJECTIVE

1. Discuss and demonstrate the use of twelve points to consider for style revisions.

You know the difference between cloudy and clear water, but can you tell when your writing is cloudy, when meaning is hidden in shadows, when the message you are trying to communicate is obscured by the style you use to present it? Water filtration involves removing particulates, harmful inorganic and organic materials, and clarifying the water. In the same way, the revision process requires filtration. You may come across word choices you thought were appropriate at the time or notice words you thought you wrote but are absent, and the revision process will start to produce results. Some words and sentence constructions will be harmful to the effective delivery and require attention. Some transitions fail to show the connections between thoughts and need to be changed.

Another way of conceptualizing the revision process in general and the clarifying process specifically is the common reference to a diamond in the rough. Like muddy water, diamonds do not come to have significant value until they have had their rough edges removed, have received expert polish, and been evaluated for clarity. Your attention to this important process will bring the value quotient of your writing up as it begins to more accurately communicate intended meaning. As we've discussed before, now is not the time to lose momentum. Just the opposite, now is the time to make your writing shine.

Here we will discuss several strategies to help clarify your writing style. If you have made wise word choices, the then next step to clarifying your document is to take it sentence by sentence. Each sentence should stand on its own, but each sentence is also interdependent on all other sentences in your document. These strategies will require significant attention to detail and an awareness of grammar that might not be your area of strength, but the more you practice them the more they will become good habits that will enhance your writing. Break Up Long Sentences

By revising long sentences you can often increase the overall clarity of your document. To do this, let's start off with one strategy that will produce immediate results. Count the number of conjunctions in your document. Word processing programs will often perform a search for a specific a word and for our use, "and" will do just fine. Simple sentences often become compound and complex through the use of the word "and." The further the subject, the action, and the modifiers or descriptions are from one another is directly related to the complexity of the sentence, increasing the probability of reader error and misunderstandings. Look for the word "and" and evaluate whether the sentence has two complete thoughts or ideas. Does it try to join two dissimilar ideas or ones better off on their own?

In prose, and your expository writing classes, you may have learned that complex sentences can communicate emotions, settings, and scenes that evoke a sense of place and time with your reading audience. In business writing, our goals aim more toward precision and the elimination of error; a good business document won't read like a college essay. A professor may have advised you to avoid short, choppy writing. Are we asking you to do something along those lines? No. Choppy writing is hard to follow, but simple, clear writing does the job with a minimum of fuss and without decoration.

In their best-selling book *The Elements of Style*, William Strunk Jr. and E. B. White [1] emphasize clarity as a central goal. However, the following is one of their rules: "Do not break sentences in two." As effective business writers we would agree with this rule, and while it may seem to contradict the preceding paragraph, let's consider what they mean by that rule. They encourage writers to avoid sentence fragments by refraining from using a period where the sentence needs a comma. That means that an independent clause should be connected to a dependent clause when necessary, and as we've discussed previously, a comma and a conjunction are appropriate for the task. The sentence fragment cannot stand alone, so we would agree with the rule as written.

But we would also qualify its use: when you have two long and awkward independent clauses that form an unwieldy sentence, it may indeed be better to divide the clauses into two independent sentences. Your skill as a business writer is required to balance the needs of the sentence to communicate meaning with your understanding of audience expectations, and clarity often involves concise sentences.

Revise Big Words and Long Phrases
Big words can clutter your writing with needless jargon that may be a barrier to many readers. Even if you know your audience has significant education and training in a field, you may need to include definitions and examples as effective strategies to communicate meaning. Don't confuse simple writing with simplistic writing. Your task will almost certainly not require an elementary approach for new readers, but it may very well require attention to words and the degree to which they contribute to, or detract from, the communication of your intended message. Long noun sequences, often used as descriptive phrases, can be one example of how writing can reduce clarity. If you need to describe a noun, use a phrase that modifies the noun clearly, with commas to offset for example, to enhance clarity.

Another long phrase to watch out for is often located in the introduction. Long preambles can make the sentence awkward and will require revision. Sentences that start with "It is" or "There are" can often be shortened or made clearer through revision.

Evaluate Long Prepositional Phrases

A prepositional phrase is a phrase composed of a preposition (a "where" word; a word that indicates location) and its object, which may be a noun, a pronoun, or a clause. Some examples of simple prepositional phrases include "with Tom," "before me," and "inside the building security perimeter."

Prepositional phrases are necessary—it would be difficult to write without them—but some add to the bottom line word count without adding much to the sentence. Bureaucratic writing often uses this technique in an attempt to make a sentence sound important, but the effort usually has the undesirable dual effects of obscuring meaning and sounding pompous.

Examples
The 1040 Form will *in all certainty* serve the majority of our customers.
The 1040 Form will *certainly* serve the majority of our customers.

The revision places an adverb in place of a long prepositional phrase and allows for a reduction in the word count while strengthening the sentence.

Delete Repetitious Words

Some level of repetition is to be expected and can be beneficial. It is also important to be consistent in your use of words when precise terminology is appropriate. However, needless repetition can make your document less than vigorous and discourage readers. For example, use of the word "said" when attributing dialogue is acceptable a couple of times, but if it is the only word you use, it will lose its impact quickly. People can "indicate," "point out," "share," and "mention" as easily as they can "say" words or phrases. Synonyms are useful in avoiding the boredom of repetition.

Eliminate Archaic Expressions or References

Some writing has been ritualized to the point of cliché and has lost its impact. For example, consider "Heretofore, we have discussed the goal of omitting needless words." *Heretofore* is an outdated word that could easily be cut from the previous sentence. Another example is "as per your request for documents that emphasize clarity and reduce reader error." Feel free to eliminate *as per your request* from your word choices.

Similar to outdated words and phrases, some references are equally outdated. While it is important to recognize leaders in a field, and this text does include references to pioneers in the field of communication, it also focuses on current research and concepts. Without additional clarification and examples, readers may not understand references to an author long since passed even though he or she made an important contribution to the field. For example, Shannon and Weaver pioneered the linear model of communication that revolutionized our understanding of interaction and contributed to computer interfaces as we know them today. [2] However, if we mention them without explaining how their work relates to our current context, we may lose our readers. Similarly, references to films like *My Fair Lady* may well be less understood than the use of *The Princess Diaries* as an example of the transformative process the lead characters undergo, from rough, street-smart women to formally educated, polished members of the elite.

Avoid Fillers

Like, you know, like, you know what I mean, ahh, umm, and all the fillers you may use or hear in oral communication have, well, little or no place in the written representation of the spoken word. Review your writing for extra words that serve the written equivalent of "like" and omit them. They do not serve you as an author, and do not serve the reading audience.

Eliminate Slang

Many college professors can give examples of e-mails they have received from students that use all the modern characteristics of instant message and text abbreviation combined with a complete disregard for any norms of grammar or spelling, resulting in nearly incomprehensible messages. If your goal is to be professional, and the audience expectations do not include the use of slang, then it is inappropriate to include it in your document. Eliminate slang as you would a jargon term that serves as a barrier to understanding meaning. Not everyone will understand your slang word no more than they would a highly specialized term, and it will defeat your purpose. Norms for capitalization and punctuation that are routinely abandoned in efficient text messages or tweets are necessary and required in professional documents. Finally, there is no place in reputable business writing for offensive slang or profanity.

Evaluate Clichés

Clichés are words or phrases that through their overuse have lost their impact. That definition does not imply they have lost their meaning, and sometimes a well-placed cliché can communicate a message effectively. "Actions speak louder than words" is a cliché, but its five words speak volumes that many of your readers will recognize. This appeal to familiarity can be an effective strategy to communicate, but use it carefully. Excessive reliance on clichés will make your writing trite, while eliminating them altogether may not serve you well either. As an effective business writer, you will need to evaluate your use of clichés for their impact versus detraction from your message.

Emphasize Precise Words

Concrete words that are immediately available to your audience are often more effective than abstract terms that require definitions, examples, and qualifications. All these strategies have their place, but excessive use of abstractions will make your document less than precise, requiring additional clarification that can translate to work for you as the author and, more importantly, for your readers. Qualifiers deserve special mention here. Some instructors may indicate that words like "may," "seems," or "apparently" make your writing weak. Words are just words and it is how we use them that creates meaning. Some qualifiers are necessary, particularly if the document serves as record or may be the point of discussion in a legal issue. In other cases direct language is required, and qualifiers must be eliminated. Too many qualifiers can weaken your writing, but too few can expose you to liability. As a business writer, your understanding of audience expectations and assignment requirements will guide you to the judicious use of qualifiers.

Evaluate Parallel Construction

When you are writing in a series or have more than one idea to express, it is important to present them in similar ways to preserve and promote unity across your document. Parallel construction refers to the use of same grammatical pattern; it can be applied to words, phrases, and sentences. For example, "We found the seminar interesting, entertaining, and inspiring" is a sentence with parallel construction, whereas "We found the seminar interesting, entertaining, and it inspired us" is not. If your sentences do not seem to flow well, particularly when you read them out loud, look for misplaced parallels and change them to make the construction truly parallel.

Obscured Verbs

Business writing should be clear and concise. If the meaning is obscured, then revision is required. One common problem is the conversion of verbs into nouns with the addition of suffixes like: -ant,-ent, -ion, -tion, -sion, -ence, -ance, and ing. Instead of hiding meaning within the phrase "through the consolidation of," consider whether to use the verb forms "consolidated" or "consolidating." Similarly, instead of "the inclusion of," consider using "including," which will likely make the sentence more active and vigorous.

The "Is It Professional?" Test

Finally, when revising your document with an attention to detail, you simply need to ask the question: is it professional? If a document is too emphatic, it may seem like an attempt at cheerleading. If it uses too much jargon, it may be appropriate for "nerds" but may limit access to the information by a nontechnical audience. If the document appears too simplistic, it may seem to be "talking down" to the audience, treating the readers more like children than adults. Does your document represent you and your organization in a professional manner? Will you be proud of the work a year from now? Does it accomplish its mission, stated objectives, and the audience's expectations? Business writing is not expository, wordy, or decorative, and the presence of these traits may obscure meaning. Business writing is professional, respectful, and clearly communicates a message with minimal breakdown.

KEY TAKEAWAY

Revising for style can increase a document's clarity, conciseness, and professionalism.

EXERCISES

1. Which of the following sentences are examples of good business writing in standard English? For the sentences needing improvement, make revisions as you see fit and explain what was wrong with the original sentence. Discuss your results with your classmates.
    a. Caitlin likes gardening, golfing, hiking, and to swim.
    b. At any given point in time, well, there is a possibility that we could, like, be called upon for help.
    c. The evaluation of writing can be done through the examination and modification of each sentence.
    d. While in the meeting, the fire alarm rang.
    e. Children benefit from getting enough sleep, eating a balanced diet, and outdoor playtime.
    f. Yee has asked us to maximize the department's ka-ching by enhancing the bling-bling of our merchandise; if we fail to do this the darn president may put the kibosh on our project.
    g. Ortega's memo stated in no uncertain terms that all employees need to arrive for work on time every day.
    h. Although there are many challenges in today's market and stock values have dropped considerably since last year, but we can hope to benefit from strategic thinking and careful decision making.
    i. If you are unable to attend the meeting, please let Steve or I know as soon as possible.
    j. One of the shipping containers are open.

Find an example of a good example of effective business writing, review it, and share it with your classmates.

Find an example of a bad example of effective business writing, review it, and share it with your classmates.

Revision requires attention to detail, and you may be under pressure to produce quality results within a deadline. How do you communicate your need for time for the revision process to those who are waiting on you to complete the document? Share and discuss your responses with your classmates.

[1] Strunk, W., Jr., & White, E. B. (1979). *The elements of style* (3rd ed.). New York, NY: Macmillian.

[2] McLean, S. (2005). *The basics of interpersonal communication*. Boston, MA: Allyn & Bacon.

7.4 Evaluating the Work of Others
LEARNING OBJECTIVES

1. Describe five elements of critical analysis to use in evaluating someone else's writing.
2. Demonstrate how to deliver an evaluation constructively and respectfully.

As an experienced business writer, you may be called upon to review others' work. Having a clear understanding of the process will help you be efficient in your review, producing constructive advice that would benefit the essay while resisting change for change's sake.

Five Steps in Evaluation
By following a sequence of orderly steps, you can increase the likelihood that your evaluation of someone else's writing will be fair, constructive, and useful. Below are the five steps in evaluation:

1. Understand the assignment.
2. Evaluate how well the writing carries out the assignment.
3. Evaluate assertions.
4. Check facts.
5. Look for errors.

First, review the instructions that were given to the writer. Make sure you understand the assignment and the target audience. What resources did the writer have access to, and how much time was allotted for completing the assignment? What purpose did the document need to fulfill, and what role will this document have in future business activities or decisions?

Second, evaluate how well the document fulfills its stated goals. As a reader, do you see the goals carried out in the document? If you didn't know the writer and you were to find the document next year in a file where you were searching for information, would it provide you with the information it aims to convey? For example, suppose the document refers to the sales history of the past five years. Does the writer provide the sales history for the reader's reference, or indicate where the reader can get this information?

Evaluate the assertions made in the document. An assertion is a declaration, statement, or claim of fact. Suppose the writer indicates that the sales history for the past five years is a significant factor. Does the writer explain why this history is significant? Is the explanation logical and sufficient?

Evaluate the facts cited in the document. Does the writer credit the sources of facts, statistics, and numbers? For example, suppose the writer mentions that the population of the United States is approximately three hundred million. Obviously, the writer did not count all U.S. residents to arrive at this number. Where did it come from? If you have access to sources where you can independently verify the accuracy of these details, look them up and note any discrepancies. Finally, check the document for proper format and for errors in spelling, punctuation, and grammar. Word processing spell checkers do not catch all errors.

Delivering the Evaluation
If you are asked to evaluate someone else's written work, keep in mind that not everyone can separate process from product, or product from personality. Many authors, particularly those new to the writing process, see the written word as an extension of self. To help the recipient receive your evaluation as professional advice, rather than as personal criticism, use strategies to be tactful and diplomatic.

Until you know the author and have an established relationship, it is best to use "I" statements, as in "I find this sentence difficult to understand." The sentence places the emphasis on the speaker rather than the sentence, and further distances the author from the sentence. If you were to say, "This sentence is awful," all the author may hear is, "I am an awful writer" and fail to pay attention to your message, the sentence under examination, or ways to improve it. Business writing produces products, and all products can be improved, but not all authors can separate messenger from message.

Avoid the use of the word *you* in your evaluation, oral or written, as it can put the recipient on the defensive. This will inhibit listening and decrease the probability of effective communication. [1] If you phrase an evaluation point as, "Why did you include this word here?" it can be interpreted as a personal attack. Just as speakers are often quite self-conscious of their public speaking abilities, writers are often quite attached to the works they have produced. Anticipating and respecting this relationship and the anxiety it sometimes carries can help you serve as a better evaluator.

Phrasing disagreement as a question is often an effective response strategy. Let's rephrase that previous question to, "What is this sentence intended to communicate?" This places the emphasis on the sentence, not the author, and allows for dialogue. Phrasing your evaluation as a question emphasizes your need to understand, and provides the author with space to respond in a collaborative fashion.

Focus on the document as a product, an "it," and avoid associating the author or authors with it. There may be times when the social rank or status of the individual involved with work requires respectful consideration, and choosing to focus on the document as a work in progress, distinct from authors themselves, can serve you well. This also means that at times you may notice a glaring error but be reluctant to challenge the author directly as you anticipate a less than collaborative response. By treating the document as a product, and focusing on ways to strengthen it, keeping in mind our goals of clear and concise as reference points, you can approach issues without involving personalities.

KEY TAKEAWAY

When evaluating the work of others, make sure you understand the assignment, evaluate how well the writing carries out the assignment, evaluate assertions, check facts, and watch for errors. Deliver your evaluation with tact and diplomacy.

EXERCISES

1. Select a piece of writing from a Web site, book, newspaper, or magazine. Imagine that you are delivering an evaluation to the author of the piece. Using the strategies in this section, write a tactful and diplomatic critique. Your instructor may choose to make this a class exercise, asking students to exchange papers and evaluate each others' writing.
2. Select a piece of writing from a Web site, book, newspaper, or magazine. Imagine that you are editing it half its original length. Share the article and your revised copy with your classmates.
3. What responsibility do you have to point out the need for correction in a document when the author or team leader outranks you at work? Does it make a difference if you anticipate they will take the feedback negatively? How do you reconcile these concerns with your responsibility to the organization? Share and discuss your responses with your classmates.

[1] McLean, S. (2005). *The basics of interpersonal communication.* Boston, MA: Allyn & Bacon.

7.5 Proofreading and Design Evaluation
LEARNING OBJECTIVES

1. Understand the difference between revising and proofreading, and how to use proofreading marks.
2. Describe six design elements for evaluation.

In traditional publishing, proofreading and design are the final stages a book undergoes before it is published. If the earlier steps of research, organizing, writing, revising, and formatting have been done carefully, proofreading and design should go smoothly. Now is not the time to go back and revise a document's content, or to experiment with changes in format. Instead, the emphasis is on catching any typographical errors that have slipped through the revision process, and "pouring" the format into a design that will enhance the writer's message.

Proofreading

By now you have completed a general and specific review of the document, with attention to detail. You may have made changes, and most word processing programs will allow you to track those changes across several versions and authors.

If you work in an environment where a document exists as a hard copy during the revision process, you may use or see handwritten proofreading symbols. Professional proofreaders often use standard markings that serve to indicate where changes needed to be made on a physical document. Some of today's word processing programs incorporate many proofreading symbols in their menus. It is useful to be familiar with the various proofreading marks that were traditionally used to review and revise hard copy documents. Even if you never use the symbols in a document, your awareness of them—and the points of emphasis under review—will serve you well. Do you need to insert a word, delete a word, capitalize a letter, or start a new paragraph? There are specific symbols for each of these actions because the review and revision process has common and consistent elements that need to be addressed.

Design Evaluation

If you are asked to review a document, design an element that deserves consideration. While most of our attention has focused on words (i.e., sentence construction and common errors), design can have a strong impact on the representation and presentation of information.

Framing

Framing refers to how information is presented, including margins, line justifications, and template expectations. Just as frame creates a border around a painting, highlighting part of the image while hiding the margins, the frame of a page influences how information is received. Margins create space around the edge and help draw attention to the content. One-inch margins are standard, but differences in margin widths will depend on the assignment requirements. A brief letter, for example, may have margins as wide as two inches so that the body of the letter fills up the stationery in a more balanced fashion. Template expectations are distinct from audience expectation, though they are often related. Most software programs have templates for basic documents, including letters, reports, and résumés.

Templates represent the normative expectations for a specific type of document. Templates have spaces that establish where a date should be indicated and where personal contact information should be represented. They also often allow you to "fill in the blank," reflecting each document's basic expectations of where information is presented.

For example, line justification involves where the text lines up on the page. Letters often have a left justify, lining up the text on the left side of the page while allowing the ends of each line on the right side to be "ragged," or not aligned. This creates even spaces between words and gives the appearance of organization while promoting white space, the space on the page free of text. Balance between text (often black) and white space creates contrast and allows for areas of emphasis. Left justify often produces the appearance of balance, as the words are evenly spaced, while left and right justify can produce large gaps between words, making the sentences appear awkward and hard to read.

Typefaces

Typeface refers to design of symbols, including letters and numbers. [1] The creation of the face of the type, as in a typing machine or printing press, has long been both an art and a science. In past centuries, carvings of the face of the type in copperplate, where ink was applied and then pressed to paper, created intricate and intriguing images designed to communicate style, prestige, status, and formality with the communication of words and symbols. We no longer use copper or hot lead type, but the typeface still exists as a medium for communication in addition to the word itself. There are two general categories of typeface: serif and sans serif. "Sans" means without, so the emphasis here is on whether the face of the type has a serif or not. A serif is a small cross line, often perpendicular to the stroke of the letter, that is decorative but also serves the useful purpose of differentiating characters that could otherwise look similar (e.g., "m" and "rn," "d" and "cl," or "3" and "8"). For this reason, serif typefaces, such as Times New Roman and

Garamond, are often easier to read, especially when the font size is small. Sans serif fonts, such as Arial and Helvetica, lack the serif and can be harder to read in long text sequences. They are most commonly used for headings. However, when text is to be read electronically (on the screen of a computer or other device), serifs can tend to break up, so sans serif typefaces can be a better choice.

The rule of thumb, or common wisdom, is to limit your document to two typefaces, contrasting sans serif (headings) with text (serif). Take care not to use a font that is hard to read, creating an unnecessary barrier for your reader. Also, use a font that conveys the tone of your professional message to enhance your effectiveness.

Paragraphs

Paragraphs are the basic organizational unit for presenting and emphasizing the key points in a document. Effective paragraphs can provide an effective emphasis strategy, but the placement within the page can also influence recall and impact. The first point presented is often the second in importance, the second point is the least important, and the third point in a series of three is often the most important. People generally recall the last point presented, and tend to forget or ignore the content in the middle of a sequence. Use this strategy to place your best point in the most appropriate location.

A lengthy document that consists of paragraph after paragraph can become monotonous, making reading a chore and obscuring pieces of information that need to stand out. To give the document visual variety and to emphasize key information, consider the following strategies:

- Bullets
- Numbers
- Boldface
- Italics
- Underlining
- Capitalization (all caps)

Remember, however, that using all caps (all capitals) for body text (as opposed to headings) is often considered rude, like shouting, particularly in electronic communications.

Visual Aids

If you have the luxury of including visual aids, such as graphics and pictures, in your document, take care to make sure that the verbal and visual messages complement each other. The visual should illustrate the text, and should be placed near the words so that the relationship is immediately clear. Sometimes during editing, a photograph will get pushed to the next page, leaving the relevant text behind and creating discontinuity. This creates a barrier for your reader, so avoid it if possible.

Designing Interactive Documents

Finally, documents increasingly have an interactivity component that can lead the reader in many directions. Providing links can facilitate interactivity, and that depth of resources can be a distinct advantage when writing documents to be read on a computer. However, be careful when integrating a web link within your document, as your audience may leave your message behind and not return. If you create a link associated with clicking on a photograph or icon, make sure that the scroll-over message is clear and communicates whether the reader will leave the current page. As we have seen in many design elements, there are strengths and weaknesses associated with each option and it requires a skilled business writer to create and deliver an effective message.

KEY TAKEAWAY

Proofreading and design put the finishing touches on a completed document.

EXERCISES

1. Using proofreading marks, mark the errors in the following paragraph:

   I never wanted to bacome a writer, but when I decidedon a career in sales, I found out that being able to write was a skill that would help me. So much of my daily work involved Writing that I sometimes thought i'd fallen asleep and woken up in someone else's life. Messages, about actual sales, were the least of it. In order to attract customers, I have to send notes to people I already knew, asking them for sales leads. Then when I got a lead, I'd write to the contact asking for a few munutes of their time.If I got to meet with them or even have a phote conversation, my next task was to write them a thank—you not. Oh, and the reports-I was always filing out reports; for my sales manager, tracking my progress with each customer and each lead. If someone had tell me how much writing sails would involve, I think I would of paid more attention to my writing courses en school.

2. With a writing assignment in draft form from your class, swap with a classmate and review the spelling, grammar, and punctuation, using proofreading marks where applicable.

[1] Kostelnick, C., & Roberts, D. (1998). *Designing visual language: Strategies for professional communicators.* Needham Heights, MA: Allyn & Bacon.

7.6 Additional Resources

- Online Writing Laboratory (OWL) at Purdue University provides a comprehensive guide to the revision process. OWL is open access, free, and an excellence resource for any writer. Please feel free to consult it anytime during our discussion to go more in depth on a grammatical point or writing tip. http://owl.english.purdue.edu/owl/resource/561/05

- Visit this YourDictionary.com page for a useful article about punctuation marks. http://www.yourdictionary.com/grammar-rules/Fourteen-Punctuation-Marks.html

- Visit this site for a useful list of irregular verbs in English. http://www.englishpage.com/irregularverbs/irregularverbs.html

- This site from Capital Community College in Connecticut provides a menu of English grammar resources. http://grammar.ccc.commnet.edu/grammar

- EnglishClub.com is dedicated to English learners and those for whom English is a second language—but it can be useful for all of us. http://www.englishclub.com/grammar

- The original (1918) edition of the famous style guide *The Elements of Style* is available online at Bartleby.com. http://www.bartleby.com/141

- The Writers and Editors site presents an article on tact and tone in editing the work of others. http://www.writersandeditors.com/tips_on_tact_and_tone_30805.htm

- Merriam-Webster provides a chart of proofreader's marks and their meanings. http://www.merriam-webster.com/mw/table/proofrea.htm

- Visit this About.com site for information on designing a document. http://desktoppub.about.com/od/designprinciples/Principles_of_Design.htm

- For in-depth information on how to present visuals effectively, visit the Web site of Edward Tufte, a Professor Emeritus at Yale University, where he taught courses in statistical evidence, information design, and interface design. http://www.edwardtufte.com/tufte/index

- For a wealth of articles and information about typefaces and other aspects of document design, explore the Web site of AIGA, the professional association for design. http://www.aiga.org/content.cfm/about

Chapter 8:
Feedback in the Writing Process

Criticism may not be agreeable, but it is necessary. It fulfills the same function as pain in the human body. It calls attention to an unhealthy state of things.
  Winston Churchill
Any fool can criticize, condemn, and complain but it takes character and self-control to be understanding and forgiving.
  Dale Carnegie
He has a right to criticize, who has a heart to help.
  Abraham Lincoln
Speaking is silver, listening is gold.
  Turkish proverb

Getting Started

INTRODUCTORY EXERCISES

1. Find a news Web site that includes a forum for reader comments on the articles. Read an article that interests you and the comments readers have posted about it. Please share your results with classmates.
2. Interview a colleague, coworker, or someone in a business or industry you are involved or interested in. Ask them how they receive feedback about their work. Please share your results with classmates.
3. Review a document (online or offline) and create at least two different examples of how a reader may respond to the content and presentation. Please share your results with classmates.

The feedback loop is your connection to your audience. It's always there, even if you haven't noticed it. In today's business environment, across a variety of careers and industries, people are taking serious note of the power of feedback. How does a viral marketing campaign take off? How does an article get passed along Twitter? How does a movie review, and its long list of discussion thread comments, influence your viewing decisions? How do Wikipedia, the Global Business Network, or customer book reviews on Amazon.com impact us, alter our views, or motivate us to write?

"The feedback loop provides you with an open and direct channel of communication with your community, and that represents a never-available-before opportunity." [1] The feedback on what you write has never been as direct and interactive as today's online environment can provide, and the need to anticipate, lead, listen, and incorporate lessons learned has never been greater. This chapter examines feedback in its many forms and how it can and will have an impact on what you write, and how you write it.

What you write does not exist in a vacuum, unaffected by the world around it. It may be that what you write is read by a relatively small group of readers, or by a large target audience who may have only read a few of your messages. Either way, what you write is part of the communication process, and it makes an impact whether you know it or not.

This chapter recognizes the writing process and its components with an emphasis on feedback. Do you know the difference between indirect and direct feedback? Are you aware of effective strategies to elicit valuable feedback? How do you know if the feedback is valid? To what extent, and in what ways, should you adapt and adjust your writing based on feedback? These are central questions in the writing process, and any skilled business writer recognizes the need for improvement based on solid feedback. You may not always enjoy receiving feedback, but you should always give it due thought and consideration. Failure to change and adapt has many unfortunate consequences. [2] It is up to you to seek good information and to separate the reliable from the unreliable in your goal of improving your business writing.

[1] Powel, J. (2009). *33 million people in the room: How to create, influence, and a run a successful business with social networking.* Upper Saddle River, NJ: FT Press/Pearson Education.
[2] Johnson, S. (1998). *Who moved my cheese? An amazing way to deal with change in your work and in your life.* New York, NY: Penguin Books.

8.1 Diverse Forms of Feedback
LEARNING OBJECTIVES

1. Describe feedback as part of the writing process.
2. Compare and contrast indirect and direct feedback.
3. Understand internal and external feedback.
4. Discuss diverse forms of feedback.

Just as you know that religion and politics are two subjects that often provoke emotional responses, you also recognize that once you are aware of someone's viewpoint you can choose to refrain from discussing certain topics, or may change the way you address them. The awareness of bias and preference, combined with the ability to adapt the message before it is sent, increases the probability of reception and successful communication. Up until now we have focused on knowing the audience's expectation and the assignment directions, as well as effective strategies for writing and production. Now, to complete the communication process, to close the writing process, we need to gather and evaluate feedback.

You may receive feedback from peers, colleagues, editors, or supervisors, but actual feedback from the intended audience can be rare. Imagine that you work in the marketing department of an engineering company and have written an article describing a new kind of water pump that operates with little maintenance and less energy consumption than previous models. Your company has also developed an advertising campaign introducing this new pump to the market and has added it to their online sales menu. Once your article has been reviewed and posted, it may be accessed online by a reader in another country who is currently researching water pumps that fall within your product range. That reader will see a banner ad displayed across the header of the Web page, with the name of your company prominently displayed in the reader's native language, even if your article is in English. Ads of this nature are called contextually relevant ads. An example is Google's Feedback Ad function, which incorporates the content of the site and any related search data to provide information to potential customers. If the reader found your article through the German version of Google, Google.de, the ad will display the Adwords, or text in an advertisement, in German.

As the author, you may never receive direct feedback on your article, but you may receive significant indirect feedback. Google can report the "hits" and links to your Web site, and your company's information technology department can tell you about the hits on your Web site from Germany, where they originated, and whether the visitor initiated a sales order for the pump. If the sale was left incomplete, they will know when the basket or order was abandoned or became inactive in the purchase process. If the sale was successful, your sales department can provide feedback in the form of overall sales as well as information on specific customers. This in turn allows you an opportunity for post-sales communication and additional feedback.

The communication process depends on a series of components that are always present. If you remove one or more, the process disintegrates. You need a source and a receiver, even if those roles alternate and blur. You need a message and a channel, or multiples of each in divergent ratios of signal strength and clarity. You also need context and environment, including both the psychological expectations of the interaction as well as the physical aspects present. Interference is also part of any communication process. Because interference—internal or external—is

always present, as a skilled business writer, you have learned how to understand and anticipate it so that you can get your message across to your audience.

The final step in the communication process is feedback. It contributes to the transactional relationship in communication, and serves as part of the cycling and recycling of information, content, negotiations, relationships, and meaning between the source and receiver. Because feedback is so valuable to a business writer, you will welcome it and use strategies to overcome any interfering factors that may compromise reception and limit feedback.

Feedback is defined as a receiver's response to a source, and can come in many forms. From the change in the cursor arrow as you pass over a link as a response to the reader's indication, via the mouse, touch screen, or similar input device, as a nonverbal response, to one spoken out loud during the course of a conversation, feedback is always present, even if we fail to capture or attend to the information as it is displayed. Let's examine several diverse types of feedback.

Indirect Feedback

If you have worked in an office you may have heard of the grapevine, and may already be aware that it often carries whines instead of wine. The grapevine is the unofficial, informal communication network within an organization, and is often characterized by rumor, gossip, and innuendo. The grapevine often involves information that is indirect, speculative, and not immediately verifiable. That makes it less than reliable, but understandably attractive and interesting to many.

In the same way, indirect feedback is a response that does not directly come from the receiver or source. The receiver may receive the message, and may become the source of the response, but they may not communicate that response directly to you, the author. Your ability to track who accesses your Web page, what they read, and how long their visit lasts can be a source of feedback that serves to guide your writing. You may also receive comments, e-mails, or information from individuals within your organization about what customers have told them; this is another source of indirect feedback. The fact that the information is not communicated directly may limit its use or reliability, but it does have value. All forms of feedback have some measure of value.

Direct Feedback

You post an article about your company's new water pump and when you come back to it an hour later there are 162 comments. As you scroll through the comments you find that ten potential customers are interested in learning more, while the rest debate the specifications and technical abilities of the pump. This direct response to your writing is another form of feedback.

Direct feedback is a response that comes from the receiver. Direct feedback can be both verbal and nonverbal, and it may involve signs, symbols, words, or sounds that are unclear or difficult to understand. You may send an e-mail to a customer who inquired about your water pump, offering to send a printed brochure and have a local sales representative call to evaluate how suitable your pump would be for the customer's particular application. In order to do so, you will need the customer's mailing address, physical location, and phone number. If the customer replies simply with "Thanks!"—no address, no phone number—how do you interpret this direct feedback? Communication is dynamic and complex, and it is no easy task to understand or predict. One aspect of the process, however, is predictable: feedback is always part of the communication process.

Just as nonverbal gestures do not appear independent of the context in which the communication interaction occurs, and often overlap, recycle, and repeat across the interaction, the ability to identify clear and direct feedback can be a significant challenge. In face-to-face communication, yawns and frequent glances at the clock may serve as a clear signal (direct feedback) for lack of interest, but direct feedback for the writer is often less obvious. It is a rare moment when the article you wrote is read in your presence and direct feedback is immediately available. Often feedback comes to the author long after the article is published.

Internal Feedback

We usually think of feedback as something that can only come from others, but in the case of internal feedback, we can get it from ourselves. Internal feedback is generated by the source in response to the message created by that same source. You, as the author, will be key to the internal feedback process. This may involve reviewing your document before you send it or post it, but it also may involve evaluation from within your organization.

On the surface, it may appear that internal feedback cannot come from anyone other than the author, but that would be inaccurate. If we go back to the communication process and revisit the definitions of source and receiver, we can clearly see how each role is not defined by just one person or personality, but instead within the transactional nature of communication by function. The source creates and the receiver receives. Once the communication interaction is initiated, the roles often alternate, as in the case of an e-mail or text message "conversation" where two people take turns writing.

When you write a document for a target audience—for example, a group of farmers who will use the pumps your company produces to move water from source to crop—you will write with them in mind as the target receiver. Until they receive the message, the review process is internal to your organization, and feedback is from individuals and departments other than the intended receiver.

You may have your company's engineering department confirm the technical specifications of the information you incorporated into the document, or have the sales department confirm a previous customer's address. In each case, you as the author are receiving internal feedback about content you produced, and in some ways, each department is contributing to the message prior to delivery.

Internal feedback starts with you. Your review of what you write is critical. You are the first and last line of responsibility for your writing. As the author, it is your responsibility to insure your content is

- correct,
- clear,
- concise,
- ethical.

When an author considers whether the writing in a document is correct, it is important to interpret correctness broadly. The writing needs to be appropriate for the context of audience's expectations and assignment directions. Some writing may be technically correct, even polished, and still be incorrect for the audience or the assignment. Attention to what you know about your reading audience (e.g., their reading levels and educational background) can help address the degree to which what you have written is correct for its designated audience and purpose.

Correctness also involves accuracy: questions concerning true, false, and somewhere in between. A skilled business writer verifies all sources for accuracy and sleeps well knowing that no critic can say his or her writing is inaccurate. If you allow less than factual information into your writing, you open the door to accusations of false information that could be interpreted as a fraudulent act with legal ramifications. Keep notes on where and when you accessed Web sites, where you found the information you cite or include, and be prepared to back up your statements with a review of your sources.

Writing correctly also includes providing current, up-to-date information. Most business documents place an emphasis on the time-sensitivity of the information. It doesn't make sense to rely on sales figures from two years ago when you can use sales figures from last year. Neither does citing old articles, outdated materials, and sources that may or may not apply to the given discussion. Information that is not current can and does serve useful purposes, but often requires qualification on why it is relevant, with particular attention to a current context.

Business writing also needs to be clear, otherwise it will fail in its purpose to inform or persuade readers. Unclear writing can lead to misunderstandings that consume time and effort to undo. An old saying in military communications is "Whatever *can* be misunderstood, *will* be misunderstood." To give yourself valuable internal feedback about the clarity of your document, try to pretend you know nothing more about the subject than your least informed reader does. Can you follow the information provided? Are your points supported? In the business environment, time is money, and bloated writing wastes time. The advice from the best-selling style guide by William Strunk Jr. and E. B. White [1] to "omit needless words" is always worth bearing in mind.

Finally, a skilled business writer understands he or she does not stand alone. Ethical consideration of the words you write, what they represent, and their possible consequences are part of the responsibility of a business writer. The writer offers information to a reading audience and if their credibility is lost, future interactions are far less likely to occur. Customer relationship management requires consideration of the context of the interaction, and all communication occurs with the context of community, whether that relationship is readily apparent or not. Brand management reinforces the associations and a relationship with the product or services that would be negatively compromised should the article, and by association, author and company, be found less than truthful. Advertising may promote features, but false advertising can and does lead to litigation. The writer represents a business or organization, but also represents a family and a community. For a family or community to function, there has to be a sense of trust amid the interdependence.

External Feedback

How do you know what you wrote was read and understood? Essentially, how do you know communication interaction has occurred? Writing, reading, and action based on the exchange of symbolic information is a reflection of the communication process. Assessment of the feedback from the receiver is part of a writer's responsibility. Increasingly Web-based documents allow for interaction and enhancement of feedback, but you will still be producing documents that may exist as hard copies. Your documents may travel to places you don't expect and cannot predict. Feedback comes in many forms and in this part of our discussion we focus on answering that essential question, assessing interaction, and gathering information from it. External feedback involves a response from the receiver. Receivers, in turn, become a source of information themselves. Attention to the channel they use (how they communicate feedback), as well as nonverbal aspects like time (when they send it), can serve you on this and future documents.

Hard Copy Documents and External Feedback

We'll start this discussion with traditional, stand-alone hard copy documents in mind before we discuss electronic documents, including Web-based publications. Your business or organization may communicate in written forms across time zones and languages via electronic communication, but some documents are still produced on paper. Offline technologies like a copy machine or a printer are still the tools you will be using as a normal course of business.

Letters are a common way of introducing information to clients and customers, and you may be tasked to produce a document that is printed and distributed via "snail mail," or the traditional post mail services. Snail mail is a term that reflects the time delay associated with the physical production, packaging, and delivery of a document. Legal documents are still largely in hard copy print form. So too are documents that address the needs of customers and clients that do not, or prefer not to, access information electronically.

Age is one characteristic of an audience that may be tempting to focus on when considering who may need to receive a letter in hard copy form, but you may be surprised about this. In a 2009 study of U.S. Internet use, the Pew Research Center [2] found that between 2008 and 2009, broadband Internet use by senior citizens increased from 20 percent to 30 percent, and broadband use by baby boomers (people born 1945–1963) increased from 50 percent to 61 percent. Socioeconomic status is a better characteristic to focus on when considering hard copy documents. Lack of access to a computer and the Internet is a reality for most of the world's population. It's often stated that half of the world's population will never make a phone call in their lifetime, and even though the references for the claims are widespread and diverse, the idea that there are people without access to a phone is striking for many Westerners. While cell phones are increasingly allowing poor and rural populations to skip the investment in landline networks and wireless Internet is a leapfrog technology that changes everything, cell phones and computers are still prohibitively expensive for many.

Let's say you work for a major bank on the West Coast of the United States. You have been assigned to write a letter offering a refinance option to a select, previously screened audience composed of individuals who share several common characteristics: high-wage earners with exceptional credit scores. How will you best get the attention of this audience? If you sent an e-mail it might get deleted as spam, or unwanted e-mail that often lacks credibility and may even be dangerous. The audience is small and you have a budget for hard copy production of documents that includes a line item for mailing costs. If the potential customer receives the letter from your department delivered by an overnight courier like FedEx, they may be more likely to receive your message. In 2005, Wells Fargo Bank did exactly that. They mailed a letter of introduction outlining an opportunity to refinance at no cost to the consumer, targeting a group identified as high profit and low risk. The channels selected—print-based documents on letterhead with the mode of delivery sure to get attention—were designed to prompt a response. The letter introduced the program, highlighted the features, and discussed why the customers were among a group of individuals to whom this offer was being extended. [3]

In the letter, the bank specifically solicited a customer response, a form of feedback, via e-mail and/or phone to establish dialogue. One could measure feedback in terms of response rate; in terms of verification of data on income, debt outstanding on loans, and current home appraisal values; and in terms of channel and how customers chose to respond. All these forms of feedback have value to the author.

Hard copy documents can be a challenge when it comes to feedback, but that doesn't mean it is impossible to involve them in the feedback process. It's important to remember that even in the late 1990s, most business documents were print-based. From sales reports to product development reports, they were printed, copied, bound, and distributed, all at considerable cost.

If one purpose of your letter is to persuade the client or customer to reply by e-mail or phone, one way to assess feedback is the response rate, or the number of replies in relation to the number of letters sent. If your report on a new product is prepared for internal use and is targeted to a specific division within your company, their questions in relation to the document may serve as feedback. If your memo produces more questions than the one it was intended to address in terms of policy, the negative feedback may highlight the need for revision. In each case, hard copy documents are often assessed through oral and written feedback.

External Feedback in a Virtual Environment

Rather than focus on the dust on top of documents once produced, perhaps read, and sometimes forgotten, let's examine document feedback from the interactive world that gathers no dust. One challenge when the Web was young involved the accurate assessment of audience. Why is that relevant to a business writer? Because you produce content for a specific audience with a specific purpose, and the degree to which it is successful has some relation to its value. Imagine that you produced a pilot television program with all the best characters, excellent dialogue, and big name stars portraying the characters, only to see the pilot flop. If you had all the right elements in a program, how could it fail? It failed to attract an audience. Television often uses ratings, or measurements of the estimated number of viewers, to measure success. Nielsen is the leading market research company associated with television ratings and online content. Programs that get past a pilot or past a first season do so because they have good ratings and are ranked above other competing programs. All programs compete with each other within a time slot or across a genre. Those that are highly ranked—those that receive the largest number of viewers—can command higher budgets, and often receive more advertising dollars. Those programs that reach few people are often canceled and replaced with other programs that have great characters, solid writing, and hopeful stars as the cycle continues.

Business writers experience a process of competition, ratings, feedback, and renewal within the world of online publishing. Business writers want their content to be read. Just as companies developed ways to measure the number of viewers of a given television program, which led to rankings that influenced which programs survived and prospered and which were canceled, the Web has a system of keeping track of what gets read and by whom. Perhaps you've heard of hits, as in how many hits a Web site receives, but have you stopped to consider what hits represent within our discussion of feedback?

First, let's examine what a hit is. When a browser, like Internet Explorer or Firefox, receives a file from a Web server, it is considered a hit. Your document may be kept on our company's Web server, or a computer dedicated to serving the online requests for information via the Internet. The Web server receives a request from the user and sends the files associated with the page; every Web page contains several files including graphics, images, and text. Each file request and receipt between server and browser counts as a hit, regardless of how many files each page contains. So let's say you created an online sales catalog with twenty images per page, twenty boxed text descriptions, and all the files for indicating color, size, and quantity. Your document could have quite a few hits with just one page request and only one viewer.

Does a large number of hits on your document mean that it was successful? Not necessarily. Hits or page views have largely been discredited as a reliable measure of a document's effectiveness, popularity, or audience size. In fact, the word "hits" is sometimes humorously referred to as being the acronym for *how idiots track success*.

Page views are a count of how many times a Web page is viewed, irrespective of the number of files it contains. Each time a user or reader views the page counts as one page view. Nielsen Online and Source.com are two companies that provide Web traffic rating services, and Google has also developed services to better enable advertisers to target specific audiences [4]. They commonly track the number of unique visits a reader makes to a Web site, and use cookies, or small, time-encoded files that identify specific users, as a means to generate data.

Another way to see whether a document has been read online is to present part of the article with a "reveal full article" button after a couple of paragraphs. If someone wants to read the entire article, the button needs to be clicked in order to display the remainder of the content. Because this feature can be annoying for readers, many content providers also display a "turn off reveal full article" button to provide an alternative; Yahoo! News is an example of a site that gives readers this option.

Jon Kleinberg's HITS (hyperlink-induced topic search) algorithm has become a popular and more effective way to rate Web pages. [5] HITS ranks documents by the links within the document, presuming that a good document is one that incorporates and references, providing links to, other Web documents while also being frequently cited by other documents. Hubs, or documents with many links, are related to authority pages, or frequently cited documents. This relationship of hubs and authority is mutually reinforcing, and if you can imagine a Web universe of one hundred pages, the one with the most links and which is most frequently referred to wins.

As a business writer you will naturally want to incorporate authoritative sources and relevant content, but you will also want to attract and engage your audience, positioning your document as hub and authority within that universe. Feedback in the form of links and references may be one way to assess your online document.

User-Generated Feedback

Moving beyond the Web tracking aspects of feedback measurement in terms of use, let's examine user-generated responses to your document. Let's say you have reviewed the posts left by unique users to the comments section of the article. This, in some ways, serves the same purpose as letters to the editor in traditional media. In newspapers, magazines, and other offline forms of print media, an edition is produced with a collection of content and then delivered to an audience. The audience includes members of a subscriber-based group with common interests, as well as those who read a magazine casually while waiting in the doctor's office. If an article generated interest, enjoyment, or outrage (or demanded correction), people would write letters in response to the content. Select responses would be published in the next edition. There is a time delay associated with this system that reflects the preparation, production, and distribution cycle of the medium. If the magazine is published once a month, it takes a full month for user feedback to be presented in print—for example, letters commenting on an article in the March issue would appear in the "Letters" section of the May issue.

With the introduction of online media, the speed of this feedback loop has been greatly increased. Public relations announcements, product reviews, and performance data of your organization are often made available internally or externally via electronic communication. If you see a factual error in an article released internally, within minutes you may be able to respond with an e-mail and a file attachment with a document that corrects the data. In the same way, if the document is released externally, you can expect that feedback from outside your organization will be quick. Audience members may debate your description of the water pump, or openly question its effectiveness in relation to its specifications; they may even post positive comments. Customer comments, like letters to the editor, can be a valuable source of feedback.

Customer reviews and similar forms of user-generated content are increasingly common across the Internet. Written communication is often chosen as the preferred format; from tweets to blogs and commentary pages, to threaded, theme-based forums, person-to-person exchange is increasingly common. Still, as a business writer, you will note that even with the explosion of opinion content, the tendency for online writers to cite a Web page with a link can and does promote interaction.

It may sound strange to ask this question, but is all communication interaction good? Let's examine examples of interaction and feedback and see if we can arrive at an answer. You may have heard that one angry customer can influence several future customers, but negative customer reviews in the online information age can make a disproportionate impact in a relatively short time. While the online environment can be both fast and effective in terms of distribution and immediate feedback, it can also be quite ineffective, depending on the context. "Putting ads in front of Facebook users is like hanging out at a party and interrupting conversations to hawk merchandise," according to Newsweek journalist Daniel Lyons. [6] Relationships between users, sometimes called social graphs, are a reflection of the dynamic process of communication, and they hold value, but translating that value into sales can be a significant challenge.

Overall, as we have seen, your goal as a business writer is to meet the audience and employer's expectations in a clear and concise way. Getting your content to a hub position, and including authoritative references, is a great way to make your content more relevant to your readers. Trying to facilitate endless discussions may be engaging and generate feedback, but may not translate into success. Facebook serves as a reminder that you want to provide solid content and attend to the feedback. People who use Google already have something in mind when they perform a search, and if your content provides what readers are looking for, you may see your page views and effectiveness increase.

Interviews

Interviews provide an author with the opportunity to ask questions of, and receive responses from, audience members. Since interviews take considerable time and cannot easily be scaled up to address large numbers of readers, they are most often conducted with a small, limited audience. An interview involves an interviewer, and interviewee, and a series of questions. It can be an employment interview, or an informational interview in preparation of document production, but in this case we're looking for feedback. As a business writer, you may choose to schedule time with a supervisor to ask a couple of questions about how the document you produced could be improved. You may also schedule time with the client or potential customer and try to learn more. You may interact across a wide range of channels, from face-to-face to an e-mail exchange, and learn more about how your document was received. Take care not to interrupt the interviewee, even if there is a long pause, as some of the best information comes up when people feel the need to fill the silence. Be patient and understanding, and thank them for taking the time to participate in the interview.

Relationships are built over time and the relationship you build through a customer interview, for example, may have a positive impact on your next writing project.

Surveys

At some point, you may have answered your phone to find a stranger on the other end asking you to take part in a survey for a polling organization like Gallup, Pew, or Roper. You may have also received a consumer survey in the mail, with a paper form to fill out and return in a postage-paid envelope. Online surveys are also becoming increasingly popular. For example, SurveyMonkey.com is an online survey tool that allows people to respond to a set of questions and provide responses. This type of reader feedback can be valuable, particularly if some of the questions are open-ended. Closed questions require a simple yes or no to respond, making them easier to tabulate as "votes," but open-ended questions give respondents complete freedom to write their thoughts. As such, they promote the expression of new and creative ideas and can lead to valuable insights for you, the writer.

Surveys can take place in person, as we discussed in an interview format, and this format is common when taking a census. For example, the U.S. government employs people for a short time to go door to door for a census count of everyone. Your organization may lack comparable resources and may choose to mail out surveys on paper with postage-paid response envelopes or may reduce the cost and increase speed by asking respondents to complete the survey online.

Focus Groups

Focus groups involve a representative sample of individuals, brought together to represent a larger group or audience. If you know your target audience, and the range of characteristics they represent, you would look for participants who can represent more than one of those characteristics. As we've discussed in an interview setting, the interaction involves a question-and-answer format, but may also introduce other ways to facilitate interaction. If your company is looking to launch a new product, you may introduce that product to this select audience to see how they react. As a business writer, what they say and express may help you in writing your promotional materials. In terms of feedback, you may assemble a group of individuals who use your product or service, and then ask them a series of questions in a group setting. The responses may have bearing on your current and future documents.

Normally we'd think of focus groups in a physical setting, but again modern technology has allowed for innovative adaptations. Forums, live Webcasts, and other virtual gatherings allow groups to come together across time and distance to discuss specific topics. A Web camera, a microphone, and an Internet connection are all it takes. There are a number of software programs and online platforms for bringing individuals together. Anticipate that focus groups will increasingly gather via computer-mediated technologies in the future as the costs of bringing people together for a traditional meeting increase.

KEY TAKEAWAY

Feedback may be indirect or direct, internal or external, and may be mediated electronically in many different ways.

EXERCISES

1. Design a market survey that asks your friends at least three questions that have to do with their attitudes, preferences, or choices. Prepare and present your results, noting the number of respondents, and any characteristics that you requested or can offer, like age or level of education, for example.

2. How does the online world affect the process of feedback on written documents? Does it improve feedback, or lead to self-censorship? Discuss your thoughts with classmates.

3. In your opinion, are traditional print publications still viable with daily, weekly, or monthly publication cycles? Why or why not?

4. Research online survey programs and review two competitors. Compare the features and the apparent ease of use. Which would you recommend and why? Report your results and compare with classmates.

[1] Strunk, W., Jr., & White, E. B. (1979). *The elements of style* (3rd ed.). New York, NY: Macmillian.

[2] Horrigan, J. B. (2009, June 17). Home broadband adoption 2009. *Pew Internet & American Life Project*. Retrieved

from http://pewresearch.org/pubs/1254/home-broadband-adoption-2009

[3] Diaz de Leon, M. (2005, September 1). Personal communication.

[4] http://googleblog.blogspot.com/2012/01/search-plus-your-world.html (06/28/12)

[5] Kleinberg, J. M. (1998). Authoritative sources in a hyperlinked environment. In *Proceedings of the ninth annual ACM-SIAM symposium on discrete algorithms* (pp. 668–677). Philadelphia, PA: Society for Industrial and Applied Mathematics. Retrieved

from http://portal.acm.org/citation.cfm?id=315045

[6] Lyons, D. (2008, October 20). Facebook's roar becomes a meow. *Newsweek*, E.22.

8.2 Qualitative and Quantitative Research

LEARNING OBJECTIVES

1. Compare and contrast the feedback that can be obtained with qualitative and quantitative research.

2. Discuss validity, reliability, and statistical significance.

Perhaps you have heard the term "market research" or have taken a class on statistics. Whether your understanding of the gathering of credible, reliable information is emerging or developed, a general awareness of research is essential for business writing. Many businesses use research as a preproduct, postproduct, and service development method of obtaining feedback. Understanding the feedback from research can influence your writing as you learn more about your target audience. Ralph Rosnow and Robert Rosenthal offer a solid introductory discussion into basic research terms in their text *Beginning Behavioral Research: A Conceptual Primer* that serves our discussion well. [1]

We can divide research into two basic categories:

1. *Qualitative research* focuses on *quality* in the sense of "what is it like?" or "how does it feel?"

2. *Quantitative research* focuses on *quantity* in the sense of "how many customers?" or "what percentage?"

Let's examine the advantages and disadvantages of each of these kinds of research.

Obtaining Feedback with Qualitative Research

Qualitative research involves investigative methods that cross subjects and academic disciplines to gain in-depth information. If quantitive research explores "what," qualitative research explores "how" and "why." From interviews to focus groups, many of the face-to-face strategies used to gather information are qualitative in nature.

You have five senses, and you may be able to distinguish between sweet and salty foods, but can you describe what you taste and smell? Let's say you work for a vineyard, and have been tasked to write a paragraph describing a new wine. Could you? Capturing fine data points and representing them in words and symbols can be a significant challenge for researchers. When testing the wine with a focus group, you might want information on how it is perceived, and the responses may be varied and unusual. What do you do with the information you gather? You may be able to identify trends among the varied responses, and create groups that indicate a woody or earthy flavor, but numbers will fail to capture the nuances of flavor and body of the wines in the information.

Some information—like the way consumers characterize the taste of a wine—is a challenge to obtain, and qualitative research often serves well in this capacity. If quantitative research handles large audiences well, qualitative research allows for in-depth interpersonal interviews that produce rich and meaningful results. The information may not be as reliable, and your ability to produce the same results over time may be limited, but humans are emotional, irrational, and unpredictable. They are also, each in his or her own way, unique. As you increase the level of perspective in terms of abstraction, all humans may eventually come to look similar, even the same. We all possess some similar characteristics, such as the use of language, or the composition of our bodies. But when you look more closely, you see the diverse range of languages, and learn that not everyone has 206 bones in an adult body. Between these two views we find the range of information that quantitative and qualitative research attempt to address.

Suppose we want to determine who has greater lifetime risk of developing heart disease, a man or a woman? If we are talking about an individual man and an individual woman, our answer might be quite different from what it would be if we were talking about men in general versus women in general. A survey may work well to capture the data about men versus women, but a face-to-face interview with a man and a woman will allow for interaction, follow-up questions, and a much better picture of the question: between this individual woman and this individual man, who is more likely to be at risk? The risk and protective factors we learn from broad research projects involving thousands of subjects have value, but there are times when a broad brushstroke will fail to capture the fine data that is needed or desired.

Imagine that you are involved with a direct observation of buying behavior by reviewing video recordings of security cameras that clearly show your company's product in relation to other products on the shelf. You may find, particularly after a review of the literature, that product placement makes a significant impact on purchase decisions. In addition, you may be involved with some level of participation in the setting. Serving as a participant observer means you are part of the process, involved in action, and not separated from the interaction. You look at the sales experience through the eyes of a participant, and view others through the eyes of an observer. You may find that interviews and focus groups serve to teach you more about your audience, but may also find that others have conducted similar interviews and learn from their findings.

As a business writer, you should be familiar with qualitative research and its relative strengths and weaknesses. You may use some of its techniques to gather information about your audience, may cite research that involves qualitative methods, and may utilize its strategies with an audience post document, product, or service.

Obtaining Feedback with Quantitative Research

Quantitative research involves investigation and analysis of data and relationships between data that can be represented by numbers. It is often used to test a hypothesis, and normally involves large volumes of data. Where a qualitative research project may involve a dozen interviews, a quantitative one would involve hundreds or thousands. Since each interview carries a cost—and a thousand or ten thousand interviews may exceed the research budget of your organization—a more cost-effective alternative must be found. By limiting the number of questions and limiting the ways in which participants can respond, the data can be gathered at a lower cost with often a higher level of statistical validity.

In qualitative research, you may ask an open-ended question like "What does the wine taste like?" In quantitative research, you may limit the response options: "Does the wine taste (a) woody, (b) fruity, or (c) both?" You may find that 90 percent of respondents indicate answer (c); you can represent it with numbers and a graph, but it may not serve your investigation the way you planned.

Research methodologies involve examining and evaluating the methods used in investigation or soliciting feedback. They are used to address and improve poorly worded questions, and to help the investigator match the research goal to the method. Quantitative research serves us well when we ask, does vitamin C, taken at a dosage of 500 mg daily for five years, lower the incidence of the common cold? We could track a thousand participants in the study who provide intake prescreening information, confirm daily compliance, and participate in periodic interviews. We also know that part of our group is taking a placebo (sugar pill) as part of the requirements of a double-blind study. At the end of the term, we have certain numbers that may be able to indicate the degree to which vitamin C affects the incidence rate of illness.

Advertisers often conduct research to learn more about preference and attitudes, two areas that are not easily captured. Sometimes preference studies use Likert scales, which give respondents a preset scale to rate their answers. An example of a Likert item might be, "Please indicate to what degree you agree or disagree with this statement: I enjoy drinking brand X wine. Do you (1) strongly agree, (2) agree, (3) neither agree nor disagree, (4) disagree, or (5) strongly disagree?"

There is a tendency for some attitudinal and preferential research that may be more accurately described as qualitative, to be described in numerical terms. For example, you have probably heard the claim that "four out of five dentists prefer brand X," when in itself, the number or representation of preference is meaningless. As an astute business writer, you will be able to understand pre (before) and post (after) document, product, or service research investigations and distinguish between the two main approaches.

What Is Validity?

How do you know the results presented in a study or article have value? How do you know they are valid? Validity involves the strength of conclusions, inferences or assertions. Thomas Cook and Dan Campbell [2] indicate that validity is often the best available approximation of the truth or falseness of an inference, proposition, or conclusion. Readers want to know that your information has value and that there is confidence in its points, supporting information, and conclusions. They want to know you are right and not making false statements.

One way you can address the value of validity is to cite all your sources clearly. As a writer, you may certainly include information from authorities in the field when the attribution is relevant and the citation is clear. Giving credit where credit is due is one way to make your information more valuable, and by referencing the sources clearly, you enable the reader to assess the validity of the information you have provided. Does all feedback have validity? Just as there are many threats to validity in research applications, you cannot always be sure that the feedback you receive is accurate or truthful. Have students ever evaluated professors negatively because of the required work in the course? Of course. In the same way, some readers may have issues with the topic or your organization. Their feedback post may be less than supportive, and even openly hostile. Assess the validity of the feedback, respond with professionalism at all times, and learn how to let go of the negative messages that offer little opportunity to improve understanding.

What Is Reliability?

Reliability is the consistency of your measurements. The degree to which an instrument gives the same measurement each and every time with the same subjects, in the same context, is a measure of its reliability. For example, if you took your temperature three times within fifteen minutes, and your thermometer gave a different reading each time—say, 98.6, 96.6, and 100.2—you would conclude that your thermometer was unreliable.

How does this apply to feedback in business writing? Let's say you have three sales agents who will complete follow-up interactions with three customers after you have sent a report to each customer on their purchases to date with suggestions for additional products and services. All three sales agents have the same information about the products and services, but will they perform the same? Of course not. Each one, even if they are trained to stay on script and follow specific

protocols, will not be identical in their approach and delivery. Each customer is also different, so the context is different in each case. As business professionals, we need to learn about our environment and adapt to it. This requires feedback and attention to the information in many forms. We need to assess the degree of strength or weakness of the information, its reliability, or validity, and be prepared to act on that information. Successful businesses, and by extension successful business communicators, recognize that communication is a two-way process in which we need to listen, learn, and respond to feedback. We need to meet and exceed the expectations of our customers.

Inter-rater reliability involves the degree to which each evaluator evaluates the same in similar contexts. One can think of a college essay, for example, to better understand this concept. Let's say you write an essay on customer relationship management and submit it to the instructor of your business communication class. At the same time, you submit the same essay to your English professor, and you submit a copy to your marketing professor. Will all three professors evaluate your essay the same? Of course not. They will each have their own set of expectations and respective disciplines that will influence what they value and how the evaluate. Still, if your essay is thoroughly researched, logically organized, and carefully written, each professor may give it a better than average grade. If this is the case, inter-rater reliability would indicate that you did a good job on the essay.

What Is Statistically Significant?

This is a research term that is often used and commonly misunderstood. Not every research finding is statistically significant, and many of those that are considered significant are only slightly more likely than pure chance. Statistically significant findings are those that have a high level of reliability, in that if the same test is applied in the same context to the same subjects, the results will come out the same time and time again. [3] You may see a confidence level of +/− (plus or minus) three percentage points as a common statement of reliability and confidence in a poll. It means that if the poll were repeated, there is confidence that the results would be within three points above or below the percentages in the original results. When statements of statistical significance are made, you will know that it means a difference or a relationship was established with confidence by the study. That confidence gives the results credibility.

KEY TAKEAWAY

Research can be qualitative or quantitative, and it is important to assess the validity, reliability, and statistical significance of research findings.

EXERCISES

1. Visit the Web site of a major polling organization such as Gallup, Pew, Roper, or Zogby. What can you learn about how the organization conducts polls? How valid, reliable, and statistically significant are the results of this organization's polls, and how do you know? Discuss your findings with your classmates.

2. Find an example where information is presented to support a claim, but you perceive it to be less than valid or reliable. Share your observations and review the results of your classmates' similar efforts.

[1] Rosnow, R., & Rosenthal, R. (1999). *Beginning behavioral research: A conceptual primer* (3rd ed.). Englewood Cliffs, NJ: Prentice Hall.

[2] Cook, T. D., & Campbel, D. T. (1979). *Quasi-experimentation: Design and analysis issues for field settings.* Chicago, IL: Rand McNally.

[3] Stone-Romero, E. F. (2002). The relative validity and usefulness of various empirical research designs. In S. G. Rogelberg (Ed.), *Handbook of research methods in industrial and organizational psycology* (pp. 77–98). Malden, MA: Blackwell.

8.3 Feedback as an Opportunity
LEARNING OBJECTIVE

1. Describe the five types of feedback identified by Carl Rogers.

Writing is a communicative act. It is a reflection of the communication process and represents each of the process's components in many ways. Yet, because many people tend to think of writing as a one-way communication, feedback can be particularly challenging for a writer to assess. The best praise for your work may be the sound of silence, of the document having fulfilled its purpose without error, misinterpretation, or complaint. Your praise may come in the form of increased referrals, or sales leads, or outright sales, but you may not learn of the feedback unless you seek it out. And that is what this section is about: seeking out feedback because it is an opportunity—an opportunity to engage with your audience, stimulate your thinking, and ultimately improve your writing.

You ask a colleague, "How was your weekend?" and he glances at the floor. Did he hear you? Was his nonverbal response to your question one of resignation that the weekend didn't go well, or is he just checking to make sure his shoes are tied? Feedback, like all parts of the communication model, can be complex and puzzling. Do you ask again? Do you leave him alone? It is hard to know what

an action means independent of context, and even harder to determine without more information. Feedback often serves the role of additional information, allowing the source to adapt, adjust, modify, delete, omit, or introduce new messages across diverse channels to facilitate communication. One point of reference within the information or response we define as feedback may, in itself, be almost meaningless, but taken together with related information can indicate a highly complex response, and even be used to predict future responses.

Carl Rogers, the famous humanistic psychologist, divides feedback into five categories:

1. Evaluative
2. Interpretive
3. Supportive
4. Probing
5. Understanding

These five types of feedback vary in their frequency and effectiveness. [1], [2] This framework highlights aspects of feedback that serve as opportunities for the business writer, as he or she recognizes feedback as an essential part of writing and the communication process. Let's examine the five types of feedback, as presented by Rogers, [3], [4] in their order of frequency.

Evaluative Feedback

This type of feedback is the most common. Evaluative feedback often involves judgment of the writer and his or her ethos (or credibility). We look for credibility clues when we examine the letterhead; feel the stationery; or read the message and note the professional language, correct grammar, and lack of spelling errors. Conversely, if the writer's credibility is undermined by errors, is perceived to be inappropriately informal, or presents questionable claims, the reader's view of the writer will be negative. The reader is less likely to read or respond to the message communicated by a source judged to lack credibility. In an interpersonal context, evaluative feedback may be communicated as a lack of eye contact, a frequent glance at a cell phone, or an overt act to avoid communication, such as walking away from the speaker. In written communication, we don't have the opportunity to watch the reader "walk away." As a business writer, your ethos is an important part of the message.

In aspects of interpersonal interaction, behavioral evaluations are one type of evaluative feedback. A behavioral evaluation assesses the action and not the actor, but the business writer lacks this context. You don't always know when or where your content will be read and evaluated, so it is in your best interest to be consistently professional. Fact checking, elimination of errors, and a professional image should be habits, not efforts of will. They should be an automatic part of the writing process for any business writer.

Interpretive Feedback

In the course of a conversation, you may not be completely sure you heard correctly, so it is often a good idea to paraphrase or restate what you heard as a way of requesting confirmation or clarification. You may also understand what was said, but restate the main point as a way of communicating attention. Listening is hard to assess in any conversation, and interpretive feedback allows the speaker to hear a clear demonstration of feedback that confirms that the message was understood or needs correction. Interpretive feedback requests confirmation or clarification of a message, and is often expressed in the form of a question.

In hard copy documents, we normally lack this feedback loop, but online documents increasingly allow for this form of exchange. You may find a "Comments" button at the end of an online article. When you click on the button, a text box will appear, providing a space and a medium for feedback from readers to the author, allowing an opportunity to respond with opinions, interpretations, and questions sparked by the article. Blogs incorporated this feature early in the development of Web content, but you can see variations of this feedback style all over the Web. This form of feedback is increasingly common in Facebook's wall and even in an article published in the online version of the *Wall Street Journal*.

Supportive Feedback

You come in second in a marathon to which you have dedicated the better part of a year in training. It was a challenging race and you are full of mixed emotions. The hug from your partner communicates support and meets your need in ways that transcend language and the exchange of symbolic meaning. In an interpersonal context it is easy to identify, describe, and even predict many representations of supportive feedback, but in other communication contexts it can prove a significant challenge.

You may give yourself encouragement as you mentally prepare for the race, and may receive backslaps and hugs after the race, but when you write about your experience, how do you experience supportive feedback? In the same way you receive evaluative or interpretive feedback via comments or to your Facebook wall, you may receive supportive feedback. Supportive feedback communicates encouragement in response to a message.

Probing Feedback

As you've read an article, have you ever wanted to learn more? Increasingly, embedded links allow a reader to explore related themes and content that give depth and breadth to content, but require the reader to be self-directed. Probing feedback communicates targeted requests for specific information. As an author, you've crafted the message and defined what information is included and what is beyond the scope of your document, but not every reader may agree with your framework. Some may perceive that a related idea is essential to the article, and specifically request additional information as a way of indicating that it should be included. Rather than responding defensively to requests for specific information and interpreting them as challenges to your authority as the author, see them for what they are: probing feedback. They are opportunities that you should respond to positively with the view that each is an opportunity to interact, clarify, and promote your position, product, or service.

Keeping a positive attitude is an important part of writing in general and feedback in particular. Not everyone is as skilled with words as you are, so their probing feedback may appear on the surface to be less than diplomatic; it may even come across as rude, ignorant, or unprofessional. But it will be to your advantage to see through the poor packaging of their feedback for the essential request, and respond in a positive, professional fashion.

Understanding Feedback

Rogers discussed the innate tendency for humans to desire to be understood. [5], [6] We, at times, may express frustration associated with a project at work. As we express ourselves to those we choose to share with, we seek not only information or solutions, but also acceptance and respect. We may not even want a solution, or need any information, but may simply want to be heard. Understanding feedback communicates sympathy and empathy for the source of the message.

As a business writer, you want your writing to be understood. When you receive feedback, it may not always be supportive or encouraging. Feedback is not always constructive, but it is always productive. Even if the feedback fails to demonstrate understanding or support for your cause or point, it demonstrates interest in the topic.

As a skilled communicator, you can recognize the types of feedback you are likely to receive from readers and can recognize that your readers may also desire feedback. Sometimes an author may communicate respect and understanding in a follow-up message. By providing a clarification, the writer can develop the relationship with the reader. Being professional involves keeping your goals in mind, and in order for your writing to be successful, you will need a positive relationship with your readers.

KEY TAKEAWAY

Feedback may be evaluative, interpretive, supportive, probing, or understanding, and it is always an opportunity for growth.

EXERCISES

1. Select a piece of writing such as an article from a Web site, newspaper, or magazine. Write at least one sentence of feedback in each of the five types described in this section. Do you find one type of feedback easier to give than another? If you were the author, how would you feel receiving this feedback? Discuss your thoughts with your classmates.

2. Review a Web site, article, or similar presentation of information. Focus on strengths and weaknesses from your perception and write a brief analysis and review. Please post your results and compare with classmates.

3. Find a blog or online article with comments posted after the document. Choose one example of feedback from the comments and share it with your classmates. Note any trends or themes that present themselves as you explore the comments.

4. Create a blog and post an opinion or editorial article. What kinds of feedback do you get from your readers? Compare and contrast your experiences with those of your classmates.

[1] Rogers, C. R. (1961). *On becoming a person: A therapist's view of psychotherapy.* Boston, MA: Houghton Mifflin.
[2] Rogers, C. R. (1970). *On encounter groups.* New York, NY: Harper & Row.
[3] Rogers, C. R. (1961). *On becoming a person: A therapist's view of psychotherapy.* Boston, MA: Houghton Mifflin.
[4] Rogers, C. R. (1970). *On encounter groups.* New York, NY: Harper & Row.
[5] Rogers, C. R. (1961). *On becoming a person: A therapist's view of psychotherapy.* Boston, MA: Houghton Mifflin.
[6] Rogers, C. R. (1970). *On encouter groups.* New York, NY: Harper & Row.

8.4 Additional Resources

- Online Writing Laboratory (OWL) at Purdue has a comprehensive guide to the writing process. http://owl.english.purdue.edu

- The newsletter *Managing Work Relations* offers an article on the grapevine and workplace gossip. http://www.workrelationships.com/site/newsletter/issue1.htm

- Visit this About.com page for an informative article for managers on how to deliver feedback to subordinates.http://humanresources.about.com/cs/communication/ht/Feedbackimpact.htm

- Read an inspiring story about feedback on this Helium.com page.http://www.helium.com/items/1231747-communication-skills-providing-feedback-that-has-an-impact

- Read more about how to accept and benefit from feedback in this e-zine article. http://ezinearticles.com/?Workplace-Communication---Accepting-Feedback&id=2147532

- Study Guides and Strategies presents an article on how to benefit from feedback when working with a tutor. http://www.studygs.net/feedback.htm

- AllBusiness presents an article on the five main methods of market research. http://www.allbusiness.com/marketing/market-research/1287-1.html

- Free Management Library presents an in-depth article on market research. http://managementhelp.org/mrktng/mk_rsrch/mk_rsrch.htm

- Explore the home page of SurveyMonkey and learn about some of the decisions that need to be made in the process of designing a survey. http://www.surveymonkey.com

- Read an article on how to organize a focus group by Carter McNamara, MBA, PhD. http://managementhelp.org/evaluatn/focusgrp.htm

- Writers often receive feedback by having their documents edited. Read about what an editor does on the home page of KOK Edit. http://www.kokedit.com

- ChangingMinds.org discusses Rogers's five feedback types with examples.http://changingminds.org/techniques/conversation/reflecting/rogers_feedback.htm

NOTES:

NOTES:

Chapter 9:
Business Writing in Action

If you call failures experiments, you can put them in your résumé and claim them as achievements.
   Mason Cooley
Volunteer—not so you can build your résumé, but so you can build yourself.
   Author Unknown

Getting Started

INTRODUCTORY EXERCISES

1. Review the different kinds of common business communication writing covered by the main headings in this chapter. Make a note of which kinds of documents you have produced in the past and which you have not. For example, have you written many memos but not a business report? Share and compare with classmates.
2. Conduct an online search for job descriptions associated with your chosen career and think about what tasks are accomplished in a typical day or week. If possible, also talk to someone who is employed in that career. Note the kinds of writing skills that are involved in carrying out job duties or tasks. Share your results with the class.

Business communication in written form requires skill and expertise. From text messages to reports, how you represent yourself with the written word counts. Writing in an online environment requires tact and skill, and an awareness that what you write may be there forever. From memos to letters, from business proposals to press releases, your written business communication represents you and your company: your goal is to make it clear, concise, and professional.

9.1 Text, E-mail, and Netiquette
LEARNING OBJECTIVES

1. Discuss the role of text messaging in business communication.
2. Write effective e-mails for both internal and external communication.
3. Demonstrate the appropriate use of netiquette.

Text messages and e-mails are part of our communication landscape, and skilled business communicators consider them a valuable tool to connect. Netiquette refers to etiquette, or protocols and norms for communication, on the Internet.

Texting

Whatever digital device you use, written communication in the form of brief messages, or texting, has become a common way to connect. It is useful for short exchanges, and is a convenient way to stay connected with others when talking on the phone would be cumbersome. Texting is not useful for long or complicated messages, and careful consideration should be given to the audience.

It is often said that you can tell how old someone is by how he or she inputs a phone number on a cell phone. If the person uses his or her thumb while holding the digital device, that person may have been raised on video games and be adept at one-handed interfaces. If he holds the digital device with one hand and inputs the number with the other, he may be over thirty, or may be less comfortable with some technological devices. Of course, there is no actual correlation between input and age, but it is a useful example to use when considering who your audience is when writing a text message. If the person is a one-hander, and knows all the abbreviations common to texting, you may be able to use similar codes to communicate effectively. If the person is a two-hander, you are better off using fewer words and spelling them out. Texting can be a great tool for connecting while on the go, but consider your audience and your company, and choose words, terms, or abbreviations that will deliver your message.

Tips for Effective Business Texting

- Know your recipient; "? % dsct" may be an understandable way to ask a close associate what the proper discount is to offer a certain customer, but if you are writing a text to your boss, it might be wiser to write, "what % discount does Murray get on $1K order?"
- Anticipate unintentional misinterpretation. Texting often uses symbols and codes to represent thoughts, ideas, and emotions. Given the complexity of communication, and the useful but limited tool of texting, be aware of its limitation and prevent misinterpretation with brief messages.
- Contacting someone too frequently can border on harassment. Texting is a tool. Use it when appropriate but don't abuse it.
- Unplug yourself once in a while. Do you feel constantly connected? Do you feel lost or "out of it" if you don't have your cell phone and cannot connect to people, even

for fifteen minutes? Sometimes being unavailable for a time can be healthy—everything in moderation, including texting.

- Don't text and drive. Research shows that the likelihood of an accident increases dramatically if the driver is texting behind the wheel. [1] Being in an accident while conducting company business would reflect poorly on your judgment as well as on your employer.

E-mail

Electronic mail, usually called e-mail, is quite familiar to most students and workers. It may be used like text, or synchronous chat, and it can be delivered to a cell phone. In business, it has largely replaced print hard copy letters for external (outside the company) correspondence, as well as taking the place of memos for internal (within the company) communication. [2] E-mail can be very useful for messages that have slightly more content than a text message, but it is still best used for fairly brief messages.

Many businesses use automated e-mails to acknowledge communications from the public, or to remind associates that periodic reports or payments are due. You may also be assigned to "populate" a form e-mail in which standard paragraphs are used but you choose from a menu of sentences to make the wording suitable for a particular transaction.

E-mails may be informal in personal contexts, but business communication requires attention to detail, awareness that your e-mail reflects you and your company, and a professional tone so that it may be forwarded to any third party if needed. E-mail often serves to exchange information within organizations. Although e-mail may have an informal feel, remember that when used for business, it needs to convey professionalism and respect. Never write or send anything that you wouldn't want read in public or in front of your company president.

Tips for Effective Business E-mails

- Proper salutations should demonstrate respect and avoid mix-ups in case a message is accidentally sent to the wrong recipient. For example, use a salutation like "Dear Ms. X" (external) or "Hi Barry" (internal).
- Subject lines should be clear, brief, and specific. This helps the recipient understand the essence of the message. For example, "Proposal attached" or "Your question of 10/25."
- Close with a signature. Identify yourself by creating a signature block that automatically contains your name and business contact information.
- Avoid abbreviations. An e-mail is not a text message, and the audience may not find your wit cause to ROTFLOL (roll on the floor laughing out loud).
- Be brief. Omit unnecessary words.
- Use a good format. Include line breaks between sentences or divide your message into brief paragraphs for ease of reading. A good e-mail should get to the point and conclude in three small paragraphs or less.
- Reread, revise, and review. Catch and correct spelling and grammar mistakes before you press "send." It will take more time and effort to undo the problems caused by a hasty, poorly written e-mail than to get it right the first time.
- Reply promptly. Watch out for an emotional response—never reply in anger—but make a habit of replying to all e-mails within twenty-four hours, even if only to say that you will provide the requested information in forty-eight or seventy-two hours.
- Use "Reply All" sparingly. Do not send your reply to everyone who received the initial e-mail unless your message absolutely needs to be read by the entire group.
- Avoid using all caps. Capital letters are used on the Internet to communicate emphatic emotion or yelling and are considered rude.
- Test links. If you include a link, test it to make sure it is complete.
- E-mail ahead of time if you are going to attach large files (audio and visual files are often quite large) to prevent exceeding the recipient's mailbox limit or triggering the spam filter.
- Give feedback or follow up. If you don't get a response in twenty-four hours, e-mail or call. Spam filters may have intercepted your message, so your recipient may never have received it.

Let's look at two examples of business e-mail. In Figure 9.1, we have an e-mail form. In Figure 9.2, we have a letter written specifically for the situation and audience.

Figure 9.1

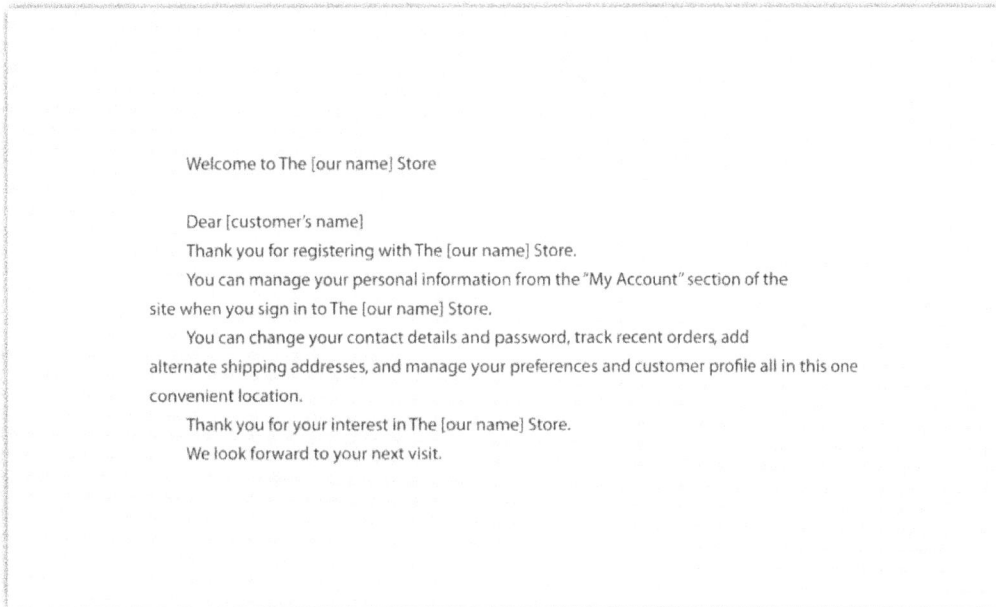

Welcome to The [our name] Store

Dear [customer's name]
Thank you for registering with The [our name] Store.
You can manage your personal information from the "My Account" section of the
site when you sign in to The [our name] Store.
You can change your contact details and password, track recent orders, add
alternate shipping addresses, and manage your preferences and customer profile all in this one
convenient location.
Thank you for your interest in The [our name] Store.
We look forward to your next visit.

Figure 9.2

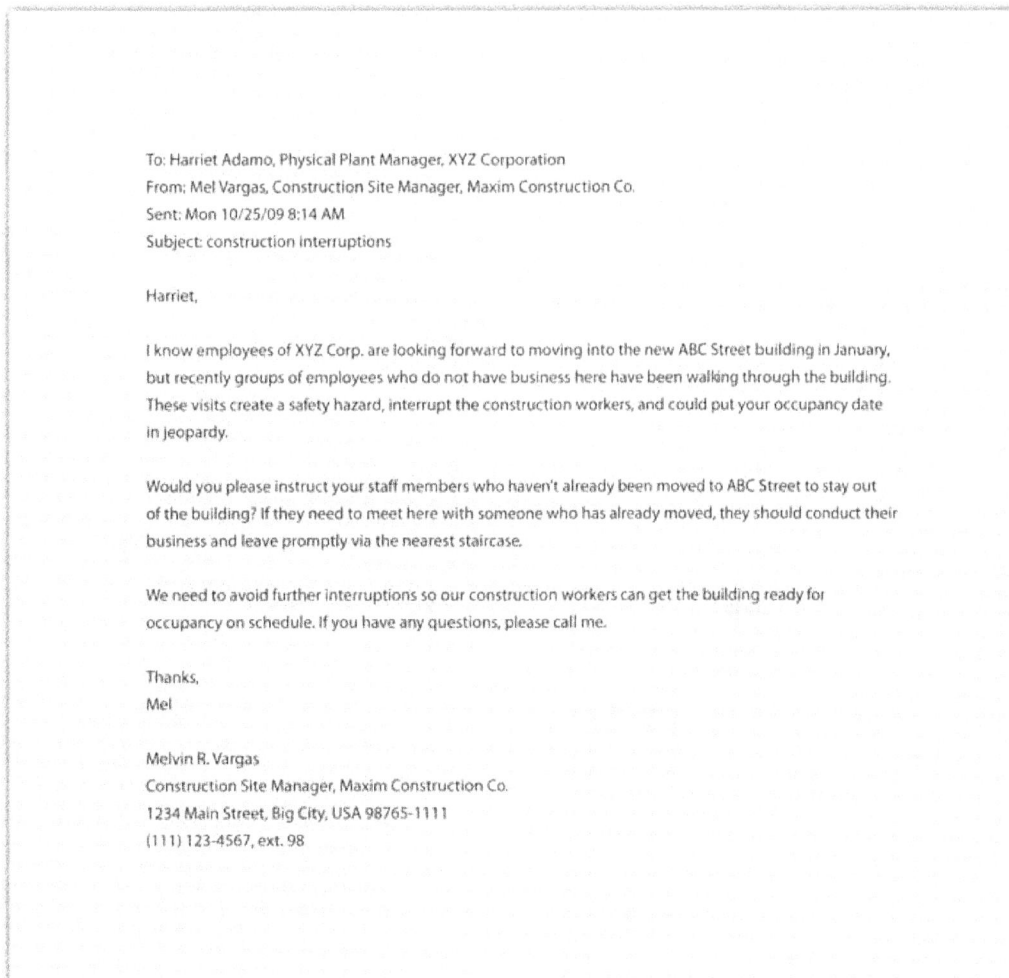

To: Harriet Adamo, Physical Plant Manager, XYZ Corporation
From: Mel Vargas, Construction Site Manager, Maxim Construction Co.
Sent: Mon 10/25/09 8:14 AM
Subject: construction interruptions

Harriet,

I know employees of XYZ Corp. are looking forward to moving into the new ABC Street building in January,
but recently groups of employees who do not have business here have been walking through the building.
These visits create a safety hazard, interrupt the construction workers, and could put your occupancy date
in jeopardy.

Would you please instruct your staff members who haven't already been moved to ABC Street to stay out
of the building? If they need to meet here with someone who has already moved, they should conduct their
business and leave promptly via the nearest staircase.

We need to avoid further interruptions so our construction workers can get the building ready for
occupancy on schedule. If you have any questions, please call me.

Thanks,
Mel

Melvin R. Vargas
Construction Site Manager, Maxim Construction Co.
1234 Main Street, Big City, USA 98765-1111
(111) 123-4567, ext. 98

Netiquette

We create personal pages, post messages, and interact via mediated technologies as a normal part of our careers, but how we conduct ourselves can leave a lasting image, literally. The photograph you posted on your Facebook page may have been seen by your potential employer, or that nasty remark in a post may come back to haunt you later. Some fifteen years ago, when the Internet was a new phenomenon, Virginia Shea laid out a series of ground rules for communication online that continue to serve us today.

Virginia Shea's Rules of Netiquette

- Remember the human on the other side of the electronic communication.
- Adhere to the same standards of behavior online that you follow in real life.
- Know where you are in cyberspace.
- Respect other people's time and bandwidth.
- Make yourself look good online.
- Share expert knowledge.
- Keep flame wars under control.
- Respect other people's privacy.
- Don't abuse your power.
- Be forgiving of other people's mistakes. [3]

Her rules speak for themselves and remind us that the golden rule (treat others as you would like to be treated) is relevant wherever there is human interaction.

KEY TAKEAWAYS

- A text message is a brief written message sent and received using a digital device. It is useful for informal, brief, time-sensitive communication.
- E-mail is useful for both internal and external business communications. The content and formatting of an e-mail message should reflect professionalism and follow the rules of netiquette.
- Social customs that exist in traditional, live, human interaction also influence the rules and customs by which we interact with each other in the online environment.

EXERCISES

1. Write a text message in your normal use of language. It should use all your normal abbreviations (e.g., FWIW, IMHO, LOL), even if not everyone understands them.
2. Find an example of an e-mail that you wish you had never sent or received. Rewrite it to eliminate the characteristics that you find problematic. Share it with your classmates.
3. Choose at least three e-mails you have sent or received that are good examples of business communication.

What makes them good examples? Could they be improved in any way? Share your suggestions with classmates.
4. When is e-mail inappropriate? Why?
5. Find a "flame war," or heated discussion in an online forum and note how it is handled. Compare the results with your classmates.
6. In your experience, how do people behave when they interact online? Share your observations with your classmates.

---

[1] Houston Chronicle. (2009, September 23). Deadly distraction: Texting while driving, twice as risky as drunk driving, should be banned. *Houston Chronicle* (3 STAR R.O. ed.), p. B8. Retrieved fromhttp://www.chron.com/CDA/archives/archive.mpl?id=2009_4791006
[2] Guffey, M. (2008). *Essentials of business communication* (7th ed.). Mason, OH: Thomson/Wadsworth.
[3] Shea, V. (1994). *Netiquette*. San Francisco, CA: Albion Books.

9.2 Memorandums and Letters
LEARNING OBJECTIVES

1. Discuss the purpose and format of a memo.
2. Understand effective strategies for business memos.
3. Describe the fifteen parts of a standard business letter.
4. Access sample business letters and write a sample business letter.

Memos

A memo (or memorandum, meaning "reminder") is normally used for communicating policies, procedures, or related official business within an organization. It is often written from a one-to-all perspective (like mass communication), broadcasting a message to an audience, rather than a one-on-one, interpersonal communication. It may also be used to update a team on activities for a given project, or to inform a specific group within a company of an event, action, or observance.

Memo Purpose

A memo's purpose is often to inform, but it occasionally includes an element of persuasion or a call to action. All organizations have informal and formal communication networks. The unofficial, informal communication network within an organization is often called the grapevine, and it is often characterized by rumor, gossip, and innuendo. On the grapevine, one person may hear that someone else is going to be laid off and start passing the news around. Rumors change and transform as they are passed from person to person, and before you know it, the word is that they are shutting down your entire department.

One effective way to address informal, unofficial speculation is to spell out clearly for all employees what is going on with a particular issue. If budget cuts are a concern, then it may be wise to send a memo explaining the changes that are imminent. If a company wants employees to take action, they may also issue a memorandum. For example, on February 13, 2009, upper management at the Panasonic Corporation issued a declaration that all employees should buy at least $1,600 worth of Panasonic products. The company president noted that if everyone supported the company with purchases, it would benefit all. [1]

While memos do not normally include a call to action that requires personal spending, they often represent the business or organization's interests. They may also include statements that align business and employee interest, and underscore common ground and benefit.

Memo Format

A memo has a header that clearly indicates who sent it and who the intended recipients are. Pay particular attention to the title of the individual(s) in this section. Date and subject lines are also present, followed by a message that contains a declaration, a discussion, and a summary.

In a standard writing format, we might expect to see an introduction, a body, and a conclusion. All these are present in a memo, and each part has a clear purpose. The declaration in the opening uses a declarative sentence to announce the main topic. The discussion elaborates or lists major points associated with the topic, and the conclusion serves as a summary.

Let's examine a sample memo.

Figure 9.3

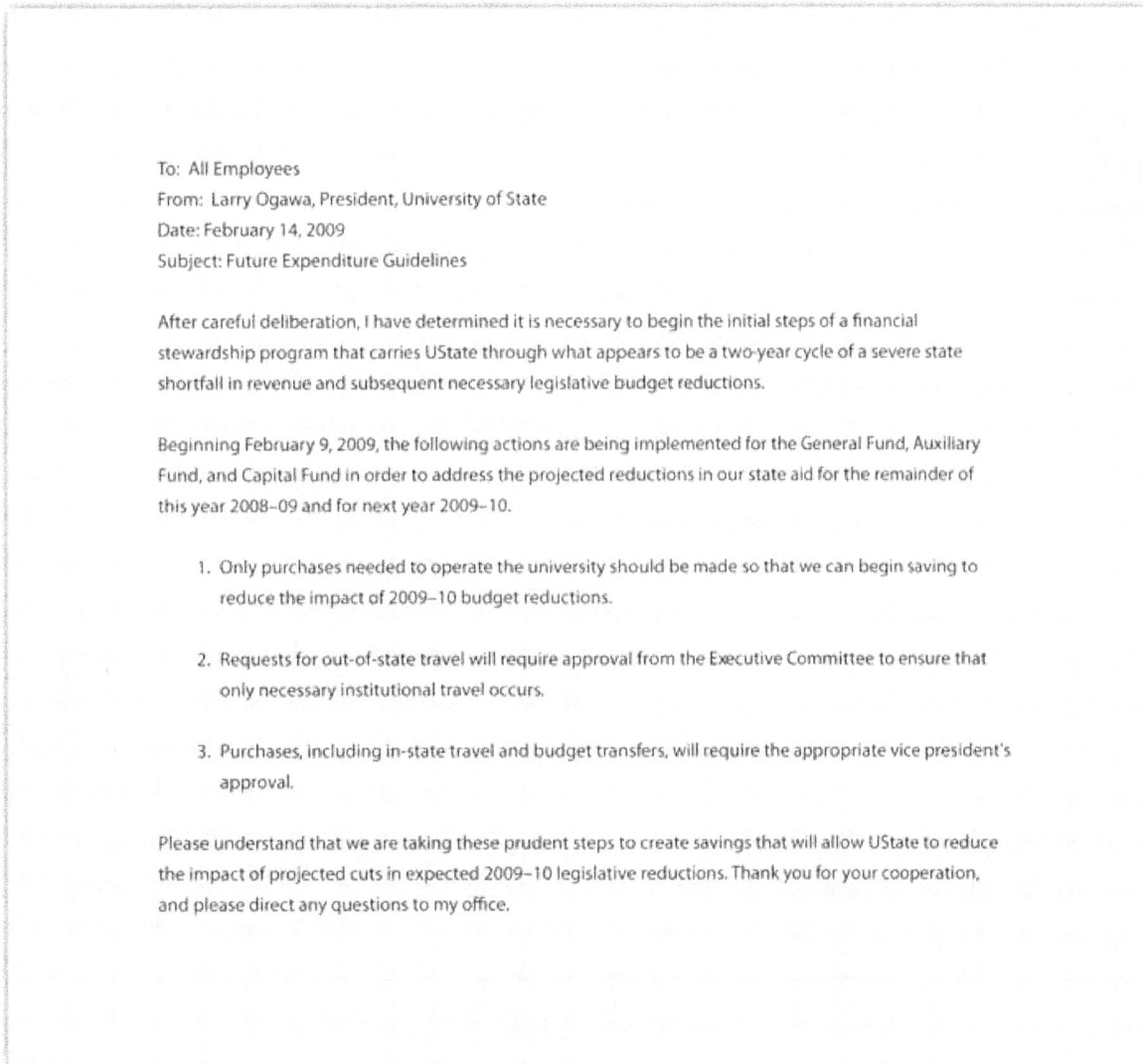

To: All Employees
From: Larry Ogawa, President, University of State
Date: February 14, 2009
Subject: Future Expenditure Guidelines

After careful deliberation, I have determined it is necessary to begin the initial steps of a financial stewardship program that carries UState through what appears to be a two-year cycle of a severe state shortfall in revenue and subsequent necessary legislative budget reductions.

Beginning February 9, 2009, the following actions are being implemented for the General Fund, Auxiliary Fund, and Capital Fund in order to address the projected reductions in our state aid for the remainder of this year 2008–09 and for next year 2009–10.

1. Only purchases needed to operate the university should be made so that we can begin saving to reduce the impact of 2009–10 budget reductions.

2. Requests for out-of-state travel will require approval from the Executive Committee to ensure that only necessary institutional travel occurs.

3. Purchases, including in-state travel and budget transfers, will require the appropriate vice president's approval.

Please understand that we are taking these prudent steps to create savings that will allow UState to reduce the impact of projected cuts in expected 2009–10 legislative reductions. Thank you for your cooperation, and please direct any questions to my office.

Five Tips for Effective Business Memos

Audience Orientation

Always consider the audience and their needs when preparing a memo. An acronym or abbreviation that is known to management may not be known by all the employees of the organization, and if the memo is to be posted and distributed within the organization, the goal is clear and concise communication at all levels with no ambiguity.

Professional, Formal Tone

Memos are often announcements, and the person sending the memo speaks for a part or all of the organization. While it may contain a request for feedback, the announcement itself is linear, from the organization to the employees. The memo may have legal standing as it often reflects policies or procedures, and may reference an existing or new policy in the employee manual, for example.

Subject Emphasis

The subject is normally declared in the subject line and should be clear and concise. If the memo is announcing the observance of a holiday, for example, the specific holiday should be named in the subject line—for example, use "Thanksgiving weekend schedule" rather than "holiday observance."

Direct Format

Some written business communication allows for a choice between direct and indirect formats, but memorandums are always direct. The purpose is clearly announced.

Objectivity

Memos are a place for just the facts, and should have an objective tone without personal bias, preference, or interest on display. Avoid subjectivity.

Letters

Letters are brief messages sent to recipients that are often outside the organization. [2] They are often printed on letterhead paper, and represent the business or organization in one or two pages. Shorter messages may include e-mails or memos, either hard copy or electronic, while reports tend to be three or more pages in length.

While e-mail and text messages may be used more frequently today, the effective business letter remains a common form of written communication. It can serve to introduce you to a potential employer, announce a product or service, or even serve to communicate feelings and emotions. We'll examine the basic outline of a letter and then focus on specific products or writing assignments.

All writing assignments have expectations in terms of language and format. The audience or reader may have their own idea of what constitutes a specific type of letter, and your organization may have its own format and requirements. This chapter outlines common elements across letters, and attention should be directed to the expectations associated with your particular writing assignment. There are many types of letters, and many adaptations in terms of form and content, but in this chapter, we discuss the fifteen elements of a traditional block-style letter.

Letters may serve to introduce your skills and qualifications to prospective employers, deliver important or specific information, or serve as documentation of an event or decision. Regardless of the type of letter you need to write, it can contain up to fifteen elements in five areas. While you may not use all the elements in every case or context, they are listed in Table 9.1 "Elements of a Business Letter".

Table 9.1 Elements of a Business Letter

Content	Guidelines
1. Return Address	This is your address where someone could send a reply. If your letter includes a letterhead with this information, either in the header (across the top of the page) or the footer (along the bottom of the page), you do not need to include it before the date.
2. Date	The date should be placed at the top, right or left justified, five lines from the top of the page or letterhead logo.
3. Reference (Re:)	Like a subject line in an e-mail, this is where you indicate what the letter is in reference to, the subject or purpose of the document.
4. Delivery (Optional)	Sometimes you want to indicate on the letter itself how it was delivered. This can make it clear to a third party that the letter was delivered via a specific method, such as certified mail (a legal requirement for some types of documents).

Content	Guidelines
5. Recipient Note (Optional)	This is where you can indicate if the letter is personal or confidential.
6. Salutation	A common salutation may be "Dear Mr. (full name)." But if you are unsure about titles (i.e., Mrs., Ms., Dr.), you may simply write the recipient's name (e.g., "Dear Cameron Rai") followed by a colon. A comma after the salutation is correct for personal letters, but a colon should be used in business. The salutation "To whom it may concern" is appropriate for letters of recommendation or other letters that are intended to be read by any and all individuals. If this is not the case with your letter, but you are unsure of how to address your recipient, make every effort to find out to whom the letter should be specifically addressed. For many, there is no sweeter sound than that of their name, and to spell it incorrectly runs the risk of alienating the reader before your letter has even been read. Avoid the use of impersonal salutations like "Dear Prospective Customer," as the lack of personalization can alienate a future client.
7. Introduction	This is your opening paragraph, and may include an attention statement, a reference to the purpose of the document, or an introduction of the person or topic depending on the type of letter. An emphatic opening involves using the most significant or important element of the letter in the introduction. Readers tend to pay attention to openings, and it makes sense to outline the expectations for the reader up front. Just as you would preview your topic in a speech, the clear opening in your introductions establishes context and facilitates comprehension.
8. Body	If you have a list of points, a series of facts, or a number of questions, they belong in the body of your letter. You may choose organizational devices to draw attention, such as a bullet list, or simply number them. Readers may skip over information in the body of your letter, so make sure you emphasize the key points clearly. This is your core content, where you can outline and support several key points. Brevity is important, but so is clear support for main point(s). Specific, meaningful information needs to be clear, concise, and accurate.
9. Conclusion	An emphatic closing mirrors your introduction with the added element of tying the main points together, clearly demonstrating their relationship. The conclusion can serve to remind the reader, but should not introduce new information. A clear summary sentence will strengthen your writing and enhance your effectiveness. If your letter requests or implies action, the conclusion needs to make clear what you expect to happen. It is usually courteous to conclude by thanking the recipient for his or her attention, and to invite them to contact you if you can be of help or if they have questions. This paragraph reiterates the main points and their relationship to each other, reinforcing the main point or purpose.
10. Close	"Sincerely" or "Cordially" are standard business closing statements. ("Love," "Yours Truly," and "BFF" are closing statements suitable for personal correspondence, but not for business.) Closing statements are normally placed one or two lines under the conclusion and include a hanging comma, as in Sincerely,
11. Signature	Five lines after the close, you should type your name (required) and, on the line below it, your title (optional).
12. Preparation Line	If the letter was prepared, or word-processed, by someone other than the signatory (you), then inclusion of initials is common, as in MJD or abc.
13. Enclosures/Attachments	Just like an e-mail with an attachment, the letter sometimes has additional documents that are delivered with it. This line indicates what the reader can look for in terms of documents included with the letter, such as brochures, reports, or related business documents.
14. Courtesy Copies or "CC"	The abbreviation "CC" once stood for carbon copies but now refers to courtesy copies. Just like a "CC" option in an e-mail, it indicates the relevant parties that will also receive a copy of the document.
15. Logo/Contact Information	A formal business letter normally includes a logo or contact information for the organization in the header (top of page) or footer (bottom of page).

Strategies for Effective Letters

Remember that a letter has five main areas:

1. The heading, which establishes the sender, often including address and date
2. The introduction, which establishes the purpose
3. The body, which articulates the message
4. The conclusion, which restates the main point and may include a call to action
5. The signature line, which sometimes includes the contact information

Figure 9.5 Sample Business Letter

(1 inch margins on all sides of the letter)

1. **Return Address**: (if not in letterhead logo)
2. **Date**: 01/01/201X

3. **Reference—Re**: How to write a letter

4. **Delivery** (optional): USPS Certified Mail #123456789

5. **Recipient Note** (optional): Confidential

6. **Salutation**: Dear Student X:

7. **Introduction**: This letter is to inform you that the myth of a paperless office, where you will not be required to produce hard copy letters on letterhead, is a myth.

8. **Body**: While e-mail has largely replaced letter writing for many applications, there remain several reasons for producing a hard copy letter. The first reason is that you are required to write it for this class, as many employers still produce letters as a normal part of business communication, including documentation. Next, we must consider that paper sales in business have increased across the last decade, showing no signs of the decrease we would associate with the transition to the paperless office. Finally, business letters serve many functions, and your proficiency in their efficient and effective production will contribute to your personal and professional success.

9. **Conclusion**: Letter writing is a skill that will continue to be required in the business environment of today and tomorrow.

10. **Close**: Sincerely,

11. **Signature Line**: Scott McLean

12. **Preparation Line**: GSM/ep

13. **Enclosures**: (optional, if needed)

14. **Courtesy Copies**: cc: Jenn Yee

15. **Logo/Contact Information**:   flatworld   13 N. Mill Street
Nyack, NY 10960

Always remember that letters represent you and your company in your absence. In order to communicate effectively and project a positive image,

- be clear, concise, specific, and respectful;
- each word should contribute to your purpose;
- each paragraph should focus on one idea;
- the parts of the letter should form a complete message;
- the letter should be free of errors.

KEY TAKEAWAYS

- Memos are brief business documents usually used internally to inform or persuade employees concerning business decisions on policy, procedure, or actions.
- Letters are brief, print messages often used externally to inform or persuade customers, vendors, or the public.
- A letter has fifteen parts, each fulfilling a specific function.

EXERCISES

1. Find a memo from your work or business, or borrow one from someone you know. Share it with your classmates, observing confidentiality by blocking out identifying details such as the name of the sender, recipient, and company. Compare and contrast.
2. Create a draft letter introducing a product or service to a new client. Post and share with classmates.
3. Write a memo informing your class that an upcoming holiday will be observed. Post and share with classmates.
4. Find a business letter (for example, an offer you received from a credit card company or a solicitation for a donation) and share it with your classmates. Look for common elements and points of difference.
5. Now that you have reviewed a sample letter, and learned about the five areas and fifteen basic parts of any business letter, write a business letter that informs a prospective client or customer of a new product or service.

[1] Lewis, L. (2009, February 13). *Panasonic orders staff to buy £1,000 in products.* Retrieved fromhttp://business.timesonline.co.uk/tol/business/markets/japan/article5723942.ece
[2] Bovee, C., & Thill, J. (2010). *Business communication essentials: a skills-based approach to vital business English* (4th ed.). Upper Saddle River, NJ: Prentice Hall.

9.3 Business Proposal
LEARNING OBJECTIVES

1. Describe the basic elements of a business proposal.
2. Discuss the main goals of a business proposal.
3. Identify effective strategies to use in a business proposal.

An effective business proposal informs and persuades efficiently. It features many of the common elements of a report, but its emphasis on persuasion guides the overall presentation.

Let's say you work in a health care setting. What types of products or services might be put out to bid? If your organization is going to expand and needs to construct a new wing, it will probably be put out to bid. Everything from office furniture to bedpans could potentially be put out to bid, specifying a quantity, quality, and time of delivery required. Janitorial services may also be bid on each year, as well as food services, and even maintenance. Using the power of bidding to lower contract costs for goods and services is common practice.

In order to be successful in business and industry, you should be familiar with the business proposal. Much like a report, with several common elements and persuasive speech, a business proposal makes the case for your product or service. Business proposals are documents designed to make a persuasive appeal to the audience to achieve a defined outcome, often proposing a solution to a problem.

Common Proposal Elements

Idea

Effective business proposals are built around a great idea or solution. While you may be able to present your normal product, service, or solution in an interesting way, you want your document and its solution to stand out against the background of competing proposals. What makes your idea different or unique? How can you better meet the needs of the company that other vendors? What makes you so special? If the purchase decision is made solely on price, it may leave you little room to underscore the value of service, but the sale follow-through has value. For example, don't consider just the cost of the unit but also its maintenance. How can maintenance be a part of your solution, distinct from the rest? In addition, your proposal may focus on a common product where you can anticipate several vendors at similar prices. How can you differentiate yourself from the rest by underscoring long-term relationships, demonstrated ability to deliver, or the ability to anticipate the company's needs? Business proposals need to have an attractive idea or solution in order to be effective.

Table 9.2 Business Proposal Format

Cover Page	Title page with name, title, date, and specific reference to request for proposal if applicable.
Executive Summary	Like an abstract in a report, this is a one- or two-paragraph summary of the product or service and how it meets the requirements and exceeds expectations.
Background	Discuss the history of your product, service, and/or company and consider focusing on the relationship between you and the potential buyer and/or similar companies.
Proposal	The idea. *Who*, *what*, *where*, *when*, *why*, and *how*. Make it clear and concise. Don't waste words, and don't exaggerate. Use clear, well-supported reasoning to demonstrate your product or service.
Market Analysis	What currently exists in the marketplace, including competing products or services, and how does your solution compare?
Benefits	How will the potential buyer benefit from the product or service? Be clear, concise, specific, and provide a comprehensive list of immediate, short, and long-term benefits to the company.
Timeline	A clear presentation, often with visual aids, of the process, from start to finish, with specific, dated benchmarks noted.
Marketing Plan	Delivery is often the greatest challenge for Web-based services—how will people learn about you? If you are bidding on a gross lot of food service supplies, this may not apply to you, but if an audience is required for success, you will need a marketing plan.
Finance	What are the initial costs, when can revenue be anticipated, when will there be a return on investment (if applicable)? Again, the proposal may involve a one-time fixed cost, but if the product or service is to be delivered more than once, and extended financial plan noting costs across time is required.
Conclusion	Like a speech or essay, restate your main points clearly. Tie them together with a common them and make your proposal memorable.

Traditional Categories

You can be creative in many aspects of the business proposal, but follow the traditional categories. Businesses expect to see information in a specific order, much like a résumé or even a letter. Each aspect of your proposal has its place and it is to your advantage to respect that tradition and use the categories effectively to highlight your product or service. Every category is an opportunity to sell, and should reinforce your credibility, your passion, and the reason why your solution is simply the best.

In the same way, if you are not enthusiastic about the product or service, why should the potential client get excited? How does your solution stand out in the marketplace? Why should they consider you? Why should they continue reading? Passion and enthusiasm are not only communicated through "!" exclamation points. Your thorough understanding, and your demonstration of that understanding, communicates dedication and interest.

Each assertion requires substantiation, each point clear support. It is not enough to make baseless claims about your product or service—you have to show why the claims you make are true, relevant, and support your central assertion that your product or service is right for this client. Make sure you cite sources and indicate "according to" when you support your points. Be detailed and specific.

Professional

A professional document is a base requirement. If it is less than professional, you can count on its prompt dismissal. There should be no errors in spelling or grammar, and all information should be concise, accurate, and clearly referenced when appropriate. Information that pertains to credibility should be easy to find and clearly relevant, including contact information. If the document exists in a hard copy form, it should be printed on a letterhead. If the document is submitted in an electronic form, it should be in a file format that presents your document as you intended. Word processing files may have their formatting changed or adjusted based on factors you cannot control—like screen size—and information can shift out of place, making it difficult to understand. In this case, a portable document format (PDF)—a format for electronic documents—may be used to preserve content location and avoid any inadvertent format changes when it is displayed.

Effective, persuasive proposals are often brief, even limited to one page. "The one-page proposal has been one of the keys to my business success, and it can be invaluable to you too. Few decision-makers can ever afford to read more than one page when deciding if they are interested in a deal or not. This is even more true for people of a different culture or language," said Adnan Khashoggi, a successful multibillionaire. [1] Clear and concise proposals serve the audience well and limit the range of information to prevent confusion.

Two Types of Business Proposals

Solicited
If you have been asked to submit a proposal it is considered solicited. The solicitation may come in the form of a direct verbal or written request, but normally solicitations are indirect, open-bid to the public, and formally published for everyone to see. A request for proposal (RFP), request for quotation (RFQ), and invitation for bid (IFB) are common ways to solicit business proposals for business, industry, and the government.

RFPs typically specify the product or service, guidelines for submission, and evaluation criteria. RFQs emphasize cost, though service and maintenance may be part of the solicitation. IRBs are often job-specific in that they encompass a project that requires a timeline, labor, and materials. For example, if a local school district announces the construction of a new elementary school, they normally have the architect and engineering plans on file, but need a licensed contractor to build it.

Unsolicited
Unsolicited proposals are the "cold calls" of business writing. They require a thorough understanding of the market, product and/or service, and their presentation is typically general rather than customer-specific. They can, however, be tailored to specific businesses with time and effort, and the demonstrated knowledge of specific needs or requirement can transform an otherwise generic, brochure-like proposal into an effective sales message. Getting your tailored message to your target audience, however, is often a significant challenge if it has not been directly or indirectly solicited. Unsolicited proposals are often regarded as marketing materials, intended more to stimulate interest for a follow-up

contact than make direct sales. Sue Baugh and Robert Hamper encourage you to resist the temptation to "shoot at every target and hope you hit at least one." [2] A targeted proposal is your most effective approach, but recognize the importance of gaining company, service, or brand awareness as well as its limitations.

Sample Business Proposal
The Writing Help Tools Center is a commercial enterprise, and offers a clear (and free) example of a business proposal here: http://www.writinghelptools.com/proposal-sample.html

KEY TAKEAWAY

Business proposals need to target a specific audience.

EXERCISES

1. Click on this link to see a sample request for proposal from the American Institute of Public Accounts. http://www.aicpa.org/audcommctr/toolkitsnpo/SampleRFP_for_CPA_Services.htm

2. Prepare a business proposal in no more than two pages. Follow the guidelines provided in the sample letter for CPA services on the American Institute of Public Accountants Web site. Do not include actual contact information. Just as the example has employees named after colors, your (imaginary) company should have contact information that does not directly link to real businesses or you as an individual. Do not respond to point 12.

3. Search for an RFP (request for proposal) or similar call to bid, and post it to your class. Compare the results with your classmates, focusing on what is required to apply or bid.

4. Identify a product or service you would like to produce or offer. List three companies that you would like to sell your product or service to and learn more about them. Post your findings, making the link between your product or service and company needs. You may find the Web site on creating a business plan (http://www.myownbusiness.org/s2/#3) useful when completing this exercise.

[1] Riley, P. G. (2002). *The one-page proposal: How to get your business pitch onto one persuasive page* (p. 2). New York, NY: HarperCollins.
[2] Baugh, L. S., & Hamper, R. J. (1995). *Handbook for writing proposals* (p. 3). New York, NY: McGraw-Hill.

9.4 Report
LEARNING OBJECTIVES

1. Discuss the main parts of a report.
2. Understand the different types of reports.
3. Write a basic report.

What Is a Report?

Reports are documents designed to record and convey information to the reader. Reports are part of any business or organization; from credit reports to police reports, they serve to document specific information for specific audiences, goals, or functions. The type of report is often identified by its primary purpose or function, as in an accident report, a laboratory report, a sales report, or even a book report. Reports are often analytical, or involve the rational analysis of information. Sometimes they simply "report the facts" with no analysis at all, but still need to communicate the information in a clear and concise format. Other reports summarize past events, present current data, and forecast future trends. While a report may have conclusions, propositions, or even a call to action, the demonstration of the analysis is the primary function. A sales report, for example, is not designed to make an individual sale. It is, however, supposed to report sales to date, and may forecast future sales based on previous trends. This chapter is designed to introduce you to the basics of report writing.

Types of Reports

Reports come in all sizes, but are typically longer than a page and somewhat shorter than a book. The type of report depends on its function. The function of the report is its essential purpose, often indicated in the thesis or purpose statement. The function will also influence the types of visual content or visual aids, representing words, numbers, and their relationships to the central purpose in graphic, representational ways that are easy for the reader to understand. The function may also contribute to parameters like report length (page or word count) or word choice and readability. "Focusing on the content of your longer business documents is not only natural but necessary because doing so helps ensure complete, correct information." [1]

Reports vary by function, and they also vary by style and tradition. Within your organization, there may be employer-specific expectations that need to be addressed to meet audience expectations. This chapter discusses reports in general terms, focusing on common elements and points of distinction, but reference to similar documents where you work or additional examination of specific sample reports may serve you well as you prepare your own report.

Informational or Analytical Report?

There are two main categories for reports, regardless of their specific function or type. An informational report informs or instructs and presents details of events, activities, individuals, or conditions without analysis. An example of this type of "just the facts" report is a police accident report. The report will note the time, date, place, contributing factors like weather, and identification information for the drivers involved in an automobile accident. It does not establish fault or include judgmental statements. You should not see "Driver was falling down drunk" in a police accident report. Instead, you would see "Driver failed sobriety tests and breathalyzer test and was transported to the station for a blood sample." The police officer is not a trained medical doctor and is therefore not licensed to make definitive diagnoses, but can collect and present relevant information that may contribute to that diagnosis.

The second type of report is called an analytical report. An analytical report presents information with a comprehensive analysis to solve problems, demonstrate relationships, or make recommendations. An example of this report may be a field report by a Center for Disease Control (CDC) physician from the site of an outbreak of the H1N1 virus, noting symptoms, disease progression, steps taken to arrest the spread of the disease, and to make recommendations on the treatment and quarantine of subjects.

Table 9.3 "Types of Reports and Their Functions" includes common reports that, depending on the audience needs, may be informational or analytical.

Table 9.3 Types of Reports and Their Functions

Type	Function
1. Laboratory Report	Communicate the procedures and results of laboratory activities
2. Research Report	Study problems scientifically by developing hypotheses, collecting data, analyzing data, and indicating findings or conclusions
3. Field Study Report	Describe one-time events, such as trips, conferences, seminars, as well as reports from branch offices, industrial and manufacturing plants
4. Progress Report	Monitor and control production, sales, shipping, service, or related business process

Type	Function
5. Technical Report	Communication process and product from a technical perspective
6. Financial Report	Communication status and trends from a finance perspective
7. Case Study	Represent, analyze, and present lessons learned from a specific case or example
8. Needs Assessment Report	Assess the need for a service or product
9. Comparative Advantage Report	Discuss competing products or services with an analysis of relative advantages and disadvantages
10. Feasibility Study	Analyze problems and predict whether current solutions or alternatives will be practical, advisable, or produced the desired outcome(s)
11. Instruction Manuals	Communicate step-by-step instructions on the use of a product or service
12. Compliance Report	Document and indicate the extent to which a product or service is within established compliance parameters or standards
13. Cost-Benefit Analysis Report	Communicate costs and benefits of products or services.
14. Decision Report	Make recommendations to management and become tools to solve problems and make decisions
15. Benchmark Report	Establish criteria and evaluate alternatives by measuring against the establish benchmark criteria
16. Examination Report	Report or record data obtained from an examination of an item or conditions, including accidents and natural disasters
17. Physical Description report	Describe the physical characteristics of a machine, a device, or object
18. Literature Review	Present summaries of the information available on a given subject

How Are Reports Organized?

Reports vary by size, format, and function. You need to be flexible and adjust to the needs of the audience while respecting customs and guidelines. Reports are typically organized around six key elements:

1. Whom the report is about and/or prepared for
2. What was done, what problems were addressed, and the results, including conclusions and/or recommendations
3. Where the subject studied occurred
4. When the subject studied occurred
5. Why the report was written (function), including under what authority, for what reason, or by whose request
6. How the subject operated, functioned, or was used

Pay attention to these essential elements when you consider your stakeholders, or those who have an interest in the report. That may include the person(s) the report is about, whom it is for, and the larger audience of the business, organization, or industry. Ask yourself who the key decision makers are

who will read your report, who the experts or technicians will be, and how executives and workers may interpret your words and images. While there is no universal format for a report, there is a common order to the information. Each element supports the main purpose or function in its own way, playing an important role in the representation and transmission of information.

Here is a checklist for ensuring that a report fulfills its goals:

1. Report considers the audience's needs
2. Format follows function of report
3. Format reflects institutional norms and expectations
4. Information is accurate, complete, and documented
5. Information is easy to read
6. Terms are clearly defined
7. Figures, tables, and art support written content
8. Figures, tables, and art are clear and correctly labeled
9. Figures, tables, and art are easily understood without text support

10. Words are easy to read (font, arrangement, organization)
11. Results are clear and concise
12. Recommendations are reasonable and well-supported
13. Report represents your best effort

14. Report speaks for itself without your clarification or explanation

Table 9.4 Ten Common Elements of a Report

Page	Element	Function	Example
1. Cover	Title and image	Like the cover of a book, sometimes a picture, image, or logo is featured to introduce the topic to the reader.	
2. Title Fly	Title only	This page is optional.	Feasibility Study of Oil Recovery from the X Tarpit Sands Location
3. Title Page	Label, report, features title, author, affiliation, date, and sometimes for whom the report was prepared		Feasibility Study of Oil Recovery from the X Tarpit Sands Location Peak Oilman, X Energy Corporation Prepared for X
4. Table of Contents	A list of the main parts of the report and their respective page numbers		Abstract......1 Introduction......2 Background......3
5. Abstract	Informational abstract: highlight topic, methods, data, and results Descriptive abstract: (All of the above without statements of conclusion or recommendations)		This report presents the current status of the X tarpit sands, the study of oil recoverability, and the findings of the study with specific recommendations.
6. Introduction	Introduces the topic of the report		*Oil sands recovery* processes include ways to extract and separate the bitumen from the clay, *sand*, and water that make up the tar *sands. This study analyzes the feasibility of extraction and separation, including a comprehensive cost/benefits analysis, with specific recommendations.*
7. Body	Key elements of body include: Background Methodology Results Analysis and Recommendations		Background: History of oil extraction and separation from tarpit sands. Methodology: Specific analysis of the site based on accepted research methods. Results: Data from the feasibility study. Analysis and Recommendations: Analysis of the data and recommendations based on that analysis.
8. Conclusion	Concise presentation of findings	This portion clearly indicates the main results and their relation to recommended action or outcome.	
9. References	Bibliography or Works Cited	This part contains a list of citations.	
10. Appendix	Related supporting materials	This may include maps, analysis of soil samples, and field reports.	

KEY TAKEAWAY

Informational and analytical reports require organization and a clear purpose.

EXERCISES

1. Find an annual report for a business you would like to learn more about. Review it with the previous reading in mind and provide examples. Share and compare with classmates.
2. Write a report on a trend in business that you've observed, and highlight at least the main finding. Draw from your experience as you bring together sources of information to illustrate a trend. Share and compare with classmates.

---

[1] Bovee, C., & Thill, J. (2010). *Business communication essentials: A skills-based approach to vital business English* (4th ed.). Upper Saddle River, NJ: Prentice Hall.

9.5 Résumé

LEARNING OBJECTIVES

1. Describe the differences among functional, reverse chronological, combination, targeted, and scannable résumés.
2. Discuss what features are required in each type of résumé.
3. Prepare a one-page résumé.

A résumé is a document that summarizes your education, skills, talents, employment history, and experiences in a clear and concise format for potential employers. The résumé serves three distinct purposes that define its format, design, and presentation:

1. To represent your professional information in writing
2. To demonstrate the relationship between your professional information and the problem or challenge the potential employer hopes to solve or address, often represented in the form of a job description or duties
3. To get you an interview by clearly demonstrating you meet the minimum qualifications and have the professional background help the organization meet its goals

An online profile page is similar to a résumé in that it represents you, your background and qualifications, and adds participation to the publication. People network, link, and connect in new ways via online profiles or professional sites like LinkedIn. In many ways, your online profile is an online version of your résumé with connections and friends on public display. Your Facebook page is also often accessible to the public, so never post anything you wouldn't want your employer (current or future) to read, see, or hear. This chapter covers a traditional résumé, as well as the more popular scannable features, but the elements and tips could equally apply to your online profile.

Main Parts of a Résumé

Regardless of the format, employers have expectations for your résumé. They expect it to be clear, accurate, and up to date. [1] This document represents you in your absence, and you want it to do the best job possible. You don't want to be represented by spelling or grammatical errors, as they may raise questions about your education and attention to detail. Someone reading your résumé with errors will only wonder what kind of work you might produce that will poorly reflect on their company. There is going to be enough competition that you don't want to provide an easy excuse to toss your résumé at the start of the process. Do your best work the first time.

Résumés have several basic elements that employers look for, including your contact information, objective or goal, education and work experience, and so on. Each résumé format may organize the information in distinct ways based on the overall design strategy, but all information should be clear, concise, and accurate. [2]

Contact Information

This section is often located at the top of the document. The first element of the contact information is your name. You should use your full, legal name even if you go by your middle name or use a nickname. There will plenty of time later to clarify what you prefer to be called, but all your application documents, including those that relate to payroll, your social security number, drug screenings, background checks, fingerprint records, transcripts, certificates or degrees, should feature your legal name. Other necessary information includes your address, phone number(s), and e-mail address. If you maintain two addresses (e.g., a campus and a residential address), make it clear where you can be contacted by indicating the primary address. For business purposes, do not use an unprofessional e-mail address like sexiluvr93@hotmale.com or tutifruti@yafoo.com. Create a new e-mail account if needed with an address suitable for professional use.

Objective

This is one part of your résumé that is relatively simple to customize for an individual application. Your objective should reflect the audience's need to quickly understand how you will help the organization achieve its goals.

Education

You need to list your education in reverse chronological order, with your most recent degree first. List the school, degree, and grade point average (GPA). If there is a difference between the GPA in your major courses and your overall GPA, you may want to list them separately to demonstrate your success in your chosen field. You may also want to highlight relevant coursework that directly relate to the position.

Work Experience

List in reverse chronological order your employment history, including the positions, companies, locations, dates, duties and skills demonstrated or acquired. You may choose to use active, descriptive sentences or bullet lists, but be consistent. Emphasize responsibilities that involved budgets, teamwork, supervision, and customer service when applying for positions in business and industry, but don't let emphasis become exaggeration. This document represents you in your absence, and if information is false, at a minimum you could lose your job.

Figure 9.6 Sample Work Experience

WORK EXPERIENCE

Dolle Company, Yuma, AZ, August 2005–May 2009
Shift Manager, Lettuce Processing and Packaging
- Supervise 30 team members
- Develop, coordinate, implement, and evaluate shift schedule
- Address quality-control improvements, including employee training

Saveway Grocery, Yuma, AZ, August 2004–August 2005
Assistant Produce Manager, Vegetables
- Stock, order, and manage display of vegetables in produce department
- Supervise part-time staff as needed
- Manage produce budget, including purchase orders

Table 9.5 Types of Résumés

Type	Function	Advantage	Disadvantage
1. Reverse Chronological	Reverse chronological résumés (also called reverse time order) focus on work history.	Demonstrates a consistent work history	It may be difficult to highlight skills and experience.
2. Functional	Functional résumés (also called competency-based résumés) focus on skills.	Demonstrates skills that can clearly link to job functions or duties	It is often associated with people who have gaps in their employment history.
3. Combination	A combination résumé lists your skills and experience first, then employment history and education.	Highlights the skills you have that are relevant to the job and provides a reverse chronological work history	Some employers prefer a reverse chronological order.
4. Targeted	A targeted résumé is a custom document that specifically highlights the experience and skills that are relevant to the job.	Points out to the reader how your qualifications and experience clearly match the job duties	Custom documents take additional time, preparation, analysis of the job announcement, and may not fit the established guidelines.
5. Scannable	A scannable résumé is specifically formatted to be read by a scanner and converted to digital information.	Increasingly used to facilitate search and retrieval, and to reduce physical storage costs	Scanners may not read the résumé correctly.

You may choose to include references at the end of your résumé, though "references upon request" is common. You may also be tempted to extend your résumé to more than one page, but don't exceed that limit unless the additional page will feature specific, relevant information that represents several years of work that directly relates to the position. The person reading your résumé may be sifting through many applicants and will not spend time reading extra pages. Use the one-page format to put your best foot forward, remembering that you may never get a second chance to make a good first impression.

Maximize Scannable Résumé Content

Use Key Words

Just as there are common search terms, and common words in relation to each position, job description, or description of duties, your scannable résumé needs to mirror these common terms. Use of nonstandard terms may not stand out, and your indication of "managed employees" may not get the same attention as the word "supervision" or "management."

Follow Directions

If a job description uses specific terms, refers to computer programs, skills, or previous experience, make sure you incorporate that language in your scannable résumé. You know that when given a class assignment, you are expected to follow directions; similarly, the employer is looking for specific skills and experience. By mirroring the employer's language and submitting your application documents in accord with their instructions, you convey a spirit of cooperation and an understanding of how to follow instructions.

Insert a Key Word Section

Consider a brief section that lists common words associated with the position as a skills summary: customer service, business communication, sales, or terms and acronyms common to the business or industry.

Make It Easy to Read

You need to make sure your résumé is easy to read by a computer, including a character recognition program. That means no italics, underlining, shading, boxes, or lines. Choose a sans serif (without serif, or decorative end) font like Arial or Tahoma that won't be misread. Simple, clear fonts that demonstrate no points at which letters may appear to overlap will increase the probability of the computer getting it right the first time. In order for the computer to do this, you have to consider your audience—a computer program that will not be able to interpret your unusual font or odd word choice. A font size of eleven or twelve is easier to read for most people, and while the computer doesn't care about font size, the smaller your font, the more likely the computer is to make the error of combining adjacent letters.

Printing, Packaging and Delivery

Use a laser printer to get crisp letter formation. Inkjet printers can have some "bleed" between characters that may make them overlap, and therefore be misunderstood. Folds can make it hard to scan your document. E-mail your résumé as an attachment if possible, but if a paper version is required, don't fold it. Use a clean, white piece of paper with black ink; colors will only confuse the computer. Deliver the document in a nine-by-twelve-inch envelope, stiffened with a sheet of cardstock (heavy paper or cardboard) to help prevent damage to the document.

KEY TAKEAWAY

A résumé will represent your skills, education, and experience in your absence. Businesses increasingly scan résumés into searchable databases.

EXERCISES

1. Find a job announcement with specific duties that represents a job that you will be prepared for upon graduation. Choose a type of résumé and prepare your résumé to submit to the employer as a class assignment. Your instructor may also request a scannable version of your résumé.
2. Conduct an online search for a functional or chronological résumé. Please post and share with your classmates.
3. Conduct an online search for job advertisements that detail positions you would be interested in, and note the key job duties and position requirements. Please post one example and share with your classmates.
4. When is a second page of your résumé justified? Explain.
5. Conduct an online search for resources to help you prepare your own résumé. Please post one link and a brief review of the Web site, noting what features you found useful and at least one recommendation for improvement.

[1] Bennett, S. A. (2005). *The elements of résumé style: Essential rules and eye-opening advice for writing résumés and cover letters that work.* AMACOM.
[2] Simons, W., & Curtis, R. (2004). *The Résumé.com guide to writing unbeatable résumés.* New York, NY: McGraw-Hill.

Figure 9.7 Sample Format for Chronological Résumé

Name
Street Address
City, State, Zip Code
Cell Phone
Home Phone/Office Phone
E-mail Address

Objective or Statement of Interest

Clear and concise statement of professional goal that may include job or position and may also indicate a field (financial services, human resources).

Employment Experience

- List in reverse chronological order (i.e., put the most recent position first).
- Note the job title, the company, and dates of employment.
- Include clear statements of work performed as part of your job responsibilities, using language similar to the job announcement.
- If the job announcement emphasizes supervisory experience, for example, this should be an area of emphasis in your descriptions of tasks performed.
- Indicate the most important or relevant job responsibilities or skills involved with those tasks first in priority order.
- Include awards, citations, or commendations that relate to your objective or statement of interest.

Education

List earned degrees and incomplete education if applicable:

- Undergraduate Studies, 86 credits, University of State
- Associate of Applied Science (AAS) in Computer Information Systems, Community College of State, 2005
- High School Diploma, City High School, GPA or class rank
- Include technical certificates and completed trainings if they directly relate to your objective or statement of interest.

Community Service

List activities, your role, and, if applicable and space is available, your accomplishments:

- Eagle Scout, Troop #12345, 1998–2001
- Youth Choir Leader, Community Interfaith Church, 1995–2001
- Students in Free Enterprise Team, City High School, 1998–2001

References

List names of references, their positions, and their contact information or include "references upon request."

Figure 9.8 Sample Format for Functional Résumé

Name
Street Address
City, State, Zip Code
Cell Phone
Home Phone/Office Phone
E-mail Address

Objective
Clear and concise statement of professional goal (job or position)

Qualification Highlights
Experience that directly relates to job description
- You may choose to highlight a specific skill that relates to the position (e.g., bilingual, computer and technology proficient, certified diesel technician).
- Only highlight specific skills, certifications, or license(s) that indicate you meet (or exceed) the minimum qualifications.
- Only highlight personal traits if they clearly meet the position description (e.g., if a sales position requires an outgoing personality, highlight theater experience and previous sales experience).

Professional Skills
- You may want to list skills with clear "because" statements, demonstrating your mastery of a skill because of your volunteer work, internship, previous employment, or similar accomplishment.

Sales
You may also want to use a key skill as the focal point (e.g., sales) and include a series of brief statements that demonstrate range or depth of experience in that skill:
- Fundraising for your youth group (name of organization, date)
- Customer service call experience
- Voter recruitment initiative participation
- Census bureau work

Skill 2

Employment History
You may not need this category if you covered it in the skill summaries above.

Education
List earned degrees and incomplete education if applicable:
- Undergraduate Studies, 86 credits, University of State

References
List names of references, their positions, and their contact information or include "references upon request."

Figure 9.9 Sample Format for Scannable Résumé

Name
Street Address
City, State, Zip Code
Cell Phone
Home Phone/Office Phone
E-mail Address

Objective

Clear and concise statement of professional goal (job or position)

Education

List earned degrees and incomplete education if applicable:

Bachelor of Science (BS) in Computer Information Systems
City State University, Hometown, State, June 2007

Associates of Applied Science (AAS) in Computer Information Systems
Community College of State, Hometown

Employment

Customer Service Representative, Quickcare Computer Repair
Hometown, State, August 2007–December 2007

List skills and certifications clearly:

Diagnostic Assessment
Computer Repair
Onsite Customer Service
Materials Handling
Computer Skills
Adobe Certified Associate ACA
Alcatel-Lucent Network Routing Specialist I NRS I
Certified Technical Trainer CTT+
Digital Home Technology Integrator DHTI+
Linux+
Network+
PDI+
Project+
Security+
Server+
Microsoft: MCTS, MCA

References

List names of references, their positions, and their contact information or include "references upon request."

9.6 Sales Message
LEARNING OBJECTIVES

1. Discuss a basic sales message and identify its central purpose
2. Detail the main parts of a sales message and understand strategies for success

A sales message is the central persuasive message that intrigues, informs, persuades, calls to action, and closes the sale. Not every sales message will make a direct sale, but the goal remains. Whether your sales message is embedded in a letter, represented in a proposal, or broadcast across radio or television, the purpose stays the same.

Sales messages are often discussed in terms of reason versus emotion. Every message has elements of ethos, or credibility; pathos, or passion and enthusiasm; and logos, or logic and reason. If your sales message focuses exclusively on reason with cold, hard facts and nothing but the facts, you may appeal to some audience, but certainly not the majority. Buyers make purchase decisions on emotion as well as reason, and even if they have researched all the relevant facts about competing products, the decision may still come down to impulse, emotion, and desire. If your sales message focuses exclusively on emotion, with little or no substance, it may not be taken seriously. Finally, if your sales message does not appear to have credibility, the message will be dismissed. In the case of the sales message, you need to meet the audience's needs that vary greatly.

In general, appeals to emotion pique curiosity and get our attention, but some attention to reason and facts should also be included. That doesn't mean we need to spell out the technical manual on the product on the opening sale message, but basic information about design or features, in specific, concrete ways can help an audience make sense of your message and the product or service. Avoid using too many abstract terms or references, as not everyone will understand these. You want your sales message to do the work, not the audience.

Format for a Common Sales Message
A sales message has the five main parts of any persuasive message.

Getting Attention
Your sales message will compete with hundreds of other messages and you want it to stand out. [1] One effective way to do that is to make sure your attention statement(s) and introduction clearly state how the reader or listener will benefit.

- Will the product or service save time or money?
- Will it make them look good?
- Will it entertain them?
- Will it satisfy them?

Table 9.6 Five Main Parts of a Persuasive Message

Attention Statement	Use humor, novelty, surprise, or the unusual to get attention.
Introduction	Build interest by appealing to common needs and wants, and include a purpose statement to set up expectations.
Body	Establish credibility, discuss attractive features, and compare with competitors, addressing concerns or potential questions before they are even considered.
Conclusion	Sum it up and offer solution steps or calls to action, motivating the audience to take the next step. The smaller the step, the more likely the audience will comply. Set up your audience for an effective closing.
Residual Message	Make the sale, make them remember you, and make sure your final words relate to the most important information, like a contact phone number.

Regardless of the product or service, the audience is going to consider first what is in it for them. A benefit is what the buyer gains with the purchase and is central to your sales message. They may gain social status, popularity, sex appeal, or even reduce or eliminate something they don't want. Your sales message should clearly communicate the benefits of your product or service. [2]

Sales Message Strategies for Success
Your product or service may sell itself, but if you require a sales message, you may want to consider these strategies for success:

1. **Start with your greatest benefit**. Use it in the headline, subject line, caption, or attention statement. Audiences tend to remember the information from the beginning and end of a message, but have less recall about the middle points. Make your first step count by highlighting the best feature first.
2. **Take baby steps**. One thing at a time. Promote, inform, and persuade on one product or service at a time. You want to hear "yes" and make the associated sale, and if you confuse the audience with too much information,

too many options, steps to consider, or related products or service, you are more likely to hear "no" as a defensive response as the buyer tries not to make a mistake. Avoid confusion and keep it simple.

3. **Know your audience**. The more background research you can do on your buyer, the better you can anticipate their specific wants and needs and individualize your sales message to meet them.

4. **Lead with emotion, follow with reason**. Gain the audience's attention with drama, humor, or novelty and follow with specific facts that establish your credibility, provide more information about the product or service, and lead to your call to action to make the sale.

These four steps can help improve your sales message, and your sales. Invest your time in planning and preparation, and consider the audience's needs as you prepare your sales message.

Figure 9.14 Sample E-mail Sales Message

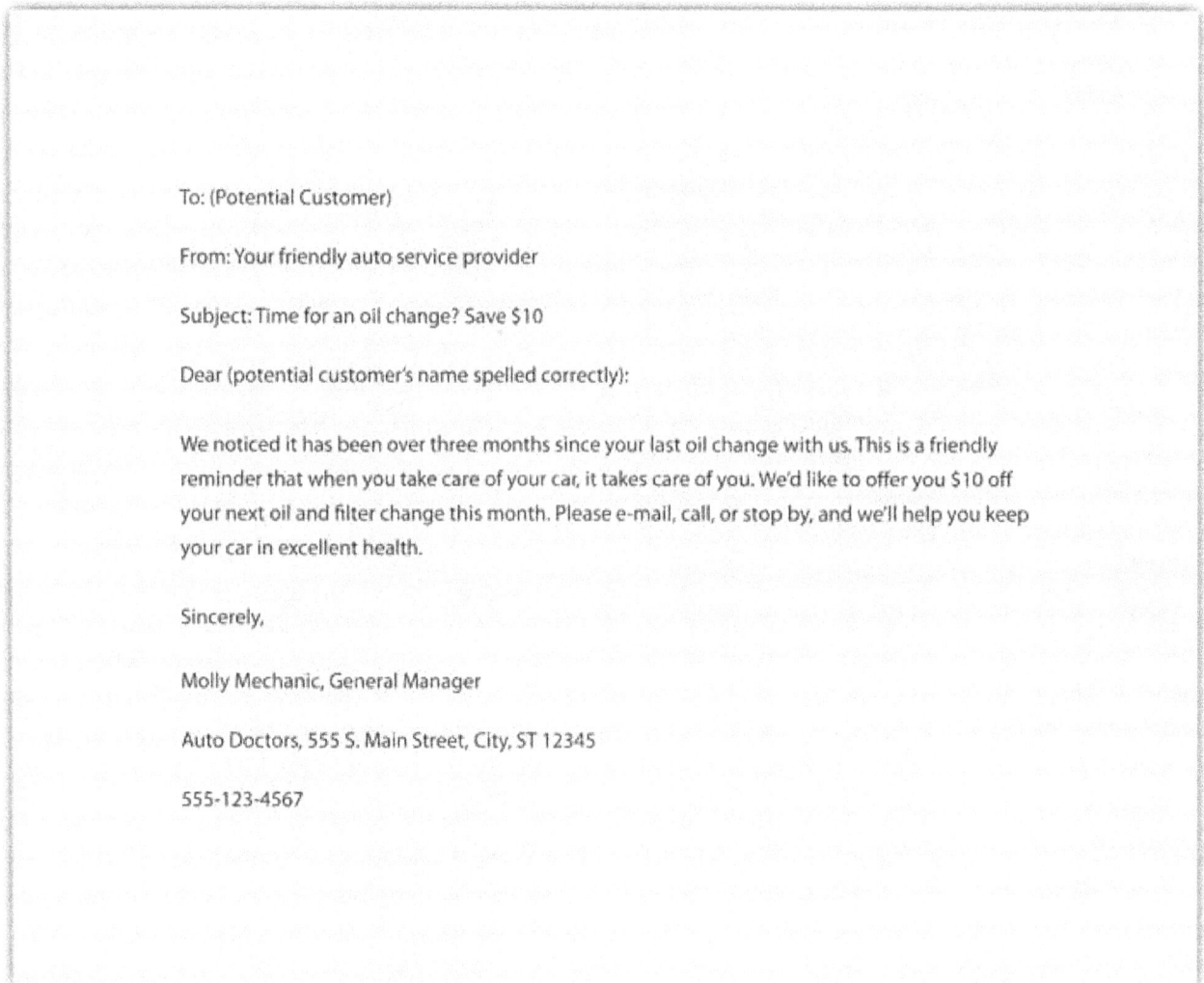

To: (Potential Customer)

From: Your friendly auto service provider

Subject: Time for an oil change? Save $10

Dear (potential customer's name spelled correctly):

We noticed it has been over three months since your last oil change with us. This is a friendly reminder that when you take care of your car, it takes care of you. We'd like to offer you $10 off your next oil and filter change this month. Please e-mail, call, or stop by, and we'll help you keep your car in excellent health.

Sincerely,

Molly Mechanic, General Manager

Auto Doctors, 555 S. Main Street, City, ST 12345

555-123-4567

KEY TAKEAWAY

A sales message combines emotion and reason, and reinforces credibility, to create interest in a product or service that leads to a sale.

EXERCISES

1. Create your own e-mail sales message in a hundred words or less. Share it with the class.

2. Identify one sales message you consider to be effective. Share it with classmates and discuss why you perceive it to be effective.

3. Please consider one purchase you made recently. What motivated you to buy and why did you choose to complete the purchase? Share the results with your classmates.

4. Are you more motivated by emotion or reason? Ask ten friends that question and post your results.

[1] Price, D. (2005, October 30). *How to communicate your sales message so buyers take action now!* Retrieved June 14, 2009, from ezinearticles.com: http://ezinearticles.com/?How-To-Communicate-Your-Sales-Message-So-Buyers-Take-Action-Now!&id=89569

[2] Winston, W., & Granat, J. (1997). *Persuasive advertising for entrepreneurs and small business owners: How to create more effective sales messages.* New York, NY: Routledge.

9.7 Additional Resources

- Visit NetLingo for some common texting abbreviations. http://www.netlingo.com/acronyms.php

- The Online Writing Lab (OWL) at Purdue University includes an area on e-mail etiquette. http://owl.english.purdue.edu/owl/resource/636/01

- Shea's Netiquette online is another useful source. http://www.albion.com/netiquette/book/index.html

- The *New York Times* blog "Gadgetwise: Getting Smart About Personal Technology" discusses an ever-changing variety of questions related to netiquette. http://gadgetwise.blogs.nytimes.com

- The OWL at Purdue also includes pages on memo writing and a sample memo.http://owl.english.purdue.edu/owl/resource/590/01;http://owl.english.purdue.edu/owl/resource/590/04

- For 642 sample letters, from cover letters to complaints, go to this site. http://www.4hb.com/letters

- Visit this Negotiations.com page for information on writing a request for proposal, quotation, and information. http://www.negotiations.com/articles/procurement-terms

- Visit this site for additional proposal writing tips. http://www.4hb.com/0350tipwritebizproposal.html

- TechSoup offers a sample Request for Proposal.http://www.techsoup.org/toolkits/rfp/RFP_client_mgmt2.pdf

- Your online profile counts as much as your résumé.http://www.npr.org/templates/story/story.php?storyId=105483848&sc=nl&cc=es-20090628

- Read a *Forbes* article on "Ten Ways to Torpedo Your Sales Pitch." http://www.forbes.com/2007/08/01/microsoft-ebay-symantec-ent-sales-cx_mf_0801byb07_torpedo.html

- Direct mail and other sales copy written by Susanna Hutcheson. http://www.powerwriting.com/port.html

- Visit this site for tips on how to write a public service announcement (PSA). http://www.essortment.com/all/tiphowtowrite_rjbk.htm

- The National Institute of Justice provides guidelines on writing a PSA.http://www.ojp.usdoj.gov/nij/topics/courts/restorative-justice/marketing-media/psa.htm

- The AdCouncil provides a range of examples. http://www.adcouncil.org/default.aspx?id=15

NOTES:

NOTES:

Chapter 10:
Developing Business Presentations

It usually takes me more than three weeks to prepare a good impromptu speech.

   Mark Twain

Being in the right does not depend on having a loud voice.

   Chinese Proverb

Getting Started

INTRODUCTORY EXERCISES

1. Complete the following self-inventory by brainstorming as many items as you can for each category. Think about anything you know, find interesting, or are involved in which relates to the topics below. Have you traveled to a different city, state, or country? Do you have any projects in other classes you find interesting? List them in the questions below.

- What do you read?
- What do you play or do for fun?
- What do you watch (visual media)?
- Where do you live or have you lived?
- What places have you visited (travel)?
- Whom do you know?
- What's important to you?
- If you could change one thing in the world, what would it be?

Choose your three favorite categories from the list above and circle them. Then ask a friend what they would be most interested in hearing about. Ask more than one friend, and keep score of which item attracts the most attention. Make sure you keep track of who likes which category.

INTRODUCTORY EXERCISES (CONT.)

2. What do you know about the world?

a.   What is the most populous country on the planet?
   1.   United States
   2.   India
   3.   China
   4.   Brazil

b.   The United States is home to more foreign-born residents than any other country. Which country has the next-highest number of foreign-born residents? [1]
   1.   Russia
   2.   England
   3.   India
   4.   Argentina

c.   As of 2008, what percentage of the world's population lived in an urban setting?
   1.   15 percent
   2.   30 percent
   3.   50 percent
   4.   60 percent

d.   The world's population was about 6.5 billion in early 2009. In what year is this figure expected to double to 13 billion? [2]
   1.   2090
   2.   2027
   3.   2067
   4.   2109

Answers: a. 3, b. 1, c. 3, d. 3.

Mark Twain makes a valid point that presentations require preparation. If you have the luxury of time to prepare, take full advantage of it. Speeches don't always happen when or how we envision them. Preparation becomes especially paramount when the element of unknown is present, forcing us to improvise. One mistake or misquote can and will be quickly rebroadcast, creating lasting damage. Take full advantage of the time to prepare for what you can anticipate, but also consider the element of surprise. In this chapter we discuss the planning and preparation necessary to prepare an effective presentation. You will be judged on how well you present yourself, so take the time when available to prepare.

Now that you are concerned with getting started and preparing a speech for work or class, let's consider the first step. It may be that you are part of a team developing a sales presentation, preparing to meet with a specific client in a one-on-one meeting, or even setting up a teleconference. Your first response may be that a meeting is not a speech, but your part of the conversation has a lot in common with a formal presentation. You need to prepare, you need to organize your message, and you need to consider audience's expectations, their familiarity with the topic, and even individual word choices that may improve your effectiveness. Regardless whether your presentation is to one individual (interpersonal) or many (group), it has as its foundation the act of communication. Communication itself is a dynamic and complex process, and the degree to which you can prepare and present effectively across a range of settings will enhance your success as a business communicator.

If you have been assigned a topic by the teacher or your supervisor, you may be able to go straight to the section on narrowing your topic. If not, then the first part of this chapter will help you. This chapter will help you step by step in preparing for your speech or oral presentation. By the time you have finished this chapter, you will have chosen a topic for your speech, narrowed the topic, and analyzed the appropriateness of the topic for yourself as well as the audience. From this basis, you will have formulated a general purpose statement and specific thesis statement to further define the topic of your speech. Building on the general and specific purpose statements you formulate, you will create an outline for your oral presentation.

Through this chapter, you will become more knowledgeable about the process of creating a speech and gain confidence in your organizational abilities. Preparation and organization are two main areas that, when well-developed prior to an oral presentation, significantly contribute to reducing your level of speech anxiety. If you are well prepared, you will be more relaxed when it is time to give your speech. Effective business communicators have excellent communication skills that can be learned through experience and practice. In this chapter we will work together to develop your skills in preparing clear and concise messages to reach your target audience.

[1] Bremner, J., Haub, C., Lee, M., Mather, M., & Zuehlke, E. (2009, September). World population highlights: Key findings from PRB's 2009 world population data sheet. *Population Bulletin, 64*(3). Retrieved from http://www.prb.org/pdf09/64.3highlights.pdf
[2] Rosenberg, M. (2009, October 15). Population growth rates and doubling time. *About.com Guide*. Retrieved from http://geography.about.com/od/populationgeography/a/population grow.htm

10.1 Before You Choose a Topic
LEARNING OBJECTIVE

1. Describe the steps in the process of planning a speech.

As you begin to think about choosing your topic, there are a few key factors to consider. These include the purpose of the speech, its projected time length, the appropriateness of the topic for your audience, and your knowledge or the amount of information you can access on the topic. Let's examine each of these factors.

Determine the General and Specific Purpose

It is important for you to have a clear understanding of your purpose, as all the other factors depend on it. Here's a brief review of the five general purposes for speaking in public:

1. *Speech to inform.* Increase the audience's knowledge, teach about a topic or issue, and share your expertise.

2. *Speech to demonstrate.* Show the audience how to use, operate, or do something.
3. *Speech to persuade.* Influence the audience by presenting arguments intended to change attitudes, beliefs, or values.
4. *Speech to entertain.* Amuse the audience by engaging them in a relatively light-hearted speech that may have a serious point or goal.
5. *Ceremonial speech.* Perform a ritual function, such as give a toast at a wedding reception or a eulogy at a funeral.

You should be able to choose one of these options. If you find that your speech may fall into more than one category, you may need to get a better understanding of the assignment or goal. Starting out with a clear understanding of why you are doing what you are supposed do will go a long way in helping you organize, focus, prepare, and deliver your oral presentation.

Once you have determined your general purpose—or had it determined for you, if this is an assigned speech—you will still need to write your specific purpose. What specifically are you going to inform, persuade, demonstrate, or entertain your audience with? What type of ceremony is your speech intended for? A clear goal makes it much easier to develop an effective speech. Try to write in just one sentence exactly what you are going to do.

Examples
To inform the audience about my favorite car, the Ford Mustang
To persuade the audience that global warming is a threat to the environment

Notice that each example includes two pieces of information. The first is the general purpose (to inform or to persuade) and the second is the specific subject you intend to talk about.

Can I Cover the Topic in Time?

Your next key consideration is the amount of time in which you intend to accomplish your purpose. Consider the depth, scope, and amount of information available on the topic you have in mind. In business situations, speeches or presentations vary greatly in length, but most often the speaker needs to get the message across as quickly as possible—for example, in less than five minutes. If you are giving a speech in class, it will typically be five to seven minutes; at most it may be up to ten minutes. In those ten minutes, it would be impossible to tell your audience about the complete history of the Ford Mustang automobile. You could, however, tell them about four key body style changes since 1965. If your topic is still too broad, narrow it down into something you can reasonably cover in the time allotted. For example, focus on just the classic Mustangs, the individual differences by year, and how to tell them apart.

You may have been assigned a persuasive speech topic, linking global warming to business, but have you been given enough time to present a thorough speech on why human growth and consumption is clearly linked to global warming? Are you supposed to discuss "green" strategies of energy conservation in business, for example? The topic of global warming is quite complex, and by definition involves a great deal of information, debate over interpretations of data, and analysis on the diverse global impacts. Rather than try to explore the chemistry, the corporate debates, or the current government activities that may be involved, you can consider how visual aids may make the speech vivid for the audience. You might decide to focus on three clear examples of global warming to capture your audience's attention and move them closer to your stated position: "green" and energy-saving strategies are good for business.

Perhaps you'll start with a brownie on a plate with a big scoop of ice cream on top, asking your audience what will happen when the ice cream melts. They will probably predict that the melted ice cream will spread out over the plate in a puddle, becoming a deeper puddle as the ice cream continues to melt. Next, you might display a chart showing that globally, temperatures have risen, followed by a map of the islands that have lost beaches due to rising tides. To explain how this had happened, you may show two pictures of Antarctica—one taken in 1993 and the other in 2003, after it lost over 15 percent of its total mass as the Ross Ice Shelf melted, cracked, and broke off from the continent. You may then make a transition to what happens when water evaporates as it goes into the atmosphere. Show a picture of the hole in the ozone over Chile and much of South America, and hold up a bottle of sunscreen, saying that even SPF 45 isn't strong enough to protect you. Finally, you may show a pie graph that illustrates that customers are aware of the environmental changes and the extent of their purchase decision is based on the perception of a product's "green" features or support of related initiatives. In just a few minutes, you've given seven visual examples to support your central position and meet your stated purpose.

Will My Topic Be Interesting to My Audience?
Remember that communication is a two-way process; even if you are the only one speaking, the audience is an essential part of your speech. Put yourself in their place and imagine how to make your topic relevant for them. What information will they actually use once your speech is over?

For example, if you are speaking to a group of auto mechanics who specialize in repairing and maintaining classic cars, it might make sense to inform them about the body features of the Mustang, but they may already be quite knowledgeable about these features. If you represent a new rust treatment product used in the restoration process, they may be more interested in how it works than any specific model of car. However, if your audience belong to a general group of students or would-be car buyers, it would be more useful to inform them about how to buy a classic car and what to look for. General issues of rust may be more relevant, and can still be clearly linked to your new rust treatment product.

For a persuasive speech, in addition to considering the audience's interests, you will also want to gauge their attitudes and beliefs. If you are speaking about global warming to a group of scientists, you can probably assume that they are familiar with the basic facts of melting glaciers, rising sea levels, and ozone depletion. In that case, you might want to focus on something more specific, such as strategies for reducing greenhouse gases that can be implemented by business and industry. Your goal might be to persuade this audience to advocate for such strategies, and support or even endorse the gradual implementation of the cost- and energy-saving methods that may not solve all the problems at once, but serve as an important first step.

In contrast, for a general audience, you may anticipate skepticism that global warming is even occurring, or that it poses any threat to the environment. Some audience members may question the cost savings, while others may assert that the steps are not nearly enough to make a difference. The clear, visual examples described above will help get your point across, but if you are also prepared to answer questions—for example, "If the earth is heating up, why has it been so cold here lately?" or "Isn't this just part of a warming and cooling cycle that's been happening for millions of years?"—you may make your speech ultimately more effective. By asking your listeners to consider what other signs they can observe that global warming is occurring, you might highlight a way for them to apply your speech beyond the classroom setting. By taking small steps as you introduce your assertions, rather than advocating a complete overhaul of the system or even revolution, you will more effectively engage a larger percentage of your audience.

How Much Information about My Topic Is Readily Available?

For a short speech, especially if it is a speech to entertain, you may be able to rely completely on your knowledge and ideas. But in most cases you will need to gather information so that you can make your speech interesting by telling the audience things they don't already know. Try to choose a topic that can be researched in your college or university libraries. You may need to do some initial checking of sources to be sure the material is available.

Putting It All Together

When you have determined your general purpose, the amount of material appropriate to the time allowed for your speech, and the appropriateness for your audience, then you should be well on your way to identifying the topic for your speech. As a double-check, you should be able to state your specific purpose in one sentence. For example, the specific purpose of our "Classic Cars" speech could be stated as, "By the end of my speech, I want my audience to be more informed about the three ways in which they can determine whether a classic car is a rust bucket or diamond in the rough, and be aware of one product solution."

KEY TAKEAWAY

Speech planning begins with knowing your general and specific purpose, your time allotment, your audience, and the amount of information available.

EXERCISES

1. Complete the following sentence for your speech: By the end of my speech, I want the audience to be more informed (persuaded, have a better understanding of, entertained by) about _____.

If you can't finish the sentence, you need to go back and review the steps in this section. Make sure you have given them sufficient time and attention. An effective speech requires planning and preparation, and that takes time. Know your general and specific purpose, and make sure you can write it in one sentence. If you don't know your purpose, the audience won't either.

2. Make a list of topic that interest you and meet the objectives of the assignment. Trade the list with a classmate and encircle three topics that you would like to learn more about on their list. Repeat this exercise. What topic received the most interest and why? Discuss the results with your classmates.

10.2 Choosing a Topic
LEARNING OBJECTIVE

1. Identify the general purpose and specific purpose of a speech

Now that you have a clear idea of your general and specific purpose, the allotted time, your audience's expectations, and the amount of information available, you are ready to commit to a topic. We have several strategies you can use to help select and narrow the topic appropriately.

Know Yourself and Your Audience

The first strategy is to identify an area of knowledge or an issue that deeply interests you. If you have not already completed the first of the Note 10.1 "Introductory Exercises" for this chapter, please work with it, identifying as many activities, areas of interest, places you've traveled to, and things you find interesting as possible. Once you have completed the exercise, identify three broad subject areas where you have some knowledge or experience and consider at least one link to business and industry for each area. Talking about what you know will make you a more credibility speaker but it must clearly connect with your employer's goals for your presentation. If, for example, you like doing a scrapbook, what kind of glue do you prefer and why? That may make for a natural speech topic that calls on your previous experience while requiring you to learn more about the glue and its properties. You may need to compare and contrast several types of glues as part of your preparation. Your in-depth awareness of scrapbooking and glue as a necessary ingredient will make you a more credible speaker.

In the first of the Note 10.1 "Introductory Exercises" for this chapter, you were asked to choose three questions from the list and then survey people you know to find out which of the three they prefer to hear about. Make sure you keep score by writing down factors like age, gender, and any other elements you think your audience may have in common. This exercise serves to reinforce the idea of being audience-centered, or tailoring your message to your specific audience. Our third of the Note 10.1 "Introductory Exercises" for this chapter should highlight that our perception of the world is not always accurate, and there is no substitute for thorough, objective research when preparing a speech. The more you know, about yourself and your audience, the better you can prepare to meet their needs and accomplish your goals as a speaker.

You have now utilized the Note 10.1 "Introductory Exercises" to help identify some broad topic areas that might work for you. If you find the topic interesting, your enthusiasm will show and your audience will become interested, too. Next, you will want to decide which of these areas would work best for your speech, and how to narrow it down.

Saving Time

Here are some strategies you can use to save yourself time in selecting a speech topic.

First, consider the information you already have close at hand. Do you already have a project you are working on, perhaps in another course? What are you currently studying in your other classes? What topics do you want to know more about? Which issues or aspects initially drew you to this topic or area? Chances are that whatever piqued your interest the first time will also get your audience interested.

Next, conduct a search (online, in the library, or interview people you know) in your subject area to get an overview of the subject. Explore topics, issues, places, or people that fascinate you.

Appeal, Appropriateness, and Ability

These are three main factors to consider when choosing a topic. All three factors are related to one another, but by systematically focusing on each one you will help address the strengths and weaknesses of your chosen topic.

Appeal involves the attractive power of arousing a sympathetic, stimulated response from the audience. Your audience will have expectations of you as a speaker and of your purpose for speaking. We all tend to seek novelty and find interesting, attractive, or appealing, or something that is not part of everyday life. A good example is the melting ice cream used in the speech on global warming. The elements are nothing new. We've all seen plates, brownies, and ice cream before, but how many of us have seen a speaker use them together to symbolize the melting ice caps associated with global warming? There is an inherent novelty present when we adapt something from its original purpose in order to make it appealing. You will need to consider an appealing way to start your speech, and will look for ways throughout your speech to reaffirm that appeal to the audience. When considering a topic, also think about the visual or auditory images that come to mind, or how you might represent it to an audience in ways other than your words. This can guide you as you proceed to select your topic, thinking about what you can make appealing to your audience.

It also follows that appeal applies to the speaker as well as the audience. You may find the prospect of discussing global warming not very interesting, and if you feel this way, it will come through in your speech. You need to be attracted, interested or find your topic appealing in order to convey this appeal to your audience. Find something that catches your interest, and that same spark is what you will cultivate to develop ways to stimulate the spark of curiosity in your audience.

Appropriateness involves a topic that is especially suitable or compatible with your audience's interest, expectations, norms, or customs. Everyone will have expectations about roles and outcomes associated with your speech. Some may be looking for information, while others may already know something about your topic and want to learn more. You will need to reach both groups within the audience. As we saw earlier in the Ford Mustang example, a highly technical speech may lose the more novice members of your audience. Appropriateness is important because some topics do not work as well in a classroom setting as others. Will everyone find a new rust treatment product interesting? Will everyone find a car speech interesting? Whether you are in the classroom or business office setting, consider your audience and the appropriateness of your topic.

Regardless where you give a speech, you should always choose topics that will not promote harmful or illegal actions. It is also important to consider whether your topic might offend members of the audience. If this is a possibility, can you find a way to present the topic that will minimize offense? Similarly, if your topic is controversial and you know that your audience has strong feelings about it, consider how you can convey your message without alienating or antagonizing your listeners. Finally, it is usually wise to avoid topics, which the audience already knows a lot about.

Ability involves the natural aptitude or acquired proficiency to be able to perform. If you have a lot of prior information on flying, gained over years of experience being at the controls of an aircraft, you may have a natural aptitude and knowledge base to use to your advantage. If, however, you've never flown before, you may need to gather information and go visit an airport to be able to approach a proficient level of understanding to discuss the topic.

In addition to your ability to draw on your natural strengths, you'll also want to consider your ability to research a topic where you are located. If you want to develop a speech on a particular topic but you find information hard to come by, this will make your job even harder and could possibly have a detrimental impact on your speech. You may find that two similar topics interest you but your ability to gather information from more diverse sources, from places that are more readily available, or from your background and experience make one topic more attractive than the other.

Consider topics that are,

- new,
- possibly controversial,
- clear,
- supported by information you can find in outside sources,
- interesting to you.

Individual course guidelines vary, so make sure that your instructor approves your topic, and that your topic is appropriate for your audience. At some colleges and universities, broad topics are designated as part of the curriculum including, for example, environment, diversity, and technology. In your class, you may be challenged to link any of those topics to business, and to prepare an informative or persuasive speech. Some colleges and university instructors may also encourage you not to choose topics that have been done repeatedly over the years, like abortion or the death penalty, unless you can connect the issue to a current event or new perspective. Don't avoid all controversial topics, as they often intrigue your audience and help maintain interest. Just make sure to consider the pre-existing attitudes of your audience when attempting to create an effective, engaging speech.

In a business setting, you will rarely be given complete freedom to choose your topic. You may even have a script and visual aids prepared in advance. In the real world the luxury of time for preparation and topic selection are rare, but in a classroom setting you are often given more of an opportunity to choose. That choice should not be taken lightly, and should be viewed as an opportunity. The classroom is a training ground, and your freedom to explore and experiment is designed to build skills and strengths. When you join an employer, you will be asked to prepare a presentation as part of the job; more often than not, there are clear guidelines on what is acceptable and your professionalism is expected.

Use Your Self-Inventory

Choosing a topic can be difficult, but your self-inventory of things you already know should get you started. By doing a little exploring, you can often help yourself come up with several possible topics. The topic itself will not exclusively make a "good" or "bad" speech. How you develop that topic and discuss its points and issues, however, will make a significant impact. Before moving on to the next step in this chapter, make sure you have a topic in which you are relatively confident. If you have trouble selecting a topic, take your self-inventory to your instructor or librarian. They may be able to help guide you to a topic that works for you.

Here are some examples to get you started. Let's say your self-inventory response from the first of the Note 10.1 "Introductory Exercises" for this chapter to the question, "**What do you play or do for fun**?" is to play sports, and it also happens to be one way you are earning your way through school on a scholarship. You could consider a topic like the history of your sport for an informative speech, or how to tell the difference between three classic types of pitches in baseball, and which you can involve an audience member for a demonstrative speech. You could also consider stereotypes of athletes in college and some of the common misperceptions and persuade the audience that athletes often handle the issues of time management well, can get good grades (provide statistics as evidence and ask a coach for examples), and are actively developing both their minds and their bodies through participation in sports. You might even take on a topic of why basketball is more interesting than football, or vice versa. You might decide instead to entertain the audience, and tell stories associated with game travel, buses breaking down, or road trips gone bad. Finally, you might put together a ceremonial speech honoring an Academic All-American player, recognizing his or her excellence both in academics and in athletics.

If you are not a student athlete, but a college student, you may have answered that same question by indicating you are taking classes for a degree as well as for fun. You could put together an informative speech on the steps involved in applying for financial aid, or produce a demonstrative speech on how to gather the information required and complete the application process. You might persuade the audience to apply for financial aid, even if they think they might not be eligible, and cover the options within the program. You might entertain the audience with funny stories about the challenges of registering for classes, completing financial aid, and completing the classes you need to graduate. (There is always just one more class, right?) You might also draft a ceremonial speech as if you were presenting the commencement speech at your graduation.

These two scenarios should stimulate some ideas, or you might already have a clear purpose and topic in mind. It's important to be clear on both your purpose and your topic as you begin to put pencil to paper, or keystroke to computer, and begin the process of writing your general purpose and thesis statements.

Writing Your Thesis Statement

Earlier in the chapter you wrote a statement expressing the general and specific purpose of your speech. Now that you have explored further and identified a definite topic, it's time to write a thesis statement. This thesis statement should be a short, specific sentence capturing the central idea of your speech. Steven Beebe and Susan Beebe [1] recommend five guiding principles when considering your thesis statement. The thesis statement should

1. be a declarative statement;
2. be a complete sentence;
3. use specific language, not vague generalities;
4. be a single idea;
5. reflect consideration of the audience.

For example, if you plan to inform a general audience about the Ford Mustang, a good thesis statement might be, "Ford produced five 'generations' of the Mustang, each with a distinctive body style that audience members can learn to recognize." If you plan to persuade a group of investors that a beachfront property could be threatened by rising sea levels, a good thesis statement might be, "Sea levels are predicted to rise because of global warming, and if these predictions are correct, the beachfront property my audience is considering investing in may be threatened."

The thesis statement is key to the success of your speech. If your audience has to work to find out what exactly you are talking about, or what your stated purpose or goal is, they will be less likely to listen, be impacted, or recall your speech. By stating your point clearly in your introduction, and then referring back to it during your speech, you promote the cognitive strategies of emphasis, clarity, and conciseness, and help your audience to listen while meeting the expectations of the rhetorical context.

KEY TAKEAWAY

Choosing a speech topic involves knowing yourself and your audience; using efficient strategies; and understanding appeal, appropriateness, and ability. When you have accomplished these steps, you will be able to write a good thesis statement.

EXERCISES

1. Which of the following qualify as good thesis statements? Take any that are faulty and rewrite them to remedy their weaknesses.
    a. Living in the desert as we do, my listeners and I can grow many beautiful and interesting plants in our gardens without using large amounts of water.
    b. To inform patients about how the medical insurance claims process works.
    c. Because recent research suggests children develop positive self-esteem through recognition for their achievements, not from indiscriminate praise, I will persuade the parents and teachers in my audience to modify their behavior toward children.
    d. Tourists can learn a lot from visiting the European battlefields of World War II, and unexploded land mines from past wars are a serious problem throughout the world.
    e. As a student attending this college on an athletic scholarship, I lead a very busy life because I am responsible for working hard at my sport as well as being held to the same academic standards as the nonathlete students in my audience.

Answers: Examples a, c, and e are good thesis statements. Example b is not a complete sentence. Example d contains more than one main idea.

From your list of possible topics, write several sample purpose or thesis statements. Share and compare your results with classmates.

Write a general purpose statement and thesis statement for a speech to inform. Now adapt these statements for a speech to persuade.

[1] Beebe, S. [Steven], & Beebe, S. [Susan]. (1997). *Public speaking: An audience-centered approach* (3rd ed.). Boston, MA: Allyn & Bacon.

10.3 Finding Resources

LEARNING OBJECTIVES

1. Understand the importance of research in developing your topic.
2. Use resources to gather information effectively.
3. Document your sources correctly and avoid plagiarism.

Now that you know your general purpose, have committed to a topic, and have written your thesis statement, it's time to gather information. If you have chosen the topic from your list, you probably already know a lot about it. But in most cases you will still need information from sources other than yourself, to establish credibility, create a more comprehensive speech, and to make sure no important aspect of your topic is left out.

Your time is valuable and you'll need to plan ahead to avoid a rushed frenzy right before your due date. You'll feel more confident if you budget your time wisely and give yourself an opportunity to reflect on what you have prepared, and this will help you feel more relaxed as you deliver your speech, reducing your speech anxiety.

Narrow Your Topic and Focus on Key Points

By now you have developed an idea of your topic, but even with your purpose and thesis statement, you may still have a broad subject that will be a challenge to cover within the allotted time. You might want to revisit your purpose and thesis statement and ask yourself: how specific is my topic? If flying an airplane is your topic area and you are going to inform your audience on the experience, discuss the history and basic equipment, and cover the basic requirements necessary to go on your first flight. Plus, look at reference information on where your audience could go locally to take flying lessons, you might find that five to seven minutes simply is not enough time. Rather than stating that you need more time, or that you'll just rush through it, consider your audience and what they might want to learn. How can you narrow your topic to better consider their needs? As you edit your topic, considering what is essential information and what can be cut, you'll come to focus on the key points naturally and reduce the pressure on yourself to cover too much information in a short amount of time.

If you haven't presented many speeches, five to seven minutes may seem like an eternity, but when you are in front of the audience, the time will pass quickly. Consider how you feel about the areas of your speech and you'll soon see how it could easily turn into an hour-long presentation. You need to work within the time limits, and show your audience respect as you stay within them, recognizing that they too will be presenting speeches in the same time frame. For yourself and your audience, narrow your topic to just the key points. Perhaps you will begin with a description and a visual image of your first flight, followed by a list of the basic equipment and training needed. Finally, a reference to local flying schools may help you define your speech. While the history of flying may be fascinating, and may serve as a topic in itself for another speech, it would add too much information to this particular brief speech.

As you begin this process, keep an open mind for the reference materials available. The access to information on the Internet is amazing, but not all the information has equal value. Try not to just go with the first three examples, Web sites or sources you run across but instead skim, rather than read in-depth, the information at that relates to your topic and what you find of interest. Look for abstracts, or brief summaries of information, before you commit time to reading an article all the way through. Look for indexes to identify key terms you might want to cover before eliminating them as you narrow your topic. Take notes as you search or bookmark pages with your Web browser in order to go back to a site or source that at first you passed over, but now think may make a relevant contribution to your speech. Consider the source and their credibility. While a high school Web page assignment may prove interesting, the link to the research in the field, the author of a study, or a university source may provide much credible information. Once you have identified sources you consider to be valuable, you will assemble the information and key points needed to make your speech effective much better.

Plan Your Search for Information

When preparing a speech, it is important to gather information from books, magazines, newspapers, electronic sources, and interviews from people who know a lot about your topic. With information from a variety of sources, you will have many possibilities when it comes to developing your speech. If you keep in mind the key information you need to support your thesis, you will save yourself time, as you can choose and edit information as you go along. Also, consider your other responsibilities in other classes or with work and family. You'll have to schedule time for your investigation and make it a priority, but it will necessarily compete with other priorities. Perhaps scheduling for yourself time in the library, a visit to the local flight school to interview a flight instructor, and some Internet search time in the evenings may help you create a to-do list that you can use to structure your research. Remember that this investigation will be more fun if your topic is one in which you are actually interested.

Before you go to the library, look over your information sources. Do you read a magazine that relates to the topic? Did you read a recent news article that might be relevant? Is there a book, CD-ROM, or music that has information you can use? Think of what you want your audience to know, and how you could show it to them. Perhaps cover art from a CD, or line from a poem may make an important contribution to your speech. You might even know someone who has experience in the area you want to research.

As you begin to investigate your topic, make sure you consider several sides of an issue. Let's say you are going to make an informative speech at a town council meeting about the recent history of commuter rail service in your town. At first, you may have looked at two sides, rail versus private cars. Automobile dealers, oil companies, and individual drivers wanted the flexibility of travel by car, while rail advocates argued that commuter trains would lower costs and energy consumption. If you take another look, you see that several other perspectives also have bearing on this issue. Many workers commuted by bus prior to the railroad, so the bus companies would not want the competition. Property owners objected to the noise of trains and the issue of eminent domain (i.e., taking of private property by the government). To serve several towns that are separated by open space, the rail lines cut through wildlife habitat and migration corridors. We now have five perspectives to the central issue, which makes the topic all the more interesting. Make sure, as you start your investigation for information, that you always question the credibility of the information. Sources may have no review by peers or editor, and the information may be misleading, biased, or even false. Be a wise information consumer.

Ethics, Content Selection, and Avoiding Plagiarism

An aspect of sifting and sorting information involves how you will ethically present your material. You may be tempted to omit information that may be perceived as negative or may not be well received. For example, you may be tempted to omit mention of several train accidents that have occurred, or of the fact that train fares have risen as service has been cut back. If your purpose is to inform, you owe it to your audience to give an honest presentation of the available facts. By omitting information, you are not presenting an accurate picture, and may mislead your audience. Even if your purpose is to persuade, omitting the opposing points will present a one-sided presentation. The audience will naturally consider what you are not telling them as well as what you are presenting, and will raise questions. Instead, consider your responsibility as a speaker to present all the information you understand to be complete, and do it honestly and ethically.

As another example, suppose you work for a swimming pool construction company and are speaking to inform a neighborhood group about pool safety. You have photos of pools you have worked on, but they aren't very exciting. There are many more glamorous swimming pool photos on free Internet sites. Who can really tell if the pool in the picture is yours or not? Furthermore, the "Terms of Use" on the site state that photos may be downloaded for personal use. Wouldn't this speech to inform be considered personal use? In fact, it probably would not, even if your informative speech is not a direct sales pitch. And even if you don't actually tell your audience, "My company built this pool," it would be reasonable for them to assume you did unless you specifically tell them otherwise.

As a student, you are no doubt already aware that failing to cite sources or including a sentence or paragraph you copied from a blog on the Internet for an English essay is called plagiarism and is grounds for an F on your paper. At many schools, plagiarism can even be grounds for expulsion. Similarly, in your professional life it behooves you to be truthful with your audience and give credit where credit is due for several reasons. First, misrepresenting your employer's work could be illegal under statutes related to fraud; it could put not only your job but also your employer's contractor

license in jeopardy. Second, someone in your audience could recognize one of the photos (after all, they can browse the Internet as easily as you can) and embarrass you by pointing it out during your presentation. Third, by using photos that display your company's actual work you will feel more confident, reducing your speech anxiety. You have a responsibility to your audience and engaging in plagiarism fails in that responsibility.

Staying Organized

Before you start browsing on your computer, go to the library, or make the trip for an interview, make sure you have designated a space where you can keep all your materials in one place. Decide on a name for the project and use it to set up a subdirectory in your computer as well as a physical receptacle, such as a cardboard box or a manila folder.

As you gather information online, open a new document in whatever writing program you use and save it as "Sources." Every time you find information that may prove useful, copy the Web address or reference/citation information and paste it into your document. If you are gathering information from books or periodicals, use one sheet of paper as your "Sources" document. This will save you a lot of time later when you are polishing your speech.

Plan to use your time effectively. What information do you hope to find in the library? Make a list. Try to combine tasks and get your investigation completed efficiently. Go to the library once with a list, rather than three times without one. Ask the research librarian for assistance in grouping information and where to find it.

As you search through articles, books, Web sites, and images for your presentation, consider how each element relates specifically to the key points in your speech. Don't just look for the first citation or reference that fits your list. Rushing through the research process can result in leaving out key areas of support or illustration in your speech, an outcome you may not be happy with. Instead, enjoy the fun of searching for material for your speech—but be aware that it is easy for your list under each key point to grow and grow with "must include" information. As we discussed earlier, narrowing your topic is a key strategy in crafting a good speech. Try not to "commit" to information until you have gathered more than you need, then go back and choose the most relevant and most interesting facts, quotations, and visual aids.

You might think of this as the "accordion phase" of preparing your speech, as the amount of material first gets bigger and then smaller. You'll feel a sense of loss as you edit and come to realize that your time frame simply does not allow for all the great information you found—but remember that nobody else will know what *didn't* go into your speech, they will just appreciate the good material you did choose. As you sift through information, look for the promising, effective elements to include and omit the rest. In your English class, you often need to edit and revise a paper to produce a rough draft before your final draft. This process parallels the production of a rough draft. By taking notes with your key point in mind, you'll begin to see your speech come together.

Searching for Information on the Internet

Finding information on the Internet or in electronic databases can decrease your search time, but you will still need to budget time to accomplish the tasks associated with reviewing, selecting, interpreting, and incorporating information to your particular use.

The World Wide Web is an amazing source of information, but for that very reason, it is difficult to get information you actually need. Let's look at two issues that can make searching online easier: where and how to search for information.

Knowing where to go for information is as important as knowing key words and concepts related to your topic. Do you need general information? Do you need to survey what's available quickly? Do you prefer searching only reviewed sites? Is your topic education-related? Depending on your answer, you may want to consider where to start your search. Table 10.1 "Some Examples of Internet Search Sites" presents a summary of main search engines and how they might work for you.

At the end of this chapter under "Additional Resources," you will find a list of many Web sites that may be useful for public speaking research.

Evaluating Your Sources

It is important to be aware of how much online information is incomplete, outdated, misleading, or downright false. Anyone can put up a Web site, and once it is up the owner may or may not enter updates or corrections on a regular basis. Anyone can write a blog on any subject, whether or not that person actually knows much about that subject. Anyone who wishes to contribute to a Wikipedia article can do so—although the postings are moderated by editors who have to register and submit their qualifications. In the United States, the First Amendment to the Constitution guarantees freedom of expression. This freedom is restricted by laws against libel (false accusations against a person) and indecency, especially child pornography, but those laws can be difficult to enforce.

It is always important to look beyond the surface of a site to who sponsors it, where the information displayed came from, and whether the site owner has a certain agenda.

Table 10.1 Some Examples of Internet Search Sites

Description	URL
General Web searches that can also be customized according to categories like news, maps, images, video	http://www.google.com http://go.com http://www.itools.com/research-it http://www.metacrawler.com http://www.search.com http://www.yahoo.com
Dictionaries and encyclopedias	http://www.britannica.com http://dictionary.reference.com http://encarta.msn.com http://www.encyclopedia.com http://www.merriam-webster.com http://en.wikipedia.org/wiki/Main_Page
Very basic information on a wide range of topics	http://www.about.com http://www.answers.com
To find people or businesses in white pages or yellow pages listings	http://www.switchboard.com http://www.anywho.com http://www.whitepages.com http://www.yellowpages.com
Specialized databases—may be free, require registration, or require a paid subscription	http://www.apa.org/psycinfo http://www.northernlight.com http://www.zillow.com http://clinicaltrials.gov/ct/screen/AdvancedSearch http://www.peoplelookup.com

In gathering information for your speech, you will want to draw on reputable, reliable sources—printed ones as well as electronic ones—because they reflect on the credibility of the message, and the messenger. Analyzing and assessing information is an important skill in speech preparation, and here are six main points to consider when evaluating a document, presentation, or similar source of information. [1] In general, documents that represent quality reasoning have:

- a clearly articulated purpose and goal;
- a question, problem, or issue to address;

- information, data, and evidence that is clearly relevant to the stated purpose and goals;
- inferences or interpretations that lead to conclusions based on the presented information, data, and evidence;
- a frame of reference or point of view that is clearly articulated;
- assumptions, concepts, and ideas that are clearly articulated

An additional question to ask is *how credible the source* is. This question can be hard to answer even with years of training and expertise. Academic researchers have been trained in the objective, impartial use of the scientific method to determine validity and reliability. But as research is increasingly dependent on funding, and funding often brings specific points of view and agendas with it, pure research can be—and has been—compromised. You can no longer simply assume that "studies show" something without finding out who conducted the study, how it was conducted, and who funded the effort. This may sound like a lot of investigation and present quite a challenge, but again it is worth the effort.

Information literacy is an essential skill set in the process of speech preparation. As you learn to spot key signs of information that will not serve to enhance your credibility and contribute to your presentation, you can increase your effectiveness as you research and analyze your resources. For example, suppose you are preparing an informative speech on safety in the workplace. You might come upon a site owned by a consulting company that specializes in safety analysis. The site might give many statistics, illustrating the frequency of on-the-job accidents, repetitive motion injuries, workplace violence, and so on. But the sources of these percentage figures may not be credited. As an intelligent researcher, you need to ask yourself whether the consulting company that owns the site performed its own research to get these numbers. Most likely it did not—so why are the sources not cited? Moreover, such a site would unlikely mention any free workplace safety resources available and free from sources such as the U.S. Occupational Safety and Health Administration (OSHA). Less biased sources of information would be the American Management Association, the U.S. Department of Labor, and other not-for-profit organizations that study workplace safety.

The Internet also encompasses thousands of interactive sites where readers can ask and answer questions. Some sites, like Askville by Amazon.com, WikiAnswers, and Yahoo! Answers, are open to almost any topic. Others, like ParentingQuestions and WebMD, deal with specific topics. Chat rooms on bridal Web sites allow couples who are planning a wedding to share advice and compare prices for gowns, florists, caterers, and so on. Reader comment sites like Newsvine facilitate discussions about current events. Customer reviews are available for just about everything imaginable, from hotels and restaurants to personal care products, home improvement products, and sports equipment. These contributors are not experts, nor do they pretend to be. Some may have extreme opinions that are not based in reality. Then, too, it is always possible for a vendor to "plant" favorable customer reviews on the Internet to make its product look good. Although the "terms of use," which contributors must agree to usually forbid the posting of advertisements, profanity, or personal attacks, some sites do a better job than others in monitoring and deleting such material. Nevertheless, if your speech research involves finding out how the "average person" feels about an issue in the news, or whether a new type of home exercise device really works as advertised, these comment and customer review sites can be very useful indeed.

It may seem like it's a hard work to assess your sources, to make sure your information is accurate and truthful, but the effort is worth it. Business and industry rely on reputation and trust, just as we individuals do, in order to maintain healthy relationships. Your speech is an important part of that reputation and interaction.

Compiling Your Information

When you have investigated and narrowed your topic, it's time to compile your information. Compiling involves composing your speech out of materials from the documents and other sources you have collected. This process has seven major steps, adapted from a model by Anderson, Anderson and Williams: sensitivity, exposure, assimilation and accommodation, incubation, incorporation, production and revision. [2]

Sensitivity refers to your capacity to respond to stimulation, be excited, be responsive, or be susceptible to new information. This starts with your self-inventory of what you are interested or involved in as you did in the first of the Note 10.1 "Introductory Exercises" for this chapter. If you are intrigued by a topic or area of interest, your enthusiasm will carry through to your speech and make it more stimulating for your audience. You may not have considered, or even noticed, elements or ideas associated with your topic, but now that you have begun the process of investigation, you see them everywhere. For example, have you ever heard someone say a word or phrase that you never heard before, but now that you are familiar with it, you hear it everywhere? This same principle applies to your sensitivity to ideas related to your topic. You'll notice information and it will help you as you develop your awareness of your topic and the many directions you could take the speech. Cognitive psychologist use the term "priming" to refer to this excited state of awareness. [3]

Exposure involves your condition of being presented views, ideas, experiences, or made known to you through direct experience. If you are thinking of giving an informative speech on flying an airplane but have never flown before, your level of exposure may be low. Your level of awareness may be high, however, in terms of the importance of security on commercial airlines after reading about, watching on television, or hearing on the radio stories after the events of September 11, 2001. You may decide to expose yourself to more information through a range of sources as you investigate the topic of airline security. The more you become exposed to the issues, processes and goals of your topic, the more likely you are to see areas of interest, think of new ideas that might fit in your speech, and form patterns of awareness you did not perceive previously.

Assimilation and accommodation refers to the process by which you integrate (assimilate) new ideas into your thinking patterns, and adopt (accommodate) or filter out new sources of information as they relate to your goal. You may have had preconceived notions or ideas about airline security before you began your investigation, but new information has changed the way you view your topic. You might also find issues (e.g., right to privacy) that may be points of conflict with your beliefs as you review information. This stage is important to the overall process of developing your topic and takes time. You need time to be able to contemplate, review, and reflect on how the new information fits or fails to connect clearly to your chosen topic.

Incubation is the process by which you cause an idea or ideas to develop in your mind. This might not happen all at once, and you might spend time thinking about the new information, directions, or ways you might develop or focus your topic. Consider the meaning of the word "incubation" as it relates to chickens and eggs. An egg may look ready to hatch as soon as the hen lays it, but it needs time and a warm environment to develop. You might have an idea but need to create an environment for it to develop. This might involve further investigation and exploration, or it may involve removing yourself from active research to "digest" what you have already learned. If you feel "stuck" on an idea or perceive an inability to move on in the development of your ideas or topic, giving it a rest may be the best course of action. You may also find that just when you least expect it, an idea, fully formed, flashes into your mind and you ask yourself,

"Why didn't I see that before?" Before the idea escapes you, write it down and make sure you can refer to it later.

Incorporation refers to the process by which you bring the information into a whole or complete topic. By now you have investigated, chosen some information over others, and have started to see how the pieces will come together. Your perceptions of how the elements come together will form the basis for the organization of your speech. It will contribute to the logic of your message and help you produce a coherent, organized speech that your audience can follow clearly.

Production involves the act of creating your speech from the elements you have gathered. You may start to consider what comes first, what goes last, and how you will link your ideas and examples together. You may find that you need additional information, and can go back to your notes that you take to find the source quickly and easily. You may also start to communicate with friends, sharing some of the elements or even practicing the first drafts of your speech, learning where the connections are clear and where they need work.

Revision is the process by which you look over your speech again in order to correct or improve it. You will notice elements that need further investigation, development, or additional examples and visual aids as your produce your speech. This is an important step to the overall production of your speech, much like revising an essay for an English course. The first time you said, thought, or wrote something it may have made sense to you, but upon reflection and after trying an idea out, you need it to be revised in order to work effectively as part of your speech. You may revisit the place in which you started, and start all speeches, by reconsidering the rhetorical situation and see if what you have produces is in line with the expectations of the audience. Your awareness of the content, audience, and purpose of the rhetorical situation will guide you through the revision process and contribute to the production of a more effective speech.

KEY TAKEAWAY

To find resources for your speech, narrow your topic and plan your search for information. Be aware of ethics, selecting reliable content, and avoiding plagiarism. Stay organized, and be a wise consumer of Internet information. Last, compile your information into a coherent series of main points.

EXERCISES

1. Find at least one example of an Internet site that is sponsored by each of the following:

o   Local, state, or federal government in the United States or another country

o   For-profit corporation that sells a product or service to the general public

o   Not-for-profit organization

o   Private or public college, university, or other school

2. Describe the type of information available on each of your chosen sites. How do they differ from one another? What do they have in common? Discuss your findings with your classmates.

3. Find a Web site you find particularly useful in terms of information. Write a brief review and then share with classmates.

4. Find a Web site you find particularly poor in terms of your ability to access information. Write a brief review and then share with classmates.

5. When creating a speech, is it appropriate to omit certain information? Explain and discuss your thoughts with a classmate.

6. How can a persuasive speech be ethical? Explain your opinion and give some examples. Compare and share in class.

---

[1] Paul, R., & Elder, L. (2007). *The miniature guide to critical thinking: Concepts and tools.* Dillon Beach, CA: The Foundation for Critical Thinking Press.
[2] Andrews, P., Andrews, J., & Williams, G. (1999). *Public speaking: Connecting you and your audience.* Boston, MA: Houghton Mifflin Company.
[3] Yaniv, I., & Meyer, D. (1987). Activation and metacognition of inaccesible stored information: Potential bases for incubation effects in problem loving. *Journal of Experimental Psychology Learning, Memory, and Cognition, 13,* 187–205.

10.4 Myths and Realities of Public Speaking
LEARNING OBJECTIVE

1. Describe common myths and realities of public speaking.

Now that you have identified your purpose, chosen your topic and thesis statement, gathered and organized your material, you are almost ready to put your speech into its final form. At this juncture, let's examine some common public speaking myths and outline the guidelines you'll need to consider as you prepare to face your audience. There are a lot of myths associated with public speaking. In many ways these guidelines dispel common perceptions of public speaking and may lead you to be more open with yourself and your audience as you prepare and present your speech.

Speaking in Public Is Not Like Killing Lions
From an evolutionary biology perspective, our bodies have developed to respond to stress in advantageous ways. When we needed to run from a bear, hunt a lion, or avoid a snake, our bodies predictably got us prepared with a surge of adrenaline. [1] Hunters who didn't respond well to stress or failed at hunting were less likely to live long enough to reach maturity and reproduce. So we have the successful hunter to thank for our genes, but people in developed countries today do not need hunting skills to feed their families.

While food is still an issue in many parts of the world, our need to respond to threats and stress has shifted from our evolutionary roots to concern over our job, our relationships, and how we negotiate a modern economy. Communication is a great resource and tool, and we can apply the principles and lessons to ourselves. We can create the perception that the speech is like defeating the lion and really get ourselves worked up. Or we can choose to see it as a natural extension of communication with others.

Speaking in public itself is not inherently stressful, but our response to the stimulus can contribute to or reduce our level of stress. We all will have a stress response to a new, unknown, or unfamiliar stimulus. Nevertheless, the butterflies in our stomach are a response we can choose to control by becoming more familiar with the expectations, preparation, and performance associated with speaking in public.

You Don't Have to Be Perfect
Letting go of perfection can be the hardest guideline to apply to ourselves. It's also in our nature to compare ourselves to others and ourselves. You might forgive a classmate for the occasional "umm" during a speech, but then turn right around and spend a lot of mental effort chastising yourself for making the same error in your presentation. We all have distinct strengths and weaknesses. Knowing yourself and where you need to improve is an important first step. Recognizing that Rome wasn't built in a day, and that you won't become a world-class speaker overnight, may be easier said than done.

It may help to recognize that your listeners don't want to see you fail; on the contrary, they want you to do well, because when you do, they will be able to relax and enjoy your presentation. You might be surprised to know that not everyone counts each time you say "umm." However, if "umm," "ahhh," or "you know what I mean" are phrases that you tend to repeat, they will distract your audience from your message. Eliminating such distracting habits can become a goal for improvement. Improvement is a process, not an end in itself; in fact, many people believe that learning to speak in public is more about the journey than the destination. Each new setting, context, and audience will present new challenges, and your ability to adapt, learned through your journey of experience, will help you successfully meet each new challenge.

Organization Is Key to Success

Have you ever thought of a great comeback to something someone said a while after they said it? Wouldn't it have been nice to be quick and articulate and able to deliver your comeback right then and there? Speaking in public gives you a distinct advantage over "off the cuff" improvisation and stumbling for the right comeback. You get to prepare and be organized. You know you'll be speaking to an audience in order to persuade them to do, think, or consider an idea or action.

What issues might they think of while you are speaking? What comebacks or arguments might they say if it were a debate? You get to anticipate what the audience will want to know, say, or hear. You get to prepare your statements and visual aids to support your speech and create the timing, organization, and presentation of each point. Many times in life we are asked to take a position and feel unprepared to respond. Speaking in public gives you the distinct opportunity to prepare and organize your ideas or points in order to make an impact and respond effectively.

Speaking in Public Is Like Participating in a Conversation

This may sound odd at first, but consider the idea of an "enlarged conversation" described by Julia T. Wood. [2] She expresses a clear connection between everyday speech and public dialogue. Sometimes we take a speech turn, while at other times we remain silent while others take their turn. We do this all day long and think nothing of it. We are often the focus of attention from friends and colleagues and it hardly ever makes us nervous. When we get on a stage, however, some people perceive that the whole game has changed. It hasn't. We still take turns, and the speaker will take a longer turn as part of an enlarged conversation. People in the audience will still communicate feedback and the speaker will still negotiate his or her turn just the way they would in an everyday conversation. The difference is all about how we, as the speaker, perceive the context.

Some people feel that the level of expectations, the need for perfection, or the idealistic qualities we perceive in eloquent speakers are required, and then focus on deficiencies, fears, and the possibility of failing to measure up. By letting go of this ideal, we can approach the challenge with a more pragmatic frame of mind. The rules we play comfortably by in conversation every day are the same as we shift to a larger conversation within the context of public speaking. This viewpoint can offer an alternative as you address your apprehensions, and help you let go of unrealistic expectations.

KEY TAKEAWAY

Public speaking does not have to be a "fright or flight" experience; it can be like holding a half of a friendly conversation. This will especially be true if you do a good job of preparing and organizing your presentation ahead of time.

EXERCISES

1. Have you ever done a creative visualization exercise? Try this one and see how it helps you prepare your speech. Choose a quiet place, sit in a comfortable position, and close your eyes. Picture yourself getting up to give your oral presentation. Picture what you want to happen—you will speak confidently, clearly, and engagingly. Your audience will listen attentively and consider the merit of your points. When you are finished, they will applaud and express appreciation for the good job you have done.

2. Write out a series of goal statements, one for each part or point of your presentation. What do you want to accomplish with each section, visual aid, or statement? Share your results with classmates.

3. Consider the elements of a speech to inform and adapt them for a speech to persuade. In what ways would you adjust key points or issues?

[1] Burnham, T., & Phelan, J. (2000). *Mean genes: From sex to money to food: Taming our primal instincts.* Cambridge, MA: Perseus.
[2] Woods, J. (2001). *Communication mosaics: An introduction to the field of communication* (2nd ed.). Belmont, CA: Wadsworth.

10.5 Overcoming Obstacles in Your Presentation
LEARNING OBJECTIVE

1. Overcome common obstacles in public speaking.

We have examined steps to help you investigate and build an effective speech, and discussed some myths, and realities, associated with public speaking. In order to prepare you for success, let's revisit some obstacles you'll want to avoid in order to make your content as accessible to your audience as possible. To build on what we covered, let's examine three key barriers to an effective speech: language, perception, and ethnocentrism. As a speaker, you will need to make an effort to consider each one and how you will create a bridge, rather than contribute to a barrier, with your audience.

Language

Language serves both to bring us together and to help us reinforce our group status. Language can include established languages, like Spanish or French; dialects; or even subtle in-group language styles within a larger language context. Have you ever been part of a group that has its own words or phrases, expressions that have meanings understood only by the members of your group? It is not unusual for families, groups of close friends, classmates, and romantic couples to develop these kinds of "private language." When a group communicates in its own way, it can create a sense of belonging, reinforcing your membership and place in that group.

People often tell each other stories, which often communicate a value or meaning in the culture. Perhaps you have heard the saying, "The early bird gets the worm," with its underlying meaning that the one who is prepared and ready gets the reward. In North America, this saying is common, and reflects a cultural value about promptness and competition. Diverse cultures have diverse sayings that reflect differences in values, customs, and traditions

Judy Pearson, Paul Nelson, [1] and Joseph DeVito [2] describe two key areas of language that serve to bring us together, but because they involve a specialized knowledge unique to the group or community, they can create barriers to outsiders. These are often called co-languages, because they exist and interact with a dominant language but are nonetheless distinct from it. Jargon is an occupation-specific language used by people in a given profession. Think of the way medical caregivers speak to one another, frequently using abbreviations for procedures and medications. Slang is the use of existing or newly invented words to take the place of standard or traditional words with the intent of adding an unconventional, nonstandard, humorous, or rebellious effect. Think of how the words "cool," "glitzy," or "scam" are used in casual conversation. In addition to language-based barriers, there are also several factors, many of which we have visited in previous chapters, which can act as barriers to effective intercultural communication.

Nature of Perception

Perception is an important part of the communication process, and it is important to recognize that other people's perceptions may be different from our own in several ways.

Your cultural value system, what you value and pay attention to, will significantly affect your speech and how your listeners perceive it. North American culture places an emphasis on space, with an "appropriate" distance while shaking hands, for example. If a North American travels to France, Spain, or Chile, he or she will find that a much smaller sense of personal space is the norm, and may receive a kiss on the cheek as a greeting from a new acquaintance. If the North American is uncomfortable, the person from France may not attribute his or her discomfort to personal space, and they may have a miscommunication. Learning about other cultures can help you adapt your speech in diverse settings,

and make you more comfortable as you enter new situations where others' perceptions are different from your own.

Role identities, which involve expected social behavior, are another aspect of intercultural communication that can act as a barrier to effective communication. How does your culture expect men and women to act and behave? How about children, or elders, and older citizens? The word "role" implies an expectation of how one is supposed to act in certain settings and scenes; just like in a play or a movie, each person has a culturally bound set of role expectations. Who works as a doctor, a lawyer, a nurse, or a welder? As times and cultures change, so do role identities. Business management was once perceived as a profession dominated by men, but in recent decades women have become actively involved in starting, developing, and facilitating the growth of businesses. As a speaker, your role will necessarily involve preparation and practice, and to a degree an element of leadership as you present your content and guide your audience through it. Your audience also has a role, which involves active listening and displays of interest. Your overlapping roles of interest in the topic are keys to an effective speech.

Goals reflect what we value and are willing to work for and vary widely across cultures. In some cultures, an afternoon lunch is the main meal of the day, a time with the family, which is followed by a siesta or resting period. In the United States and northern Europe, people often have a quick lunch or even a "working lunch," with the emphasis on continuing productivity and the goal of personal and organizational achievement. The differences in values, such as family time versus work time, establish themselves in how we lead our lives. To a European who is accustomed to a full month of vacation each year, the thought of someone from the United States spending a few intense, three-day power weekends hiking, skiing, or sailing might seem stressful. To a goal-oriented North American, the power weekend may be just the rejuvenation required to get "back in the game." Time, and limits on it, will be an important goal in your speech.

Geert Hofstede has spent decades researching the concepts of individualism versus collectivism across diverse cultures. He characterized U.S. culture as strongly individualistic: people perceive things primarily from their own viewpoint, see themselves as individuals capable of making his or her own decisions, and feel responsible for their actions and solving their own problems. [3] He also found many countries in Asia and South America to be much more collectivistic, focusing on the needs of the family, community, or larger group. In this context, cultural background can become a barrier to an effective speech if your fail to consider your audience and their needs.

In addition, there are other cultural dimensions that influence how we relate to the world that impact our intercultural communication. Carley Dodd discusses the degree to which cultures communicate rules explicitly or implicitly. [4] In an explicit context, the rules are discussed before we hold a meeting, negotiate a contract, or even play a game. In the United States, we want to make sure everyone knows the rules beforehand and get frustrated if people do not follow the rules. In the Middle East and Latin America, the rules are generally understood by everyone, and people from these cultures tend to be more accommodating to small differences and are less concerned about whether or not everyone plays by the same rules. Our ability to adapt to contexts that are explicit or implicit is related to our ability to tolerate uncertainty. [5]

In the United States, we often look to guiding principles rather than rules for every circumstance, and believe that with hard work, we can achieve our goals even though we do not know the outcome. In Peru, Chile, and Argentina, however, people prefer to reduce ambiguity and uncertainty, and like to know exactly what is expected and what the probable outcome will be. [6]

Table 10.2 Cultural Dimensions

Individualistic Cultures. People value individual freedom and personal independence.	**Collectivistic Cultures.** People value the family or community over the needs of the individual.
Explicit-Rule Cultures. People discuss rules and expectations clearly to make sure the rules are known.	**Implicit-Rule Cultures.** People's customs are implied and known by everyone, but not always clearly stated.
Uncertainty-Accepting Cultures. People often focus on principles, rather than having rules for every circumstance, and accept that the outcome is not always known.	**Uncertainty-Rejecting Cultures.** People often focus on rules for every circumstance and do not like ambiguity or not knowing what the outcome will be.

When we consider whether a culture as a whole places more emphasis on the individual or the community, we must be careful to recognize that individual members of the culture may hold beliefs or customs that do not follow a cultural norm. Stereotypes, defined as generalizations about a group of people that oversimplify their culture, [7] can be one significant barrier to effective intercultural communication. Gordon Allport, a pioneer in the field of communication

research, examined how and when we formulate or use stereotypes to characterize distinct groups or communities. He found that we tend to stereotype people and cultures with which we have little contact. [8]

In addition, your first-hand experience will provide you with an increased understanding of prejudice. Prejudice involves a negative preconceived judgment or opinion that guides conduct or social behavior. Within the United States, can you make a list of people or groups that may be treated with prejudice by the majority group? Your list may include specific ethnic, racial, or cultural groups that are stereotyped in the media, but it could also include socioeconomic groups or even different regions of the United States. For example, Native Americans were long treated with prejudice in early Western films. Can you imagine, in other countries they may also treat groups with prejudice? In many parts of South America, indigenous people are treated poorly and their rights as citizens are sometimes not respected. Has treatment of Native Americans changed in North America? It has also changed, and continues to change in North and South America.

People who treat other with prejudice often make judgments about the group or communities. As Allport illustrated for us, we often assume characteristics about groups with which we have little contact. By extension, we can sometimes assume similarity that people are all basically similar, in effect denying cultural, racial, or ethnic differences. We sometimes describe the United States as a "melting pot," where individual and cultural differences blend to become a homogeneous culture. This "melting pot" often denies cultural differences. The metaphor of a "salad bowl," where communities and cultures retain their distinctive characteristics or "flavor," serves as more equitable model. In this "salad bowl," we value the differences and what they contribute to the whole.

We can also run the risk of assuming familiarity with cultures when we attribute characteristics of one group to everyone who has connections to the larger culture. For example, people may assume that we are familiar with all Native Americans if we know one tribe in our community, forgetting the distinct differences that exist between tribes and even between individual Native Americans who live either in urban areas or on reservations.

Ethnocentrism

Finally, your experience may help you to not view the world and its diversity of cultures in an ethnocentric way. Ethnocentrism means you go beyond pride in your culture, heritage or background and hold the "conviction that (you) know more and are better than those of different cultures." [9] This belief in the superiority of one's own group can guide individual and group behavior. If you visit a new country where people do things differently, you would be considered ethnocentric if you viewed their way as wrong because it is not the same way you were taught. Groups are considered ethnocentric if they prejudge individuals or other groups of people based on negative preconceptions.

KEY TAKEAWAY

For a successful oral presentation, do your best to avoid obstacles to understanding, such as language expressions (i.e., unknown to other listeners), cultural perceptions, and ethnocentrism.

EXERCISES

1. Consider the vocabulary that you and your classmates generally use in casual conversations. Are there slang expressions that you often use? Is there a jargon related to your career or major field of study? Make a list of slang and jargon words that you might want to use in a speech. Now, consider whether you can substitute standard English words that will be better understood by all your listeners, remembering that in a business context it is often best to avoid slang and jargon.

2. Pretend you were going to invite someone from a completely different culture to come home with you for a break or holiday. Make a list of ideas, words, or places you would want to share with them to gain insight of you, your family, or your community.

3. How can a speaker prepare a speech for a diverse audience? Explain and give some specific examples. Discuss your thoughts with a classmate.

4. Observe someone presenting a speech. Given the discussion in this chapter, what elements of their speech could you use in your speech? What elements would you not want to use? Why? Compare with a classmate.

10.6 Additional Resources

- Oral communication skill is key to success in politics. Visit the C-SPAN Web site to watch and listen to speeches, interviews, and other public speaking events. http://www.c-span.org/Topics/Politics.aspx

- Schooltube.com offers a video archive of student government speeches. http://www.schooltube.com/video/27713/2009-Student-Government-Campaign-Speeches

- The Nation's Forum Collection of the Library of Congress consists of recordings of dozens of speeches from the period 1918 to 1920. http://memory.loc.gov/ammem/nfhtml

- The Copyright Office of the Library of Congress offers a wide variety of resources for understanding copyright law and how to avoid plagiarism. http://www.copyright.gov

- Thunderbird School of Global Management operates Thunderbird Knowledge Network, an interactive forum on contemporary business issues delivered in stories, columns, videos, podcasts, and blogs. http://knowledgenetwork.thunderbird.edu/research

- The U.S. Department of Labor's Occupational Safety and Health Administration (OSHA) sets the standards and conducts inspections to ensure safety and prevent accidents in the workplace. http://www.osha.gov

- Watch an informative speech on "Avoiding Stereotypes in Public Speaking" on eHow.com. http://www.ehow.com/video_4401072_avoiding-stereotypes-public-speaking.html

NOTES:

[1] Pearson, J., & Nelson, P. (2000). *An introduction to human communication: Understanding and sharing.* Boston, MA: McGraw-Hill.

[2] DeVito, J. (1986). *The communication handbook: A dictionary.* New York, NY: Harper & Row.

[3] Hofstede, G. (1982). *Culture's consequences* (2nd ed.). Newbury Park, CA: Sage.

[4] Dodd, C. (1998). *Dynamics of intercultural communication* (5th ed.). New York, NY: Harper & Row.

[5] Hofstede, G. (1982). *Culture's consequences* (2nd ed.). Newbury Park, CA: Sage.

[6] Samovar, L., Porter, R., & Stefani, L. (1998). *Communication between cultures* (3rd ed.). Belmont, CA: Wadsworth.

[7] Rogers, E., & Steinfatt, T. (1999). *Intercultural communication.* Prospect Heights, IL: Waveland Press.

[8] Allport, G. (1958). *The nature of prejudice.* New York, NY: Doubleday.

[9] Seiler, W., & Beall, M. (2000). *Communication: Making connections* (4th ed.). Boston, MA: Allyn & Bacon.

NOTES:

Chapter 11:
Nonverbal Delivery

The most important thing in communication is hearing what isn't said.
  Peter F. Drucker
But behavior in the human being is sometimes a defense, a way of concealing motives and thoughts.
  Abraham Maslow
Electric communication will never be a substitute for the face of someone who with their soul encourages another person to be brave and true.
  Charles Dickens

Getting Started

INTRODUCTORY EXERCISES

1. It's not just what you say but how you say it. Choose a speech to watch. Examples may include famous speeches by historical figures like Martin Luther King Jr. or Winston Churchill, current elected officials, or perhaps candidates for local and state office that may be televised. Other examples could be from a poetry slam, a rap performance, or a movie. Watch the presentation without sound and see what you observe. Does the speaker seem comfortable and confident? Aggressive or timid? If possible, repeat the speech a second time with the sound on. Do your perceptions change? What patterns do you observe?

2. Invasion of space. When someone "invades" your space, how do you feel? Threatened, surprised, interested, or repulsed? We can learn a lot from each other as we come to be more aware of the normative space expectations and boundaries. Set aside ten minutes where you can "people watch" in a public setting. Make a conscious effort to notice how far apart they stand from people they communicate. Record your results. Your best estimate is fine and there is no need to interrupt people, just watch and record. Consider noting if they are male or female, or focus only on same-sex conversations. When you have approximate distances for at least twenty conversations or ten minutes have passed, add up the results and look for a pattern. Compare your findings with those of a classmate.

In the first of the Note 11.1 "Introductory Exercises" for this chapter, we focus on how a speaker presents ideas, not the ideas themselves. Have you ever been in class and found it hard to listen to the professor, not because he or she wasn't well informed or the topic wasn't interesting or important to you, but because the style of presentation didn't engage you

as a listener? If your answer is yes, then you know that you want to avoid making the same mistake when you give a presentation. It's not always what you say, but how you say it that makes a difference. We sometimes call this "body language," or "nonverbal communication," and it is a key aspect of effective business communication.

How do you know when your boss or instructors are pleased with your progress (or not)? You might know from the smiles on their faces, from the time and attention they give you, or perhaps in other nonverbal ways, like a raise, a bonus, or a good grade. Whether the interaction takes place face-to-face, or at a distance, you can still experience and interpret nonverbal responses.

Sometimes we place more emphasis on nonverbal aspects of communication that they warrant. Suppose you have just gotten home from your first date with Amanda and you feel it went very well. How soon should afterward should you call Amanda? There are lots of advice columns, informal rules and customs, and friends with opinions to offer you suggestions, but you know what is right for you. You also know that texting her at five o'clock the next morning might be a bit early. You may choose to wait until a coffee break around 10 a.m. to send a short text message, and realize that you might not get a response until later that afternoon.

Does the lack of an immediate response have any meaning? Does it mean Amanda is less interested in you than you are in her? While you might give it more attention than it deserves, and maybe let it weigh on your mind and distract you from other tasks, the time interval for responding may not have as much intentional meaning as you think. It might mean that Amanda has a different sense of time urgency than you do, or that she simply didn't receive your message until later.

Timing is an important aspect of nonverbal communication, but trying to understand what a single example of timing means is challenging. Context may make a difference. For example, if you have known someone for years who has always responded promptly to your e-mails or texts, but now that person hasn't responded in over a day, you may have reason for concern. That person's behavior doesn't match what you are familiar with, and this sudden, unexplained change in the established pattern may mean that you need to follow up.

11.1 Principles of Nonverbal Communication
LEARNING OBJECTIVES

1. Demonstrate nonverbal communication and describe its role in the communication process.
2. Understand and explain the principles of nonverbal communication.

Nonverbal Communication Is Fluid

Chances are you have had many experiences where words were misunderstood, or where the meaning of words was unclear. When it comes to nonverbal communication, meaning is even harder to discern. We can sometimes tell what people are communicating through their nonverbal communication, but there is no foolproof "dictionary" of how to interpret nonverbal messages. Nonverbal communication is the process of conveying a message without the use of words. It can include gestures and facial expressions, tone of voice, timing, posture and where you stand as you communicate. It can help or hinder the clear understanding of your message, but it doesn't reveal (and can even mask) what you are really thinking. Nonverbal communication is far from simple, and its complexity makes our study and our understanding a worthy but challenging goal.

Where does a wink start and a nod end? Nonverbal communication involves the entire body, the space it occupies and dominates, the time it interacts, and not only what is not said, but how it is not said. Confused? Try to focus on just one element of nonverbal communication and it will soon get lost among all the other stimuli. Let's consider eye contact. What does it mean by itself without context, chin position, or eyebrows to flag interest or signal a threat? Nonverbal action flows almost seamlessly from one to the next, making it a challenge to interpret one element, or even a series of elements.

We perceive time as linear, flowing along in a straight line. We did one task, we're doing another task now, and we are planning on doing something else all the time. Sometimes we place more emphasis on the future, or the past, forgetting that we are actually living in the present moment whether we focus on "the now" or not. Nonverbal communication is always in motion, as long as we are, and is never the same twice.

Nonverbal communication is irreversible. In written communication, you can write a clarification, correction, or retraction. While it never makes the original statement go completely away, it does allow for correction. Unlike written communication, oral communication may allow "do-overs"

on the spot: you can explain and restate, hoping to clarify your point. You can also dig the hole you are in just a little bit deeper. The old sayings "when you find yourself in a hole, stop digging" and "open mouth, insert foot" can sometimes apply to oral communications. We've all said something we would give anything to take back, but we all know we can't. Oral communication, like written communication, allows for some correction, but it still doesn't erase the original message or its impact. Nonverbal communication takes it one step further. You can't separate one nonverbal action from the context of all the other verbal and nonverbal communication acts, and you can't take it back.

In a speech, nonverbal communication is continuous in the sense that it is always occurring, and because it is so fluid, it can be hard to determine where one nonverbal message starts and another stops. Words can be easily identified and isolated, but if we try to single out a speaker's gestures, smile, or stance without looking at how they all come together in context, we may miss the point and draw the wrong conclusion. You need to be conscious of this aspect of public speaking because, to quote another old saying, "Actions speak louder than words." This is true in the sense that people often pay more attention to your nonverbal expressions more than your words. As a result, nonverbal communication is a powerful way to contribute to (or detract from) your success in communicating your message to the audience.

Nonverbal Communication Is Fast

Let's pretend you are at your computer at work. You see that an e-mail has arrived, but you are right in the middle of tallying a spreadsheet whose numbers just don't add up. You see that the e-mail is from a coworker and you click on it. The subject line reads "pink slips." You could interpret this to mean a suggestion for a Halloween costume, or a challenge to race for each other's car ownership, but in the context of the workplace you may assume it means layoffs.

Your emotional response is immediate. If the author of the e-mail could see your face, they would know that your response was one of disbelief and frustration, even anger, all via your nonverbal communication. Yes, when a tree falls in the forest it makes a sound, even if no one is there to hear it. In the same way, you express yourself via nonverbal communication all the time without much conscious thought at all. You may think about how to share the news with your partner, and try to display a smile and a sense of calm when you feel like anything but smiling.

Nonverbal communication gives our thoughts and feelings away before we are even aware of what we are thinking or how we feel. People may see and hear more than you ever anticipated. Your nonverbal communication includes both intentional and unintentional messages, but since it all happens so fast, the unintentional ones can contradict what you know you are supposed to say or how you are supposed to react.

Nonverbal Communication Can Add to or Replace Verbal Communication

People tend to pay more attention to how you say it than what you actually say. In presenting a speech this is particularly true. We communicate nonverbally more than we engage in verbal communication, and often use nonverbal expressions to add to, or even replace, words we might otherwise say. We use a nonverbal gesture called an illustrator to communicate our message effectively and reinforce our point. Your coworker Andrew may ask you, "Barney's Bar after work?" as he walks by, and you simply nod and say "yeah." Andrew may respond with a nonverbal gesture, called an emblem, by signaling with the "OK" sign as he walks away.

In addition to illustrators or emblematic nonverbal communication, we also use regulators. "Regulators are nonverbal messages which control, maintain or discourage interaction." [1] For example, if someone is telling you a message that is confusing or upsetting, you may hold up your hand, a commonly recognized regulator that asks the speaker to stop talking.

Let's say you are in a meeting presenting a speech that introduces your company's latest product. If your audience members nod their heads in agreement on important points and maintain good eye contact, it is a good sign. Nonverbally, they are using regulators encouraging you to continue with your presentation. In contrast, if they look away, tap their feet, and begin drawing in the margins of their notebook, these are regulators suggesting that you better think of a way to regain their interest or else wrap up your presentation quickly.

"Affect displays are nonverbal communication that express emotions or feelings." [2] An affect display that might accompany holding up your hand for silence would be to frown and shake your head from side to side. When you and Andrew are at Barney's Bar, smiling and waving at coworkers who arrive lets them know where you are seated and welcomes them.

"Adaptors are displays of nonverbal communication that help you adapt to your environment and each context, helping you feel comfortable and secure." [3] A self-adaptor involves you meeting your need for security, by playing with your hair for example, by adapting something about yourself in way for which it was not designed or for no apparent purpose. Combing your hair would be an example of a purposeful action, unlike a self-adaptive behavior. An object-adaptor involves the use of an object in a way for which it was not designed. You may see audience members tapping their pencils, chewing on them, or playing with them, while ignoring you and your presentation. Or perhaps someone pulls out a comb and repeatedly rubs a thumbnail against the comb's teeth. They are using the comb or the pencil in a way other than its intended design, an object-adaptor that communicates a lack of engagement or enthusiasm in your speech.

Intentional nonverbal communication can complement, repeat, replace, mask, or contradict what we say. When Andrew invited you to Barney's, you said, "Yeah" and nodded, complementing and repeating the message. You could have simply nodded, effectively replacing the "yes" with a nonverbal response. You could also have decided to say no, but did not want to hurt Andrew's feelings. Shaking your head "no" while pointing to your watch, communicating work and time issues, may mask your real thoughts or feelings. Masking involves the substitution of appropriate nonverbal communication for nonverbal communication you may want to display. [4] Finally, nonverbal messages that conflict with verbal communication can confuse the listener. Table 11.1 "Some Nonverbal Expressions" summarizes these concepts.

Nonverbal Communication Is Universal

Consider the many contexts in which interaction occurs during your day. In the morning, at work, after work, at home, with friends, with family, and our list could go on for quite a while. Now consider the differences in nonverbal communication across these many contexts. When you are at work, do you jump up and down and say whatever you want? Why or why not? You may not engage in that behavior because of expectations at work, but the fact remains that from the moment you wake until you sleep, you are surrounded by nonverbal communication.

If you had been born in a different country, to different parents, and perhaps as a member of the opposite sex, your whole world would be quite different. Yet nonverbal communication would remain a universal constant. It may not look the same, or get used in the same way, but it will still be nonverbal communication in its many functions and displays.

Table 11.1 Some Nonverbal Expressions

Term	Definition
Adaptors	Help us feel comfortable or indicate emotions or moods
Affect Displays	Express emotions or feelings
Complementing	Reinforcing verbal communication
Contradicting	Contradicting verbal communication
Emblems	Nonverbal gestures that carry a specific meaning, and can replace or reinforce words
Illustrators	Reinforce a verbal message
Masking	Substituting more appropriate displays for less appropriate displays
Object-Adaptors	Using an object for a purpose other than its intended design
Regulators	Control, encourage or discourage interaction
Repeating	Repeating verbal communication
Replacing	Replacing verbal communication
Self-Adaptors	Adapting something about yourself in a way for which it was not designed or for no apparent purpose

Nonverbal Communication Is Confusing and Contextual

Nonverbal communication can be confusing. We need contextual clues to help us understand, or begin to understand, what a movement, gesture, or lack of display means. Then we have to figure it all out based on our prior knowledge (or lack thereof) of the person and hope to get it right. Talk about a challenge. Nonverbal communication is everywhere, and we all use it, but that doesn't make it simple or independent of when, where, why, or how we communicate.

Nonverbal Communication Can Be Intentional or Unintentional

Suppose you are working as a salesclerk in a retail store, and a customer communicated frustration to you. Would the nonverbal aspects of your response be intentional or unintentional? Your job is to be pleasant and courteous at all times, yet your wrinkled eyebrows or wide eyes may have been unintentional. They clearly communicate your negative feelings at that moment. Restating your wish to be helpful and displaying nonverbal gestures may communicate "no big deal," but the stress of the moment is still "written" on your face.

Can we tell when people are intentionally or unintentionally communicating nonverbally? Ask ten people this question and compare their responses. You may be surprised. It is clearly a challenge to understand nonverbal communication in action. We often assign intentional motives to nonverbal communication when in fact their display is unintentional, and often hard to interpret.

Nonverbal Messages Communicate Feelings and Attitudes

Steven Beebe, Susan Beebe, and Mark Redmond offer us three additional principals of interpersonal nonverbal communication that serve our discussion. One is that you often react faster than you think. Your nonverbal responses communicate your initial reaction before you can process it through language or formulate an appropriate response. If your appropriate, spoken response doesn't match your nonverbal reaction, you may give away your true feelings and attitudes. [5]

Albert Mehrabian asserts that we rarely communicate emotional messages through the spoken word. According to Mehrabian, 93 percent of the time we communicate our emotions nonverbally, with at least 55 percent associated with facial gestures. Vocal cues, body position and movement, and normative space between speaker and receiver can also be clues to feelings and attitudes. [6]

Is your first emotional response always an accurate and true representation of your feelings and attitudes, or does your emotional response change across time? We are all changing all the time, and sometimes a moment of frustration or a flash of anger can signal to the receiver a feeling or emotion that existed for a moment, but has since passed. Their response to your communication will be based on that perception, even though you might already be over the issue. This is where the spoken word serves us well. You may need to articulate clearly that you were frustrated, but not anymore. The words spoken out loud can serve to clarify and invite additional discussion.

We Believe Nonverbal Communication More than Verbal

Building on the example of responding to a situation with facial gestures associated with frustration before you even have time to think of an appropriate verbal response, let's ask the question: what would you believe, someone's actions or their words? According to William Seiler and Melissa Beall, most people tend to believe the nonverbal message over the verbal message. People will often answer that "actions speak louder than words" and place a disproportionate emphasis on the nonverbal response. [7] Humans aren't logical all the time, and they do experience feelings and attitudes that change. Still, we place more confidence in nonverbal communication, particularly when it comes to lying behaviors. According to Miron Zuckerman, Bella DePaulo, and Robert Rosenthal, there are several behaviors people often display when they are being deceptive: [8]

- Reduction in eye contact while engaged in a conversation
- Awkward pauses in conversation
- Higher pitch in voice
- Deliberate pronunciation and articulation of words
- Increased delay in response time to a question
- Increased body movements like changes in posture
- Decreased smiling
- Decreased rate of speech

If you notice one of more of the behaviors, you may want to take a closer look. Over time we learn people's patterns of speech and behavior, and form a set of expectations. Variation from their established patterns, combined with the clues above, can serve to alert you to the possibility that something deserves closer attention.

Our nonverbal responses have a connection to our physiological responses to stress, such as heart rate, blood pressure, and skin conductivity. Polygraph machines (popularly referred to as "lie detectors") focus on these physiological responses and demonstrate anomalies, or variations. While movies and TV crime shows may make polygraphs look foolproof, there is significant debate about whether they measure dishonesty with any degree of accuracy.

Can you train yourself to detect lies? It is unlikely. Our purpose in studying nonverbal communication is not to uncover dishonesty in others, but rather to help you understand how to use the nonverbal aspects of communication to increase understanding.

Nonverbal Communication Is Key in the Speaker/Audience Relationship

When we first see each other, before anyone says a word, we are already sizing each other up. Within the first few seconds we have made judgments about each other based on what we wear, our physical characteristics, even our posture. Are these judgments accurate? That is hard to know without context, but we can say that nonverbal communication certainly affects first impressions, for better or worse. When a speaker and the audience first meet, nonverbal communication in terms of space, dress, and even personal characteristics can contribute to assumed expectations. The expectations might not be accurate or even fair, but it is important to recognize

that they will be present. There is truth in the saying, "You never get a second chance to make a first impression." Since beginnings are fragile times, your attention to aspects you can control, both verbal and nonverbal, will help contribute to the first step of forming a relationship with your audience. Your eye contact with audience members, use of space, and degree of formality will continue to contribute to that relationship.

As a speaker, your nonverbal communication is part of the message and can contribute to, or detract from, your overall goals. By being aware of them, and practicing with a live audience, you can learn to be more aware and in control.

KEY TAKEAWAYS

- Nonverbal communication is the process of conveying a message without the use of words; it relates to the dynamic process of communication, the perception process and listening, and verbal communication.
- Nonverbal communication is fluid and fast, universal, confusing, and contextual. It can add to or replace verbal communication and can be intentional or unintentional.
- Nonverbal communication communicates feelings and attitudes, and people tend to believe nonverbal messages more than verbal ones.

EXERCISES

1. Does it limit or enhance our understanding of communication to view nonverbal communication as that which is not verbal communication? Explain your answer and discuss with the class.
2. Choose a television personality you admire. What do you like about this person? Watch several minutes of this person with the sound turned off, and make notes of the nonverbal expressions you observe. Turn the sound back on and make notes of their tone of voice, timing, and other audible expressions. Discuss your results with a classmate.
3. Find a program that focuses on microexpressions and write a brief summary of how they play a role in the program. Share and compare with classmates.
4. Create a survey that addresses the issue of which people trust more, nonverbal or verbal messages. Ask an equal number of men and women and compare your results with those of your classmates.
5. Search for information on the reliability and admissibility of results from polygraph (lie detector) tests. Share your findings with classmates.
6. See how long and how much you can get done during the day without the use of verbal messages.

[1] McLean, S. (2003). *The basics of speech communication*. Boston, MA: Allyn & Bacon.

[2] McLean, S. (2003). *The basics of speech communication* (p. 77). Boston, MA: Allyn & Bacon.

[3] McLean, S. (2003). *The basics of speech communication* (p. 77). Boston, MA: Allyn & Bacon.

[4] McLean, S. (2003). *The basics of speech communication* (p. 77). Boston, MA: Allyn & Bacon.

[5] Beebe, S. [Steven], Beebe, S. [Susan], & Redmond, M. (2002). *Interpersonal communication relating to others* (3rd ed.). Boston, MA: Allyn & Bacon.

[6] Mehrabian, A. (1972). *Nonverbal communication*. Chicago, IL: Aldine Atherton.

[7] Seiler, W., & Beall, M. (2000). *Communication: Making connections* (4th ed.). Boston, MA: Allyn & Bacon.

[8] Zuckerman, M., DePaulo, B., & Rosenthal, R. (1981). Verbal and nonverbal communication of deception. *Advances in Experimental Social Psychology, 14*, 1–59.

11.2 Types of Nonverbal Communication

LEARNING OBJECTIVE

1. Describe the similarities and differences among eight general types of nonverbal communication.

Now that we have discussed the general principles that apply to nonverbal communication, let's examine eight types of nonverbal communication to further understand this challenging aspect of communication:

1. Space
2. Time
3. Physical characteristics
4. Body movements
5. Touch
6. Paralanguage
7. Artifacts
8. Environment

Space

When we discuss space in a nonverbal context, we mean the space between objects and people. Space is often associated with social rank and is an important part of business communication. Who gets the corner office? Why is the head of the table important and who gets to sit there?

People from diverse cultures may have different normative space expectations. If you are from a large urban area, having people stand close to you may be normal. If you are from a rural area or a culture where people expect more space, someone may be standing "too close" for comfort and not know it.

Edward T. Hall, serving in the European and South Pacific Regions in the Corps of Engineers during World War II, traveled around the globe. As he moved from one place to another, he noticed that people in different countries kept different distances from each other. In France, they stood closer to each other than they did in England. Hall wondered why that was and began to study what he called proxemics, or the study of the human use of space and distance in communication. [1]

In *The Hidden Dimension*, he indicated there are two main aspects of space: territory and personal space. Hall drew on anthropology to address the concepts of dominance and submission, and noted that the more powerful person often claims more space. This plays an important role in modern society, from who gets the corner office to how we negotiate space between vehicles. Road rage is increasingly common where overcrowding occurs, and as more vehicles occupy the same roads, tensions over space are predictable.

Territory is related to control. As a way of establishing control over your own room, maybe you painted it your favorite color, or put up posters that represent your interests or things you consider unique about yourself. Families or households often mark their space by putting up fences or walls around their houses. This sense of a right to control your space is implicit in territory. Territory means the space you claim as your own, are responsible for, or are willing to defend.

The second aspect Hall highlights is personal space, or the "bubble" of space surrounding each individual. As you walk down a flight of stairs, which side do you choose? We may choose the right side because we've learned that is what is expected, and people coming up the same stair choose their right. The right choice insures that personal space is not compromised. But what happens when some comes up the wrong side? They violate the understood rules of movement and often correct themselves. But what happens if they don't change lanes as people move up and down the stairs? They may get dirty looks or even get bumped as people in the crowd handle the invasion of "their" space. There are no lane markers, and bubbles of space around each person move with them, allowing for the possibility of collision.

We recognize the basic need for personal space, but the normative expectations for space vary greatly by culture. You may perceive that in your home people sleep one to each bed, but in many cultures people sleep two or more to a bed and it is considered normal. If you were to share that bed, you might feel uncomfortable, while someone raised with group sleeping norms might feel uncomfortable sleeping alone. From where you stand in an aerobics class in relation to others, to where you place your book bag in class, your personal expectations of space are often at variance with others.

As the context of a staircase has norms for nonverbal behavior, so does the public speaking context. In North America, eye contact with the audience is expected. Big movements and gestures are not generally expected and can be distracting. The speaker occupies a space on the "stage," even if it's in front of the class. When you occupy that space, the audience will expect to behave in certain ways. If you talk to the screen behind you while displaying a PowerPoint presentation, the audience may perceive that you are not paying attention to them. Speakers are expected to pay attention to, and interact with, the audience, even if in the feedback is primarily nonverbal. Your movements should coordinate with the tone, rhythm, and content of your speech. Pacing back and forth, keeping your hands in your pockets, or crossing your arms may communicate nervousness, or even defensiveness, and detract from your speech.

Figure 11.2 Space: Four Main Categories of Distance

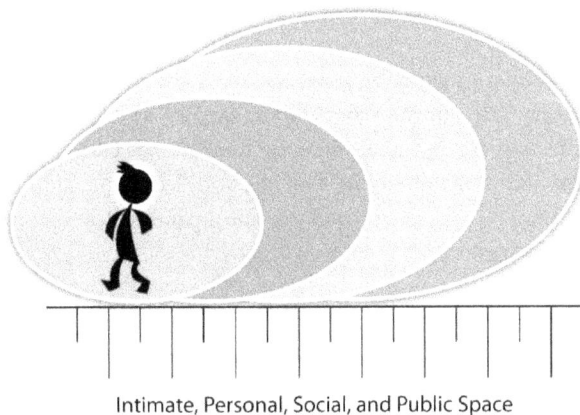

Intimate, Personal, Social, and Public Space

As a general rule, try to act naturally, as if you were telling a friend a story, so that your body will relax and your nonverbal gestures will come more naturally. Practice is key to your level of comfort; the more practice you get, the more comfortable and less intimidating it will seem to you.

Hall articulated four main categories of distance used in communication as shown in Figure 11.2 "Space: Four Main Categories of Distance". [2]

Time

Do you know what time it is? How aware you are of time varies by culture and normative expectations of adherence (or ignorance) of time. Some people, and the communities and cultures they represent, are very time-oriented. The Euro Railways trains in Germany are famous for departing and

arriving according to the schedule. In contrast, if you take the train in Argentina, you'll find that the schedule is more of an approximation of when the train will leave or arrive.

"Time is money" is a common saying across many cultures, and reveals a high value for time. In social contexts, it often reveals social status and power. Who are you willing to wait for? A doctor for an office visit when you are sick? A potential employer for a job interview? Your significant other or children? Sometimes we get impatient, and our impatience underscores our value for time.

When you give a presentation, does your audience have to wait for you? Time is a relevant factor of the communication process in your speech. The best way to show your audience respect is to honor the time expectation associated with your speech. Always try to stop speaking before the audience stops listening; if the audience perceives that you have "gone over time," they will be less willing to listen. This in turn will have a negative impact on your ability to communicate your message.

Suppose you are presenting a speech that has three main points. Your audience expects you to regulate the time and attention to each point, but if you spend all your time on the first two points and rush through the third, your speech won't be balanced and will lose rhythm. The speaker occupies a position of some power, but it is the audience that gives them that position. By displaying respect and maintaining balance, you will move through your points more effectively.

Chronemics is the study of how we refer to and perceive time. Tom Bruneau at Radford University has spent a lifetime investigating how time interacts in communication and culture. [3], [4], [5] As he notes, across Western society, time is often considered the equivalent of money. The value of speed is highly prized in some societies. [6] In others, there is a great respect for slowing down and taking a long-term view of time.

When you order a meal at a fast food restaurant, what are your expectations for how long you will have to wait? When you order a pizza online for delivery, when do you expect it will arrive? If you order cable service for your home, when do you expect it might be delivered? In the first case, you might measure the delivery of a hamburger in a matter of seconds or minutes, and perhaps thirty minutes for pizza delivery, but you may measure the time from your order to working cable in days or even weeks. You may even have to be at your home from 8 a.m. to noon, waiting for its installation. The expectations vary by context, and we often grow frustrated in a time-sensitive culture when the delivery does not match our expectations.

In the same way, how long should it take to respond to a customer's request for assistance or information? If they call on the phone, how long should they be on hold? How soon should they expect a response to an e-mail? As a skilled business communicator, you will know to anticipate normative expectations and do your best to meet those expectations more quickly than anticipated. Your prompt reply or offer of help in response to a request, even if you cannot solve the issue on the spot, is often regarded positively, contributing to the formation of positive communication interactions.

Across cultures the value of time may vary. Some Mexican American friends may invite you to a barbecue at 8 p.m., but when you arrive you are the first guest, because it is understood that the gathering actually doesn't start until after 9 p.m. Similarly in France, an 8 p.m. party invitation would be understood to indicate you should arrive around 8:30, but in Sweden 8 p.m. means 8 p.m., and latecomers may not be welcome. Some Native Americans, particularly elders, speak in well-measured phrases and take long pauses between phrases. They do not hurry their speech or compete for their turn, knowing no one will interrupt them. [7] Some Orthodox Jews observe religious days when they do not work, cook, drive, or use electricity. People around the world have different ways of expressing value for time.

Physical Characteristics

You didn't choose your birth, your eye color, the natural color of your hair, or your height, but people spend millions every year trying to change their physical characteristics. You can get colored contacts; dye your hair; and if you are shorter than you'd like to be, buy shoes to raise your stature a couple of inches. You won't be able to change your birth, and no matter how much you stoop to appear shorter, you won't change your height until time and age gradually makes itself apparent. If you are tall, you might find the correct shoe size, pant length, or even the length of mattress a challenge, but there are rewards. Have you ever heard that taller people get paid more? [8] There is some truth to that idea. There is also some truth to the notion that people prefer symmetrical faces (where both sides are equal) over asymmetrical faces (with unequal sides; like a crooked nose or having one eye or ear slightly higher than the other). [9]

We often make judgments about a person's personality or behavior based on physical characteristics, and researchers are quick to note that those judgments are often inaccurate.[10], [11] Regardless of your eye or hair color, or even how tall you are, being comfortable with yourself is an important part of your presentation. Act naturally and consider aspects of your presentation you can control in order to maximize a positive image for the audience.

Body Movements

The study of body movements, called kinesics, is key to understanding nonverbal communication. Since your actions will significantly contribute to the effectiveness of your business interactions, let's examine four distinct ways body movements that complement, repeat, regulate, or replace your verbal messages.

Body movements can complement the verbal message by reinforcing the main idea. For example, you may be providing an orientation presentation to a customer about a software program. As you say, "Click on this tab," you may also initiate that action. Your verbal and nonverbal messages reinforce each other. You can also reinforce the message by repeating it. If you first say, "Click on the tab," and then motion with your hand to the right, indicating that the customer should move the cursor arrow with the mouse to the tab, your repetition can help the listener understand the message.

In addition to repeating your message, body movements can also regulate conversations. Nodding your head to indicate that you are listening may encourage the customer to continue asking questions. Holding your hand up, palm out, may signal them to stop and provide a pause where you can start to answer.

Body movements also substitute or replace verbal messages. Ekman and Friesen found that facial features communicate to others our feelings, but our body movements often reveal how intensely we experience those feelings. [12] For example, if the customer makes a face of frustration while trying to use the software program, they may need assistance. If they push away from the computer and separate themselves physically from interacting with it, they may be extremely frustrated. Learning to gauge feelings and their intensity as expressed by customers takes time and patience, and your attention to them will improve your ability to facilitate positive interactions.

Touch

Touch in communication interaction is called haptics, and William Seiler and Meliss Beall[13] identify five distinct types of touch, from impersonal to intimate, as listed in Table 11.2 "Types of Touch".

Before giving your presentation, you may interact with people by shaking hands and making casual conversation. This interaction can help establish trust before you take the stage. While speaking in public we do not often touch people in the audience, but we do interact with visual aids, our note cards, and other objects. How we handle them can communicate our comfort level. It's always a good idea to practice using the technology, visual aids, or note cards you will use in a speech during a practice session. Using the technology correctly by clicking the right button on the mouse or pressing the right switch on the overhead projector can contribute to your credibility.

Table 11.2 Types of Touch

Term	Definition
1. Functional-Professional Touch	Medical examination, physical therapy, sports coach, music teacher
2. Social-Polite Touch	Handshake
3. Friendship-Warmth Touch	Hug
4. Love-Intimacy Touch	Kiss between family members or romantic partners
5. Sexual-Arousal Touch	Sexual caressing and intercourse

Paralanguage

Paralanguage is the exception to the definition of nonverbal communication. You may recall that we defined nonverbal communication as not involving words, but paralanguage exists when we are speaking, using words. Paralanguage involves verbal and nonverbal aspects of speech that influence meaning, including tone, intensity, pausing, and even silence.

Perhaps you've also heard of a pregnant pause, a silence between verbal messages that is full of meaning. The meaning itself may be hard to understand or decipher, but it is there nonetheless. For example, your coworker Jan comes back from a sales meeting speechless and with a ghost-white complexion. You may ask if the meeting went all right. "Well, ahh…" may be the only response you get. The pause speaks volumes. Something happened, though you may not know what. It could be personal if Jan's report was not well received, or it could be more systemic, like the news that sales figures are off by 40 percent and pink slips may not be far behind.

Silence or vocal pauses can communicate hesitation, indicate the need to gather thought, or serve as a sign of respect. Keith Basso quotes an anonymous source as stating, "It is not the case that a man who is silent says nothing." [14] Sometimes we learn just as much, or even more, from what a person does not say as what they do say. In addition, both Basso and Susan Philips found that traditional speech among Native Americans places a special emphasis on silence. [15]

Artifacts

Do you cover your tattoos when you are at work? Do you know someone who does? Or perhaps you know someone who has a tattoo and does not need to cover it up on their job? Expectations vary a great deal, but body art or tattoos are still controversial in the workplace. According to the *San Diego Union-Tribune,* [16]

- 20 percent of workers indicated their body art had been held against them on the job.
- 42 percent of employers said the presence of visible body art lowered their opinion of workers.
- 44 percent of managers surveyed have body art.
- 52 percent of workers surveyed have body art.
- 67 percent of workers who have body art or piercings cover or remove them during work hours.

In your line of work, a tattoo might be an important visual aid, or it might detract from your effectiveness as a business communicator. Body piercings may express individuality, but you need to consider how they will be interpreted by employers and customers.

Artifacts are forms of decorative ornamentation that are chosen to represent self-concept. They can include rings and tattoos, but may also include brand names and logos. From clothes to cars, watches, briefcases, purses, and even eyeglasses, what we choose to surround ourselves with communicates something about our sense of self. They may project gender, role or position, class or status, personality, and group membership or affiliation. Paying attention to a customer's artifacts can give you a sense of the self they want to communicate, and may allow you to more accurately adapt your message to meet their needs.

Environment

Environment involves the physical and psychological aspects of the communication context. More than the tables and chairs in an office, environment is an important part of the dynamic communication process. The perception of one's environment influences one's reaction to it. For example, Google is famous for its work environment, with spaces created for physical activity and even in-house food service around the clock. The expense is no doubt considerable, but Google's actions speak volumes. The results produced in the environment, designed to facilitate creativity, interaction, and collaboration, are worth the effort.

EXERCISE

1. Do a Google search on space and culture. Share your findings with your classmates.

2. Note where people sit on the first day of class, and each class session thereafter. Do students return to the same seat? If they do not attend class, do the classmates leave their seat vacant? Compare your results.

3. What kind of value do you have for time, and what is truly important to you? Make a list of what you spend your time on, and what you value most. Do the lists match? Are you spending time on what is truly important to you? Relationships take time, and if you want them to succeed in a personal or business context, you have to make them a priority.

4. To what degree is time a relevant factor in communication in the information age? Give some examples. Discuss your ideas with a classmate.

5. How many people do you know who have chosen tattoos or piercings as a representation of self and statement of individuality? Survey your friends and share your findings with your classmates.

[1] Hall, E. T. (1963). Proxemics: The study of man's spacial relations and boundaries. In Iago Galdston (Ed.), *Man's image in medicine and anthropology* (pp. 422–445). New York, NY: International Universities Press.

[2] Hall, E. (1966). *The hidden dimension*. New York, NY: Doubleday.

[3] Bruneau, T. (1974). Time and nonverbal communication. *Journal of Poplular Culture, 8*, 658–666.

[4] Bruneau, T. (1990). Chronemics: The study of time in human interaction. In J. DeVito & M. Hecht (Eds.), *The nonverbal reader* (pp. 301–311). Prospect Heights, IL: Waveland Press.

[5] Bruneau, T., & Ishii, S. (1988). Communicative silence: East and west. *World Communication, 17*, 1–33.

[6] Schwartz, T. (1989, January/February). Acceleration syndrome: Does everyone live in the fast lane? *Utne Reader, 31*, 36–43.

[7] McLean, S. (1998). Turn-taking and the extended pause: A study of interpersonal communication styles across generations on the Warm Springs Indian reservation. In K. S. Sitaram & M. Prosser (Eds.), *Civic discourse: Multiculturalism, cultural diversity, and global communication* (pp. 213–227). Stamford, CT: Ablex Publishing Company.

[8] Burnham, T., & Phelan, J. (2000). *Mean genes: From sex to money to food: Taming our primal instincts*. Cambridge, MA: Perseus.

[9] Burnham, T., & Phelan, J. (2000). *Mean genes: From sex to money to food: Taming our primal instincts*. Cambridge, MA: Perseus.

[10] Wells, W., & Siegel, B. (1961). Stereotypes somatypes. *Psychological Reports, 8*, 77–78.

[11] Cash, T., & Kilcullen, R. (1985). The eye of the beholder: Susceptibility to sexism and beautyism in the evaluation of managerial applicants. *Journal of Applied Social Psychology, 15*, 591–605.

[12] Ekman, P., & Friesen, W. (1967). Head and body cures in the judgment of emotions: A reformulation. *Perceptual and Motor Skills, 24*, 711–724.

[13] Seiler, W., & Beall, M. (2000). *Communication: Making connections* (4th ed.). Boston, MA: Allyn & Bacon.

[14] Basso, K. A. (1970). To give up on words: Silence in western Apache culture. In D. Carbaugh (Ed.), *Cultural communication and intercultural contact* (pp. 301–318). Hillsdale, NJ: Laurence Erlbaum.

[15] Philips, S. (1983). *The invisible culture: Communication in the classroom and community on the Warm Springs Indian Reservation*. Chicago, IL: Waveland Press.

[16] Kinsman, M. (2001, August 20). Tattoos and nose rings. *San Diego Union-Tribune*, p. C1.

11.3 Movement in Your Speech
LEARNING OBJECTIVE

1. Demonstrate how to use movement to increase the effectiveness of your presentation.

At some point in your business career you will be called upon to give a speech. It may be to an audience of one on a sales floor, or to a large audience at a national meeting. You already know you need to make a positive first impression, but do you know how to use movement in your presentation? In this section we'll examine several strategies for movement and their relative advantages and disadvantages.

Customers and audiences respond well to speakers who are comfortable with themselves. Comfortable doesn't mean overconfident or cocky, and it doesn't mean shy or timid. It means that an audience is far more likely to forgive the occasional "umm" or "ahh," or the nonverbal equivalent of a misstep, if the speaker is comfortable with themselves and their message.

Let's start with behaviors to avoid. Who would you rather listen to: a speaker who moves confidently across the stage or one who hides behind the podium; one who expresses herself nonverbally with purpose and meaning or one who crosses his arms or clings to the lectern?

Audiences are most likely to respond positively to open, dynamic speakers who convey the feeling of being at ease with their bodies. The setting, combined with audience expectations, will give a range of movement. If you are speaking at a formal event, or if you are being covered by a stationary camera, you may be expected to stay in one spot. If the stage allows you to explore, closing the distance between yourself and your audience may prove effective. Rather than focus on a list of behaviors and their relationship to environment and context, give emphasis to what your audience expects and what you yourself would find more engaging instead.

Novice speakers are often told to keep their arms at their sides, or to restrict their movement to only that which is absolutely necessary. If you are in formal training for a military presentation, or a forensics (speech and debate) competition, this may hold true. But in business and industry, "whatever works" rules the day. You can't say that expressive gestures—common among many cultural groups, like arm movement while speaking—are not appropriate when they are, in fact, expected.

The questions are, again, what does your audience consider appropriate and what do you feel comfortable doing during your presentation? Since the emphasis is always on meeting the needs of the customer, whether it is an audience of one on a sales floor or a large national gathering, you may need to stretch outside your comfort zone. On that same note, don't stretch too far and move yourself into the uncomfortable range. Finding balance is a challenge, but no one ever said giving a speech was easy.

Movement is an important aspect of your speech and requires planning, the same as the words you choose and the visual aids you design. Be natural, but do not naturally shuffle your feet, pace back and forth, or rock on your heels through your entire speech. These behaviors distract your audience from your message and can communicate nervousness, undermining your credibility.

Positions on the Stage

Figure 11.3 Speaker's Triangle

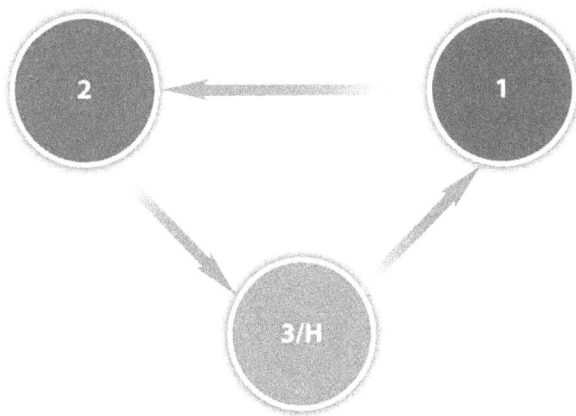

In a classical speech presentation, positions on the stage serve to guide both the speaker and the audience through transitions. The speaker's triangle (see Figure 11.3 "Speaker's Triangle") indicates where the speaker starts in the introduction, moves to the second position for the first point, across for the second point, then returns to the original position to make the third point and conclusion. This movement technique can be quite effective to help you remember each of your main points. It allows you to break down your speech into manageable parts, and putting tape on the floor to indicate position is a common presentation trick. Your movement will demonstrate purpose and reinforce your credibility.

Gestures
Gestures involve using your arms and hands while communicating. Gestures provide a way to channel your nervous energy into a positive activity that benefits your speech and gives you something to do with your hands. For example, watch people in normal, everyday conversations. They frequently use their hands to express themselves. Do you think *they* think about how they use their hands? Most people do not. Their arm and hand gestures come naturally as part of their expression, often reflecting what they have learned within their community.

For professional speakers this is also true, but deliberate movement can reinforce, repeat, and even regulate an audience's response to their verbal and nonverbal messages. You want to come across as comfortable and natural, and your use of your arms and hands contributes to your presentation. We can easily recognize that a well-chosen gesture can help make a point memorable or lead the audience to the next point.

As professional speakers lead up to a main point, they raise their hand slightly, perhaps waist high, often called an anticipation step. The gesture clearly shows the audience your anticipation of an upcoming point, serving as a nonverbal form of foreshadowing.

The implementation step, which comes next, involves using your arms and hands above your waist. By holding one hand at waist level pointing outward, and raising it up with your palm forward, as in the "stop" gesture, you signal the point. The nonverbal gesture complements the spoken word, and as students of speech have noted across time, audiences respond to this nonverbal reinforcement. You then slowly lower your hand down past your waistline and away from your body, letting go of the gesture, and signaling your transition.

The relaxation step, where the letting go motion complements your residual message, concludes the motion.

Facial Gestures
As you progress as a speaker from gestures and movement, you will need to turn your attention to facial gestures and expressions. Facial gestures involve using your face to display feelings and attitudes nonverbally. They may reinforce, or contradict, the spoken word, and their impact cannot be underestimated. As we have discussed, people often focus

more on how we say something than what we actually say, and place more importance on our nonverbal gestures. [1] As in other body movements, your facial gestures should come naturally, but giving them due thought and consideration can keep you aware of how you are communicating the nonverbal message.

Facial gestures should reflect the tone and emotion of your verbal communication. If you are using humor in your speech, you will likely smile and wink to complement the amusement expressed in your words. Smiling will be much less appropriate if your presentation involves a serious subject such as cancer or car accidents. Consider how you want your audience to feel in response to your message, and identify the facial gestures you can use to promote those feelings. Then practice in front of a mirror so that the gestures come naturally.

The single most important facial gesture (in mainstream U.S. culture) is eye contact. [2]Eye contact refers to the speaker's gaze that engages the audience members. It can vary in degree and length, and in many cases, is culturally influenced. Both in the speaker's expectations and the audience member's notion of what is appropriate will influence normative expectations for eye contact. In some cultures, there are understood behavioral expectations for male gaze directed toward females, and vice versa. In a similar way, children may have expectations of when to look their elders in the eye, and when to gaze down. Depending on the culture, both may be nonverbal signals of listening. Understanding your audience is critical when it comes to nonverbal expectations.

When giving a presentation, avoid looking over people's heads, staring at a point on the wall, or letting your eyes dart all over the place. The audience will find these mannerisms unnerving. They will not feel as connected, or receptive, to your message and you will reduce your effectiveness. Move your eyes gradually and naturally across the audience, both close to you and toward the back of the room. Try to look for faces that look interested and engaged in your message. Do not to focus on only one or two audience members, as audiences may respond negatively to perceived favoritism. Instead, try to give as much eye contact as possible across the audience. Keep it natural, but give it deliberate thought.

KEY TAKEAWAY

To use movement strategically in your presentation, keep it natural and consider using the speaker's triangle, the three-step sequence, facial gestures, and eye contact.

EXERCISES

1. Think of a message you want to convey to a listener. If you were to dance your message, what would the dance look like? Practice in front of a mirror.
2. Ask a friend to record you while you are having a typical conversation with another friend or family member. Watch the video and observe your movements and facial gestures. What would you do differently if you were making a presentation? Discuss your thoughts with a classmate.
3. Play "Lie to Me," a game in which each person creates three statements (one is a lie) and tells all three statements to a classmate or group. The listeners have to guess which statement is a lie.

[1] Mehrabian, A. (1981). *Silent messages: Implicit communication of emotions and attitudes* (2nd ed.). Belmont, CA: Wadsworth.

[2] Seiler, W., & Beall, M. (2000). *Communication: Making connections* (4th ed.). Boston, MA: Allyn & Bacon.

11.4 Visual Aids

LEARNING OBJECTIVE

1. Demonstrate how to use visual aids effectively in your presentation.

Almost all presentations can be enhanced by the effective use of visual aids. These can include handouts, overhead transparencies, drawings on the whiteboard, PowerPoint slides, and many other types of props. Visual aids are an important nonverbal aspect of your speech that you can control. Once you have chosen a topic, you need to consider how you are going to show your audience what you are talking about.

Have you ever asked for driving directions and not understood someone's response? Did the person say, "Turn right at Sam's Grocery Store, the new one" or "I think you will turn at the second light, but it might be the third one"? Chances are that unless you know the town well or have a map handy, the visual cue of a grocery store or a traffic light might be insufficient to let you know where to turn. Your audience experiences the same frustration, or sense of accomplishment, when they get lost or find their way during your speech. Consider how you can express yourself visually, providing common references, illustrations, and images that lead the audience to understand your point or issue.

Visual aids accomplish several goals:
- Make your speech more interesting
- Enhance your credibility as a speaker

- Serve as guides to transitions, helping the audience stay on track
- Communicate complex or intriguing information in a short period of time
- Reinforce your verbal message
- Help the audience use and retain the information

Purpose, Emphasis, Support, and Clarity

When you look at your own presentation from an audience member's perspective, you might consider how to distinguish the main points from the rest of the information. You might also consider the relationships being presented between ideas or concepts, or how other aspects of the presentation can complement the oral message.

Your audience naturally will want to know why you are presenting the visual aid. The purpose for each visual aid should be clear, and almost speak for itself. If you can't quickly grasp the purpose of a visual aid in a speech, you have to honestly consider whether it should be used in the first place. Visual aids can significantly develop the message of a speech, but they must be used for a specific purpose the audience can easily recognize.

Perhaps you want to highlight a trend between two related issues, such as socioeconomic status and educational attainment. A line graph might show effectively how, as socioeconomic status rises, educational attainment also rises. This use of a visual aid can provide emphasis, effectively highlighting key words, ideas, or relationships for the audience.

Visual aids can also provide necessary support for your position. Audience members may question your assertion of the relationship between socioeconomic status and educational attainment. To support your argument, you might include on the slide, "According to the U.S. Department of Education Study no. 12345," or even use an image of the Department of Education Web page projected on a large screen. You might consider showing similar studies in graphic form, illustrating similarities across a wide range of research.

Clarity is key in the use of visual aids. One way to improve clarity is to limit the number of words on a PowerPoint slide. No more than ten words per slide, with a font large enough to be read at the back of the room or auditorium, is a good rule of thumb. Key images that have a clear relationship to the verbal message can also improve clarity. You may also choose to illustrate the same data successively in two distinct formats, perhaps a line graph followed by two pie graphs. Your central goal is to ensure your visual aid is clear.

Methods and Materials

If you have been asked to give a presentation on a new product idea that a team within your organization is considering, how might you approach the challenge? You may consider a chronological organization pattern, starting with background, current market, and a trend analysis of what is to come—fair enough, but how will you make it vivid for your audience? How to represent information visually is a significant challenge, and you have several options.

You may choose to use a chart or diagram to show a timeline of events to date, from the first meeting about the proposed product to the results from the latest focus group. This timeline may work for you, but let's say you would like to get into the actual decision-making process that motivated your team to design the product with specific features in the first place. You may decide to use decision trees (or tree diagrams) showing the variables and products in place at the beginning of your discussions, and how each decision led to the next, bringing you to the decision-making point where you are today.

To complement this comprehensive guide and help make a transition to current content areas of questions, you may use a bar or pie graph to show the percentage of competing products in the market. If you have access to the Internet and a projector, you may use a topographical map showing a three-dimensional rendering of the local areas most likely to find your product attractive. If actual hills and valleys have nothing to do with your project, you can still represent the data you have collected in three dimensions. Then you may show a comparable graph illustrating the distribution of products and their relative degree of market penetration.

Finally, you may move to the issue of results, and present the audience with a model of your product and one from a competitor, asking which they prefer. The object may be just the visual aid you need to make your point and reinforce the residual message. When we can see, feel, touch, or be in close proximity to an object it often has a greater impact. In a world of digital images and special effects, objects presented in real time can still make a positive effect on the audience.

Additional visual aids you may choose include—but are not limited to—sound and music, video, and even yourself. If your speech is about how to use the product, your demonstration may just be the best visual aid.

You will want to give some thought to how to portray your chart, graph, or object when it's time to use your visual aids. The chalk or white board is common way of presenting visual aids, but it can get messy. Your instructor may write key words or diagrams on the boards while discussing a textbook chapter, but can you read his or her writing? The same lesson holds true for you. If you are going to use a white board and have a series of words on it, write them out clearly before you start your presentation.

Flip charts on a pedestal can also serve to show a series of steps or break a chart down into its basic components. A poster board is another common way of organizing your visual aids before a speech, but given its often one-time use, it is losing out to the computer screen. It is, however, portable and allows you a large "blank page" with which to express your ideas.

Handouts may also serve to communicate complex or detailed information to the audience, but be careful never to break handout rule number one: never give handouts to the audience at the beginning of your speech. Where do you want the audience to look—at you or at the handout? Many novice speakers might be tempted to say the handout, but you will no doubt recognize how that diverts and divides the audience's attention. People will listen to the words from the handout in their minds and tune you out. They will read at their own pace and have questions. They may even be impolite enough to use them as fans or paper airplanes. Handouts can be your worst enemy. If you need to use one, state at the beginning of the speech that you will be providing one at the conclusion of your presentation. This will alleviate the audience's worry about capturing all your content by taking notes, and keep their attention focused on you while you speak.

Transparencies and slides have been replaced by computer-generated slide show programs like PowerPoint by Microsoft, which we will discuss in greater detail later in this section. These programs can be very helpful in presenting visual information, but because computers and projectors sometimes break down and fail to work as planned, you need a plan B. You may need a poster board, or to write on the whiteboard or to have a handout in reserve, but a Plan B is always a good idea when it comes to presentations that integrate technology. You may arrive at your destination and find the equipment is no longer available, is incompatible with your media storage device, or is simply not working, but the show must go on.

Video clips, such as those you might find on YouTube, can also be effective visual aids. However, as with handouts, there is one concern: You don't want the audience to want to watch the video more than they want to tune into your presentation. How do you prevent this? Keep the clip short and make sure it reinforces the central message of your presentation. Always stop speaking before the audience stops listening, and the same holds true for the mesmerizing force of moving images on a screen. People are naturally attracted to them and will get "sucked into" your video example rather quickly. Be a good editor, introduce the clip and state what will happen out loud, point out a key aspect of it to the audience while it plays (overlap), and then make a clear transitional statement as you turn it off. Transitions are often the hardest part of any speech as the audience can get off track, and video clips are one of the most challenging visual aids you can choose because of their power to attract attention. Use that power wisely.

Preparing Visual Aids

Get started early so that you have time to create or research visual aids that will truly support your presentation, not just provide "fluff." Make sure you use a font or image large enough to be legible for those in the back of the room, and that you actually test your visual aids before the day of your presentation. Ask a friend to stand at the back of the room and read or interpret your visual aid. If you are using computer-generated slides, try them out in a practice setting, not just on your computer screen. The slides will look different when projected. Allow time for revision based on what you learn.

Your visual aids should meet the following criteria:
- *Big.* They should be legible for everyone, and should be "back row certified."
- *Clear.* Your audience should "get it" the first time they see it.
- *Simple.* They should serve to simplify the concepts they illustrate.
- *Consistent.* They should reinforce continuity by using the same visual style.

Using Visual Aids

Here are three general guidelines to follow when using visual aids. [1] Here are some *do*s and *don't*s:
1. Do make a clear connection between your words and the visual aid for the audience.
2. Do not distract the audience with your visual aid, blocking their view of you or adjusting the visual aid repeatedly while trying to speak.
3. Do speak to your audience—not to the whiteboard, the video, or other visual aids.

The timing of your presentation, and of your visual aids, can also have good or bad consequences. According to a popular joke, a good way to get your boss to approve just about anything is to schedule a meeting after lunch, turn the lights down, and present some boring PowerPoint slides. While the idea of a drowsy boss signing off on a harebrained project is amusing, in reality you will want to use visual aids not as a sleeping potion but as a strategy to keep your presentation lively and interesting.

Becoming proficient at using visual aids takes time and practice, and the more you practice before your speech, the more comfortable you will be with your visual aids and the role they serve in illustrating your points. Planning ahead before speaking will help, but when it comes time to actually give your speech, make sure they work for the audience as they should. Speaking to a visual aid (or reading it with your back to the audience) is not an effective strategy. You should know your material well enough that you refer to a visual aid, not rely on it.

Using PowerPoint as a Visual Aid

PowerPoint and similar visual representation programs can be an effective tool to help audiences remember your message, but they can also be an annoying distraction to your speech. How you prepare your slides and use the tool will determine your effectiveness.

PowerPoint is a slideware program that you have no doubt seen used in class, presentation at work, or perhaps used yourself to support a presentation. PowerPoint and similar slideware programs provide templates for creating electronic slides to present visual information to the audience, reinforcing the verbal message. You'll be able to import, or cut and paste, words from text files, images, or video clips to create slides to represent your ideas. You can even incorporate Web links. When using any software program, it's always a good idea to experiment with it long before you intend to use it, explore its many options and functions, and see how it can be an effective tool for you.

At first, you might be overwhelmed by the possibilities, and you might be tempted to use all the bells, whistles, and sound effects, not to mention the tumbling, flying, and animated graphics. If used wisely, a dissolve or key transition can be like a well-executed scene from a major motion picture film and lead your audience to the next point. But if used indiscriminately, it can annoy the audience to the point where they cringe in anticipation of the sound effect at the start of each slide. This danger is inherent in the tool, but you are in charge of it and can make wise choices that enhance the understanding and retention of your information.

The first point to consider is what is the most important visual aid? The answer is you, the speaker. You will facilitate the discussion, give life to the information, and help the audience correlate the content to your goal or purpose. You don't want to be in a position where the PowerPoint presentation is the main focus and you are on the side of the stage, simply helping the audience follow along. It should support you in your presentation, rather than the other way around. Just as there is a number one rule for handouts, there is also one for PowerPoints: do not use PowerPoints as a read-aloud script for your speech. The PowerPoints should amplify and illustrate your main points, not reproduce everything you are going to say.

Your pictures are the second area of emphasis you'll want to consider. The tool will allow you to show graphs, charts and illustrate relationships that words may only approach in terms of communication, but your verbal support of the visual images will make all the difference. Dense pictures or complicated graphics will confuse more than clarify. Choose clear images that have an immediate connection to both your content and the audience, tailored to their specific needs. After images, consider only key words that can be easily read to accompany your pictures. The fewer words the better: try to keep each slide to a total word count of less than ten words. Do not use full sentences. Using key words provides support for your verbal discussion, guiding you as well as your audience. The key words can serve as signposts or signal words related to key ideas.

A natural question at this point is, "How do I communicate complex information simply?" The answer comes with several options. The visual representation on the screen is for support and illustration. Should you need to communicate more technical, complex, or in-depth information in a visual way, consider preparing a handout to distribute at the conclusion of your speech. You may also consider using a printout of your slide show with a "notes" section, but if you distribute it at the beginning of your speech, you run the risk of turning your presentation into a guided reading exercise and possibly distracting or losing members of the audience. Everyone reads at a different pace and takes notes in their own way. You don't want to be in the position of going back and forth between slides to help people follow along.

Another point to consider is how you want to use the tool to support your speech and how your audience will interpret its presentation. Most audiences wouldn't want to read a page of text—as you might see in this book—on the big screen. They'll be far more likely to glance at the screen and assess the information you present in relation to your discussion. Therefore, it is key to consider one main idea, relationship, or point per slide. The use of the tool should be guided with the idea that its presentation is for the audience's benefit, not yours. People often understand pictures and images more quickly and easily than text, and you can use this to your advantage, using the knowledge that a picture is worth a thousand words.

Use of Color
People love color, and understandably your audience will appreciate the visual stimulation of a colorful presentation. If you have ever seen a car painted a custom color that just didn't attract you, or seen colors put together in ways that made you wonder what people were thinking when they did that, you will recognize that color can also distract and turn off an audience.

Color is a powerful way to present information, and the power should be used wisely. You will be selecting which color you want to use for headers or key words, and how they relate the colors in the visual images. Together, your images, key words, and the use of color in fonts, backgrounds, table, and graphs can have a significant impact on your audience. You will need to give some thought and consideration to what type of impact you want to make, how it will contribute or possibly distract, and what will work well for you to produce an effective and impressive presentation.

There are inherent relationships between colors, and while you may have covered some of this information in art classes you have taken, it is valuable to review here. According to the standard color wheel, colors are grouped into primary, secondary, and tertiary categories. Primary colors are the colors from which other colors are made through various combinations. Secondary colors represent a combination of two primary colors, while tertiary colors are made from combinations of primary and secondary colors.

- *Primary colors.* Red, blue and yellow
- *Secondary colors.* Green, violet, and orange
- *Tertiary colors.* Red-orange, red-violet, blue-violet, blue-green, yellow-orange, and yellow-green

Colors have relationships depending on their location on the wheel. Colors that are opposite each other are called complementary and they contrast, creating a dynamic effect. Analogous colors are located next to each other and promote harmony, continuity, and sense of unity.

Your audience comes first: when considering your choice of colors to use, legibility must be your priority. Contrast can help the audience read your key terms more easily. Also,

focus on the background color and its relation to the images you plan to incorporate to insure they complement each other. Consider repetition of color, from your graphics to your text, to help unify each slide. To reduce visual noise, try not to use more than two or three additional colors. Use colors sparingly to make a better impact, and consider the use of texture and reverse color fonts (the same as a background or white) as an option.

Be aware that many people are blue-green colorblind, and that red-green colorblindness is also fairly common. With this in mind, choose colors that most audience members will be able to differentiate. If you are using a pie chart, for example, avoid putting a blue segment next to a green one. Use labeling so that even if someone is totally colorblind they will be able to tell the relative sizes of the pie segments and what they signify.

Color is also a matter of culture. Some colors may be perceived as formal or informal, or masculine or feminine. Recognize that red is usually associated with danger, while green signals "go." Make sure the color associated with the word is reflected in your choice. If you have a key word about nature, but the color is metallic, the contrast may not contribute to the rhetorical situation and confuse the audience.

Seeking a balance between professionalism and attractiveness may seem to be a challenge, but experiment and test your drafts with friends to see what works for you. Also consider examining other examples, commonly available on the Internet, but retain the viewpoint that not everything online is effective nor should it be imitated. There are predetermined color schemes already incorporated into PowerPoint that you can rely on for your presentation.

We've given consideration to color in relation to fonts and the representation of key words, but we also need to consider font size and selection. PowerPoint will have default settings for headlines and text, but you will need to consider what is most appropriate for your rhetorical situation. Always think about the person sitting in the back of the room. The title size should be at least forty points, and the body text (used sparingly) should be at least thirty-two points.

In *Designing Visual Language: Strategies for Professional Communicators*, [2] Charles Kostelnick and David Roberts provide a valuable discussion of fonts, font styles, and what to choose to make an impact depending on your rhetorical situation. One good principle they highlight is that sans serif fonts such as Arial work better than serif fonts like Times New Roman for images projected onto a screen. The thin lines and extra aspects to serif the font may not portray themselves well on a large screen or contribute to clarity. To you this may mean that you choose Arial or a similar font to enhance clarity and ease of reading. Kostelnick and Roberts also discuss the use of grouping strategies to improve the communication of information. [3] Bullets, the use of space, similarity, and proximity all pertain to the process of perception, which differs from one person to another.

Helpful Hints for Visual Aids

As we've discussed, visual aids can be a powerful tool when used effectively, but can also run the risk of dominating your presentation. As a speaker, you will need to consider your audience and how the portrayal of images, text, graphic, animated sequences, or sound files will contribute or detract from your presentation. Here is a brief list of hints to keep in mind as you prepare your presentation:

- Keep visual aids simple.
- Use one key idea per slide.
- Avoid clutter, noise, and overwhelming slides.
- Use large, bold fonts that the audience can read from at least twenty feet from the screen.
- Use contrasting colors to create a dynamic effect.
- Use analogous colors to unify your presentation.
- Use clip art with permission and sparingly.
- Edit and proofread each slide with care and caution.
- Use copies of your visuals available as handouts after your presentation.
- Check the presentation room beforehand.
- With a PowerPoint presentation, or any presentation involving technology, have a backup plan, such as your visuals printed on transparencies, should unexpected equipment or interface compatibility problems arise

Becoming proficient at using visual aids takes time and practice. The more you practice before your speech, the more comfortable you will be with your visual aids and the role they serve in illustrating your message. Giving thought to where to place visual aids before speaking helps, but when the time comes to actually give your speech, make sure you reassess your plans and ensure that they work for the audience as they should. Speaking to a visual aid (or reading it to the audience) is not an effective strategy. Know your material well enough that you refer to your visual aids, not rely on them.

KEY TAKEAWAY

Strategically chosen visual aids will serve to illustrate, complement, and reinforce your verbal message.

EXERCISES

1. Look at the picture of the blankets above. Write copy for the left part of the slide and decide what colors would best complement the message. Share your results with the class.
2. Create your own presentation of three to five slides with no less than three images and three words per slide. Share the results with the class.
3. Explore PowerPoint or a similar slideware program and find your favorite feature. Write a series of steps on how to access and use it. Share your results with the class.
4. Create a slide presentation that defines and explains your favorite feature in the program and include at least one point on its advantage for the audience. Share the results with the class.

[1] McLean, S. (2003). *The basics of speech communication*. Boston, MA: Allyn & Bacon.

[2] Kostelnick, C., & Roberts, D. (1998). *Designing visual language: Strategies for professional communicators*. Needham Heights, MA: Allyn & Bacon.

[3] Kostelnick, C., & Roberts, D. (1998). *Designing visual language: Strategies for professional communicators*. Needham Heights, MA: Allyn & Bacon.

11.5 Nonverbal Strategies for Success with Your Audience

LEARNING OBJECTIVE

1. Demonstrate three ways to improve nonverbal communication.

Nonverbal communication is an important aspect of business communication, from the context of an interpersonal interaction to a public presentation. It is a dynamic, complex, and challenging aspect of communication. We are never done learning and adapting to our environment and context, and improving our understanding of nonverbal communication comes with the territory.

When your audience first sees you, they begin to make judgments and predictions about you and your potential, just as an employer might do when you arrive for a job interview. If you are well dressed and every crease is ironed, your audience may notice your attention to detail. Wearing jeans with holes, a torn T-shirt, and a baseball cap would send a different message. Neither style of dress is "good" or "bad, but simply appropriate or inappropriate depending on the environment and context. Your skills as an effective business communicator will be called upon when you contemplate your appearance. As a speaker, your goal is to create common ground and reduce the distance between the audience and yourself. You want your appearance to help establish and reinforce your credibility.

In order to be a successful business communicator, you will need to continually learn about nonverbal communication and its impact on your interactions. Below are three ways to examine nonverbal communication.

Watch Reactions

Market research is fundamental to success in business and industry. So, too, you will need to do a bit of field research to observe how, when, and why people communicate the way they do. If you want to be able to communicate effectively with customers, you will need to anticipate not only their needs, but also how they communicate. They are far more likely to communicate with someone whom they perceive as being like them, than with a perceived stranger. From dress to mannerisms and speech patterns, you can learn from your audience how to be a more effective business communicator.

Enroll an Observer

Most communication in business and industry involves groups and teams, even if the interpersonal context is a common element. Enroll a coworker or colleague in your effort to learn more about your audience, or even yourself. They can observe your presentation and note areas you may not have noticed that could benefit from revision. Perhaps the gestures you make while speaking tend to distract rather than enhance your presentations. You can also record a video of your performance and play it for them, and yourself, to get a sense of how your nonverbal communication complements or detracts from the delivery of your message.

Focus on a Specific Type of Nonverbal Communication

What is the norm for eye contact where you work? Does this change or differ based on gender, age, ethnicity, cultural background, context, environment? Observation will help you learn more about how people communicate; looking for trends across a specific type of nonverbal communication can be an effective strategy. Focus on one behavior you exhibit on your videotape, like pacing, body movements across the stage, hand gestures as you are making a point, or eye contact with the audience.

KEY TAKEAWAY

To use nonverbal communication to enhance your message, watch reactions and consider enrolling an observer to help you become aware of your nonverbal habits and how your audience receives nonverbal messages.

EXERCISES

1. Watch a television program without the sound. Can you understand the program? Write a description of the program and include what you found easy to understand, and what presented a challenge, and present it to the class.

2. Observe communication in your environment. Focus on specific actions like face touching, blink rate, or head nodding and write a brief description of what you observe. Share with classmates.

3. In a group, play charades. Pull words from a hat or envelope and act out the words without verbal communication.

4. Interview someone from a different culture than your own and ask them to share a specific cultural difference in nonverbal communication—for example, a nonverbal gesture that is not used in polite company. Write a brief description and present it to the class.

5. What do you think are the assumptions (explicit or underlying) about nonverbal communication in this chapter? Discuss your thoughts with a classmate.

11.6 Additional Resources

- Visit this site for a library of University of California videotapes on nonverbal communication produced by Dane Archer of the University of California at Santa Cruz. http://nonverbal.ucsc.edu

- Read "Six Ways to Improve Your Nonverbal Communications" by Vicki Ritts, St. Louis Community College at Florissant Valley and James R. Stein, Southern Illinois University, Edwardsville. http://honolulu.hawaii.edu/intranet/committees/Fac DevCom/guidebk/teachtip/commun-1.htm

- Read "Listen With Your Eyes: Tips for Understanding Nonverbal Communication," an About.com article by Susan Heathfield. http://humanresources.about.com/od/interpersonalco mmunicatio1/a/nonverbal_com.htm

- Presentation Magazine offers a wealth of ideas, tips, and templates for designing effective visual aids. http://www.presentationmagazine.com

- The National Center for Education Statistics offers an easy-to-use "Create a Graph" tutorial including bar, line, area, pie, and other types of graphs. The site is made for kids, but it's worthwhile for adults too. http://nces.ed.gov/nceskids/graphing/classic

- Read "The Seven Sins of Visual Presentations" from Presentation Magazine. http://www.presentationmagazine.com/7sinsvisual.ht m

- Yale emeritus professor Edward Tufte is one of the top authorities on the visual presentation of data. Learn about his books on data presentation and a one-day course he teaches. http://www.edwardtufte.com/tufte/courses

- Greg Conley has produced an excellent discussion of color, contrast, and tips for the use of color on his Web site and has gracefully allowed it to be included here for your benefit. Check out his site for more in-depth information and consider taking an art course to further develop your awareness of color. http://www.watercolorpainting.com/color.htm
- Visit "Presenting Effective Presentations with Visual Aids" from the U.S. Department of Labor, OSHA Office of Training and Education. http://www.osha.gov/doc/outreachtraining/htmlfiles/traintec.html
- The American Psychological Association provides guidelines for making presentations accessible for persons with disabilities. http://www.apa.org/pi/disability/resources/convention/index.aspx
- Read "Using Visual Aids and Props for Giving More Powerful Presentations" by Larry M. Lynch. http://ezinearticles.com/?Using-Visual-Aids-and-Props-for-Giving-More-Powerful-Presentations&id=100871
- Is "how you say it" really more important than what you say? Read an article by communications expert Dana Bristol-Smith that debunks a popular myth. http://www.sideroad.com/Public_Speaking/how-you-say-not-more-important-what-you-say.html

NOTES:

NOTES:

Chapter 12:
Organization and Outlines

Speech is power; speech is to persuade, to convert, to compel.
  Ralph Waldo Emerson

Getting Started

INTRODUCTORY EXERCISES

1. Please read the following paragraph and rearrange the sentences in logical order:
A. I saw "The Day After Tomorrow" recently. **B**. The Northern Seas got very cold, very quickly. **C**. People in the United States fled to Mexico. **D**. Have you ever seen a movie you just couldn't forget? **E**. Soon it was hailing, snowing, and raining all around the world. **F**. In the movie there was a scientist who forecast a sudden change in the climate. **G**. They were declared illegal aliens and not allowed in the country. **H**. The film made me think about global warming and global politics. **I**. The U.S. president forgave their debts, and the Mexican president allowed U.S. citizens to cross the border.

2. Consider the following words and find at least two ways to organize the words into groups.
    o   Knife
    o   Fork
    o   Spoon
    o   Corkscrew

Answers
1. D, A, F, B, E, C, G, I, H
2. Table service (knife, fork, spoon), sharp implements (knife, fork, corkscrew), Tools (all). Can you think of any other organizational principles by which to group these items?

In earlier stages of preparation for a speech, you have gained a good idea of who your audience is and what information you want to focus on. This chapter will help you consider how to organize the information to cover your topic. You may be tempted to think that you know enough about your topic that you can just "wing it" or go "freestyling." Your organization might be something like this: "First, I'll talk about this, then I'll give this example, and I'll wrap it up with this." While knowledge on your topic is key to an effective speech, do not underestimate the importance of organization. You may start to give your speech thinking you'll follow the "outline" in your mind, and then suddenly your mind will go blank. If it doesn't go blank, you may finish what was planned

as a five-minute speech with three minutes remaining, sit down, and then start to remember all the things you intended to say but didn't. To your listeners, your presentation may have sounded like the first of the Note 12.1 "Introductory Exercises" for this chapter—a bunch of related ideas that were scattered and unorganized.

Organization in your speech is helpful both to you and to your audience. Your audience will appreciate hearing the information presented in an organized way, and being well organized will make the speaking situation much less stressful for you. You might forget a point and be able to glance at your outline and get back on track. Your listeners will see that you took your responsibility as a speaker seriously and will be able to listen more attentively. They'll be able to link your key points in their minds, and the result will be a more effective speech.

An extemporaneous speech involves flexibility and organization. You know your material. You are prepared and follow an outline. You do not read a script or PowerPoint presentation, you do not memorize every single word in order (though some parts may be memorized), but you also do not make it up as you go along. Your presentation is scripted in the sense that it is completely planned from start to finish, yet every word is not explicitly planned, allowing for some spontaneity and adaptation to the audience's needs in the moment. This extemporaneous approach is the most common form used in business and industry today.

Your organization plan will serve you and your audience as a guide, and help you present a more effective speech. If you are concerned with grades, it will no doubt help you improve your score as well. If you work in a career where your "grades" are sales, and a sales increase means getting an "A," then your ability to organize will help you make the grade. Just as there is no substitute for practice and preparation, there is no substitute for organization and an outline when you need it the most: on stage. Do yourself and the audience a favor and create an outline with an organization pattern that best meets your needs.

In the 1991 film *What about Bob?* a psychiatrist presents the simple idea to the patient, played by actor Bill Murray. If the patient takes whatever he needs to do step by step, the process he once perceived as complex becomes simple. In this same way, your understanding of giving business presentations will develop step by step, as the process and its important elements unfold. Read and reflect on how each area might influence your speech, how it might involve or impact your audience, and how your purpose guides your strategies as you plan your speech.

If you take it step by step, presenting a speech can be an exhilarating experience not unlike winning a marathon or climbing a high peak. Every journey begins with a first step, and in terms of communication, you've already taken countless steps in your lifetime. Now we'll take the next step and begin to analyze the process of public speaking.

12.1 Rhetorical Situation
LEARNING OBJECTIVE

1. Label and discuss the three main components of the rhetorical situation.

In the classical tradition, the art of public speaking is called rhetoric; the circumstances in which you give your speech or presentation are the rhetorical situation. By understanding the rhetorical situation, you can gauge the best ways to reach your listeners and get your points across. In so doing, you'll make the transition from your viewpoint to that of your audience members. Remember that without an audience to listen and respond to you, it's really not much of a speech. The audience gives you the space and time as a speaker to fulfill your role and, hopefully, their expectations. Just as a group makes a leader, an audience makes a speaker. By looking to your audience, you shift your attention from an internal focus (you) to an external (them/others) emphasis. This "other-orientation" is key to your success as an effective speaker.

Several of the first questions any audience member asks himself or herself are, "Why should I listen to you?" "What does what you are saying have to do with me?" and "How does this help me?" We communicate through the lens of personal experience and it's only natural that we would relate what others say to our own needs and wants, but by recognizing that we share in our humanity many of the same basic motivations, we can find common ground of mutual interest. Generating interest in your speech is only the first step as you guide perception through selection, organization, and interpretation of content and ways to communicate your point. Your understanding of the rhetorical situation will guide you as you plan how to employ various strategies to guide your listeners as they perceive and interpret your message. Your awareness of the overall process of building a speech will allow you to take it step by step and focus on the immediate task at hand.

The rhetorical situation involves three elements: the set of expectations inherent in the context, audience, and the purpose of your speech or presentation. [1] This means you need to consider, in essence, the "who, what, where, when, why, and how" of your speech from the audience's perspective.

Context

As we consider the rhetorical situation, we need to explore the concept in depth. Your speech is not given in a space that has no connection to the rest of the world. If you are going to be presenting a speech in class, your context will be the familiar space of your classroom. Other contexts might include a business conference room, a restaurant where you are the featured speaker for a dinner meeting, or a podium that has been set up outdoors for a sports award ceremony. The time of your speech will relate to people's natural patterns of behavior. If you give a speech right after lunch, you can expect people to be a bit sleepy. Knowing this, you can take steps to counter this element of the context by making your presentation especially dynamic, such as having your audience get up from their seats or calling on them to answer questions at various points in your speech.

You can also place your topic within the frame of reference of current events. If you are presenting a speech on the importance of access to health care for everyone, and you are presenting it in October of an election year, the current events that exist outside your speech may be used to enhance it. Your listeners might be very aware of the political climate, and relating your topic to a larger context may effectively take into consideration the circumstances in which your readers will use, apply, or contemplate your information.

Audience

The receiver (i.e., listener or audience) is one of the basic components of communication. Without a receiver, the source (i.e., the speaker) has only himself or herself in which to send the message. By extension, without an audience you can't have a speech. Your audience comes to you with expectations, prior knowledge, and experience. They have a purpose that makes them part of the audience instead of outside playing golf. They have a wide range of characteristics like social class, gender, age, race and ethnicity, cultural background, and language that make them unique and diverse. What kind of audience will you be speaking to? What do you know about their expectations, prior knowledge or backgrounds, and how they plan to use your information? Giving attention to this aspect of the rhetorical situation will allow you to gain insight into how to craft your message before you present it.

Purpose

A speech or oral presentation may be designed to inform, demonstrate, persuade, motivate, or even entertain. You may also overlap by design and both inform and persuade. The purpose of your speech is central to its formation. You should be able to state your purpose in one sentence or less, much like an effective thesis statement in an essay. You also need to consider alternate perspectives, as we've seen previously in this chapter. Your purpose may be to persuade, but the audience after lunch may want to be entertained, and your ability to adapt can make use of a little entertainment that leads to persuasion.

KEY TAKEAWAY

The rhetorical situation has three components: the context, the audience, and the purpose of the speech.

EXERCISES

1. Is it important to consider the rhetorical situation? Why or why not? Discuss your opinion with a classmate.

2. Think of an example (real or hypothetical) of a speech, a sales presentation, a news broadcast or television program. Using the elements listed in this section of the chapter, describe the rhetorical situation present in your example. Present your example to the class.

3. Let's take the topic of tattoos. Imagine you are going to present two informative speeches about tattoos: one to a group of middle school children, and the other to a group of college students. How would you adapt your topic for each audience and why? Write your results, provide an example or explanation, and discuss with classmates.

4. Examine a communication interaction and identify the context, the audience, and the purpose of the exchange. Write a brief description and share with classmates.

5. You've been assigned the task of arranging a meeting for your class to discuss an important topic. How do context, audience, and purpose influence your decisions? Write a brief statement of what you would want in terms of time, location, setting, and scene and why. Please share your results with classmates.

[1] Kostelnick, C., & Roberts, D. (1998). *Designing visual language: Strategies for professional communicators.* Needham Heights, MA: Allyn & Bacon.

12.2 Strategies for Success
LEARNING OBJECTIVE

1. Identify and provide examples of at least five of the nine basic cognate strategies in communication.

Given the diverse nature of audiences, the complexity of the communication process, and the countless options and choices to make when preparing your speech, you may feel overwhelmed. One effective way to address this is to focus on ways to reach, interact, or stimulate your audience. Humans share many of the same basic needs, and meeting those needs provides various strategies for action.

Charles Kostelnick and David Roberts outline several cognate strategies, or ways of framing, expressing, and representing a message to an audience, in *Designing Visual Language: Strategies for Professional Communicators.* [1] The word "cognate" refers to knowledge, and these strategies are techniques to impart knowledge to your audience. Kostelnick and Roberts's strategies are cross-disciplinary in that they can be applied to writing, graphic design, and verbal communication. They help the writer, designer, or speaker answer questions like "Does the audience understand how I'm arranging my information?" "Am I emphasizing my key points effectively?" and "How does my expression and representation of information contribute to a relationship with the audience?" They can serve you to better anticipate and meet your audience's basic needs.

Aristotle outlined three main forms of rhetorical proof: ethos, logos, and pathos. Ethos involves the speaker's character and expertise. Logos is the logic of the speaker's presentation—something that will be greatly enhanced by a good organizational plan. Aristotle discussed pathos as the use of emotion as a persuasive element in the speech, [2] or "the arousing of emotions in the audience." We don't always make decisions based on clear thinking. Sometimes we are moved by words, by a scene in a movie, or by other mediated forms of communication. As the speaker, you may create a message by selecting some aspects and rejecting others. A close-up picture of a child starving to death can capture attention and arouse emotions. If you use pathos in a strategic way, you are following Aristotle's notion of rhetorical proof as the available means of persuasion. If logic and expertise don't move the audience, a tragic picture may do so.

The cognate strategies are in many ways expressions of these three elements, but by focusing on individual characteristics, can work towards being more effective in their preparation and presentation. Many of these strategies build on basic ideas of communication, such as verbal and nonverbal delivery. By keeping that in mind, you'll be more likely to see the connections and help yourself organize your presentation effectively.

Here we adapt and extend Kostelnick and Roberts' strategies in order to highlight ways to approach the preparation and presentation of your message. Across the cognate strategies, we can see Aristotle's rhetorical elements through a range of strategies to communicate better with our audience. There is a degree of overlap, and many of the strategies draw on related elements, but by examining each strategy as a technique for engaging your audience, you can better craft your message to meet their expectations.

Tone

From the choice of your words, to the choice of your dress, you contribute to the tone of the speech. Tone, or the general manner of expression of the message, will contribute to the context of the presentation. First, consider your voice. Is it relaxed, or shaky and nervous? Your voice is like a musical instrument that, when played expressively, fulfills a central role in your ability to communicate your message to your audience. Next consider how your tone is expressed through your body language. Are your arms straight down at your sides, or crossed in front of you, or are they moving in a natural flow to the rhythm and cadence of your speech? Your dress, your use of space, and the degree to which you are comfortable with yourself will all play a part in the expression of your message.

Emphasis

If everyone speaks at the same time, it's hard for anyone to listen. In the same way, if all your points are equally presented, it can be hard to distinguish one from another, or to focus on the points that are most important. As the speaker, you need to consider how you place emphasis—stress, importance, or prominence—on some aspects of your speech, and how you lessen the impact of others. Perhaps you have a visual aid to support your speech in the form of a visually arresting picture. Imagine that you want to present a persuasive speech on preventing skin cancer and you start with a photo of two people wearing very little clothing. While the image may capture attention, clearly placing emphasis on skin, it may prove to be more of a distraction than an addition. Emphasis as a cognate strategy asks you to consider relevance, and the degree to which your focal point of attention contributes to or detracts from your speech. You will need to consider how you link ideas through transitions, how you repeat and rephrase, and how you place your points in hierarchical order to address the strategy of emphasis in your presentation.

Engagement

Before you start thinking about weddings, consider what key element is necessary for one to occur? If you guessed a relationship you were correct. Just as a couple forms an interpersonal relationship, the speaker forms a relationship with the audience members. Eye contact can be an engaging aspect of this strategy, and can help you form a connection—an engagement—with individual audience members. Looking at the floor or ceiling may not display interest to the audience.

Engagement strategies develop the relationship with the audience, and you will need to consider how your words, visuals, and other relevant elements of your speech help this relationship grow.

Clarity

As a speaker, you may have excellent ideas to present, but if they are not made clear to the audience, your speech will be a failure. "Clarity strategies help the receiver (audience) to decode the message, to understand it quickly and completely, and when necessary, to react without ambivalence." [3] Your word choices, how you say them, and in what order all relate to clarity. If you use euphemisms, or indirect expressions, to communicate a delicate idea, your audience may not follow you. If you use a story, or an arresting image, and fail to connect it clearly to your main point or idea, your audience will also fail to see the connection. Depending on the rhetorical situation, the use of jargon may clarify your message or confuse your audience. You'll also need to consider the visual elements of your presentation and how they clarify your information. Is the font sufficiently large on your PowerPoint slide to be read in the back of the room? Is your slide so packed with words that they key ideas are lost in a noise of text? Will it be clear to your listeners how your pictures, motion clips, or audio files relate to topic?

Conciseness

Being clear is part of being concise. Conciseness refers to being brief and direct in the visual and verbal delivery of your message, and avoiding unnecessary intricacy. It involves using as many words as necessary to get your message across, and no more. If you only have five to seven minutes, how will you budget your time? Being economical with your time is a pragmatic approach to insuring that your attention, and the attention of your audience, is focused on the point at hand.

Arrangement

As the speaker, you will gather and present information in some form. How that form follows the function of communicating your message involves strategically grouping information. "Arrangement means order, the organization of visual (and verbal) elements [4] "in ways that allow the audience to correctly interpret the structure, hierarchy, and relationships among points of focus in your presentation. We will discuss the importance of hierarchy, and which point comes first and last, as we explore arguments and their impact on the perception of your message.

Credibility

Here we can clearly see Aristotle's ethos—character and expertise. You will naturally develop a relationship with your audience, and the need to make trust an element is key to that development. The word "credibility" comes from the word "credence," or belief. Credibility involves your qualities, capabilities, or power to elicit from the audience belief in your character. Cultivating a sense of your character and credibility may involve displaying your sense of humor, your ability to laugh at yourself, your academic or profession-specific credentials, or your personal insight into the topic you are discussing.

For example, if you are going to present a persuasive speech on the dangers of drinking and driving, and start with a short story about how you helped implement a "designated driver" program, the audience will understand your relationship to the message, and form a positive perception of your credibility. If you are going to persuade the audience to give blood, practice safe sex, or get an HIV test, your credibility on the subject may come from your studies in the medical or public health field, from having volunteered at a blood drive, or perhaps from having had a loved one who needed a blood transfusion. Consider persuasive strategies that will appeal to your audience, build trust, and convey your understanding of the rhetorical situation.

Expectation

Your audience, as we've addressed previously, will have inherent expectations of themselves and of you depending on the rhetorical situation. Expectations involve the often unstated, eager anticipation of the norms, roles and outcomes of the speaker and the speech. If you are giving an after-dinner speech at a meeting where the audience members will have had plenty to eat and drink immediately before you get up to speak, you know that your audience's attention may be influenced by their state of mind. The "after-dinner speech" often incorporates humor for this very reason, and the anticipation that you will be positive, lighthearted and funny is implicit in the rhetorical situation. If, on the other hand, you are going to address a high school assembly on the importance of graduating from high school and pursuing a college education, you may also be motivational, funny, and lighthearted, but there will be an expectation that you will also discuss some serious issues as a part of your speech.

Reference

No one person knows everything all the time at any given moment, and no two people have experienced life in the same way. For this reason, use references carefully. Reference involves attention to the source and way you present your information. If you are a licensed pilot and want to inform your audience about the mistaken belief that flying is more dangerous than driving, your credibility will play a role. You might also say "according to the Federal Aviation Administration" as you cite mortality statistics associated

with aviation accidents in a given year. The audience won't expect you to personally gather statistics and publish a study, but they will expect you to state where you got your information. If you are talking to a group of children who have never flown before, and lack a frame of reference to the experience of flying, you will need to consider how to reference key ideas within their scope of experience.

A good way to visualize this is as a frame, where some information you display to the audience is within the frame, and other information (that you do not display) lies outside the frame. You focus the information to improve clarity and conciseness, and the audience will want to know why the information you chose is included and where you got it. That same frame may also be related to experience, and your choice of terms, order or reliance on visual aids to communicate ideas. If you are giving a speech on harvesting crops on an incline, and your audience is made up of rural Bolivians who farm manually, talking about a combine may not be as effective as showing one in action in order to establish a frame of reference.

Table 12.1 "Nine Cognate Strategies" summarizes the nine cognate strategies in relation to Aristotle's forms of rhetorical proof; it also provides areas on which to focus your attention as you design your message.

Table 12.1 Nine Cognate Strategies

Aristotle's Forms of Rhetorical Proof	Cognate Strategies	Focus
Pathos	Tone Emphasis Engagement	Expression Relevance Relationship
Logos	Clarity Conciseness Arrangement	Clear understanding Key points Order, hierarchy, placement
Ethos	Credibility Expectation Reference	Character, trust Norms and anticipated outcomes Sources and frames of reference

You'll want to consider the cognate strategies and how to address each area to make your speech as effective as possible, given your understanding of the rhetorical situation.

KEY TAKEAWAY

The nine cognate strategies all contribute to your success in conveying the speech to the audience.

EXERCISES

1. Make a copy of Table 12.2 "How I Will Apply the Cognate Strategies" and use it to help get yourself organized as you start to prepare your speech. Fill in the far right column according to how each rhetorical element, cognate strategy, and focus will apply to the specific speech you are preparing.

2. In a group with your classmates, complete the above exercise using Table 12.2 "How I Will Apply the Cognate Strategies" and demonstrate your results.

3. Find an example where a speaker was lacking ethos, pathos, or logos. Write a brief summary of the presentation, and make at least one suggestion for improvement. Compare your results with classmates.

4. Does organizing a presentation involve ethics? Explain your response and discuss it with the class.

TABLE 12.2 HOW I WILL APPLY THE COGNATE STRATEGIES

Aristotle's Forms of Rhetorical Proof	Cognate Strategies	Focus	My speech will address each element and strategy by (verbal and visual)
Pathos	o Tone o Emphasis o Engagement	o Expression o Relevance o Relationship	
Logos	o Clarity o Conciseness o Arrangement	o Clear understanding o Key points o Order, hierarchy, placement	
Ethos	o Credibility o Expectation o Reference	o Character, trust o Norms and anticipated outcomes o Sources and frames of reference	

[1] Kostelnick, C., & Roberts, D. (1998). *Designing visual language: Strategies for professional communicators.* Needham Heights, MA: Allyn & Bacon.

[2] Wisse, J. (1989). *Ethos and pathos: From Aristotle to Cicero.* Amsterdam, Netherlands: Adolph M. Hakkert.

[3] Kostelnick, C., & Roberts, D. (1998). *Designing visual language: Strategies for professional communicators* (p. 17). Needham Heights, MA: Allyn & Bacon.

[4] Kostelnick, C., & Roberts, D. (1998). *Designing visual language: Strategies for professional communicators* (p. 14). Needham Heights, MA: Allyn & Bacon.

12.3 Building a Sample Speech

LEARNING OBJECTIVES

1. Demonstrate how to build a sample speech by expanding on the main points you wish to convey.

2. Demonstrate how to use the five structural parts of any speech.

As you begin to investigate your topic, make sure you consider several sides of an issue. Let's say you are going to do a speech to inform on the history of the First Transcontinental Railroad. At first you may have looked at just two sides, railroaders versus local merchants. Railroad tycoons wanted to bring the country together—moving people, goods, and services in a more efficient way—and to make money. Local merchants wanted to keep out competition and retain control of their individual markets.

Take another look at this issue and you see that several other perspectives have bearing on this issue. Shipping was done primarily by boat prior to the railroad, so shippers would not want the competition. Recent Chinese immigrants were in need of work. Native Americans did not want to lose their culture or way of life, and a railroad that crossed the country would cut right through the buffalo's migration patterns. We now have five perspectives to the central issue, which makes the topic all the more interesting.

The general purpose is to inform the audience on the First Transcontinental Railroad and its impact on a young but developing United States. The thesis statement focuses on shipping, communication, and cultures across America.

- *Topic.* First Transcontinental Railroad
- *General purpose statement.* I want the audience to be more informed about the impact of the First Transcontinental Railroad.

- *Thesis statement.* The First Transcontinental Railroad changed shipping, communication, and cultures across America.

With the information we have so far, we can now list three main points:
1. Change in shipping
2. Change in communication
3. Change in cultures

Think of each one of these main points as a separate but shorter speech. The point is to develop each of these main points like you have developed your overall speech. What do you want to focus on? The major types of shipping at the time of the First Transcontinental Railroad? One aspect you may want consider is to what degree is your audience familiar with this time in history. If they are not very familiar, a little background and context can help make your speech more meaningful and enhance its relevance to your thesis statement. By taking time to consider what you want to accomplish with each point, you will help yourself begin to address how you need to approach each point. Once you have thought about what you want to focus on for each point, list each subheading next to the main points.

By now you've identified your key points and are ready to start planning your speech in more detail. While your organizational structure will vary from speech to speech, there are nonetheless five main parts of any speech: attention statement, introduction, body, conclusion, and residual message. These are basic to the rhetorical process and you will see time and time again, regardless of audience or culture, these same elements in some form utilized to communicate in public. They will serve to guide you, and possibly even save you should you get a last minute request to do a speech or presentation.

Place your hand on the table or desk and you'll more likely see a thumb and four fingers. Associate your hand with these five elements. Each digit is independently quite weak, but together they make a powerful fist. Your thumb is quite versatile and your most important digit. It's a lot like your attention statement. If you don't gain the audience's attention, the rest of the speech will be ineffective.

Each successive digit can represent the remaining four parts of any speech. One day you will be asked to speak with little or no time for preparation. By focusing on this organizational model, and looking down at your hand, you can quickly and accurately prepare your speech. With the luxury of time for preparation, each step can even be further developed. Remember the five-finger model of public speaking, as

summarized in Table 12.3 "Five-Finger Model of Public Speaking", and you will always stand out as a more effective speaker.

Table 12.3 Five-Finger Model of Public Speaking

Attention Statement	The attention statement is the way you focus the audience's attention on you and your speech.
Introduction	Your introduction introduces you and your topic, and should establish a relationship with your audience and state your topic clearly.
Body	In the body, or main content area of your speech, you will naturally turn to one of the organizational patterns.
Conclusion	You conclusion should provide the audience with a sense of closure by summarizing the main points and relating the points to the overall topic.
Residual Message	The residual message is an idea or thought that stays with your audience well after the speech.

KEY TAKEAWAY

Speeches are built by identifying the main points to be communicated and by following five structural elements (attention statement, introduction, body, conclusion, and residual message).

EXERCISES

1. By visiting the library or doing an Internet search, find a speech given by someone you admire. The speech may be published in a book or newspaper, recorded in an audio file, or recorded on video. It may be a political speech, a business speech, or even a commercial sales pitch. Read or listen to the speech and identify the five structural elements as this speaker has used them. Post your results, discuss with classmates, and if a link to the speech is available, please be sure to include it.
2. By visiting the library or doing an Internet search, find a speech that would benefit from significant improvement. The speech may be published in a book or newspaper, recorded in an audio file, or recorded on video. It may be a political speech, a business speech, or even a commercial sales pitch. Read or listen to the speech and identify the five structural elements as this speaker has used them, noting specifically where they could improve their performance. Post your results, discuss with classmates, and if a link to the speech is available, please be sure to include it.
3. What functions does organization serve in a speech? Can organization influence or sway the audience? Explain your response and position.

12.4 Sample Speech Outlines
LEARNING OBJECTIVE

1. Understand how to create two different styles of outlines for a speech.

Chances are you have learned the basic principles of outlining in English writing courses: an outline is a framework that organizes main ideas and subordinate ideas in a hierarchical series of roman numerals and alphabetical letters. The center column of Table 12.4 "Speech Outline A" presents a generic outline in a classical style. In the left column, the five main structural elements of a speech are tied to the outline. Your task is to fill in the center column outline with the actual ideas and points you are making in your speech. Feel free to adapt it and tailor it to your needs, depending on the specifics of your speech. Next, fill in the right column with the verbal and visual delivery features of your speech.

There is no law that says a speech outline has to follow a classical outline format, however, Table 12.5 "Speech Outline B" is an alternate outline form you may want to use to develop your speech. As you can see, this outline is similar to the one above in that it begins with the five basic structural elements of a speech. In this case, those elements are tied to the speech's device, thesis, main points, summary, and recap of the thesis. In the right column, this outline allows you to fill in the cognate strategies you will use to get your points across to your audience. You may use this format as a model or modify it as needed.

Table 12.4 Speech Outline A

Attention Statement	Device	Verbal and Visual Delivery
Introduction	Main idea Common ground	
Body	I. Main idea: Point 1 Subpoint 1 A.1 specific information 1 A.2 specific information 2 II. Main idea: Point 2 Subpoint 1 B.1 specific information 1 B.2 specific information 2 III. Main idea: Point 3 Subpoint 1 C.1 specific information 1 C.2 specific information 2	
Conclusion	Summary, main points 1–3	
Residual Message	Main idea	

Table 12.5 Speech Outline B

Attention Statement	Device	Cognate Strategies, Verbal and Visual
Introduction	General purpose statement or thesis statement Common ground	
Body	Point 1: Point 2: Point 3:	
Conclusion	Summarize main points and reinforce common ground	
Residual Message	Reiterate thesis	

An outline is a framework that helps the speaker to organize ideas and tie them to the main structural elements of the speech.

EXERCISES

1. The next time you attend a class lecture, try to take notes in outline form, using the sample outlines in this chapter as a guide. You may want to do this as a class project: have all your classmates put their notes into outline form and then compare the different student outlines with the outline your professor began with in planning the lecture.
2. Create an outline of your day, with main headings and detail points for your main tasks of the day. At the end of the day, review the outline and write a brief summary of your experience. Share with classmates.
3. Diagram or create an outline from a sample speech. Do you notice any patterns? Share and compare your results with classmates.

12.5 Organizing Principles for Your Speech
LEARNING OBJECTIVE

1. Identify and understand how to use at least five different organizing principles for a speech.

There are many different ways to organize a speech, and none is "better" or "more correct" than the others. The choice of an organizing principle, or a core assumption around which everything else is arranged, depends on the subject matter, the rhetorical situation, and many other factors, including your preference as speaker.

The left column of Table 12.6 "Sample Organizing Principles for a Speech" presents seventeen different organizing principles to consider. The center column explains how the principle works, and the right column provides an applied example based on our sample speech about the First Transcontinental Railroad. For example, using a biographical organizing principle, you might describe the journey of the Lewis and Clark expedition in 1804; the signing of the Pacific Railroad Act in 1862, and the completion of the first Transcontinental Express train trip in 1876. As another example, using a spatial organizing principle, you might describe the mechanics of how a steam locomotive engine works to turn the train wheels, which move on a track to travel across distances.

As you read each organizational structure, consider how the main points and subheadings might change or be adapted to meet each pattern.

Table 12.6 Sample Organizing Principles for a Speech

Organizing Principle	Explanation	Applied Example
1. Time (Chronological)	Structuring your speech by time shows a series of events or steps in a process, which typically has a beginning, middle, and end. "Once upon a time stories" follow a chronological pattern.	Before the First Transcontinental Railroad, the events that led to its construction, and its impact on early America…
2. Comparison	Structuring your speech by comparison focuses on the similarities and/or differences between points or concepts.	A comparison of pre– and post–First Transcontinental Railroad North America, showing how health and life expectancy remained the same.
3. Contrast	Structure your speech by using contrasting points highlights the differences between items and concepts.	A contrast of pre– and post–First Transcontinental Railroad North America, by shipping times, time it took to communicate via letter, or how long it took to move out West.
4. Cause and Effect	Structuring your speech by cause and effect establishes a relationship between two events or situations, making the connection clear.	The movement of people and goods out West grew considerably from 1750 to 1850. With the availability of a new and faster way to go West, people generally supported its construction.
5. Problem and Solution	Structuring your speech by problem and solution means you state the problem and detail how it was solved. This approach is effective for persuasive speeches.	Manufacturers were producing better goods for less money at the start of the Industrial Revolution, but they lack a fast, effective method of getting their goods to growing markets. The First Transcontinental Railroad gave them speed, economy, and access to new markets.

Organizing Principle	Explanation	Applied Example
6. Classification (Categorical)	Structuring your speech by classification establishes categories.	At the time the nation considered the First Transcontinental Railroad, there were three main types of transportation: by water, by horse, and by foot.
7. Biographical	Structuring your speech by biography means examining specific people as they relate to the central topic.	1804: Lewis and Clark travel 4,000 miles in over two years across America 1862: President Lincoln signs the Pacific Railroad Act 1876: The Transcontinental Express from New York arrives in San Francisco with a record-breaking time of 83 hours and 39 minutes 2009: President Obama can cross America by plane in less than 5 hours
8. Space (Spatial)	Structuring your speech by space involves the parts of something and how they fit to form the whole.	A train uses a heat source to heat water, create stream, and turn a turbine, which moves a lever that causes a wheel to move on a track.
9. Ascending and Descending	Structuring your speech by ascending or descending order involves focusing on quantity and quality. One good story (quality) leads to the larger picture, or the reverse.	A day in the life of a traveler in 1800. Incremental developments in transportation to the present, expressed through statistics, graphs, maps and charts.
10. Psychological	It is also called "Monroe's Motivated Sequence." [1]Structuring your speech on the psychological aspects of the audience involves focusing on their inherent needs and wants. See Maslow [2] and Shutz. [3]The speaker calls *attention* to a *need*, then focuses on the satisfaction of the need, *visualization* of the solution, and ends with a proposed or historical *action*. This is useful for a persuasive speech.	When families in the year 1800 went out West, they rarely returned to see family and friends. The country as a whole was an extension of this distended family, separated by time and distance. The railroad brought families and the country together.
11. Elimination	Structuring your speech using the process of elimination involves outlining all the possibilities.	The First Transcontinental Railroad helped pave the way for the destruction of the Native American way of life in 1870. After examining treaties, relocation and reservations, loss of the buffalo, disease and war, the railroad can be accurately considered the catalyst for the end of an era.
12. Ceremonial: Events, Ceremonies, or Celebrations	Structure your speech by focusing on the following: Thank dignitaries and representatives. Mention the importance of the event. Mention the relationship of the event to the audience. Thank the audience for their participation in the event, ceremony, or celebration.	Thanking the representatives, builders, and everyone involved with the construction of the Transcontinental Railroad. The railroad will unite America, and bring us closer in terms of trade, communication and family. Thank you for participating in today's dedication.
13. Awards	Structure your speech by focusing on the following: Thank everyone for coming together. Discuss the history and importance of the award. Give a brief biography of the person who will receive the award (often nonspecific to keep people guessing and to build suspense). Announce the name of the award recipient. Present the award (present award with left hand, shake with right). Award recipient may give a speech.	>Thank everyone for coming together. The Golden Spike Award was created in honor of all the great men and women that made today possible. The person receiving this award needs no introduction. His/her tireless efforts to build partnerships, coalitions, and raise support for the railroad have been unwavering. (Name), please come and receive the Golden Spike Award. (Speech/no speech.) Thank you, everyone, for coming.

Organizing Principle	Explanation	Applied Example
	Transition to the next item or thank everyone for participating.	
14. Toast: Weddings or Similar Gatherings	Structure your speech by focusing on the following: Thank everyone for coming together. Discuss the importance of the event (wedding). Mention the relationship of the couple to the audience or the speaker to the person being celebrated. Add one short sentence. Optional: Conclude, thanking the audience for participation in the event, ceremony, or celebration.	Thank everyone for coming together. I've know the groom since he played with toy trains and only now, with (partner's name), can I see how far his involvement in our new cross-country train got him. "All the best of health and happiness." Thank you everyone for joining us in this celebration of (name) and (name) (point 5 is optional).
15. Speaker Introductions	Structure your speech by focusing on the following: Thank everyone for coming together. Provide a brief biography of the person who will speak or establish their credibility. Discuss the speaker and his or her topic. Announce the name of the speaker, and possibly once their speech has concluded. Transition to the next item or thank everyone for participating.	Thank everyone for coming together. Today's speaker has a long history in the development of the train, including engineering technical aspects of steam locomotion. Today he/she will address the steps that lead to our very own cross-country railroad. Please help me welcome (name). (Optional after speech: Thank you, everyone. Next we have…)
16. After-Dinner Speech	Structure your speech by focusing on the following: Thank everyone for coming together. Provide a fun or humorous attention statement. Discuss the topic in a light-hearted manner with connected stories, anecdotes, or even a joke or two. Connect the humor to the topic of importance Thank everyone for participating.	Thank you for coming together to celebrate the driving of the Golden Spike. There have been many challenging moments along the way that I would like to share tonight (stories, anecdotes, or even a joke). While it's been a long journey, we've made it. Thank you for coming tonight.
17. Oral Interpretation	Structure your speech by focusing on the following: Draw attention to the piece of literature. Explain its significance, context, and background. Interpret the manuscript for the audience. Conclude with key points from the reading. Reiterate the main point of the piece of literature.	Today I would like to share with you the proclamation that led to the railroad you see before you today. (Interpret the proclamation, using your voice to bring the written word alive.) Without the foresight, vision and leadership we can now see, this railroad might still be a dream.

KEY TAKEAWAY

A speech may be organized according to any of many different organizing principles.

EXERCISES

1. Choose at least three different organizing principles from the left column of Table 12.6 "Sample Organizing Principles for a Speech". Take the thesis of a speech you are preparing and write an applied example, similar to the ones provided about the First Transcontinental Railroad that shows how you would apply each of your chosen organizing principles to your speech.
2. Think of one technology or application that you perceive has transformed your world. Choose two organizing principles and create two sample outlines for speeches about your topic. Share and compare with classmates.

[1] Ayres, J., & Miller, J. (1994). *Effective public speaking* (4th ed., p 274). Madison, WI: Brown & Benchmark.
[2] Maslow, A. (1970). *Motivation and personality* (2nd ed.). New York, NY: Harper & Row.
[3] Shutz, W. (1966). *The interpersonal underworld*. Palo Alto, CA: Science and Behavior Books.

12.6 Transitions
LEARNING OBJECTIVE

1. Understand and demonstrate how to use transitions effectively within your speech.

By now you have identified your main points, chosen your organizational model, and are ready to begin putting your speech together. If you were going to build a house, you would need a strong foundation. Could the columns and beams hold your roof in place without anything to keep them from falling down? Of course not. In the same way, the columns or beams are like the main ideas of your speech, and identifying them is one important step. Another is to consider how to position them securely to rest on a solid foundation, have sufficient connection to each other that they become interdependent, and to make sure they stay where you want them to so your house, or your speech, doesn't come crashing down.

Transitions are words, phrases, or visual devices that help the audience follow the speaker's ideas, connect the main points to each other, and see the relationships you've created in the information you are presenting. They are often described as bridges between ideas, thought or concepts, providing some sense of where you've been and where you are going with your speech. Transitions are used by the speaker to guide the audience in the progression from one significant idea, concept or point to the next issue. They can also show the relationship between the main point and the support the speaker uses to illustrate, provide examples for, or reference outside sources. Depending your purpose, transitions can serve different roles as you help create the glue that will connect your points together in a way the audience can easily follow.

Table 12.7 Types of Transitions in Speeches

Type	Definition	Examples
1. Internal Previews	An internal preview is a brief statement referring to a point you are going to make. It can forecast or foreshadow a main point coming in your speech.	If we look ahead to, next we'll examine, now we can focus our attention on, first we'll look at, then we'll examine
2. Signposts	A signpost alerts the audience that you are moving from one topic to the next. Signposts or signal words draw attention to themselves and focus the audience's attention.	Stop and consider, we can now address, next I'd like to explain, turning from/to, another, this reminds me of, I would like to emphasize
3. Internal Summaries	An internal summary briefly covers information or alludes to information introduced previously. It can remind an audience of a previous point and reinforce information covered in your speech.	As I have said, as we have seen, as mentioned earlier, in any event, in other words, in short, on the whole, therefore, to summarize, as a result, as I've noted previously, in conclusion
4. Sequence Transition	A sequence transition outlines a hierarchical order or series of steps in your speech. It can illustrate order or steps in a logical process.	First...second...third, furthermore, next, last, still, also, and then, besides, finally
5. Time	A time transition focuses on the chronological aspects of your speech order. Particularly useful in a speech utilizing a story, this transition can illustrate for the audience progression of time.	Before, earlier, immediately, in the meantime, in the past, lately, later, meanwhile, now, presently, shortly, simultaneously, since, so far, soon as long as, as soon as, at last, at length, at that time, then, until, afterward
6. Addition	An addition or additive transition contributes to a previous point. This transition can build on a previous point and extend the discussion.	In addition to, furthermore, either, neither, besides, moreover, in fact, as a matter of fact, actually, not only, but also, as well as, not to mention
7. Similarity	A transition by similarity draws a parallel between two ideas, concepts, or examples. It can indicate a common area between points for the audience.	In the same way, by the same token, equally, similarly, just as we have seen, in the same vein
8. Comparison	A transition by comparison draws a distinction between two ideas, concepts, or examples. It can indicate a common or divergent area between points for the audience.	Like, in relation to, bigger than, smaller than, the fastest, than any other, is greater than, both, either...or, likewise, even more important

Type	Definition	Examples
9. Contrast	A transition by contrast draws a distinction of difference, opposition, or irregularity between two ideas, concepts, or examples. This transition can indicate a key distinction between points for the audience.	But, neither…nor, however, on the other hand, although, even though, in contrast, in spite of, despite, on the contrary, conversely, unlike, while, instead, nevertheless, nonetheless, regardless, still, though, yet
10. Cause and Effect or Result	A transition by cause and effect or result illustrates a relationship between two ideas, concepts, or examples and may focus on the outcome or result. It can illustrate a relationship between points for the audience.	As a result, because, consequently, for this purpose, accordingly, so, then, therefore, thereupon, thus, to this end, for this reason, as a result, because, therefore, consequently, as a consequence, and the outcome was
11. Examples	A transition by example illustrates a connection between a point and an example or examples. You may find visual aids work well with this type of transition.	In fact, as we can see, after all, even, for example, for instance, of course, specifically, such as, in the following example, to illustrate my point
12. Place	A place transition refers to a location, often in a spatially organized speech, of one point of emphasis to another. Again, visual aids work well when discussing physical location with an audience.	Opposite to, there, to the left, to the right, above, below, adjacent to, elsewhere, far, farther on, beyond, closer to, here, near, nearby, next to
13. Clarification	A clarification transition restates or further develops a main idea or point. It can also serve as a signal to a key point.	To clarify, that is, I mean, in other words, to put it another way, that is to say, to rephrase it, in order to explain, this means
14. Concession	A concession transition indicates knowledge of contrary information. It can address a perception the audience may hold and allow for clarification.	We can see that while, although it is true that, granted that, while it may appear that, naturally, of course, I can see that, I admit that even though

Table 12.7 "Types of Transitions in Speeches" is a summary of fourteen distinct types of transitions. As you contemplate how to bring together your information, consider how you will use various transitions, and note them on your outline.

KEY TAKEAWAY

A speech needs transitions to help the audience understand how the speaker's main ideas are connected to one another.

EXERCISES

1. By visiting the library or doing an Internet search, find a speech that teaches you one new skill or idea. The speech may be published in a book or newspaper, recorded in an audio file, or recorded on video. Read or listen to the speech and identify the transitions the speaker has used.
2. Listen to your favorite comedian. Write a brief summary of how they transition from topic to topic. Share and compare with classmates.
3. Listen to a conversation with friends and observe how they transition from topic to topic. Write a brief summary. Share and compare with classmates.

12.7 Additional Resources

- The commercial site from *Inc.* magazine presents an article on organizing your speech by Patricia Fripp, former president of the National Speakers Association. http://www.inc.com/articles/2000/10/20844.html
- Read a straightforward tutorial on speech organization by Robert Gwynne on this University of Central Florida site. http://pegasus.cc.ucf.edu/~rbrokaw/organizing.html
- Read a straightforward tutorial on speech organization on the University of Tennessee Toastmasters website. http://www.uttoastmasters.com/organizespeech.html
- View an eHow video on how to organize a speech. How does the advice in this video differ from organizing advice given in this chapter? http://www.ehow.com/video_4401082_organizing-speech-parts.html
- Read more about how to outline a speech on this site from John Jay College of Criminal Justice. http://www.lib.jjay.cuny.edu/research/outlining.html
- Learn more about how to outline a speech from the Six Minutes public speaking and presentation skills blog. http://sixminutes.dlugan.com/2008/02/29/speech-preparation-3-outline-examples

NOTES:

NOTES:

Chapter 13:
Presentations to Inform

After all, the ultimate goal of all research is not objectivity, but truth.
  Helene Deutsch

Getting Started

INTRODUCTORY EXERCISES

1. Please make a list of five activities you have participated in recently. Choose one and create a time order list, from start to finish, of at least five major steps involved in accomplishing the activity.
2. From the list of five activities above, please consider which of the activities the audience (or your class) has probably had the least experience with. Now make a list from that activity of at least three things you would explain to them so that they could better understand it. From that new list, consider how you might show those three things, including visual aids.

Storytelling is a basic part of human communication. You've probably told several short stories just today to relate to friends what the drive to school was like, how your partner has been acting, what your boss said to a customer, or even what your speech teacher did in class. With each story you were sharing information, but is sharing the same as informing? At first you might be tempted to say "sure," but consider whether you had a purpose for telling a friend about another friend's actions, or if the words you used to discuss your boss communicated any attitude.

At some point in your business career you will be called upon to teach someone something. It may be a customer, coworker, or supervisor, and in each case you are performing an informative speech. It is distinct from a sales speech, or persuasive speech, in that your goal is to communicate the information so that your listener understands. For example, let's say you have the task of teaching a customer how to use a remote control (which button does what) to program a DVD/R to record. Easy, you say? Sure, it's easy for you. But for them it is new, so take a moment and consider their perspective. You may recommend this unit versus that unit, and aim for a sale, but that goal is separate from first teaching them to be successful at a task they want to learn to perform. You may need to repeat yourself several times, and they may not catch on as fast as you expect, but their mastery of the skill or task they want to learn can directly lead to a sale. They will have more confidence in you and in themselves once

they've mastered the task, and will be more receptive to your advice about the competing products available.

While your end goal may be a sale, the relationship you form has more long-term value. That customer may tell a friend about the experience, show their family what they learned, and before you know it someone else comes in asking for you by name. Communicating respect and focusing on their needs is a positive first step. The informative speech is one performance you'll give many times across your career, whether your audience is one person, a small group, or a large auditorium full of listeners. Once you master the art of the informative speech, you may mix and match it with other styles and techniques.

13.1 Functions of the Presentation to Inform
LEARNING OBJECTIVES

1. Describe the functions of the speech to inform.
2. Explain the difference between exposition and interpretation.

Informative presentations focus on helping the audience to understand a topic, issue, or technique more clearly. You might say, "Is that all?" and the answer is both yes and no. An affirmative response underscores the idea that informative speeches do not seek to motivate the audience to change their minds, adopt a new idea, start a new habit, or get out there and vote. They may, however, inform audiences on issues that may be under consideration in an election or referendum. On the other hand, a negative response reaffirms the idea that to communicate a topic, issue, or subject clearly is a challenge in itself and shouldn't be viewed as a simplistic process. There are distinct functions inherent in a speech to inform, and you may choose to use one or more of these functions in your speech. Let's take a look at the functions and see how they relate to the central objective of facilitating audience understanding.

Share
The basic definition of communication highlights the process of understanding and sharing meaning. An informative speech follows this definition in the aspect of sharing content and information with an audience. You won't be asking the audience to actually do anything in terms of offering a response or solving a problem. Instead you'll be offering to share with the audience some of the information you have

gathered relating to a topic. This act of sharing will reduce ignorance, increase learning, and facilitate understanding of your chosen topic.

Increase Understanding

How well does your audience grasp the information? This should be a guiding question to you on two levels. The first involves what they already know—or don't know—about your topic, and what key terms or ideas might be necessary for someone completely unfamiliar with your topic to grasp the ideas you are presenting. The second involves your presentation and the illustration of ideas. A bar chart, a pie graph, and a video clip may all serve you and the audience well, but how will each ingredient in your speech contribute to their understanding? The audience will respond to your attention statement and hopefully maintain interest, but how will you take your speech beyond superficial coverage of content and effectively communicate key relationships that increase understanding? These questions should serve as a challenge for your informative speech, and by looking at your speech from an audience-oriented perspective, you will increase your ability to increase the audience's understanding.

Change Perceptions

How you perceive stimuli has everything to do with a range of factors that are unique to you. We all want to make sense of our world, share our experiences, and learn that many people face the same challenges we do. Many people perceive the process of speaking in public as a significant challenge, and in this text, we have broken down the process into several manageable steps. In so doing, we have to some degree changed your perception of public speaking. When you present your speech to inform, you may want to change the audience member's perceptions of your topic. You may present an informative speech on air pollution and want to change common perceptions such as the idea that most of North America's air pollution comes from private cars, or that nuclear power plants are a major source of air pollution. You won't be asking people to go out and vote, or change their choice of automobiles, but you will help your audience change their perceptions of your topic.

Gain Skills

Just as you want to increase the audience's understanding, you may want to help the audience members gain skills. If you are presenting a speech on how to make salsa from fresh ingredients, your audience may thank you for not only the knowledge of the key ingredients and their preparation but also the product available at the conclusion. If your audience members have never made their own salsa, they may gain a new skill from your speech. In the same way, perhaps you decide to inform your audience about eBay, a person-to-

person marketplace much like a garage sale in which items are auctioned or available for purchase over the Internet. You may project onto a screen in class the main Web site and take the audience through a step-by-step process on how to sell an item. The audience may learn an important skill, clean out the old items in their garage, and buy new things for the house with their newfound skills. Your intentions, of course, are not to argue that salsa is better than ketchup or that eBay is better than Amazon, but to inform the audience, increasing their understanding of the subject, and in this case, gaining new skills.

Exposition versus Interpretation

When we share information informally, we often provide our own perspective and attitude for our own reasons. But when we set out to inform an audience, taking sides or using sarcasm to communicate attitude may divide the audience into groups that agree or disagree with the speaker. The speech to inform the audience on a topic, idea, or area of content is not intended to be a display of attitude and opinion. Consider the expectations of people who attend a formal dinner. Will they use whatever fork or spoon they want, or are there expectations of protocol and decorum? In any given communication context there are expectations, both implicit and explicit. If you attend a rally on campus for health care reform, you may expect the speaker to motivate you to urge the university to stop investing in pharmaceutical companies, for example. On the other hand, if you enroll in a biochemistry course, you expect a teacher to inform you about the discipline of biochemistry—not to convince you that pharmaceutical companies are a good or bad influence on our health care system.

The speech to inform is like the classroom setting in that the goal is to inform, not to persuade, entertain, display attitude, or create comedy. If you have analyzed your audience, you'll be better prepared to develop appropriate ways to gain their attention and inform them on your topic. You want to communicate thoughts, ideas, and relationships and allow each listener specifically, and the audience generally, to draw their own conclusions. The speech to inform is all about sharing information to meet the audience's needs, not your own. While you might want to inform them about your views on politics in the Middle East, you'll need to consider what they are here to learn from you and let your audience-oriented perspective guide you as you prepare.

Exposition

This relationship between informing as opposed to persuading your audience is often expressed in terms of exposition versus interpretation. Exposition means a public exhibition or display, often expressing a complex topic in a way that makes the relationships and content clear. Expository prose is writing to inform; you may have been asked to write an expository essay in an English course or an expository report in a journalism course. The goal is to communicate the topic and content to your audience in ways that illustrate, explain, and reinforce the overall content to make your topic more accessible to the audience. The audience wants to learn about your topic and may have some knowledge on it as you do. It is your responsibility to consider ways to display the information effectively.

Interpretation and Bias

Interpretation involves adapting the information to communicate a message, perspective, or agenda. Your insights and attitudes will guide your selection of material, what you focus on, and what you delete (choosing what not to present to the audience). Your interpretation will involve personal bias. Bias is an unreasoned or not-well-thought-out judgment. Bias involves beliefs or ideas held on the basis of conviction rather than current evidence. Beliefs are often called "habits of the mind" because we come to rely on them to make decisions. Which is the better, cheapest, most expensive, or the middle-priced product? People often choose the middle-priced product and use the belief "if it costs more it must be better" (and the opposite: "if it is cheap it must not be very good"). The middle-priced item, regardless of actual price, is often perceived as "good enough." All these perceptions are based on beliefs, and they may not apply to the given decision or even be based on any evidence or rational thinking.

By extension, marketing students learn to facilitate the customer "relationship" with the brand. If you come to believe a brand stands for excellence, and a new product comes out under that brand label, you are more likely to choose it over an unknown or lesser-known competitor. Again, your choice of the new product is based on a belief rather than evidence or rational thinking. We take mental shortcuts all day long, but in our speech to inform, we have to be careful not to reinforce bias.

Bias is like a filter on your perceptions, thoughts, and ideas. Bias encourages you to accept positive evidence that supports your existing beliefs (regardless of whether they are true) and reject negative evidence that does not support your beliefs. Furthermore, bias makes you likely to reject positive support for opposing beliefs and accept negative evidence (again, regardless of whether the evidence is true). So what is positive and what is negative? In a biased frame of mind, that which supports your existing beliefs is positive and likely to be accepted, while that which challenges your beliefs is likely to be viewed as negative and rejected. There is the clear danger

in bias. You are inclined to tune out or ignore information, regardless of how valuable, useful, or relevant it may be, simply because it doesn't agree with or support what you already believe.

Point of View

Let's say you are going to present an informative speech on a controversial topic like same-sex marriage. Without advocating or condemning same-sex marriage, you could inform your audience about current laws in various states, recent and proposed changes in laws, the number of same-sex couples who have gotten married in various places, the implications of being married or not being able to marry, and so on. But as you prepare and research your topic, do you only read or examine information that supports your existing view? If you only choose to present information that agrees with your prior view, you've incorporated bias into your speech. Now let's say the audience members have different points of view, even biased ones, and as you present your information you see many people start to fidget in their seats. You can probably anticipate that if they were to speak, the first word they would say is "but" and then present their question or assertion. In effect, they will be having a debate with themselves and hardly listening to you.

You can anticipate the effects of bias and mitigate them to some degree. First, know the difference between your point of view or perspective and your bias. Your point of view is your perception of an idea or concept from your previous experience and understanding. It is unique to you and is influenced by your experiences and also factors like gender, race, ethnicity, physical characteristics, and social class. Everyone has a point of view, as hard as they may try to be open-minded. But bias, as we've discussed previously, involves actively selecting information that supports or agrees with your current belief and takes away from any competing belief. To make sure you are not presenting a biased speech, frame your discussion to inform from a neutral stance and consider alternative points of view to present, compare and contrast, and diversify your speech. The goal of the speech to inform is to present an expository speech that reduces or tries to be free from overt interpretation.

This relates to our previous discussion on changing perceptions. Clearly no one can be completely objective and remove themselves from their own perceptual process. People are not modern works of minimalist art, where form and function are paramount and the artist is completely removed from the expression. People express themselves and naturally relate what is happening now to what has happened to them in the past. You are your own artist, but you also control your creations.

Objectivity involves expressions and perceptions of facts that are free from distortion by your prejudices, bias, feelings or interpretations. For example, is the post office box blue? An objective response would be yes or no, but a subjective response might sound like "Well, it's not really blue as much as it is navy, even a bit of purple, kind of like the color of my ex-boyfriend's car, remember? I don't care for the color myself." Subjectivity involves expressions or perceptions that are modified, altered, or impacted by your personal bias, experiences, and background. In an informative speech, your audience will expect you to present the information in a relatively objective form. The speech should meet the audience's need as they learn about the content, not your feelings, attitudes, or commentary on the content.

Here are five suggestions to help you present a neutral speech:

1. Keep your language neutral and not very positive for some issues while very negative for others.
2. Keep your sources credible and not from biased organizations. The National Rifle Association (NRA) will have a biased view of the Second Amendment, for example, as will the American Civil Liberties Union (ACLU) on civil rights.
3. Keep your presentation balanced. If you use a source that supports one clear side of an issue, include an alternative source and view. Give each equal time and respectful consideration.
4. Keep your audience in mind. Not everyone will agree with every point or source of evidence, but diversity in your speech will have more to offer everyone.
5. Keep who you represent in mind: Your business and yourself.

KEY TAKEAWAYS

- The purpose of an informative speech is to share ideas with the audience, increase their understanding, change their perceptions, or help them gain new skills.
- An informative speech incorporates the speaker's point of view but not attitude or interpretation.

EXERCISES

1. Consider the courses you have taken in the past year or two, and the extent to which each class session involved an informative presentation or one that was more persuasive. Do some disciplines lend themselves more to informing rather than interpretation and attitude? Discuss your findings with your classmates.

2. Visit a major network news Web site and view a video of a commentator such as Rachel Maddow or Keith Olbermann (MSNBC) or Glenn Beck or Bill O'Reilly (Fox News). Identify the commentator's point of view. If you were giving a presentation to inform, would you express your point of view in a similar style?

3. On the same network news Web site you used for Exercise no. 2, view a video reporting a news event (as opposed to a commentator's commentary). Do you feel that the reporter's approach conveys a point of view, or is it neutral? Explain your feelings and discuss with your classmates.

4. What is the difference between an informative presentation and a persuasive one? Provide an example in your response.

5. Consider a sample speech to inform on a topic where you have a strong opinion. In what ways would you adjust your key points so as not to persuade your listeners? Discuss your ideas with a classmate.

13.2 Types of Presentations to Inform
LEARNING OBJECTIVE

1. Provide examples of four main types of speech to inform.

Speaking to inform may fall into one of several categories. The presentation to inform may be:

- an explanation,
- a report,
- a description, or
- a demonstration of how to do something.

Let's explore each of these types of informative speech.

Explanation

Have you ever listened to a lecture or speech where you just didn't get it? It wasn't that you weren't interested, at least not at first. Perhaps the professor used language and jargon, or gave a confusing example, or omitted something that would have linked facts or concepts together. Soon you probably lost interest and sat there, attending the speech or lecture in body but certainly not in mind. An effective speech to inform will take a complex topic or issue and *explain* it to the audience in ways that increase audience understanding. Perhaps the speech where you felt lost lacked definitions upfront, or a clear foundation in the introduction. You certainly didn't learn much, and that's exactly what you want to avoid when you address your audience. Consider how you felt and then find ways to explain your topic—visually, using definitions and examples, providing a case study—that can lay a foundation on common ground with your audience and build on it.

No one likes to feel left out. As the speaker, it's your responsibility to ensure that this doesn't happen. Also know that to teach someone something new—perhaps a skill that they did not possess or a perspective that allows them to see new connections—is a real gift, both to you and the audience members. You will feel rewarded because you made a difference and they will perceive the gain in their own understanding.

Report

As a business communicator, you may be called upon to give an informative report where you communicate status, trends, or relationships that pertain to a specific topic. You might have only a few moments to speak, and you may have to prepare within a tight time frame. Your listeners may want "just the highlights," only to ask pointed questions that require significant depth and preparation on your part. The informative report is a speech where you organize your information around key events, discoveries, or technical data and provide context and illustration for your audience. They may naturally wonder, "Why are sales up (or down)?" or "What is the product leader in your lineup?" and you need to anticipate their perspective and present the key information that relates to your topic. If everyone in the room knows the product line, you may not need much information about your best seller, but instead place emphasis on marketing research that seems to indicate why it is the best seller.

Perhaps you are asked to be the scout and examine a new market, developing strategies to penetrate it. You'll need to orient your audience and provide key information about the market and demonstrate leadership as you articulate your strategies. You have a perspective gained by time and research, and your audience wants to know why you see things the way you do, as well as learn what you learned. A status report may be short or long, and may be an update that requires little background, but always consider the audience and what common ground you are building your speech on.

Description

Have you ever listened to a friend tell you about their recent trip somewhere and found the details fascinating, making you want to travel there or visit a similar place? Or perhaps you listened to your chemistry teacher describe a chemical reaction you were going to perform in class and you understood the process and could reasonably anticipate the outcome. Describing information requires emphasis on language that is vivid, captures attention, and excites the imagination. Your audience will be drawn to your effective use of color, descriptive language, and visual aids. An informative speech that focuses description will be visual in many ways. You may choose to illustrate with images, video and audio clips, and maps. Your first-person experience combined with your content will allow the audience to come to know a topic, area, or place through you, or secondhand. Their imagination is your ally, and you should aim to stimulate it with attention-getting devices and clear visual aids. Use your imagination to place yourself in their perspective: how would you like to have someone describe the topic to you?

Demonstration

You want to teach the audience how to throw a fast pitch in softball or a curveball in baseball. You want to demonstrate how to make salsa or how to program the applications on a smartphone. Each of these topics will call on your kindergarten experience of "show and tell." A demonstrative speech focuses on clearly showing a process and telling the audience important details about each step so that they can imitate, repeat, or do the action themselves. If the topic is complicated, think of ways to simplify each step.

Consider the visual aids or supplies you will need. You may have noticed that cooking shows on television rarely show the chef chopping and measuring ingredients during the demonstration. Instead, the ingredients are chopped and measured ahead of time and the chef simply adds each item to the dish with a brief comment like, "Now we'll stir in half a cup of chicken stock." If you want to present a demonstration speech on the ways to make a paper airplane, one that will turn left or right, go up, down or in loops, consider how best to present your topic. Perhaps by illustrating the process of making one airplane followed by example on how to make adjustments to the plane to allow for different flight patterns would be effective. Would you need additional paper airplanes made in advance of your speech? Would an example of the paper airplane in each of the key stages of production be helpful to have ready before the speech? Having all your preparation done ahead of time can make a world of difference, and your audience will appreciate your thoughtful approach.

By considering each step and focusing on how to simplify it, you can understand how the audience might grasp the new information and how you can best help them. Also, consider the desired outcome; for example, will your listeners be able to actually do the task themselves or will they gain an appreciation of the complexities of a difficult skill like piloting an airplane to a safe landing? Regardless of the sequence or pattern you will illustrate or demonstrate, consider how people from your anticipated audience will respond, and budget additional time for repetition and clarification.

Informative presentations come in all sizes, shapes, and forms. You may need to create an "elevator speech" style presentation with the emphasis on brevity, or produce a comprehensive summary of several points that require multiple visual aids to communicate complex processes or trends. The main goal in an informative presentation is to inform, not to persuade, and that requires an emphasis on credibility, for the speaker and the data or information presented. Extra attention to sources is required and you'll need to indicate what reports, texts, or Web sites were sources for your analysis and conclusions.

Here are additional, more specific types of informative presentations:

- Biographical information
- Case study results
- Comparative advantage results
- Cost-benefit analysis results
- Feasibility studies
- Field study results
- Financial trends analysis
- Health, safety, and accident rates
- Instruction guidelines
- Laboratory results
- Product or service orientations
- Progress reports
- Research results
- Technical specifications

Depending on the rhetorical situation, the audience, and the specific information to be presented, any of these types of presentation may be given as an explanation, a report, a description, or a demonstration.

KEY TAKEAWAY

An informative speech may explain, report, describe, or demonstrate how to do something.

EXERCISES

1. Watch a "how-to" television show, such as one about cooking, home improvement, dog training, or crime solving. What informative techniques and visual aids are used in the show to help viewers learn the skills that are being demonstrated?
2. Prepare a simple "how-to" presentation for the class. Present and compare your results.
3. Compare and contrast two television programs, noting how each communicates the meaning via visual communication rather than words or dialogue. Share and compare with classmates.

13.3 Adapting Your Presentation to Teach
LEARNING OBJECTIVES

1. Articulate and demonstrate an audience-centered perspective.
2. Provide and demonstrate examples of ways to facilitate active listening.

Successfully delivering an informative speech requires adopting an audience-centered perspective. Imagine that you are in the audience. What would it take for the speaker to capture and maintain your attention? What would encourage you to listen? In this section we present several techniques for achieving this, including motivating your audience to listen, framing your information in meaningful ways, and designing your presentation to appeal to diverse learning styles.

Motivating the Listener

In an ideal world, every audience member would be interested in your topic. Unfortunately, however, not everyone will be equally interested in your informative speech. The range of interest might extend from not at all interested to very interested, with individual audience members all across this continuum. So what is a speaker to do in order to motivate the listener?

The perception process involves selection or choice, and you want your audience to choose to listen to you. You can have all the "bells and whistles" of a dramatic, entertaining or engaging speech and still not capture everyone's attention. You can, however, use what you know to increase their chances of paying attention to you. Begin with your attention statement at the beginning of your speech and make sure it is dynamic and arresting. Remember what active listening involves, and look for opportunities throughout your speech to encourage active listening.

Let's highlight seven strategies by posing questions that audience members may think, but not actually say out loud, when deciding whether to listen to your speech. By considering each question, you will take a more audience-centered approach to developing your speech, increasing your effectiveness.

How Is Your Topic Relevant to Me?

A natural question audience members will ask themselves is, what does the topic have to do with me? Why should I care about it? Your first response might be because it's your turn to speak, so the least they can do is be respectful. Instead, consider the idea that you can lead a horse to water but you can't make her drink. If you are in a class, the audience is part of the class and they may be present in body, but they may arrive wishing they were somewhere else. You can put a stop to that wish by making your topic relevant for your audience. Relevance means that the information applies, relates, or has significance to the listener. Find areas of common ground and build on them.

If you are going to present an informative speech about the drinking and driving laws in your state, you can be assured that many people in the audience drive automobiles, some may consume alcohol, and according to psychologist Abraham Maslow, [1] everyone needs safety. You may also consider that some of your listeners have had experiences with people who have consumed too much alcohol or people who have driven under the influence; they may have even had a loved one injured by an intoxicated driver. You may use the issue of safety to underscore relevance. You might consider briefly alluding to the effects of alcohol, asking rhetorically if audience members have ever seen someone try to walk, talk, or even drive after a drinking binge. All these strategies will reinforce the relevance of your topic and highlight connections across common ground.

What Will I Learn from You?
This question involves several issues. How much does the audience already know about your subject? What areas do you think they might not know? If you know that many people are aware of the laws in your state that pertain to intoxicated driving, you may consider informing them about proposed changes to these laws in your state legislature. Another approach might be to describe the impact of the laws on families and individuals. The consequences can be discussed in terms of annual statistics of motor vehicle accidents involving alcohol, the age and gender distribution of those involved, and the individual consequences in terms of financial penalties, impact on employment, and a criminal record. By building on the information the audience knows, briefly reviewing it and then extending it, illustrating it, and demonstrating the impact, you inform them of things they didn't already know.

Why Are You Interested in This Topic?
Your interest in your topic is an excellent way to encourage your audience to listen. Interest involves qualities that arouse attention, stimulate curiosity, or move an individual to a more excited state of mind. You probably selected your topic with your audience in mind, but also considered your interest in the topic. Why did you choose it over other topics? What about your topic aroused your attention? Did it stimulate your curiosity? Did it make you excited about researching and preparing a speech on it? These questions will help you clarify

your interest, and by sharing the answers with your listeners, you will stimulate excitement on their part.

How Can I Use the Knowledge or Skills You Present to Me?
In an informative speech you are not asking your listeners to go out and vote, or to quit smoking tomorrow, as you would in a persuasive speech. Nevertheless, you need to consider how they will apply their new understanding. Application involves the individual's capacity for practical use of the information, skill, or knowledge. As a result of your speech, will your listeners be able to do something new like set up an auction on eBay? Will they better understand the importance of saving money and know three new ways to save for retirement?

For example, as a result of your informative speech on drunk driving laws, they may reflect on what a conviction would mean to them financially, think about how they would get to work if their driver's license was suspended, or imagine the grief of a family when an innocent person is killed in a drunk driving accident. Although your goal is not to persuade but inform, the new knowledge gained by your audience may motivate them to make new decisions about their lives.

When you prepare your presentation, consider ways you can actively show application of your material or content. Incorporate messages into your speech to highlight the practical use of the knowledge or skill. A couple of helpful comments about how the audience will actually use the information will go a long way toward encouraging listening and gaining attention.

What Is New about What You Propose to Present?
Sometimes humans seem like a mass of contradictions. We are naturally attracted to novelty, yet we appreciate predictability. We like clear organization, yet there are times when we enjoy a little controlled chaos. Novelty involves something new, unusual, or unfamiliar. As a speaker, how do you meet the two contrasting needs for familiarity and novelty?

Address both. You may want to start by forming a clear foundation on what you have in common with the audience. Present the known elements of your topic and then extend into areas where less is known, increasing the novelty or new information as you progress. People will feel comfortable with the familiar, and be intrigued by the unfamiliar.

You might also invert this process, starting from a relatively unfamiliar stance and working your way back to the familiar. This is a technique often used in cinema, where the opening shot is an extreme close-up of something and you can't guess what it is for lack of perspective. As the camera pulls back or pans left or right, you get more clues and eventually are able to see what it is. It is intriguing, yet familiar. Consider ways to reinforce the novelty of your material to your audience to encourage listening.

Are You Going to Bore Me?

You have probably sat through your fair share of boring lectures where the speaker, teacher, or professor talks at length in a relatively monotone voice, fails to alternate his or her pace, incorporates few visual aids or just reads from a PowerPoint show for an hour in a dimly lighted room. Recall how you felt. Trapped? Tired? Did you wonder why you had to be there? Then you know what you need to avoid.

Being bored means the speaker failed to stimulate you as the listener, probably increased your resistance to listening or participating, and became tiresome. To avoid boring your audience, speak with enthusiasm, and consider ways to gain, and keep gaining, their attention. You don't have to be a standup comedian, however, to avoid being a boring speaker. Consider the rhetorical situation, and let the audience's needs guide you as you prepare. Adjust and adapt as they give you feedback, nonverbal or verbal. Consider the question, "What's in it for me?" from the audience's perspective and plan to answer it specifically with vivid examples. If your presentation meets their expectations and meets their needs, listeners are more likely to give you their attention.

You may also give some thought and consideration to the organizational principle and choose a strategy that promises success. By organizing the information in interesting ways within the time frame, you can increase your effectiveness. The opposite of boring is not necessarily entertaining. Variety in your speech, from your voice to your visual aids, will help stimulate interest.

Is This Topic Really as Important as You Say It Is?

No one wants to feel like his or her time is being wasted. That trapped, tired, or bored feeling is often related to a perception that the topic is not relevant or important. What is important to you and what is important to your audience may be two different things. Take time and plan to reinforce in your speech how the topic is important to your audience. Importance involves perceptions of worth, value, and usefulness.

How can you express that the topic is worthy of their attention? We've discussed the importance of considering why you chose the topic in the first place as a strategy to engage your audience. They will want to know why the topic was worthy of your time, and by extension, their time.

Consider how to express through images, examples, or statistics the depth, breadth, and impact of your topic. Tell the audience how many drivers under the age of twenty-one lose their lives each year in alcohol-related accidents, or what percentage of all under-twenty-one deaths in your state are related to a combination of drinking and driving. Remember, too, that because statistics may sound impersonal or overwhelming, focusing on a specific case may provide more depth. As a final tip, be careful not to exaggerate the importance of your topic, as you may run the risk of having the audience mentally call your bluff. If this happens, you will lose some credibility and attention.

Framing

The presentation of information shapes attitudes and behavior. This is done through framing and content. Framing involves placing an imaginary set of boundaries, much like a frame around a picture or a window, around a story, of what is included and omitted, influencing the story itself. What lies within the frame that we can see? What lies outside the frame that we cannot see? Which way does the window face? All these variables impact our perspective, and by the acts of gatekeeping and agenda setting, the media frames the stories we see and information we learn.

Suppose you are presenting an informative speech about media effects on viewers. You might cite the case of the 1993 movie *The Program* about college football players. [2] In one scene, to demonstrate their "courage," the football players lie on the divider line of a busy highway at night as cars rush past. After viewing the film, several teenagers imitated the scene; some were seriously injured and one died as a result. [3] How will you frame this incident in the context of your speech? You might mention that the production studio subsequently deleted the highway sequence from the film, that the sequence clearly indicated the actors were stunt men, or that *The Program* ultimately argues that such behavior is destructive and unwarranted. Or you might cite additional incidents where people have been injured or killed by trying a stunt they saw in the media.

One form of framing is gatekeeping. Gatekeeping, according to Pearson and Nelson, is "a process of determining what news, information, or entertainment will reach a mass audience." [4] The term "gatekeeping" was originally used by psychologist Kurt Lewin as a metaphor, featuring a series of gates that information must pass through before ever reaching the audience. [5] In the context of journalism and mass media, gates and gatekeepers may include media owners, editors, or even the individual reporter in the context of mass communication. In the context of public speaking, you as the speaker are the gatekeeper to the information.

Another function of gatekeeping is agenda setting. Setting the agenda, just like the agenda of a meeting, means selecting what the audience will see and hear and in what order. Who decides what the top story on the evening news is? Throughout the twentieth century, professional communicators working in the media industry set the agenda for readers, listeners, and viewers; today widespread Internet access has greatly broadened the number of people who can become agenda setters. In giving a speech, you select the information and set the agenda. You may choose to inform the audience on a topic that gets little press coverage, or use a popular story widely covered in a new way, with a case example and local statistics.

Another aspect of framing your message is culture. According to Pearson and Nelson, culture within the context of communication is "a set of beliefs and understandings a society has about the world, its place in it, and the various activities used to celebrate and reinforce those beliefs." [6] Themes of independence, overcoming challenging circumstances, and hard-fought victory are seen repeatedly in American programming and national speeches. They reflect an aspect of American culture. In the case of football, it is sometimes viewed as the quintessentially male American sport, and its importance on Thanksgiving Day is nothing short of a ritual for many Americans. If you went to a country in Latin America, you would probably find the television set tuned to a soccer game, where soccer is the revered sport. What do these sports say about culture?

One might argue that American football is aggressive and that, while the team is important, the individual's effort and record are celebrated in all the time between plays. Significant attention is given to the salary each individual player makes. In South American football, or soccer, the announcer's emphasis is on the team and at breaks, some discussion of key players is present, but not to the same degree, though this is changing.

What do these differences tell us? Our interpretation of these differences may point toward ways in which the media reinforces national culture and its values. However, since you are speaking to inform, take care not to overgeneralize. To state that American football is a male-viewer-dominated sport may be an accurate observation, but to exclude women when discussing the sport would lead to a generalization that is not accurate, and may even perpetuate a stereotype.

The media and its public communication is an active participant in the perpetuation of stereotypes in many ways. In the mid-1990s, Julia Wood [7] made an interesting observation of the world according to television: "It is a world in which males make up two-thirds of the population. The women are fewer in number perhaps because less than 10 percent live beyond 35. Those who do, like their male counterparts and the younger females, are nearly all white and heterosexual. In addition to being young, the majority of women are beautiful, very thin, passive, and primarily concerned with relationships and getting rings out of collars and commodes." [8]

This limited view, itself a product of gatekeeping, agenda setting, and the profit motive, has little connection to the "real world." Most people in the world are not white, and the majority of U.S. adults are either overweight or obese. There are more women than men in the adult populations of most countries. Women do not tend to die off at age thirty-five, in fact women on average live longer than men. Many people, particularly in a diverse country that is undergoing dramatic demographic changes, are not members of just one racial, ethnic, or cultural group but rather a member of many groups. Consider culture when selecting content and note that diversity of information and sources will strengthen your speech and relate to more members of your audience.

Additional Tips

Andrews, Andrews, and Williams [9] offer eight ways to help listeners learn that are adapted and augmented here.

Limit the Number of Details

While it may be tempting to include many of the facts you've found in your research, choose only those that clearly inform your audience. Try to group the information and then choose the best example to reduce your list of details. You don't want the audience focusing on a long list of facts and details only to miss your main points.

Focus on Clear Main Points

Your audience should be able to discern your main points clearly the first time. You'll outline them in your introduction and they will listen for them as you proceed. Connect supporting information to your clear main points to reinforce them, and provide verbal cues of points covered and points to come.

Use internal summaries, where you state, "Now that we've discussed X point, let's examine its relationship to Y point. This will help your audience follow your logic and organization and differentiate between supporting material and main points. You may also want to foreshadow points by stating, "We'll examine Z point in a moment but first let's consider Y point."

Pace Yourself Carefully

Talking too fast is a common expression of speech anxiety. One way to reduce your anxiety level is to practice and know your information well. As you practice, note where you are in terms of time at the completion of each point. After a few practice rounds, you should begin to see some consistency in your speed. Use these benchmarks of time to pace yourself. When you deliver your speech, knowing you have time, are well prepared, and are familiar with your speech patterns will help you to pace yourself more effectively.

Speak with Concern for Clarity

Not everyone speaks English as his or her first language, and even among English speakers, there is a wide discrepancy in speaking style and language use. When you choose your language, consider challenging terms and jargon, and define them accordingly. You may assume that everyone knows "NIH" stands for "National Institutes of Health," but make sure you explain the acronym the first time you use it, just as you would if you were writing a formal article. Also pay attention to enunciation and articulation. As your rate of speech picks up, you may tend to slur words together and drop or de-emphasize consonants, especially at the ends of words. Doing this will make you harder to understand, discouraging listening.

Use Restatement and Repetition

There is nothing wrong with restating main points or repeating key phrases. The landmark speech titled "I have a dream," which Martin Luther King Jr. delivered on August 28, 1963, on the steps of the Lincoln Memorial, used that phrase multiple times to reinforce the main message effectively.

Provide Visual Reinforcement

We've discussed the importance of visual aids to support and illustrate your content. As a speaker giving a prepared presentation, you have the luxury of preparing your visual aids with your audience in mind. In an impromptu speech, or a media interview, you may lack this luxury and find the effort challenging to appropriately reinforce your content. Take advantage of the known time frame before your speech to prepare effective visual aids and your speech will be more effective.

Include Time for Questions

You can't possibly cover all the information about a topic that every audience member would want to know in the normal five to seven minutes of a speech. You may do an excellent job of supporting and reinforcing your points, but many listeners may have questions. Take this as a compliment—after all, if you hadn't piqued their interest, they wouldn't have any questions to ask. Answering questions is an opportunity to elaborate on a point, reinforcing what you presented and relying on your thorough preparation to illustrate the point with more depth.

In some situations, the speaker will accept and answer questions during the body of the presentations, but it is more typical to ask listeners to hold their questions until the end. Depending on your instructor's guidelines, you may advise the class at the beginning of your presentation which of these formats you will follow.

Look for Ways to Involve Listeners Actively

Instead of letting your audience sit passively, motivate them to get involved in your presentation. You might ask for a show of hands as you raise a question like, "How many of you have wondered about…?" You might point out the window, encouraging your audience to notice a weather pattern or an example of air pollution. Even stepping away from the podium for a moment can provide variety and increase active listening.

Assess Learning, If Possible

Questions during a speech can help assess understanding, but also run the risk of derailing your speech as the audience pursues one point while you have two more to present. Make time for dialogue after the conclusion of your speech and encourage your audience to write down their questions and ask them at that time. Perhaps asking your audience to reflect on a point, and then to write a few sentences at the conclusion of your speech, might reinforce your central message.

KEY TAKEAWAY

To present a successful informative speech, motivate your audience by making your material relevant and useful, finding interesting ways to frame your topic, and emphasizing new aspects if the topic is a familiar one.

EXERCISES

1. Visit an online news Web site such as CNN, MSNBC, or PBS News Hour. Select a news video on a topic that interests you and watch it a few times. Identify the ways in which the speaker(s) adapt the presentation to be informative and frame the topic. Discuss your results with your classmates.

2. Watch a news program and write down the words that could be considered to communicate values, bias, or opinion. Share and compare with the class.

3. Watch a news program and find an example that you consider to be objective, "just the facts," and share it with the class.

4. Note how television programs (or other media) use novelty to get your attention. Find at least three headlines, teaser advertisements for television programs, or similar attempts to get attention and share with the class.

5. How can an audience's prior knowledge affect a speech? What percentage of an informative presentation do you expect an audience to remember? Why?

[1] Maslow, A. (1970). *Motivation and personality* (2nd ed.). New York, NY: Harper & Row.

[2] James, C. (1993, October 24). If Simon says, 'Lie down in the road,' should you? *New York Times*. Retrieved

from http://www.nytimes.com/1993/10/24/weekinreview/the-nation-if-simon-says-lie-down-in-the-road-should-you.html

[3] Wilson, J., & Wilson, S. (1998). *Mass media/mass culture* (4th ed.). New York, NY: McGraw-Hill.

[4] Pearson, J., & Nelson, P. (2000). *An introduction to human communication: Understanding and sharing* (p. 133). Boston, MA: McGraw-Hill.

[5] Wilson, J., & Wilson, S. (1998). *Mass media/mass culture* (4th ed.). New York, NY: McGraw-Hill.

[6] Pearson, J., & Nelson, P. (2000). *An introduction to human communication: Understanding and sharing* (p. 132). Boston, MA: McGraw-Hill.

[7] Wood, J. (1994). *Gendered lives: Communication, gender, and culture* (2nd ed.). New York, NY: Random House.

[8] Pearson, J., & Nelson, P. (2000). *An introduction to human communication: Understanding and sharing* (p.136). Boston, MA: McGraw-Hill.

[9] Andrews, P. H., Andrews, J., & Williams, G. (1999). *Public speaking: Connecting you and your audience*. Boston, MA: Houghton Mifflin Company.

13.4 Diverse Types of Intelligence and Learning Styles
LEARNING OBJECTIVE

1. Define the concepts of multiple intelligences and learning styles, and identify different types of intelligence and learning styles that audience members may have.

Psychologist Howard Gardner [1] is known for developing the theory of multiple intelligences in which he proposes that different people are intelligent in different domains. For example, some people may excel in interpersonal intelligence, or the ability to form and maintain relationships. Other people may excel in bodily-kinesthetic intelligence, or physical coordination and control. Still others have a high degree of musical intelligence or of logico-mathematical intelligence. While some psychologists argue that these are actually talents or aptitudes rather than forms of intelligence, the point remains that individual audience members will receive information differently, depending on the types of intelligence (or talent) they possess.

An outgrowth of the theory of multiple intelligences is the theory of learning styles, the idea that people learn better if the message is presented in a strategy that fits with the types of intelligence in which they are strongest. Consider each style when preparing your speech. What styles might work best with your particular audience?

For example, suppose you work for a do-it-yourself home improvement store and part of your job is to give an informative seminar once a month on how to renovate a previously wallpapered wall. Your topic is specified for you, and you are very familiar with your subject matter, having worked in a variety of homes where old wallpaper needed to be removed or replaced. However, you never know from one month to the next how many people will come to your seminar or what their interests and level of prior knowledge are.

If you begin by going around the room and asking each person to describe the wallpaper situation they plan to work on, this will help you determine what kinds of questions your audience hopes to have answered, but it won't tell you anything about their learning styles. Suppose instead that you ask them to state why they decided to attend and what their career or occupation is. Now you can gauge your presentation according to the likely learning styles of your audience. For example, if you have ten attendees and five of them work in the banking or information technology field, it is probably safe to assume they are fairly strong in the logical or mathematical area. This will help you decide how to talk about measuring the wall, calculating product quantities, and estimating cost. If another attendee is a psychologist, he or she may be able to relate on the intrapersonal and interpersonal level. You may decide to strengthen your remarks about the importance of being comfortable with one's choices for renovating the room, seeking consensus from family members, and considering how the finished room will be suitable for guests. If some attendees work in the arts, they may be especially attentive to your advice about the aesthetic qualities of a well-executed wall surface renovation.

Table 13.1 "Diverse Learning Styles and Strategies" provides a summary of the seven styles and some suggested strategies to help you design your speech to align with each learning style.

Table 13.1 Diverse Learning Styles and Strategies

Learning Style	Examples	Strategies
Linguistic	Language, reading, verbal expression, speaking, writing, memorizing words (names, places, and dates)	Reading, oral presentations such as debates, reports, or storytelling
Logical/Mathematical	Use of numbers, perceiving relationships, reasoning (sequential, deductive, inductive), computation	Problem solving, graphic organizers, categorizing, classifying, working with patterns and relationships
Spatial	Think in three dimensions, mental imagery, design color, form and line within space	Maps, charts, graphic organizers, painting or drawing, visual aids, working with pictures or colors
Musical	Discern rhythm, pitch and tone, interpret music, identify tonal patterns, compose music	Rhythmic patterns and exercises, singing, music performance
Bodily/Kinesthetic	Sense of timing and balance, athletics, dance, work that takes physical skill	Drama, role playing, touching and manipulating objects, demonstrating
Interpersonal	Organizing, leading others, communicating, collaboration, negotiating, mediating	Group projects, interaction, debates, discussions, cooperative learning, sharing ideas
Intrapersonal	Reflection, thinking strategies, focusing/concentration	Individual projects, self-paced instruction, note-taking, reflection

KEY TAKEAWAY

An informative speech can be more effective when the learning styles of the audience members are addressed.

EXERCISES

1. Make a list of several people you know well, including family members, lifelong friends, or current roommates. Opposite each person's name, write the types of intelligence or the learning styles in which you believe that person is especially strong. Consider making this a reciprocal exercise by listing your strongest learning styles and asking family and friends to guess what is on your list.
2. How do you learn best? What works for you? Write a short paragraph and share with the class.
3. Write a review of your best teacher, noting why you think they were effective. Share with the class.
4. Write a review of your worst teacher, noting why you think they were ineffective. Share with the class.

[1] Gardner, H. (1993). *Frames of mind: The theory of multiple intelligences.* New York, NY: Basic Books.

13.5 Preparing Your Speech to Inform
LEARNING OBJECTIVES

1. Discuss and provide examples of ways to incorporate ethics in a speech.

2. Construct an effective speech to inform.

Now that we've covered issues central to the success of your informative speech, there's no doubt you want to get down to work. Here are five final suggestions to help you succeed.

Start with What You Know

Are you taking other classes right now that are fresh in your memory? Are you working on a challenging chemistry problem that might lend itself to your informative speech? Are you reading a novel by Gabriel García Márquez that might inspire you to present a biographical speech, informing your audience about the author? Perhaps you have a hobby or outside interest that you are excited about that would serve well. Regardless of where you draw the inspiration, it's a good strategy to start with what you know and work from there. You'll be more enthusiastic, helping your audience to listen intently, and you'll save yourself time. Consider the audience's needs, not just your need to cross a speech off your "to-do" list. This speech will be an opportunity for you to take prepared material and present it, gaining experience and important feedback. In the "real world," you often lack time and the consequences of a less than effective speech can be serious. Look forward to the opportunity and use what you know to perform an effective, engaging speech.

Consider Your Audience's Prior Knowledge

You don't want to present a speech on the harmful effects of smoking when no one in the audience smokes. You may be more effective addressing the issue of secondhand smoke, underscoring the relationship to relevance and addressing the issue of importance with your audience. The audience will want to learn something from you, not hear everything they have heard before. It's a challenge to assess what they've heard before, and often a class activity is conducted to allow audience members to come to know each other. You can also use their speeches and topic selection as points to consider. Think about age, gender, and socioeconomic status, as well as your listeners' culture or language. Survey the audience if possible, or ask a couple of classmates what they think of the topics you are considering.

In the same way, when you prepare a speech in a business situation, do your homework. Access the company Web site, visit the location and get to know people, and even call members of the company to discuss your topic. The more information you can gather about your audience, the better you will be able to adapt and present an effective speech.

Adapting Jargon and Technical Terms

You may have a topic in mind from another class or an outside activity, but chances are that there are terms specific to the area or activity. From wakeboarding to rugby to a chemical process that contributes to global warming, there will be jargon and technical terms. Define and describe the key terms for your audience as part of your speech and substitute common terms where appropriate. Your audience will enjoy learning more about the topic and appreciate your consideration as you present your speech.

Using Outside Information

Even if you think you know everything there is to know about your topic, using outside sources will contribute depth to your speech, provide support for your main points, and even enhance your credibility as a speaker. "According to _____" is a normal way of attributing information to a source, and you should give credit where credit is due. There is nothing wrong with using outside information as long as you clearly cite your sources and do not present someone else's information as your own.

Presenting Information Ethically

A central but often unspoken expectation of the speaker is that we will be ethical. This means, fundamentally, that we perceive one another as human beings with common interests and needs, and that we attend to the needs of others as well as our own. An ethical informative speaker expresses respect for listeners by avoiding prejudiced comments against any group, and by being honest about the information presented, including information that may contradict the speaker's personal biases. The ethical speaker also admits it when he or she does not know something. The best salespersons recognize that ethical communication is the key to success, as it builds a healthy relationship where the customer's needs are met, thereby meeting the salesperson's own needs.

Reciprocity

Tyler [1] discusses ethical communication and specifically indicates reciprocity as a key principle. Reciprocity, or a relationship of mutual exchange and interdependence, is an important characteristic of a relationship, particularly between a speaker and the audience. We've examined previously the transactional nature of communication, and it is important to reinforce this aspect here. We exchange meaning with one another in conversation, and much like a game, it takes more than one person to play. This leads to interdependence, or the dependence of the conversational partners on one another. Inequality in the levels of dependence can negatively impact the communication and, as a result, the relationship. You as the speaker will have certain expectations and roles, but dominating your audience will not encourage them to fulfill their roles in terms of participation and active listening. Communication involves give and take, and in a public speaking setting, where the communication may be perceived as "all to one," don't forget that the audience is also communicating in terms of feedback with you. You have a responsibility to attend to that feedback, and develop reciprocity with your audience. Without them, you don't have a speech.

Mutuality

Mutuality means that you search for common ground and understanding with the audience, establishing this space and building on it throughout the speech. This involves examining viewpoints other than your own, and taking steps to insure the speech integrates an inclusive, accessible format rather than an ethnocentric one.

Nonjudgmentalism

Nonjudgmentalism underlines the need to be open-minded, an expression of one's willingness to examine diverse perspectives. Your audience expects you to state the truth as you perceive it, with supporting and clarifying information to support your position, and to speak honestly. They also expect you to be open to their point of view and be able to negotiate meaning and understanding in a constructive way. Nonjudgmentalism may include taking the perspective that being different is not inherently bad and that there is common ground to be found with each other.

While this characteristic should be understood, we can see evidence of breakdowns in communication when audiences perceive they are not being told the whole truth. This does not mean that the relationship with the audience requires honesty and excessive self-disclosure. The use of euphemisms and displays of sensitivity are key components of effective communication, and your emphasis on the content of your speech and not yourself will be appreciated. Nonjudgmentalism does underscore the importance of approaching communication from an honest perspective where you value and respect your audience.

Honesty

Honesty, or truthfulness, directly relates to trust, a cornerstone in the foundation of a relationship with your audience. Without it, the building (the relationship) would fall down. Without trust, a relationship will not open and develop the possibility of mutual understanding. You want to share information and the audience hopefully wants to learn from you. If you "cherry-pick" your data, only choosing the best information to support only your point and ignore contrary or related issues, you may turn your informative speech into a persuasive one with bias as a central feature.

Look at the debate over the U.S. conflict with Iraq. There has been considerable discussion concerning the cherry-picking of issues and facts to create a case for armed intervention. To what degree the information at the time was accurate or inaccurate will continue to be a hotly debated issue, but the example holds in terms on an audience's response to a perceived dishonestly. Partial truths are incomplete and often misleading, and you don't want your audience to turn against you because they suspect you are being less than forthright and honest.

Respect

Respect should be present throughout a speech, demonstrating the speaker's high esteem for the audience. Respect can be defined as an act of giving and displaying particular attention to the value you associate with someone or a group. This definition involves two key components. You need to give respect in order to earn from others, and you need to show it. Displays of respect include making time for conversation, not interrupting, and even giving appropriate eye contact during conversations.

Trust

Communication involves sharing and that requires trust. Trust means the ability to rely on the character or truth of someone, that what you say you mean and your audience knows it. Trust is a process, not a thing. It builds over time, through increased interaction and the reduction of uncertainty. It can be lost, but it can also be regained. It should be noted that it takes a long time to build trust in a relationship and can be lost in a much shorter amount of time. If your audience suspects you mislead them this time, how will they approach your next presentation? Acknowledging trust and its importance in your relationship with the audience is the first step in focusing on this key characteristic.

Avoid Exploitation

Finally, when we speak ethically, we do not intentionally exploit one another. Exploitation means taking advantage, using someone else for one's own purposes. Perceiving a relationship with an audience as a means to an end and only focusing on what you get out of it, will lead you to treat people as objects. The temptation to exploit others can be great in business situations, where a promotion, a bonus, or even one's livelihood are at stake.

Suppose you are a bank loan officer. Whenever a customer contacts the bank to inquire about applying for a loan, your job is to provide an informative presentation about the types of loans available, their rates and terms. If you are paid a commission based on the number of loans you make and their amounts and rates, wouldn't you be tempted to encourage them to borrow the maximum amount they can qualify for? Or perhaps to take a loan with confusing terms that will end up costing much more in fees and interest than the customer realizes? After all, these practices are within the law; aren't they just part of the way business is done? If you are an ethical loan officer, you realize you would be exploiting customers if you treated them this way. You know it is more valuable to uphold your long-term relationships with customers than to exploit them so that you can earn a bigger commission.

Consider these ethical principles when preparing and presenting your speech, and you will help address many of these natural expectations of others and develop healthier, more effective speeches.

Sample Informative Presentation

Here is a generic sample speech in outline form with notes and suggestions.

Attention Statement
Show a picture of a goldfish and a tomato and ask the audience, "What do these have in common?"
Introduction
1. Briefly introduce genetically modified foods.

2. State your topic and specific purpose: "My speech today will inform you on genetically modified foods that are increasingly part of our food supply."

3. Introduce your credibility and the topic: "My research on this topic has shown me that our food supply has changed but many people are unaware of the changes."

4. State your main points: "Today I will define genes, DNA, genome engineering and genetic manipulation, discuss how the technology applies to foods, and provide common examples."

Body

1. *Information*. Provide a simple explanation of the genes, DNA and genetic modification in case there are people who do not know about it. Provide clear definitions of key terms.

2. *Genes and DNA*. Provide arguments by generalization and authority.

3. *Genome engineering and genetic manipulation*. Provide arguments by analogy, cause, and principle.

4. *Case study*. In one early experiment, GM (genetically modified) tomatoes were developed with fish genes to make them resistant to cold weather, although this type of tomato was never marketed.

5. Highlight other examples.

Conclusion

Reiterate your main points and provide synthesis, but do not introduce new content.

Residual Message

"Genetically modified foods are more common in our food supply than ever before."

KEY TAKEAWAY

In preparing an informative speech, use your knowledge and consider the audience's knowledge, avoid unnecessary jargon, give credit to your sources, and present the information ethically.

EXERCISES

1. Identify an event or issue in the news that interests you. On at least three different news networks or Web sites, find and watch video reports about this issue. Compare and contrast the coverage of the issue. Do the networks or Web sites differ in their assumptions about viewers' prior knowledge? Do they give credit to any sources of information? To what extent do they each measure up to the ethical principles described in this section? Discuss your findings with your classmates.

2. Find an example of reciprocity in a television program and write two to three paragraphs describing it. Share and compare with your classmates.

3. Find an example of honesty in a television program and write two to three paragraphs describing it. Share and compare with your classmates.

4. Find an example of exploitation depicted in the media. Describe how the exploitation is communicated with words and images and share with the class.

5. Compose a general purpose statement and thesis statement for a speech to inform. Now create a sample outline. Share with a classmate and see if he or she offers additional points to consider.

[1] Tyler, V. (1978). Report of the working groups of the second SCA summer conference on intercultural communication. In N. C. Asuncio-Lande (Ed.), *Ethical Perspectives and Critical Issues in Intercultural Communication* (pp. 170–177). Falls Church, VA: SCA.

13.6 Creating an Informative Presentation
LEARNING OBJECTIVES

1. Discuss the parts of an informational presentation.
2. Understand the five parts of any presentation.

An informational presentation is common request in business and industry. It's the verbal and visual equivalent of a written report. Information sharing is part of any business or organization. Informative presentations serve to present specific information for specific audiences for specific goals or functions. The type of presentation is often identified by its primary purpose or function. Informative presentations are often analytical or involve the rational analysis of information. Sometimes they simply "report the facts" with no analysis at all, but still need to communicate the information in a clear and concise format. While a presentation may have conclusions, propositions, or even a call to action, the demonstration of the analysis is the primary function.

A sales report presentation, for example, is not designed to make a sale. It is, however, supposed to report sales to date and may forecast future sales based on previous trends.

An informative presentation does not have to be a formal event, though it can be. It can be generic and nonspecific to the audience or listener, but the more you know about your audience, the better. When you tailor your message to that audience, you zero in on your target and increase your effectiveness. The emphasis is on clear and concise communication, but it may address several key questions:

- Topic: Product or Service?
- Who are you?
- Who is the target market?
- What is the revenue model?
- What are the specifications?

- How was the information gathered?
- How does the unit work?
- How does current information compare to previous information?

Table 13.2 "Presentation Components and Their Functions" lists the five main parts or components of any presentation. [1]

You will need to address the questions to establish relevance and meet the audience's needs. The five parts of any speech will serve to help you get organized.

Sample Speech Guidelines

Imagine that you have been assigned to give an informative presentation lasting five to seven minutes. Follow the guidelines in Table 13.3 "Sample Speech Guidelines" and apply them to your presentation.

Table 13.2 Presentation Components and Their Functions

Component	Function
Attention Statement	Raise interest and motivate the listener
Introduction	Communicate a point and common ground
Body	Address key points
Conclusion	Summarize key points
Residual Message	Communicate central theme, moral of story, or main point

Table 13.3 Sample Speech Guidelines

1. Topic	Choose a product or service that interests you, research it, and report your findings in your speech.
2. Purpose	Your general purpose, of course, is to inform. But you need to formulate a more specific purpose statement that expresses a point you have to make about your topic—what you hope to accomplish in your speech.
3. Audience	Think about what your audience might already know about your topic and what they may not know, and perhaps any attitudes toward or concerns about it. Consider how this may affect the way that you will present your information.
4. Supporting Materials	Using the information gathered in your search for information, determine what is most worthwhile, interesting, and important to include in your speech. Time limits will require that you be selective about what you use. **Use visual aids!**
5. Organization	a. Write a central idea statement that expresses the message, or point, that you hope to get across to your listeners in the speech. Determine the two to three main points that will be needed to support your central idea. c. Finally, prepare a complete sentence outline of the body of the speech.
6. Introduction	Develop an opening that will get the attention and interest of your listeners, express your central idea or message, lead into the body of your speech.
7. Conclusion	The conclusion should review and/or summarize the important ideas in your speech and bring it to a smooth close.
8. Delivery	The speech should be delivered extemporaneously (not reading but speaking), using speaking notes and not reading from the manuscript. Work on maximum eye contact with your listeners. Use any visual aids or handouts that may be helpful.

KEY TAKEAWAY

Informative presentations illustrate, explain, describe, and instruct the audience on topics and processes.

EXERCISES

1. Write a brief summary of a class or presentation you personally observed recently; include what you learned. Compare with classmates.
2. Search online for an informative speech or presentation that applies to business or industry. Indicate one part or aspect of the presentation that you thought was effective and one you would improve. Provide the link to the presentation in your post or assignment.
3. Pick a product or service and come up with a list of five points that you could address in a two-minute informative speech. Place them in rank order and indicate why.
4. With the points discussed in this chapter in mind, observe someone presenting a speech. What elements of their speech could you use in your speech? What elements would you not want to use? Why? Compare with a classmate.

---

[1] McLean, S. (2003). *The basics of speech communication.* Boston: Allyn & Bacon.

13.7 Additional Resources

- To listen to speeches from great figures in history, visit the History Channel's audio speech archive. http://www.history.com/video.do?name=speeches
- What were the greatest speeches of the twentieth century? Find out here. http://gos.sbc.edu/top100.html
- Visit this eHow link for a great video demonstrating how to remove ink stains from clothing. http://www.ehow.com/video_2598_remove-ink-stains.html
- To improve your enunciation, try these exercises from the Mount Holyoke College site. http://www.mtholyoke.edu/acad/intrel/speech/enunciation.htm
- The Merriam-Webster dictionary site provides a wealth of resources on words, their meanings, their origins, and audio files of how to pronounce them. http://www.merriam-webster.com
- For information on adapting your speech for an audience or audience members with special needs, explore this index of resources compiled by Ithaca College. http://www.ithaca.edu/wise/topics/speech_language.htm

- Dr. Richard Felder of North Carolina State University presents this questionnaire to assess your learning styles. http://www.engr.ncsu.edu/learningstyles/ilsweb.html
- The American Speech-Language-Hearing Association offers an array of Web resources on ethics. http://www.asha.org/practice/ethics
- Visit this site for a list of more than thirty informative topics for a business speech. http://www.speech-topics-help.com/informative-business-speech-topics.html
- Visit this eHow site to get ideas for an audience-oriented informative speech topic. http://www.ehow.com/how_2239702_choose-topic-informative-speech.html

NOTES:

NOTES:

Chapter 14:
Presentations to Persuade

We are more easily persuaded, in general, by the reasons that we ourselves discover than by those which are given to us by others.
    Pascal
For every sale you miss because you're too enthusiastic, you will miss a hundred because you're not enthusiastic enough.
    Zig Ziglar

Getting Started

INTRODUCTORY EXERCISES

1. Please list three things that you recently purchased, preferably in the last twenty-four hours—the things can be items or services. Decide which purchase on your list stands out as most important to you and consider why you made that purchase decision. See if you can list three reasons. Now pretend you are going to sell that same item or service to a friend—would the three reasons remain the same, or would you try additional points for them to consider? Compare your results with a classmate.

2. Please think of one major purchase you made in the past year. It should be significant to you, and not a daily or monthly purchase. Once you made the purchase decision and received the item (e.g., a car), did you notice similar cars on the roads? Did you pay attention to details like color, modifications, or reports in the popular press about quality? Did you talk to your friends about it? What kind of information did you pay attention to— information that reinforced your purchase decision, or information that detracted from your appreciation of your newly acquired possession? Discuss your responses with classmates.

No doubt there has been a time when you wanted something from your parents, your supervisor, or your friends, and you thought about how you were going to present your request. But do you think about how often people—including people you have never met and never will meet—want something from you? When you watch television, advertisements reach out for your attention, whether you watch them or not. When you use the Internet, pop-up advertisements often appear. Living in the United States, and many parts of the world, means that you have been surrounded, even inundated, by persuasive messages. Mass media in general and television in particular make a significant impact you will certainly recognize.

Consider these facts:

- The average person sees between four hundred and six hundred ads per day—that is forty million to fifty million by the time he or she is sixty years old. One of every eleven commercials has a direct message about beauty. [1]
- By age eighteen, the average American teenager will have spent more time watching television—25,000 hours— than learning in a classroom. [2]
- An analysis of music videos found that nearly one-fourth of all MTV videos portray overt violence, with attractive role models being aggressors in more than 80 percent of the violent videos. [3]
- Forty percent of nine- and ten-year-old girls have tried to lose weight, according to an ongoing study funded by the National Heart, Lung and Blood Institute. [4]
- A 1996 study found that the amount of time an adolescent watches soaps, movies, and music videos is associated with their degree of body dissatisfaction and desire to be thin. [5]
- Identification with television stars (for girls and boys), models (girls), or athletes (boys) positively correlated with body dissatisfaction. [6]
- At age thirteen, 53 percent of American girls are "unhappy with their bodies." This grows to 78 percent by the time they reach seventeen. [7]
- By age eighteen, the average American teenager will witness on television 200,000 acts of violence, including 40,000 murders. [8]

Mass communication contains persuasive messages, often called propaganda, in narrative form, in stories and even in presidential speeches. When President Bush made his case for invading Iraq, his speeches incorporated many of the techniques we'll cover in this chapter. Your local city council often involves dialogue, and persuasive speeches, to determine zoning issues, resource allocation, and even spending priorities. You yourself have learned many of the techniques by trial and error and through imitation. If you ever wanted the keys to your parents' car for a special occasion, you used the principles of persuasion to reach your goal.

[1] Raimondo, M. (2010). About-face facts on the media. *About-face*. Retrieved fromhttp://www.about-face.org/r/facts/media.shtml
[2] Ship, J. (2005, December). Entertain. Inspire. Empower. How to speak a teen's language, even if you're not one. *Change This*. Retrieved fromhttp://www.changethis.com/pdf/20.02.TeensLanguage.pdf

[3] DuRant, R. H. (1997). Tobacco and alcohol use behaviors portrayed in music videos: Content analysis. *American Journal of Public Health, 87*, 1131–1135.

[4] Body image and nutrition: Fast facts. (2009). *Teen Health and the Media*. Retrieved from http://depts.washington.edu/thmedia/view.cgi?section=bodyimage&page=fastfacts

[5] Tiggemann, M., & Pickering, A. S. (1996). Role of television in adolescent women's body: Dissatisfaction and drive for thinness. *International Journal of Eating Disorders, 20*, 199–203.

[6] Hofschire, L. J., & Greenberg, B. S. (2002). Media's impact on adolescent's body dissatisfaction. In D. Brown, J. R. Steele, & K. Walsh-Childers (Eds.), *Sexual Teens, Sexual Media*. NJ: Lawrence Erlbaum Associates, Inc.

[7] Brumberg, J. J. (1997). *The body project: An intimate history of American girls*. New York, NY: Random House.

[8] Huston, A. C., et al. (1992). *Big world, small screen: The role of television in American society*. Lincoln: University of Nebraska Press.

14.1 What Is Persuasion?
LEARNING OBJECTIVES

1. Demonstrate an understanding of the importance of persuasion.
2. Describe similarities and differences between persuasion and motivation.

Persuasion is an act or process of presenting arguments to move, motivate, or change your audience. Aristotle taught that rhetoric, or the art of public speaking, involves the faculty of observing in any given case the available means of persuasion. [1] In the case of President Obama, he may have appealed to your sense of duty and national values. In persuading your parents to lend you the car keys, you may have asked one parent instead of the other, calculating the probable response of each parent and electing to approach the one who was more likely to adopt your position (and give you the keys). Persuasion can be implicit or explicit and can have both positive and negative effects. In this chapter we'll discuss the importance of ethics, as we have in previous chapters, when presenting your audience with arguments in order to motivate them to adopt your view, consider your points, or change their behavior.

Motivation is distinct from persuasion in that it involves the force, stimulus, or influence to bring about change. Persuasion is the process, and motivation is the compelling stimulus that encourages your audience to change their beliefs or behavior, to adopt your position, or to consider your arguments. Why think of yourself as fat or thin? Why should you choose to spay or neuter your pet? Messages about what is beautiful, or what is the right thing to do in terms of your pet, involve persuasion, and the motivation compels you to do something.

Another way to relate to motivation also can be drawn from the mass media. Perhaps you have watched programs like *Law and Order*, *Cold Case*, or *CSI* where the police detectives have many of the facts of the case, but they search for motive. They want to establish motive in the case to provide the proverbial "missing piece of the puzzle." They want to know why someone would act in a certain manner. You'll be asking your audience to consider your position and provide both persuasive arguments and motivation for them to contemplate. You may have heard a speech where the speaker tried to persuade you, tried to motivate you to change, and you resisted the message. Use this perspective to your advantage and consider why an audience should be motivated, and you may find the most compelling examples or points. Relying on positions like "I believe it, so you should too," "Trust me, I know what is right," or "It's the right thing to do" may not be explicitly stated but may be used with limited effectiveness. Why should the audience believe, trust, or consider the position "right?" Keep an audience-centered perspective as you consider your persuasive speech to increase your effectiveness.

You may think initially that many people in your audience would naturally support your position in favor of spaying or neutering your pet. After careful consideration and audience analysis, however, you may find that people are more divergent in their views. Some audience members may already agree with your view, but others may be hostile to the idea for various reasons. Some people may be neutral on the topic and look to you to consider the salient arguments. Your audience will have a range of opinions, attitudes, and beliefs across a range from hostile to agreement.

Rather than view this speech as a means to get everyone to agree with you, look at the concept of measurable gain, a system of assessing the extent to which audience members respond to a persuasive message. You may reinforce existing beliefs in the members of the audience that agree with you and do a fine job of persuasion. You may also get hostile members of the audience to consider one of your arguments, and move from a hostile position to one that is more neutral or ambivalent. The goal in each case is to move the audience members toward your position. Some change may be small but measurable, and that is considered gain. The next time a hostile audience member considers the issue, they may be more open to it. Figure 14.1 "Measurable Gain" is a useful diagram to illustrate this concept.

Figure 14.1 Measurable Gain

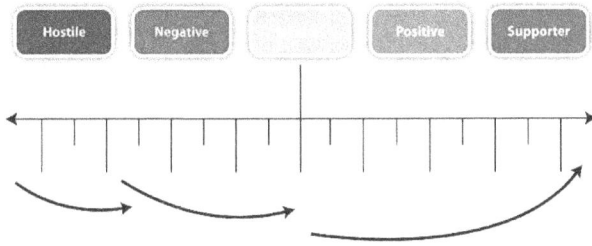

Edward Hall [2] also underlines this point when discussing the importance of context. The situation in which a conversation occurs provides a lot of meaning and understanding for the participants in some cultures. In Japan, for example, the context, such as a business setting, says a great deal about the conversation and the meaning to the words and expressions within that context. In the United States, however, the concept of a workplace or a business meeting is less structured, and the context offers less meaning and understanding.

Cultures that value context highly are aptly called high-context cultures. Those that value context to a lesser degree are called low-context cultures. These divergent perspectives influence the process of persuasion and are worthy of your consideration when planning your speech. If your audience is primarily high-context, you may be able to rely on many cultural norms as you proceed, but in a low-context culture, like the United States, you'll be expected to provide structure and clearly outline your position and expectations. This ability to understand motivation and context is key to good communication, and one we will examine throughout this chapter.

KEY TAKEAWAY

Persuasion is the act of presenting arguments for change, while motivation involves the force to bring about change. The concept of measurable gain assesses audience response to a persuasive message.

EXERCISES

1. Select an online advertisement that you find particularly effective or ineffective. Why does it succeed, or fail, in persuading you to want to buy the advertised product? Discuss your ideas with your classmates.
2. Think of a social issue, widely held belief, or political position where change has occurred in your lifetime, or where you would like to see change happen. What kinds of persuasion and motivation were involved—or would need to happen—to produce measurable gain? Explain your thoughts to a classmate.

3. Think of a time when someone tried to persuade you to do something you did not want to do. Did their persuasion succeed? Why or why not? Discuss the event with a classmate.

[1] Covino, W. A., & Jolliffe, D. A. (1995). *Rhetoric: Concepts, definitions, boundaries.* Boston, MA: Allyn & Bacon.
[2] Hall, E. (1966). *The hidden dimension.* New York, NY: Doubleday.

14.2 Principles of Persuasion
LEARNING OBJECTIVE

1. Identify and demonstrate how to use six principles of persuasion.

What is the best way to succeed in persuading your listeners? There is no one "correct" answer, but many experts have studied persuasion and observed what works and what doesn't. Social psychologist Robert Cialdini [1] offers us six principles of persuasion that are powerful and effective:
1. Reciprocity
2. Scarcity
3. Authority
4. Commitment and consistency
5. Consensus
6. Liking

You will find these principles both universal and adaptable to a myriad of contexts and environments. Recognizing when each principle is in operation will allow you to leverage the inherent social norms and expectations to your advantage, and enhance your sales position.

Principle of Reciprocity
Reciprocity is the mutual expectation for exchange of value or service. In all cultures, when one person gives something, the receiver is expected to reciprocate, even if only by saying "thank you." There is a moment when the giver has power and influence over the receiver, and if the exchange is dismissed as irrelevant by the giver the moment is lost. In business this principle has several applications. If you are in customer service and go out of your way to meet the customer's need, you are appealing to the principle of reciprocity with the knowledge that all humans perceive the need to reciprocate—in this case, by increasing the likelihood of making a purchase from you because you were especially helpful. Reciprocity builds trust and the relationship develops, reinforcing everything from personal to brand loyalty. By taking the lead and giving, you build in a moment where people will feel compelled from social norms and customs to give back.

Principle of Scarcity

You want what you can't have, and it's universal. People are naturally attracted to the exclusive, the rare, the unusual, and the unique. If they are convinced that they need to act now or it will disappear, they are motivated to action. Scarcity is the perception of inadequate supply or a limited resource. For a sales representative, scarcity may be a key selling point—the particular car, or theater tickets, or pair of shoes you are considering may be sold to someone else if you delay making a decision. By reminding customers not only of what they stand to gain but also of what they stand to lose, the representative increases the chances that the customer will make the shift from contemplation to action and decide to close the sale.

Principle of Authority

Trust is central to the purchase decision. Whom does a customer turn to? A salesperson may be part of the process, but an endorsement by an authority holds credibility that no one with a vested interest can ever attain. Knowledge of a product, field, trends in the field, and even research can make a salesperson more effective by the appeal to the principle of authority. It may seem like extra work to educate your customers, but you need to reveal your expertise to gain credibility. We can borrow a measure of credibility by relating what experts have indicated about a product, service, market, or trend, and our awareness of competing viewpoints allows us insight that is valuable to the customer. Reading the manual of a product is not sufficient to gain expertise—you have to do extra homework. The principal of authority involves referencing experts and expertise.

Principle of Commitment and Consistency

Oral communication can be slippery in memory. What we said at one moment or another, unless recorded, can be hard to recall. Even a handshake, once the symbol of agreement across almost every culture, has lost some of its symbolic meaning and social regard. In many cultures, the written word holds special meaning. If we write it down, or if we sign something, we are more likely to follow through. By extension, even if the customer won't be writing anything down, if you do so in front of them, it can appeal to the principle of commitment and consistency and bring the social norm of honoring one's word to bear at the moment of purchase.

Principle of Consensus

Testimonials, or first person reports on experience with a product or service, can be highly persuasive. People often look to each other when making a purchase decision, and the herd mentality is a powerful force across humanity: if "everybody else" thinks this product is great, it must be great.

We often choose the path of the herd, particularly when we lack adequate information. Leverage testimonials from clients to attract more clients by making them part of your team. The principle of consensus involves the tendency of the individual to follow the lead of the group or peers.

Principle of Liking

Safety is the twin of trust as a foundation element for effective communication. If we feel safe, we are more likely to interact and communicate. We tend to be attracted to people who communicate to us that they like us, and who make us feel good about ourselves. Given a choice, these are the people with whom we are likely to associate. Physical attractiveness has long been known to be persuasive, but similarity is also quite effective. We are drawn to people who are like us, or who we perceive ourselves to be, and often make those judgments based on external characteristics like dress, age, sex, race, ethnicity, and perceptions of socioeconomic status. The principle of liking involves the perception of safety and belonging in communication.

KEY TAKEAWAY

A persuasive message can succeed through the principles of reciprocity, scarcity, authority, commitment and consistency, consensus, and liking.

EXERCISES

1. Think of a real-life example of the principle of scarcity being used in a persuasive message. Were you the one trying to persuade someone, or were you the receiver of the scarcity message? Was the message effective? Discuss your thoughts with a classmate.

2. Do you think the principle of consensus often works—are people often persuaded to buy things because other people own that item, or are going to buy it? Are you susceptible to this kind of persuasion? Think of some examples and discuss them with classmates.

3. Do people always use reason to make decisions? Support your opinion and discuss it with classmates.

4. Make a list of five or six people you choose to associate with—friends, neighbors, and coworkers, for example. Next to each person's name, write the characteristics you have in common with that person. Do you find that the principle of liking holds true in your choice of associates? Why or why not? Discuss your findings with your classmates.

[1] Cialdini, R. (1993). *Influence*. New York, NY: Quill.

14.3 Functions of the Presentation to Persuade
LEARNING OBJECTIVE

1. Identify and demonstrate the effective use of five functions of speaking to persuade.

What does a presentation to persuade do? There is a range of functions to consider, and they may overlap or you may incorporate more than one as you present. We will discuss how to:

- stimulate,
- convince,
- call to action,
- increase consideration, and
- develop tolerance of alternate perspectives.

We will also examine how each of these functions influences the process of persuasion.

Stimulate

When you focus on stimulation as the goal or operational function of your speech, you want to reinforce existing beliefs, intensify them, and bring them to the forefront. Perhaps you've been concerned with global warming for quite some time. Many people in the audience may not know about the melting polar ice caps and the loss of significant ice shelves in Antarctica, including part of the Ross Ice Shelf, an iceberg almost 20 miles wide and 124 miles long, more than twice the size of Rhode Island. They may be unaware of how many ice shelves have broken off, the 6 percent drop in global phytoplankton (the basis of many food chains), and the effects of the introduction of fresh water to the oceans. By presenting these facts, you will reinforce existing beliefs, intensify them, and bring the issue to the surface. You might consider the foundation of common ground and commonly held beliefs, and then introduce information that a mainstream audience may not be aware of that supports that common ground as a strategy to stimulate.

Convince

In a persuasive speech, the goal is to change the attitudes, beliefs, values, or judgments of your audience. If we look back at the idea of motive, in this speech the prosecuting attorney would try to convince the jury members that the defendant is guilty beyond reasonable doubt. He or she may discuss motive, present facts, all with the goal to convince the jury to believe or find that his or her position is true. In the film *The Day After Tomorrow*, Dennis Quaid stars as a paleoclimatologist who unsuccessfully tries to convince the U.S. vice president that a sudden climate change is about to occur. In the film, much like real life, the vice president listens to Quaid's position with his own bias in mind, listening for only points that reinforce his point of view while rejecting points that do not.

Audience members will also hold beliefs and are likely to involve their own personal bias. Your goal is to get them to agree with your position, so you will need to plan a range of points and examples to get audience members to consider your topic. Perhaps you present Dennis Quaid's argument that loss of the North Atlantic Current will drastically change our climate, clearly establishing the problem for the audience. You might cite the review by a professor, for example, who states in reputable science magazine that the film's depiction of a climate change has a chance of happening, but that the timetable is more on the order of ten years, not seven days as depicted in the film. You then describe a range of possible solutions. If the audience comes to a mental agreement that a problem exists, they will look to you asking, "What are the options?" Then you may indicate a solution that is a better alternative, recommending future action.

Call to Action

In this speech, you are calling your audience to action. You are stating that it's not about stimulating interest to reinforce and accentuate beliefs, or convincing an audience of a viewpoint that you hold, but instead that you want to see your listeners change their behavior. If you were in sales at Toyota, you might incorporate our previous example on global warming to reinforce, and then make a call to action (make a purchase decision), when presenting the Prius hybrid (gas-electric) automobile. The economics, even at current gas prices, might not completely justify the difference in price between a hybrid and a nonhybrid car. However, if you as the salesperson can make a convincing argument that choosing a hybrid car is the right and responsible decision, you may be more likely to get the customer to act. The persuasive speech that focuses on action often generates curiosity, clarifies a problem, and as we have seen, proposes a range of solutions. They key difference here is there is a clear link to action associated with the solutions.

Solutions lead us to considering the goals of action. These goals address the question, "What do I want the audience to do as a result of being engaged by my speech?" The goals of action include adoption, discontinuance, deterrence, and continuance.

Adoption means the speaker wants to persuade the audience to take on a new way of thinking, or adopt a new idea. Examples could include buying a new product, voting for a new candidate, or deciding to donate blood. The key is that the audience member adopts, or takes on, a new view, action, or habit.

Discontinuance involves the speaker persuading the audience to stop doing something what they have been doing, such as smoking. Rather than take on a new habit or action, the speaker is asking the audience member to stop an existing behavior or idea. As such, discontinuance is in some ways the opposite of adoption.

Deterrence is a call action that focuses on persuading audience not to start something if they haven't already started. Perhaps many people in the audience have never tried illicit drugs, or have not gotten behind the wheel of a car while intoxicated. The goal of action in this case would be to deter, or encourage the audience members to refrain from starting or initiating the behavior.

Finally, with continuance, the speaker aims to persuade the audience to continue doing what they have been doing, such as reelect a candidate, keep buying product, or staying in school to get an education.

A speaker may choose to address more than one of these goals of action, depending on the audience analysis. If the audience is largely agreeable and supportive, you may find continuance to be one goal, while adoption is secondary.

These goals serve to guide you in the development of solution steps. Solution steps involve suggestions or ways the audience can take action after your speech. They often proceed from national to personal level, or the inverse. Audience members appreciate a clear discussion of the problem in a persuasive speech, but they also appreciate solutions. You might offer a national solution that may be viewed as unworkable, but your solution on a personal level may be more realistic, such as considering an alternate point of view or making a small donation to a worthy cause.

Increase Consideration

Perhaps you know that your audience is not open to emotional appeals that involve the fear of global warming, so you choose to base your persuasive speech on something they are more open to: the economic argument and the relative cost of car ownership. In this speech, you want to increase consideration on the part of the audience whose members either hold hostile views or perhaps are neutral and simply curious. You might be able to compare and contrast competing cars and show that the costs over ten years are quite similar, but that the Prius has additional features that are the equivalent of a bonus, including high gas mileage. You might describe tax incentives for ownership, maintenance schedules and costs, and resale value. Your arguments and their support aim at increasing the audience's consideration of your position. You won't be asking for action in this presentation, but a corresponding increase of consideration may lead the customer to that point at a later date.

Develop Tolerance of Alternate Perspectives

Finally, you may want to help your audience develop tolerance of alternate perspectives and viewpoints. Perhaps your audience, as in the previous example, is interested in purchasing a car and you are the lead salesperson on that model. As you listen, and do your informal audience analysis, you may learn that horsepower and speed are important values to this customer. You might raise the issue of torque versus horsepower and indicate that the "uumph" you feel as you start a car off the line is torque. Many hybrid and even electric vehicles have great torque, as their systems involve fewer parts and less friction than a corresponding internal combustion-transaxle system. You goal is to help your audience develop tolerance, but not necessarily acceptance, of alternate perspectives. A traditional way of measuring speed has always been how fast a car can go from zero to sixty miles per hour.

You are essentially indicating that there are two relevant factors to consider when discussing speed (horsepower and torque), and asking the customer to consider the alternate perspective. Lots of horsepower might be all right for high speeds, but by raising the issue of their normal driving, they might learn that what counts day in and day out for driving is torque, not horsepower. By starting from common ground, and introducing a related idea, you are persuading your audience to consider an alternate perspective.

KEY TAKEAWAY

A persuasive speech may stimulate thought, convince, call to action, increase consideration, or develop tolerance of alternate perspectives.

EXERCISES

1. Select a commercial for a product or service you do not believe you would ever buy. Evaluate the commercial according to the principles of persuasion described in this section. Does it use more than one principle? Is any principle effective on you as an audience member? If you could change the commercial to increase its persuasive appeal to yourself as a customer, what changes would you make? Discuss your findings with your classmates.

2. Which do you think is a more difficult challenge, discontinuance or deterrence? Why? Give some examples and discuss them with your classmates.

3. Do you think persuasion by continuance is necessary? Or would people continue a given behavior regardless of any persuasive messages? Think of an example and discuss it with your classmates.

14.4 Meeting the Listener's Basic Needs
LEARNING OBJECTIVE

1. Identify and describe several basic needs that people seek to fulfill when they communicate.

In this section we will examine why we communicate, illustrating how meeting the listener's basic needs is central to effective communication. It's normal for the audience to consider why you are persuading them, and there is significant support for the notion that by meeting the audience's basic needs, whether they are a customer, colleague, or supervisor, you will more effectively persuade them to consider your position.

Not all oral presentations involve taking a position, or overt persuasion, but all focus on the inherent relationships and basic needs within the business context. Getting someone to listen to what you have to say involves a measure of persuasion, and getting that person to act on it might require considerable skill. Whether you are persuading a customer to try a new product or service, or informing a supplier that you need additional merchandise, the relationship is central to your communication. The emphasis inherent in our next two discussions is that we all share this common ground, and by understanding that we share basic needs, we can better negotiate meaning and achieve understanding.

Table 14.1 "Reasons for Engaging in Communication" presents some reasons for engaging in communication. As you can see, the final item in the table indicates that we communicate in order to meet our needs. What are those needs? We will discuss them next.

Table 14.1 Reasons for Engaging in Communication

Review	Why We Engage in Communication
Gain Information	We engage in communication to gain information. This information can involve directions to an unknown location, or a better understanding about another person through observation or self-disclosure.
Understand Communication Contexts	We also want to understand the context in which we communication, discerning the range between impersonal and intimate, to better anticipate how to communicate effectively in each setting.
Understand Our Identity	Through engaging in communication, we come to perceive ourselves, our roles, and our relationships with others.
Meet Our Needs	We meet our needs through communication.

Maslow's Hierarchy

If you have taken courses in anthropology, philosophy, psychology, or perhaps sociology in the past, you may have seen Maslow's hierarchy of needs (Figure 14.3 "Maslow's Hierarchy"). Psychologist Abraham Maslow [1] provides seven basic categories for human needs, and arranges them in order of priority, from the most basic to the most advanced.

In this figure, we can see that we need energy, water, and air to live. Without any of these three basic elements, which meet our physiological needs (1), we cannot survive. We need to meet them before anything else, and will often sacrifice everything else to get them. Once we have what we need to live, we seek safety (2). A defensible place, protecting your supply lines for your most basic needs, could be your home.

For some, however, home is a dangerous place that compromises their safety. Children and victims of domestic violence need shelter to meet this need. In order to leave a hostile living environment, people may place the well-being and safety of another over their own needs, in effect placing themselves at risk.

Figure 14.3 Maslow's Hierarchy [2]

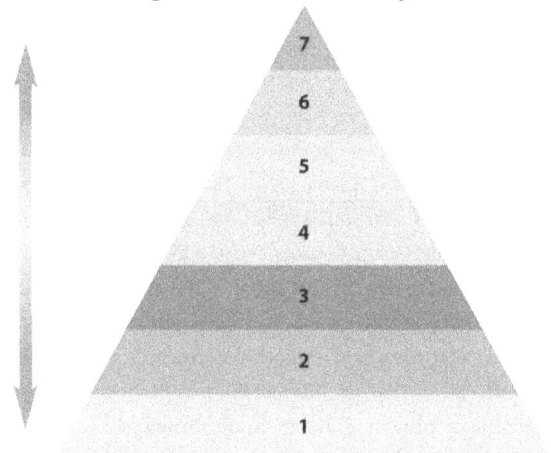

An animal would fight for its own survival above all else, but humans can and do acts of heroism that directly contradict their own self-interest. Our own basic needs motivate us, but sometimes the basic needs of others are more important to us than our own.

We seek affection from others once we have the basics to live and feel safe from immediate danger. We look for a sense of love and belonging (3). All needs in Maslow's model build on the foundation of the previous needs, and the third level reinforces our need to be a part of a family, community, or group. This is an important step that directly relates to business communication. If a person feels safe at your place of business, they are more likely to be open to communication. Communication is the foundation of the business relationship, and without it, you will fail. If they feel on edge, or that they might be pushed around, made to feel stupid, or even unwanted, they will leave and your business will disappear. On the other hand, if you make them feel welcome, provide multiple ways for them to learn, educate themselves, and ask questions in a safe environment, you will form relationships that transcend business and invite success.

Once we have been integrated in a group, we begin to assert our sense of self and self-respect, addressing our need for self-esteem (4). Self-esteem is essentially how we feel about ourselves. Let's say you are a male, but you weren't born with a "fix-it" gene. It's nothing to be ashamed of, but for many men it can be hard to admit. We no longer live in a time when we have to build our own houses or learn about electricity and plumbing as we grow up, and if it is not part of your learning experience, it is unreasonable to expect that you'll be handy with a wrench from the first turn.

The do-it-yourself chain Home Depot may have recognized how this interest in home repair is paired with many men's reluctance to admit their lack of experience. They certainly turned it into an opportunity. Each Saturday around the country, home repair clinics on all sorts of tasks, from cutting and laying tile to building a bird house, are available free to customers at Home Depot stores. You can participate, learn, gain mastery of a skill set, and walk out of the store with all the supplies you need to get the job done. You will also now know someone (the instructor, a Home Depot employee) whom you can return to for follow-up questions. Ultimately, if you don't succeed in getting the job done right, they will help you arrange for professional installation. This model reinforces safety and familiarity, belonging to a group or perceiving a trustworthy support system, and the freedom to make mistakes. It's an interactive program that squarely addresses one of customers' basic of human needs.

Maslow discusses the next level of needs in terms of how we feel about ourselves and our ability to assert control and influence over our lives. Once we are part of a group and have begun to assert ourselves, we start to feel as if we have reached our potential and are actively making a difference in our own world. Maslow calls this self-actualization (5). Self-actualization can involve reaching your full potential, feeling accepted for who you are, and perceiving a degree of control or empowerment in your environment. It may mean the freedom to go beyond building the bird house to the tree house, and to design it yourself as an example of self-expression.

As we progress beyond these levels, our basic human curiosity about the world around us emerges. When we have our basic needs met, we do not need to fear losing our place in a group or access to resources. We are free to explore and play, discovering the world around us. Our need to know (6) motivates us to grow and learn. You may have taken an elective art class that sparked your interest in a new area, or your started a new sport or hobby, like woodworking. If you worked at low-paying jobs that earned you barely enough to meet your basic needs, you may not be able to explore all your interests. You might be too exhausted after sixty or seventy hours a week on a combination of the night shift and the early morning shift across two jobs. If you didn't have to work as many hours to meet your more basic needs, you'd have time to explore your curiosity and address the need to learn. Want to read a good book? You'd have the time. Want to take a watercolor class? Sounds interesting. If, however, we are too busy hunting and gathering food, there is little time for contemplating beauty.

Beyond curiosity lies the aesthetic need to experience beauty (7). Form is freed from function, so that a wine bottle opener can be appreciated for its clever design that resembles a rabbit's head instead of simply how well it works to remove the cork. The appreciation of beauty transcends the everyday, the usual; it becomes exceptional. You may have walked in a building or church and become captivated by the light, the stained-glass windows, or the design. That moment that transcends the mundane, that stops you in your tracks, comes close to describing the human appreciation for the aesthetic, but it's really up to you.

We can see in Maslow's hierarchy how our most basic needs are quite specific, and as we progress through the levels, the level of abstraction increases until ultimately we are freed from the daily grind to contemplate the meaning of a modern painting. As we increase our degree of interconnectedness with others, we become interdependent and, at the same time, begin to express independence and individuality. As a speaker, you may seek the safety of the familiar, only to progress with time and practice to a point where you make words your own.

Your audience will share with you a need for control. You can help meet this need by constructing your speech with an effective introduction, references to points you've discussed, and a clear conclusion. The introduction will set up audience expectations of points you will consider, and allow the audience to see briefly what is coming. Your internal summaries, signposts, and support of your main points all serve to remind the audience what you've discussed and what you will discuss. Finally, your conclusion answers the inherent question, "Did the speaker actually talk about what they said they were going to talk about?" and affirms to the audience that you have fulfilled your objectives.

Social Penetration Theory

The field of communication draws from many disciplines, and in this case, draws lessons from two prominent social psychologists. Irwin Altman and Dalmas Taylor articulated the social penetration theory, which describes how we move from superficial talk to intimate and revealing talk. [3] Altman and Taylor discuss how we attempt to learn about others so that we can better understand how to interact. [4] With a better understanding of others and with more information, we are in a better position to predict how they may behave, what they may value, or what they might feel in specific situations. We usually gain this understanding of others without thinking about it through observation or self-disclosure. In this model, often called the "onion model," we see how we start out on superficial level, but as we peel away the layers, we gain knowledge about the other person that encompasses both breadth and depth.

Figure 14.4 Altman and Taylor's Social Penetration Model

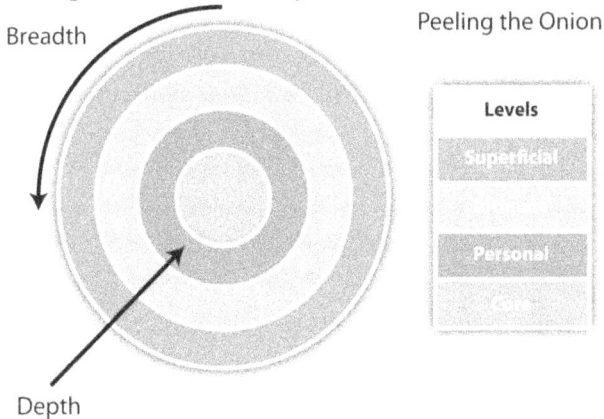

Source: Adapted from Altman and Taylor's social penetration model. [5]

We come to know more about the way a person perceives a situation (breadth), but also gain perspective into how they

see the situation through an understanding of their previous experiences (depth). Imagine these two spheres, which represent people, coming together. What touches first? The superficial level. As the two start to overlap, the personal levels may touch, then the intimate level, and finally the core levels may even touch. Have you ever known a couple— perhaps your parents or grandparents—who have been together for a very long time? They know each other's stories and finish each other's sentences. They might represent the near overlap, where their core values, attitudes, and beliefs are similar through a lifetime of shared experiences.

Figure 14.5 American Foreign Service Manual Iceberg Model

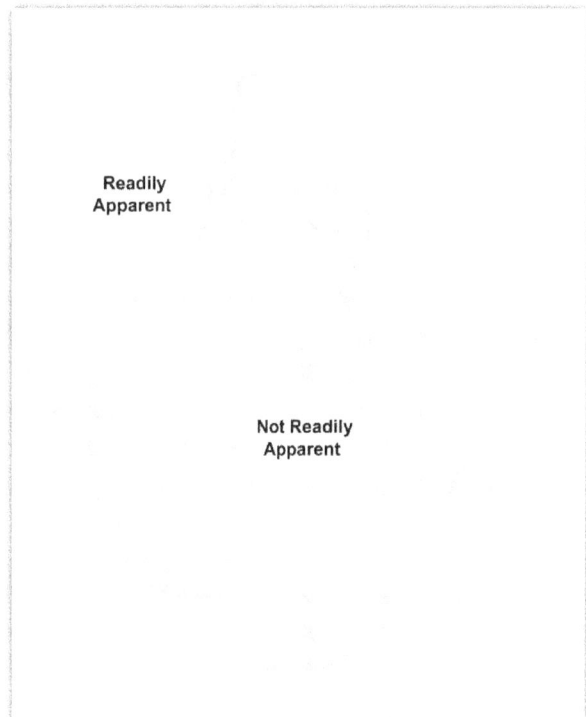

We move from public to private information as we progress from small talk to intimate conversations. Imagine an onion. The outer surface can be peeled away, and each new layer reveals another until you arrive at the heart of the onion. People interact on the surface, and only remove layers as trust and confidence grows.

Another way to look at it is to imagine an iceberg. How much of the total iceberg can you see from the surface of the ocean? Not much. But once you start to look under the water, you gain an understanding of the large size of the iceberg, and the extent of its depth. We have to go beyond superficial understanding to know each other, and progress through the process of self-disclosure to come to know and understand one another. See Figure 14.5 "American Foreign Service Manual Iceberg Model" for an illustration of an "iceberg model" adapted from the American Foreign Service Manual. [6] This model has existed in several forms since the 1960s, and serves as a useful illustration of how little we perceive of each other with our first impressions and general assumptions.

KEY TAKEAWAY

We are motivated to communicate in order to gain information, get to know one another, better understand our situation or context, come to know ourselves and our role or identity, and meet our fundamental interpersonal needs.

EXERCISES

1. Consider your life in relation to Maslow's hierarchy of needs. To what degree do you feel you have attained the different levels in the hierarchy? Two or three years ago, were you at the same level where you currently are, or has your position in the hierarchy changed? In what ways do you expect it to change in the future? Discuss your thoughts with your classmates.

2. Think of someone you have met but do not know very well. What kinds of conversations have you had with this person? How might you expect your conversations to change if you have more opportunities to get better acquainted? Discuss your thoughts with a classmate.

3. Think of a conversation you have had within the past day. What were the reasons for having that conversation? Can you relate it to the reasons for engaging in conversation listed in Table 14.1 "Reasons for Engaging in Communication"? Discuss your thoughts with a classmate.

4. Write a brief paragraph about getting to know someone. Discuss whether, in your experience, it followed the social penetration theory. Share and compare with classmates.

[1] Maslow, A. (1970). *Motivation and personality* (2nd ed.). New York, NY: Harper & Row.

[2] Maslow, A. (1970). *Motivation and personality* (2nd ed.). New York, NY: Harper & Row.

[3] Altman, I., & Taylor, D. (1973). *Social penetration: The development of interpersonal relationships.* New York, NY: St. Martin's Press.

[4] Altman, I., & Taylor, D. (1973). *Social penetration: The development of interpersonal relationships.* New York, NY: St. Martin's Press.

[5] Altman, I., & Taylor, D. (1973). *Social penetration: The development of interpersonal relationships.* New York, NY: St. Martin's Press.

[6] American Foreign Service Manual. (1975).

14.5 Making an Argument
LEARNING OBJECTIVES

1. Label and discuss three components of an argument.
2. Identify and provide examples of emotional appeals.

According to the famous satirist Jonathan Swift, "Argument is the worst sort of conversation." You may be inclined to agree. When people argue, they are engaged in conflict and it's usually not pretty. It sometimes appears that way because people resort to fallacious arguments or false statements, or they simply do not treat each other with respect. They get defensive, try to prove their own points, and fail to listen to each other.

But this should not be what happens in persuasive argument. Instead, when you make an argument in a persuasive speech, you will want to present your position with logical points, supporting each point with appropriate sources. You will want to give your audience every reason to perceive you as an ethical and trustworthy speaker. Your audience will expect you to treat them with respect, and to present your argument in way that does not make them defensive. Contribute to your credibility by building sound arguments and using strategic arguments with skill and planning.

In this section, we will briefly discuss the classic form of an argument, a more modern interpretation, and finally seven basic arguments you may choose to use. Imagine that each is a tool in your toolbox, and that you want to know how to use each effectively. Know that people who try to persuade you, from telemarketers to politics, usually have these tools at hand.

Let's start with a classical rhetorical strategy, as shown in Table 14.2 "Classical Rhetorical Strategy". It asks the rhetorician, speaker, or author to frame arguments in six steps.

Table 14.2 Classical Rhetorical Strategy

1. Exordium	Prepares the audience to consider your argument
2. Narration	Provides the audience with the necessary background or context for your argument
3. Proposition	Introduces your claim being argued in the speech
4. Confirmation	Offers the audience evidence to support your argument
5. Refutation	Introduces to the audience and then discounts or refutes the counterarguments or objections
6. Peroration	Your conclusion of your argument

The classical rhetorical strategy is a standard pattern and you will probably see it in both speech and English courses. The pattern is useful to guide you in your preparation of your speech and can serve as a valuable checklist to ensure that you are prepared. While this formal pattern has distinct advantages, you may not see it used exactly as indicated here on a daily basis. What may be more familiar to you is Stephen Toulmin's [1] rhetorical strategy that focuses on three main elements, shown in Table 14.3 "Toulmin's Three-Part Rhetorical Strategy".

Table 14.3 Toulmin's Three-Part Rhetorical Strategy

Element	Description	Example
1. Claim	Your statement of belief or truth	It is important to spay or neuter your pet.
2. Data	Your supporting reasons for the claim	Millions of unwanted pets are euthanized annually.
3. Warrant	You create the connection between the claim and the supporting reasons	Pets that are spayed or neutered do not reproduce, preventing the production of unwanted animals.

Toulmin's rhetorical strategy is useful in that it makes the claim explicit, clearly illustrating the relationship between the claim and the data, and allows the listener to follow the speaker's reasoning. You may have a good idea or point, but your audience will be curious and want to know how you arrived at that claim or viewpoint. The warrant often addresses the inherent and often unspoken question, "Why is this data so important to your topic?" and helps you illustrate relationships between information for your audience. This model can help you clearly articulate it for your audience.

Argumentation Strategies: GASCAP/T

Here is useful way of organizing and remembering seven key argumentative strategies:

1. Argument by **G**eneralization
2. Argument by **A**nalogy
3. Argument by **S**ign
4. Argument by **C**onsequence
5. Argument by **A**uthority
6. Argument by **P**rinciple
7. Argument by **T**estimony

Richard Fulkerson [2] notes that a single strategy is sufficient to make an argument some of the time, but more common is an effort to combine two or more strategies to increase your powers of persuasion. He organized the argumentative strategies in this way to compare the differences, highlight the similarities, and allow for their discussion. This model, often called by its acronym GASCAP, is a useful strategy to summarize six key arguments and is easy to remember. In Table 14.4 "GASCAP/T Strategies" we have adapted it, adding one more argument that is often used in today's speeches and presentations: the argument by testimony. This table presents each argument, provides a definition of the strategy and an example, and examines ways to evaluate each approach.

Table 14.4 GASCAP/T Strategies

	Argument by	Claim	Example	Evaluation
G	Generalization	Whatever is true of a good example or sample will be true of everything like it or the population it came from.	If you can vote, drive, and die for your country, you should also be allowed to buy alcohol.	STAR System: For it to be reliable, we need a (S) sufficient number of (T) typical, (A) accurate, and (R) reliable examples.
A	Analogy	Two situations, things or ideas are alike in observable ways and will tend to be alike in many other ways	Alcohol is a drug. So is tobacco. They both alter perceptions, have an impact physiological and psychological systems, and are federally regulated substances.	Watch for adverbs that end in "ly," as they qualify, or lessen the relationship between the examples. Words like "probably," "maybe," "could, "may," or "usually" all weaken the relationship.
S	Sign	Statistics, facts or cases indicate meaning, much like a stop sign means "stop."	Motor vehicle accidents involving alcohol occur at significant rates among adults of all ages in the United States	Evaluate the relationship between the sign and look for correlation, where the presenter says what a facts "means." Does the sign say that? Does is say more, or what is not said? Is it relevant?

	Argument by	Claim	Example	Evaluation
C	Cause	If two conditions always appear together, they are causally related.	The U.S. insurance industry has been significantly involved in state and national legislation requiring proof of insurance, changes in graduated driver's licenses, and the national change in the drinking age from age 18 to age 21.	Watch out for "after the fact, therefore because of the fact" (*post hoc, ergo propter hoc*) thinking. There might not be a clear connection, and it might not be the whole picture. Mothers Against Drunk Driving might have also been involved with each example of legislation.
A	Authority	What a credible source indicates is probably true.	According to the National Transportation and Safety Board, older drivers are increasingly involved in motor vehicle accidents.	Is the source legitimate and is their information trustworthy? Institutes, boards and people often have agendas and distinct points of view.
P	Principle	An accepted or proper truth	The change in the drinking age was never put to a vote. It's not about alcohol, it's about our freedom of speech in a democratic society.	Is the principle being invoked generally accepted? Is the claim, data or warrant actually related to the principle stated? Are there common exceptions to the principle? What are the practical consequences of following the principle in this case?
T	Testimony	Personal experience	I've lost friends from age 18 to 67 to alcohol. It impacts all ages, and its effects are cumulative. Let me tell you about two friends in particular.	Is the testimony authentic? Is it relevant? Is it representative of other's experiences? Use the STAR system to help evaluate the use of testimony.

Evidence

Now that we've clearly outlined several argument strategies, how do you support your position with evidence or warrants? If your premise or the background from which you start is valid, and your claim is clear and clearly related, the audience will naturally turn their attention to "prove it." This is where the relevance of evidence becomes particularly important. Here are three guidelines to consider in order to insure your evidence passes the "so what?" test of relevance in relation to your claim. Make sure your evidence is:

1. **Supportive** Examples are clearly representative, statistics accurate testimony authoritative, and information reliable.
2. **Relevant** Examples clearly relate to the claim or topic, and you are not comparing "apples to oranges."
3. **Effective** Examples are clearly the best available to support the claim, quality is preferred to quantity, there are only a few well-chosen statistics, facts or data.

Appealing to Emotions

While we've highlighted several points to consider when selecting information to support your claim, know that Aristotle [3] strongly preferred an argument based in logic over emotion. Can the same be said for your audience, and to what degree is emotion and your appeal to it in your audience a part of modern life?

Emotions are a psychological and physical reaction, such as fear or anger, to stimuli that we experience as a feeling. Our feelings or emotions directly impact our own point of view and readiness to communicate, but also influence how, why, and when we say things. Emotions influence not only how you say what you say, but also how you hear and what you hear. At times, emotions can be challenging to control. Emotions will move your audience, and possibly even move you, to change or act in certain ways. Marketing experts are famous for creating a need or associating an emotion with a brand or label in order to sell it. You will speak the language of your audience in your document, and may choose to appeal to emotion, but you need to consider the strategic use as a tool that has two edges.

Aristotle indicated the best, and most preferable, way to persuade an audience was through the use of logic, free of emotion. He also recognized that people are often motivated, even manipulated, by the exploitation of their emotions. In our modern context, we still engage this debate, demanding to know the facts separate from personal opinion or agenda, but see the use of emotion used to sell products. If we think of the appeal to emotion as a knife, we can see it has two edges. One edge can cut your audience, and the other can cut you. If you advance an appeal to emotion in your document on spaying and neutering pets, and discuss the millions of unwanted pets that are killed each year, you may elicit an emotional response. If you use this approach repeatedly, your audience may grow weary of it, and it will lose its effectiveness. If you change your topic to the use of animals in research, the same strategy may apply, but repeated attempts at engaging an emotional response may backfire on you, in essence "cutting" you, and produce a negative response, called emotional resistance.

Emotional resistance involves getting tired, often to the point of rejection, of hearing messages that attempt to elicit an emotional response. Emotional appeals can wear out the audience's capacity to receive the message. As Aristotle outlined, ethos (credibility), logos (logic) and pathos (passion, enthusiasm and emotional response) constitute the building blocks of any document. It's up to you to create a balanced document, where you may appeal to emotion, but choose to use it judiciously.

On a related point, the use of an emotional appeal may also impair your ability to write persuasively or effectively. If you choose to present an article to persuade on the topic of suicide, and start with a photo of your brother or sister that you lost to suicide, your emotional response may cloud your judgment and get in the way of your thinking. Never use a personal story, or even a story of someone you do not know, if the inclusion of that story causes you to lose control. While it's important to discuss relevant topics, including suicide, you need to assess you own relationship to the message. Your documents should not be an exercise in therapy and you will sacrifice ethos and credibility, even your effectiveness, if you "lose it" because you are really not ready to discuss the issue. As we saw in our discussion of Altman and Taylor, [4] most relationships form from superficial discussions and grow into more personal conversations. Consider these levels of self-disclosure when planning your speech to persuade in order to not violate conversational and relational norms.

Now that we've outlined emotions and their role in a speech in general and a speech to persuade specifically, it's important recognize the principles about emotions in communication that serve us well when speaking in public. DeVito [5] offers us five key principles to acknowledge the role emotions play in communication and offer guidelines for their expression.

Emotions Are Universal
Emotions are a part of every conversation or interaction that we have. Whether or not you consciously experience them while communicating with yourself or others, they influence how you communicate. By recognizing that emotions are a component in all communication interactions, we can place emphasis on understanding both the content of the message and the emotions that influence how, why, and when the content is communicated.

The context, which includes your psychological state of mind, is one of the eight basic components of communication.

Expression of emotions is important, but requires the three Ts: tact, timing, and trust. If you find you are upset and at risk of being less than diplomatic, or the timing is not right, or you are unsure about the level of trust, then consider whether you can effectively communicate your emotions. By considering these three Ts, you can help yourself express your emotions more effectively.

Emotional Feelings and Emotional Expression Are Not the Same
Experiencing feelings and actually letting someone know you are experiencing them are two different things. We experience feeling in terms of our psychological state, or state of mind, and in terms of our physiological state, or state of our body. If we experience anxiety and apprehension before a test, we may have thoughts that correspond to our nervousness. We may also have an increase in our pulse, perspiration, and respiration (breathing) rate. Our expression of feelings by our body influences our nonverbal communication, but we can complement, repeat, replace, mask, or even contradict our verbal messages. Remember that we can't tell with any degree of accuracy what other people are feeling simply through observation, and neither can they tell what we are feeling. We need to ask clarifying questions to improve understanding. With this in mind, plan for a time to provide responses and open dialogue after the conclusion of your speech.

Emotions Are Communicated Verbally and Nonverbally
You communicate emotions not only through your choice of words but also through the manner in which you say those words. The words themselves communicate part of your message, but the nonverbal cues, including inflection, timing, space, and paralanguage can modify or contradict your spoken message. Be aware that emotions are expressed in both ways and pay attention to how verbal and nonverbal messages reinforce and complement each other.

Emotional Expression Can Be Good and Bad
Expressing emotions can be a healthy activity for a relationship and build trust. It can also break down trust if expression is not combined with judgment. We're all different, and we all experience emotions, but how we express our emotions to ourselves and others can have a significant impact on our relationships. Expressing frustrations may help the audience realize your point of view and see things as they have never seen them before. However, expressing frustrations combined with blaming can generate defensiveness and decrease effective listening. When you're expressing yourself, consider the audience's point of view, be specific about your concerns, and emphasize that your relationship with your listeners is important to you.

Emotions Are Often Contagious

Have you ever felt that being around certain people made you feel better, while hanging out with others brought you down? When we interact with each other, some of our emotions can be considered contagious. If your friends decide to celebrate, you may get caught up in the energy of their enthusiasm. Thomas Joiner noted that when one college roommate was depressed, it took less than three weeks for the depression to spread to the other roommate. [6] It is important to recognize that we influence each other with our emotions, positively and negatively. Your emotions as the speaker can be contagious, so use your enthusiasm to raise the level of interest in your topic. Conversely, you may be subject to "catching" emotions from your audience. Your listeners may have just come from a large lunch and feel sleepy, or the speaker who gave a speech right before you may have addressed a serious issue like suicide. Considering the two-way contagious action of emotions means that you'll need to attend to the emotions that are present as you prepare to address your audience.

KEY TAKEAWAY

Everyone experiences emotions, and as a persuasive speaker, you can choose how to express emotion and appeal to the audience's emotions.

EXERCISES

1. Think of a time when you have experienced emotional resistance. Write two or three paragraphs about your experience. Share your notes with the class.
2. Which is the more powerful, appeal to reason or emotion? Discuss your response with an example.
3. Select a commercial or public service announcement that uses an emotional appeal. Using the information in this section, how would you characterize the way it persuades listeners with emotion? Is it effective in persuading you as a listener? Why or why not? Discuss your findings with your classmates.
4. Find an example of an appeal to emotion in the media. Review and describe it in two to three paragraphs and share with your classmates.

[1] Toulmin, S. (1958). *The uses of argument*. New York, NY: Cambridge University Press.

[2] Fulkerson, R. (1996). The Toulmin model of argument and the teaching of composition. In B. Emmel, P. Resch, & D. Tenney (Eds.), *Argument revisited: Argument redefined: Negotiating meaning the composition classroom* (pp. 45–72). Thousand Oaks, CA: Sage.

[3] Aristotle. (1991). *On rhetoric* (G. A. Kennedy, Trans.). New York, NY: Oxford University Press.

[4] Altman, I., & Taylor, D. (1973). *Social penetration: The development of interpersonal relationships*. New York, NY: St. Martin's Press.

[5] DeVito, J. (2003). *Messages: Building interpersonal skills*. Boston, MA: Allyn & Bacon.

[6] Joiner, T. (1994). Contagious depression: Existence, specificity to depressed symptoms, and the role or reassuracne seeking. *Journal of Personality and Social Psychology, 67*, 287.

14.6 Speaking Ethically and Avoiding Fallacies
LEARNING OBJECTIVES

1. Demonstrate the importance of ethics as part of the persuasion process.
2. Identify and provide examples of eight common fallacies in persuasive speaking.

What comes to mind when you think of speaking to persuade? Perhaps the idea of persuasion may bring to mind propaganda and issues of manipulation, deception, intentional bias, bribery, and even coercion. Each element relates to persuasion, but in distinct ways. In a democratic society, we would hope that our Bill of Rights is intact and validated, and that we would support the exercise of freedom to discuss, consider and debate issues when considering change. We can recognize that each of these elements in some ways has a negative connotation associated with it. Why do you think that deceiving your audience, bribing a judge, or coercing people to do something against their wishes is wrong? These tactics violate our sense of fairness, freedom, and ethics.

Manipulation involves the management of facts, ideas or points of view to play upon inherent insecurities or emotional appeals to one's own advantage. Your audience expects you to treat them with respect, and deliberately manipulating them by means of fear, guilt, duty, or a relationship is unethical. In the same way, deception involves the use of lies, partial truths, or the omission of relevant information to deceive your audience. No one likes to be lied to, or made to believe something that is not true. Deception can involve intentional bias, or the selection of information to support your position while framing negatively any information that might challenge your belief.

Bribery involves the giving of something in return for an expected favor, consideration, or privilege. It circumvents the normal protocol for personal gain, and again is a strategy that misleads your audience. Coercion is the use of power to compel action. You make someone do something they would not choose to do freely. You might threaten punishment, and people may go along with you while the "stick" is present, but once the threat is removed, they will revert to their previous position, often with new antagonism toward the person or agency that coerced them. While you may raise the issue that the ends justify the means, and you are "doing it for the audience's own good," recognize the unethical nature of coercion.

As Martin Luther King Jr. stated in his advocacy of nonviolent resistance, two wrongs do not make a right. They are just two wrongs and violate the ethics that contribute to community and healthy relationships. Each issue certainly relates to persuasion, but you as the speaker should be aware of each in order to present an ethical persuasive speech. Learn to recognize when others try to use these tactics on you, and know that your audience will be watching to see if you try any of these strategies on them.

Eleven Points for Speaking Ethically

In his book *Ethics in Human Communication*, [1] Richard Johannesen offers eleven points to consider when speaking to persuade. His main points reiterate many of the points across this chapter and should be kept in mind as you prepare, and present, your persuasive message.

Do not:

- use false, fabricated, misrepresented, distorted or irrelevant evidence to support arguments or claims.
- intentionally use unsupported, misleading, or illogical reasoning.
- represent yourself as informed or an "expert" on a subject when you are not.
- use irrelevant appeals to divert attention from the issue at hand.
- ask your audience to link your idea or proposal to emotion-laden values, motives, or goals to which it is actually not related.
- deceive your audience by concealing your real purpose, by concealing self-interest, by concealing the group you represent, or by concealing your position as an advocate of a viewpoint.
- distort, hide, or misrepresent the number, scope, intensity, or undesirable features of consequences or effects.
- use "emotional appeals" that lack a supporting basis of evidence or reasoning.
- oversimplify complex, gradation-laden situations into simplistic, two-valued, either-or, polar views or choices.
- pretend certainty where tentativeness and degrees of probability would be more accurate.
- advocate something which you yourself do not believe in.

Aristotle said the mark of a good person, well-spoken was a clear command of the faculty of observing in any given case the available means of persuasion. He discussed the idea of perceiving the many points of view related to a topic, and their thoughtful consideration. While it's important to be able to perceive the complexity of a case, you are not asked to be a lawyer defending a client.

In your speech to persuade, consider honesty and integrity as you assemble your arguments. Your audience will appreciate your thoughtful consideration of more than one view, your understanding of the complexity, and you will build your ethos, or credibility, as you present your document. Be careful not to stretch the facts, or assemble them only to prove yourself, and instead prove the argument on its own merits. Deception, coercion, intentional bias, manipulation and bribery should have no place in your speech to persuade.

Avoiding Fallacies

Fallacies are another way of saying false logic. These rhetorical tricks deceive your audience with their style, drama, or pattern, but add little to your speech in terms of substance and can actually detract from your effectiveness. There are several techniques or "tricks" that allow the speaker to rely on style without offering substantive argument, to obscure the central message, or twist the facts to their own gain. Here we will examine the eight classical fallacies. You may note that some of them relate to the ethical cautions listed earlier in this section. Eight common fallacies are presented in Table 14.5 "Fallacies". Learn to recognize these fallacies so they can't be used against you, and so that you can avoid using them with your audience.

Avoid false logic and make a strong case or argument for your proposition. Finally, here is a five-step motivational checklist to keep in mind as you bring it all together:

1. Get their attention
2. Identify the need
3. Satisfy the need
4. Present a vision or solution
5. Take action

This simple organizational pattern can help you focus on the basic elements of a persuasive message when time is short and your performance is critical.

KEY TAKEAWAY

Speaking to persuade should not involve manipulation, coercion, false logic, or other unethical techniques.

EXERCISES

1. Can persuasion be ethical? Why or why not? Discuss your opinion with a classmate.
2. Select a persuasive article or video from a Web site that you feel uses unethical techniques to persuade the audience. What techniques are being used? What makes

them unethical? Discuss your findings with your classmates.

3. Find an example of a particularly effective scene where a character in your favorite television program is persuaded to believe or do something. Write a two- to three-paragraph description of the scene and why it was effective. Share and compare with classmates.

4. Find an example of a particularly ineffective scene where a character in your favorite television program is not persuaded to believe or do something. Write a two- to three-paragraph description of the scene and why it was ineffective. Share and compare with classmates.

5. Find an example of a fallacy in an advertisement and share it with the class.

6. Find an example of an effective argument in an advertisement and share it with the class.

7. Write a two- to three-paragraph description of a persuasive message that caused you to believe or do something. Share and compare your description with classmates.

[1] Johannesen, R. (1996). *Ethics in human communication* (4th ed.). Prospect Heights, IL: Waveland Press.

Table 14.5 Fallacies

Fallacy	Definition	Example
1. Red Herring	Any diversion intended to distract attention from the main issue, particularly by relating the issue to a common fear.	It's not just about the death penalty; it's about the victims and their rights. You wouldn't want to be a victim, but if you were, you'd want justice.
2. Straw Man	A weak argument set up to be easily refuted, distracting attention from stronger arguments	What if we released criminals who commit murder after just a few years of rehabilitation? Think of how unsafe our streets would be then!
3. Begging the Question	Claiming the truth of the very matter in question, as if it were already an obvious conclusion.	We know that they will be released and unleashed on society to repeat their crimes again and again.
4. Circular Argument	The proposition is used to prove itself. Assumes the very thing it aims to prove. Related to begging the question.	Once a killer, always a killer.
5. Ad Populum	Appeals to a common belief of some people, often prejudicial, and states everyone holds this belief. Also called the Bandwagon Fallacy, as people "jump on the bandwagon" of a perceived popular view.	Most people would prefer to get rid of a few "bad apples" and keep our streets safe.
6. Ad Hominem	"Argument against the man" instead of against his message. Stating that someone's argument is wrong solely because of something about the person rather than about the argument itself.	Our representative is a drunk and philanderer. How can we trust him on the issues of safety and family?
7. Non Sequitur	"It does not follow." The conclusion does not follow from the premises. They are not related.	Since the liberal antiwar demonstrations of the 1960s, we've seen an increase in convicts who got let off death row.
8. Post Hoc Ergo Propter Hoc	"After this, therefore because of this," also called a coincidental correlation. It tries to establish a cause-and-effect relationship where only a correlation exists.	Violent death rates went down once they started publicizing executions.

14.7 Sample Persuasive Speech
LEARNING OBJECTIVE

1. Understand the structural parts of a persuasive speech.

Here is a generic, sample speech in an outline form with notes and suggestions.

Attention Statement

Show a picture of a person on death row and ask the audience: does an innocent man deserve to die?

Introduction

Briefly introduce the man in an Illinois prison and explain that he was released only days before his impending death because DNA evidence (not available when he was convicted), clearly established his innocence.

A statement of your topic and your specific stand on the topic: "My speech today is about the death penalty, and I am against it."

Introduce your credibility and the topic: "My research on this controversial topic has shown me that deterrence and retribution are central arguments for the death penalty, and today I will address each of these issues in turn."

State your main points: "Today I will address the two main arguments for the death penalty, deterrence and retribution, and examine how the governor of one state decided that since some cases were found to be faulty, all cases would be stayed until proven otherwise."

Body

Information: Provide a simple explanation of the death penalty in case there are people who do not know about it. Provide clear definitions of key terms.

Deterrence: Provide arguments by generalization, sign, and authority.

Retribution: Provide arguments by analogy, cause, and principle.

Case study: State of Illinois, Gov. George Ryan. Provide an argument by testimony and authority by quoting: "You have a system right now…that's fraught with error and has innumerable opportunities for innocent people to be executed," Dennis Culloton, spokesman for the Governor, told the *Chicago Tribune*. "He is determined not to make that mistake."

Solution steps:

1. *National level.* "Stay all executions until the problem that exists in Illinois, and perhaps the nation, is addressed."
2. *Local level.* "We need to encourage our own governor to examine the system we have for similar errors and opportunities for innocent people to be executed."
3. *Personal level.* "Vote, write your representatives, and help bring this issue to the forefront in your community."

Conclusion

Reiterate your main points and provide synthesis; do not introduce new content.

Residual Message

Imagine that you have been assigned to give a persuasive presentation lasting five to seven minutes. Follow the guidelines in Table 14.6 "Sample Speech Guidelines" and apply them to your presentation.

Table 14.6 Sample Speech Guidelines

1.Topic	Choose a product or service that interests you so much that you would like to influence the audience's attitudes and behavior toward it.
2. Purpose	Persuasive speakers may plan to secure behavioral changes, influence thinking, or motivate action in their audience. They may state a proposition of fact, value, definition, or policy. They may incorporate appeals to reason, emotion, and/or basic needs.
3. Audience	Think about what your audience might already know about your topic and what they may not know, and perhaps any attitudes toward or concerns about it. Consider how this may affect the way that you will present your information. You won't be able to convert everyone in the audience from a "no" to a "yes," but you might encourage a couple to consider "maybe." Audiences are more likely to change their behavior if it meets their needs, saves them money, involves a small change, or if the proposed change is approached gradually in the presentation.
4. Supporting Materials	Using the information gathered in your search for information, determine what is most worthwhile, interesting, and important to include in your speech. Time limits will require that you be selective about what you use. Consider information that the audience might want to know that contradicts or challenges your claims and be prepared for questions. Use visual aids to illustrate your message.
5. Organization	Write a central idea statement, which expresses the message, or point, that you hope to get across to your listeners in the speech. Determine the two to three main points that will be needed to support your central idea. Prepare a complete sentence outline of the body of the speech, including solution steps or action items.
6. Introduction	Develop an opening that will get the attention and interest of your listeners, express your central idea/message, and lead into the body of your speech.
7. Conclusion	The conclusion should review and/or summarize the important ideas in your speech and bring it to a smooth close.
8. Delivery	The speech should be delivered extemporaneously, using speaking notes and not reading from the manuscript. Work on maximum eye contact with your listeners. Use any visual aids or handouts that may be helpful.

A speech to persuade presents an attention statement, an introduction, the body of the speech with main points and supporting information, a conclusion, and a residual message.

EXERCISES

1. Apply this framework to your persuasive speech.
2. Prepare a three- to five-minute presentation to persuade and present it to the class.
3. Review an effective presentation to persuade and present it to the class.
4. Review an ineffective presentation to persuade and present it to the class

14.8 Elevator Speech
LEARNING OBJECTIVES

1. Discuss the basic parts of an elevator speech.
2. Create an effective elevator speech.

An elevator speech is to oral communication what a Twitter message (limited to 140 characters) is to written communication. It has to engage and interest the listener, inform and/or persuade, and be memorable. [1] An elevator speech is a presentation that persuades the listener in less than thirty seconds, or around a hundred words. It takes its name from the idea that in a short elevator ride (of perhaps ten floors), carefully chosen words can make a difference. In addition to actual conversations taking place during elevator rides, other common examples include the following:

- An entrepreneur making a brief presentation to a venture capitalist or investor
- A conversation at the water cooler
- Comments during intermission at a basketball game
- A conversation as you stroll across the parking lot

Creating an Elevator Speech

An elevator speech does not have to be a formal event, though it can be. An elevator speech is not a full sales pitch and should not get bloated with too much information. The idea is not to rattle off as much information as possible in a short time, nor to present a "canned" thirty-second advertising message, but rather to give a relaxed and genuine "nutshell" summary of one main idea. The speech can be generic and nonspecific to the audience or listener, but the more you know about your audience, the better. When you tailor your message to that audience, you zero in on your target and increase your effectiveness. [2] The emphasis is on brevity, but a good elevator speech will address several key questions:

1. What is the topic, product or service?
2. Who are you?
3. Who is the target market? (if applicable)
4. What is the revenue model? (if applicable)
5. What or who is the competition and what are your advantages?

Table 14.7 "Parts of an Elevator Speech" adapts the five parts of a speech to the format of the elevator speech.

Table 14.7 Parts of an Elevator Speech

Speech Component	Adapted to Elevator Speech
Attention Statement	Hook + information about you
Introduction	What you offer
Body	Benefits; what's in it for the listener
Conclusion	Example that sums it up
Residual Message	Call for action

Example:
1. How are you doing?
2. Great! Glad you asked. I'm with (X Company) and we just received this new (product x)—it is amazing. It beats the competition hands down for a third of the price. Smaller, faster, and less expensive make it a winner. It's already a sales leader. Hey, if you know anyone who might be interested, call me! (Hands business card to the listener as visual aid)

You often don't know when opportunity to inform or persuade will present itself, but with an elevator speech, you are prepared!

EXERCISES

1. Pick a product or service and prepare an elevator speech (less than a hundred words, no more than thirty seconds). Rehearse the draft out loud to see how it sounds and post or present it in class.
2. Find an example of an elevator speech online (YouTube, for example) and review it. Post the link and a brief summary of strengths and weaknesses. Share and compare with classmates.
3. Prepare an elevator speech (no more than thirty seconds) and present to the class.

[1] Howell, L. (2006). *Give your elevator speech a lift*. Bothell, WA: Publishers Network.

[2] Albertson, E. (2008). *How to open doors with a brilliant elevator speech*. New Providence, NJ: R. R. Bowker.

NOTES:

14.9 Additional Resources

- Robert Cialdini, author of *Influence: The Psychology of Persuasion*, asks, "Which messages spur citizens to protect the environment?" January 25, 2007, at the Royal Society for the encouragement of Arts, Manufactures and Commerce (RSA); free downloads of MP3 and PDF transcripts are available. http://www.thersa.org/events/audio-and-past-events/which-messages-spur-citizens-to-protect-the-environment-the-secret-impact-of-social-norms

- Justthink.org promotes critical thinking skills and awareness of the impact of images in the media among young people. http://www.justthink.org

- Watch a YouTube video of a persuasive speech on becoming a hero. http://www.youtube.com/watch?v=KYtm8uEo5vU

- Watch a YouTube video of a persuasive speech on same-sex marriage. http://www.youtube.com/watch?v=cR4N8oEQR3c&feature=related

- Professional speaker Ruth Sherman speaks persuasively about her book, *Get Them to See It Your Way, Right Away*. http://www.ruthsherman.com/video.asp

- Visit this site for a video and other resources about Maslow's hierarchy of needs. http://www.abraham-maslow.com/m_motivation/Hierarchy_of_Needs.asp

- Read an informative article on negotiating face-to-face across cultures called "Cross-Cultural Face-Negotiation: An Analytical Overview" by Stella Ting-Toomey, presented on April 15, 1992, at Simon Fraser University, Vancouver. http://www.cic.sfu.ca/forum/ting-too.html

- Purdue University's Online Writing Lab (OWL) provides a guide to persuasive speaking strategies. http://owl.english.purdue.edu/owl/resource/588/04

- Visit the Web site of talk show host Sean Hannity and assess his persuasive speaking techniques. http://www.hannity.com

- Visit the Web site of National Public Radio and assess the persuasive message of various radio programs. http://www.npr.org

- This site from Western Washington University provides information about persuasive techniques and fallacies. http://www.ac.wwu.edu/~gmyers/esssa/rhetoric.html

NOTES:

Chapter 15:
Business Presentations in Action

Personnel directors have described their needs in prospective employers as follows:

"Send me people who know how to speak, listen, and think, and I'll do the rest. I can train people in their specific job responsibilities, as long as they listen well, know how to think, and can express themselves well."[1]

"For better or worse, our culture relies on quotations—literary passages, Bible verses, movie lines, song lyrics, catchphrases, proverbs—to transmit the wit and wisdom of the past and the present and to lend resonance to our everyday discourse. Perhaps the most important are the political quotes, the sound bites, slogans, zingers and bloopers that can win or lose elections and shape our arguments and opinions. —Fred R. Shapiro" [2]

Getting Started

INTRODUCTORY EXERCISES

1. Prepare a short summary of your experience in public speaking. Include one example and one goal you would like to set for yourself for improvement. Share and compare with classmates.
2. Who is your favorite speaker? Write a brief introduction for them and include why you find them particularly talented. Share and compare with classmates.

No matter what career you pursue or what level of success you achieve, on some occasions you will certainly find it necessary to introduce yourself or another speaker, accept an award, serve as master of ceremonies at a meeting, or make a comment to the media. Each task requires preparation and practice, and a solid understanding of the roles and responsibilities associated with the many activities you may perform as a successful business communicator. In this chapter we explore many of these common activities with brief discussions and activities to prepare you for the day when the responsibility falls to you.

[1] Seiler, W., & Beall, M. (2000). *Communication: Making connections* (4th ed., p. 7). Boston, MA: Allyn & Bacon.
[2] Shapiro, Fred R. (2008, July 21). Quote…misquote [Commentary]. *New York Times Magazine*. Retrieved from http://www.nytimes.com/2008/07/21/magazine/27wwwl-guestsafire-t.html?pagewanted=all

15.1 Sound Bites and Quotables
LEARNING OBJECTIVES

1. Discuss elements that make a sound bite effective.
2. Choose a sound bite or quote from a written or verbal message.
3. Prepare a quote that is memorable.

Sometimes the words with the most impact are succinct, memorable statements. Sound bites, brief statements that zero in on the point of a larger or longer message, are often excised from interviews and articles, and presented apart from the context in which they were originally written or spoken. Slogans are phrases that express the goals, aims or nature of a product, service, person, or company. Quotes are memorable sayings extracted from written or verbal messages. Some move armies, while others make armies laugh. All are memorable and quickly become part of our cultural literacy, expressing a common sentiment or perception, and reinforcing our image of the speaker, business, product, or service. [1]

Common Elements of Effective Sound Bites
Whether you are writing a document, preparing a presentation, or both, you will want to consider how others will summarize your main point. If you can provide a clear sound bite or quote, it is more likely to get picked up and repeated, reinforcing your message. By preparing your sound bites, you help control the interpretation of your message. [2] Here are four characteristics of effective sound bites:
1. Clear and concise
2. Use vivid, dynamic language
3. Easy to repeat
4. Memorable

Your goal when writing a sound bite or quote is to make sure your idea represents all four characteristics. You won't always be creating the message; in some cases you may be asked to summarize someone else's written or verbal message, such as an interview, with a quote or a sound bite. Look for one or more sentences or phrases that capture these elements and test them out on your classmates or colleagues. Can the sound bite, slogan, or quote be delivered without stumbling? Is it easy to read? Does it get the job done?

KEY TAKEAWAY

Sound bites are brief statements that are often quoted.

EXERCISES

1. Choose a product or service that you find appealing. Try to come up with several sound bites, slogans, or quotes that meet all four criteria. You may look to company sales materials or interviews as a source for this exercise, and if you pull a quote from an online interview, please post the link when you complete your assignment. Discuss how the sound bite, slogan, or quote meets all four criteria in your response.

2. Match these phrases with their sources.

Product, Business or Person	Sound Bite, Slogan, or Memorable Quote
A. Nike	1. Where's the beef?
B. Barack Obama	2. Ask not what your country can do for you, but what you can do for your country.
C. Homer Simpson	3. Huge. That's huge, or huge.
D. Wendy's	4. Just do it!
E. John F. Kennedy	5. It's amazing how much you can get done when you're not trying to take credit for it.
F. Neil Armstrong	6. D'oh!
G. Paris Hilton	7. That's one small step for a man; one giant leap for mankind.
H. Franklin D. Roosevelt	8. A diamond is forever.
I. De Beers Consolidated	9. The only thing we have to fear is fear itself.

3. Answers: A-4, B-5, C-6, D-1, E-2, F-7, G-3, H-9, I-8

4. Indicate at least one sound bite or memorable quote and who said it. Please share your results with classmates and compare your results.

---

[1] Taylor, I. (2004). *Mediaspeak: Strategy. Sound-Bites. Spin: The plain-talking guide to issures, reptuation and message management.* Toronto, Canada: Hushion House Publishing.

[2] Kerchner, K. (1997). *Soundbites: A business guide for working with the media.* Superior, WI: Savage Press.

15.2 Telephone/VoIP Communication
LEARNING OBJECTIVES

1. Demonstrate the five stages in a telephone conversation.
2. Understand delivery strategies to increase comprehension and reduce misunderstanding.

Talking on the phone or producing an audio recording lacks an interpersonal context with the accompanying nonverbal messages. Unless you use vivid language, crisp, and clear descriptions, your audience will be left to sort it out for themselves. They may create mental images that don't reflect your intention that lead to miscommunication. Conversations follow predictable patterns and have main parts or stages we can clearly identify. While not every conversation is the same, many will follow a variation of a standard pattern composed by David Taylor and Alyse Terhune: [1]

1. Opening
2. Feedforward
3. Business
4. Feedback
5. Closing

Table 15.1 "A Five-Stage Telephone Conversation" [2] provides an example of how a conversation might go according to these five stages.

Cell phones are a part of many, if not most, people's lives in the industrialized world and, increasingly, in developing nations as well. Computer users can also utilize voice interaction and exchange through voice over Internet protocol (VoIP) programs like Skype. With the availability of VoIP, both audio and visual images are available to the conversation participants. But in our discussion, we'll focus primarily on voice exchanges.

Since you lack the nonverbal context, you need to make sure that your voice accurately communicates your message. Your choice of words and how you say them, including spacing or pausing, pace, rhythm, articulation, and pronunciation are relevant factors in effective delivery. Here are five main points to consider:

1. Speak slowly and articulate your words clearly.
2. Use vivid terms to create interest and communicate descriptions.
3. Be specific.
4. Show consideration for others by keeping your phone conversations private.
5. Silence cell phones, pagers, and other devices when you are in a meeting or sharing a meal with colleagues.

Table 15.1 A Five-Stage Telephone Conversation

Stage	Subevents	Example
Opening	Both parties identify themselves Greetings are reciprocated	[phone rings] Ken: Hello, Ken Reilly. Val: Hi, Ken. This is Val Martin from [company or department]. How are you? Ken: Fine, and you? Val: Fine, I'm doing great.
Feedforward	Purpose and tone of conversation are established Permission is given to continue (or not)	Val: I hate to bother you, but I wonder if you have five minutes to give me some advice. Ken: Sure, Val. What's happening? [or: I'm tied up right now. Can I call you back in an hour?]
Business	Substance of conversation Parties exchange roles	Val: Here's the situation. [explains] I know you are good at resolving these kinds of issues, so I was wondering what you think I should do. Ken: Wow, I can understand how this has you concerned. Considering what you've told me, here's what I think I would do. [explains]
Feedback	Signal that business is concluded	Val: Hmm, that makes sense. I'll certainly keep your ideas in mind. Thank you so much, Ken! Ken: Hey, you're welcome. Let me know how it turns out.
Closing	Both parties say goodbye	Val: Yes, I will. Have a good weekend, Ken. Ken: You too, Val. Bye. Val: Bye. [they hang up]

You don't have to slow down your normal pattern of speech by a large degree, but each word needs time and space to be understood or the listener may hear words that run together, losing meaning and creating opportunities for misunderstanding. Don't assume that they will catch your specific information the first time and repeat any as necessary, such as an address or a phone number.

Feedback, the response from the receiver to the sender, is also an essential element of phone conversations. Taking turns in the conversation can sometimes be awkward, especially if there is an echo or background noise on the line. With time and practice, each "speaker's own natural, comfortable, expressive repertoire will surface." [3]

KEY TAKEAWAY

A telephone conversation typically includes five stages: opening, feed forward, business, feedback, and closing. Because telephone conversations lack nonverbal cues, they require additional attention to feedback.

EXERCISES

1. Write an outline of a script for a telephone conversation that introduces a new product or service to an existing client. Partner with a classmate to role-play the conversation and note points that could use improvement. Compare your results with classmates.
2. Think of a phone conversation you had recently. Write a brief summary and include at least one example of what worked or what did not. Share and compare with classmates.
3. Take notes during a telephone conversation and write a brief description, labeling the parts of the conversation and providing examples. Share and compare with classmates.

[1] Taylor, D., & Terhune, A. D. (2000). Doing e-business: Strategies for thriving in an electronic marketplace. New York, NY: John Wiley & Sons. Retrieved from http://www.wiley.com/WileyCDA/WileyTitle/productCd-0471380652.html

[2] Adapted from Taylor, D., & Terhune, A. D. (2000). Doing e-business: Strategies for thriving in an electronic marketplace. New York, NY: John Wiley & Sons. Retrieved from http://www.wiley.com/WileyCDA/WileyTitle/productCd-0471380652.html

[3] Mayer, K. (1980). Developing delivery skills in oral business communication. *Business Communication Quarterly, 43*(3), 21–24.

15.3 Meetings

LEARNING OBJECTIVES

1. Discuss meetings and their role in business communication.
2. Describe the main parts of an agenda.
3. Discuss several strategies for effective meetings.

A meeting is a group communication in action around a defined agenda, at a set time, for an established duration. Meetings can be effective, ineffective, or a complete waste of time. If time is money and effectiveness and efficiency are your goals, then if you arrange a meeting, lead a meeting, or participate in one, you want it to be worth your time. [1]

Meetings can occur face-to-face, but increasingly business and industry are turning to teleconferencing and videoconferencing options as the technology improves, the cost to participate is reduced, and the cost of travel including time is considered. Regardless how you come together as a team, group, or committee, you will need to define your purpose in advance with an agenda. [2] The main parts of an agenda for a standard meeting are listed in Table 15.2 "Meeting Agenda Elements".

Table 15.2 Meeting Agenda Elements

Term	Definition
Title Header	Title, time, date, location, phone number, e-mail contact, and any other information necessary to get all participants together.
Participants	Expected participants
Subject Line	Purpose statement
Call to Order	Who will call the meeting to order?
Introductions	If everyone is new, this is optional. If even one person is new, everyone should briefly introduce themselves with their name and respective roles.
Roll Call	This may quietly take place while introductions are made.
Reading of the minutes	Notes from the last meeting are read (if applicable) with an opportunity to correct. These are often sent out before the meeting so participants have the opportunity to review them and note any needed corrections.
Old Business	List any unresolved issues from last time or issues that were "tabled," or left until this meeting.
New Business	This is a list of items for discussion and action.
Reports	This is optional and applies if there are subcommittees or groups working on specific, individual action items that require reports to the group or committee.
Good of the Order	This is the time for people to offer any news that relates to the topic of the meeting that was otherwise not shared or discussed.
Adjournment	Note time, date, place meeting adjourned and indicate when the next meeting is scheduled.

Strategies for Effective Meetings

You want an efficient and effective meeting, but recognize that group communication by definition can be chaotic and unpredictable. To stay on track, consider the following strategies:

- Send out the last meeting's minutes one week before the next meeting.
- Send out the agenda for the current meeting at least one week in advance.
- Send out reminders for the meeting the day before and the day of the meeting.

- Schedule the meeting in Outlook or a similar program so everyone receives a reminder.
- Start and end your meetings on time.
- Make sure the participants know their role and requirements prior to the meeting.
- Make sure all participants know one another before discussion starts.
- Formal communication styles and reference to the agenda can help reinforce the time frame and tasks.
- Follow Robert's Rules of Order when applicable, or at least be familiar with them.

- Make sure notes taken at the meeting are legible and can be converted to minutes for distribution later.
- Keep the discussion on track, and if you are the chair, or leader of a meeting, don't hesitate to restate a point to interject and redirect the attention back to the next agenda point.
- If you are the chair, draw a clear distinction between on-topic discussions and those that are more personal, individual, or off topic.
- Communicate your respect and appreciation for everyone's time and effort.
- Clearly communicate the time, date, and location or means of contact for the next meeting.

KEY TAKEAWAY

With good planning and preparation, meetings can be productive, engaging, and efficient.

EXERCISE

1. Create a sample agenda for a business meeting to discuss the quarterly sales report and results from the latest marketing campaign. Decide what information is needed, and what position might normally be expected to produce that information. Note in your agenda all the elements listed above, even if some elements (such as "good of the order") only serve as a placeholder for the discussion that will take place.
2. Write a brief description of a meeting you recently attended and indicate one way you perceived it as being effective. Compare with classmates.
3. Write a brief description of a meeting you recently attended and indicate one way you perceived it as being ineffective. Compare with classmates.

[1] Mosvick, R. K. (1996). *We've got to start meeting like this: A guide to successful meeting management.* New York, NY: Park Avenue Productions.
[2] Deal, T., & Kennedy, A. (1982). *Corporate cultures: The rites and rituals of corporate life.* Reading, MA: Addison-Wesley Publishing Company, Inc.

15.4 Celebrations: Toasts and Roasts
LEARNING OBJECTIVES

1. Discuss the role, function, and importance of a toast.
2. Discuss the elements of an effective toast.

Toasts are formal expressions of goodwill, appreciation, or calls for group attention to an issue or person in a public setting, often followed by synchronous consumption of beverages. Examples often include a toast at a wedding congratulating the couple, toasts at a bar after a tournament win to congratulate the team or an individual player, or a general toast to health for everyone on a holiday or other special occasion.

Toasts serve to unify the group, acknowledge a person or event, mark a special occasion, or simply to encourage the consumption of alcohol. These can range from serious to silly but are normally words that point out something that is commonly known. For example, a toast to the most valuable player in a game may serve to publicly acknowledge him or her for achievements that are already known by the community. The verbal recognition, followed by ritualistic drinking, serves as a public acknowledgement. Belonging is a basic human need that requires reinforcement, and a toast can be characterized as a reinforcement ritual, acknowledging respect for the individual or team, and also reinforcing group affiliation, common symbols and terms, beliefs and values, goals and aspirations. [1]

Toasts, while common in many societies, are relatively rare in daily life. They are normally associated with informal and formal gatherings of the group, team, or community. Since you may only perform a couple of toasts in your lifetime, you no doubt want to get them right the first time. We will address toasts and one variation in particular, the roast.

Proposing a Toast
One proposes a toast, rather than "making" a toast or simply "toasting," because for it to truly be a toast, everyone in the group, team, or community must participate. If you propose a toast to someone and no one responds, even if you raise your glass to them as a nonverbal sign or respect and take a sip, it doesn't count as a toast. Only the community can publicly acknowledge someone with a toast, but it takes an individual to make the proposition.

Sometimes the person who is supposed to make that proposition is already known by function or role. The best man and maid of honor at a wedding, the host of a party, and the highest-ranking manager at a business meal are common roles that are associated with ritualistic toasts.

Standing with proper posture to address the group is normally associated with acts of public speaking, including toasts. If you are understood to be a person who will be proposing a toast, you may not need to say anything to get the group's attention. As you rise and raise your glass, the room will grow quiet in anticipation of your words. If the group does not expect you to propose a toast, you may need to say, "May I propose a toast?" in a voice above the level of the group. Nonverbal displays also work to capture attention, [2] such as standing on a chair. While that may be nonstandard, your context will give you clues about how best to focus attention. Striking a glass with spoon to produce a ring, while common, is sometimes considered less than educated and a poor reflection of etiquette. The group norms determine what is expected and accepted, and it may be a custom that is considered normal. Etiquette is a conventional social custom or rule for behavior, but social customs and rules for behavior vary across communities and cultures.

You will raise your glass, raise your voice, and make a brief statement complimenting the person being honored. Your toast should be brief. If you write it out in advance, use thirty words as your upper limit. Common mistakes are for toast-givers to ramble on too long and to talk about themselves instead of the honoree. The toast is not as much about the words you use, though they carry weight and importance, but it's about the toast ritual as a group expression of acknowledgement and respect. People then raise their glasses to indicate agreement, often repeating "hear, hear!" or a word or phrase from the toast, such as "to success!" They then sip from their cup, possibly touching glasses first.

One common toast that always serves to unify the group is the toast to health. To propose a toast to health is common, well understood, and serves both the role and function of a toast. "Live long and prosper" is a common variation of "to your health" in English. Table 15.3 "Toasts to Health" lists toasts to health in other languages.

Table 15.3 Toasts to Health

Language	Toast
Chinese	Wen lie
French	A votre santé
Gaelic	Sláinte
German	Zum Wohl
Greek	Stin ygia sou
Hebrew	L'chiam
Italian	Alla salute
Japanese	Kanpai
Polish	Na zdrowie
Portuguese	Saúde
Spanish	Salud

Sometimes a best man at a wedding will be expected to tell a short story as part of their toast. A common story is how the couple met from the best man's perspective. While this may be your choice, remember to keep it quite brief, positive, and focused on the honorees, not on yourself. Important occasions require you to play your part like everyone else, and your role is to focus attention on the individual, team, couple, or group as you honor them.

Alcohol is not a requirement for a toast, nor is draining one's glass. The beverage and the quantity to be swallowed are a reflection of group norms and customs. Often alternatives, such as nonalcoholic sparkling cider, are served. If you are expected to perform a toast, one that requires tact, grace, and a clear presence of mind, you should refrain from drinking alcohol until after you've completed your obligation. Your role has responsibilities, and you have a duty to perform.

Roasts

Roasts are public proclamations that ridicule or criticize someone to honor them. That may sound awkward at first, but consider the targets most commonly associated with roasts: those in positions of power or prestige. Knocking someone off their pedestal is a special delight for the group or community, but it requires special care and attention to social dynamics, sensitivities, rank, and roles.

A common context for a round of roasts, or a series of public statements intended to poke fun at someone, is at a retirement party. Individuals in the room tell brief stories that may have some basis in truth, but which through word choice and clear communication of exaggeration, allow everyone to look back upon the episode with light humor and laughter. Time has passed and the absurd is worthy of group laughter. A roast is not an opportunity to say something mean. If you don't think the target will laugh it off, don't say it. Roasts can hurt feelings, and that misses the point. A roast honors someone in a position of power or influence by allowing them to demonstrate they can take a joke at their own expense gracefully. It is not intended to do harm to the individual or create divisions in the community. Ritual public speaking is supposed to unify groups, teams, and communities, and not create division or rival internal groups.

KEY TAKEAWAY

Toasts and roasts honor a member of the community.

EXERCISES

1. You are called upon to propose a toast to your team leader after your group has just completed a large contract. Work on this project wasn't always easy, but now is the time for celebration and recognition. Write a sample toast in no more than thirty words. Compare your results with your classmates.

2. What should someone propose a toast to? How should they propose it? Write your response and include an example. Compare with classmates.

3. If you were the subject of a roast, what would you feel comfortable having people say, do, or show to make fun of you in public? Write your response and include an example. Compare with classmates.

---

[1] McLean, S. (2005). *The basics of interpersonal communication.* Boston, MA: Allyn & Bacon.

[2] McLean, S. (2005). *The basics of interpersonal communication.* Boston, MA: Allyn & Bacon.

15.5 Media Interviews
LEARNING OBJECTIVES

1. Discuss the purpose of the media interview.
2. Understand ways to prepare for the media interview.

At some point in your business career it's likely that you will be interviewed by a representative of the media. It may be a camera and microphone in your face as you leave a building, or a scheduled interview where you have an opportunity to prepare. A press interview is both a challenge and an opportunity. Like a speech, it may make you nervous, but you have the advantage of being the center of attention and having the opportunity to have your say. This chapter addresses the basics for preparing and participating in a press interview.

A media interview is a discussion involving questions and answers for the purpose of broadcast. It is distinct from an informational interview, [1] where you might be asked questions to learn background on a story, but you will still need to observe the three hallmark rules of interviews:

1. Anything you say can and often will be used against you.
2. Never say anything you would not feel comfortable hearing quoted out of context on the evening news.
3. Be prepared for the unexpected as well as the expected.

At first, those rules may sound extreme, but let's examine them in the context of today's media realities. In a press interview setting you will be recorded in some fashion, whether audio, video, or handwritten notes on a reporter's notepad. With all the probability for errors and misinterpretation, you want your words and gestures to project the best possible image to the press. There was a time when news programs didn't have to justify themselves with advertising dollars, but today all news is news entertainment and has to pay its own way. That means your interview will be used to attract viewers. You also have to consider the possibility that the person interviewing you is not a trained professional journalist, but rather an aspiring actor or writer

who happened to land a job with the media. From their perspective, your quote in an audio, video, or print content package is dinner. It may also serve the public good, and inform, or highlight an important cause, but news has a bottom line just like business.

Because of these factors, you need to be proactive in seeing the press interview as part of the overall spectacle that is media, devoted to revenue. The six-second quote that is taken from the interview may not represent the tone, range, or even substance of your comments, but it will have been chosen to grab attention. It will also go viral if it catches on. Your interviewer may ask you a question that is off-the-wall, inappropriate, outside the scope of the interview, or unusual just to catch you off guard and get that attention-worthy quote. Independent journalism with a nonprofit, inform-the-public orientation still exists in some forms, but even those media outlets have to support themselves with an audience. So consider your role in the interview: to provide information and represent your business or organization with honor and respect. In sports, business, and press interviews, a good defense is required.

That said, a press interview is a positive opportunity, whether it is planned in advance or catches you off guard in public. You are the focus of the interview, and many people believe that if you are on television, for example, that you have something to say, that you have special insight, or that you are different from the viewing audience. That can give you an edge of credibility that can serve your business or company as you share your knowledge and experience.

When asked to give an interview, before you agree, learn as much as you can about the topic, the timing, the format, and the background. Table 15.4 "Interview Preparation Factors" summarizes how to approach these factors.

These four areas will serve you well as you begin to define the range and content of the interview for yourself. You will also need to pay attention to the setting and scene, how you want to present yourself (dress or suit?), and how well you answer anticipated questions. Mock interviews with colleagues can help, and a comprehensive knowledge of your talking points is essential.

You want to be well rested, if at all possible, on the day of the interview. With a clear mind you will be agile and responsive, and you will be able to present yourself well. You'll be calm in the knowledge of your preparation, and not be thrown if an unexpected question comes your way. You'll be ready on time, understanding that most journalists have to package the story as quickly as possible, demonstrating respect for the interviewer. You'll also know that it is not just about what you say but how you say it. Audiences respond to emotional cues, and you want to project an image of credibility and integrity. You'll anticipate the question-and-answer pattern and limit your responses to ones that are clear and concise. You'll have visual aids ready if needed to make a point.

Table 15.4 Interview Preparation Factors

Topic	What will be the range or scope of the interview? How can you prepare yourself so you are better able to address specific questions? Ask for the list of questions in advance, and anticipate that you will be asked questions that are not listed. Prepare for the unexpected and you won't be caught off guard.
Time	What's the time frame or limit? A 15-minute interview may not require as much depth as one that lasts an hour or more.
Format	How will you be interviewed? Will it be through audio or video, over the Internet, over the telephone, or in person?
Background	What's the backstory on the interview? Is there a specific issue or incident? Is there a known agenda? Why is the interview now and not earlier or not at all? Why is it important?

Naturally, however, you may not have the luxury of time to prepare. Press interviews are often requested at the last minute, and you may not be the first person this reporter asked for an interview that day. They have a story in mind, and they are looking for you to be part of that story. If the opportunity to be interviewed arises on the spur of the moment, you will need to make a quick judgment on whether to agree or decline. Your decision will rest on a multitude of factors, such as how much you know about the topic, whether someone else in your organization is better qualified to answer, whether your employer would appreciate your agreeing to speak to the media, and so on. If something newsworthy occurs at your workplace, start thinking about how you would make this decision before you are put on the spot. Finally, if the topic of the media inquiry is not time urgent, remember that you can always ask to postpone the interview to allow time to prepare.

KEY TAKEAWAY

A press interview is both a challenge and an opportunity.

EXERCISES

1. How does the press interview serve the business or organization? List two ways and provide examples. Discuss your ideas with classmates.

2. Consider the following scenario. Your large company is opening a new office in a new town and you have been designated to be part of the team that will be on the front lines. You want to establish goodwill, but also recognize that, being an outsider, you and your company may not be welcomed with open arms by the local business community. Your company produces a product and provides a service (feel free to choose; a coffee shop for example) that is currently offered in the town, but your organization perceives room for market growth as well as market share. Describe how you would handle relations with the local media. Compare your ideas with those of a classmate.

3. Form a team in class of interviewee and interviewer. Take ten-minute turns, having one person play the role of interviewee and the other the interviewer. Record your exchange and post as a file attachment in your class (if applicable), or post to YouTube or a similar Web hosting site and post the link. Write a report of your experience in no less than two hundred words.

4. Observe a press interview. How do they take turns? Does the interviewee ever look nervous? What could he or she have done to improve their performance? Write a brief suggestion and provide the link to the interview.

5. Find a sample press interview on a video Web site such as YouTube and evaluate it based on the guidelines in this chapter. Was it effective? Why or why not? Present your findings to the class.

6. Find at least one example of an interview gone bad. It may involve a misquotation, expressions of frustration or anger, or even an interview cut short. What happened? Provide a brief summary and provide the link to the interview.

[1] McLean, S. (2005). *The basics of interpersonal communication*. Boston, MA: Allyn & Bacon.

15.6 Introducing a Speaker
LEARNING OBJECTIVE

1. Understand how to introduce a speaker in a courteous and professional manner.

A speaker introduction involves establishing the person's credibility, motivating audience interest, and saying what the speaker could not say. Not many speakers will jump to the stage and share their list of accomplishments, as this would appear arrogant and could quickly turn off an audience. At the same time, if you are able to share that they have turned two companies around and would like to share lessons learned, your audience may see the value in giving their attention. Being designated to introduce a speaker is an honor and an important duty that requires planning and preparation.

Scot Ober states, "Remarks should be directed at welcoming the speaker and establishing his or her qualifications to speak on the topic." [1] You may start with a quote from their work, or a quote from a publication or colleague describing them. You may decide to use humor. All these options are available, but whatever you choose, let respect and dignity be your overriding goal. The function and role of the introduction is to focus the spotlight squarely on the speaker. You should not distract the audience from that task with your dress, gestures, antics, or by talking about yourself.

The person you are introducing may already be well known to the audience, but you can always find some new information to share. You may need to consider the unusual, or the little known, when introducing someone who is famous. You may also consider mentioning their most recent work or activity as it relates to the topic of the presentation. Avoid the "laundry list" approach to a summary of their education and experience, as this may bore the audience. Instead, focus on something specific and relevant. Your range of options is almost limitless, but your time frame and overall function are not. You need to be brief, and you need to establish the speaker's credibility while motivating interest. According to Bonnie Devet, "Performing the role of introducer also reinforces the rhetorical principles seminal to any business writing course: the need for ethos (credibility of both speakers and introducers), for audience-based discourse, and for accuracy." [2] Think of an introduction as a speech in miniature. Your purpose is to inform, your time frame is (typically) one to three minutes, and your specific purpose is to inform the audience about the speaker's qualifications, credibility, and enthusiasm for the topic he or she will cover.

KEY TAKEAWAY

To introduce a speaker is an honor and requires preparation and practice.

EXERCISES

1. Introduce a classmate who is about to present a report, document, or speech to the class. You can draw information from the Web (Facebook, Twitter), the person's résumé, or even a personal interview. You will need to prepare your introduction in advance and may want to consider incorporating a quote from the document they will discuss. Keep your remarks to thirty seconds and your written introduction to no more than a hundred words.
2. Watch an introduction of a speaker—televised award ceremonies offer plenty of examples—and note one example that you consider effective, and one that you

consider ineffective. Explain why you rated them this way. Report your response and the Web links.
3. List five facts, points, or things about yourself and your career that you would want an audience to know. Post your results and compare with classmates.

---

[1] Ober, S. (1995). *Contemporary business communication* (2nd ed., p. 478). Boston, MA: Houghton Mifflin.
[2] Devet, B. (1995). Introducing a speaker: An assingment for students in business communication. *Business Communication Quarterly, 58,* 57–58.

15.7 Presenting or Accepting an Award
LEARNING OBJECTIVES

1. Discuss the purpose of an award.
2. Describe the process of presenting an award.
3. Describe the process of accepting an award.

There is nothing more gratifying than recognition from your peers and colleagues for a job well done. We all strive for acceptance, and recognition is a reflection of belonging, a basic human need. [1] In this chapter we will discuss how to present or accept an award tactfully, graciously, and professionally.

First, make sure that you have all the information correct before you get up to speak: the honoree's correct name and how it is pronounced, the correct title of the award, and the details about the honoree's accomplishments that you are about to share. The spotlight will be on you, and your accurate delivery will be crucial to the happiness of the occasion.

When presenting an award, the key is to focus attention on the honor and the person receiving it—not on yourself. You may have been part of the committee that chose the winner, or involved in some other way, but your role should never upstage that of the person being honored.

You can focus the attention on the recipient in two ways: surprise or direct acknowledgement. In the surprise approach, you mention characteristics of the person receiving the award without initially mentioning their name—allowing the audience to start guessing who it might be. You may mention a list of accomplishments, or perhaps a positive story. With the surprise approach, you share the information that is sure to reveal the recipient's identity right before you present the award.

You may prefer, however, a direct acknowledgement of the honoree's performance or service and simply announce his or her name. The direct acknowledgement approach is typically followed by the reasons for choosing this person to receive the award, or include his or her past accomplishments. This direct strategy may be preferred if the audience is not familiar with the recipient.

Table 15.5 "Presenting an Award" summarizes the process of presenting an award.

Table 15.5 Presenting an Award

Preparation	Verify the recipient's name, the correct title of the award, and details about the recipient.
Focus	Keep the focus on the honoree, not on yourself or the awards committee.
Surprise Approach	Build suspense by listing the winner's accomplishments from general to more and more specific; end by disclosing a unique accomplishment that identifies the winner, and finally announcing his or her name.
Direct Approach	Announce the award winner and follow with a list of his or her accomplishments.
Exit	Step aside and let the honoree have the spotlight.

If you are the award recipient, be aware that the acceptance of an award often provides a moment of influence on the audience that can serve to advance your position or cause. Use of the limelight is an important skill, and much like any speech or presentation, it requires planning and preparation. You don't want to be caught speechless, and you want to project a professional presence that corresponds to the award or recognition.

If you know you are being considered for an award, first consider what the award recognizes within your professional community. An award is a symbol of approval, recognition, or distinction that honors the recipient in public. As the recipient, it is your role to convey recognition of that honor with your gracious acceptance.

Perhaps you have seen an awards ceremony on television, where a producer, composer, actor, or musician has received public recognition. Sometimes the acceptance unifies the community and serves as an inspiration to others. Other times the recipient stumbles, talks as fast as they can to list all the people who helped them reach their goal (often forgetting several, which can hurt feelings), or they use the spotlight to address an unrelated issue, like a political protest. They may mumble, and their nervousness may be so obvious that it impacts their credibility. Accepting an award is an honor, an opportunity, and a challenge.

The first step in accepting an award is to say thank you. You can connect with the audience with your heartfelt emotional displays and enthusiasm. Raised arms, clasped hands, and a bow are universal symbols of respect and gratitude. Note that rambunctious displays of emotion such as jumping up and down or large, sweeping gestures are better left for the athletic fields. An award ceremony is a formal event, and your professionalism will be on display for all to see.

Next, you should consider giving credit where credit is due, noting its relevance to your field or community. If you name one person, you have to be sure to not leave anyone out, or you run the risk of hurting feelings and perhaps even making professional enemies. If you confine your credit list to a couple of key people, it is wise to extend the credit beyond the individual mentions by saying something like, "There are so many people who made this possible. Thank you all!" You should link your response to the award organization and your field, industry, or business. Don't apologize or use terms that can be interpreted as negative. The acceptance of an award is a joyous, uplifting affair, and your role is to maintain and perpetuate that perception.

You may also consider linking your award to a motivational anecdote. A brief, personal story about how a teacher or neighbor in your community motivated you to do better than you thought you could and how you hope this can serve to motivate up-and-coming members to strive for their very best, can often stimulate an audience. Don't exaggerate or stretch the story. The simple facts speak for themselves and the award serves as a powerful visual aid.

Say "thank you again" as you leave the stage, facilitating the transition to the next part of the ceremony while acknowledging the honor. You may need to take note where previous recipients have exited the stage to proceed without error, or simply return to your seat. Your brief comments combined with a graceful entrance and exit will communicate professionalism. Table 15.6 "Accepting an Award" summarizes the steps we have outlined.

Table 15.6 Accepting an Award

Acceptance	Say "thank you."
Relevance	Indicate where credit is due, what the award means to you, and how it relates to the awarding organization or your community.
Acknowledgment	Show your honor with dignity and respect as you say "thank you" again and exit the stage.

KEY TAKEAWAY

Awards are public recognitions of success, and tact and grace are required both in presenting and receiving them.

EXERCISES

1. Who needs to be prepared to present an award in a business and why? Discuss your ideas with the class.

2. This can be a fun two-minute oral communication exercise. In the exercise, you will alternate between the role of the award announcer and the recipient. You will be paired up into teams where you will need to create a business or industry award, prepare a brief script and notes on acceptance, and then demonstrate your results for your class. The introduction of the speaker should last no more than thirty seconds and the acceptance should also be completed in less than a minute. If you are at a distance from your class, you may be assigned a particular role that fits your situation. Record your performance and post it in class.

3. Find one example of an award acceptance speech that you perceive as particularly effective. Indicate why and share the link. Compare with your classmates.

4. Find one example of an award acceptance speech that you perceive as particularly ineffective. Indicate why and share the link. Compare with classmates.

[1] Schutz, W. (1966). *The interpersonal underworld.* Palo Alto, CA: Science and Behavior Books.

15.8 Serving as Master of Ceremonies
LEARNING OBJECTIVES

1. Discuss the role of master of ceremonies.
2. Understand the responsibilities of the master of ceremonies.

A master of ceremonies is the conductor of ritual gatherings. The master of ceremonies (or MC for short, often written as "emcee") has the poise and stage presence to start, conduct, and conclude a formal ceremony for a group or community. Typically emcees will be full members of the community, recognized for their credibility, integrity, service, and sense of humor. The emcee sets the intellectual and emotional tone for the event.

At a conference or other business function, the master of ceremonies is often the first person to take the stage and the last one to leave it. They come completely prepared to make sure the agenda is followed, nothing is forgotten, all transitions go smoothly, and the event starts and ends on time. While many business conferences are not humorous affairs, a sense of humor can go a long way in helping defuse tension when unavoidable delays, problems, or errors occur. The emcee is required to help an unprepared speaker accept an award, move to their conclusion, and exit the stage. While a shepherd's crook might seem like an attractive tool for that role, often eye contact and a nonverbal gesture, such as a couple of steps toward the podium, will do the trick. If not, a gentle hand on a shoulder might be required, or even an interjected word about the schedule. The speaker knows and the audience expects the master of ceremonies to keep the ceremony on track with honor and respect.

If you are assigned to act as emcee for an event, you should have an agenda that includes all the components of the event, from start to finish, with estimations of time, roles, functions, and notes concerning responsibility. If this is not provided for you, you will need to compile it yourself. In either case, make sure the agenda is available far enough in advance that you can study it, become familiar with the key components and transitions, and anticipate any challenges that are likely to arise. If possible, you should also communicate with the people who will be joining you on stage: featured speakers, award presenters, and the like. You need to confirm their availability and understanding of their roles, with special attention to reinforcing time commitments.

One trick of the trade is to incorporate time as transitions. If you have a one-hour ceremony involving several awards and one featured speaker, indicate on the agenda that the speaker has seven minutes for their presentation. Communicate this to them before the event so they can prepare their remarks around this time frame. Then budget three minutes as a transition to the next event. It won't take you three minutes to make the transition, but by building this time window into the schedule you allow for a degree of overlap that may be required to keep the event on track in case the speaker speaks for nine minutes.

It is especially important to observe the schedule if you are emceeing a multipart event with breakout sessions and/or segments on different topics of interest to different audiences. Imagine an all-day conference for which some attendees registered only for the afternoon session and some only for the morning. Now imagine that the morning speaker was delayed due to a travel mishap. As emcee, would you decide to postpone the morning topic and have the afternoon speaker give his presentation in the morning? If so, you would need to be prepared to give refunds to afternoon attendees who missed the speaker they signed up to hear—and even if their registration fees were refunded, they might still be upset about having spent time and money traveling to the event. The solution? Have a "Plan B," such as a substitute speaker who is qualified to present on the topic of the "top billed" speaker.

A professional master of ceremonies is expected to keep the event running on time while "making it look easy." The audience will appreciate the seamless progression as the event proceeds.

KEY TAKEAWAY

Serving as the master of ceremonies is an honor that involves a great deal of responsibility and preparation.

EXERCISES

1. Create a sample awards ceremony that incorporates the acceptance speech assignment as well as the introducing a speaker assignment. This assignment then combines three functions into one, where each person plays their role. One person will need to serve as master of ceremonies. If the class is large enough, you may be able to subdivide into groups and hold separate ceremonies in more than one classroom. Planning and preparing a ceremony takes time and attention to detail. It also never goes as planned. Remain calm and relaxed as you perform your awards ceremony.
2. Evaluate a master of ceremonies and post your results. Share and compare with classmates.

15.9 Viral Messages

LEARNING OBJECTIVES

1. Discuss the elements of viral messages.
2. Understand strategies to develop effective viral messages.

What was once called "word of mouth" advertising has gone viral with the introduction of social marketing via the Internet. What was once called a "telephone chain," where one person called another in order to pass along news or a request in a linear model, has now gone global. One tweet from Twitter gets passed along and the message is transmitted exponentially. The post to the Facebook page is seen before the nightly news on television. Text messages are often real time. Radio once beat print media to the news, and then television trumped both. Now person-to-person, computer-mediated communication trumps them all at the speed of light—if the message is attractive, relevant, dramatic, sudden, or novel. If no one bothers to pass along the message, or the tweet isn't very interesting, it will get lost in the noise. What, then, makes a communication message viral?

Let's look at the June 2009 death of Michael Jackson for an example of a viral message and see what we can learn.

According to Jocelyn Noveck, news of his death spread via Twitter, text messages, and Facebook before the traditional media could get the message out. People knew about the 911 call from Jackson's home before it hit the mainstream media. By the time the story broke, it was already old. [1]

People may not have had all the facts, but the news was out. Communities, represented by families, groups of friends, employees at organizations, had been mobilized to spread the news. They were motivated to share the news, but why?

Effective Viral Messages

Viral messages are words, sounds, or images that compel the audience to pass them along. They prompt people to act, and mobilize communities. Community mobilization has been studied in many ways and forms. [2] We mobilize communities to leave areas of disaster, or to get out and walk more as part of an exercise program. If we want people to consider and act on a communication message, we first have to gain the audience's attention. In our example, communities were mobilized to share word of Jacksons' passing. Attention statements require sparks and triggers. A spark topic "has an appeal to emotion, a broad base of impact and subsequent concern, and results in motivating a consensus about issues, planning, and action." [3]

In the example of Michael Jackson, the consensus may be that he died under suspicious circumstances, but in other examples, it could be that the product or service being discussed is the next cool thing. The message in social marketing and viral messages does not exist apart from individuals or communities. They give it life and attention, or ignore it.

If you want to design a message to go viral, you have to consider three factors:
1. Does it have an emotional appeal that people will feel compelled to share?
2. Does it have a trigger (does it challenge, provide novelty, or incorporate humor to motivate interest)?
3. Is it relevant to the audience?

An appeal to emotion is a word, sound, or image that arouses an emotional response in the audience. Radio stations fill the airwaves with the sounds of the 1980s to provoke an emotional response and gain a specific demographic within the listening audience. The day after the announcement of Michael Jackson's death broke, you could hear his music everywhere. Many people felt compelled to share the news because of an emotional association to his music, the music's association to a time in their lives, and the fact that it was a sudden, unanticipated, and perhaps suspicious death.

A trigger is a word, sound, or image that causes an activity, precipitates an event or interaction, or provokes a reaction between two or more people. In the case of Michael Jackson, the triggers included all three factors and provoked an observable response that other forms of media will not soon forget. His death at a young age challenged the status quo. In the same way, videos on YouTube have earned instant fame (wanted or unwanted) for a few with hilarious antics, displays of emotion, or surprising news.

The final ingredient to a viral message is relevance. It must be immediately accessible to the audience, salient, and important. If you want someone to stop smoking, graphs and charts may not motivate them to action. Show them someone like them with post-surgery scars across their throat and it will get attention. Attention is the first step toward pre-contemplation in a change model that [4] may lead to action.

KEY TAKEAWAY

Viral messages are contagious.

EXERCISES

1. Design a viral message about a hypothetical product or service you would like to promote. Incorporate the elements listed above in no more than a hundred words. Post your viral message in class and compare with classmates.
2. Identify a company that is relevant to your major or interests and locate an example of their marketing material about a specific product or service. Write a viral message as if you were an employee presenting to a potential client. Share and compare with classmates.
3. Consider a message you passed along recently. Write a brief description and include discussion on why you passed it along.
4. What motivates you to pay attention? Make a list of five ideas, images, or words that attract your attention. Post and compare with classmates.

[1] Noveck, J. (2009, June). *Jackson death was twittered, texted, and Facebooked.* Retrieved from http://news.yahoo.com/s/ap/20090627/ap_en_ot/us/michael_jackson_the_media_moment

[2] Freire, P. (1970). *Pedagogy of the oppressed.* New York, NY: Seabury Press.

[3] McLean, S. (1997). A communication analysis of community mobilization on the Warm Springs Indian Reservation. *Journal of Health Communication, 2,* 113–125.

[4] Prochaska, J., & DiClemente, C. (1982). Transtheoretical therapy: Toward a more integrative model of change. *Psychotherapy: Theory, Research, and Practice, 19*(3), 276–288.

15.10 Additional Resources

- Visit this site for an "elevator speech" template. http://www.2020.co.uk/downloads/elevator_speech.doc
- Entertonement provides videos of the current "Most Popular Sound Bites." http://www.entertonement.com/clips/browse/popularity_day
- "Good quotes/sound bites are the salsa on the nacho chip of our narrative." http://knightpoliticalreporting.syr.edu/teachingfiles/Choosing%20Good%20Quotes-Soundbites.pdf
- "Getting Maximum Value From The Six Touch Points Of Communications" by Nancy Friedman. http://www.telephonedoctor.com/newsletter/200404.asp
- Visit this University of Chicago site for information on succeeding in an employment interview. https://caps.uchicago.edu/resourcecenter/handouts/interviews.pdf
- "How to conduct a meeting." http://www.ascls.org/leadership/ldc/conduct_howto.pdf
- The Official Robert's Rules of Order Web Site: Robert's Rules Association is an unincorporated membership association representing Robert's Rules of Order, the guide to parliamentary procedure. http://www.robertsrules.com
- A ten-step article from eHow on how to propose a toast. http://www.ehow.com/how_1383_propose-toast.html
- Read an e-zine article by the Advanced Public Speaking Institute. "Being roasted is an honor, but you must be careful to honor people while you are roasting them during a public speaking engagement." http://ezinearticles.com/?Public-Speaking:-Roast-Humor-and-Insults&id=100203
- "Preparing For Your Media Interview" by Judy Jernudd. http://www.streetdirectory.com/travel_guide/1578/business_and_finance/preparing_for_your_media_interview.html
- "How to prepare yourself for a media interview: Fears of being misquoted or having their research oversimplified scares scientists away from media interviews," an article from the American Psychological Association. http://www.apa.org/monitor/mar98/prep.html
- "7 Tips on How to Prepare For Mainstream News and Feature Media Interviews" by Amelia Brazell from EzineArticles.com. http://ezinearticles.com/?News-Media-Interviews---7-   Tips-on-How-to-Prepare-For-

Mainstream-News-and-Feature-Media-Interviews&id=1178440

- Read the Code of Ethics of the Society of Professional Journalists. http://www.spj.org/ethicscode.asp
- "How to introduce a speaker" by Marijane Suttor from Helium. http://www.helium.com/items/670256-how-to-introduce-a-speaker
- "How to Give an Acceptance Speech" by Patricia Fripp from The Sideroad. http://www.sideroad.com/Public_Speaking/acceptance_speech.html

- Visit this site for a pamphlet on how to serve as a master of ceremonies. http://www.usda.org/trifold/IS04503.pdf
- "Why Pass on Viral Messages? Because They Connect Emotionally," a *Harvard Business Online* article by Angela Dobele, Adam Lindgreen, Michael Beverland, Joelle Vanhamme, and Robert Van Wijk. http://harvardbusinessonline.hbsp.harvard.edu/b02/en/common/item_detail.jhtml?id=BH239&_requestid=38978

NOTES:

Chapter 16:
Intrapersonal and Interpersonal Business Communication

Identity is the essential core of who we are as individuals, the conscious experience of the self inside.
   Kauffman

Getting Started

INTRODUCTORY EXERCISES

1. Define yourself in five words or less.
2. Describe yourself in no less than twenty words and no more than fifty.
3. List what is important to you in priority order. List what you spend your time on in rank order. Compare the results.

What are you doing? This simple question is at the heart of an application that allows user to stay hyper connected. Before we consider the social media and its implications on business communication, let's first examine the central question Twitter asks its users to address in 140 characters or less.

What are you doing right now? Are you reading, learning, or have you already tuned out this introduction and skipped over to Twitter to see what your friends are up to? We often define ourselves through action, but the definition doesn't work very well. When you are a newborn baby, your actions represented a small percentage of your potential—now that you're older, you are more than an eating machine that requires constant care and feeding—but what are you? A common response may be "human," but even that can be challenging to define. If we say humans are the tool makers and then note that several nonhuman species from primates to otters make and use tools, where does that leave us? You could say that a human has two arms, two legs, or two eyes, but not everyone has these, so the definition fails yet again. You may want to say that you can communicate, but we don't all speak the same language, and communication is a universal process across species. You may be tempted to respond to the question "what are you?" by saying something along the lines of "I think, therefore I am"—but what is thinking, and are humans the only species with the ability to think? Again, defining yourself through your ability to think may not completely work. Finally, you may want to raise the possibility of your ability to reason and act, recall the past, be conscious of the present, and imagine the future; or your

ability to contemplate the abstract, the ironic, even the absurd. Now we might be getting somewhere.

What does the word "party" mean to you? Most cultures have rituals where people come together in a common space for conversation and sharing. Such gatherings often include food, music, and dancing. In our modern society, we increasingly lack time to connect with others. It may be too expensive or time-consuming to travel across the country for Thanksgiving, but we may meet on Skype and talk (audio/video) at relatively little or no cost. Some of your instructors may have traveled to a designated location for a professional conference each year, seeing colleagues and networking; but in recent years, time, cost, and competition for attention has shifted priorities for many. We may have two (or three or four) jobs that consume much of our time, but you'll notice that in the breaks and pauses of life people reach for their cell phones to connect. We instant message (IM), text message, tweet, e-mail, and interact. As humans, we have an innate need to connect with each other, even when that connection can (and does) sometimes produce conflict.

When we ask the question, "What are you doing?" the answer invariably involves communication; communication with self, with others, in verbal (oral and written) and nonverbal ways. How do we come to this and how does it influence our experience within the business environment? How do we come to enter a new community through a rite of initiation, often called a job interview, only to find ourselves lost as everyone speaks a new language, the language of the workplace? How do we negotiate relationships, demands for space and time, across meetings, collaborative efforts, and solo projects? This chapter addresses several of these issues as we attempt to answer the question, "What are you doing?" with the answer: communicating.

16.1 Intrapersonal Communication
LEARNING OBJECTIVE

1. Discuss intrapersonal communication.

When you answer the question, "What are you doing?" what do you write? Eating at your favorite restaurant? Working on a slow evening? Reading your favorite book on a Kindle? Preferring the feel of paper to keyboard? Reading by candlelight? In each case you are communicating what you are doing, but you may not be communicating why, or what it means to you. That communication may be internal, but is it only an internal communication process?

Intrapersonal communication can be defined as communication with one's self, and that may include self-talk, acts of imagination and visualization, and even recall and memory. [1] You read on your cell phone screen that your friends are going to have dinner at your favorite restaurant. What comes to mind? Sights, sounds, and scents? Something special that happened the last time you were there? Do you contemplate joining them? Do you start to work out a plan of getting from your present location to the restaurant? Do you send your friends a text asking if they want company? Until the moment when you hit the "send" button, you are communicating with yourself.

Communications expert Leonard Shedletsky examines intrapersonal communication through the eight basic components of the communication process (i.e., source, receiver, message, channel, feedback, environment, context, and interference) as transactional, but all the interaction occurs within the individual. [2] Perhaps, as you consider whether to leave your present location and join your friends at the restaurant, you are aware of all the work that sits in front of you. You may hear the voice of your boss, or perhaps of one of your parents, admonishing you about personal responsibility and duty. On the other hand, you may imagine the friends at the restaurant saying something to the effect of "you deserve some time off!"

At the same time as you argue with yourself, Judy Pearson and Paul Nelson would be quick to add that intrapersonal communication is not only your internal monologue but also involves your efforts to plan how to get to the restaurant. [3] From planning to problem solving, internal conflict resolution, and evaluations and judgments of self and others, we communicate with ourselves through intrapersonal communication.

All this interaction takes place in the mind without externalization, and all of it relies on previous interaction with the external world. If you had been born in a different country, to different parents, what language would you speak? What language would you think in? What would you value, what would be important to you, and what would not? Even as you argue to yourself whether the prospect of joining your friends at the restaurant overcomes your need to complete your work, you use language and symbols that were communicated to you. Your language and culture have given you the means to rationalize, act, and answer the question, "What are you doing?" but you are still bound by the expectations of yourself and the others who make up your community.

In intrapersonal communication, we communicate with ourselves.

EXERCISES

1. Describe what you are doing, pretending you are another person observing yourself. Write your observations down or record them with a voice or video recorder. Discuss the exercise with your classmates.
2. Think of a time when you have used self-talk—for example, giving yourself "I can do this!" messages when you are striving to meet a challenge, or "what's the use?" messages when you are discouraged. Did you purposely choose to use self-talk, or did it just happen? Discuss your thoughts with classmates.
3. Take a few minutes and visualize what you would like your life to be like a year from now, or five years from now. Do you think this visualization exercise will influence your actions and decisions in the future? Compare your thoughts with those of your classmates.

[1] McLean, S. (2005). *The basics of interpersonal communication.* Boston, MA: Allyn & Bacon.
[2] Shedletsky, L. J. (1989). Meaning and mind: An interpersonal approach to human communication. *ERIC Clearinghouse on reading and communication skills.* Bloomington, IN: ERIC.
[3] Pearson, J., & Nelson, P. (1985). *Understanding and sharing: An introduction to speech communication* (3rd ed.). Dubuque, IA: William C. Brown.

16.2 Self-Concept and Dimensions of Self
LEARNING OBJECTIVE

1. Define and discuss self-concept.

Again we'll return to the question "what are you doing?" as one way to approach self-concept. If we define ourselves through our actions, what might those actions be, and are we no longer ourselves when we no longer engage in those activities? Psychologist Steven Pinker defines the conscious present as about three seconds for most people. Everything else is past or future. [1] Who are you at this moment in time, and will the self you become an hour from now be different from the self that is reading this sentence right now?

Just as the communication process is dynamic, not static (i.e., always changing, not staying the same), you too are a dynamic system. Physiologically your body is in a constant state of change as you inhale and exhale air, digest food, and cleanse waste from each cell. Psychologically you are constantly in a state of change as well. Some aspects of your personality and character will be constant, while others will shift and adapt to your environment and context. That complex combination contributes to the self you call you. We may choose to define self as one's own sense of individuality, personal characteristics, motivations, and actions, [2] but any definition we create will fail to capture who you are, and who you will become.

Self-Concept

Our self-concept is "what we perceive ourselves to be," [3] and involves aspects of image and esteem. How we see ourselves and how we feel about ourselves influences how we communicate with others. What you are thinking now and how you communicate impacts and influences how others treat you. Charles Cooley [4] calls this concept the looking-glass self. We look at how others treat us, what they say and how they say it, for clues about how they view us to gain insight into our own identity. Leon Festinger added that we engage in social comparisons, evaluating ourselves in relation to our peers of similar status, similar characteristics, or similar qualities. [5]

The ability to think about how, what, and when we think, and why, is critical to intrapersonal communication. Animals may use language and tools, but can they reflect on their own thinking? Self-reflection is a trait that allows us to adapt and change to our context or environment, to accept or reject messages, to examine our concept of ourselves and choose to improve.

Internal monologue refers to the self-talk of intrapersonal communication. It can be a running monologue that is rational and reasonable, or disorganized and illogical. It can interfere with listening to others, impede your ability to focus, and become a barrier to effective communication. Alfred Korzybski suggested that the first step in becoming conscious of how we think and communicate with ourselves was to achieve an inner quietness, in effect "turning off" our internal monologue. [6] Learning to be quiet inside can be a challenge. We can choose to listen to others when they communicate through the written or spoken word while refraining from preparing our responses before they finish their turn is essential. We can take mental note of when we jump to conclusions from only partially attending to the speaker's or writer's message. We can choose to listen to others instead of ourselves.

One principle of communication is that interaction is always dynamic and changing. That interaction can be internal, as in intrapersonal communication, but can also be external. We may communicate with one other person and engage in interpersonal communication. If we engage two or more

individuals (up to eight normally), group communication is the result. More than eight normally results in subdivisions within the group and a reversion to smaller groups of three to four members [7] due to the ever-increasing complexity of the communication process. With each new person comes a multiplier effect on the number of possible interactions, and for many that means the need to establish limits.

Dimensions of Self

Who are you? You are more than your actions, and more than your communication, and the result may be greater than the sum of the parts, but how do you know yourself? In the first of the Note 16.1 "Introductory Exercises" for this chapter, you were asked to define yourself in five words or less. Was it a challenge? Can five words capture the essence of what you consider yourself to be? Was your twenty to fifty description easier? Or was it equally challenging? Did your description focus on your characteristics, beliefs, actions, or other factors associated with you? If you compared your results with classmates or coworkers, what did you observe? For many, these exercises can prove challenging as we try to reconcile the self-concept we perceive with what we desire others to perceive about us, as we try to see ourselves through our interactions with others, and as we come to terms with the idea that we may not be aware or know everything there is to know about ourselves.

Joseph Luft and Harry Ingram [8], [9] gave considerable thought and attention to these dimensions of self, which are represented in Figure 16.1 "Luft and Ingram's Dimensions of Self". In the first quadrant of the figure, information is known to you and others, such as your height or weight. The second quadrant represents things others observe about us that we are unaware of, like how many times we say "umm" in the space of five minutes. The third quadrant involves information that you know, but do not reveal to others. It may involve actively hiding or withholding information, or may involve social tact, such as thanking your Aunt Martha for the large purple hat she's given you that you know you will never wear. Finally, the fourth quadrant involves information that is unknown to you and your conversational partners. For example, a childhood experience that has been long forgotten or repressed may still motivate you. As another example, how will you handle an emergency after you've received first aid training? No one knows because it has not happened.

These dimensions of self serve to remind us that we are not fixed—that freedom to change combined with the ability to reflect, anticipate, plan, and predict allows us to improve, learn, and adapt to our surroundings. By recognizing that we are not fixed in our concept of "self," we come to terms with the responsibility and freedom inherent in our potential humanity.

Figure 16.1 Luft and Ingram's Dimensions of Self

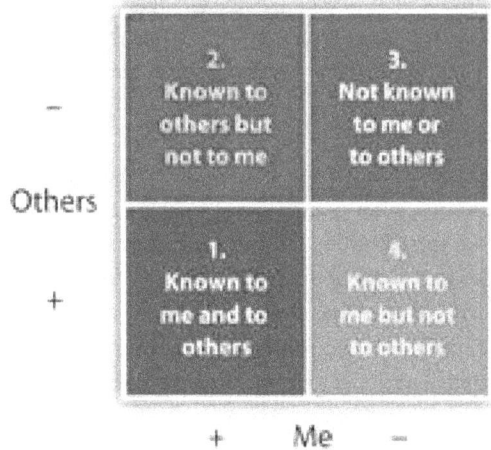

In the context of business communication, the self plays a central role. How do you describe yourself? Do your career path, job responsibilities, goals, and aspirations align with what you recognize to be your talents? How you represent "self," through your résumé, in your writing, in your articulation and presentation—these all play an important role as you negotiate the relationships and climate present in any organization.

KEY TAKEAWAY

Self-concept involves multiple dimensions and is expressed in internal monologue and social comparisons.

EXERCISES

1. Examine your academic or professional résumé—or, if you don't have one, create one now. According to the dimensions of self-described in this section, which dimensions contribute to your résumé? Discuss your results with your classmates.
2. How would you describe yourself in terms of the dimensions of self as shown in Figure 16.1 "Luft and Ingram's Dimensions of Self"? Discuss your thoughts with a classmate.
3. Can you think of a job or career that would be a good way for you to express yourself? Are you pursuing that job or career? Why or why not? Discuss your answer with a classmate.

[1] Pinker, S. (2009). *The stuff of thought: Language as a window to human nature.* New York, NY: Penguin Books.

[2] McLean, S. (2005). *The basics of interpersonal communication.* Boston, MA: Allyn & Bacon.

[3] McLean, S. (2005). *The basics of interpersonal communication* (p. 97). Boston, MA: Allyn & Bacon.

[4] Cooley, C. (1922). *Human nature and the social order* (Rev. ed.). New York, NY: Scribners.

[5] Festinger, L. (1954). A theory of soical comparison processes. *Human Relationships*, 7, 117–140.

[6] Korzybski, A. (1933). *Science and sanity.* Lancaster, PA: International Non-Aristotelian Library Publish Co.

[7] McLean, S. (2005). *The basics of interpersonal communication.* Boston, MA: Allyn & Bacon.

[8] Luft, J., & Ingham, H. (1955). *The Johari Window: A graphic model for interpersonal relations.* Los Angeles: University of California Western Training Lab.

[9] Luft, J. (1970). *Group processes: An introduction to group dynamics* (2nd ed.). Palo Alto, CA: National Press Group.

16.3 Interpersonal Needs

LEARNING OBJECTIVE

1. Understand the role of interpersonal needs in the communication process.

You may have had no problem answering the question, "What are you doing?" and simply pulled a couple of lines from yesterday's Twitter message or reviewed your BlackBerry calendar. But if you had to compose an entirely original answer, would it prove to be a challenge? Perhaps at first this might appear to be a simple task. You have to work and your job required your participation in a meeting, or you care about someone and met him or her for lunch.

Both scenarios make sense on the surface, but we have to consider the *why* with more depth. Why that meeting, and why that partner? Why not another job, or a lunch date with someone else? If we consider the question long enough, we'll come around to the conclusion that we communicate with others in order to meet basic needs, and our meetings, interactions, and relationships help us meet those needs. We may also recognize that not all our needs are met by any one person, job, experience, or context; instead, we diversify our communication interactions in order to meet our needs. At first, you may be skeptical of the idea that we communicate to meet our basic needs, but let's consider two theories on the subject and see how well they predict, describe, and anticipate our tendency to interact.

Abraham Maslow's hierarchy of needs, represented in Figure 16.2 "Maslow's Hierarchy of Needs", may be familiar to you. [1] Perhaps you saw it in negotiation or international business classes and came to recognize its universal applicability. We need the resources listed in level one (i.e., air, food, and water) to survive. If we have met those basic needs, we move to level two: safety. We want to make sure we are safe and that our access to air, food, and water is secure. A job may represent this level of safety at its most basic level. Regardless of how much satisfaction you may receive from a job well done, a paycheck ultimately represents meeting basic needs for many. Still, for others, sacrifice is part of the job. Can you think of any professions that require individuals to make decisions where the safety of others comes first? "First responders" and others who work in public safety often place themselves at risk for the benefit of those they serve.

If we feel safe and secure, we are more likely to seek the companionship of others. Humans tend to form groups naturally, and if basic needs are met, love and belonging occur in level three. Perhaps you've been new at work and didn't understand the first thing about what was really going on. It's not that you weren't well trained and did not receive a solid education, but rather that the business or organization is made up of groups and communities that communicate and interact in distinct and divergent ways. You may have known how to do something, but not how it was done at your new place of work. Colleagues may have viewed you as a stranger or "newbie" and may have even declined to help you. Conflict may have been part of your experience, but if you were lucky, a mentor or coworker took the first step and helped you find your way.

As you came to know what was what and who was who, you learned how to negotiate the landscape and avoid landmines. Your self-esteem (level four) improved as you perceived a sense of belonging, but still may have lacked the courage to speak up.

Over time, you may have learned your job tasks and the strategies for succeeding in your organization. Perhaps you even came to be known as a reliable coworker, one who did go the extra mile, one who did assist the "newbies" around the office. If one of them came to you with a problem, you would know how to handle it. You are now looked up to by others and by yourself within the role, with your ability to make a difference. Maslow calls this "self-actualization" (level five), and discusses how people come to perceive a sense of control or empowerment over their context and environment. Where they look back and see that they once felt at the mercy of others, particularly when they were new, they can now influence and direct aspects of the work environment that were once unavailable.

Beyond self-actualization, Maslow recognizes our innate need to know (level six) that drives us to grow and learn, explore our environment, or engage in new experiences. We come to appreciate a sense of self that extends beyond our immediate experiences, beyond the function, and into the community and the representational. We can take in beauty for its own sake, and value aesthetics (level seven) that we previously ignored or had little time to consider.

Figure 16.2 Maslow's Hierarchy of Needs

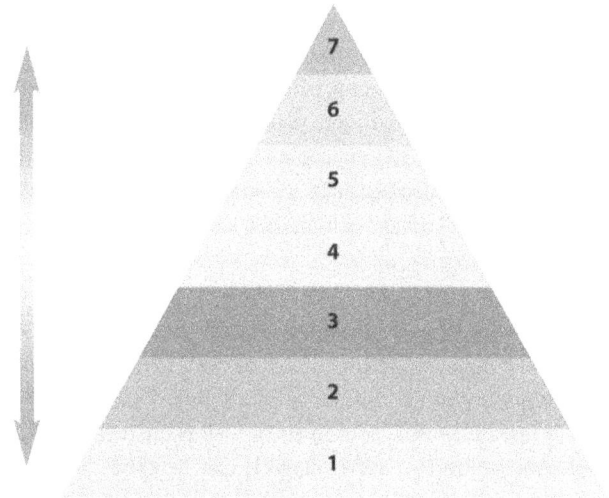

Now that you have reached a sense of contentment in your job and can take in a museum tour, the news of a possible corporate merger is suddenly announced in the mainstream media. It may have been just gossip before, but now it is real. You may feel a sense of uncertainty and be concerned about your status as a valued employee. Do you have reason to worry about losing your job? How will you handle the responsibilities that you've acquired and what about the company and its obligations to those who have sacrificed over time for common success? Conflict may be more frequent in the workplace, and you may feel compelled to go over your personal budget and reprioritize your spending. You may eliminate museum visits and donations, and you may decide to start saving money as the future is less certain. You may dust off your résumé and start communicating with colleagues in related fields as you network, reaching out to regain that sense of stability, of control, that is lost as you feel your security threatened. You will move through Maslow's hierarchy as you reevaluate what you need to survive.

This theory of interpersonal needs is individualistic, and many cultures are not centered on the individual, but it does serve to start our discussion about interpersonal needs. What do we need? Why do we communicate? The answers to both questions are often related.

William Schutz offers an alternate version of interpersonal needs. Like Maslow, he considers the universal aspects of our needs, but he outlines how they operate within a range or continuum for each person. [2] According to Schutz, the need for affection, or appreciation, is basic to all humans. We all need to be recognized and feel like we belong, but may have differing levels of expectations to meet that need. When part of the merger process is announced and the news of layoffs comes, those coworkers who have never been particularly outgoing and have largely kept to themselves may become even more withdrawn. Schutz describes underpersonals as people who seek limited interaction. On the opposite end of the spectrum, you may know people where you work that are often seeking attention and affirmation. Schutz describes overpersonals as people who have a strong need to be liked and constantly seek attention from others. The person who strikes a healthy balance is called a personal individual.

Humans also have a need for control, or the ability to influence people and events. But that need may vary by the context, environment, and sense of security. You may have already researched similar mergers, as well as the forecasts for the new organization, and come to realize that your position and your department are central to the current business model. You may have also of taken steps to prioritize your budget, assess your transferable skills, and look for opportunities beyond your current context. Schutz would describe your efforts to control your situation as autocratic, or self-directed. At the same time there may be several employees who have not taken similar steps who look to you and others for leadership, in effect abdicating their responsibility. Abdicrats shift the burn of responsibility from themselves to others, looking to others for a sense of control. Democrats share the need between the individual and the group, and may try to hold a departmental meeting to gather information and share.

Finally, Schutz echoes Maslow in his assertion that belonging is a basic interpersonal need, but notes that it exists within a range or continuum, where some need more and others less. Undersocials may be less likely to seek interaction, may prefer smaller groups, and will generally not be found on center stage. Oversocials, however, crave the spotlight of attention and are highly motivated to seek belonging. A social person is one who strikes a healthy balance between being withdrawn and being the constant center of attention. Schutz describes these three interpersonal needs of affection, control, and belonging as interdependent and variable. In one context, an individual may have a high need for control, while in others he or she may not perceive the same level of motivation or compulsion to meet that need. Both Maslow and Schutz offer us two related versions of interpersonal needs that begin to address the central question: why communicate?

We communicate with each other to meet our needs, regardless how we define those needs. From the time you are a newborn infant crying for food or the time you are a toddler learning to say "please" when requesting a cup of milk, to the time you are an adult learning the rituals of the job interview and the conference room, you learn to communicate in order to gain a sense of self within the group or community, meeting your basic needs as you grow and learn.

KEY TAKEAWAY

Through communication, we meet universal human needs.

EXERCISES

1. Review the types of individuals from Schutz's theory described in this section. Which types do you think fit you? Which types fit some of your coworkers or classmates? Why? Share your opinions with your classmates and compare your self-assessment with the types they believe describe you.
2. Think of two or more different situations and how you might express your personal needs differently from one situation to the other. Have you observed similar variations in personal needs in other people from one situation to another? Discuss your thoughts with a classmate.

[1] Maslow, A. (1970). *Motivation and personality* (2nd ed.). New York, NY: Harper & Row.
[2] Schutz, W. (1966). *The interpersonal underworld.* Palo Alto, CA: Science and Behavior Books.

16.4 Social Penetration Theory
LEARNING OBJECTIVES

1. Discuss social penetration theory and self-disclosure and its principles.
2. Describe interpersonal relations.

How do you get to know other people? If the answer springs immediately to mind, we're getting somewhere: communication. Communication allows us to share experiences, come to know ourselves and others, and form relationships, but it requires time and effort. You don't get to know someone in a day, a month, or even a year. At the same time you are coming to know them, they are changing, adapting, and growing—and so are you. Irwin Altman and Dalmas Taylor describe this progression from superficial to intimate levels of communication in social penetration theory, which is often called the Onion Theory because the model looks like an onion and involves layers that are peeled away. [1] According to social penetration theory, we fear that which we do not know. That includes people. Strangers go from being unknown to known through a series of steps that we can observe through conversational interactions.

If we didn't have the weather to talk about, what would we say? People across cultures use a variety of signals to indicate neutral or submissive stances in relation to each other. A wave, a nod, or a spoken reference about a beautiful day can indicate an open, approachable stance rather than a guarded, defensive posture. At the outermost layer of the onion, in this model, there is only that which we can observe. We can observe characteristics about each other and make judgments, but they are educated guesses at best. Our nonverbal displays of affiliation, like a team jacket, a uniform, or a badge, may communicate something about us, but we only peel away a layer when we engage in conversation, oral or written.

As we move from public to private information we make the transition from small talk to substantial, and eventually intimate, conversations. Communication requires trust and that often takes time. Beginnings are fragile times and when expectations, roles, and ways of communicating are not clear, misunderstandings can occur. Some relationships may never proceed past observations on the weather, while others may explore controversial topics like politics or religion. A married couple that has spent countless years together may be able to finish each other's sentences, and as memory fades, the retelling of stories may serve to bond and reinforce the relationship. Increasingly, intimate knowledge and levels of trust are achieved over time, involving frequency of interaction as well as length and quality. Positive interactions may lead to more positive interactions, while negative ones may lead to less overall interaction.

This may appear to be common sense at first, but let's examine an example. You are new to a position and your supervisor has been in his or her role for a number of years. Some people at your same level within the organization enjoy a level of knowledge and ease of interaction with your supervisor that you lack. They may have had more time and interactions with the supervisor, but you can still use this theory to gain trust and build a healthy relationship. Recognize that you are unknown to your supervisor and vice versa. Start with superficial conversations that are neutral and nonthreatening, but demonstrate a willingness to engage in communication. Silence early in a relationship can be a sign of respect, but it can also send the message that you are fearful, shy, or lack confidence. It can be interpreted as an unwillingness to communicate, and may actually discourage interaction. If the supervisor picks up the conversation, keep your responses short and light. If not, keep an upbeat attitude and mention the weather.

Over time, the conversations may gradually grow to cross topics beyond the scope of the office, and a relationship may form that involves trust. To a degree, you and your coworkers learn to predict one another's responses and relax in the knowledge of mutual respect. If, however, you skip from superficial to intimate topics too quickly, you run risk of violating normative expectations. Trust takes time, and with that comes empathy and understanding. But if you share with your supervisor your personal struggles on day one, it may erode your credibility. According to the social penetration theory, people go from superficial to intimate conversations as trust develops through repeated, positive interactions. Self-disclosure is "information, thoughts, or feelings we tell others about ourselves that they would not otherwise know." [2] Taking it step by step, and not rushing to self-disclose or asking personal questions too soon, can help develop positive business relationships.

Principles of Self-Disclosure

Write down five terms that describe your personal self, and five terms that describe your professional self. Once you have completed your two lists, compare the results. They may have points that overlap, or may have words that describe you in your distinct roles that are quite different. This difference can be easy to address, but at times it can be a challenge to maintain. How much of "you" do you share in the workplace? Our personal and professional lives don't exist independently, and in many ways are interdependent.

How do people know more about us? We communicate information about ourselves, whether or not we are aware of it. You cannot *not* communicate. [3]From your internal monologue and intrapersonal communication, to verbal and nonverbal communication, communication is constantly occurring. What do you communicate about yourself by the clothes (or brands) you wear, the tattoos you display, or the piercing you remove before you enter the workplace? Self-disclosure is a process by which you intentionally communicate information to others, but can involve unintentional, but revealing slips. Steven Beebe, Susan Beebe, and Mark Redmond offer us five principles of self-disclosure that remind us that communication is an integral part of any business or organizational setting. Let's discuss them one by one. [4]

Self-Disclosure Usually Moves in Small Steps

Would you come to work on your first day wearing a large purple hat? If you knew that office attire was primarily brown and gray suits? Most people would say, "Of course not!" as there is a normative expectation for dress, sometimes called a dress code. After you have worked within the organization, earned trust and established credibility, and earned your place in the community, the purple hat might be positively received with a sense of humor. But if you haven't yet earned your place, your fashion statement may be poorly received. In the same way, personal information is normally reserved for those of confidence, and earned over time. Take small steps as you come to know your colleagues, taking care to make sure who you are does not speak louder than what you say.

Self-Disclosure Moves from Impersonal to Intimate Information

So you decided against wearing the purple hat to work on your first day, but after a successful first week you went out with friends from your college days. You shut down the bar late in the evening and paid for it on Sunday. At work on Monday, is it a wise strategy to share the finer tips of the drinking games you played on Saturday night? Again, most people would say, "Of course not!" It has nothing to do with work, and only makes you look immature. Some people have serious substance abuse issues, and your stories could sound insensitive, producing a negative impact. How would you know, as you don't really know your coworkers yet? In the same way, it is not a wise strategy to post photos from the weekend's escapades on your Facebook or similar social networking Web page. Employers are increasingly aware of their employees' Web pages, and the picture of you looking stupid may come to mind when your supervisor is considering you for a promotion. You represent yourself, but you also represent your company and its reputation. If you don't represent it well, you run the risk of not representing it at all.

Self-Disclosure Is Reciprocal

Monday morning brings the opportunity to tell all sorts of stories about the weekend, and since you've wisely decided to leave any references to the bar in the past, you may instead choose the wise conversational strategy of asking questions. You may ask your coworkers what they did, what it was like, who they met, and where they went, but eventually all conversations form a circle that comes back to you. The dance between source and receiver isn't linear, it's transactional. After a couple of stories, sooner or later, you'll hear the question, "What did you do this weekend?" It's now your turn. This aspect of conversation is universal. We expect when we reveal something about ourselves that others will reciprocate. The dyadic effect is the formal term for this process, and is often thought to meet the need to reduce uncertainty about conversational partners. If you stay quiet or decline to answer after everyone else has taken a turn, what will happen? They may be put off at first, they may invent stories and let their imaginations run wild, or they may reject you. It may be subtle at first, but reciprocity is expected.

You have the choice of what to reveal and when. You may choose to describe your weekend by describing the friends and conversations while omitting any reference to the bar. You may choose to focus on your Sunday afternoon gardening activities. You may just say you read a good book

and mention the title of the one you are reading. Regardless of what option you choose, you have the freedom and responsibility within the dyadic effect to reciprocate, but you have a degree of control. You can learn to anticipate when your turn will come, and to give some thought to what you will say before the moment arrives.

Self-Disclosure Involves Risk

If you decided to go with the "good book" option, or perhaps mention that you watched a movie, you just ran the risk that whatever you are reading or watching may be criticized. If the book you are enjoying is controversial, you might anticipate a bit of a debate, but if you mentioned a romance novel, or one that has a science fiction theme, you may have thought it wouldn't generate criticism. Sometimes the most innocent reference or comment can produce conflict when the conversational partners have little prior history. At the same time, nothing ventured, nothing gained. How are you going to discover that the person you work with appreciates the same author or genre if you don't share that information? Self-disclosure involves risk, but can produce positive results.

Self-Disclosure Involves Trust

Before you mention the title of the book or movie you saw this weekend, you may consider your audience and what you know about them. If you've only known them for a week, your awareness of their habits, quirks, likes and dislikes may be limited. At the same time, if you feel safe and relatively secure, you may test the waters with a reference to the genre but not the author. You may also decide that it is just a book, and they can take it or leave it.

"Trust is the ability to place confidence in or rely on the character or truth of someone." [5] Trust is a process, not a badge to be earned. It takes time to develop, and can be lost in a moment. Even if you don't agree with your coworker, understand that self-revelation communicates a measure of trust and confidence. Respect that confidence, and respect yourself.

Also, consider the nature of the information. Some information communicated in confidence must see the light of day. Sexual harassment, fraud, theft, and abuse are all issues in the workplace, and if you become aware of these behaviors you will have a responsibility to report them according to your organization's procedures. A professional understands that trust is built over time, and understands how valuable this intangible commodity can be to success.

Interpersonal Relationships

Interpersonal communication can be defined as communication between two people, but the definition fails to capture the essence of a relationship. This broad definition is useful when we compare it to intrapersonal communication, or communication with ourselves, as opposed to mass communication, or communication with a large audience, but it requires clarification. The developmental view of interpersonal communication places emphasis on the relationship rather than the size of the audience, and draws a distinction between impersonal and personal interactions.

For example, one day your coworker and best friend, Iris, whom you've come to know on a personal as well as a professional level, gets promoted to the position of manager. She didn't tell you ahead of time because it wasn't certain, and she didn't know how to bring up the possible change of roles. Your relationship with Iris will change as your roles transform. Her perspective will change, and so will yours. You may stay friends, or she may not have as much time as she once did. Over time, you and Iris gradually grow apart, spending less time together. You eventually lose touch. What is the status of your relationship?

If you have ever had even a minor interpersonal transaction such as buying a cup of coffee from a clerk, you know that some people can be personable, but does that mean you've developed a relationship within the transaction process? For many people the transaction is an impersonal experience, however pleasant. What is the difference between the brief interaction of a transaction and the interactions you periodically have with your colleague, Iris, who is now your manager?

The developmental view places an emphasis on the prior history, but also focuses on the level of familiarity and trust. Over time and with increased frequency we form bonds or relationships with people, and if time and frequency are diminished, we lose that familiarity. The relationship with the clerk may be impersonal, but so can the relationship with the manager after time has passed and the familiarity is lost. From a developmental view, interpersonal communication can exist across this range of experience and interaction.

Review the lists you made for the third of the Note 16.1 "Introductory Exercises" for this chapter. If you evaluate your list of what is important to you, will you find objects or relationships? You may value your home or vehicle, but for most people relationships with friends and family are at the top of the list. Interpersonal relationships take time and effort to form, and they can be challenging. All relationships are dynamic, meaning that they transform and adapt to changes within the context and environment. They require effort and sacrifice, and at times, give rise to the question, why bother?

A short answer may be that we, as humans, are compelled to form bonds. But it still fails to answer the question, why?

Uncertainty theory states that we choose to know more about others with whom we have interactions in order to reduce or resolve the anxiety associated with the unknown. [6], [7], [8] The more we know about others, and become accustomed to how they communicate, the better we can predict how they will interact with us in future contexts. If you learn that Monday mornings are never a good time for your supervisor, you quickly learn to schedule meetings later in the week. The predicted outcome value theory asserts that not only do we want to reduce uncertainty, we also want to maximize our possible benefit from the association. [9], [10], [11] This theory would predict that you would choose Tuesday or later for a meeting in order to maximize the potential for positive interaction and any possible rewards that may result. One theory involves the avoidance of fear while the other focuses on the pursuit of reward. Together, they provide a point of reference as we continue our discussion on interpersonal relationships.

Regardless of whether we focus on collaboration or competition, we can see that interpersonal communication is necessary in the business environment. We want to know our place and role within the organization, accurately predict those within our proximity, and create a sense of safety and belonging. Family for many is the first experience in interpersonal relationships, but as we develop professionally, our relationships at work may take on many of the attributes we associate with family communication. We look to each other with similar sibling rivalries, competition for attention and resources, and support. The workplace and our peers can become as close, or closer, than our birth families, with similar challenges and rewards.

KEY TAKEAWAYS

- Interpersonal relationships are an important part of the work environment.
- We come to know one another gradually.
- Self-disclosure involves risk and reward, and is a normal part of communication.

EXERCISES

1. Write down five terms that describe your personal self, and five terms that describe your professional self. Compare your results with a classmate.
2. Think of someone you trust and who trusts you. How did you come to have a mutually trusting relationship? Did it take effort on both people's part? Discuss your thoughts with a classmate.

3. How important do you think self-disclosure is in business settings? Give some examples. Discuss your thoughts with a classmate.

[1] Altman, I., & Taylor, D. (1973). *Social penetration: The development of interpersonal relationships*. New York, NY: St. Martin's Press.

[2] McLean, S. (2005). *The basics of interpersonal communication* (p. 112). Boston, MA: Allyn & Bacon.

[3] Watzlawick, P. (1993). *The language of change: Elements of therapeutic communication*. New York, NY: W. W. Norton & Company.

[4] Beebe, S. [Steven], Beebe, S. [Susan], & Redmond, M. (2002). *Interpersonal communication relating to others* (3rd ed.). Boston, MA: Allyn & Bacon.

[5] McLean, S. (2005). *The basics of interpersonal communication* (p 114). Boston, MA: Allyn & Bacon.

[6] Berger, C., & Calabrese, R. (1975). Some explorations in initial interactions and beyond: Toward a developmental theory of interpersonal communication. *Human Communication Research, 1*, 99–112.

[7] Berger, C. (1986). Uncertain outcome values in predicted relationships: Uncertainty reduction theory then and now. *Human Communication Research, 13*(1), 34–38.

[8] Gudykunst, W. (1995) Anxiety/uncertainty management theory. In R. W. Wiseman (Ed.), *Intercultural communication theory* (pp. 8–58). Thousand Oaks, CA: Sage.

[9] Sunnafrank, M. (1986). Predicted outcome value during initial interactions: A reformulation of uncertainty reduction theory. *Human Communication Research*, 3–33.

[10] Sunnafrank, M. (1990). Predicted outcome value and uncertainty reduction theory: A test of competing perspective. *Human Communication Theory, 17*, 76–150.

[11] Kellerman, K., & Reynolds, R. (1990). When ignorance is bliss: The role of motivation to reduce uncertainty in uncertainty reduction theory. *Human Communication Research, 17*, 5–75.

16.5 Rituals of Conversation and Interviews
LEARNING OBJECTIVES

1. Understand the five steps in any conversation.
2. Discuss employment interviewing.

You no doubt have participated in countless conversations throughout your life, and the process of how to conduct a conversation may seem so obvious that it needs no examination. Yet, all cultures have rituals of various kinds, and conversation is one of these universal rituals. A skilled business communicator knows when to speak, when to remain silent, and to always stop speaking before the audience stops listening. Further, understanding conversation provides a solid foundation for our next discussion on employment interviewing. Employment interviews follow similar ritual patterns and have their own set of expectations. Expectations may differ based on field, level, knowledge, and experience, but they generally follow the five steps of a basic conversation.

Conversation as a Ritual
Why discuss the ritual of conversation? Because it is one of the main ways we interact in the business environment, and it is ripe for misunderstandings. Our everyday familiarity with conversations often makes us blind to the subtle changes that take place during the course of a conversation. Examining it will allow you to consider its components, predict the next turn, anticipate an opening or closing, and make you a better conversationalist. Steven Beebe, Susan Beebe, and Mark Redmond offer us five stages of conversation that are adapted here for our discussion. [1]

Initiation
The first stage of conversation is called initiation, and requires you to be open to interact. How you communicate openness is up to you; it may involve nonverbal signals like eye contact or body positions, such as smiling or even merely facing the other person and making eye contact. A casual reference to the weather, a light conversation about the weekend, or an in-depth conversation about how the financial markets are performing this morning requires a source to start the process: someone has to initiate the exchange. For some, this may produce a degree of anxiety. If status and hierarchical relationships are present, it may be a question of who speaks when according to cultural norms. The famous anthropologist Bronislaw Malinowski called small talk "phatic communion," [2] reinforcing the idea that there is a degree of ritual across cultures on how we initiate, engage, and conclude conversations.

Preview
The preview is an indication, verbal or nonverbal, of what the conversation is about, both in terms of content and in terms of the relationship. A word or two in the subject line of an e-mail may signal the topic, and the relationship between individuals, such as an employee-supervisor relationship, may be understood. A general reference to a topic may approach a topic indirectly, allowing the recipient to either pick up on the topic and to engage in the discussion or to redirect the conversation away from a topic they are not ready to talk about. People are naturally curious, and also seek certainty. A preview can serve to reduce uncertainty and signal intent.

Talking Point(s)
Joseph DeVito characterizes this step as getting down to business, reinforcing the goal orientation of the conversation. [3] In business communication, we often have a specific goal or series of points to address, but we cannot lose sight of the relationship messages within the discussion of content. You may signal to your conversation partner that there are three points to address, much like outlining an agenda at a meeting. This may sound formal at first, but if you listen to casual conversations you'll often find there is an inherent list or central point where the conversational partners arrive. By clearly articulating, either in written or oral

form, the main points, you provide an outline or structure to the conversation.

Feedback

Similar to a preview step, this stage allows the conversational partners to clarify, restate, or discuss the points of the conversation to arrive a sense of mutual understanding. In some cultures the points and their feedback may recycle several times, which may sound repetitious to Western ears. In Western cultures we often get to the point rather quickly and once we've arrived at an understanding, we move quickly to the conclusion. Communication across cultures often requires additional cycles of statement and restatement to insure transmission of information as well as reinforcement of the relationship. Time may be money in some cultures, but time is also a representation of respect. Feedback is an opportunity to make sure the interaction was successful the first time. Failure to attend to this stage can lead to the need for additional interactions, reducing efficiency across time.

Closing

The acceptance of feedback on both sides of the conversation often signals the transition to the conclusion of the conversation. Closings are similar to the initiation step, [4] and often involve ritual norms. [5] Verbal clues are sometimes present, but you may also notice the half step back as conversational partners create additional space in preparation to disengage.

There are times when a conversational partner introduces new information in the conclusion, which can start the process all over again. You may also note that if words like "in conclusion" or "oh—one more thing" are used, a set of expectations is now in force. A conclusion has been announced and the listener expects it. If the speaker continues to recycle at this point, the listener's listening skills are often not as keen as they were during the heat of the main engagement, and it may even produce frustration. People mentally shift to the next order of business and this transition must be negotiated successfully.

By mentioning a time, date, or place for future communication you can clearly signal that the conversation, although currently concluded, will continue later. In this way, you can often disengage successfully while demonstrating respect.

Employment Interviewing

We all join communities, teams, and groups across our lifetimes. [6] We go from an unknown outsider to a new member and eventually a full member. Businesses and organizations are communities consisting of teams and groups, and if we decide to switch teams or communities, or if that decision is made for us with a reduction in force layoff, for example, we'll be back on the job market. In order to make the transition from an outsider to an insider, you'll have to pass a series of tests, both informal and formal. One of the most common tests is otherwise known as an employment interview. An employment interview is an exchange between a candidate and a prospective employer (or their representative). It is a formal process with several consistent elements that you can use to guide your preparation.

Employment interviews come in all shapes and sizes, and may not be limited to only one exchange but one interaction. A potential employee may very well be screened by a computer (as the résumé is scanned) and interviewed online or via the telephone before the applicant ever meets a representative or panel of representatives. The screening process may include formal tests that include personality tests, background investigations, and consultations with previous employers. Depending on the type of job you are seeking, you can anticipate answering questions, often more than once, to a series of people as you progress through a formal interview process. Just as you have the advantage of preparing for a speech with anticipation, you can apply the same research and public speaking skills to the employment interview.

The invitation to interview means you have been identified as a candidate who meets the minimum qualifications and demonstrate potential as a viable candidate. Your cover letter, résumé, or related application materials may demonstrate the connection between your preparation and the job duties, but now comes the moment where you will need to articulate those points out loud.

If we assume that you would like to be successful in your employment interviewing, then it makes sense to use the communication skills gained to date with the knowledge of interpersonal communication to maximize your performance. There is no one right or wrong way to prepare and present at your interview, just as each audience is unique, but we can prepare and anticipate several common elements.

Preparation

The right frame of mind is an essential element for success in communication, oral or written. For many if not most, the employment interview is surrounded with mystery and a degree of fear and trepidation. Just as giving a speech may produce a certain measure of anxiety, you can expect that a job interview will make you nervous. Anticipate this normal response, and use your nervous energy to your benefit. To place your energies where they will be put to best use, the first step is preparation.

Would you prepare yourself before writing for publication or speaking in public? Of course. The same preparation applies to the employment interview. Briefly, the employment interview is a conversational exchange (even if it is in writing at first) where the participants try to learn more about each other. Both conversational partners will have goals in terms of content, and explicitly or implicitly across the conversational exchange will be relational messages. Attending to both points will strengthen your performance. On the content side, if you have been invited for an interview, you can rest assured that you have met the basic qualifications the employer is looking for. Hopefully, this initiation signal means that the company or organization you have thoroughly researched is one you would consider as a potential employer. Perhaps you have involved colleagues and current employees of the organization in your research process and learned about several of the organization's attractive qualities as well as some of the challenges experienced by the people working there.

Businesses hire people to solve problems, so you will want to focus on how your talents, expertise, and experience can contribute to the organization's need to solve those problems. The more detailed your analysis of their current challenges, the better. You need to be prepared for standard questions about your education and background, but also see the opening in the conversation to discuss the job duties, the challenges inherent in the job, and the ways in which you believe you can meet these challenges. Take the opportunity to demonstrate the fact that you have "done your homework" in researching the company. Table 16.1 "Interview Preparation Checklist" presents a checklist of what you should try to know before you consider yourself prepared for an interview.

Table 16.1 Interview Preparation Checklist

What to Know	Examples
Type of Interview	Will it be a behavioral interview, where the employer watches what you do in a given situation? Will you be asked technical questions or given a work sample? Or will you be interviewed over lunch or coffee, where your table manners and social skills will be assessed?
Type of Dress	Office attire varies by industry, so stop by the workplace and observe what workers are wearing if you can. If this isn't possible, call and ask the human resources office what to wear—they will appreciate your wish to be prepared.
Company or Organization	Do a thorough exploration of the company's Web site. If it doesn't have one, look for business listings in the community online and in the phone directory. Contact the local chamber of commerce. At your library, you may have access to subscription sites such as Hoover's Online (http://www.hoovers.com).
Job	Carefully read the ad you answered that got you the interview, and memorize what it says about the job and the qualifications the employer is seeking. Use the Internet to find sample job descriptions for your target job title. Make a written list of the job tasks and annotate the list with your skills, knowledge, and other attributes that will enable you to perform the job tasks with excellence.
Employer's Needs	Check for any items in the news in the past couple of years involving the company name. If it is a small company, the local town newspaper will be your best source. In addition, look for any advertisements the company has placed, as these can give a good indication of the company's goals.

Performance

You may want to know how to prepare for an employment interview, and we're going to take it for granted that you have researched the company, market, and even individuals in your effort to learn more about the opportunity. From this solid base of preparation, you need to begin to prepare your responses. Would you like some of the test questions before the test? Luckily for you, employment interviews involve a degree of uniformity across their many representations. Here are eleven common questions you are likely to be asked in an employment interview: [7]

1.   Tell me about yourself.
2.   Have you ever done this type of work before?
3.   Why should we hire you?
4.   What are your greatest strengths? Weaknesses?
5.   Give me an example of a time when you worked under pressure.
6.   Tell me about a time you encountered (X) type of problem at work. How did you solve the problem?
7.   Why did you leave your last job?
8.   How has your education and/or experience prepared you for this job?

9. Why do you want to work here?
10. What are your long-range goals? Where do you see yourself three years from now?
11. Do you have any questions?

When you are asked a question in the interview, look for its purpose as well as its literal meaning. "Tell me about yourself" may sound like an invitation for you to share your text message win in last year's competition, but it is not. The employer is looking for someone who can address their needs. Telling the interviewer about yourself is an opportunity for you make a positive professional impression. Consider what experience you can highlight that aligns well with the job duties and match your response to their needs. In the same way, responses about your strengths are not an opening to brag, and your weakness not an invitation to confess. If your weakness is a tendency towards perfectionism, and the job you are applying for involves a detail orientation, you can highlight how your weaknesses may serve you well in the position.

Consider using the "because" response whenever you can. A "because" response involves the restatement of the question followed by a statement of how and where you gained education or experience in that area. For example, if you are asked about handling difficult customers, you could answer that you have significant experience in that area because you've served as a customer service representative with X company for X years. You may be able to articulate how you were able to turn an encounter with a frustrated customer into a long-term relationship that benefited both the customer and the organization. Your specific example, and use of a "because" response, can increase the likelihood that the interviewer or audience will recall the specific information you provide.

You may be invited to participate in a conference call, and be told to expect it will last around twenty minutes. The telephone carries your voice and your words, but doesn't carry your nonverbal gestures. If you remember to speak directly into the telephone, look up and smile, your voice will come through clearly and you will sound competent and pleasant. Whatever you do, don't take the call on a cell phone with an iffy connection—your interviewers are guaranteed to be unfavorably impressed if you keep breaking up during the call. Use the phone to your advantage by preparing responses on note cards or on your computer screen before the call. When the interviewers ask you questions, keep track of the time, limiting each response to about a minute. If you know that a twenty-minute call is scheduled for a certain time, you can anticipate that your phone may ring may be a minute or two late, as interviews are often scheduled in a series while

the committee is all together at one time. Even if you only have one interview, your interviewers will have a schedule and your sensitivity to it can help improve your performance. You can also anticipate that the last few minutes will be set aside for you to ask your questions. This is your opportunity to learn more about the problems or challenges that the position will be addressing, allowing you a final opportunity to reinforce a positive message with the audience. Keep your questions simple, your attitude positive, and communicate your interest.

At the same time as you are being interviewed, know that you too are interviewing the prospective employer. If you have done your homework you may already know what the organization is all about, but you may still be unsure whether it is the right fit for you. Listen and learn from what is said as well as what is not said, and you will add to your knowledge base for wise decision making in the future.

Above all, be honest, positive, and brief. You may have heard that the world is small and it is true. As you develop professionally, you will come to see how fields, organizations, and companies are interconnected in ways that you cannot anticipate. Your name and reputation are yours to protect and promote.

Postperformance

You completed your research of the organization, interviewed a couple of employees, learned more about the position, were on time for the interview (virtual or in person), wore neat and professional clothes, and demonstrated professionalism in your brief, informative responses. Congratulations are in order, but so is more work on your part.

Remember that feedback is part of the communication process: follow up promptly with a thank-you note or e-mail, expressing your appreciation for the interviewer's time and interest. You may also indicate that you will call or e-mail next week to see if they have any further questions for you. (Naturally, if you say you will do this, make sure you follow through!) In the event that you have decided the position is not right for you, the employer will appreciate your notifying them without delay. Do this tactfully, keeping in mind that communication occurs between individuals and organizations in ways you cannot predict.

After you have communicated with your interviewer or committee, move on. Candidates sometimes become quite fixated on one position or job and fail to keep their options open. The best person does not always get the job, and the prepared business communicator knows that networking and research is a never-ending, ongoing process. Look over the horizon at the next challenge and begin your research process again. It may be hard work, but getting a job is your job. Budget time and plan on the effort it will take to make the next contact, get the next interview, and continue to explore alternate paths to your goal.

You may receive a letter, note, or voice mail explaining that another candidate's combination of experience and education better matched the job description. If this happens, it is only natural for you to feel disappointed. It is also only natural to want to know why you were not chosen, but be aware that for legal reasons most rejection notifications do not go into detail about why one candidate was hired and another was not. Contacting the company with a request for an explanation can be counterproductive, as it may be interpreted as a "sore loser" response. If there is any possibility that they will keep your name on file for future opportunities, you want to preserve your positive relationship.

Although you feel disappointed, don't focus on the loss or all the hard work you've produced. Instead, focus your energies where they will serve you best. Review the process and learn from the experience, knowing that each audience is unique and even the most prepared candidate may not have been the right "fit." Stay positive and connect with people you who support you. Prepare, practice, and perform. Know that you as a person are far more than just a list of job duties. Focus on your skill sets: if they need improvement, consider additional education that will enhance you knowledge and skills. Seek out local resources and keep networking. Have your professional interview attire clean and ready, and focus on what you can control—your preparation and performance.

KEY TAKEAWAY

Conversations have universal aspects we can predict and improve. We can use the dynamics of the ritual of conversation to learn to prepare for employment interviews and evaluations, both common contexts of communication in the work environment. Employment interviews involve preparation, performance, and feedback.

EXERCISES

1. How does the employment interview serve both interviewer and interviewee? Explain and present your thoughts to the class.
2. Identify a company that you might be interested in working for. Use the resources described in this section to research information about the company, the kinds of

jobs it hires people to do, and the needs and goals of the organization. Share your findings with your classmates.
3. Find a job announcement of a position that might interest you after you graduate or reach your professional goal. Write a brief statement of what experience and education you currently have that applies to the position and note what you currently lack.
4. What are the common tasks and duties of a job you find interesting? Create a survey, identify people who hold a similar position, and interview them (via e-mail or in person). Compare your results with your classmates.
5. What has been your employment interview experience to date? Write a brief statement and provide examples.
6. What employment-related resources are available on your campus or in your community? Investigate and share your findings.
7. Prepare for a job that you would like to do by finding a job announcement, preparing sample responses, and enlisting a friend or colleague in playing the role of a mock interviewer. Limit your interview to fifteen minutes and record it (audio or audio/visual) and post it in class. If your instructor indicates this exercise will be an in-class exercise or assessment, dress the part and be completely prepared. Use this exercise to prepare you for the moment when you will be required to perform and when you want the job.

[1] Beebe, S. [Steven], Beebe, S. [Susan], & Redmond, M. (2002). *Interpersonal communication relating to others* (3rd ed.). Boston, MA: Allyn & Bacon.
[2] Malinowski, B. (1935). *The language and magic of gardening*. London, England: Allen & Unwin.
[3] DeVito, J. (2003). *Messages: Building interpersonal skills*. Boston, MA: Allyn & Bacon.
[4] Knapp, M., & Vangelisti, A. (2000). *Interpersonal communication and relationships* (4th ed.). Boston: Allyn & Bacon.
[5] Malinowski, B. (1935). *The language and magic of gardening*. London, England: Allen & Unwin.
[6] McLean, S. (2005). *The basics of interpersonal communication*. Boston, MA: Allyn & Bacon.
[7] McLean, S. (2005). *The basics of interpersonal communication*. Boston, MA: Allyn & Bacon.

16.6 Conflict in the Work Environment
LEARNING OBJECTIVE

1. Understand evaluations and criticism in the workplace, and discuss several strategies for resolving workplace conflict.

The word "conflict" produces a sense of anxiety for many people, but it is part of the human experience. Just because conflict is universal does not mean that we cannot improve how we handle disagreements, misunderstandings, and struggles to understand or make ourselves understood. Joyce

Hocker and William Wilmot [1] offer us several principles on conflict that have been adapted here for our discussion:

- Conflict is universal.
- Conflict is associated with incompatible goals.
- Conflict is associated with scarce resources.
- Conflict is associated with interference.
- Conflict is not a sign of a poor relationship.
- Conflict cannot be avoided.
- Conflict cannot always be resolved.
- Conflict is not always bad.

Conflict is the physical or psychological struggle associated with the perception of opposing or incompatible goals, desires, demands, wants, or needs. [2] When incompatible goals, scarce resources, or interference are present, conflict is a typical result, but it doesn't mean the relationship is poor or failing. All relationships progress through times of conflict and collaboration. How we navigate and negotiate these challenges influences, reinforces, or destroys the relationship. Conflict is universal, but how and when it occurs is open to influence and interpretation. Rather than viewing conflict from a negative frame of reference, view it as an opportunity for clarification, growth, and even reinforcement of the relationship.

Conflict Management Strategies

As professional communicators, we can acknowledge and anticipate that conflict will be present in every context or environment where communication occurs. To that end, we can predict, anticipate, and formulate strategies to address conflict successfully. How you choose to approach conflict influences its resolution. Joseph DeVito [3] offers us several conflict management strategies that we have adapted and expanded for our use.

Avoidance

You may choose to change the subject, leave the room, or not even enter the room in the first place, but the conflict will remain and resurface when you least expect it. Your reluctance to address the conflict directly is a normal response, and one which many cultures prize. In cultures where independence is highly valued, direct confrontation is more common. In cultures where the community is emphasized over the individual, indirect strategies may be more common. Avoidance allows for more time to resolve the problem, but can also increase costs associated with problem in the first place. Your organization or business will have policies and protocols to follow regarding conflict and redress, but it is always wise to consider the position of your conversational partner or opponent and to give them, as well as yourself, time to explore alternatives.

Defensiveness versus Supportiveness

Jack Gibb [4] discussed defensive and supportive communication interactions as part of his analysis of conflict management. Defensive communication is characterized by control, evaluation, and judgments, while supportive communication focuses on the points and not personalities. When we feel judged or criticized, our ability to listen can be diminished, and we may only hear the negative message. By choosing to focus on the message instead of the messenger, we keep the discussion supportive and professional.

Face-Detracting and Face-Saving

Communication is not competition. Communication is the sharing of understanding and meaning, but does everyone always share equally? People struggle for control, limit access to resources and information as part of territorial displays, and otherwise use the process of communication to engage in competition. People also use communication for collaboration. Both competition and collaboration can be observed in communication interactions, but there are two concepts central to both: face-detracting and face-saving strategies.

Face-detracting strategies involve messages or statements that take away from the respect, integrity, or credibility of a person. Face-saving strategies protect credibility and separate message from messenger. For example, you might say that "sales were down this quarter," without specifically noting who was responsible. Sales were simply down. If, however, you ask, "How does the sales manager explain the decline in sales?" you have specifically connected an individual with the negative news. While we may want to specifically connect tasks and job responsibilities to individuals and departments, in terms of language each strategy has distinct results.

Face-detracting strategies often produce a defensive communication climate, inhibit listening, and allow for little room for collaboration. To save face is to raise the issue while preserving a supportive climate, allowing room in the conversation for constructive discussions and problem solving. By using a face-saving strategy to shift the emphasis from the individual to the issue, we avoid power struggles and personalities, providing each other space to save face. [5]

In collectivist cultures, where the community's well-being is promoted or valued above that of the individual, face-saving strategies are a common communicative strategies. In Japan, for example, to confront someone directly is perceived as humiliation, a great insult. In the United States, greater emphasis is placed on individual performance, and responsibility may be more directly assessed. If our goal is to solve a problem, and preserve the relationship, then consideration of a face-saving strategy should be one option a skilled business communicator considers when addressing negative news or information.

Empathy

Communication involves not only the words we write or speak, but how and when we write or say them. The way we communicate also carries meaning, and empathy for the individual involves attending to this aspect of interaction. Empathetic listening involves listening to both the literal and implied meanings within a message. For example, the implied meaning might involve understanding what has led this person to feel this way. By paying attention to feelings and emotions associated with content and information, we can build relationships and address conflict more constructively. In management, negotiating conflict is a common task and empathy is one strategy to consider when attempting to resolve issues.

Gunnysacking

George Bach and Peter Wyden [6] discuss gunnysacking (or backpacking) as the imaginary bag we all carry into which we place unresolved conflicts or grievances over time. If your organization has gone through a merger, and your business has transformed, there may have been conflicts that occurred during the transition. Holding onto the way things used to be can be like a stone in your gunnysack, and influence how you interpret your current context.

People may be aware of similar issues but might not know your history, and cannot see your backpack or its contents. For example, if your previous manager handled issues in one way, and your new manage handles them in a different way, this may cause you some degree of stress and frustration. Your new manager cannot see how the relationship existed in the past, but will still observe the tension. Bottling up your frustrations only hurts you and can cause your current relationships to suffer. By addressing, or unpacking, the stones you carry, you can better assess the current situation with the current patterns and variables.

We learn from experience, but can distinguish between old wounds and current challenges, and try to focus our energies where they will make the most positive impact.

Managing Your Emotions

Have you ever seen red, or perceived a situation through rage, anger, or frustration? Then you know that you cannot see or think clearly when you are experiencing strong emotions. There will be times in the work environment when emotions run high. Your awareness of them can help you clear your mind and choose to wait until the moment has passed to tackle the challenge.

"Never speak or make decision in anger" is one common saying that holds true, but not all emotions involve fear, anger, or frustration. A job loss can be a sort of professional death for many, and the sense of loss can be profound. The loss of a colleague to a layoff while retaining your position can bring pain as well as relief, and a sense of survivor's guilt. Emotions can be contagious in the workplace, and fear of the unknown can influence people to act in irrational ways. The wise business communicator can recognize when emotions are on edge in themselves or others, and choose to wait to communicate, problem-solve, or negotiate until after the moment has passed.

Evaluations and Criticism in the Workplace

Mary Ellen Guffey wisely notes that Xenophon, a Greek philosopher, once said, "The sweetest of all sounds is praise." [7] We have seen previously that appreciation, respect, inclusion, and belonging are all basic human needs across all contexts, and are particularly relevant in the workplace. Efficiency and morale are positively related, and recognition of good work is important. There may come a time, however, when evaluations involve criticism. Knowing how to approach this criticism can give you peace of mind to listen clearly, separating subjective, personal attacks from objective, constructive requests for improvement. Guffey offers us seven strategies for giving and receiving evaluations and criticism in the workplace that we have adapted here.

Listen without Interrupting

If you are on the receiving end of an evaluation, start by listening without interruption. Interruptions can be internal and external, and warrant further discussion. If your supervisor starts to discuss a point and you immediately start debating the point in your mind, you are paying attention to yourself and what you think they said or are going to say, and not that which is actually communicated. This gives rise to misunderstandings and will cause you to lose valuable information you need to understand and address the issue at hand.

External interruptions may involve your attempt to get a word in edgewise, and may change the course of the conversation. Let them speak while you listen, and if you need to take notes to focus your thoughts, take clear notes of what is said, also noting points to revisit later. External interruptions can also take the form of a telephone ringing, a "text message has arrived" chime, or a coworker dropping by in the middle of the conversation.

As an effective business communicator, you know all too well to consider the context and climate of the communication interaction when approaching the delicate subject of evaluations or criticism. Choose a time and place free from interruption. Choose one outside the common space where there may be many observers. Turn off your cell phone. Choose face-to-face communication instead of an impersonal e-mail. By providing a space free of interruption, you are displaying respect for the individual and the information.

Determine the Speaker's Intent

We have discussed previews as a normal part of conversation, and in this context they play an important role. People want to know what is coming and generally dislike surprises, particularly when the context of an evaluation is present. If you are on the receiving end, you may need to ask a clarifying question if it doesn't count as an interruption. You may also need to take notes and write down questions that come to mind to address when it is your turn to speak. As a manager, be clear and positive in your opening and lead with praise. You can find one point, even if it is only that the employee consistently shows up to work on time, to highlight before transitioning to a performance issue.

Indicate You Are Listening

In mainstream U.S. culture, eye contact is a signal that you are listening and paying attention to the person speaking. Take notes, nod your head, or lean forward to display interest and listening. Regardless of whether you are the employee receiving the criticism or the supervisor delivering it, displaying listening behavior engenders a positive climate that helps mitigate the challenge of negative news or constructive criticism.

Paraphrase

Restate the main points to paraphrase what has been discussed. This verbal display allows for clarification and acknowledges receipt of the message.

If you are the employee, summarize the main points and consider steps you will take to correct the situation. If none come to mind or you are nervous and are having a hard time thinking clearly, state out loud the main point and ask if you can provide solution steps and strategies at a later date. You can request a follow-up meeting if appropriate, or indicate you will respond in writing via e-mail to provide the additional information.

If you are the employer, restate the main points to ensure that the message was received, as not everyone hears everything that is said or discussed the first time it is presented. Stress

can impair listening, and paraphrasing the main points can help address this common response.

If You Agree

If an apology is well deserved, offer it. Communicate clearly what will change or indicate when you will respond with specific strategies to address the concern. As a manager you will want to formulate a plan that addresses the issue and outlines responsibilities as well as time frames for corrective action. As an employee you will want specific steps you can both agree on that will serve to solve the problem. Clear communication and acceptance of responsibility demonstrates maturity and respect.

If You Disagree

If you disagree, focus on the points or issue and not personalities. Do not bring up past issues and keep the conversation focused on the task at hand. You may want to suggest, now that you better understand their position, a follow-up meeting to give you time to reflect on the issues. You may want to consider involving a third party, investigating to learn more about the issue, or taking time to cool off.

Do not respond in anger or frustration; instead, always display professionalism. If the criticism is unwarranted, consider that the information they have may be flawed or biased, and consider ways to learn more about the case to share with them, searching for a mutually beneficial solution. If other strategies to resolve the conflict fail, consider contacting your human resources department to learn more about due process procedures at your workplace. Display respect and never say anything that would reflect poorly on yourself or your organization. Words spoken in anger can have a lasting impact and are impossible to retrieve or take back.

Learn from Experience

Every communication interaction provides an opportunity for learning if you choose to see it. Sometimes the lessons are situational and may not apply in future contexts. Other times the lessons learned may well serve you across your professional career. Taking notes for yourself to clarify your thoughts, much like a journal, serve to document and help you see the situation more clearly.

Recognize that some aspects of communication are intentional, and may communicate meaning, even if it is hard to understand. Also, know that some aspects of communication are unintentional, and may not imply meaning or design. People make mistakes. They say things they should not have said. Emotions are revealed that are not always rational, and not always associated with the current context. A challenging morning at home can spill over into the work day and someone's bad mood may have nothing to do with you.

Try to distinguish between what you can control and what you cannot, and always choose professionalism.

KEY TAKEAWAY

Conflict is unavoidable and can be opportunity for clarification, growth, and even reinforcement of the relationship.

EXERCISES

1. Write a description of a situation you recall where you came into conflict with someone else. It may be something that happened years ago, or a current issue that just arose. Using the principles and strategies in this section, describe how the conflict was resolved, or could have been resolved. Discuss your ideas with your classmates.

2. Of the strategies for managing conflict described in this section, which do you think are the most effective? Why? Discuss your opinions with a classmate.

3. Can you think of a time when a conflict led to a new opportunity, better understanding, or other positive result? If not, think of a past conflict and imagine a positive outcome. Write a two- to three-paragraph description of what happened, or what you imagine could happen. Share your results with a classmate.

[1] Hocker, J., & Wilmot, W. (1991). *Interpersonal conflict*. Dubuque, IA: Willam C. Brown.

[2] McLean, S. (2005). *The basics of interpersonal communication*. Boston, MA: Allyn & Bacon.

[3] DeVito, J. (2003). *Messages: Building interpersonal skills*. Boston, MA: Allyn & Bacon.

[4] Gibb, J. (1961). Defensive and supportive communication. *Journal of Communication, 11*, 141–148.

[5] Donohue, W., & Klot, R. (1992). *Managing interpersonal conflict*. Thousand Oaks, CA: Sage.

[6] Bach, G., & Wyden, P. (1968). *The intimate enemy: How to fight fair in love and marriage*. New York, NY: Avon.

[7] Guffey, M. (2008). *Essentials of business communication* (7th ed., p. 320). Mason, OH: Thomson/Wadsworth.

16.7 Additional Resources

- A Literaryzone article describes the literary devices of internal monologue and stream of consciousness. http://literaryzone.com/?p=79

- For another twist on the meaning of "stream of consciousness," visit this blog from the retail merchant Gaiam. http://blog.gaiam.com

- Read an informative article on self-concept and self-esteem by Arash Farzaneh. http://psychology.suite101.com/article.cfm/impact_of_selfconcept_and_selfesteem_on_life

- PsyBlog offers an informative article on self-disclosure. Don't miss the readers' comments at the end! http://www.spring.org.uk/2007/02/getting-closer-art-of-self-disclosure.php

- The job search site Monster.com offers a menu of articles about employment interviews. http://career-advice.monster.com/job-interview/careers.aspx

- About.com offers an informative article about different types of job interviews. http://jobsearch.about.com/od/interviewsnetworking/a/interviewtypes.htm

- The Boston Globe's Boston.com site offers tips on handling conflict in the workplace from management consultant Sue Lankton-Rivas. http://www.boston.com/jobs/galleries/workplaceconflict

NOTES:

Chapter 17:
Negative News and Crisis Communication

You don't hear things that are bad about your company unless you ask.
It is easy to hear good tidings, but you have to scratch to get the bad news.
   Thomas J. Watson Sr.
One day, today, is worth two tomorrows.
   Anonymous

Getting Started

INTRODUCTORY EXERCISES

1. Write a brief description of an experience when someone shared negative news with you in person or in writing. How was it presented? How was it delivered? How did it make you feel? After all this time, how do you still feel about it? Share your response and compare with classmates.
2. Write a brief description of an experience when you shared negative news with someone in person or in writing. How did you present it? How did you deliver it? How did you feel, and what was your perception of how it was received? How do you feel about it now? How do you perceive the recipient of the negative news may feel about it today? Share your response and compare with classmates.
3. Locate the emergency plan where you work or go to school. What would you do in the case of an emergency? Discuss with classmates.
4. Can you think of one company that has had a scandal, a major problem, or a crisis in the last year? Indicate the company and your perception of how the situation was handled. Discuss with classmates.
5. Find five examples of press conferences and create a table with the product or service and the message.
6. From Introductory Exercise 5, add a third and fourth column to your table, noting whether you thought the message was effective or ineffective.

Communication is constant, but is it always effective? In times of confusion or crisis, clear and concise communication takes on an increased level of importance. When an emergency arises, rumors can spin out of control, emotions can run high, feelings can be hurt, and in some cases lives can tragically be lost. In this chapter we will examine several scenarios in which negative news is delivered or received, and examine ways to improve communication. We will conclude with a discussion of a formal crisis communication plan. Whether you anticipate the necessity of being the bearer of unpleasant or bad news, or a sudden and unexpected crisis occurs, your thoughtful preparation can make all the difference.

17.1 Delivering a Negative News Message
LEARNING OBJECTIVES

1. List and discuss seven goals of a negative news message.
2. Write an effective negative news message.

The negative news message delivers news that the audience does not want to hear, read, or receive. Delivering negative news is never easy. Whether you are informing someone they are being laid off or providing constructive criticism on their job performance, how you choose to deliver the message can influence its response. [1] Some people prefer their bad news to be direct and concise. Others may prefer a less direct approach. Regardless whether you determine a direct or indirect approach is warranted, your job is to deliver news that you anticipate will be unwelcome, unwanted, and possibly dismissed.

In this section we will examine several scenarios that can be communicated internally (within the organization) and externally (outside the organization), but recognize that the lines can be blurred as communication flows outside and through an organization or business. Internal and external communication environments often have a degree of overlap. The rumor of anticipated layoffs may surface in the local media, and you may be called upon to address the concern within the organization. In a similar way, a product that has failed internal quality control tests will require several more tests and improvements before it is ready for market, but if that information leaves the organization, it can hurt the business reputation, prospects for future contracts, and the company's ability to secure financing.

Communication is constantly present, and our ability to manage, clarify, and guide understanding is key to addressing challenges while maintaining trust and integrity with employees, stakeholders, and the public.

There are seven goals to keep in mind when delivering negative news, in person or in written form:
1. Be clear and concise in order not to require additional clarification.
2. Help the receiver understand and accept the news.

3. Maintain trust and respect for the business or organization and for the receiver.
4. Avoid legal liability or erroneous admission of guilt or culpability.
5. Maintain the relationship, even if a formal association is being terminated.
6. Reduce the anxiety associated with the negative news to increase comprehension.
7. Achieve the designated business outcome.

Let's examine our first scenario:
You are a supervisor and have been given the task of discussing repeated tardiness with an employee, Chris. Chris has frequently been late for work, and the problem has grown worse over the last two weeks. The tardiness is impairing not only Chris's performance, but also that of the entire work team. Your manager has instructed you to put an end to it. The desired result is for Chris to stop his tardiness behavior and improve his performance.

You can:
1. stop by Chris's cubicle and simply say, "Get to work on time or you are out";
2. invite Chris out to a nice lunch and let him have it;
3. write Chris a stern e-mail;
4. ask Chris to come to your office and discuss the behavior with him in private.

While there are many other ways you could choose to address the situation, let's examine each of these four alternatives in light of the goals to keep in mind when presenting negative news.

First, you could approach Chris in his work space and speak to him directly. Advantages include the ability to get right to the point right away. Disadvantages include the strain on the supervisor-employee relationship as a result of the public display of criticism, the possibility that Chris may not understand you, the lack of a formal discussion you can document, and the risk that your actions may not bring about the desired results.

The goals include the desire to be clear and concise in order not to require additional clarification. This possible response does not provide the opportunity for discussion, feedback, or confirmation that Chris has clearly understood your concern. It fails to address the performance concern, and limits the correction to the tardiness. It fails to demonstrate respect for all parties. The lack of tact apparent in the approach may reflect negatively on you as the supervisor, not only with Chris but with your manager as well.

When you need to speak to an employee about a personnel concern, it is always best to do it in private. Give thought and concern to the conversation before it occurs, and make a list of points to cover with specific information, including grievances. Like any other speech, you may need to rehearse, particularly if this type of meeting is new to you. When it comes time to have the discussion, issue the warning, back it up in writing with documentation, and don't give the impression that you might change your decision. Whether the issue at hand is a simple caution about tardiness or a more serious conversation, you need to be fair and respectful, even if the other person has been less than professional. Let's examine the next alternative.

Let's say you invite Chris to lunch at a nice restaurant. There is linen on the table, silverware is present for more than the main course, and the water glasses have stems. The environment says "good job" in its uniqueness, presentation, and luxury. Your word will contradict this nonverbal message. The juxtaposition between the environment and the verbal message will cause tension and confusion, which will probably be an obstacle to the receiver's ability to listen. If Chris doesn't understand the message, and the message requires clarification, your approach has failed. The contrast between the restaurant setting and the negative message does not promote understanding and acceptance of the bad news or correction. Furthermore, it does not build trust in the relationship, as the restaurant invitation might be interpreted as a "trap" or a betrayal. Let's examine yet another approach.

You've written Chris a stern e-mail. You've included a list of all the recent dates when he was late and made several statements about the quality of his work. You've indicated he needs to improve, and stop being late, or else. But was your e-mail harassment? Could it be considered beyond the scope of supervision and interpreted as mean or cruel? And do you even know if Chris has received it? If there was no reply, do you know whether it achieved its desired business outcome? A written message may certainly be part of the desired approach, but how it is presented and delivered is as important as what it says. Let's examine our fourth approach to this scenario.

You ask Chris to join you in a private conversation. You start the conversation with an expression of concern and an open-ended question: "Chris, I've been concerned about your work lately. Is everything all right?" As Chris answers, you may demonstrate that you are listening by nodding your head, and possibly taking notes. You may learn that Chris has been having problems sleeping, or that his living situation has changed. Or Chris may decline to share any issues, deny that anything is wrong, and ask why you are concerned. You may then state that you've observed the chronic tardiness, and name one or more specific mistakes you have found in Chris's work, ending with a reiteration that you are concerned. This statement of concern may elicit more responses and open the conversation up into a dialogue where you come to understand the situation, Chris sees your concern, and the relationship is preserved. Alternatively, in case the conversation does not go well, you will still keep a positive attitude even as you document the meeting and give Chris a verbal warning.

Regardless of how well or poorly the conversation goes, if Chris tells other employees about it, they will take note of how you handled the situation, and it will contribute to their perception of you. It guides their expectations of how you operate and how to communicate with you, as this interaction is not only about you and Chris. You represent the company and its reputation, and your professional display of concern as you try to learn more sends a positive message. While the private, respectful meeting may not be the perfect solution, it is preferable to the other approaches we have considered.

One additional point to consider as you document this interaction is the need to present the warning in writing. You may elect to prepare a memo that outlines the information concerning Chris's performance and tardiness and have it ready should you want to present it. If the session goes well, and you have the discretion to make a judgment call, you may elect to give him another week to resolve the issue. Even if it goes well, you may want to present the memo, as it documents the interaction and serves as evidence of due process should Chris's behavior fail to change, eventually resulting in the need for termination.

This combined approach of a verbal and written message is increasingly the norm in business communication. In the next two sections, we'll compare and contrast approaches, verbal and written, and outline several best practices in terms of approach. But first, we'll outline the four main parts of a negative news message:
1. Buffer or cushion
2. Explanation
3. Negative news
4. Redirect

The first part of a negative news message, verbal or written, involves neutral or positive information. This sets the tone and often serves as a buffer or cushion for the information to come. Next, an explanation discusses why there is an issue in the first place. This may be relatively simple, quite complex, or uncomfortable. In a journal article titled "Further Conceptualization of Explanations in Negative

News Messages," [2] Mohan Limaye makes the clear case that not only is an explanation a necessary part of any negative news message, it is an ethical and moral requirement. While an explanation is important, never admit or imply responsibility without written authorization from your company cleared by legal counsel. The third part of the negative news message involves the bad news itself, and the emphasis here is on clarity and accuracy. Finally, the redirect may refocus attention on a solution strategy, an alternative, or the subsequent actions that will take place. Table 17.1 "Negative News Message Sample Script" provides an example that might apply in an external communication situation.

Table 17.1 Negative News Message Sample Script

Parts of the Negative News Message	Example
Buffer or Cushion	Thank you for your order. We appreciate your interest in our product.
Explanation	We are writing to let you know that this product has been unexpectedly popular, with over 10,000 requests on the day you placed your order.
Negative News	This unexpected increase in demand has resulted in a temporary out-of-stock/backorder situation. We will fulfill your order, received at 11:59 p.m. on 09/09/2009, in the order it was received.
Redirect	We anticipate that your product will ship next Monday. While you wait, we encourage you to consider using the enclosed $5 off coupon toward the purchase of any product in our catalog. We appreciate your business and want you to know that our highest priority is your satisfaction.

In Table 17.1 "Negative News Message Sample Script", the neutral or positive news comes first and introduces the customer to the overall topic. The explanation provides an indication of the purpose of the communication, while the negative message directly addresses how it affects the customer. The redirect discusses specific actions to take place. In this case, it also includes a solution strategy enhanced with a soft sell message, a subtle, low-pressure method of selling, cross-selling, or advertising a product or service. Whether you are delivering negative news in person or in writing, the four main parts of a negative message can help you meet all seven goals.

Before we move to the verbal and written delivery of the negative news message, we need to offer a word of counsel. You want to avoid legal problems when communicating bad news. You cannot always predict how others are going to respond, but you can prepare for and deliver your response in ways that lower the risk of litigation in four ways:

1. Avoid abusive language or behavior.
2. Avoid contradictions and absolutes.
3. Avoid confusion or misinterpretation.
4. Maintain respect and privacy.

Sarcasm, profanity, shouting, or abusive or derogatory language is an obstacle to clear communication. Furthermore, such language can be interpreted as defamatory, or harming the reputation of the person, possibly having a negative impact on their future earnings. In written form, it is called libel. If you say it out loud, it is called slander. While slander may be harder to prove, no defamatory remarks should be part of your negative news message. Cell phones increasingly serve to record conversations, and you simply never know if your words will come back to you in short order. Represent yourself, the business, and the receiver of your message with professionalism and avoid abusive or defamatory language.

You also want to avoid contradictions, as they only serve to invite debate. Make sure your information is consistent and in agreement with the general information in the conversation. If one part of the information stands out as a contradiction, its importance will be magnified in the context and distract from your main message. Don't provide more information that is necessary. Polarizing, absolute terms like "always" and "never" are often part of sweeping generalizations that are open to debate. Instead of saying, "You are always late," choose to say, "You were late sixteen times in May." To avoid confusion or misinterpretation, be precise and specific.

Always maintain respect and privacy. Making a negative statement about an employee in front of a group of coworkers can be considered ridicule or harm, and in the coming cases may be actionable and involve legal ramifications. In addition to the legal responsibility, you have the overall goal of demonstrating professionalism as you represent yourself and your company in maintaining the relationship with the employee, even if the end goal is termination. Employees have retaliated against their organizations in many ways, from discouraging remarks to vandalism and computer viruses. Your goal is to avoid such behavior, not out of fear, but out of professionalism and respect for yourself and your organization. Open lines of communication present in a relationship can help reduce the risk of relational deterioration or animosity. The sidebar below provides a checklist for delivering a negative message.

Negative Message Checklist

1. Clear goal in mind
2. Clear instructions from supervisor (legal counsel)
3. Clear understanding of message
4. Clear understanding of audience/reader
5. Clear understanding of procedure and protocol
6. Clear, neutral opening
7. Clear explanation without admission of guilt or culpability
8. Clear statement of impact or negative news
9. Clear redirect with no reminders of negative news
10. Clear results with acceptance or action on negative news

Presenting Negative News in Person

Most of us dislike conflict. It may be tempting to avoid face-to-face interaction for fear of confrontation, but delivering negative news in person can be quite effective, even necessary, in many business situations. When considering a one-on-one meeting or a large, formal meeting, consider the preparation and implementation of the discussion.

The first step involves a clear goal. Stephen Covey (1989) recommends beginning with the end in mind. [3] Do you want your negative news to inform, or to bring about change, and if so what kind of change and to what degree? A clear conceptualization of the goal allows you to anticipate the possible responses, to plan ahead, and to get your emotional "house" in order.

Your emotional response to the news and the audience, whether it is one person or the whole company, will set the tone for the entire interaction. You may feel frustrated, angry, or hurt, but the display of these emotions is often more likely to make the problem worse than to help solve it. Emotions can be contagious, and people will respond to the emotional tone of the speaker.

If your response involves only one other person, a private, personal meeting is the best option, but it may not be available. Increasingly people work and contribute to projects from a distance, via the Internet, and may only know each other via e-mail, phone, or videophone/videoconferencing services. A personal meeting may be impractical or impossible. How then does one deliver negative news in person? By the best option available to both parties. Written feedback may be an option via e-mail, but it takes time to prepare, send, receive, process, and respond—and the written word has its disadvantages. Miscommunication and misinterpretation can easily occur, with little opportunity for constructive feedback to check meanings and clarify perceptions.

The telephone call allows both parties to hear each other's voices, including the words, the inflection, the disfluencies, and the emotional elements of conversation. It is immediate in that the possibility of overlap is present, meaning not only is proximity in terms of voice as close as possible, but both parties may experience overlaps as they take turns and communicate. Telephone calls allow for quick feedback and clarification questions, and allow both parties an opportunity to recycle and revisit topics for elaboration or a better understanding. They also can cover long distances with reasonable clarity. Voice over Internet protocol (VoIP) allows you to do the same with relatively little cost.

While there are distinct advantages, the telephone lacks part of the nonverbal spectrum available to speakers in a live setting. On the telephone, proximity is a function of response time rather than physical space and the degree to which one person is near another. Time is also synchronous, though the telephone crosses time zones and changes the context as one party may have just arrived at work while the other party is leaving for lunch. Body language gets lost in the exchange as well, although many of us continue to make hand gestures on the phone, even when our conversational partners cannot see us. Paralanguage, or the sounds we hear that are not verbal, including pitch, tone, rate, rhythm, pace, articulation, and pronunciation are all available to the listener. As we can see, the telephone call allows for a richer communication experience than written communication, but cannot convey as much information as would be available in person. Just as a telephone interview may be used for screening purposes while a live interview is reserved for the final candidates, the live setting is often considered the best option for delivering negative news.

Live and in person may be the best option for direct communication with immediate feedback. In a live setting time is constant. The participants may schedule a breakfast meeting, for example, mirroring schedules and rhythms. Live, face-to-face communication comes in many forms. The casual exchange in the hallway, the conversation over coffee, and the formal performance review meeting all have interpersonal communication in common.

If you need to share the message with a larger audience, you may need to speak to a group, or you might even have to make a public presentation or speech. If it needs a feedback loop, we often call it a press conference, as the speech is followed by a question and answer session. From meeting in the hallway to live, onstage, under camera lights and ready for

questions, the personal delivery of negative news can be a challenging task.

Presenting Negative News in Writing

Writing can be intrapersonal, between two people, group communication, public communication, or even mass communication. One distinct advantage of presenting negative news in writing is the planning and preparation that goes into the message, making the initial communication more predictable. When a message is delivered orally in an interpersonal setting, we may interrupt each other, we sometimes hear what we want to, and it often takes negotiation and listening skills to grasp meaning. While a written message, like all messages, is open to interpretation, the range of possibilities is narrowed and presented within the frame and format designed by the source or author.

The written message involves verbal factors like language and word choice, but it can also involve nonverbal factors like timing and presentation. Do you communicate the message on letterhead, do you choose the channel of e-mail over a hard copy letter, or do you compose your written message in your best penmanship? Each choice communicates meaning, and the choice of how you present your written message influences its reception, interpretation, and the degree to which it is understood. In this section we consider the written message that delivers negative news.

Let's consider several scenarios:
1. A community disaster such as illness (e.g., a swine flu epidemic), earthquake, wildfire, plane crash, or a terrorism incident
2. An on-the-job accident with injuries or even death
3. A product defect resulting in injuries, illness, or even death to consumers
4. An unsuccessful product test (e.g., a new software system that isn't going to be ready for launch as planned)
5. A company merger that may result in reductions in force or layoffs

In business communication we often categorize our communication as internal or external. Internal communication is the sharing and understanding of meaning between individuals, departments, or representatives of the same business. External communication is the sharing and understanding of meaning between individuals, departments, or representatives of the business and parties outside the organization. Across the five scenarios we'll consider each of these categories in turn.

The confirmation of swine flu (H1N1) may first occur with a laboratory report (itself a written document), but it is normally preceded by conversations between health care professionals concerned over the symptoms exhibited by patients, including a high fever, a cough, sore throat, and a headache. According to Sally Redman, a registered nurse at Student Health Services at Washington State University–Pullman, over two thousand students (of nineteen thousand total student population) presented symptoms on or around August 21, 2009. [4]

Communication will predictably occur among students, health care professionals, and the community, but parents at a distance will want to know not only the status of their child, but also of the university. A written message that necessarily contains negative news may be written in the form of a press release, for example, noting important information like the number of students affected, the capacity of the health care system to respond, the experience to date, and whom to contact for further details and updates. This message will be read over and over as parents, reporters, and people across the country want to learn more about the situation. Like all business communication, it needs to be clear and concise.

Our next scenario offers a learning opportunity as well. An on-the-job accident affects employees and the company, and like our previous example, there will be considerable interest. There may be interpersonal communication between company representatives and the individual's family, but the company will want to communicate a clear record of the occurrence with an assurance, or statement that the contributing factors that gave rise to the situation has been corrected or were beyond the control of the company and its representatives.

In addition to a statement of record, and an assurance, the company will certainly want to avoid the implication or indication of guilt or culpability. In the case of a product defect resulting in injuries, illness, or even death to consumers, this will be a relevant point of consideration. Perhaps a voluntary recall will be ordered, proactively addressing the risk before an accident occurs. It may also be the case that the recall order is issued by a government agency. Again, a written statement delivering negative news, in this case the recall of a product that presents a risk, must be written with care and consultation of legal counsel.

If your company is publicly traded, the premature announcement of a software program full of bugs, or programming errors that result in less than perfect performance, can send the company's stock price plummeting. How you release this information within the organization will influence how it is received. If your written internal memo briefly states that the software program development process has been extended to incorporate additional improvements, the emphasis shifts from the negative to the positive. While the negative news, the delay of release, remains, the focus on the benefits of the additional time can influence employees' views, and can make a difference in how the message is received outside the organization.

The awareness of a merger, and the possibility of a reduction in force or layoffs, will be discussed along the grapevine at work, and will give rise to tension and anticipation of negative news. You could simply write a short memo "To All Employees," not include any contact information, and have an assistant walk around and place copies on everyone's chair or desk during the lunch hour. But let's look at the message this would send to employees. The written communication includes nonverbal aspects like timing and presentation as well as verbal aspects like language and word choice. The timing itself suggests avoidance of conflict, and a reluctance to address the issue with transparency. The presentation of a memo in hard copy form on your chair from an unidentified company representative will certainly cause confusion, may be mistaken for a prank, and could cause considerable stress. It will contribute to increased tensions rather than solidarity, and if trust is the foundation for all effective communication, it violates this principle.

Negative news may not be easy to deliver, but it is necessary at times and should be done with clarity and brevity. All parties should be clearly identified. The negative news itself should be clear and concise. The presentation should be direct, with authority and credibility. Communication occurs between people, and all humans experience concern, fear, and trepidation of the unknown. The negative news message, while it may be unwelcome, can bring light to an issue.
As we mentioned at the beginning of the chapter, some people prefer their bad news to be direct and concise, while others prefer a less direct approach. Let's weigh the pros and cons of each approach. Table 17.2 "Direct and Indirect Delivery" contrasts the elements of the two approaches.

The direct approach places the negative news at the beginning of the message, while the indirect approach packages the negative news between a positive introduction, sometimes called a "buffer" or cushion, and a conclusion. Your negative message may include the rationale or reasons for the decision.

The direct approach is often associated with a message where the audience values brevity and the message needs to be concise. A positive introduction often introduces the topic but not the outcome. An effective negative news statement clearly states the message while limiting the possibility of misinterpretation. An effective closing statement may provide reasons, reference a policy, or indicate a procedure to follow for more information.

Table 17.2 Direct and Indirect Delivery

Direct Delivery	Direct Example	Indirect Delivery	Indirect Example
		Positive introduction	Thank you for your request for leave.
Negative news message as introduction	Your request for leave has been denied.	Negative news message	We regret to inform you that your request has been denied.
Conclusion	Please contact your supervisor if you need more information.	Conclusion	Please contact your supervisor if you need more information.

KEY TAKEAWAY

Delivering negative news involves a buffer or cushion statement, an explanation, the negative news itself, and a redirecting statement. Whether you choose a direct or an indirect approach, the message should be delivered clearly and concisely, with respect for the receiver and the organization.

EXERCISES

1. When should you use an indirect approach in delivering a negative news message? Explain your answer to the class.
2. Ask five friends which they would prefer: negative news in a direct or indirect format? Why? Discuss your results with a classmate.
3. Sales have decreased for two consecutive quarters at your business. You have been instructed to inform your sales team that their hours, and base pay, will be reduced by 20 percent. While you may have a few members of your sales team that are underperforming, you want to retain the entire team. Write a negative news message in a direct or indirect approach informing your sales team of the news.
4. You have observed and documented an employee being late and taking long breaks for the past two weeks. Write out a brief summary of the conversation you need to have. You may be assigned to another classmate for a role-playing exercise. Share and compare with your classmates.

[1] Bovee, C., & Thill, J. (2010). *Business communication essentials: A skills-based approach to vital business English* (4th ed.). Upper Saddle River, NJ: Prentice Hall.
[2] Limaye, Mohan R. (1997, June 1). Further conceptualization of explanation in negative messages. *Business Communication Quarterly, 60*(2), 38–50.
[3] Covey, S. (1989). *The seven habits of highly effective people*. New York, NY: Simon & Schuster.
[4] Yardley, William. (2009, September 6). 2,000 Washington state students report signs of swine flu. *New York Times*. Retrieved from http://www.nytimes.com/2009/09/06/health/06flu.html?_r=1

17.2 Eliciting Negative News
LEARNING OBJECTIVES

1. Understand the importance of feedback, even if it is negative.
2. Describe and demonstrate the effective use of open- and closed-ended questions.

How do you know when you are doing a good job? How do you know when, where, and how you could do a better job? What makes the difference between a business or organization that is stagnant and one that is dynamic? Often the response to all these questions involves one key, but often overlooked, company resource: feedback. Feedback is the verbal and/or nonverbal response to a message, and that message may involve a company product or service.

Employee surveys, for example, may be completed online, in written form, in small focus groups, and can involve both oral and written communication. In the same way, customer satisfaction surveys may involve similar options and both provide a valuable opportunity to take a critical look at what we are doing, how it is perceived, and what areas we can identify for improvement. They often measure opinions, satisfaction, attitude, brand affiliation, preference, and engagement of customers and employees. In this section we will consider negative news as a valuable tool in self, team, company, product, and service improvement.

Across the years there have been extensive studies on how to improve businesses and companies, from Total Quality Improvement to the Six Sigma approach to excellence. Regardless of the theory, approach, or label, they all rest on a foundation of effective communication. One way that communication is often described involves customer relationship management, [1] or the relationship between the organization (sometimes represented by the product or service itself) and the customer.

This leads us to our first point: who is the customer? You might be tempted to say the end-user, the purchaser, or the decision-maker, but customers are often categorized as internal and external. Employees themselves represent internal customers, and their relationship with the business, product, or service has value to the organization. External customers may include the end-user, but can also include vendors and related businesses that are part of the supply chain. This expanded, global view of communication and customer service relationships will guide our discussion as we explore ways to effectively elicit negative news, critical feedback, and praise for a job well done.

Positive news is part of feedback, and indeed the difference between positive and negative news often lies more in the interpretation of information than the information itself. For example, if a software product that your company has been testing for some time, scheduled for a release date in the near future, has failed several tests, the tendency to view the news as negative is understood. The fact that the problems and issues were identified prior to release, however, provides an opportunity to correct them before their impact is magnified by negative news in the press, customer rejection of an inferior product, and a diminished view of your brand, all of which could ultimately damage customer loyalty and even your stock value. The chain reaction doesn't stop there; these effects could in turn limit your ability to get additional financing as an organization, the perceived risk could elevate interest rates on your company debts, and this could reduce budgets across the organization, limiting the very research and development budget that gives rise to the new, innovative, or breakout products that will gain market share.

Viewed in this light, it could be a very positive development that the faults in the software were detected before release. In addition, by learning to view information in a dispassionate way, noting that there is more than one way to interpret much of what we gather as data, you as a business professional can enhance your ability to see new approaches to products or services.

Thomas Kuhn, author of *The Structure of Scientific Revolutions* (1996), [2] states that communities operate on a set of beliefs. These beliefs form the foundation of the community, business, and organization. Employees and customers alike become socialized, learning the values, meaning, behaviors, cultural customs, expectations for excellence, and brand associations through interaction with the community. In business, we can clearly see the example of new employees becoming socialized into the company culture; they are training, learning about their jobs, and getting to know their coworkers.

We can also see how a customer interacts with a product or service, and comes to associate feelings, ideas, and expectations with a brand or company. This foundation or set of actualized beliefs becomes the norm or the status quo, and can become static or fixed. If a certain process is successful and an individual or company is rewarded, the process is often repeated. If a customer buys a certain product that works as they anticipate it will, they are more likely to make a similar purchase decision in the future.

Kuhn discusses research and the scientific method as a process that can affirm the status quo, but can also produce an anomaly, or something that doesn't fit, challenges the existing norm, or stands apart from the anticipated results. [3]This anomaly can challenge the status quo, and may not be greeted with open arms. Instead, it may be ignored or dismissed as irrelevant, but nothing could be further from the truth. As Kuhn (1996) [4] notes, this outlying information that challenges the norm is precisely the necessary ingredient for a paradigm shift, or a change in overall view. The view itself can be as simple as the new awareness that a product has more uses than originally anticipated, or as significant as a new awareness of the brand and the company focus.
Is there a better way to produce a product? Is there a new feature that customers want? You'll never know if you don't ask, and you'll never improve or change if you don't listen to the feedback.

One story that articulates this power of the anomaly, of unanticipated information that results in a change in view, involves a common business product. A research chemist for the 3M Company, Spencer Silver, was used to trial and error as he pursued his goal of a new superglue. [5] By mixing simple organic compounds in unusual ratios, he tried to create this super strong glue, but one result in particular was a spectacular failure. This particular result, a polymer, would stick to many surfaces, but it was also easy to remove, leaving no trace of itself. This odd substance was considered useless until Arthur Fry, a fellow 3M scientist, found a new use for it: removable paper notes that could be used to mark pages in his hymnal when he sang in his church choir. Minor modifications resulted in sample note pads that were passed around at 3M, and soon a new form of written communication and information organization was created: the now-famous Post-it brand note. [6] Silver and Fry could have dismissed the negative result as a failure to reach the established goal of inventing a super glue, but by undergoing a paradigm shift, they revolutionized business communication. Learning to be open to information that challenges your views is a key business skill.

This now brings us to the question of how we elicit negative news, critical feedback, and assessment information. How do you learn more about the people around you? You watch, listen, and ask questions. Asking questions while watching, listening, and learning is the foundation of eliciting feedback. We can ask questions in interpersonal interviews, in small groups, and even large groups in person. We can use technology to help gather and process information, categorizing and classifying it. We can also create surveys with questions designed to elicit specific types of information.

Academic research often uses the terms "qualitative" and "quantitative" to categorize two types of information gathering. Qualitative research involves interactions, which by their very nature are subject to interpretation and, as a result, are less reliable and statistically valid. Their strength is in the raw data, the proximity to the source, and the possibility of unexpected results. The weakness in the results is often the inability to replicate the results the same way again. An example may be a focus group, where participants try a new beverage and report their experience in words and nonverbal expressions. By recording the group, we can replay and study their response to the new drink, and learn that many of the participants perceive it to be sour from their facial gestures. The written responses may not indicate this response to the same degree, and the recorded responses may portray a different story. If you replicate the focus group with new participants, you may very well have a different outcome. Over time, patterns may emerge that produce reliable results, and indeed double-blind studies for many pharmaceuticals use a similar approach, but the number of participants has to be significantly increased while the confounding factors, or factors that can alter the results, must be anticipated and controlled. All of this involves a cost, and not every product, service, or study needs this type of investigation.

Quantitative research involves investigation and analysis of data and relationships between data that can be represented by numbers. The categorization and classification from the moment the investigation means that some aspects of the raw data will be necessarily lost in the process, but the information that remains will have a reliability and validity that compensates for this loss. Indeed, quantitative measures and representations of data are increasingly the norm in business communication, and are used to make decisions at all levels.

If your company produces automobiles, you may want qualitative information from potential consumers on their impression of the placement of the cup holders, but you will probably prefer quantitative information when it comes to engineering and safety. As you stress-test the steel in crash tests, assessing the force of the impact, the displacement of parts of the car as the crumple zones deform to absorb the energy, and the relative location of the crash-test dummy driver to the crush zone, you will measure it in terms of numbers. Each time your repeat the test, you should see similar results. If you don't, you may need to test the welds and examine the production process to determine why there is an inconsistency. You may even need to test the steel itself to see if it is a materials issue, rather than a process and production problem. All this information would be measured in terms of numbers and symbols, representing velocity, tensile strength, and related factors.

Another factor in gathering feedback is confidentiality. Before you consider how to ask questions, you may want to consider to what degree you want identifying information in the process. If you are designing a campaign where employees submit suggestions to save the company money, increase production, or improve quality, and want to offer a financial incentive for ideas that are adopted, you will need to be able to identify the contributing employee for the reward. On the other hand, if you want a feedback system for employees to report coworkers who are under the influence or have substance abuse problems on the job, threatening the safety of all, then you would want an anonymous 1-800 number to give out, and to encourage its use by assuring employees that it carries no identifying markers.

Anonymous surveys can elicit information that would not be revealed otherwise, but they can also be a place for employees to vent, exaggerate, or invent responses. The validity is an issue, but the opportunity for insight may outweigh the risks. You can also provide an optional opportunity for the employee or customer to self-identify by providing a place where they could indicate contact information. A customer that completes a postpurchase survey may be offered a coupon if they register, and that contact information may be useful for follow-up contacts. Some customers will prefer, however, to write a direct complaint without identifying themselves. When designing a survey, brochure, or procedure to elicit feedback, you need to consider identification and anonymity.

In order to gather information, we often ask questions. For this application there are two types of questions: open and closed. [7] Open-ended questions allow for interpretation and a range of responses in the respondent's own words. Closed-ended questions limit the responses to a preselected range of options or choices. Your choice of open or closed questions depends on what type of information you plan to gather. Open-ended questions may sound like the following:

1. What do you like about the product?

2. How was the service today?
3. How does the product make you feel?
4. What does our brand mean to you?
5. Why did you choose our product?

In each case, the question can be answered many ways, depending on the word choice of the respondent. The value is placed on the personal response and the range of data gathered may well be quite diverse, presenting challenge to categorize and group. Open-ended questions cannot be answered with a simple yes or no response.

Closed-ended questions, however, can be answered with a yes/no response. Here are five examples of closed-ended questions:

1. Have you purchased our product previously?
   ___ Yes
   ___ No
2. Why did you choose our product?
   a. Price/low cost
b. Quality
c. Reputation
d. Previous experience

How was the service today?

1	2	3	4	5
Poor	Below average	Neutral	Good	Excellent

What do you like about the product? (Please indicate in rank order.)
___ Low cost
___ Quality
___ Reputation
___ Features
___ Low maintenance

Please indicate the year you were born. _____

The first closed-ended question is simply a closed question with its yes/no response options, but it is also an example of a categorical question. Categorical questions limit the responses to two categories. For example, you may ask a customer to indicate their sex in the response survey, allowing them to choose from two categories: male or female. Multiple choice questions allow for specific choices and limit the range of options. Likert Scale questions allow for the conversion of feelings, attitudes, and perceptions into numbers in a range. Ordinal questions request the respondent to rank order specific options. Numerical questions request a specific number, often a birth date or a serial number, that

itself carries meaning. For example, age may be correlated to disposable income, and while the respondent may not be willing to respond to a direct question about their income level, they may be willing to indicate their year of birth.

To summarize the pros and cons of the two basic question types: open-ended questions are best when you want all possible responses in the respondent's own words. Closed-ended questions limit the responses to a few choices, and they can be categorized, placed in order, assess degrees of attitudes and feelings, and request specific information. [8]

KEY TAKEAWAY

Eliciting negative news through feedback is an important way to avert problems, safeguard valuable relationships, and achieve paradigm shifts. Feedback may be qualitative or quantitative and may be requested through open-ended or closed-ended questions.

EXERCISES

1. Describe a time when you received negative feedback in time to correct your error. How did you feel about the correction at the time? Looking back, how do you feel about it in retrospect? Discuss your thoughts with a classmate.
2. Find a negative message online and write a brief review. Share and compare with classmates.
3. Prepare a sample customer satisfaction survey with at least ten questions. Make sure you include a couple of questions to learn more about your audience as well as their opinions of the product or service. Post your results in class and compare them with classmates.

[1] Bauer, J. E., Duffy, G. L., & Westcott, R. T. (2006). *The quality improvement handbook*. New York, NY: ASQ Quality Press.
[2] Kuhn, T. (1996). *The structure of scientific revolutions* (3rd ed.). Chicago, IL: University of Chicago Press.
[3] Kuhn, T. (1996). *The structure of scientific revolutions* (3rd ed.). Chicago, IL: University of Chicago Press.
[4] Kuhn, T. (1996). *The structure of scientific revolutions* (3rd ed.). Chicago, IL: University of Chicago Press.
[5] Kuhn, T. (1996). *The structure of scientific revolutions* (3rd ed.). Chicago, IL: University of Chicago Press.
[6] 3M Company. (2009). A NOTE-able achievement. Retrieved fromhttp://www.3m.com/US/office/postit/pastpresent/history_ws.html
[7] Fink, A. (1995). *How to ask survey questions*. Thousand Oaks, CA: Sage.
[8] Fink, A. (1995). *How to ask survey questions*. Thousand Oaks, CA: Sage.

17.3 Crisis Communication Plan
LEARNING OBJECTIVE

1. Understand how to prepare a crisis communication plan.

A rumor that the CEO is ill pulls down the stock price. A plant explosion kills several workers and requires evacuating residents on several surrounding city blocks. Risk management seeks to address these many risks, including prevention as well as liability, but emergency and crisis situations happen nevertheless. In addition, people make errors in judgment that can damage the public perception of a company. The mainstream media does not lack stories involving infidelity, addiction, or abuse that require a clear a response from a company's standpoint. In this chapter we address the basics of a crisis communication plan.

Focus on key types of information during an emergency: [1]

- What is happening?
- Is anyone in danger?
- How big is the problem?
- Who reported the problem?
- Where is the problem?
- Has a response started?
- What resources are on-scene?
- Who is responding so far?
- Is everyone's location known?

You will be receiving information from the moment you know a crisis has occurred, but without a framework or communication plan to guide you, valuable information may be ignored or lost. These questions help you quickly focus on the basics of "who, what, and where" in the crisis situation.

Developing Your Crisis Communication Plan

A crisis communication plan is the prepared scenario document that organizes information into responsibilities and lines of communication prior to an event. With a plan in place, if an emergency arises, each person knows his or her role and responsibilities from a common reference document. Overall effectiveness can be enhanced with a clear understanding of roles and responsibilities for an effective and swift response.

The plan should include four elements:

1. Crisis communication team members with contact information
2. Designated spokesperson
3. Meeting place/location
4. Media plan with procedures
   A crisis communication team includes people who can
   a. decide what actions to take,
   b. carry out those actions,
   c. offer expertise or education in the relevant areas.

By designating a spokesperson prior to an actual emergency, your team addresses the inevitable need for information in a proactive manner. People will want to know what happened and where to get further details about the crisis. Lack of

information breeds rumors, which can make a bad situation worse. The designated spokesperson should be knowledgeable about the organization and its values; be comfortable in front of a microphone, camera, and media lights; and be able to stay calm under pressure.

Part of your communication crisis plan should focus on where you will meet to coordinate communicate and activities. In case of a fire in your house, you might meet in the front yard. In an organization, a designated contingency building or office some distance away from your usual place of business might serve as a central place for communication in an emergency that requires evacuating your building. Depending on the size of your organization and the type of facilities where you do business, the company may develop an emergency plan with exit routes, hazardous materials procedures, and policies for handling bomb threats, for example. Safety, of course, is the priority, but in terms of communication, the goal is to eliminate confusion about where people are and where information is coming from.

Whether or not evacuation is necessary, when a crisis occurs, your designated spokesperson will gather information and carry out your media plan. He or she will need to make quick judgments about which information to share, how to phrase it, and whether certain individuals need to be notified of facts before they become public. The media and public will want to know information and reliable information is preferable to speculation. Official responses help clarify the situation for the public, but an unofficial interview can make the tragedy personal, and attract unwanted attention. Remind employees to direct all inquiries to the official spokesperson and to never speak "off the record."

Enable your spokesperson to have access to the place you indicated as your crisis contingency location to coordinate communication and activities, and allow that professional to prepare and respond to inquiries. When crisis communication is handled in a professional manner, it seeks not to withhold information or mislead, but to minimize the "spin damage" from the incident by providing necessary facts, even if they are unpleasant or even tragic.

KEY TAKEAWAY

Because crises are bound to happen despite the best planning, every organization should have a crisis communication plan, which includes designating a crisis communication team and spokesperson.

EXERCISES

1. Locate the crisis communication plan where you go to school or work, or find one online. Briefly describe the

overall plan and please note at least one part, element, or point of emphasis we have not discussed. Post and compare with classmates.

2. When people don't know what to do in a crisis situation, what happens? How can you address probable challenges before the crisis occurs? Discuss your ideas with classmates.

3. As a case study, research one crisis that involves your area of training or career field. What communication issues were present and how did they affect the response to the crisis? Compare your results with classmates.

4. Locate a crisis communication online and review it. Share and compare with classmates.

5. Do you always have to be on guard with members of the media? Why or why not? Explain your answer to the class as if they were members of the media.

[1] Mallet, L., Vaught, C., & Brinch, M. (1999). *The emergency communication triangle*. Centers for Disease Control and Prevention, National Institute for Occupational Saftey and Health, U.S. Department of Health and Human Services. Pittsburgh, PA: Pittsburgh Research Laboratory.

17.4 Press Conferences
LEARNING OBJECTIVES

1. Discuss the purpose of a press conference.
2. Discuss how to prepare and conduct a press conference.

Holding a press conference when you are unprepared can feel like standing in front of a firing squad, where all the journalists are armed so no one will carry the guilt of the winning shot. It can make you nervous, scared, and reluctant to speak at all. It can take your fear of a misquote, or a stumble, or a misstatement replayed across the Internet thousands of times in the next twenty-four hours and make you wish for a blindfold and a cigarette, but that won't help. The way to calm your nerves is to be confident in your material. This section discusses the press conference, from preparation to execution (pun intended).

A press conference is a presentation of information to the media. It normally involves a written statement that is read exactly as written and is followed by questions and answers. The press conference normally requires a seasoned representative of the company or business with established credibility and integrity. It also requires a sense of calm in the confidence that you know your material, know how to tactfully say you don't know or don't wish to comment, and a sense of humor to handle the "gotcha" questions.

Press conferences can be held for positive news like the announcement of a new hospital wing that will increase the health care services available to the community. It can also be held to clarify information regarding the CEO's trip to Chile with an alleged mistress, the recent law enforcement sting operation on the illegal sale of controlled substances from the hospital, or to announce the layoff of employees as part of a reduction in force.

Positive or negative, your role as a speaker at a press conference is to deliver the prepared message and to represent the business or organization in a professional manner. You understand that there may be moments of tension, but you also know you have a choice in how to respond. First we'll examine preparation, then discuss the actual press conference.

You should have a good reason for holding a press conference. Wasting the media's time on a frivolous issue will only set you up for challenges later on. You should also have a brief prepared statement that you will read and restate if necessary. Today's press conference messages are often drafted by someone in public relations or media, and reviewed by legal counsel when warranted. If the task falls to you, keep it short and simple, addressing the following:

- Who?
- What?
- Where?
- When?
- How?
- Why?

As a follow-up to why the press conference needs to occur in the first place, you need to consider the location. If it is a ribbon-cutting ceremony, the choice is obvious. If the announcement is less than positive, and you've been instructed by your supervisors or counsel to not offer additional remarks, you'll want a podium strategically located next to a stage exit. Your press release or invitation to the media will contain the time, date, and location of the press conference, and may contain a title or subject line as well as contact information for follow-up information.

As you prepare your background materials, learning as much as needed for the announcement, you may also want to consider using a moderator. Perhaps that will be your role as you introduce senior management to read the prepared statement. A moderator can serve to influence the process and redirect if questions go off topic or if a transition is needed. A moderator can also call a formal close the press conference and thank everyone for attending.

Finally, visual aids are an excellent way to reinforce and communicate your message. They need to be big, they need to be relevant (not just decorative), and (from a technical standpoint) they need to work. If they will be projected onto a screen, make sure the screen is available (not stuck), the laptop has power (as well as battery backup), the presentation or visual aid is on the laptop, and that the projector can and does project what you want it to. Don't forget sound equipment if necessary, and make sure everything works the day of the presentation.

Holding a Press Conference

Someone should be designated as the greeter for the media. Be ready at least fifteen minutes before the scheduled time of the event. Provide each member of the media with a print copy of the actual statement that will be read before or after the event. If there is an element of surprise, you may want to hold the copies of the statement back until after the press conference has been concluded, but otherwise distributing them beforehand is standard.

The moderator opens the press conference with a welcome, indicates the purpose of the press conference and reminds everyone that there will (or will not) be an opportunity for questions following the press conference. The moderator introduces the spokesperson who will read the statement and welcomes him or her to the podium. The moderator may need to assist with sound equipment but otherwise stands back but near the speaker.

The speaker will read the statement. If there are to be no questions, the moderator will retake the podium and indicate that press kits, containing background material, fact sheets, the news release, sample photos, or related materials will be available; or simply indicate that copies of the press release are available at the back of the room. If there are questions, the moderator may still take the podium and outline ground rules for questions such as: they should pertain to the subject, be brief, and may or may not include follow-up questions. Members of the media will often ask a question and state that they have a follow-up question as a way of reserving two turns.

The moderator may indicate which member of the media is to ask a question, and typically they will stand and address the speaker directly. The speaker can take notes, but this isn't common. Instead, they should be aware that every movement is being recorded and that by maintaining eye contact, they are demonstrating that they are listening. They may reiterate the statement from the press release or refer to the background material, but should limit the scope of their response. Your team may have anticipated several questions and the speaker may have several sound bites ready to deliver. Visual media will want it visual, audio will want clarity, and print will want descriptive quotes. Meet the needs of your audience as you deliver your message.

Invariably the "gotcha" question, or the question that attempts to catch the speaker off guard, will be asked. "We're not ready to discuss the matter at this time," "When more information becomes available we will let you know," "Our company has no position on that issue," or "We're not prepared to speculate on that issue at this time" are all common response phrases. Don't use "I think," "I believe," or "I don't know" comments as they invite speculation, and refrain from "no comment" if at all possible as it is increasingly perceived as if the company or representative is "hiding something."

You want to appear professional, knowledgeable, and credible—not as if you are sneaking or hiding something. Don't display a nonverbal gesture or make a face at a question, as this can also be misinterpreted. Keep your poise and balance at all times, and if you are the speaker and the question puts you off, establish eye contact with the moderator. Their role is to step in and they may move to the conclusion.

Never say anything you wouldn't want the world to hear, as microphones are increasingly powerful, video captures lips movement, and there will be a communication professional available to analyze your nonverbal gestures on the evening news. Being cool, calm, and collected is the best policy whether you are delivering positive or negative news.

KEY TAKEAWAY

A press conference is an important presentation of information that requires you to anticipate questions and prepare possible responses.

EXERCISES

Your role as spokesperson is to write and present a prepared statement, and respond to no less than five questions. You will select one of the scenarios below based on your birth month, and prepare your statement. You are allowed to improve on facts, but should recognize that each scenario is serious and treat the assignment with professionalism.

1. January—Healthcare, Inc.

A hacker illegally accessed thousands of the new digital health care records on file with Healthcare, Inc. and posted them directly to the Internet in an early morning protest against invasion of privacy. The hacker has not been identified, but local law enforcement is on the scene investigating the incident and the offending Web sites have been taken offline.

Your company has received hundreds of calls concerning the incident. The federal government required the conversion to digital records last year, and your company complied with the order. Your company used a government-approved vendor for a no-bid installation of hardware and software to secure the digital records. You represent Healthcare, Inc.

2. February—Educational Services, Inc.

Half the senior class in your private magnet high school cheated on the graduation exam, and the rest were apparently aware of the cheating, as were many of the parents. An employee, a secretary with several employee passwords, allegedly gained access to the exam before its release and provided the questions and responses to her son, who then provided it to his friends. The employee was often provided login names and passwords to facilitate records processing for several administrators when they were off site, often at conferences. Headquarters wants to minimize the publicity but cannot in good faith issue diplomas to students who cheated. The employee has been dismissed for conduct, and an investigation is underway, but graduation is next week and the evidence against the cheating seniors is clear. They won't be receiving their diplomas unless they pass an alternate version of the test that won't be ready for sixty days. You represent Educational Services, Inc.

3. March—Software, Inc.

Your company recently released its latest version of a popular business and industry software program. Programs always have a few bugs or problems upon release, even after the most rigorous laboratory testing, but this program is apparently infested with bugs. Stories are popping up across the Internet about how the program doesn't work, or specific features don't work, and your customer service team has been responding to customer complaints. The software designers report it is an exaggeration to say "infested," and point out that in all the trial tests it has worked perfectly. Your company is working on finding and addressing the issues, and is ready to create patch programs and issue refunds if necessary, but wants to prevent a recall and a loss of consumer confidence. You represent Software, Inc.

4. April—Electric Company, Inc.

An employee was consuming alcohol on the job and failed to adjust the voltage regulator. The voltage was increased by a considerable amount, causing several house fires, significant loss of property (appliances) and the death of an eleven-year-old child. The local media interviewed the employee's spouse who stated the employee was working a double shift, that they had called someone to relieve them, and no one came.

Your company is investigating, but has no new information. You represent Electric Company, Inc.

5. May—Online Market, Inc.

An online marketplace company has been accused by law enforcement of knowingly allowing users to sell stolen goods on their Web site. Since the company never handles any of the goods themselves, and simply facilitates the exchange of goods between buyer and seller via the short-term creation of a Web page with text and images provided by the seller, the company denies all responsibility. You represent Online Market, Inc.

6. June—ABC Engineering, Inc.

A 4.2-million-dollar, two-lane bridge recently completed collapsed into the local Blue River, taking with it three vehicles. The loss of life included four men, three women, and one unborn baby. Local media has interviewed workers who indicated they were rushed to complete the bridge to get a bonus for the construction firm. The construction firm indicates that their internal investigation points to a faulty design, but the architects, engineers, and government inspectors deny the charge. You represent ABC Engineering.

7. July—Package Delivery, Inc.

A class-action lawsuit has been filed in federal court against Package Delivery, Inc. A group of employees, all female, allege sexual harassment and discriminatory promotion practices against the company. They cite photos and calendars of a sexual nature hung in the workplace and allege that male colleagues with less seniority were promoted ahead of the female workers. You represent Package Delivery, Inc.

8. August—Hamburgers, Inc.

Hamburgers, Inc. is pleased to announce a new menu practice where the nutritional information and the calorie counts will be prominently displayed, helping consumers make healthy choices from the menu. Your supervisors have heard that there may be representatives of the Cow Liberation Group (which advocates vegetarianism) and several nutritionists (who perceive the company has not done enough to improve its products) at the press conference. You represent Hamburgers, Inc.

9. September—Headache Pills, Inc.

A person in New York died of cyanide poisoning, supposedly after taking a 200-mg Headache Pill made by your company. Your headache pills come in sealed, tamper-resistant packaging with child-proof protective caps. Some stores are voluntarily taking your product off the market. The U.S. Food and Drug Administration has announced an investigation, and the family of the person who died has threatened to sue. You represent Headache Pills, Inc.

10. October—Maisy Mayflower, Star Actress

You represent Maisy Mayflower as her spokesperson. She has recently returned from Bolivia where she adopted a two-year-old child. She already has three adopted children representing several countries. She is not married. Upon her return, a man claiming to be the child's father came forward to the media in La Paz, Bolivia protesting the adoption, and the U.S. media has picked up on it. It is all over the Internet. The Bolivian government issued a statement that while they cannot confirm the legitimacy of his claim, the father of the child did not present himself at court during the announced hearing, nor did he present himself in the six months preceding the adoption. The child was legally declared abandoned, and legally adopted. You represent Maisy Mayflower.

11. November—Fast Food Restaurants, Inc.

A customer reported finding a severed human fingertip in soup purchased from Fast Food Restaurants, Inc. The soup and sandwich package was purchased at a Fast Food Restaurant as a take-out order. Your company has several quality controls in place to prevent accidents like this. Local law enforcement is investigating. The customer has taken pictures and posted them all over the Web, and made both libelous and slanderous comments against your company in media interviews and blogs. The customer has never been an employee of Fast Food Restaurants or its affiliates. You represent Fast Food Restaurants, Inc.

12. December—Congressman "Honest" Abe Johnson.

The honorable Congressman from the State of Denial was apprehended in Ecuador for solicitation of a minor. The local media reports that a young girl approached him when he was with his traveling group and he offered to take a picture of her. The mother appeared, spoke to him, and slapped him in the face. She says the congressman offered her money for time alone with her daughter. The congressman stated to local law enforcement, according to a conversation with his spouse from jail, that all he did was compliment her on her daughter, something like "what a fine daughter you have," in his best Spanish. You represent the Congressman.

17.5 Additional Resources

- "Good Ways to Deliver Bad News" by Curtis Sittenfeld from *Fast Company*. http://www.fastcompany.com/magazine/23/buckman.html
- "How to Deliver Bad News to a Group" by Kevin Daley, a Harvard Business article. http://blogs.harvardbusiness.org/cs/2009/10/how_to_deliver_bad_news_to_a_g.html
- "How to Deliver Bad News" from SmallBiz.com. http://www.smsmallbiz.com/bestpractices/How_to_Deliver_Bad_News.html
- Development by Design offers an article on how to elicit feedback. http://www.development-by-design.com/article_Tips.htm
- "Top 7 Ways To Elicit Constructive Web site Feedback" by Adam Senour. http://top7business.com/?id=555
- Visit this Northern Illinois University site for a guide to preparing a generic crisis communication plan and adapting it to your needs. http://www3.niu.edu/newsplace/crisis.html
- To see an actual crisis communication plan, visit this North Carolina State University Web site. http://www2.ncsu.edu/ncsu/univ_relations/crisis.html
- See the Crisis Communication Plan of Meredith College at this site. http://www.meredith.edu/marketing/crisis-plan.doc
- Western Organization of Research Councils presents "How to Hold a Press Conference." http://www.npaction.org/resources/WORC/pressconf12.pdf
- "How to Hold a Press Conference" by Kori Rodley Irons. Press conferences aren't just for the rich and famous. http://www.associatedcontent.com/article/60465/how_to_hold_a_press_conference.html

NOTES:

NOTES:

Chapter 18:
Intercultural and International Business Communication

We should never denigrate any other culture but rather help people to understand the relationship between their own culture and the dominant culture. When you understand another culture or language, it does not mean that you have to lose your own culture.

   Edward T. Hall

I've been traveling all over the world for 25 years, performing, talking to people, studying their cultures and musical instruments, and I always come away with more questions in my head than can be answered.

   Yo-Yo Ma

Getting Started

INTRODUCTORY EXERCISES

1. Find a film where one person overcomes all obstacles. Make notes of your observations on how he or she approaches the world, solves problems, and rises triumphant

2. Find a film where a group of people overcomes obstacles through joint effort. Make notes of your observations on how they approach the world, solve problems, and rise triumphant.

3. Consider a culture with which you have had little interaction. Write down at least five terms to describe that culture.

As a professional in the modern business community, you need to be aware that the very concept of community is undergoing a fundamental transformation. Throughout the world's history—until recently—a community was defined by its geographic boundaries. A merchant supplied salt and sugar, and people made what they needed. The products the merchant sold were often produced locally because the cost of transportation was significant. A transcontinental railroad brought telegraph lines, shipping routes, and brought ports together from coast to coast. Shipping that once took months and years was now measured in days. A modern highway system and cheap oil products allowed for that measurement unit to be reduced to days and minutes. Just in time product delivery reduced storage costs, from renting a warehouse at the port to spoilage in transit. As products sold, bar code and RDIF (radio frequency identification) tagged items instantly updated inventories and initiated orders at factories all over the world.

Communication, both oral and written, linked communities in ways that we failed to recognize until economic turmoil in one place led to job loss, in a matter of days or minutes, thousands of miles away. A system of trade and the circulation of capital and goods that once flowed relatively seamlessly have been challenged by change, misunderstanding, and conflict. People learn of political, economic, and military turmoil that is instantly translated into multiple market impacts. Integrated markets and global networks bind us together in ways we are just now learning to appreciate, anticipate, and understand. Intercultural and international communication are critical areas of study with readily apparent, real-world consequences.

Agrarian, industrial, and information ages gave way to global business and brought the importance of communication across cultures to the forefront. The Pulitzer Prize–winning journalist Thomas Friedman calls this new world "flat," [1] noting how the integration of markets and community had penetrated the daily lives of nearly everyone on the planet, regardless of language or culture. While the increasing ease of telecommunications and travel have transformed the nature of doing business, Friedman argues that "the dawning 'flat world' is a jungle pitting 'lions' and 'gazelles,' where 'economic stability is not going to be a feature' and 'the weak will fall farther behind.'" [2] Half of the world's population that earn less than $2 (USD) a day felt the impact of a reduction in trade and fluctuations in commodity prices even though they may not have known any of the details. Rice, for example, became an even more valuable commodity than ever; to the individuals who could not find it, grow it, or earn enough to buy it, the hunger felt was personal and global. International trade took on a new level of importance.

Intercultural and international business communication has taken on a new role for students as well as career professionals. Knowing when the European and Asian markets open has become mandatory; so has awareness of multiple time zones and their importance in relation to trade, shipping, and the production cycle. Managing production in China from an office in Chicago has become common. Receiving technical assistance for your computer often means connecting with a well-educated English speaker in New Delhi. We compete with each other via Elance.com or oDesk.com for contracts and projects, selecting the currency of choice for each bid as we can be located anywhere on the planet. Communities are no longer linked as simply "brother" and "sister" cities in symbolic partnerships. They are linked in the daily trade of goods and services.

In this chapter, we explore this dynamic aspect of communication. If the foundation of communication is important, its application in this context is critical. Just as Europe once formed intercontinental alliances for the trade of metals—leading to the development of a common currency, trade zone, and new concept of nation-state—now North and South America are following with increased integration. Major corporations are no longer affiliated with only one country or one country's interests but instead perceive the integrated market as team members across global trade. "Made in X" is more of a relative statement as products, from cars to appliances to garments, now come with a list of where components were made and assembled and what percentage corresponds to each nation.

Global business is more than trade between companies located in distinct countries; indeed, that concept is already outdated. Intercultural and international business focuses less on the borders that separate people and more on the communication that brings them together. Business communication values clear, concise interaction that promotes efficiency and effectiveness. You may perceive your role as a business communicator within a specific city, business, or organization, but you need to be aware that your role crosses cultures, languages, value and legal systems, and borders.

[1] Friedman, T. (2005). *The world is flat: A brief history of the twenty-first century.* New York, NY: Farrar, Straus, and Giroux.
[2] Publishers Weekly. (2009). The world is flat: A brief history of the twenty-first century [Starred review]. Retrieved from http://www.thomaslfriedman.com/bookshelf/the-world-is-flat

18.1 Intercultural Communication
LEARNING OBJECTIVES

1. Define and discuss how to facilitate intercultural communication.
2. Define and discuss the effects of ethnocentrism.

Communication is the sharing of understanding and meaning, [1] but what is intercultural communication? If you answered, "The sharing of understanding and meaning across cultures," you'd be close, but the definition requires more attention. What is a culture? Where does one culture stop and another start? How are cultures created, maintained, and dissolved? Donald Klopf described culture as "that part of the environment made by humans." [2] From the building we erect that represents design values to the fences we install that delineate borders, our environment is a representation of culture, but it is not all that is culture.

Culture involves beliefs, attitudes, values, and traditions that are shared by a group of people. Thus, we must consider more than the clothes we wear, the movies we watch, or the video games we play, all representations of environment, as culture. Culture also involves the psychological aspects of our expectations of the communication context. For example, if we are raised in a culture where males speak while females are expected to remain silent, the context of the communication interaction governs behavior, which in itself is a representation of culture. From the choice of words (message), to how we communicate (in person, or by e-mail), to how we acknowledge understanding with a nod or a glance (nonverbal feedback), to the internal and external interference, all aspects of communication are influenced by culture.

In defining intercultural communication, we only have eight components of communication to work with and yet we must bridge divergent cultures with distinct values across languages and time zones to exchange value, a representation of meaning. It may be tempting to consider only the source and receiver within a transaction as a representation of intercultural communication, but if we do that, we miss the other six components—the message, channel, feedback, context, environment, and interference—in every communicative act. Each component influences and is influenced by culture. Is culture context? Environment? Message? Culture is represented in all eight components every time we communicate. All communication is intercultural.

We may be tempted to think of intercultural communication as interaction between two people from different countries. While two distinct national passports may be artifacts, or nonverbal representations of communication, what happens when two people from two different parts of the same country communicate? From high and low Germanic dialects, to the perspective of a Southerner versus a Northerner in the United States, to the rural versus urban dynamic, our geographic, linguistic, educational, sociological, and psychological traits influence our communication.

It is not enough to say that someone from rural Southern Chile and the capital, Santiago, both speak *Castellano* (the Chilean word for the Spanish language), so that communication   between   them   must be intracultural communication, or communication within the same culture. What is life like for the rural Southerner? For the city dweller? Were their educational experiences the same? Do they share the same vocabulary? Do they value the same things? To a city dweller, all the sheep look the same. To the rural Southerner, the sheep are distinct, with unique markings; they have value as a food source, a source of wool with which to create sweaters and socks that keep the cold winters at bay, and in their numbers they represent wealth. Even if both Chileans speak the same language, their socialization will influence how they communicate and what they value, and their vocabulary will reflect these differences. Let's take this intranational comparison a step further. Within the same family, can there be intercultural communication? If all communication is intercultural, then the answer would be yes, but we still have to prove our case. Imagine a three-generation family living in one house. The grandparents may represent another time and different values from the grandchildren. The parents may have a different level of education and pursue different careers from the grandparents; the schooling the children are receiving may prepare them for yet another career. From music, to food preferences, to how work is done may vary across time; Elvis Presley may seem like ancient history to the children. The communication across generations represents intercultural communication, even if only to a limited degree.

But suppose we have a group of students who are all similar in age and educational level. Do gender and the societal expectations of roles influence interaction? Of course. And so we see that among these students not only do the boys and girls communicate in distinct ways but also not all boys and girls are the same. With a group of sisters, there may be common characteristics, but they will still have differences, and these differences contribute to intercultural communication. We are each shaped by our upbringing and it influences our worldview, what we value, and how we interact with each other. We create culture, and it creates us.

Everett Rogers and Thomas Steinfatt define intercultural communication as the exchange of information between individuals who are "unalike culturally." [3] If you follow our discussion and its implications, you may arrive at the idea that ultimately we are each a "culture of one"—we are simultaneously a part of a community and its culture(s) and separate from it in the unique combination that represents us as an individual. All of us are separated by a matter of degrees from each other even if we were raised on the same street or by parents of similar educational background and profession, and yet, we have many other things in common.

Communication with yourself is called intrapersonal communication, which may also be intracultural, as you may only represent one culture. But most people belong to many groups, each with their own culture. Within our imaginary intergenerational home, how many cultures do you think we might find? If we only consider the parents and consider work one culture, and family another,

we now have two. If we were to examine the options more closely, we would find many more groups, and the complexity would grow exponentially. Does a conversation with yourself ever involve competing goals, objectives, needs, wants, or values? How did you learn of those goals, or values? Through communication within and between individuals, they themselves representatives of many cultures. We struggle with the demands of each group and their expectations and could consider this internal struggle intercultural conflict or simply intercultural communication.

Culture is part of the very fabric of our thought, and we cannot separate ourselves from it, even as we leave home, defining ourselves anew in work and achievements. Every business or organization has a culture, and within what may be considered a global culture, there are many subcultures or co-cultures. For example, consider the difference between the sales and accounting departments in a corporation. We can quickly see two distinct groups with their own symbols, vocabulary, and values. Within each group, there may also be smaller groups, and each member of each department comes from a distinct background that in itself influences behavior and interaction.

Intercultural communication is a fascinating area of study within business communication, and it is essential to your success. One idea to keep in mind as we examine this topic is the importance of considering multiple points of view. If you tend to dismiss ideas or views that are "unalike culturally," you will find it challenging to learn about diverse cultures. If you cannot learn, how can you grow and be successful?

Ethnocentrism is the tendency to view other cultures as inferior to one's own. Having pride in your culture can be healthy, but history has taught us that having a predisposition to discount other cultures simply because they are different can be hurtful, damaging, and dangerous. Ethnocentrism makes us far less likely to be able to bridge the gap with others and often increases intolerance of difference. Business and industry are no longer regional, and in your career, you will necessarily cross borders, languages, and cultures. You will need tolerance, understanding, patience, and openness to difference. A skilled business communicator knows that the process of learning is never complete, and being open to new ideas is a key strategy for success.

KEY TAKEAWAY

Intercultural communication is an aspect of all communicative interactions, and attention to your perspective is key to your effectiveness. Ethnocentrism is a major obstacle to intercultural communication.

EXERCISES

1. Please list five words to describe your dominant culture. Please list five words to describe a culture with which you are not a member, have little or no contact, or have limited knowledge. Now, compare and contrast the terms noting their inherent value statements.

2. Identify a country you would like to visit. Research the country and find one interesting business fact and share it with the class.

3. Write a brief summary about a city, region, state, or country you have visited that is not like where you live. Share and compare with classmates.

[1] Pearson, J., & Nelson, P. (2000). *An introduction to human communication: Understanding and sharing.* Boston, MA: McGraw-Hill.
[2] Klopf, D. (1991). *Intercultural encounters: The fundamentals of intercultural communication* (2nd ed.). Inglewood, CA: Morton Publishing Company.
[3] Rogers, E., & Steinfatt, T. (1999). *Intercultural communication.* Prospect Heights, IL: Waveland Press.

18.2 How to Understand Intercultural Communication
LEARNING OBJECTIVE

1. Describe strategies to understand intercultural communication, prejudice, and ethnocentrism.

The American anthropologist Edward T. Hall is often cited as a pioneer in the field of intercultural communication. [1] Born in 1914, Hall spent much of his early adulthood in the multicultural setting of the American Southwest, where Native Americans, Spanish-speakers, and descendants of pioneers came together from diverse cultural perspectives. He then traveled the globe during World War II and later served as a U.S. State Department official. Where culture had once been viewed by anthropologists as a single, distinct way of living, Hall saw how the perspective of the individual influences interaction. By focusing on interactions rather than cultures as separate from individuals, he asked us to evaluate the many cultures we ourselves belong to or are influenced by as well as those with whom we interact. While his view makes the study of intercultural communication far more complex, it also brings a healthy dose of reality to the discussion. Hall is generally credited with eight contributions to our study of intercultural communication: [2], [3], and [4]

1. *Compare cultures.* Focus on the interactions versus general observations of culture.

2. *Shift to local perspective.* Local level versus global perspective.

3. *You don't have to know everything to know something.* Time, space, gestures, and gender roles can be studied, even if we lack a larger understanding of the entire culture.

4. *There are rules we can learn.* People create rules for themselves in each community that we can learn from, compare, and contrast.

5. *Experience counts.* Personal experience has value in addition to more comprehensive studies of interaction and culture.

6. *Perspectives can differ.* Descriptive linguistics serves as a model to understand cultures, and the U.S. Foreign Service adopted it as a base for training.

7. *Intercultural communication can be applied to international business.* U.S. Foreign Service training yielded applications for trade and commerce and became a point of study for business majors.

8. *It integrates the disciplines.* Culture and communication are intertwined and bring together many academic disciplines.

Hall [5] shows us that emphasis on a culture as a whole, and how it operates, may lead us to neglect individual differences. Individuals may hold beliefs or practice customs that do not follow their own cultural norm. When we resort to the mental shortcut of a stereotype, we lose these unique differences. Stereotypes can be defined as a generalization about a group of people that oversimplifies their culture. [6]

The American psychologist Gordon Allport [7] explored how, when, and why we formulate or use stereotypes to characterize distinct groups. His results may not surprise you. Look back at the third of the Note 18.1 "Introductory Exercises" for this chapter and examine the terms you used to describe a culture with which you are unfamiliar. Were the terms flattering or pejorative? Did they reflect respect for the culture or did they make unfavorable value judgments? Regardless of how you answered, you proved Allport's main point. When we do not have enough contact with people or their cultures to understand them well, we tend to resort to stereotypes. [8]

As Hall [9] notes, experience has value. If you do not know a culture, you should consider learning more about it firsthand if possible. The people you interact with may not be representative of the culture as a whole, but that is not to say that what you learn lacks validity. Quite the contrary; Hall asserts that you can, in fact, learn something without understanding everything, and given the dynamic nature of communication and culture, who is to say that your lessons will not serve you well? Consider a study abroad experience if that is an option for you, or learn from a classmate who comes from a foreign country or an unfamiliar culture. Be open to new ideas and experiences, and start investigating. Many have gone before you, and today, unlike in generations past, much of the information is accessible. Your experiences will allow you to learn about another culture and yourself, and help you to avoid prejudice.

Prejudice involves a negative preconceived judgment or opinion that guides conduct or social behavior. [11] As an example, imagine two people walking into a room for a job interview. You are tasked to interview both, and having read the previous section, you know that Allport rings true when he says we rely on stereotypes when encountering people or cultures with which we have had little contact. Will the candidates' dress, age, or gender influence your opinion of them? Will their race or ethnicity be a conscious or subconscious factor in your thinking process? Allport's work would indicate that those factors and more will make you likely to use stereotypes to guide your expectations of them and your subsequent interactions with them.

People who treat other with prejudice often make assumptions, or take preconceived ideas for granted without question, about the group or communities. As Allport illustrated for us, we often assume characteristics about groups with which we have little contact. Sometimes we also assume similarity, thinking that people are all basically similar. This denies cultural, racial, ethnic, socioeconomic, and many other valuable, insightful differences.

KEY TAKEAWAY

Ethnocentric tendencies, stereotyping, and assumptions of similarity can make it difficult to learn about cultural differences.

EXERCISES

1. People sometimes assume that learning about other cultures is unnecessary if we simply treat others as we would like to be treated. To test this assumption, try answering the following questions.
    a. When receiving a gift from a friend, should you open it immediately, or wait to open it in private?
    b. When grocery shopping, should you touch fruits and vegetables to evaluate their freshness?
    c. In a conversation with your instructor or your supervisor at work, should you maintain direct eye contact?

    Write down your answers before reading further. Now let's explore how these questions might be answered in various cultures.
    d. In Chile, it is good manners to open a gift immediately and express delight and thanks. But in Japan it is a traditional custom to not open a gift in the giver's presence.

    e. In the United States, shoppers typically touch, hold, and even smell fruits and vegetables before buying them. But in northern Europe this is strongly frowned upon.
    f. In mainstream North American culture, people are expected to look directly at each other when having a conversation. But a cultural norm for many Native Americans involves keeping one's eyes lowered as a sign of respect when speaking to an instructor or supervisor.

No one can be expected to learn all the "dos and don'ts" of the world's myriad cultures; instead, the key is to keep an open mind, be sensitive to other cultures, and remember that the way you'd like to be treated is not necessarily the way others would appreciate.

Please write a short paragraph where your perception of someone was changed once you got to know them. Share and compare with your classmates

[1] Chen, G., & Starosta, W. (2000). *Foundations of intercultural communication.* Boston, MA: Allyn & Bacon.

[2] Chen, G., & Starosta, W. (2000). *Foundations of intercultural communication.* Boston, MA: Allyn & Bacon.

[3] Leeds-Hurwitz, W. (1990). Notes in the history of intercultural communication: The foreign service institute and the mandate for intercultral training. *Quarterly Journal of Speech, 76,* 268–281.

[4] McLean, S. (2005). *The basics of interpersonal communication.* Boston, MA: Allyn & Bacon.

[5] Hall, E. (1966). *The hidden dimension.* New York, NY: Doubleday.

[6] Rogers, E., & Steinfatt, T. (1999). *Intercultural communication.* Prospect Heights, IL: Waveland Press.

[7] Allport, G. (1958). *The nature of prejudice.* New York, NY: Doubleday.

[8] Allport, G. (1958). *The nature of prejudice.* New York, NY: Doubleday.

[9] Hall, E. (1966). *The hidden dimension.* New York, NY: Doubleday.

[10] McLean, S. (2005). *The basics of interpersonal communication.* Boston, MA: Allyn & Bacon.

[11] McLean, S. (2005). *The basics of interpersonal communication.* Boston, MA: Allyn & Bacon.

18.3 Common Cultural Characteristics
LEARNING OBJECTIVE

1. Understand the concept of common cultural characteristics and list several examples of such characteristics in your life.

While we may be members of many different cultures, we tend to adhere to some more than others. Perhaps you have become friendly with several of your fellow students as you've pursued your studies in college. As you take many of the same classes and share many experiences on campus, you begin to have more and more in common, in effect forming a small group culture of your own. A similar cultural formation process may happen in the workplace, where coworkers spend many hours each week sharing work experiences and getting to know each other socially in the process.

Groups come together, form cultures, and grow apart across time. How does one become a member of a community, and how do you know when you are full member? What aspects of culture do we have in common and how do they relate to business communication? Researchers who have studied cultures around the world have identified certain characteristics that define a culture. These characteristics are expressed in different ways, but they tend to be present in nearly all cultures. Let's examine them.

Rites of Initiation

Cultures tend to have a ritual for becoming a new member. A newcomer starts out as a nonentity, a stranger, an unaffiliated person with no connection or even possibly awareness of the community. Newcomers who stay around and learn about the culture become members. Most cultures have a rite of initiation that marks the passage of the individual within the community; some of these rituals may be so informal as to be hardly noticed (e.g., the first time a coworker asks you to join the group to eat lunch together), while others may be highly formalized (e.g., the ordination of clergy in a religion). The nonmember becomes a member, the new member becomes a full member, and individuals rise in terms of responsibility and influence.

Business communities are communities first, because without communication interaction, no business will occur. Even if sales and stock are processed by servers that link database platforms to flow, individuals are still involved in the maintenance, repair, and development of the system. Where there is communication, there is culture, and every business has several cultures.

Across the course of your life, you have no doubt passed several rites of initiation but may not have taken notice of them. Did you earn a driver's license, register to vote, or acquire the permission to purchase alcohol? In North American culture, these three common markers indicate the passing from a previous stage of life to a new one, with new rights and responsibilities. As a child, you were not allowed to have a driver's license. At age fourteen to eighteen, depending on your state and location (rural versus urban), you were allowed to drive a tractor, use farm equipment, operate a motor vehicle during daylight hours, or have full access to public roads. With the privilege of driving comes responsibility. It is your responsibility to learn what the signs and signals mean and to obey traffic laws for the common safety. In order for stop signs to work, we all have to agree

on the behavior associated with them and observe that behavior.

Sometimes people choose to ignore a stop sign, or accidentally miss one, and it places the public in danger. Law enforcement officials reinforce that common safety as representatives of the culture, empowered by the people themselves based on a common agreement of what a stop sign means and what a driver is supposed to do when approaching one. Some people may argue that law enforcement serves some while it prosecutes others. This point of debate may deserve some consideration, but across cultures, there are rules, signs, and symbols that we share.

Rites of initiation mark the transition of the role or status of the individual within the group. Your first day on the job may have been a challenge as you learned your way around the physical space, but the true challenge was to learn how the group members communicate with each other. If you graduate from college with a Master of Business Administration (MBA) degree, you will already have passed a series of tests, learned terms and theories, and possess a symbol of accomplishment in your diploma, but that only grants you the opportunity to look for a job—to seek access to a new culture.

In every business, there are groups, power struggles, and unspoken ways that members earn their way from the role of a "newbie" to that of a full member. The newbie may get the tough account, the office without a window, or the cubicle next to the bathroom, denoting low status. As the new member learns to navigate through the community—establishing a track record and being promoted—he passes the rite of initiation and acquires new rights and responsibilities.

Over time, the person comes to be an important part of the business, a "keeper of the flame." The "flame" may not exist in physical space or time, but it does exist in the minds of those members in the community who have invested time and effort in the business. It is not a flame to be trusted to a new person, as it can only be earned with time. Along the way, there may be personality conflicts and power struggles over resources and perceived scarcity (e.g., there is only one promotion and everyone wants it). All these challenges are to be expected in any culture.

Common History and Traditions

Think for a moment about the history of a business like Ford Motor Company—what are your associations with Henry Ford, the assembly line manufacturing system, or the Model T? Or the early days of McDonald's? Do you have an emotional response to mental images of the "golden arches" logo, Ronald McDonald, or the Big Mac sandwich? Traditions form as the organization grows and expands, and stories are told and retold to educate new members on how business should be conducted. The history of every culture, of every corporation, influences the present. There are times when the phrase "we've tried that before" can become stumbling block for members of the organization as it grows and adapts to new market forces. There may be struggles between members who have weathered many storms and new members, who come armed with new educational perspectives, technological tools, or experiences that may contribute to growth.

Common Values and Principles

Cultures all hold values and principles that are commonly shared and communicated from older members to younger (or newer) ones. Time and length of commitment are associated with an awareness of these values and principles, so that new members, whether they are socialized at home, in school, or at work, may not have a thorough understanding of their importance. For example, time (fast customer service) and cleanliness are two cornerstone values of the McDonald's corporation. A new employee may take these for granted, while a seasoned professional who inspects restaurants may see the continued need to reinforce these core values. Without reinforcement, norms may gradually change, and if this were the case it could fundamentally change the customer experience associated with McDonald's.

Common Purpose and Sense of Mission

Cultures share a common sense of purpose and mission. Why are we here and whom do we serve? These are fundamental questions of the human condition that philosophers and theologians all over the world have pondered for centuries. In business, the answers to these questions often address purpose and mission, and they can be found in mission and vision statements of almost every organization. Individual members will be expected to acknowledge and share the mission and vision, actualize them, or make them real through action. Without action, the mission and vision statements are simply an arrangement of words. As a guide to individual and group behavioral norms, they can serve as a powerful motivator and a call to action.

Common Symbols, Boundaries, Status, Language, and Rituals

Most of us learn early in life what a stop sign represents, but do we know what military stripes represent on a sleeve, or a ten-year service pin on a lapel, or a corner office with two windows? Cultures have common symbols that mark them as a group; the knowledge of what a symbol stands for helps to reinforce who is a group member and who is not. You may have a brand on your arm from your fraternity, or wear a college ring—symbols that represent groups you affiliate with temporarily, while you are a student. They may or may not continue to hold meaning to you when your college experience is over. Cultural symbols include dress, such as the Western business suit and tie, the Scottish kilt, or the Islamic headscarf. Symbols also include slogans or sayings, such as "you're in good hands" or "you deserve a break today." The slogan may serve a marketing purpose but may also embrace a mission or purpose within the culture. Family crests and clan tartan patterns serve as symbols of affiliation. Symbols can also be used to communicate rank and status within the group.

Space is another common cultural characteristic; it may be a nonverbal symbol that represents status and power. In most of the world's cultures, a person occupying superior status is entitled to a physically elevated position—a throne, a dais, a podium from which to address subordinates. Subordinates may be expected to bow, curtsy, or lower their eyes as a sign of respect. In business, the corner office may offer the best view with the most space. Movement from a cubicle to a private office may also be a symbol of transition within an organization, involving increased responsibility as well as power. Parking spaces, the kind of vehicle you drive, and the transportation allowance you have may also serve to communicate symbolic meaning within an organization.

The office serves our discussion on the second point concerning boundaries. Would you sit on your boss's desk or sit in his chair with your feet up on the desk in his presence? Most people indicate they would not, because doing so would communicate a lack of respect, violate normative space expectations, and invite retaliation. Still, subtle challenges to authority may arise in the workplace. A less than flattering photograph of the boss at the office party posted to the recreational room bulletin board communicates more than a lack of respect for authority. By placing the image anonymously in a public place, the prankster clearly communicates a challenge, even if it is a juvenile one. Movement from the cubicle to the broom closet may be the result for someone who is found responsible for the prank. Again, there are no words used to communicate meaning, only symbols, but those symbols represent significant issues. Communities have their own vocabulary and way in which they communicate. Consider the person who uses a sewing machine to create a dress and the accountant behind the desk; both are professionals and both have specialized jargon used in their field. If they were to change places, the lack of skills would present an obstacle, but the lack of understanding of terms, how they are used, and what they mean would also severely limit their effectiveness. Those terms and how they are used are learned over time and through interaction. While a textbook can help, it cannot demonstrate use in live interactions. Cultures are dynamic systems that reflect the communication process itself.

Cultures celebrate heroes, denigrate villains, and have specific ways of completing jobs and tasks. In business and industry, the emphasis may be on effectiveness and efficiency, but the practice can often be "because that is the way we have always done it." Rituals serve to guide our performance and behavior and may be limited to small groups or celebrated across the entire company. A pink Cadillac has a special meaning for a Mary Kay cosmetics representative. How that car is received is ritualistic, recognizing current success while honoring past performances across the company.

Rituals can serve to bind a group together, or to constrain it. Institutions tend to formalize processes and then have a hard time adapting to new circumstances. While the core values or mission statement may hold true, the method of doing things that worked in the past may not be as successful as it once was. Adaptation and change can be difficult for individuals and companies, and yet all communities, cultures, and communication contexts are dynamic, or always changing. As much as we might like things to stay the same, they will always change—and we will change with (and be changed by) them.

KEY TAKEAWAY

All cultures have characteristics such as initiations, traditions, history, values and principles, purpose, symbols, and boundaries.

EXERCISES

1. Compile a list or group of pictures of symbols that characterize some of the cultural groups you belong to. Share and discuss your list with your classmates.
2. Compile a list of pictures or symbols that your group or community finds offensive. Share and compare with classmates.

18.4 Divergent Cultural Characteristics

LEARNING OBJECTIVE

1. Discuss divergent cultural characteristics and list several examples of such characteristics in the culture(s) you identify with.

We are not created equal. We are born light- or dark-skinned, to parents of education or parents without access to education, and we grow up short or tall, slender or stocky. Our life chances or options are in many ways determined by our birth. The Victorian "rags to riches" novels that Horatio

Alger wrote promoted the ideal that individuals can overcome all obstacles, raising themselves up by their bootstraps. Some people do have amazing stories, but even if you are quick to point out that Microsoft founder Bill Gates became fabulously successful despite his lack of a college education, know that his example is exception, not the rule. We all may use the advantages of our circumstances to improve our lives, but the type and extent of those advantages vary greatly across the planet.

Cultures reflect this inequality, this diversity, and the divergent range of values, symbols, and meanings across communities. Can you tie a knot? Perhaps you can tie your shoes, but can you tie a knot to secure a line to a boat, to secure a heavy load on a cart or truck, or to bundle a bale of hay? You may not be able to, but if you were raised in a culture that place a high value on knot-tying for specific purposes, you would learn that which your community values. We all have viewpoints, but they are shaped by our interactions with our communities. Let's examine several points of divergence across cultures.

Individualistic versus Collectivist Cultures

People in individualistic cultures value individual freedom and personal independence, and cultures always have stories to reflect their values. You may recall the story of Superman, or John McLean in the Diehard series, and note how one person overcomes all obstacles. Through personal ingenuity, in spite of challenges, one person rises successfully to conquer or vanquish those obstacles. Sometimes there is an assist, as in basketball or football, where another person lends a hand, but still the story repeats itself again and again, reflecting the cultural viewpoint.

The Dutch researcher Geert Hofstede explored the concepts of individualism and collectivism across diverse cultures. [1], [2], [3] He found that in individualistic cultures like the United States, people perceived their world primarily from their own viewpoint. They perceived themselves as empowered individuals, capable of making their own decisions, and able to make an impact on their own lives.

Cultural viewpoint is not an either/or dichotomy, but rather a continuum or range. You may belong to some communities that express individualistic cultural values, while others place the focus on a collective viewpoint. Collectivist cultures, [4] including many in Asia and South America, focus on the needs of the nation, community, family, or group of workers. Ownership and private property is one way to examine this difference. In some cultures, property is almost exclusively private, while others tend toward community ownership. The collectively owned resource returns benefits to the community. Water, for example, has long been viewed as a community resource, much like air, but that has been changing as business and organizations have purchased water rights and gained control over resources. Public lands, such as parks, are often considered public, and individual exploitation of them is restricted. Copper, a metal with a variety of industrial applications, is collectively owned in Chile, with profits deposited in the general government fund. While public and private initiatives exist, the cultural viewpoint is our topic. How does someone raised in a culture that emphasizes the community interact with someone raised in a primarily individualistic culture? How could tensions be expressed and how might interactions be influenced by this point of divergence?

Explicit-Rule Cultures versus Implicit-Rule Cultures

Do you know the rules of your business or organization? Did you learn them from an employee manual or by observing the conduct of others? Your response may include both options, but not all cultures communicate rules in the same way. Carley Dodd [5] discusses this difference and has found quite a range of difference. In an explicit-rule culture, where rules are clearly communicated so that everyone is aware of them, the guidelines and agenda for a meeting are announced prior to the gathering. In an implicit-rule culture, where rules are often understood and communicated nonverbally, there may be no agenda. Everyone knows why they are gathered and what role each member plays, even though the expectations may not be clearly stated. Power, status, and behavioral expectations may all be understood, and to the person from outside this culture, it may prove a challenge to understand the rules of the context.

Outsiders often communicate their "otherness" by not knowing where to stand, when to sit, or how to initiate a conversation if the rules are not clearly stated. While it may help to know that implicit-rule cultures are often more tolerant of deviation from the understood rules, the newcomer will be wise to learn by observing quietly—and to do as much research ahead of the event as possible.

Uncertainty-Accepting Cultures versus Uncertainty-Rejecting Cultures

When we meet each other for the first time, we often use what we have previously learned to understand our current context. We also do this to reduce our uncertainty. Some cultures, such as the United States and Britain, are highly tolerant of uncertainty, while others go to great lengths to reduce the element of surprise. Cultures in the Arab world, for example, are high in uncertainty avoidance; they tend to be resistant to change and reluctant to take risks. Whereas a U.S. business negotiator might enthusiastically agree to try a

new procedure, the Egyptian counterpart would likely refuse to get involved until all the details are worked out.

Charles Berger and Richard Calabrese [6] developed uncertainty reduction theory to examine this dynamic aspect of communication. Here are seven axioms of uncertainty:
1. There is a high level of uncertainty at first. As we get to know one another, our verbal communication increases and our uncertainty begins to decrease.
2. Following verbal communication, nonverbal communication increases, uncertainty continues to decrease, and more nonverbal displays of affiliation, like nodding one's head to indicate agreement, will start to be expressed.
3. When experiencing high levels of uncertainty, we tend to increase our information-seeking behavior, perhaps asking questions to gain more insight. As our understanding increases, uncertainty decreases, as does the information-seeking behavior.
4. When experiencing high levels of uncertainty, the communication interaction is not as personal or intimate. As uncertainty is reduced, intimacy increases.
5. When experiencing high levels of uncertainty, communication will feature more reciprocity, or displays of respect. As uncertainty decreases, reciprocity may diminish.
6. Differences between people increase uncertainty, while similarities decrease it.
7. Higher levels of uncertainty are associated with a decrease in the indication of liking the other person, while reductions in uncertainty are associated with liking the other person more.

Time Orientation

Edward T. Hall and Mildred Reed Hall [7] state that monochronic time-oriented cultures consider one thing at a time, whereas polychronic time-oriented cultures schedule many things at one time, and time is considered in a more fluid sense. In monochromatic time, interruptions are to be avoided, and everything has its own specific time. Even the multitasker from a monochromatic culture will, for example, recognize the value of work first before play or personal time. The United States, Germany, and Switzerland are often noted as countries that value a monochromatic time orientation.

Polychromatic time looks a little more complicated, with business and family mixing with dinner and dancing. Greece, Italy, Chile, and Saudi Arabia are countries where one can observe this perception of time; business meetings may be scheduled at a fixed time, but when they actually begin may be another story. Also note that the dinner invitation for 8 p.m. may in reality be more like 9 p.m. If you were to show up on time, you might be the first person to arrive and find that the hosts are not quite ready to receive you.

When in doubt, always ask before the event; many people from polychromatic cultures will be used to foreigner's tendency to be punctual, even compulsive, about respecting established times for events. The skilled business communicator is aware of this difference and takes steps to anticipate it. The value of time in different cultures is expressed in many ways, and your understanding can help you communicate more effectively.

Short-Term versus Long-Term Orientation

Do you want your reward right now or can you dedicate yourself to a long-term goal? You may work in a culture whose people value immediate results and grow impatient when those results do not materialize. Geert Hofstede [8], [9] discusses this relationship of time orientation to a culture as a "time horizon," and it underscores the perspective of the individual within a cultural context. Many countries in Asia, influenced by the teachings of Confucius, value a long-term orientation, whereas other countries, including the United States, have a more short-term approach to life and results. Native American cultures are known for holding a long-term orientation, as illustrated by the proverb attributed to the Iroquois that decisions require contemplation of their impact seven generations removed.

If you work within a culture that has a short-term orientation, you may need to place greater emphasis on reciprocation of greetings, gifts, and rewards. For example, if you send a thank-you note the morning after being treated to a business dinner, your host will appreciate your promptness. While there may be a respect for tradition, there is also an emphasis on personal representation and honor, a reflection of identity and integrity. Personal stability and consistency are also valued in a short-term oriented culture, contributing to an overall sense of predictability and familiarity.

Long-term orientation is often marked by persistence, thrift and frugality, and an order to relationships based on age and status. A sense of shame for the family and community is also observed across generations. What an individual does reflects on the family and is carried by immediate and extended family members.

Masculine versus Feminine Orientation

There was a time when many cultures and religions valued a female figurehead, and with the rise of Western cultures we have observed a shift toward a masculine ideal. Each carries with it a set of cultural expectations and norms for gender behavior and gender roles across life, including business.

Hofstede describes the masculine-feminine dichotomy not in terms of whether men or women hold the power in a given culture, but rather the extent to which that culture values certain traits that may be considered masculine or feminine. Thus, "the assertive pole has been called 'masculine' and the modest, caring pole 'feminine.' The women in feminine countries have the same modest, caring values as the men; in the masculine countries they are somewhat assertive and competitive, but not as much as the men, so that these countries show a gap between men's values and women's values." [10]

We can observe this difference in where people gather, how they interact, and how they dress. We can see it during business negotiations, where it may make an important difference in the success of the organizations involved. Cultural expectations precede the interaction, so someone who doesn't match those expectations may experience tension. Business in the United States has a masculine orientation—assertiveness and competition are highly valued. In other cultures, such as Sweden, business values are more attuned to modesty (lack of self-promotion) and taking care of society's weaker members. This range of difference is one aspect of intercultural communication that requires significant attention when the business communicator enters a new environment.

Direct versus Indirect

In the United States, business correspondence is expected to be short and to the point. "What can I do for you?" is a common question when a business person receives a call from a stranger; it is an accepted way of asking the caller to state his or her business. In some cultures it is quite appropriate to make direct personal observation, such as "You've changed your hairstyle," while for others it may be observed, but never spoken of in polite company. In indirect cultures, such as those in Latin America, business conversations may start with discussions of the weather, or family, or topics other than business as the partners gain a sense of each other, long before the topic of business is raised. Again, the skilled business communicator researches the new environment before entering it, as a social faux pas, or error, can have a significant impact.

Materialism versus Relationships

Does the car someone drives say something about them? You may consider that many people across the planet do not own a vehicle and that a car or truck is a statement of wealth. But beyond that, do the make and model reflect their personality? If you are from a materialistic culture, you may be inclined to say yes. If you are from a culture that values relationships rather than material objects, you may say no or focus on how the vehicle serves the family. From rocks that display beauty and wealth—what we call jewelry—to what you eat—will it be lobster ravioli or prime rib?—we express our values and cultural differences with our purchase decisions.

Members of a materialistic culture place emphasis on external goods and services as a representation of self, power, and social rank. If you consider the plate of food before you, and consider the labor required to harvest the grain, butcher the animal, and cook the meal, you are focusing more on the relationships involved with its production than the foods themselves. Caviar may be a luxury, and it may communicate your ability to acquire and offer a delicacy, but it also represents an effort. Cultures differ in how they view material objects and their relationship to them, and some value people and relationships more than the objects themselves. The United States and Japan are often noted as materialistic cultures, while many Scandinavian nations feature cultures that place more emphasis on relationships.

Low-Power versus High-Power Distance

How comfortable are you with critiquing your boss's decisions? If you are from a low-power distance culture, your answer might be "no problem." In low-power distance cultures, according to Hofstede, [11] people relate to one another more as equals and less as a reflection of dominant or subordinate roles, regardless of their actual formal roles as employee and manager, for example.

In a high-power distance culture, you would probably be much less likely to challenge the decision, to provide an alternative, or to give input. If you are working with people from a high-power distance culture, you may need to take extra care to elicit feedback and involve them in the discussion because their cultural framework may preclude their participation. They may have learned that less powerful people must accept decisions without comment, even if they have a concern or know there is a significant problem. Unless you are sensitive to cultural orientation and power distance, you may lose valuable information.

KEY TAKEAWAY

Cultures have distinct orientations when it comes to rules, uncertainty, time and time horizon, masculinity, directness, materialism, and power distance.

EXERCISES

1. Take a business letter or a page of a business report from a U.S. organization and try rewriting it as someone from a highly indirect, relational culture might have written it. Share and discuss your result with your classmates.

2. Conduct an online search for translated movie titles. Share and compare your results with your classmates.

3. Consider the movie you noted in the first of the Note 18.1 "Introductory Exercises" for this chapter. In what ways does it exemplify this individualistic viewpoint? Share your observations with your classmates.

4. Think of a movie where one or more characters exemplify individualism. Write a brief statement and share with classmates.

5. Think of a movie where one or more characters exemplify community-oriented values. Write a brief statement and share with classmates.

[1] Hofstede, G. (1982). *Culture's consequences* (2nd ed.). Newbury Park, CA: Sage.

[2] Hofstede, G. (2001). *Culture's consequences: Comparing values, behaviors, institutions, and organizations across nations* (2nd ed.). Thousand Oaks, CA: Sage.

[3] Hofstede, G. (2005). *Cultures and organizations: Software of the mind* (2nd ed.). New York, NY: McGraw-Hill.

[4] Hofstede, G. (1982). *Culture's consequences* (2nd ed.). Newbury Park, CA: Sage.

[5] Dodd, C. (1998). *Dynamics of intercultural communication* (5th ed.). New York, NY: Harper & Row.

[6] Berger, C., & Calabrese, R. (1975). Some explorations in initial interactions and beyond: Toward a developmental theory of interpersonal communication. *Human communication Research, 1*, 99–112.

[7] Hall, M. R., & Hall, E. T. (1987). *Hidden differences: Doing business with the Japanese*. New York, NY: Doubleday.

[8] Hofstede, G. (2001). *Culture's consequences: Comparing values, behaviors, institutions, and organizations across nations* (2nd ed.). Thousand Oaks, CA: Sage.

[9] Hofstede, G. (2005). *Cultures and organizations: Software of the mind* (Revised and expanded 2nd ed.). New York, NY: McGraw-Hill.

[10] Hofstede, G. (2009). Geert Hofstede cultural dimensions. *Itim International*. Retrieved from http://www.geert-hofstede.com

[11] Hofstede, G. (2009). Geert Hofstede cultural dimensions. *Itim International*. Retrieved from http://www.geert-hofstede.com

18.5 International Communication and the Global Marketplace
LEARNING OBJECTIVE

1. Describe international communication and the global marketplace, including political, legal, economic, and ethical systems.

People create systems that reflect cultural values. These systems reduce uncertainty for the culture, creating and perpetuating the rules and customs, but may prove a significant challenge to the entrepreneur entering a new market. Political, legal, economic, and ethical systems vary from culture to culture, and may or may not reflect formal boundaries. For example, disputes over who controls what part of their shoreline are common and are still a matter of debate, interpretation, and negotiation in many countries.

To a large extent, a country's culture is composed of formal systems. Formal systems often direct, guide, constrain, or promote some behaviors over others. A legal system, like taxation, may favor the first-time homebuyer in the United States, and as a consequence, home ownership may be pursued instead of other investment strategies. That same legal system, via tariffs, may levy import taxes on specific goods and services, and reduce their demand as the cost increases. Each of these systems reinforces or discourages actions based on cultural norms, creating regulations that reflect ways that each culture, through its constituents, views the world.

In this section, we'll examine intercultural communication from the standpoint of international communication. International communication can be defined as communication between nations, but we recognize that nations do not exist independent of people. International communication is typically government to government or, more accurately, governmental representatives to governmental representatives. It often involves topics and issues that relate to the nations as entities, broad issues of trade, and conflict resolution. People use political, legal, and economic systems to guide and regulate behavior, and diverse cultural viewpoints necessarily give rise to many variations. Ethical systems also guide behavior, but often in less formal, institutional ways. Together these areas form much of the basis of international communication, and warrant closer examination.

Political Systems

You may be familiar with democracy, or rule by the people; and theocracy, or rule of God by his or her designates; but the world presents a diverse range of how people are governed. It is also important to note, as we examine political systems, that they are created, maintained, and changed by people. Just as people change over time, so do all systems that humans create. A political climate that was once closed to market forces, including direct and indirect investment, may change over time.

Centuries ago, China built a physical wall to keep out invaders. In the twentieth century, it erected another kind of wall: a political wall that separated the country from the Western world and limited entrepreneurship due to its adherence to its interpretation of communism. In 2009, that closed market is now open for business. To what extent it is open may be a point of debate, but simple observation provides ample evidence of a country, and a culture, open to investment and trade. The opening and closing ceremonies for the 2008 Olympic Games in Beijing symbolized this openness, with symbolic representations of culture combined with notable emphasis on welcoming the world. As the nature of global trade and change transforms business, so it also transforms political systems.

Political systems are often framed in terms of how people are governed, and the extent to which they may participate. Democracy is one form of government that promotes the involvement of the individual, but even here we can observe stark differences. In the United States, people are encouraged to vote, but it is not mandatory, and voter turnout is often so low that voting minorities have great influence on the larger political systems. In Chile, voting is mandatory, so that all individuals are expected to participate, with adverse consequences if they do not. This doesn't mean there are not still voting minorities or groups with disproportionate levels of influence and power, but it does underscore cultural values and their many representations. Centralized rule of the people also comes in many forms. In a dictatorship, the dictator establishes and enforces the rules with few checks and balances, if any. In a totalitarian system, one party makes the rules. The Communist states of the twentieth century (although egalitarian in theory) were ruled in practice by a small central committee. In a theocracy, one religion makes the rules based on their primary documents or interpretation of them, and religious leaders hold positions of political power. In each case, political power is centralized to a small group over the many.

A third type of political system is anarchy, in which there is no government. A few places in the world, notably Somalia, may be said to exist in a state of anarchy. But even in a state of anarchy, the lack of a central government means that local warlords, elders, and others exercise a certain amount of political, military, and economic power. The lack of an established governing system itself creates the need for informal power structures that regulate behavior and conduct, set and promote ideals, and engage in commerce and trade, even if that engagement involves nonstandard strategies such as the appropriation of ships via piracy. In the absence of appointed or elected leaders, emergent leaders will rise as people attempt to meet their basic needs.

Legal Systems

Legal systems also vary across the planet and come in many forms. Some legal systems promote the rule of law while others promote the rule of culture, including customs, traditions, and religions. The two most common systems are civil and common law. Civil law draws from a Roman history and common law from an English tradition. In civil law the rules are spelled out in detail, and judges are responsible for applying the law to the given case. In common law, the judge interprets the law and considers the concept of precedent, or previous decisions. Common law naturally adapts to changes in technology and modern contexts as precedents accumulate, while civil law requires new rules to be written out to reflect the new context even as the context transforms and changes. Civil law is more predictable and is practiced in the majority of countries, while common law involves more interpretation that can produce conflict with multiple views on the application of the law in question. The third type of law draws its rules from a theological base rooted in religion. This system presents unique challenges to the outsider, and warrants thorough research.

Economic Systems

Economic systems vary in similar ways across cultures, and again reflect the norms and customs of people. Economies are often described on the relationship between people and their government. An economy with a high degree of government intervention may prove challenging for both internal and external businesses. An economy with relatively little government oversight may be said to reflect more of the market(s) and to be less restricted. Along these same lines, government may perceive its role as a representative of the common good, to protect individual consumers, and to prevent fraud and exploitation.

This continuum or range, from high to low degrees of government involvement, reflects the concept of government itself. A government may be designed to give everyone access to the market, with little supervision, in the hope that people will regulate transactions based on their own needs, wants, and desires; in essence, their own self-interest. If everyone operates in one's self-interest and word gets out that one business produces a product that fails to work as advertised, it is often believed that the market will naturally gravitate away from this faulty product to a competing product that works properly. Individual consumers, however, may have a hard time knowing which product to have faith in and may look to government to provide that measure of safety.

Government certification of food, for example, attempts to reduce disease. Meat from unknown sources would lack the seal of certification, alerting the consumer to evaluate the product closely or choose another product. In terms of supervision, we can see an example of this when Japan restricts the sale of U.S. beef for fear of mad cow disease. The concern may be warranted from the consumer's viewpoint, or it may be protectionist from a business standpoint, protecting the local producer over the importer.

From meat to financial products, we can see both the dangers and positive attributes of intervention and can also

acknowledge that its application may be less than consistent. Some cultures that value the community may naturally look to their government for leadership in economic areas, while those that represent an individualistic tendency may take a more "hands off" approach.

Ethical Systems

Ethical systems, unlike political, legal, and economic systems, are generally not formally institutionalized. This does not imply, however, that they are less influential in interactions, trade, and commerce. Ethics refers to a set of norms and principles that relate to individual and group behavior, including businesses and organizations. They may be explicit, in the form of an organization's code of conduct; may be represented in religion, as in the Ten Commandments; or may reflect cultural values in law. What is legal and what is ethical are at times quite distinct.

For example, the question of executive bonuses was hotly debated when several U.S. financial services companies accepted taxpayer money under the Troubled Assets Relief Program (TARP) in 2008. It was legal for TARP recipient firms to pay bonuses—indeed, some lawyers argued that failing to pay promised bonuses would violate contract law—but many taxpayers believed it was unethical.

Some cultures have systems of respect and honor that require tribute and compensation for service, while others may view payment as a form of bribe. It may be legal in one country to make a donation or support a public official in order to gain influence over a decision, but it may be unethical. In some countries, it may be both illegal and unethical. Given the complexity of human values and their expression across behaviors, it is wise to research the legal and ethical norms of the place or community where you want to do business.

Global Village

International trade has advantages and disadvantages, again based on your viewpoint and cultural reference. If you come from a traditional culture, with strong gender norms and codes of conduct, you may not appreciate the importation of some Western television programs that promote what you consider to be content that contradicts your cultural values. You may also take the viewpoint from a basic perspective and assert that basic goods and services that can only be obtained through trade pose a security risk. If you cannot obtain the product or service, it may put you, your business, or your community at risk.

Furthermore, "just in time" delivery methods may produce shortages when the systems break down due to weather, transportation delays, or conflict. People come to know each other through interactions (and transactions are fundamental to global trade), but cultural viewpoints may come into conflict. Some cultures may want a traditional framework to continue and will promote their traditional cultural values and norms at the expense of innovation and trade. Other cultures may come to embrace diverse cultures and trade, only to find that they have welcomed some who wish to do harm. In a modern world, transactions have a cultural dynamic that cannot be ignored.

Intercultural communication and business have been related since the first exchange of value. People, even from the same community, had to arrive at a common understanding of value. Symbols, gestures, and even language reflect these values. Attention to this central concept will enable the skilled business communicator to look beyond his or her own viewpoint.

It was once the privilege of the wealthy to travel, and the merchant or explorer knew firsthand what many could only read about. Now we can take virtual tours of locations we may never travel to, and as the cost of travel decreases, we can increasingly see the world for ourselves. As global trade has developed, and time to market has decreased, the world has effectively grown smaller. While the size has not changed, our ability to navigate has been dramatically decreased. Time and distance are no longer the obstacles they once were. The Canadian philosopher Marshall McLuhan, a pioneer in the field of communication, predicted what we now know as the "global village." The global village is characterized by information and transportation technologies that reduce the time and space required to interact. [1]

KEY TAKEAWAY

People create political, legal, economic, and ethical systems to guide them in transacting business domestically and internationally.

EXERCISES

1. Choose one country you would like to visit and explore its political system. How is it different from the system in your country? What are the similarities? Share your findings with classmates.
2. Think of an ethical aspect of the economic crisis of 2008 that involved you or your family. For example, did you or a relative get laid off at work, have difficulty making mortgage or rent payments, change your spending habits, or make donations to help those less fortunate? Is there more than one interpretation of the ethics of the situation? Write a short essay about it and discuss it with your classmates.
3. Choose one country you would like to visit and explore its economic system, including type of currency and its

current value in relation to the U.S. dollar. Share and compare your results with classmates.

[1] McLuhan, M. (1964). *Understanding media: The extensions of man.* New York, NY: McGraw-Hill.

18.6 Styles of Management
LEARNING OBJECTIVE

1. Understand and discuss how various styles of management, including Theory X, Y, and Z, influence workplace culture.

People and their relationships to dominant and subordinate roles are a reflection of culture and cultural viewpoint. They are communicated through experience and create expectations for how and when managers interact with employees. The three most commonly discussed management theories are often called X, Y, and Z. In this section we'll briefly discuss them and their relationship to intercultural communication.

Theory X

In an influential book titled *The Human Side of Enterprise*, M. I. T. management professor Douglas McGregor [1] described two contrasting perceptions on how and why people work, formulating Theory X and Theory Y; they are both based on Maslow's hierarchy of needs. [2], [3] According to this model, people are concerned first with physical needs (e.g., food, shelter) and second with safety. At the third level, people seek love, acceptance, and intimacy. Self-esteem, achievement, and respect are the fourth level. Finally, the fifth level embodies self-actualization.

McGregor's Theory X asserts that workers are motivated by their basic (low-level) needs and have a general disposition against labor. In this viewpoint, workers are considered lazy and predicted to avoid work if they can, giving rise to the perceived need for constant, direct supervision. A Theory X manager may be described as authoritarian or autocratic, and does not seek input or feedback from employees. The view further holds that workers are motivated by personal interest, avoid discomfort, and seek pleasure. The Theory X manager uses control and incentive programs to provide punishment and rewards. Responsibility is the domain of the manager, and the view is that employees will avoid it if at all possible to the extent that blame is always deflected or attributed to something other than personal responsibility. Lack of training, inferior machines, or failure to provide the necessary tools are all reasons to stop working, and it is up to the manager to fix these issues.

Theory Y

In contrast to Theory X, Theory Y views employees as ambitious, self-directed, and capable of self-motivation. Employees have a choice, and they prefer to do a good job as a representation of self-actualization. The pursuit of pleasure and avoidance of pain are part of being human, but work is also a reward in itself and employees take pride in their efforts. Employees want to reach their fullest potential and define themselves by their profession. A job well done is reward in and of itself, and the employee may be a valuable source of feedback. Collaboration is viewed as normal, and the worker may need little supervision.

Theory Z

Theory X and Y may seem like two extremes across the range of management styles, but in fact they are often combined in actual work settings. William Ouchi's Theory Z combines elements of both, and draws from American and Japanese management style. It promotes worker participation and emphasizes job rotation, skills development, and loyalty to the company. [4] Workers are seen as having a high need for reinforcement, and belonging is emphasized. Theory Z workers are trusted to do their jobs with excellence and management is trusted to support them, looking out for their well-being. [5]

Each of these theories of management features a viewpoint with assumptions about people and why they do what they do. While each has been the subject of debate, and variations on each have been introduced across organizational communication and business, they serve as a foundation for understanding management in an intercultural context.

KEY TAKEAWAY

Management Theories X, Y, and Z are examples of distinct and divergent views on worker motivation, need for supervision, and the possibility of collaboration.

EXERCISES

1. Imagine that you are a manager in charge of approximately a dozen workers. Would you prefer to rely primarily on Theory X, Y, or Z as your management style? Why? Write a short essay defending your preference, giving some concrete examples of management decisions you would make. Discuss your essay with your classmates.
2. Describe your best boss and write a short analysis on what type of management style you perceive they used. Share and compare with classmates.
3. Describe your worst boss and write a short analysis on what type of management style you perceive they used. Share and compare with classmates.

[1] McGregor, D. (1960). *The human side of enterprise.* New York, NY: McGraw-Hill.
[2] Maslow, A. (1954). *Motivation and personality.* New York, NY: Harper & Row.
[3] Maslow, A. (1970). *Motivation and personality* (2nd ed.). New York, NY: Harper & Row.
[4] Luthans, F. (1989). *Organisational behaviour.* New York, NY: McGraw-Hill.
[5] Massie, J., & Douglas, J. (1992). *Managing: A contemporary introduction.* Englewood Cliffs, NJ: Prentice Hall.

18.7 The International Assignment
LEARNING OBJECTIVES

1. Describe how to prepare for an international assignment.
2. Discuss the acculturation process as an expatriate.
3. Describe effective strategies for living and working abroad.

Suppose you have the opportunity to work or study in a foreign country. You may find the prospect of an international assignment intriguing, challenging, or even frightening; indeed, most professionals employed abroad will tell you they pass through all three stages at some point during the assignment. They may also share their sense of adjustment, even embrace of their host culture, and the challenges of reintegration into their native country.

An international assignment, whether as a student or a career professional, requires work and preparation, and should be given the time and consideration of any major life change. When you lose a loved one, it takes time to come to terms with the loss. When someone you love is diagnosed with a serious illness, the news may take some time to sink in. When a new baby enters your family, a period of adjustment is predictable and prolonged. All these major life changes can stress an individual beyond their capacity to adjust. Similarly, in order to be a successful "expat," or expatriate, one needs to prepare mentally and physically for the change.

International business assignments are a reflection of increased global trade, and as trade decreases, they may become an expensive luxury. As technology allows for instant face-to-face communication, and group collaboration on documents via cloud computing and storage, the need for physical travel may be reduced. But regardless of whether your assignment involves relocation abroad, supervision of managers in another country at a distance, or supervision by a foreign manager, you will need to learn more about the language, culture, and customs that are not your own. You will need to compare and contrast, and seek experiences that lend insight, in order to communicate more effectively.

An efficient, effective manager in any country is desirable, but one with international experience even more so. You will represent your company and they will represent you, including a considerable financial investment, either by your employer (in the case of a professional assignment) or by whoever is financing your education (in the case of studying abroad). That investment should not be taken lightly. As many as 40 percent of foreign-assigned employees terminate their assignments early, [1] at a considerable cost to their employers. Of those that remain, almost 50 percent are less than effective. [2]

Preparation

With this perspective in mind, let's discuss how to prepare for the international assignment and strategies to make you a more effective professional as a stranger in a strange land. First we'll dispel a couple of myths associated with an idealized or romantic view of living abroad. Next we'll examine traits and skills of the successful expatriate. Finally, we'll examine culture shock and the acculturation process.

Your experience with other cultures may have come firsthand, but for most, a foreign location like Paris is an idea formed from exposure to images via the mass media. Paris may be known for its art, as a place for lovers, or as a great place to buy bread. But if you have only ever known about a place through the lens of a camera, you have only seen the portraits designed and portrayed by others. You will lack the multidimensional view of one who lives and works in Paris, and even if you are aware of its history, its economic development, or its recent changes, these are all academic observations until the moment of experience.

That is not to say that research does not form a solid foundation in preparation for an international assignment, but it does reinforce the distinction between a media-fabricated ideal and real life. Awareness of this difference is an important step as you prepare yourself for life in a foreign culture.

If the decision is yours to make, take your time. If others are involved, and family is a consideration, you should take even more care with this important decision. Residence abroad requires some knowledge of the language, an ability to adapt, and an interest in learning about different cultures. If family members are not a part of the decision, or lack the language skills or interest, the assignment may prove overwhelming and lead to failure. Sixty-four percent of expatriate respondents who terminated their assignment early indicated that family concerns were the primary reason. [3]

Points to consider include the following:

- How flexible are you?
- Do you need everything spelled out or can you go with the flow?
- Can you adapt to new ways of doing business?
- Are you interested in the host culture and willing to dedicate the time and put forth the effort to learn more about it?
- What has been your experience to date working with people from distinct cultures?
- What are your language skills at present, and are you interested in learning a new language?
- Is your family supportive of the assignment?
- How will it affect your children's education? Your spouse's career? Your career?
- Will this assignment benefit your family?
- How long are you willing to commit to the assignment?
- What resources are available to help you prepare, move, and adjust?
- Can you stand being out of the loop, even if you are in daily written and oral communication with the home office?
- What is your relationship with your employer, and can it withstand the anticipated stress and tension that will result as not everything goes according to plan?
- Is the cultural framework of your assignment similar to—or unlike—your own, and how ready are you to adapt to differences in such areas as time horizon, masculinity versus femininity, or direct versus indirect styles of communication?

This list of questions could continue, and feel free to add your own as you explore the idea of an international assignment. An international assignment is not like a domestic move or reassignment. Within the same country, even if there are significantly different local customs in place, similar rules, laws, and ways of doing business are present. In a foreign country, you will lose those familiar traditions and institutions and have to learn many new ways of accomplishing your given tasks. What once took a five-minute phone call may now take a dozen meetings and a month to achieve, and that may cause you some frustration. It may also cause your employer frustration as you try to communicate how things are done locally, and why results are not immediate, as they lack even your limited understanding of your current context. Your relationship with your employer will experience stress, and your ability to communicate your situation will require tact and finesse.

Successful expatriates are adaptable, open to learning new languages, cultures, and skilled at finding common ground for communication. Rather than responding with frustration, they learn the new customs and find the advantage to get the job done. They form relationships and are not afraid to ask for help when it is warranted or required. They feel secure in their place as explorer, and understand that mistakes are a given, even as they are unpredictable. Being a stranger is no easy task, but they welcome the challenge with energy and enthusiasm.

Acculturation Process

Acculturation, or the transition to living abroad, is often described as an emotional rollercoaster. Steven Rhinesmith [4] provides ten steps that show the process of acculturation, including culture shock, that you may experience:
1. Initial anxiety
2. Initial elation
3. Initial culture shock
4. Superficial adjustment
5. Depression-frustration
6. Acceptance of host culture
7. Return anxiety
8. Return elation
9. Reentry shock
10. Reintegration

Humans fear the unknown, and even if your tolerance for uncertainty is high, you may experience a degree of anxiety in anticipation of your arrival. At first the "honeymoon" period is observed, with a sense of elation at all the newfound wonders. You may adjust superficially at first, learning where to get familiar foods or new ways to meet your basic needs. As you live in the new culture, divergence will become a trend and you'll notice many things that frustrate you. You won't anticipate the need for two hours at a bank for a transaction that once took five minutes, or could be handled over the Internet, and find that businesses close during midday, preventing you from accomplishing your goals. At this stage, you will feel that living in this new culture is simply exhausting. Many expats advise that this is the time to tough it out—if you give in to the temptation to make a visit back home, you will only prolong your difficult adjustment.

Over time, if you persevere, you will come to accept and adjust to your host culture, and learn how to accomplish your goals with less frustration and ease. You may come to appreciate several cultural values or traits and come to embrace some aspects of your host culture. At some point, you will need to return to your first, or home, culture, but that transition will bring a sense of anxiety. People and places change, the familiar is no longer so familiar, and you too have changed. You may once again be elated at your return and the

familiar, and experience a sense of comfort in home and family, but culture shock may again be part of your adjustment. You may look at your home culture in a new way and question things that are done in a particular way that you have always considered normal. You may hold onto some of the cultural traits you adopted while living abroad, and begin the process of reintegration.

You may also begin to feel that the "grass is greener" in your host country, and long to return. Expatriates are often noted for "going native," or adopting the host culture's way of life, but even the most confirmed expats still gather to hear the familiar sound of their first language, and find community in people like themselves who have blended cultural boundaries on a personal level.

Living and Working Abroad

In order to learn to swim you have to get in the water, and all the research and preparation cannot take the place of direct experience. Your awareness of culture shock may help you adjust, and your preparation by learning some of the language will assist you, but know that living and working abroad take time and effort. Still, there are several guidelines that can serve you well as you start your new life in a strange land:
1. *Be open and creative.* People will eat foods that seem strange or do things in a new way, and your openness and creativity can play a positive role in your adjustment. Staying close to your living quarters or surrounding yourself with similar expats can limit your exposure to and understanding of the local cultures. While the familiar may be comfortable, and the new setting may be uncomfortable, you will learn much more about your host culture and yourself if you make the effort to be open to new experiences. Being open involves getting out of your comfort zone.
2. *Be self-reliant.* Things that were once easy or took little time may now be challenging or consume your whole day. Focus on your ability to resolve issues, learn new ways to get the job done, and be prepared to do new things.
3. *Keep a balanced perspective.* Your host culture isn't perfect. Humans aren't perfect, and neither was your home culture. Each location and cultural community has strengths you can learn from if you are open to them.
4. *Be patient.* Take your time, and know a silent period is normal. The textbook language classes only provide a base from which you will learn how people who live in the host country actually communicate. You didn't learn to walk in a day and won't learn to successfully navigate this culture overnight either.

5. *Be a student and a teacher.* You are learning as the new member of the community, but as a full member of your culture, you can share your experiences as well.

6. *Be an explorer.* Get out and go beyond your boundaries when you feel safe and secure. Traveling to surrounding villages, or across neighboring borders, can expand your perspective and help you learn.

7. *Protect yourself.* Always keep all your essential documents, money, and medicines close to you, or where you know they will be safe. Trying to source a medicine in a country where you are not fluent in the language, or where the names of remedies are different, can be a challenge. Your passport is essential to your safety and you need to keep it safe. You may also consider vaccination records, birth certificates, or business documents in the same way, keeping them safe and accessible. You may want to consider a "bug-out bag," with all the essentials you need, including food, water, keys, and small tools, as an essential part of planning in case of emergency.

KEY TAKEAWAYS

Preparation is key to a successful international assignment. Living and working abroad takes time, effort, and patience.

EXERCISES

1. Research one organization in a business or industry that relates to your major and has an international presence. Find a job announcement or similar document that discusses the business and its international activities. Share and compare with classmates.

2. Conduct a search on expat networks including online forum. Briefly describe your findings and share with classmates.

3. What would be the hardest part of an overseas assignment for you and why? What would be the easiest part of an overseas assignment for you and why?

4. Find an advertisement for an international assignment. Note the qualifications, and share with classmates.

5. Find an article or other first-person account of someone's experience on an international assignment. Share your results with your classmates.

[1] Tu, H., & Sullivan, S. (1994). *Business horizons.* Retrieved fromhttp://findarticles.com/p/articles/mi_m1038/is_nl_v37/ai_1492292 6

[2] Tu, H., & Sullivan, S. (1994). *Business horizons.* Retrieved from FindArticles.com:http://findarticles.com/p/articles/mi_m1038/is_nl_v37 /ai_14922926

[3] Contreras, C. D. (2009). Should you accept the international assignment? *BNET.* Retrieved from http://findarticles.com/p/articles/mi_qa5350/is_200308/ai_n21334 696

[4] Rhinesmith, S. (1984). *Returning home.* Ottawa, Canada: Canadian Bureau for International Education.

18.8 Additional Resources

- Visit the Web site of culture scholar Edward T. Hall. http://www.edwardthall.com/index.html

- Learn about intercultural awareness in the classroom by reading this article by Mark Pedelty (2001, Spring), "Self as other: An intercultural performance exercise," published in *Multicultural Education.* http://findarticles.com/p/articles/mi_qa3935/is_2001 04/ai_n8937001

- Visit these sites to explore the history and traditions of some famous American businesses. http://www.ford.com/about-ford/heritage;http://www.aboutmcdonalds.com/mcd/ our_company/mcd_history.html

- Learn more about Geert Hofstede's research on culture by exploring his Web site. http://www.geert-hofstede.com/geert_hofstede_resources.shtml

- Read advice from the U.S. Department of State on living abroad http://travel.state.gov/travel/living/living_1243.html

- Visit ExpatExchange: A World of Friends Abroad to learn about the opportunities, experiences, and emotions of people living and working in foreign countries and cultures worldwide. http://www.expatexchange.com/newsarchiveall.cfm

NOTES:

Chapter 19:
Group Communication, Teamwork, and Leadership

Teamwork is the ability to work together toward a common vision. The ability to direct individual accomplishments toward organizational objectives. It is the fuel that allows common people to attain uncommon results.
   Andrew Carnegie
Never doubt that a small group of thoughtful, committed people can change the world. Indeed, it is the only thing that ever has.
   Margaret Mead

Getting Started

INTRODUCTORY EXERCISES

1. List the family and social groups you belong to and interact with on a regular basis—for example, within a twenty-four-hour period or within a typical week. Please also consider forums, online communities, and Web sites where you follow threads of discussion or post regularly. Discuss your results with your classmates.
2. List the professional (i.e., work-related) groups you interact with in order of frequency. Please also consider informal as well as formal groups (e.g., the 10:30 coffee club and the colleagues you often share your commute with). Compare your results with those of your classmates.
3. Identify one group to which you no longer belong. List at least one reason why you no longer belong to this group. Compare your results with those of your classmates.

As humans, we are social beings. We naturally form relationships with others. In fact, relationships are often noted as one of the most important aspects of a person's life, and they exist in many forms. Interpersonal communication occurs between two people, but group communication may involve two or more individuals. Groups are a primary context for interaction within the business community. Groups may have heroes, enemies, and sages alongside new members. Groups overlap and may share common goals, but they may also engage in conflict. Groups can be supportive or coercive and can exert powerful influences over individuals.

Within a group, individuals may behave in distinct ways, use unique or specialized terms, or display symbols that have meaning to that group. Those same terms or symbols may be confusing, meaningless, or even unacceptable to another

group. An individual may belong to both groups, adapting his or her communication patterns to meet group normative expectations. Groups are increasingly important across social media venues, and there are many examples of successful business ventures on the Web that value and promote group interaction.

Groups use words to exchange meaning, establish territory, and identify who is a stranger versus who is a trusted member. Are you familiar with the term "troll"? It is often used to identify someone who is not a member of an online group or community; does not share the values and beliefs of the group; and posts a message in an online discussion board to initiate flame wars, cause disruption, or otherwise challenge the group members. Members often use words to respond to the challenge that are not otherwise common in the discussions, and the less than flattering descriptions of the troll are a rallying point.

Groups have existed throughout human history and continue to follow familiar patterns across emerging venues as we adapt to technology, computer-mediated interaction, suburban sprawl, and modern life. We need groups, and groups need us. Our relationship with groups warrants attention on this interdependence as we come to know our communities, our world, and ourselves.

19.1 What Is a Group?
LEARNING OBJECTIVES

1. Define groups and teams.
2. Discuss how primary and secondary groups meet our interpersonal needs.
3. Discuss how groups tend to limit their own size and create group norms.

Let's get into a time machine and travel way, way back to join early humans in prehistoric times. Their needs are like ours today: they cannot exist or thrive without air, food, and water—and a sense of belonging. How did they meet these needs? Through cooperation and competition. If food scarcity was an issue, who got more and who got less? This serves as our first introduction to roles, status and power, and hierarchy within a group. When food scarcity becomes an issue, who gets to keep their spoon? In some Latin American cultures, having a job or earning a living is referred to by the slang term *cuchara*, which literally means "spoon" and figuratively implies food, safety, and security.

Now let's return to the present and enter a modern office. Cubicles define territories and corner offices denote status. In times of economic recession or slumping sales for the company, there is a greater need for cooperation, and there is competition for scarce resources. The loss of a "spoon"—or of one's cubicle—may now come in the form of a pink slip, but it is no less devastating.

We form self-identities through our communication with others, and much of that interaction occurs in a group context. A group may be defined as three or more individuals who affiliate, interact, or cooperate in a familial, social, or work context. Group communication may be defined as the exchange of information with those who are alike culturally, linguistically, and/or geographically. Group members may be known by their symbols, such as patches and insignia on a military uniform. They may be known by their use of specialized language or jargon; for example, someone in information technology may use the term "server" in reference to the Internet, whereas someone in the food service industry may use "server" to refer to the worker who takes customer orders in a restaurant. Group members may also be known by their proximity, as in gated communities. Regardless of how the group defines itself, and regardless of the extent to which its borders are porous or permeable, a group recognizes itself as a group. Humans naturally make groups a part of their context or environment.

Types of Groups in the Workplace

As a skilled business communicator, learning more about groups, group dynamics, management, and leadership will serve you well. Mergers, forced sales, downsizing, and entering new markets all call upon individuals within a business or organization to become members of groups. In the second of the Note 19.1 "Introductory Exercises" for this chapter, you were asked to list the professional (i.e., work-related) groups you interact with in order of frequency. What did your list include? Perhaps you noted your immediate coworkers, your supervisor and other leaders in your work situation, members of other departments with whom you communicate, and the colleagues who are also your personal friends during off-work times. Groups may be defined by function. They can also be defined, from a developmental viewpoint, by the relationships within them. Groups can also be discussed in terms of their relationship to the individual and the degree to which they meet interpersonal needs.

Some groups may be assembled at work to solve problems, and once the challenge has been resolved, they dissolve into previous or yet to be determined groups. Functional groups like this may be immediately familiar to you. You take a class in sociology from a professor of sociology, who is a member of the discipline of sociology. To be a member of a discipline is to be a disciple, and adhere to a common framework to for viewing the world. Disciplines involve a common set of theories that explain the world around us, terms to explain those theories, and have grown to reflect the advance of human knowledge. Compared to your sociology instructor, your physics instructor may see the world from a completely different perspective. Still, both may be members of divisions or schools, dedicated to teaching or research, and come together under the large group heading we know as the university.

In business, we may have marketing experts who are members of the marketing department, who perceive their tasks differently from a member of the sales staff or someone in accounting. You may work in the mailroom, and the mailroom staff is a group in itself, both distinct from and interconnected with the larger organization.

Relationships are part of any group, and can be described in terms of status, power, control, as well as role, function, or viewpoint. Within a family, for example, the ties that bind you together may be common experiences, collaborative efforts, and even pain and suffering. The birth process may forge a relationship between mother and daughter, but it also may not. An adoption may transform a family. Relationships are formed through communication interaction across time, and often share a common history, values, and beliefs about the world around us.

In business, an idea may bring professionals together and they may even refer to the new product or service as their "baby," speaking in reverent tones about a project they have taken from the drawing board and "birthed" into the real world. As in family communication, work groups or teams may have challenges, rivalries, and even "birthing pains" as a product is developed, adjusted, adapted, and transformed. Struggles are a part of relationships, both in families and business, and form a common history of shared challenged overcome through effort and hard work.

Through conversations and a shared sense that you and your coworkers belong together, you meet many of your basic human needs, such as the need to feel included, the need for affection, and the need for control. [1] In a work context, "affection" may sound odd, but we all experience affection at work in the form of friendly comments like "good morning," "have a nice weekend," and "good job!" Our professional lives also fulfill more than just our basic needs (i.e., air, food, and water, as well as safety). While your work group may be gathered together with common goals, such as to deliver the mail in a timely fashion to the corresponding departments and individuals, your daily interactions may well go beyond this functional perspective.

In the same way, your family may provide a place for you at the table and meet your basic needs, but they also may not meet other needs. If you grow to understand yourself and your place in a way that challenges group norms, you will be able to choose which parts of your life to share and to withhold in different groups, and to choose where to seek acceptance, affection, and control.

Primary and Secondary Groups
There are fundamentally two types of groups that can be observed in many contexts, from church to school, family to work. These two types are primary and secondary groups. The hierarchy denotes the degree to which the group(s) meet your interpersonal needs. Primary groups meet most, if not all, of one's needs. Groups that meet some, but not all, needs are called secondary groups. Secondary groups often include work groups, where the goal is to complete a task or solve a problem. If you are a member of the sales department, your purpose is to sell.

In terms of problem solving, work groups can accomplish more than individuals can. People, each of whom have specialized skills, talents, experience, or education come together in new combinations with new challenges, find new perspectives to create unique approaches that they themselves would not have formulated alone.

Secondary groups may meet your need for professional acceptance and celebrate your success, but they may not meet your need for understanding and sharing on a personal level. Family members may understand you in ways that your coworkers cannot, and vice versa.

If Two's Company and Three's a Crowd, What Is a Group? This old cliché refers to the human tendency to form pairs. Pairing is the most basic form of relationship formation; it applies to childhood best friends, college roommates, romantic couples, business partners, and many other dyads (two-person relationships). A group, by definition, includes at least three people. We can categorize groups in terms of their size and complexity.

When we discuss demographic groups as part of a market study, we may focus on large numbers of individuals that share common characteristics. If you are the producer of an ecologically innovative car such as the Smart For Two, and

know your customers have an average of four members in their family, you may discuss developing a new model with additional seats. While the target audience is a group, car customers don't relate to each other as a unified whole. Even if they form car clubs and have regional gatherings, a newsletter, and competitions at their local race tracks each year, they still subdivide the overall community of car owners into smaller groups.

The larger the group grows, the more likely it is to subdivide. Analysis of these smaller, or micro groups, is increasingly a point of study as the Internet allows individuals to join people of similar mind or habit to share virtually anything across time and distance. A micro group is a small, independent group that has a link, affiliation, or association with a larger group. With each additional group member the number of possible interactions increases. [2], [3]

Small groups normally contain between three and eight people. One person may involve intrapersonal communication, while two may constitute interpersonal communication, and both may be present within a group communication context. You may think to yourself before making a speech or writing your next post, and you may turn to your neighbor or coworker and have a side conversation, but a group relationship normally involves three to eight people, and the potential for distraction is great.

In Table 19.1 "Possible Interaction in Groups", you can quickly see how the number of possible interactions grows according to how many people are in the group. At some point, we all find the possible and actual interactions overwhelming and subdivide into smaller groups. For example, you may have hundreds of friends on Facebook, but how many of them do you regularly communicate with? You may be tempted to provide a number greater than eight, but if you exclude the "all to one" messages, such as a general tweet to everyone (but no one person in particular), you'll find the group norms will appear.

Table 19.1 Possible Interaction in Groups

Number of Group Members	2	3	4	5	6	7	8
Number of Possible Interactions	2	9	28	75	186	441	1,056

Group norms are customs, standards, and behavioral expectations that emerge as a group forms. If you post an update every day on your Facebook page and your friends stop by to post on your wall and comment, not posting for a week will violate a group norm. They will wonder if you are sick or in the hospital where you have no access to a computer to keep them updated. If, however, you only post once a week, the group will come to naturally expect your customary post. Norms involve expectations that are self and group imposed and that often arise as groups form and develop.

If there are more than eight members, it becomes a challenge to have equal participation, where everyone has a chance to speak, listen, and respond. Some will dominate, others will recede, and smaller groups will form. Finding a natural balance within a group can also be a challenge. Small groups need to have enough members to generate a rich and stimulating exchange of ideas, information, and interaction, but not so many people that what each brings cannot be shared. [4]

KEY TAKEAWAY

Forming groups fulfills many human needs, such as the need for affiliation, affection, and control; individuals also need to cooperate in groups to fulfill basic survival needs.

EXERCISES

1. Think of the online groups you participate in. Forums may have hundreds or thousands of members, and you may have hundreds of friends on Facebook, but how many do you regularly communicate with? Exclude the "all-to-one" messages, such as a general tweet to everyone (but no one person in particular). Do you find that you gravitate toward the group norm of eight or fewer group members? Discuss your answer with your classmates.
2. What are some of the primary groups in your life? How do they compare with the secondary groups in your life? Write a two- to three-paragraph description of these groups and compare it with a classmate's description.
3. What group is most important to people? Create a survey with at least two questions, identify a target sample size, and conduct your survey. Report how you completed the activity and your findings. Compare the results with those of your classmates.
4. Are there times when it is better to work alone rather than in a group? Why or why not? Discuss your opinion with a classmate.

[1] Schutz, W. (1966). *The interpersonal underworld*. Palo Alto, CA: Science and Behavior Books.

[2] Harris, T., & Sherblom, J. (1999). *Small group and team communication*. Boston, MA: Allyn & Bacon.

[3] McLean, S. (2003). *The basics of speech communication*. Boston, MA: Allyn & Bacon.

[4] Galanes, G., Adams, K., & Brilhart, J. (2000). *Communication in groups: Applications and skills* (4th ed.). Boston, MA: McGraw-Hill.

19.2 Group Life Cycles and Member Roles
LEARNING OBJECTIVES

1. Identify the typical stages in the life cycle of a group.
2. Describe different types of group members and group member roles.

Groups are dynamic systems in constant change. Groups grow together and eventually come apart. People join groups and others leave. This dynamic changes and transforms the very nature of the group. Group socialization involves how the group members interact with one another and form relationships. Just as you were once born and changed your family, they changed you. You came to know a language and culture, a value system, and set of beliefs that influence you to this day. You came to be socialized, to experience the process of learning to associate, communicate, or interact within a group. A group you belong to this year—perhaps a soccer team or the cast of a play—may not be part of your life next year. And those who are in leadership positions may ascend or descend the leadership hierarchy as the needs of the group, and other circumstances, change over time.

Group Life Cycle Patterns

Your life cycle is characterized with several steps, and while it doesn't follow a prescribed path, there are universal stages we can all recognize. You were born. You didn't choose your birth, your parents, your language, or your culture, but you came to know them through communication. You came to know yourself, learned skills, discovered talents, and met other people. You learned, worked, lived, and loved, and as you aged, minor injuries took longer to heal. You competed in ever-increasing age groups in your favorite sport, and while your time for each performance may have increased as you aged, your experience allowed you to excel in other ways. Where you were once a novice, you have now learned something to share. You lived to see some of your friends pass before you, and the moment will arrive when you too must confront death.

In the same way, groups experience similar steps and stages and take on many of the characteristics we associate with life. [1] They grow, overcome illness and dysfunction, and transform across time. No group, just as no individual, lives forever.

Your first day on the job may be comparable to the first day you went to school. At home, you may have learned some of the basics, like how to write with a pencil, but knowledge of that skill and its application are two different things. In school, people spoke and acted in different ways than at home. Gradually, you came to understand the meaning of recess, the importance of raising your hand to get the teacher's attention, and how to follow other school rules. At work, you may have had academic training for your profession, but the knowledge you learned in school only serves as your foundation—much as your socialization at home served to guide you at school. On the job they use jargon terms, have schedules that may include coffee breaks (recess), have a supervisor (teacher), and have rules, explicit and understood. On the first day, it was all new, even if many of the elements were familiar.

In order to better understand group development and its life cycle, many researchers have described the universal stages and phases of groups. While there are modern interpretations of these stages, most draw from the model proposed by Bruce Tuckman. [2] This model, shown in Table 19.2 "Tuckman's Linear Model of Group Development" [3], specifies the usual order of the phases of group development, and allows us to predict several stages we can anticipate as we join a new group.

Table 19.2 Tuckman's Linear Model of Group Development

Stages	Activities
Forming	Members come together, learn about each other, and determine the purpose of the group.
Storming	Members engage in more direct communication and get to know each other. Conflicts between group members will often arise during this stage.
Norming	Members establish spoken or unspoken rules about how they communicate and work. Status, rank, and roles in the group are established.
Performing	Members fulfill their purpose and reach their goal.
Adjourning	Members leave the group.

Tuckman begins with the forming stage as the initiation of group formation. This stage is also called the orientation stage because individual group members come to know each other. Group members who are new to each other and can't predict each other's behavior can be expected to experience the stress of uncertainty. Uncertainty theory states that we choose to know more about others with whom we have interactions in order to reduce or resolve the anxiety associated with the unknown. [4], [5], [6] The more we know about others and become accustomed to how they communicate, the better we can predict how they will interact with us in future contexts. If you learn that Monday mornings are never a good time for your supervisor, you quickly learn to schedule meetings later in the week. Individuals are initially tentative and display caution as they begin to learn about the group and its members.

If you don't know someone very well, it is easy to offend. Each group member brings to the group a set of experiences, combined with education and a self-concept. You won't be able to read this information on a nametag, but instead you will only come to know it through time and interaction. Since the possibility of overlapping and competing viewpoints and perspectives exists, the group will experience a storming stage, a time of struggles as the members themselves sort out their differences. There may be more than one way to solve the problem or task at hand, and some group members may prefer one strategy over another. Some members of the group may be more senior to the organization than you, and members may treat them differently. Some group members may be as new as you are and just as uncertain about everyone's talents, skills, roles, and self-perceptions. The wise business communicator will anticipate the storming stage and help facilitate opportunities for the members to resolve uncertainty before the work commences. There may be challenges for leadership, and conflicting viewpoints. The sociology professor sees the world differently than the physics professor. The sales agent sees things differently than someone from accounting. A manager who understands and anticipates this normal challenge in the group's life cycle can help the group become more productive.

A clear definition of the purpose and mission of the group can help the members focus their energies. Interaction prior to the first meeting can help reduce uncertainty. Coffee and calories can help bring a group together. Providing the group with what they need and opportunities to know each other prior to their task can increase efficiency.

Groups that make a successful transition from the storming stage will next experience the norming stage, where the group establishes norms, or informal rules, for behavior and interaction. Who speaks first? Who takes notes? Who is creative, who is visual, and who is detail-oriented? Sometimes our job titles and functions speak for themselves, but human beings are complex. We are not simply a list of job functions, and in the dynamic marketplace of today's business environment you will often find that people have talents and skills well beyond their "official" role or task. Drawing on these strengths can make the group more effective.

The norming stage is marked by less division and more collaboration. The level of anxiety associated with interaction is generally reduced, making for a more positive work climate that promotes listening. When people feel less threatened and their needs are met, they are more likely to focus their complete attention on the purpose of the group. If they are still concerned with who does what, and whether they will speak in error, the interaction framework will stay in the storming stage. Tensions are reduced when the normative expectations are known, and the degree to which a manager can describe these at the outset can reduce the amount of time the group remains in uncertainty. Group members generally express more satisfaction with clear expectations and are more inclined to participate.

Ultimately, the purpose of a work group is performance, and the preceding stages lead us to the performing stage, in which the group accomplishes its mandate, fulfills its purpose, and reaches its goals. To facilitate performance, group members can't skip the initiation of getting to know each other or the sorting out of roles and norms, but they can try to focus on performance with clear expectations from the moment the group is formed. Productivity is often how we measure success in business and industry, and the group has to produce. Outcome assessments may have been built into the system from the beginning to serve as a benchmark for success. Wise managers know how to celebrate success, as it brings more success, social cohesion, group participation, and a sense of job satisfaction. Incremental gains toward a benchmark may also be cause for celebration and support, and failure to reach a goal should be regarded as an opportunity for clarification.

It is generally wiser to focus on the performance of the group rather than individual contributions. Managers and group members will want to offer assistance to underperformers as well as congratulate members for their contributions. If the goal is to create a community where competition pushes each member to perform, individual highlights may serve your needs, but if you want a group to solve a problem or address a challenge as a group, you have to promote group cohesion. Members need to feel a sense of belonging, and praise (or the lack thereof) can be a sword with two edges: one stimulates and motivates while the other demoralizes and divides.

Groups should be designed to produce and perform in ways and at levels that individuals cannot, or else you should consider compartmentalizing the tasks. The performing stage is where the productivity occurs, and it is necessary to make sure the group has what it needs to perform. Missing pieces, parts, or information can stall the group, and reset the cycle to storming all over again. Loss of performance is inefficiency, which carries a cost. Managers will be measured by the group's productivity and performance. Make sure the performing stage is one that is productive and healthy for its members.

Imagine that you are the manager of a group that has produced an award-winning design for an ecologically innovative four-seat car. Their success is your success. Their celebrations are yours even if the success is not focused on you. A manager manages the process while group members perform. If you were a member of the group that helped design the belt line, you made a fundamental contribution to the style of the car. Individual consumers may never consider the line from the front fender, across the doors, to the rear taillight as they make a purchase decision, but they will recognize beauty. You will know that you could not have achieved that fundamental part of car design without help from the engineers in the group, and if the number-crunching accountants had not seen the efficiency of the production process that produced it, it may never have survived the transition from prototype to production. The group came together and accomplished its goals with amazing results.

Now, as typically happens, all groups will eventually have to move on to new assignments. In the adjourning stage, members leave the group. The group may cease to exist or it may be transformed with new members and a new set of goals. Your contributions in the past may have caught the attention of the management, and you may be assigned to redesign the flagship vehicle, the halo car of your marque or brand. It's quite a professional honor, and it's yours because of your successful work in a group. Others will be reassigned to tasks that require their talents and skills, and you may or may not collaborate with them in the future.

You may miss the interactions with the members, even the more cantankerous ones, and will experience both relief and a sense of loss. Like life, the group process is normal, and mixed emotions are to be expected. A wise manager anticipates this stage and facilitates the separation with skill and ease. We often close this process with a ritual marking its passing, though the ritual may be as formal as an award or as informal as a "thank you" or a verbal acknowledgement of a job well done over coffee and calories.

On a more sober note, it is important not to forget that groups can reach the adjourning stage without having achieved success. Some businesses go bankrupt, some departments are closed, and some individuals lose their positions after a group fails to perform. Adjournment can come suddenly and unexpectedly, or gradually and piece by piece. Either way, a skilled business communicator will be prepared and recognize it as part of the classic group life cycle.

Life Cycle of Member Roles

Just as groups go through a life cycle when they form and eventually adjourn, so the group members fulfill different roles during this life cycle. These roles, proposed by Richard Moreland and John Levine, [7] are summarized in Table 19.3 "Life Cycle of Member Roles". [8]

Table 19.3 Life Cycle of Member Roles

1. Potential Member	Curiosity and interest
2. New Member	Joined the group but still an outsider, and unknown
3. Full Member	Knows the "rules" and is looked to for leadership
4. Divergent Member	Focuses on differences
5. Marginal member	No longer involved
6. Ex-Member	No longer considered a member

Suppose you are about to graduate from school and you are in the midst of an employment search. You've gathered extensive information on a couple of local businesses and are aware that they will be participating in the university job fair. You've explored their Web sites, talked to people currently employed at each company, and learned what you can from the public information available. At this stage, you are considered a potential member. You may have an electrical, chemical, or mechanical engineering degree soon, but you are not a member of an engineering team.

You show up at the job fair in professional attire and completely prepared. The representatives of each company are respectful, cordial, and give you contact information. One of them even calls a member of the organization on the spot and arranges an interview for you next week. You are excited at the prospect and want to learn more. You are still a potential member.

The interview goes well the following week. The day after the meeting, you receive a call for a follow-up interview that leads to a committee interview. A few weeks later, the company calls you with a job offer. However, in the meantime, you have also been interviewing with other potential employers, and you are waiting to hear back from two of them. You are still a potential member.

After careful consideration, you decide to take the job offer and start the next week. The projects look interesting, you'll be gaining valuable experience, and the commute to work is reasonable. Your first day on the job is positive, and they've assigned you a mentor. The conversations are positive, but you feel lost at times, as if they are speaking a language you can't quite grasp. As a new group member, your level of acceptance will increase as you begin learning the groups' rules, spoken and unspoken. [9] You will gradually move from the potential member role to the role of new group member as you learn to fit into the group.

Over time and projects, you gradually increase your responsibilities. You are no longer looked at as the new person, and you can follow almost every conversation. You can't quite say, "I remember when" because your tenure hasn't been that long, but you are a known quantity and know your way around. You are a full member of the group. Full members enjoy knowing the rules and customs, and can even create new rules. New group members look to full members for leadership and guidance. Full group members can control the agenda and have considerable influence on the agenda and activities.

Full members of a group, however, can and do come into conflict. When you were a new member, you may have remained silent when you felt you had something to say, but now you state your case. There is more than one way to get the job done. You may suggest new ways that emphasize efficiency over existing methods. Coworkers who have been working in the department for several years may be unwilling to adapt and change, resulting in tension. Expressing different views can cause conflict and may even interfere with communication.

When this type of tension arises, divergent group members pull back, contribute less, and start to see themselves as separate from the group. Divergent group members have less eye contact, seek out each other's opinion less frequently, and listen defensively. In the beginning of the process, you felt a sense of belonging, but now you don't. Marginal group members start to look outside the group for their interpersonal needs.

After several months of trying to cope with these adjustments, you decide that you never really investigated the other two companies; that your job search process was incomplete. Perhaps you should take a second look at the options. You will report to work on Monday, but will start the process of becoming an ex-member, one who no longer belongs. You may experience a sense of relief upon making this decision, given that you haven't felt like you belonged to the group for a while. When you line up your next job and submit your resignation, you make it official.

This process has no set timetable. Some people overcome differences and stay in the group for years; others get promoted and leave the group only when they get transferred to regional headquarters. As a skilled business communicator, you will recognize the signs of divergence, just as you have anticipated the storming stage, and do your best to facilitate success.

Positive and Negative Member Roles

If someone in your group always makes everyone laugh, that can be a distinct asset when the news is less than positive. At times when you have to get work done, however, the class clown may become a distraction. Notions of positive and negative will often depend on the context when discussing groups. Table 19.4 "Positive Roles" [10], [11] and Table 19.5 "Negative Roles" [12], [13] list both positive and negative roles people sometimes play in a group setting. [14], [15]

Table 19.4 Positive Roles

Initiator-Coordinator	Suggests new ideas or new ways of looking at the problem
Elaborator	Builds on ideas and provides examples
Coordinator	Brings ideas, information, and suggestions together
Evaluator-Critic	Evaluates ideas and provides constructive criticism
Recorder	Records ideas, examples, suggestions, and critiques

Table 19.5 Negative Roles

Dominator	Dominates discussion, not allowing others to take their turn
Recognition Seeker	Relates discussion to their accomplishments; seeks attention
Special-Interest Pleader	Relates discussion to special interest or personal agenda
Blocker	Blocks attempts at consensus consistently
Joker or Clown	Seeks attention through humor and distracts group members

Now that we've examined a classical view of positive and negative group member roles, let's examine another perspective. While some personality traits and behaviors may negatively influence groups, some are positive or negative depending on the context.

Just as the class clown can have a positive effect in lifting spirits or a negative effect in distracting members, a dominator may be exactly what is needed for quick action. An emergency physician doesn't have time to ask all the group members in the emergency unit how they feel about a course of action; instead, a self-directed approach based on training and experience may be necessary. In contrast, the pastor of a church may have ample opportunity to ask members of the congregation their opinions about a change in the format of Sunday services; in this situation, the role of coordinator or elaborator is more appropriate than that of dominator.

The group is together because they have a purpose or goal, and normally they are capable of more than any one individual member could be on their own, so it would be inefficient to hinder that progress. But a blocker, who cuts off collaboration, does just that. If a group member interrupts another and presents a viewpoint or information that suggests a different course of action, the point may be well taken and serve the collaborative process. But if that same group member repeatedly engages in blocking behavior, then the behavior becomes a problem. A skilled business communicator will learn to recognize the difference, even when positive and negative aren't completely clear.

KEY TAKEAWAY

Groups and their individual members come together and grow apart in predictable patterns.

EXERCISES

1. Is it possible for an outsider (a nongroup member) to help a group move from the storming stage to the norming stage? Explain your answer and present it to the class.

2. Think of a group of which you are a member and identify some roles played by group members, including yourself. Have your roles, and those of others, changed over time? Are some roles more positive than others? Discuss your answers with your classmates.

3. In the course where you are using this book, think of yourself and your classmates as a group. At what stage of group formation are you currently? What stage will you be at when the school year ends?

4. Think of a group you no longer belong to. At what point did you become an ex-member? Were you ever a marginal group member or a full member? Write a two- to three-paragraph description of the group, how and why you became a member, and how and why you left. Share your description with a classmate.

[1] Moreland, R., & Levine, J. (1982). Socialization in small groups: Temporal changes in individual group relations. In L. Berkowitz (Ed.), *Advances in Experimental Social Psychology, 15*, 153.

[2] Tuckman, B. (1965). Developmental sequence in small groups. *Psychological Bulletin, 63*, 384–399.

[3] Tuckman, B. (1965). Developmental sequence in small groups. *Psychological Bulletin, 63*, 384–399.

[4] Berger, C., & Calabrese, R. (1975). Some explorations in initial interactions and beyond: Toward a developmental theory of interpersonal communication. *Human communication Research, 1*, 99–112.

[5] Berger, C. (1986). Response uncertain outcome values in predicted relationships: Uncertainty reduction theory then and now. *Human Communication Research, 13*, 34–38.

[6] Gudykunst, W. (1995). Anxiety/uncertainty management theory. In R. W. Wiseman (Ed.), *Intercultural communication theory* (pp. 8–58). Thousand Oaks, CA: Sage.

[7] Moreland, R., & Levine, J. (1982). Socialization in small groups: Temporal changes in individual group relations. In L. Berkowitz (Ed.), *Advances in Experimental Social Psychology, 15*, 153.

[8] Moreland, R., & Levine, J. (1982). Socialization in small groups: Temporal changes in individual group relations. In L. Berkowitz (Ed.), *Advances in Experimental Social Psychology, 15*, 153.

[9] Fisher, B. A. (1970). Decision emergence: Phases in group decision making. *Speech Monographs, 37*, 56–66.

[10] Beene, K., & Sheats, P. (1948). Functional roles of group members. *Journal of Social Issues, 37*, 41–49.

[11] McLean, S. (2005). *The basics of interpersonal communication*. Boston, MA: Allyn & Bacon.

[12] Beene, K., & Sheats, P. (1948). Functional roles of group members. *Journal of Social Issues, 37*, 41–49.

[13] McLean, S. (2005). *The basics of interpersonal communication*. Boston, MA: Allyn & Bacon.

[14] Beene, K., & Sheats, P. (1948). Functional roles of group members. *Journal of Social Issues, 37*, 41–49.

[15] McLean, S. (2005). *The basics of interpersonal communication*. Boston, MA: Allyn & Bacon.

19.3 Group Problem Solving
LEARNING OBJECTIVE

1. Identify and describe how to implement seven steps for group problem solving.

No matter who you are or where you live, problems are an inevitable part of life. This is true for groups as well as for individuals. Some groups—especially work teams—are formed specifically to solve problems. Other groups encounter problems for a wide variety of reasons. Within a family group, a problem might be that a daughter or son wants to get married and the parents do not approve of the marriage partner. In a work group, a problem might be that some workers are putting in more effort than others, yet achieving poorer results. Regardless of the problem, having the resources of a group can be an advantage, as different people can contribute different ideas for how to reach a satisfactory solution.

Once a group encounters a problem, the questions that come up range from "Where do we start?" to "How do we solve it?" While there are many ways to approach a problem, the American educational philosopher John Dewey's reflective thinking sequence has stood the test of time. This seven-step process [1] has produced positive results and serves as a handy organizational structure. If you are member of a group that needs to solve a problem and don't know where to start, consider these seven simple steps in a format adapted from Scott McLean: [2]

1. Define the problem
2. Analyze the problem
3. Establish criteria
4. Consider possible solutions
5. Decide on a solution
6. Implement the solution
7. Follow up on the solution

Let's discuss each step in detail.

Define the Problem

If you don't know what the problem is, how do you know you can solve it? Defining the problem allows the group to set boundaries of what the problem is and what it is not and to begin to formalize a description or definition of the scope, size, or extent of the challenge the group will address. A problem that is too broadly defined can overwhelm the group. If the problem is too narrowly defined, important information will be missed or ignored.

In the following example, we have a Web-based company called Favorites that needs to increase its customer base and ultimately sales. A problem-solving group has been formed, and they start by formulating a working definition of the problem.

Too broad: "Sales are off, our numbers are down, and we need more customers."

More precise: "Sales have been slipping incrementally for six of the past nine months and are significantly lower than a seasonally adjusted comparison to last year. Overall, this loss represents a 4.5 percent reduction in sales from the same time last year. However, when we break it down by product category, sales of our nonedible products have seen a modest but steady increase, while sales of edibles account for the drop off and we need to halt the decline."

Analyze the Problem

Now the group analyzes the problem, trying to gather information and learn more. The problem is complex and requires more than one area of expertise. Why do nonedible products continue selling well? What is it about the edibles that is turning customers off? Let's meet our problem solvers at Favorites.

Kevin is responsible for customer resource management. He is involved with the customer from the point of initial contact through purchase and delivery. Most of the interface is automated in the form of an online "basket model," where photographs and product descriptions are accompanied by "buy it" buttons. He is available during normal working business hours for live chat and voice chat if needed, and customers are invited to request additional information. Most Favorites customers do not access this service, but Kevin is kept quite busy, as he also handles returns and complaints. Because Kevin believes that superior service retains customers while attracting new ones, he is always interested in better ways to serve the customer. Looking at edibles and nonedibles, he will study the cycle of customer service and see if there are any common points—from the main Web page, through the catalog, to the purchase process, and to returns—at which customers abandon the sale. He has existing customer feedback loops with end-of-sale surveys, but most customers decline to take the survey and there is currently no incentive to participate.

Mariah is responsible for products and purchasing. She wants to offer the best products at the lowest price, and to offer new products that are unusual, rare, or exotic. She regularly adds new products to the Favorites catalog and culls underperformers. Right now she has the data on every product and its sales history, but it is a challenge to represent it. She will analyze current sales data and produce a report that specifically identifies how each product—edible and nonedible—is performing. She wants to highlight "winners" and "losers" but also recognizes that today's "losers" may be the hit of tomorrow. It is hard to predict constantly changing tastes and preferences, but that is part of her job. It's not all science, and it's not all art. She has to have an eye for what will catch on tomorrow while continuing to provide what is hot today.

Suri is responsible for data management at Favorites. She gathers, analyzes, and presents information gathered from the supply chain, sales, and marketing. She works with vendors to make sure products are available when needed, makes sales predictions based on past sales history, and assesses the effectiveness of marketing campaigns.

The problem-solving group members already have certain information on hand. They know that customer retention is one contributing factor. Attracting new customers is a constant goal, but they are aware of the well-known principle that it takes more effort to attract new customers than to keep existing ones. Thus, it is important to insure a quality customer service experience for existing customers and encourage them to refer friends. The group needs to determine how to promote this favorable customer behavior. Another contributing factor seems to be that customers often abandon the shopping cart before completing a purchase, especially when purchasing edibles. The group members need to learn more about why this is happening.

Establish Criteria

Establishing the criteria for a solution is the next step. At this point, information is coming in from diverse perspectives, and each group member has contributed information from their perspective, even though there may be several points of overlap.

Kevin: Customers who complete the post sale survey indicate that they want to know (1) what is the estimated time of delivery, (2) why a specific item was not in stock and when it will be available, and (3) why their order sometimes arrives with less than a complete order, with some items back-ordered, without prior notification.

He notes that a very small percentage of customers complete the post sale survey, and the results are far from scientific. He also notes that it appears the interface is not capable of cross-checking inventory to provide immediate information concerning back orders, so that the customer "buys it" only to learn several days later that it was not in stock. This seems to be especially problematic for edible products, because people may tend to order them for special occasions like birthdays and anniversaries. But we don't really know this for sure because of the low participation in the post sale survey.
Mariah: There are four edible products that frequently sell out. So far, we haven't been able to boost the appeal of other edibles so that people would order them as a second choice when these sales leaders aren't available. We also have several rare, exotic products that are slow movers. They have potential, but currently are underperformers.

Suri: We know from a zip code analysis that most of our customers are from a few specific geographic areas associated with above-average incomes. We have very few credit cards declined, and the average sale is over $100. Shipping costs represent on average 8 percent of the total sales cost. We do not have sufficient information to produce a customer profile. There is no specific point in the purchase process where basket abandonment tends to happen; it happens fairly uniformly at all steps.

Consider Possible Solutions to the Problem

The group has listened to each other and now starts to brainstorm ways to address the challenges they have addressed while focusing resources on those solutions that are more likely to produce results.

Kevin: Is it possible for our programmers to create a cross-index feature, linking the product desired with a report of how many are in stock? I'd like the customer to know right away whether it is in stock, or how long they may have to wait. As another idea, is it possible to add incentives to the purchase cycle that won't negatively impact our overall profit? I'm thinking a small volume discount on multiple items, or perhaps free shipping over a specific dollar amount.

Mariah: I recommend we hold a focus group where customers can sample our edible products and tell us what they like best and why. When the best sellers are sold out, could we offer a discount on related products to provide an instant alternative? We might also cull the underperforming products with a liquidation sale to generate interest.

Suri: If we want to know more about our customers, we need to give them an incentive to complete the post sale survey. How about a 5 percent off coupon code for the next purchase to get them to return and to help us better identify our customer base? We may also want to build in a customer referral rewards program, but it all takes better data in to get results out. We should also explore the supply side of the business by getting a more reliable supply of the leading products and trying to get discounts that are more advantageous from our suppliers, especially in the edible category.

Decide on a Solution

Kevin, Mariah, and Suri may want to implement all the solution strategies, but they do not have the resources to do them all. They'll complete a cost-benefit analysis, which ranks each solution according to its probable impact. The analysis is shown in Table 19.6 "Cost-Benefit Analysis".

Table 19.6 Cost-Benefit Analysis

Source	Proposed Solution	Cost	Benefit	Comment
Kevin	Integrate the cross-index feature	High	High	Many of our competitors already have this feature
	Volume discount	Low	Medium	May increase sales slightly
	Free shipping	Low	Low	This has a downside in making customers more aware of shipping costs if their order doesn't qualify for free shipping
Mariah	Hold a focus group to taste edible products	High	Medium	Difficult to select participants representative of our customer base
	Search for alternative products to high performers	Medium	Medium	We can't know for sure which products customers will like best
	Liquidate underperformers	Low	Low	Might create a "bargain basement" impression inconsistent with our brand
Suri	Incentive for post sale survey completion	Low	Medium	Make sure the incentive process is easy for the customer
	Incentive for customer referrals	Low	Medium	People may feel uncomfortable referring friends if it is seen as putting them in a marketing role
	Find a more reliable supply of top-selling edibles	Medium	High	We already know customers want these products
	Negotiate better discounts from vendors	Low	High	If we can do this without alienating our best vendors, it will be a win-win

Now that the options have been presented with their costs and benefits, it is easier for the group to decide which courses of action are likely to yield the best outcomes. The analysis helps the group members to see beyond the immediate cost of implementing a given solution. For example, Kevin's suggestion of offering free shipping won't cost Favorites much money, but it also may not pay off in customer goodwill. And even though Mariah's suggestion of having a focus group might sound like a good idea, it will be expensive and its benefits are questionable.

A careful reading of the analysis indicates that Kevin's best suggestion is to integrate the cross-index feature in the ordering process so that customers can know immediately whether an item is in stock or on back order. Mariah, meanwhile, suggests that searching for alternative products is probably the most likely to benefit Favorites, while Suri's two supply-side suggestions are likely to result in positive outcomes.

Implement the Solution

Kevin is faced with the challenge of designing the computer interface without incurring unacceptable costs. He strongly believes that the interface will pay for itself within the first year—or, to put it more bluntly, that Favorites' declining sales will get worse if the Web site does not have this feature soon. He asks to meet with top management to get budget approval and secures their agreement, on one condition: he must negotiate a compensation schedule with the Information Technology consultants that includes delayed compensation in the form of bonuses after the feature has been up and running successfully for six months.

Mariah knows that searching for alternative products is a never-ending process, but it takes time and the company needs results. She decides to invest time evaluating products that competing companies currently offer, especially in the edible category, on the theory that customers who find their desired items sold out on the Favorites Web site may have been buying alternative products elsewhere instead of choosing an alternative from Favorites's product lines.

Suri decides to approach the vendors of the four frequently sold-out products and ask point blank, "What would it take to get you to produce these items more reliably in greater quantities?" By opening the channel of communication with these vendors, she is able to motivate them to make modifications that will improve the reliability and quantity. She also approaches the vendors of the less popular products with a request for better discounts in return for their cooperation in developing and test-marketing new products.

Follow Up on the Solution

Kevin: After several beta tests, the cross-index feature was implemented and has been in place for thirty days. Now customers see either "in stock" or "available [mo/da/yr]" in the shopping basket. As expected, Kevin notes a decrease in the number of chat and phone inquiries to the effect of, "Will this item arrive before my wife's birthday?" However, he notes an increase in inquiries asking, "Why isn't this item in stock?" It is difficult to tell whether customer satisfaction is higher overall.

Mariah: In exploring the merchandise available from competing merchants, she got several ideas for modifying Favorites' product line to offer more flavors and other variations on popular edibles. Working with vendors, she found that these modifications cost very little. Within the first thirty days of adding these items to the product line, sales are up. Mariah believes these additions also serve to enhance the Favorites brand identity, but she has no data to back this up.

Suri: So far, the vendors supplying the four top-selling edibles have fulfilled their promise of increasing quantity and reliability. However, three of the four items have still sold out, raising the question of whether Favorites needs to bring in one or more additional vendors to produce these items. Of the vendors with which Favorites asked to negotiate better discounts, some refused, and two of these were "stolen" by a competing merchant so that they no longer sell to Favorites. In addition, one of the vendors that agreed to give a better discount was unexpectedly forced to cease operations for several weeks because of a fire.

This scenario allows us to see that the problem may have several dimensions as well as solutions, but resources can be limited and not every solution is successful. Even though the problem is not immediately resolved, the group problem-solving pattern serves as a useful guide through the problem-solving process.

KEY TAKEAWAY

Group problem solving can be an orderly process when it is broken down into seven specific stages.

EXERCISES

1. Think of a problem encountered in the past by a group of which you are a member. How did the group solve the problem? How satisfactory was the solution? Discuss your results with your classmates.
2. Consider again the problem you described in Exercise 1. In view of the seven-step framework, which steps did the group utilize? Would following the full seven-step framework have been helpful? Discuss your opinion with a classmate.
3. Research one business that you would like to know more about and see if you can learn about how they communicate in groups and teams. Compare your results with those of classmates.
4. Think of a decision you will be making some time in the near future. Apply the cost-benefit analysis framework to your decision. Do you find this method helpful? Discuss your results with classmates.

[1] Adler, R. (1996). *Communicating at work: Principles and practices for business and the professions.* Boston, MA: McGraw-Hill.

[2] McLean, S. (2005). *The basics of interpersonal communication.* Boston, MA: Allyn & Bacon.

19.4 Business and Professional Meetings
LEARNING OBJECTIVES

1. Understand how to prepare for and conduct business meetings.
2. Understand how to use technology to aid in group communications.
3. Understand the basic principles of organizational communication.

Business and professional meetings are a part of the communication climate of any business. Some view meetings as boring, pointless, and futile exercises, while others see them as opportunities to exchange information and produce results. A combination of preparation and execution makes all the difference. Remember, too, that meetings do not have to take place in a physical space where the participants meet face to face. Instead, a number of technological tools make it possible to hold virtual meetings in which the participants are half a world away from one another. Virtual meetings are formally arranged gatherings where participants, located in distinct geographic locations, come together via the Internet.

Preparation

A meeting, like a problem-solving group, needs a clear purpose statement. The specific goal for the specific meeting will clearly relate to the overall goal of the group or committee. Determining your purpose is central to an effective meeting and getting together just to get together is called a party, not a meeting. Do not schedule a meeting just because you met at the same time last month or because it is a standing committee. Members will resent the intrusion into their schedules and quickly perceive the lack of purpose.

Similarly, if the need for a meeting arises, do not rush into it without planning. A poorly planned meeting announced at the last minute is sure to be less than effective. People may be unable to change their schedules, may fail to attend, or may impede the progress and discussion of the group because of their absence. Those who attend may feel hindered because they needed more time to prepare and present comprehensive results to the group or committee.

If a meeting is necessary, and a clear purpose can be articulated, then you'll need to decide how and where to meet. Distance is no longer an obstacle to participation, as we will see later in this section when we explore some of the technologies for virtual meetings. However, there are many advantages to meeting in person. People communicate not just with words but also with their body language—facial expressions, hand gestures, head nodding or head shaking, and posture. These subtleties of communication can be key to determining how group members really feel about an issue or question. Meeting in real time can be important, too, as all group members have the benefit of receiving new information at the same time. For purposes of our present discussion, we will focus on meetings taking place face to face in real time.

If you have a purpose statement for the meeting, then it also follows that you should be able to create an agenda, or a list of topics to be discussed. You may need to solicit information from members to formulate an agenda, and this premeeting contact can serve to encourage active participation. The agenda will have a time, date, place, and method of interaction noted, as well as a list of participants. It will also have a statement of purpose, a list of points to be considered, and a brief summary of relevant information that relates to each point. Somewhere on the agenda the start and end times need to be clearly indicated, and it is always a good idea to leave time at the end for questions and additional points that individual members may want to share. If the meeting has an emotional point or theme, or the news is negative, plan for additional time for discussion, clarification, and recycling of conversations as the participants process the information.

If you are planning an intense work session, you need to consider the number of possible interactions among the participants and limit them. Smaller groups are generally more productive. If you are gathering to present information or to motivate the sales staff, a large audience, where little interaction is expected, is appropriate. Each member has a role, and attention to how and why they are interacting will produce the best results. Review the stages of group formation in view of the idea that a meeting is a short-term group. You can anticipate a "forming" stage, and if roles are not clear, there may be a bit of "storming" before the group establishes norms and becomes productive. Adding additional participants for no clear reason will only make the process more complex and may produce negative results.

Inviting the participants via e-mail has become increasingly common across business and industry. Software programs like Microsoft Outlook allow you to initiate a meeting request and receive an "accept" or "decline" response that makes the invitation process organized and straightforward. Reliance on a software program, however, may not be enough to encourage and ensure participation. A reminder on the individual's computer may go off fifteen minutes prior to the meeting, but if they are away from their computer or if Outlook is not running, the reminder will go unseen and unheard. A reminder e-mail on the day of the meeting, often early in the morning, can serve as a personal effort to highlight the activities of the day.

If you are the person responsible for the room reservation, confirm the reservation a week before the meeting and again the day before the meeting. Redundancy in the confirmation process can help eliminate double-booking a room, where two meetings are scheduled at the same time. If technology is required at the meeting, such as a microphone, conference telephone, or laptop and projector, make sure you confirm their reservation at the same time as you confirm the meeting room reservation. Always personally inspect the room and test these systems prior to the meeting. There is nothing more embarrassing than introducing a high-profile speaker, such as the company president, and then finding that the PowerPoint projector is not working properly.

Conducting the Meeting

The world is a stage and a meeting is a performance, the same as an interview or speech presentation. Each member has a part to perform and they should each be aware of their roles and responsibilities prior to the meeting. Everyone is a member of the group, ranging from new members to full members. If you can reduce or eliminate the storming stage, all the better. A clearly defined agenda can be a productive tool for this effort.

People may know each other by role or title, but may not be familiar with each other. Brief introductions can serve to establish identity, credibility, and help the group transition to performance. The purpose of the meeting should be clearly stated, and if there are rules or guidelines that require a specific protocol, they should be introduced.

Mary Ellen Guffey [1] provides a useful participant checklist that is adapted here for our use:

- Arrive on time and stay until the meeting adjourns (unless there are prior arrangements)
- Leave the meeting only for established breaks or emergencies
- Be prepared and have everything you need on hand
- Turn off cell phones and personal digital assistants
- Follow the established protocol for turn taking
- Respect time limits
- Demonstrate professionalism in your verbal and nonverbal interactions
- Communicate interest and stay engaged in the discussion
- Avoid tangents and side discussions
- Respect space and don't place your notebook or papers all around you
- Clean up after yourself
- Engage in polite conversation after the conclusion

If you are cast in the role of meeting leader, you may need to facilitate the discussion and address conflict. The agenda serves as your guide and you may need to redirect the discussion to the topic, but always demonstrate respect for each and every member. You may also need to intervene if a point has reached a stalemate in terms of conflict (this text offers specific guidelines for managing interpersonal conflict that apply here).

There has been quite a discussion on the role of seating arrangements in meeting within the field of business communication. Generally, a table that is square, rectangular, or U-shaped has a fixed point at which the attention is directed, often referred to as the head of the table. This space is often associated with power, status, and hierarchy and may play an important role in the flow of interactions across the meeting. If information is to be distributed and presented from administration to managers, for example, a table with a clear focal point for the head or CEO may be indicated. Tables that are round, or tables arranged in a circular pattern, allow for a more egalitarian model of interaction, reducing the hierarchical aspects while reinforcing the clear line of sight among all participants. If a meeting requires intense interaction and collaboration, generally a round table or a circular pattern is indicated.

Some meetings do not call for a table, but rather rows of seats all facing toward the speaker; you probably recognize this arrangement from many class lectures you have attended. For relatively formal meetings in which information is being delivered to a large number of listeners and little interaction is desired, seating in rows is an efficient use of space.

Transitions are often the hardest part of any meeting. Facilitating the transition from one topic to the next may require you to create links between each point. You can specifically note the next point on the agenda and verbally introduce the next speaker or person responsible for the content area. Once the meeting has accomplished its goals in the established time frame, it is time to facilitate the transition to a conclusion. You may conclude by summarizing what has been discussed or decided, and what actions the group members are to take as a result of the meeting. If there is a clear purpose for holding a subsequent meeting, discuss the time and date, and specifically note assignments for next time.

Feedback is an important part of any communication interaction. Minutes are a written document that serves to record the interaction and can provide an opportunity for clarification. Minutes often appear as the agenda with notes in relation to actions taken during the meeting or specific indications of who is responsible for what before the next meeting. In many organizations, minutes of the meeting are tentative, like a rough draft, until they are approved by the members of the group or committee. Normally minutes are sent within a week of the meeting if it is a monthly event, and more quickly if the need to meet more frequently has been determined. If your organization does not call for minutes, you can still benefit by reviewing your notes after a meeting and comparing them with those of others to make sure you understood what was discussed and did not miss—or misinterpret—any key information.

Using Technology to Facilitate Meetings

Given the widespread availability and increasingly low cost of electronic communication, technologies that once served to bring people together across continents and time zones are now also serving people in the same geographic area. Rather than traveling (by plane, car, or even elevator within the same building) to a central point for a face-to-face interaction, busy and cost-conscious professionals often choose to see and hear each other via one of many different electronic interface technologies. It is important to be aware of the dimensions of nonverbal communication that are lost in a virtual meeting compared to an in-person meeting. Nevertheless, these technologies are a boon to today's business organizations, and knowing how to use them is a key skill for all job seekers. We will discuss the technologies by category, beginning with audio-only, then audio-visual, and finally social media.

Audio-Only Interactions

The simplest form of audio-only interaction is, of course, a telephone call. Chances are that you have been using the phone all your life, yet did you know that some executives hire professional voice coaches to help them increase their effectiveness in phone communication? When you stop to think about it, we use a great many audio-only modes of communication, ranging from phone calls and voice-activated telephone menus to radio interviews, public address systems, dictation recording systems, and computer voice recognition technology. The importance of audio communication in the business world has increased with the availability of conference calls, Web conferences, and voice over Internet protocol (VoIP) communications.

Your voice has qualities that cannot be communicated in written form, and you can use these qualities to your advantage as you interact with colleagues. If you are sending a general informative message to all employees, an e-mail may serve you well, but if you are congratulating one employee on receiving an industry award, your voice as the channel carries your enthusiasm.

Take care to pay attention to your pronunciation of words, stating them correctly in normal ways, and avoiding words that you are not comfortable with as you may mispronounce them. Mispronunciation can have a negative impact on your reputation or perceived credibility. Instead of using complicated words that may cause you to stumble, choose a simple phrase if you can, or learn to pronounce the word correctly before you use it in a formal interactive setting.

Your voice quality, volume, and pitch also influence how your spoken words are interpreted. Quality often refers to emotional tone of your voice, from happy and enthusiastic to serious or even sad. In most business situations, it is appropriate to speak with some level of formality, yet avoid sounding stilted or arrogant. Your volume (the loudness of your voice) should be normal, but do make sure your listeners can hear you. In some situations, you may be using a directional microphone that only amplifies your voice signal if you speak directly into it.

If your audience includes English learners, remember that speaking louder (i.e., shouting) does not help them to understand you any better than speaking in a normal tone. Your word choices will make a much more significant impact when communicating across cultures; strive to use direct sentences and avoid figures of speech that do not translate literally.

Pitch refers to the frequency, high or low, of your voice. A pleasant, natural voice will have some variation in pitch. A speaker with a flat pitch, or a monotone (one-tone) voice, is often interpreted as being bored and often bores his or her listeners.

If you are leaving a voice mail, state all the relevant information in concise, clear terms, making sure to speak slowly; don't forget to include your contact information, even if you think the person already knows your phone number. Imagine you were writing down your phone number as you recite it and you will be better able to record it at a "listener-friendly" speed. Don't leave a long, rambling voice mail message. You may later wish you had said less, and the more content you provide the more you increase the possibility for misunderstandings without your being present for clarification.

Audio-Visual Interactions

Rather than call each other, we often call and interact in both audio and visual ways via the Internet. There are several ways to interface via audio and video, and new technologies in this area are being invented all the time. For example, VoIP software allows the participants to see and hear each other across time and distance with one-on-one calls and video conferencing. The audio portion of the call comes through a headset, and the callers see each other on their computer monitors, as if they were being broadcast on television. This form of audio-visual communication is quickly becoming a low- or no-cost business tool for interaction.

If you are going to interact via audio and visual signals, make sure you are prepared. Appropriate dress, setting, and attitude are all required. The integration of a visual signal to the traditional phone call means that nonverbal gestures can now be observed in real time and can both aid and detract from the message.

If you are unfamiliar with the technology, practice with it before your actual business interaction. Try out the features with a friend and know where to find and access the information. If the call doesn't go as planned, or the signal isn't what you expected or experienced in the past, keep a good attitude and try again.

Social Media

Online communities, forums, blogs, tweets, cloud computing, and avatar-activated environments are some of the continually developing means of social media being harnessed by the business world. The Internet is increasingly promoting tools and platforms for people to interact. From bulletin boards that resemble the FreeNet posts of years past, to interactive environments like Second Life, people are increasingly representing and interpreting themselves online.

Humans seek interaction, and this has led to new ways to market, advertise, and interact; however, caution is warranted when engaging in social media online. When you use these media, remember a few simple cautions:

1. Not everything is at it appears. The individuals on the forum may not all be who they represent themselves to be.
2. The words you write and the images you send, regardless of how much you trust the recipient, may become public and can remain online forever.
3. Always consider what you access and what you post, and how it represents you and your employer, even if you think others cannot know where you work or who you are.
4. Be aware that Internet service providers (ISPs) are required by law to archive information concerning the use and traffic of information that can become available under subpoena.

Forums are often theme-based Web sites that gather a community of individuals dedicated to a common interest. From owner-enthusiast Web sites that celebrate the new Mini Cooper, where owners discuss modifications and sell parts to each other, to forums that emphasize a viewpoint, such as the Life After the Oil Crash (LATOC) discussion board, affectionately called doomers, people come together to compare notes around areas of interest.

Professional networking sites such as LinkedIn allow people to link to, and interact with, others who work in their industry or related ones. More general social media sites include Facebook, which also presents threaded discussions and dynamic interfaces with groups that may or may not be limited to those that user intends. Interactive writing platforms such as blogs, wikis, and cloud computing involve having common documents stored on the Internet which can be accessed from multiple sites at once, further facilitating the interaction. Blogs are Web pages with periodic posts that may or may not feature feedback responses from readers. Wikis are collaborations on Web content that are created and edited by users. Cloud computing involves secure access of files from anywhere as information is stored remotely. Somewhere between a social networking site, where people gather virtually to interact, and a computer game lies the genre of avatar-activated virtual worlds such as Second Life. In these environments, users can meet others and make friends, participate in activities, and create and trade virtual property and services.

Business and industry organizations may also incorporate posts and threaded discussions, but often under a password-protected design on a company's intranet or other limited-access platform. Employees may use their business-provided computer equipment to access sites that are not business related (if not specifically blocked), but all information associated with each business's computer is subject to inspection, archival, and supervision.

Every computer is assigned an Internet protocol or IP address. The IP address can be specifically traced back to the original user, or at least to the computer itself and to who is responsible for its use. From an e-mail via one of the free sites (e.g., Juno, Google's Gmail, or Yahoo! Mail) to cloud computing and wikis, your movements across the Web leave clear "footprints."

Whether you maintain a personal Web page, a blog, or engage with peers and colleagues via Twitter, take care when considering what personal information to make public. Privacy is an increasing issue online and your safety is a priority. Always represent yourself and your organization with professionalism, knowing that what you search for and how you use your business computer can and often is subject to inspection.

Organizational Communication

Businesses and companies are often described in terms we normally associate with family, from relationships between siblings, to dominant-subordinate roles between parents and children, and the role of praise and correction. Organizational communication, or the study of the communication context, environment, and interaction within an organization, was once the domain of speech communication departments. Modern business schools now view the study of organizational communication as an integral part of the curriculum, noting the interdependent relationships of productivity, climate, and interaction between individuals within the organization (internal) and related to the organization (external), such as suppliers or customers.

Organizations have communication needs and challenges just like a family, a group, or a community. We can examine the study of communication within an organization, noting common interactive practices like performance reviews, newsletters, supervisor and direction, and the flow of information throughout the organization. We can also study the practices of the organization as they relate to other organizations and the media, as is public relations, crisis communication plans, and interorganizational interaction. Research into these areas often emphasizes the outcome, in terms of increased productivity and more effective strategic communication systems. [2] Change management, knowledge management, organizational culture, leaderships, and strategic planning often include elements of organizational communication, and again examine communication from the perspective of efficiency and effectiveness.

As a skilled business writer or communicator, you can see that the study of organizational communication can serve to inform you on the lessons learned by other companies, which are often represented in research publications, to improve the processes in place within your organization. For example, crisis management once was a knee-jerk reaction to a situation, one that caused businesses and companies to experience chaos and information management in unanticipated ways, leading to mistakes and damaging reputations. Crisis communication plans are now a common

feature in business, outlining roles and responsibilities, as well as central communication coordination and how to interact with media. Supervisors and employees then have a guide to serve everyone, much like a common playbook in organized sports like football, where everyone knows everyone else's position on the field once an emergency occurs.

KEY TAKEAWAY

Meetings require planning, choice of appropriate technology, and understanding of organizational communication.

EXERCISES

1. Take notes in one of your classes as if they were the official minutes of a meeting. Does the class "meeting" have a purpose? What preparations were made and what technology was used? Is there a follow-up or a plan for the next class meeting? Compare your notes with another student to see if you understood all the information conveyed in the class.

2. Collaborate with one or more classmates and contribute to a computing cloud or a wiki. What was the activity like? Did you learn new information that you would not have learned by studying individually?

3. Make an audio recording of your voice and listen to it. Are there aspects of your voice quality, pronunciation, or delivery style that you would like to improve? Practice daily and make more recordings until you notice improvement.

[1] Guffey, M. (2007). *Essentials of business communication* (7th ed.). Mason, OH: Thomson/Wadsworth.

[2] Tucker, M., Meyer, G., & Westman, J. (1986). *Thinking through communication: An introduction to the study of human communication.* Boston, MA: Allyn & Bacon.

19.5 Teamwork and Leadership
LEARNING OBJECTIVES

1. Define teamwork and explain how to overcome various challenges to group success.
2. Describe the process of leader development.
3. Describe several different leadership styles and their likely influence on followers.

Two important aspects of group communication—especially in the business environment—are teamwork and leadership. You will work in a team and at some point may be called on to lead. You may emerge to that role as the group recognizes your specific skill set in relation to the task, or you may be appointed to a position of responsibility for yourself and others. Your communication skills will be your foundation for success as a member and as a leader. Listen and seek to understand both the task and your group members as you become involved with the new effort. Have confidence in yourself and inspire the trust of others. Know that leading and following are both integral aspects of effective teamwork.

Teamwork

Teamwork is a compound word, combining team and work. Teams are a form of group normally dedicated to production or problem solving. That leaves us with the work. This is where our previous example on problem solving can serve us well. Each member of the team has skills, talents, experience, and education. Each is expected to contribute. Work is the activity, and while it may be fun or engaging, it also requires effort and commitment, as there is a schedule for production with individual and group responsibilities. Each member must fulfill his or her own obligations for the team to succeed, and the team, like a chain, is only as strong as its weakest member. In this context we don't measure strength or weakness at the gym, but in terms of productivity.

Teams can often achieve higher levels of performance than individuals because of the combined energies and talents of the members. Collaboration can produce motivation and creativity that may not be present in single-contractor projects. Individuals also have a sense of belonging to the group, and the range of views and diversity can energize the process, helping address creative blocks and stalemates. By involving members of the team in decision-making, and calling up on each member's area of contribution, teams can produce positive results.

Teamwork is not without its challenges. The work itself may prove a challenge as members juggle competing assignments and personal commitments. The work may also be compromised if team members are expected to conform and pressured to go along with a procedure, plan, or product that they themselves have not developed. Groupthink, or the tendency to accept the group's ideas and actions in spite of individual concerns, can also compromise the process and reduce efficiency. Personalities and competition can play a role in a team's failure to produce.

We can recognize that people want to belong to a successful team, and celebrating incremental gain can focus the attention on the project and its goals. Members will be more willing to express thoughts and opinions, and follow through with actions, when they perceive that they are an important part of the team. By failing to include all the team members, valuable insights may be lost in the rush to judgment or production. Making time for planning, and giving each member time to study, reflect, and contribute can allow them to gain valuable insights from each other, and may make them more likely to contribute information that challenges the

status quo. Unconventional or "devil's advocate" thinking may prove insightful and serve to challenge the process in a positive way, improving the production of the team. Respect for divergent views can encourage open discussion.

John Thill and Courtland Bovee [1] provide a valuable list to consider when setting up a team, which we have adapted here for our discussion:

- Select team members wisely
- Select a responsible leader
- Promote cooperation
- Clarify goals
- Elicit commitment
- Clarify responsibilities
- Instill prompt action
- Apply technology
- Ensure technological compatibility
- Provide prompt feedback

Group dynamics involve the interactions and processes of a team and influence the degree to which members feel a part of the goal and mission. A team with a strong identity can prove to be a powerful force, but it requires time and commitment. A team that exerts too much control over individual members can run the risk or reducing creative interactions and encourage tunnel vision. A team that exerts too little control, with attention to process and areas of specific responsibility, may not be productive. The balance between motivation and encouragement, and control and influence, is challenging as team members represent diverse viewpoints and approaches to the problem. A skilled business communicator creates a positive team by first selecting members based on their areas of skill and expertise, but attention to their style of communication is also warranted. Individuals that typically work alone or tend to be introverted may need additional encouragement to participate. Extroverts may need to be encouraged to listen to others and not dominate the conversation. Teamwork involves teams and work, and group dynamics play an integral role in their function and production.

Leadership

Whether or not there is a "natural leader," born with a combination of talents and traits that enable a person to lead others, has been a subject of debate across time. In a modern context, we have come to recognize that leadership comes in many form and representations. Once it was thought that someone with presence of mind, innate intelligence, and an engaging personality was destined for leadership, but modern research and experience shows us otherwise. Just as a successful heart surgeon has a series of skill sets, so does a dynamic leader. A television producer must both direct and provide space for talent to create, balancing control with confidence and trust. This awareness of various leadership styles serves our discussion as groups and teams often have leaders, and they may not always be the person who holds the title, status, or role.

Leaders take on the role because they are appointed, elected, or emerge into the role. The group members play an important role in this process. An appointed leader is designated by an authority to serve in that capacity, irrespective of the thoughts or wishes of the group. They may serve as the leader and accomplish all the designated tasks, but if the group does not accept their role as leader, it can prove to be a challenge. As Bruce Tuckman [2] notes, "storming" occurs as group members come to know each other and communicate more freely, and an appointed leader who lacks the endorsement of the group may experience challenges to his or her authority.

A democratic leader is elected or chosen by the group, but may also face serious challenges. If individual group members or constituent groups feel neglected or ignored, they may assert that the democratic leader does not represent their interests. The democratic leader involves the group in the decision-making process, and insures group ownership of the resulting decisions and actions as a result. Open and free discussions are representative of this process, and the democratic leader acknowledges this diversity of opinion.

An emergent leader contrasts the first two paths to the role by growing into the role, often out of necessity. The appointed leader may know little about the topic or content, and group members will naturally look to the senior member with the most experience for leadership. If the democratic leader fails to bring the group together, or does not represent the whole group, subgroups may form, each with an informal leader serving as spokesperson.

Types of Leaders

We can see types of leaders in action and draw on common experience for examples. The heart surgeon does not involve everyone democratically, is typically appointed to the role through earned degrees and experience, and resembles a military sergeant more than a politician. The autocratic leader is self-directed and often establishes norms and conduct for the group. In some settings we can see that this is quite advantageous, such as open-heart surgery or during a military exercise, but it does not apply equally to all leadership opportunities.

Contrasting the autocrat is the laissez-faire, or "live and let live" leader. In a professional setting, such as a university,

professors may bristle at the thought of an autocratic leader telling them what to do. They have earned their role through time, effort, and experience and know their job. A wise laissez-faire leader recognizes this aspect of working with professionals and may choose to focus efforts on providing the professors with the tools they need to make a positive impact. Imagine that you are in the role of a television director and you have a vision or idea of what the successful pilot program should look like. The script is set, the lighting correct, and the cameras are in the correct position. You may tell people what to do and where to stand, but you remember that your job is to facilitate the overall process. You work with talent, and creative people are interesting on camera. If you micromanage your actors, they may perform in ways that are not creative and that will not draw audiences. If you let them run wild through improvisation, the program may not go well at all. Balancing the need for control with the need for space is the challenge of the laissez-faire leader.

Not all leaders are autocrats or laissez-faire leaders. Thomas Harris and John Sherblom [3] specifically note three leadership styles that characterize the modern business or organization, and reflect our modern economy. We are not born leaders but may become them if the context or environment requires our skill set. A leader-as-technician role often occurs when we have skills that others do not. If you can fix the copy machine at the office, your leadership and ability to get it running again are prized and sought-after skills. You may instruct others on how to load the paper or how to change the toner, and even though your pay grade may not reflect this leadership role, you are looked to by the group as a leader within that context. Technical skills, from Internet technology to facilities maintenance, may experience moments where their particular area of knowledge is required to solve a problem. Their leadership will be in demand.

The leader-as-conductor involves a central role of bringing people together for a common goal. In the common analogy, a conductor leads an orchestra and integrates the specialized skills and sounds of the various components the musical group comprises. In the same way, a leader who conducts may set a vision, create benchmarks, and collaborate with a group as they interpret a set script. Whether it is a beautiful movement in music or a group of teams that comes together to address a common challenge, the leader-as-conductor keeps the time and tempo of the group.

Coaches are often discussed in business-related books as models of leadership for good reason. A leader-as-coach combines many of the talents and skills we've discussed here, serving as a teacher, motivator, and keeper of the goals of the group. A coach may be autocratic at times, give pointed direction without input from the group, and stand on the sidelines while the players do what they've been trained to do and make the points. The coach may look out for the group and defend it against bad calls, and may motivate players with words of encouragement. We can recognize some of the behaviors of coaches, but what specific traits have a positive influence on the group? Thomas Peters and Nancy Austin [4] identify five important traits that produce results:

1. Orientation and education
2. Nurturing and encouragement
3. Assessment and correction
4. Listening and counseling
5. Establishing group emphasis

Coaches are teachers, motivators, and keepers of the goals of the group. There are times when members of the team forget that there is no "I" in the word "team." At such times, coaches serve to redirect the attention and energy of the individuals to the overall goals of the group. They conduct the group with a sense of timing and tempo, and at times, they relax and let the members demonstrate their talents. Through their listening skills and counseling, they come to know each member as an individual, but keep the team focus for all to see. They set an example. Coaches, however, are human and by definition are not perfect. They can and do prefer some players over others and can display less than professional sideline behavior when they don't agree with the referee, but the style of leadership is worthy of your consideration in its multidisciplinary approach. Coaches use more than one style of leadership and adapt to the context and environment. A skilled business communicator will recognize that this approach has its merits

KEY TAKEAWAY

Teamwork allows individuals to share their talents and energy to accomplish goals. An effective leader facilitates this teamwork process.

EXERCISES

1. Do you prefer working in a group or team environment, or working individually? What are the advantages and disadvantages of each? Discuss your thoughts with classmates.
2. Imagine that you could choose anyone you wanted to be on a team with you. Who would you choose, and why? Write a two- to three-paragraph description and share it with a classmate.
3. Think of a leader you admire and respect. How did this individual become a leader—for example, by appointment, democratic selection, or emergence? How

would you characterize this leader's style—is the leader autocratic or laissez-faire, a technician, or a coach?

[1] Thill, J. V., & Bovee, C. L. (2002). *Essentials of business communication.* Upper Saddle River, NJ: Prentice Hall.
[2] Tuckman, B. (1965). Developmental sequence in small groups. *Psychological Bulletin, 63,* 384–399.
[3] Harris, T., & Sherblom, J. (1999). *Small group and team communication.* Boston, MA: Allyn & Bacon.
[4] Peters, T., & Austin, N. (1985). *A passion for excellence: The leadership difference.* New York, NY: Random House.

19.6 Additional Resources

- Read about groups and teams on the business Web site 1000 Ventures. http://www.1000ventures.com/business_guide/crossc uttings/team_main.html
- Learn more about Tuckman's linear model. http://www.infed.org/thinkers/tuckman.htm
- Learn more about Dewey's sequence of group problem solving on this site from Manatee Community College in Florida. http://faculty.mccfl.edu/frithl/SPC1600/handouts/D ewey.htm
- Read a hands-on article about how to conduct productive meetings. http://www.articlesnatch.com/Article/How-To-Conduct-Productive-Meetings-/132050
- Visit this wikiHow site to learn how to use VoIP. http://www.wikihow.com/Use-VoIP
- Watch a YouTube video on cloud computing. http://www.youtube.com/watch?v=6PNu QHUiV3Q
- Read about groups and teams, and contribute to a wiki about them, on Wikibooks. http://en.wikibooks.org/wiki/Managing_ Groups_and_Teams
- How did Twitter get started? Find out. http://twitter.com/about
- Take a (nonscientific) quiz to identify your leadership style. http://psychology.about.com/library/quiz/bl-leadershipquiz.htm

NOTES:

www.ingramcontent.com/pod-product-compliance
Lightning Source LLC
Chambersburg PA
CBHW051406200326
41520CB00023B/7135